For Reference

Not to be taken from this room

Dictionary of Literary Biography

American Writers in Paris, 1920-1939

Dictionary of Literary Biography • Volume Four

American Writers in Paris, 1920-1939

Edited by Karen Lane Rood

Foreword by Malcolm Cowley

A Bruccoli Clark Book
Gale Research Company • Book Tower • Detroit, Michigan 48226
1980

Copyright © 1980
GALE RESEARCH COMPANY

Library of Congress Cataloging in Publication Data

Main entry under title:

American writers in Paris, 1920-1939.

(Dictionary of literary biography ; v. 4)
"A Bruccoli Clark book."
Bibliography: p.
1. Authors, American--20th century--Bio-Bibliography.
2. American literature--France--Paris--Bio-Bibliography.
3. Americans in Paris--Biography. 4. Paris--Intellec-
tual life--Bibliography. I. Rood, Karen Lane.
PS129.A57   810'.9'0052 [B]   79-26101
ISBN 0-8103-0916-5

For
Sheila and Norman Lane

Vernon Sternberg, the first member of the
Dictionary of Literary Biography Planning Board,
died in 1979. He was a complete publisher
and the best of company.

Contents

*Indicates master entries

Contents

Contents

Foreword

I am delighted to have these informative brief lives of writers most of whom I knew, either in Paris or New York. Except for a few older men and women also represented in this volume, they form a coherent age group that contributed a chapter, and an important one, to the history of American letters. They are the so-called Lost Generation. It was during their heyday, and partly because of their efforts, that American writing ceased to be regarded as a provincial activity, a sort of assembly plant for British-inspired artifacts, and was recognized by the world for its inherent qualities. All the writers discussed here spent months or years in Paris during the 1920s or 1930s, and for most of them—by no means all—that sojourn (or "expatriation," as it was then called) became a decisive experience that gives this volume a dominant theme.

Most of them have now become the subjects of scholarly research. There has been a busy production of biographies, checklists, monographs, master's theses, and doctoral dissertations that present their works and days. Having lived among them and then survived most of my great contemporaries, I find myself elected against my will to the office or function of Scholarly Resource. It seems to me that everyone who studies a figure connected with the American years in Paris—almost every biographer, monographer, essayist, or candidate for a doctorate in American Studies—wants to enliven his work with information straight from the horse's mouth. "You're the horse," each of them says to me in effect. "Won't you please give me your impressions—answer the enclosed questionnaire of only six typewritten pages—give me a list of sources to consult—let me put your memories on tape?" Not one of them, I grumble to myself, offers a stall to the horse. Not one of them fills his feedbox with oats or his manger with hay. The horse is expected to forage for himself, if he has any time after answering questions. He is too old to live in comfort by—as Conrad Aiken used to say—putting himself out to stud.

Still, forgetting old Dobbin's complaints, I try to answer the queries when they seem reasonable and when I have moments to spare, or postage stamps. I refuse to follow the example of Edmund Wilson, who had a postcard printed with a list of things he refused to do: read manuscripts, for example, or furnish quotable phrases for book jackets, or provide information for researchers; the printed list included twenty or more "Mr. Wilson does not's." He simply checked the proper item, addressed the card, and dropped it in the mail. That was an efficient procedure, but it seemed to me a little unfeeling. I preferred the brief letter that Yvor Winters, not one of the Paris crowd, sometimes sent to seekers after knowledge: "Don't bother me. I'm a cranky old man." But now I have an excuse for writing letters almost as short as Winters' and at the same time more helpful. I shall say, "Consult the *Dictionary of Literary Biography*, Volume IV, *American Writers in Paris, 1920-1939.*"

For letters I have written or interviews I have given in the past, I feel partly rewarded—though not in oats or hay—when a book appears that has been in some measure strengthened or straightened by information I was able to supply. One book to which I made a contribution of sorts was *Black Sun*, a life of Harry Crosby, the poet who committed suicide in 1929 after a briefly extravagant career in Paris. I had written about Crosby, an extraordinary figure, in a long chapter of *Exile's Return*. Geoffrey Wolff, the author of *Black Sun*, says in his preface that reading the chapter was what inspired him to write his book. He also thanks me for an interview in which I suggested various sources that he might investigate. He went to all those sources and to many others, including some that proved to be vastly richer than any I had mentioned. I was gratified to find that he had presented Crosby's whole story; it is one that deserves to be told at length for the light it casts on a personality and a period.

I was less gratified to learn that he was trying to refute almost every general statement I had made in *Exile's Return*. Perhaps that was only to be expected; new authors are always tempted to controvert and abolish their predecessors. It is a normal impulse, but I suspect that Wolff has carried it to an extreme, sometimes in disregard of historical records. Thus, he denies that there was any group of American expatriates, let alone exiles, in Paris during the 1920s. Of course that is chiefly a question of nomenclature. Nobody doubts that there were hundreds or thousands of Americans in Paris vaguely connected with the arts; it doesn't matter whether they were expatriates or simply visitors who didn't want to go home. But Wolff also denies that they had any general reason for residing in Paris rather than New York, outside of the fact that living was cheaper abroad. He thereby misses the import of a widespread revolt among American artists against puritanism, prohibition, and booster clubs. He does not recognize the magnetic force that Paris exerted as—in those years—the international capital of the arts.

Wolff goes farther in smashing images and failing to see connections. He asserts that the American visitors had no relation with French life and no knowledge whatever of French fiction and poetry. Which American visitors? There were some who clearly had such relation and knowledge. Wolff denies that Harry Crosby was in any way representative of others: "The story is remarkable," he says, "not for its illustration of general principles or its symbolic burden, but for its isolation, its lonely singularity." Finally he refuses to admit that there is any such thing as a literary generation, something he dismisses as "that most convenient fabrication."

He gets down to cases. "In Cowley's thesis," he says, "much depends on one's willingness to assume that there is such an odd creature as a literary generation—to accept Faulkner, Frost, Pound, Hemingway, MacLeish and Crane as belonging together in ways that go beyond their common dedication to the execution of their various talents." But of course there are literary generations—or rather age groups, to use a more exact term— just as there are age groups in music, painting, politics, science, and other fields of human activity. One cannot get round their existence unless one holds that the nature of literary talent, for example, is completely determined by genetics and is influenced not at all by environment. People born in a given period grow up in a different world from those born in other periods; their minds are shaped by a different set of events and social customs; they have different ideals of what constitutes an admirable work or a successful life. The existence of age groups with marked characteristics can be proved by any list of writers that includes their years of birth. Any list of persons entertained by Harry and Caresse Crosby during their Paris years would make the same point. The Crosbys, like most of us at the time, did not associate with many persons much older or younger than themselves.

The age group to which Crosby belonged, the one composed of writers born between 1891, let us say, and about 1905, was clearly marked off from its predecessors (who, it must be noted, included Frost, born in 1874, and Pound, born in 1885; the mention of those two names, in this connection, shows that Wolff hasn't bothered to understand what I was talking about). As for the other names listed, they are those of writers only a little older or younger than Crosby, who was born in 1898. With others not mentioned, including Fitzgerald, Cummings, Dos Passos, and Edmund Wilson, they did have something in common, beginning with, but not confined to, "their common dedication to the execution of their various talents," a characteristic more strongly marked with them than with later age groups. For the best writers of the expatriate years, producing works of art was a moral purpose that took precedence over others. They despised the younger writers who were bent on "making it" at any price.

Harry Crosby belongs with those others by virtue of his dedication, even if his talent was less than theirs. Wolff is wrong to regard his story as remarkable chiefly for "its isolation, its lonely singularity"; everybody tried to be singular in those days. Not only was Crosby a contemporary of Scott Fitzgerald's, but one comes to regard him as a character whom Fitzgerald might have imagined, let us say a combination of the Rich Boy and Jay Gatsby, with Gatsby's pathetic belief in a Platonic ideal of himself. "The poor son-of-a-bitch," Owl-eyes says after standing by Gatsby's grave. "You poor, damned, dumb bastard," MacLeish said under his breath to Harry while watching over his corpse in Bellevue Morgue. Later he added, for the world, "I never met anyone who was so imbued with literature; he was drowned in it." That is one of the points I was trying to make in *Exile's Return*.

Did I exaggerate the extent to which the exiles—or expatriates or simple visitors—were affected by French culture and by French ideals of the literary life? Wolff has a point here, so long as he confines himself to the Americans who sat around tables outside the Cafe du Dome or the Select Bar. He says, "To read one after another the dozens of memoirs written about Paris in the Twenties is to notice immediately that very little that was French, save for food and artifacts and bodies, registered on American visitors there, least of all French fiction and poetry." Perhaps Wolff has read the wrong books. Did he read *Exile's Return* with any attention? Or Matthew Josephson's *Life Among the Surrealists*? Or John Glassco's *Memoirs of Montparnasse*? He also says, to clinch his point, "When William Carlos Williams asked Robert McAlmon, who was at the dead center of life in the American village of Montparnasse, to introduce him to some French poets, McAlmon could not, because after years in Paris he knew none." Of course Williams was asking the wrong person. Why didn't he approach Eugene Jolas, who published French poets in *transition*? Or Kitty Cannell, who was then living with one of them? McAlmon was a special case in his willed incapacity to learn anything whatever, including the French language. As for his being "at the dead center" of life in Montparnasse, there were scores of Americans in that village who obsessively didn't like McAlmon. There were scores of others—writers, artists, composers, scholars—who prided themselves on not being seen at the Cafe du Dome.

Some of them acquired an intimate knowledge of French culture on various levels, from that of criminals to that of the Faubourg Saint-Germain. I think of E. E. Cummings, an ambulance driver for the French army—like Crosby and many other future American writers—who spent weeks in a French detention barracks, the Enormous Room. I think of another ambulance driver, Julien Green, who chose to write in French and became the first member of the French Academy who was also an American citizen. I think of Kay Boyle, who married a Frenchman shortly after World War I and became a put-upon French housewife before she became a distinguished novelist. I think of her second husband, Laurence Vail, sometimes called "the King of Montparnasse," which of course had no king, any more than it had a dead center. Laurence, now a neglected figure, was born in Paris and spent his long life on the border between two cultures. I think of Sylvia Beach, whose bookstore, Shakespeare and Company, was across the street from a French bookstore owned by Adrienne Monnier, her close friend. Through Monnier she met all the great men of contemporary French literature, who helped to keep Shakespeare and Company going after most of her American clients had gone home. I think of Janet Flanner, whose letters from Paris, printed year after year in the *New Yorker*, told us what *tout Paris* was talking about. I think of many others whose names I might mention without going beyond literary circles.

But why not go beyond those circles? Paris in those days had dozens of special *milieux*, including those of the modernist poets, the rebel artists, the fashion writers, the jazz musicians, the boxers, the barmen, the gigolos, the lesbians, the entertainers, the *sportifs*, and the aristocrats of the Faubourg Saint-Germain. There were Americans in most of the circles, learning from the French and at the same time exercising a reciprocal influence. In modernist art, for example, Man Ray was a famous figure (as his longtime mistress, Kiki, was in Montparnasse cafes). Sandy Calder had even more friends among French artists than he had in New York. After he died a few years ago his studio at Sache, near Tours, was taken over as a Calder museum by the French government.

There were also American scholars, continuing their studies in various French libraries. Most of them came back to the States to offer courses in French literature, sometimes famous ones. I think of Ramon Guthrie, with his course on Proust's great novel, which he gave at Dartmouth for thirty-one years, rereading the whole novel each of those years and each time discovering something new. I think of his colleague George Diller, who helped him compile the two best anthologies of modernist French literature (*French Literature and Thought Since the Revolution* and *Prose and Poetry of Modern France*). I think of Jackson Matthews, for many years at the University of Washington before he resigned to edit a complete English translation of Paul Valery. I think of Wallace Fowlie at Duke, now the foremost expounder of modern French writing, and Warren Ramsey at Berkeley, the American authority on the life and works of Jules Laforgue; but there are dozens of others.

And what is the purpose of mentioning such names, all of former expatriates and all of persons who deserve to be remembered? I am trying to suggest that there was, in spite of Wolff's denigratory remarks, an active Franco-American culture and that Paris was its definite center between the two wars, a fact amply documented in the present volume. I am also suggesting that hundreds of Americans were more than mere visitors and—getting down to a single case—that Harry Crosby's brief career was played out against a rich background, on which it throws a special sort of light. It wasn't typical, God knows and God be thanked, but it was revelatory and in some ways representative.

—*Malcolm Cowley*

Preface

The generation of American writers who went to Paris after World War I were rebels against social and political conservatism in the United States, and they were attracted by the favorable rate of exchange that allowed them to live more cheaply in France. But they also saw Paris as a cultural center and as a place where they could find an audience for their literary experiments. In Paris they not only interacted with contemporary American and European writers and artists, but they found English-language newspapers, little magazines, and book publishers. Although they became a largely separate community in Paris, looking to each other for inspiration and literary standards, their experiments with style changed the course of American writing in this century.

American Writers in Paris, 1920-1939 provides biographical sketches of ninety-nine of the writers, journalists, editors, and publishers who went to France between the two World Wars. The entries concentrate on the writers' years in France. The full careers of many of the writers in this book will be covered in future volumes of the *Dictionary of Literary Biography.* While bibliographies in *American Writers in Paris, 1920-1939* list the writers' major works, their primary emphasis is on works written or published in France and those works influenced by the writers' years on the Continent. Periodical publications are especially selective and tend to be limited to contributions to little magazines in Europe and to major American literary magazines. All primary and secondary works have been selected by contributors to suit the focus of their entries.

There are two types of entries. Master entries provide more detailed discussions of the subjects' roles in the American literary community in Paris. These essays cover major writers whose years in France played a significant part in their literary careers, individuals who were major catalysts in establishing the milieu in which these writers worked, and important reporters of this unique period in American writing. Standard entries cover major figures whose connections with Paris were brief, as well as others whose places in American literary history are small, but who made contributions to literary life in Paris during the twenties and thirties. Much of the information about these minor figures is collected for the first time in *American Writers in Paris, 1920-1939*.

The staff of BC Research produced this book: Susan P. Allen, Pamela A. Chappell, Glenda G. Fedricci, Cynthia H. Rogers, Jean W. Ross, Theodora J. Thompson, and Nancy L. Ward.

Many of the photographs in this volume are from the Sylvia Beach Collection at the Princeton University Library. Thanks to Richard Ludwig and his staff for their assistance. The following individuals and institutions helped by providing photographs or information: John Anderson; Donna Boone; Jamie Boozer; Rodica Botoman; Mrs. William Aspenwall Bradley; Ashley Brown; Joan Crane; Maryann Curry; Donald Gallup; Elizabeth Gardiner; Diana Haskell; Michael Havener; Linda Hubbard; Roy Hubbard; Roger Mortimer; Laura Murphy; Anna Neagoe; Harriet Oglesbee; Michael Plunkett; Hilary Putnam; Jean Rhyne; Jane Thesing; Joyce Werner; Neda M. Westlake; Agence Hoffman, Paris; Collection of American Literature, Beinecke Rare Book and Manuscript Library, Yale University; Bird Library, Syracuse University; Dartmouth College Museum and Galleries; Houghton Library, Harvard University; McKeldin Library, University of Maryland; The Newberry Library, Chicago; The Poetry Collection of the University Libraries, State University of New York at Buffalo; Special Collections, Morris Library, Southern Illinois University at Carbondale; Thomas Cooper Library, University of South Carolina; Van Pelt Library, University of Pennsylvania.

Photographic work for this volume was done by Pat Crawford, Photo-Vision, Richard H. Taylor, and Richard H. Taylor, Jr.

Dictionary of Literary Biography

American Writers in Paris, 1920-1939

Dictionary of Literary Biography

Margaret Anderson

Paula R. Feldman
University of South Carolina

BIRTH: Indianapolis, Indiana, 24 November 1886.

EDUCATION: Western College for Women, Oxford, Ohio, 1903-1906.

DEATH: Le Cannet, France, 18 October 1973.

BOOKS: *My Thirty Years' War* (New York: Covici Friede, 1930; London: Knopf, 1930);
The Fiery Fountains (New York: Hermitage House, 1951; London: Rider, 1953);
The Unknowable Gurdjieff (London: Routledge & Paul, 1962);
The Strange Necessity (New York: Horizon, 1970).

As a very young woman, Margaret Anderson decided that her life was to be "Beautiful as no life had ever been." Her personal search for that beauty was eventually to take her to Paris in the twenties, but even before that she had become the friend and publisher of many of the leading writers, artists, and intellectuals of her time both in Europe and America. She defied convention throughout her life, armed with the knowledge that "the great thing to learn about life is first, not to do what you don't want to do, and second, to do what you do want to do."

In college she studied piano though she much preferred listening to performing. She read indiscriminately such writers as Ellen Key, Havelock Ellis, Dostoevski, Shelley, Keats, and Swinburne. After three years, she returned to her parents' prosperous home in Columbus, Indiana, and planned "how to escape mediocrity."

Her passion was conversation, and she believed the most stimulating sort took place only among artists. Thus, in 1906 she established herself in Chicago, then the center of Midwestern intellectual ferment. She began by writing book reviews for a religious magazine, the *Continent*, and for the Chicago *Evening Post*, and in 1912 she became a clerk in "the most beautiful bookshop in the world," the one Frank Lloyd Wright had designed in the Fine Arts Building. There she met Francis F. Browne, editor of the *Dial*. Becoming a member of the *Dial* staff, Anderson soon acquired a practical knowledge of the printing room which was to prove indispensable in her later publishing ventures.

Around 1913 she went back to work for the *Continent* as literary editor. One of her main reasons for accepting the job was that she would have the opportunity to visit New York to interview publishers about forthcoming books. Of the many she met, her favorite was Alfred Harcourt, who later founded the house of Harcourt, Brace. After another year in Chicago, she was rebuked by the editor of the *Continent* for making the aesthetic judgment that Dreiser's *Sister Carrie* (1900) was a fine piece of work rather than denouncing it as immoral. Thus ended her career with the *Continent*.

She was depressed, for she wanted a life filled with inspired conversation. Her solution was to found the *Little Review*, a magazine she vowed to fill with "the best conversation the world has to offer." During her year as literary editor of the *Continent*, she had met Floyd Dell, literary editor of the Chicago *Evening Post*, and his wife Margery Currey, who had created a sort of salon. There Anderson met Sherwood Anderson, Theodore Dreiser, Susan Glaspell, Llewellyn Jones, Arthur Davison Ficke, and a man she identifies in her memoirs as Dewitt or Dick (probably DeWitt C. Wing, an early contributor to the *Little Review*). He believed in the idea of the *Little Review* and provided her with funds for her venture. At his suggestion she also solicited her advertisements for the first number in Boston and New York.

Back in Chicago, Anderson took an office for the *Little Review* in room 917 of the Fine Arts Building. Her conviction in founding this monthly magazine was that "people who make Art are more interesting than those who don't; that they have a special illumination about life; that this illumination is the subject-matter of all inspired conversation; that one might as well be dead as to live outside this radiance." The defiant slogan of her magazine dedicated to art for art's sake was "A Magazine of the Arts, Making No Compromise with the Public Taste." In March 1914 the *Little Review* was launched with a first number which contained a poem by Nicholas Vachel Lindsay, five poems by Arthur Davison Ficke, an article by Llewellyn Jones on the meaning of Bergsonism, an article by Sherwood Anderson entitled "The New Note," the first in a series of articles on Nietzsche by George Burman Foster, an article on the "cubist literature" of Gertrude Stein by George Soule, and a review by Margery Currey and Cornelia Anderson (Sherwood Anderson's first wife) of Ellen Key's book on Rahel Varnhagen, a nineteenth-century feminist. Margaret Anderson herself contributed articles about Paderewski's playing, Galsworthy's new novel *The Dark Flower*, William Vaughn Moody's *Letters*, and the poetry of Rupert Brooke. Also included in this first number was coverage of events of literary interest in Chicago. Floyd Dell boosted sales with a long and mostly favorable review in the Chicago *Evening Post*. The second number was mainly notable for reprinting excerpts from William Butler Yeats's address to American poets.

The third number, dated May 1914, created a scandal. Anderson had heard a lecture by the anarchist Emma Goldman which inspired her to laud Goldman in the pages of the *Little Review* and to denounce ownership of private property. This article lost her the support of her backer, Dewitt. Anderson had to resort to subscription campaigns and part-time reviewing to pay the printer, but others helped too. Frank Lloyd Wright contributed money, the poet Eunice Strong Tietjens contributed a diamond ring, and the influential Bert Leston Taylor gave her valuable exposure in his famous *Chicago Tribune* column, "A Line O'Type or Two." People began coming to the studio: Maxwell Bodenheim, Ben Hecht, Carl Sandburg, Edgar Lee Masters, Sinclair Lewis, and Harriet Monroe. Amy

Lowell offered to support the magazine if she were made poetry editor, but Anderson declined, explaining she could not function "in association." Emma Goldman wrote to express her appreciation for Anderson's article, and the two women met and became good friends.

Anderson grew increasingly anarchistic. Subscriptions fell off. When rent money was no longer to be had, the *Little Review* staff, along with Anderson's sister Lois and her children, pitched tents on the Lake Michigan beach, where they lived from the middle of May until the middle of November 1914. When the *Chicago Tribune* ran a feature story on this colony of revolutionary literary nomads, new subscriptions flooded in, but the group lost the use of a house that had been promised them for the winter. A socialist friend of Goldman's rescued the beachdwellers from the cold by making a house on Indiana Avenue available to them.

In addition to her espousal of feminism and anarchism, Anderson was also publishing and defending the Imagists. Throughout 1914-1916 the magazine published poems by Amy Lowell, an article on Hilda Doolittle (H.D.), and a statement of the Imagists' tenets by Richard Aldington, along with John Cowper Powys on Henry James and on Theodore Dreiser, stories by Ben Hecht, the long poem "So We Grew Together" by Edgar Lee Masters, "Portrait of Theodore Dreiser" by Arthur Davison Ficke, stories by Sherwood Anderson, poems by Carl Sandburg, and "Letters from Prison" by Emma Goldman. Though Rupert Brooke was under contract to an English publisher and could not contribute anything, he and the *Little Review* staff spent many evenings together while he was in Chicago.

Despite the present-day celebrity of many of the early *Little Review* contributors, nearly everything included during its first years was work that would not have otherwise found publication. "I never knew what was wrong with art for art's sake," Anderson commented. "Should it be art for money's sake? Is there something the matter with art that it dare not exist for itself alone?" She accepted or rejected manuscripts on the sole basis of "art as the person." As she explained, "An artist is an exceptional person. Such a person has something exceptional to say. Exceptional matter makes an exceptional manner. This is 'style.' "

In February 1916 Anderson met Jane Heap, whom she considered "the world's best talker." Anderson later called her "the most interesting thing that had happened to the magazine"; she became associate editor and a regular contributor. In the

SHE PRACTICES EIGHTEEN HOURS A DAY AND—

BREAKFASTING

GATHERING HER OWN FIRE-WOOD

CONVERTING THE SHERIFF TO ANARCHISM AND VERS LIBRE

—TAKES HER MASON AND HAMLIN TO BED WITH HER

SWIMMING

THE STEED ON WHICH SHE HAS HER PICTURE TAKEN

SUFFERING FOR HUMANITY AT EMMA GOLDMAN'S LECTURES

THE INSECT ON WHICH SHE RIDES

Light occupations of the editor, while there is nothing to edit.

Little Review *(September 1916)*

summer of 1916, the editors moved the *Little Review* to California, where Anderson produced its most famous issue in September 1916: sixty-four pages of blank paper accompanied by the statement that since no real art was being offered and since the *Little Review* would publish nothing second-rate, it preferred to publish nothing. The most interesting period of the *Little Review*'s life began in early 1917 when Anderson moved the monthly to New York and when Ezra Pound became its European editor. In the first number after Pound joined the staff, T. S. Eliot and Wyndham Lewis appeared for the first time in the *Little Review* along with William Butler Yeats. The *Little Review* now began to publish Hart Crane and Ford Madox Ford along with more work by an earlier contributor, William Carlos Williams, and much of Pound's own work.

It was in March 1918 that the *Little Review* began the serialization of James Joyce's *Ulysses* (1922), which was to ensure the *Little Review*'s lasting reputation for excellence but was also to contribute to its eventual destruction. Pound brought the manuscript to Anderson's attention.

When she read it, she exclaimed, "This is the most beautiful thing we'll ever have! We'll print it if it's the last effort of our lives." During the three years it ran, the U. S. Post Office burned four issues for alleged obscenity, and the intellectuals who did not decry Joyce's masterpiece virtually ignored it. On 4 October 1920, the Washington Square Bookshop notified the *Little Review* that the Society for the Suppression of Vice had served them with papers for having sold to a minor a copy of the July-August issue, which contained the conclusion of Episode XIII of *Ulysses*, the Gerty MacDowell section. Defended by the eminent New York lawyer John Quinn, a friend of Pound and Joyce and a patron of the magazine, Margaret Anderson and Jane Heap were tried in the Court of Special Sessions, found guilty, and fined one hundred dollars. Not one New York newspaper spoke out in support of either the *Little Review* or of James Joyce.

However, the *Little Review* went on, though issues appeared at longer and longer intervals, publishing Djuna Barnes, Gertrude Stein, A. R. Orage, Wallace Stevens, and Malcolm Cowley. In the

Margaret Anderson   Jane Heap

Sylvia Beach Collection

autumn of 1921, the *Little Review* became a quarterly, and in the spring of 1922 it published what was considered by many the high watermark of critical writing: "Aesthetic Meditation on Painting" by Guillaume Apollinaire. About this time Anderson began, despite Jane Heap's protests, to consider giving up the *Little Review*. Shortly afterwards, according to Anderson, "I didn't know what to do about life—so I did a nervous breakdown that lasted many months."

But two events were to alter Anderson's life considerably and help bring her the changes she needed. First, her conversations with Yeats, who was in America visiting John Quinn, made her curious about travel to Europe. Second, she met Georgette Leblanc, Maurice Maeterlinck's former companion and an exceptionally fine singer who was giving a series of recitals in New York. Leblanc offered Anderson the opportunity to begin a career in piano as her accompanist on a European tour. This meeting was the beginning of a long and enduring attachment.

In late 1922 or early 1923 Georgette Leblanc, Margaret Anderson, and Jane Heap sailed for France. The first person the two editors went to see in Paris was Ezra Pound, who turned out to be completely unlike the picture Anderson had formed of him. "I am very fond of Ezra," she declared. "Only it will be more interesting to know him when he has grown up." Later, Anderson introduced Pound to composer George Antheil, whom she had known in New York. One result of this meeting was Pound's book *Antheil and the Treatise on Harmony* (1924). Another was that Pound and Anderson together were

able to convince Antheil to contribute an article on "Abstraction and Time in Music" for the Autumn/Winter 1924-1925 issue of the *Little Review*.

James Joyce and his wife came to see Anderson in Pound's studio and impressed her as "a portrait of my father as a young man—the same gentle bearing, the same kindliness, the same deprecating humor in the smile, the same quality of personal aristocracy." He gave Anderson the impression of "having less escape from suffering about irremediable things than anyone I had ever known." After meeting Nora Joyce, Anderson believed that no contemporary description of her had ever done her justice. She considered Joyce's wife charming and admired her spirit and independence which she willingly subordinated to her devotion to her husband. Still, Anderson pronounced her "one of those women a man loves forever and hopes one day to take effectively by the throat."

Anderson and Heap also went to see Gertrude Stein and Alice B. Toklas at their studio in the rue de Fleurus. Stein told Anderson that she believed no one of the younger generation now had any difficulty reading her prose, but in her autobiography, *My Thirty Years' War* (1930), Anderson confessed, "I for one still have difficulty, a difficulty that is often unrewarded by understanding. And my understanding is often unrewarded by interest." Though Anderson admired Gertrude Stein principally for Stein's warm nature and for the sound of her contagious laugh, the two did not get along, according to Janet Flanner, because they were both such egoists. Flanner observed, "One of the things that made Margaret insupportable to other women of spirit was a belief she had developed in her own infallibility which, of course, made her unbearable." When Stein and Anderson would meet for Sunday lunch at the home of a mutual friend at Orgeval, outside Paris, it was Stein who dominated. According to Flanner, "Her nature was so solid that it reduced Margaret to the two opposite elements always uppermost in her own personality—violent agreement and violent disagreement, both accompanied by characteristic spirals of her taunting laughter. She meant to taunt no one, however, as her nature was affectionate, but she had a split mentality, based on her addiction to argument. The Orgeval lunches invariably developed, by the second cups of coffee which ended them, into small verbal wars. These were Margaret's particular delight, and if she was able to say, as she drew on her topcoat to go home, that she'd never had better conversation, it was her way of acknowledging that she had been involved in battles with almost everyone at the table and felt that she had triumphed in most of them."

The Ernest Hemingway Anderson knew did not fit the legend. She found him to be soft-hearted, generous, and simple. She agreed with Jane Heap that Hemingway's animal prototype was a rabbit with "white and pink face, soft brown eyes that look at you without blinking. As for his love for boxing and bull-fighting—all that is thrashing up the ground with his hind legs." The *Little Review* was one of the earliest publishers of Hemingway's fiction. Although Anderson had earlier rejected one of Hemingway's stories, he was invited to contribute to the Spring 1923 Exile's Number of the magazine. Hemingway contributed six short prose sketches, entitled "In Our Time," which would later appear as Chapters I through VI of *in our time*, published by William Bird's Three Mountains Press in 1924. In the same issue appeared "They All Made Peace— What Is Peace?," Hemingway's poem about the Lausanne Peace Conference. Later the *Little Review* published Hemingway's short stories "Mr. and Mrs. Elliot" (Autumn-Winter 1924-1925) and "Banal Story" (Spring-Summer 1926). For the Final Number Hemingway wrote a poem, called "Valentine," addressed to a reviewer who had written a negative review of *Men Without Women* (1927), and a humorous letter asking for acknowledgement of the poem. Anderson was later to declare *A Farewell to Arms* (1929) one of America's best novels.

Anderson considered Jean Cocteau, whose poem "The Cape of Good Hope" the *Little Review*

had published in translation in 1921, the most charming man in Paris, a catalytic agent. She wrote that Cocteau was "one of those writers whose name is impressed upon his generation not so much by what he writes as by what he is. His novels are brilliant personal exposition but if he hadn't written them his poetry would have been enough. If he had written no poetry his plays would have been enough. If he had written no plays his translations would have been enough. And if he had translated nothing, written nothing, he would still have made a legend. Someone would have discovered him leaning from his window at midnight talking the most witty surrealism to stray drunkards clinging about the lamp post below."

The *Little Review* had been publishing the work of French writers such as Louis Aragon, Andre Breton, Philippe Soupault, and Paul Morand even before Anderson went to France. The French editor of the *Little Review* since 1922 had been Francis Picabia, whose vanity irritated Anderson and of whom she said rather unkindly, "We had never had anything from him except a Picabia number." There was also a Brancusi number in 1922. Anderson was personally fond of Brancusi and of his parties, where she would see Duchamp, Leger, and others of that circle. In the spring of 1923 Anderson met the younger Dadaists and Surrealists: Rene Crevel, Paul Eluard, Jacques Baron, Joseph Delteil, Tristan Tzara, Drieu de la Rochelle, and Pierre Reverdy, all of whom she had published or was soon to print.

By 1924 Anderson began to lose interest in the *Little Review*. It was now ten years old, and she felt it had fulfilled its function. Contemporary art had "arrived"; "for a hundred years, perhaps, the literary world would produce only: repetition." Before leaving for France, Anderson had offered to hand over the *Little Review* to Jane Heap. Now she carried out her promise, and during 1924-1927 Heap took over the editorship of the *Little Review* and published it from New York as a quarterly when possible and otherwise as an annual. During these years Anderson stayed in Europe—principally in France and Italy.

In the spring of 1925 or 1926 A. R. Orage fundamentally altered Anderson's outlook on life by advising her to "Act, don't be acted upon." These words brought her to the conviction that "my thirty years of fighting have been not actions but reactions. In 1929, just fifteen years after the *Little Review* had been launched as a magazine in which I could record my reactions I decided that there had been enough of this. Everyone was doing it—the artist above all. The artist organism is preeminently the acted-upon organism." She did not want the *Little Review* to die a conventional death, however, so discarding all the material that they had amassed for a final number, she and Heap drafted instead a ten item questionnaire asking the artists of the world what they were feeling and thinking about their work and lives. The questions included "What should you most like to do, to know, to be? (In case you are not satisfied); What is your attitude toward art today? Why do you go on living?" More than fifty of the foremost men and women in the arts responded, among them Sherwood Anderson, Richard Aldington, Edith Sitwell, George Antheil, Jean Cocteau, Havelock Ellis, Emma Goldman, H.D., Ernest Hemingway, Mina Loy, Jacques Lipchitz, Aldous Huxley, Marianne Moore, Bertrand Russell, Gertrude Stein, Joseph Stella, and William Carlos Williams. Their replies and an editorial by Anderson make up most of the last issue. She concluded from the answers to the questionnaires that "even the artist doesn't know what he is talking about. And I can no longer go on publishing a magazine in which no one really knows what he is talking about. It doesn't interest me."

Her search now was not for transformation but for illumination. From her summer house, the lighthouse at Tancarville, and from Paris, where she wrote the first volume of her autobiography, entitled *My Thirty Years' War*, chronicling the period of the *Little Review*, she concluded, "I am trying to become a new human being. I still make vows to achieve an increasingly beautiful life. I think of Chicago and the lighthouse sending its searchlight into my window. I no longer look out upon a lighthouse. I live in one."

Anderson's second volume of autobiography, *The Fiery Fountains* (1951), devotes itself almost entirely to her twenty-year friendship with Georgette Leblanc, singer, actress, and author of *Souvenirs* (1931), translated into English by Janet Flanner and published in the United States as *Souvenirs My Life with Maeterlinck* (1932). Jane Heap lived in England, while Anderson, Leblanc, and a woman named Monique stayed with the family of Leblanc's sister at the Chateau de Tancarville, an eleventh-century chateau in Normandy used by William the Conqueror, Richard the Lion-Hearted, Charles IX, and Elizabeth I. (Mary Stuart is supposed to have been imprisoned in its tower.) They spent their summers at the lighthouse on the estate "in a kind of incredulous delight, loving France above all other countries and each other above all others." Anderson believed that her initial meeting of Leblanc could not have been coincidental "since we knew at once that we were to join hands and advance through life together. Ah, I said, when I first saw her marvelous mystic face: this is the land I have been seeking; I left home long ago to discover it—a new continent, an unearthly place, the great world of art; not a personal but a classical world—formal, magical, mythical. At first I could not understand her language, but when I did I was not surprised to discover that she always said the matchless thing. For twenty years I listened to her words, always with the feeling that I was being blessed or rescued. Ah, I continued to say for the rest of my life."

Anderson was to consider her twenty years with Georgette Leblanc her happiest. The woman who had declared in her first volume of memoirs that she considered her greatest enemy reality now devoted herself to a personal world which would ignore the real world around it. Living for art no longer seemed appropriate. She lived now for wonder and delight. "Our lighthouse," she wrote, "was no ivory tower—it had a more attractive isolation than that. We were in a balloon, in space, looking down at the life on earth as we floated by, but finding our own the most perfect kingdom." Only part of their time was actually spent at the lighthouse, however. Poverty forced them to spend much time visiting Leblanc's wealthy but niggardly relatives at their various chateaus or to stay in small, cheap French hotels.

It was desperation for money which led Anderson to write *My Thirty Years' War*, while Leblanc wrote *Souvenirs*. Anderson's still very readable, anecdotal account of her *Little Review* years was a commercial success, and though Leblanc's *Souvenirs* was less so, their combined royalties allowed them to live in comparative comfort for a period. They bought a car and eventually went to live in a chateau called Le Palais des Muses where Louis XIV was supposed to have lived. Briefly they returned to America, where Leblanc fulfilled concert engagements from New York to San Francisco. Later, after an abortive attempt at a concert tour of Italy, they found an apartment in Paris where Anderson socialized with no Americans. This eight-month epoch Anderson later recalled "as one of the most satisfyingly unreal of my existence." She spent her days arranging new concert programs and was once amazed to find that she had not left the apartment for two weeks since life within had been so absorbing. Anderson loved Paris because she saw it as a place of personal freedom whose cafes, unlike those of any other city, provide for the life of the mind. She did not, however, consider herself an expatriate: "I felt that I had been born in Paris and that I could never, willingly or wonderfully, live anywhere else."

At the end of September 1930, Anderson and

Leblanc installed themselves in a nearly uninhabitable chateau called the Muette. They lived there for two happy years without ever succeeding in making it comfortable. Then in a small hotel in the rue Jacob in Paris, Georgette Leblanc was stricken with pneumonia, and the two went to Vernet-les-Bains in the Pyrenees Orientales for her convalescence. There Anderson came to know and love the French peasants.

In *The Fiery Fountains*, Anderson writes out of her experience with Leblanc about the varieties of human love and emotion. She also writes about their spiritual devotion to the Russo-Greek mystic George Gurdjieff. They had first heard about him from his disciple A. R. Orage, former editor of the *New Age*, and they had heard Gurdjieff himself speak in New York. In Paris they learned more of Gurdjieff's new Institute for the Harmonious Development of Man, his chateau retreat near the village of Moret at Fontainebleau-Avon. Anderson claimed that "we immediately recognized Gurdjieff as the kind of man we had never seen—a seer, a prophet, a messiah?" She, Leblanc, and Heap first went in June of 1924 to Fontainebleau-Avon, where Gurdjieff himself, absorbed in finishing his book, was virtually inaccessible to them. Nevertheless, for the next two years they lived there at intervals and afterwards encountered Gurdjieff on rare occasions.

But in 1934, while living in Vernet, Anderson and Leblanc heard that Gurdjieff was in Paris and was accepting a small group for special teaching. In April 1935 they moved once more to Paris to join Gurdjieff's group, and Anderson began in earnest a personal spiritual transformation. In the beginning, their special Gurdjieff group included Heap, Orage, Leblanc, and Solita Solano. Later it would also include Kathryn Hulme, author of *The Wild Place* and *The Nun's Story*.

For Anderson to follow Gurdjieff meant always "seeking the emotion which would allow me, compel me, to put my head in my hands," to try to stop living "as if in emulation of Rachmaninoff's 'Second Piano Concerto.' " The years 1936-1938 constituted what she has termed her "D period"—a time of depression, discouragement, disgust of self, despair, decrepitude, destruction, where life itself became a desert. Finally, according to Anderson, "for the first time I saw that I was as stupid as I was vain, and as egotistic as I was empty." In March 1938 in Paris Anderson was to write, "I saw myself—no longer sitting on a cloud, nor was I left sitting on the ground. I was no longer unhappy, nor would I be happy again. I would never again be anything but rejoicing. A blessing was upon me, I felt it on every side. I would no longer be spared, or killed, or

protected. I would be helped."

In June 1939 doctors discovered that Georgette Leblanc had a tumor, and Anderson spent the next two years, the last of Leblanc's life, nursing and comforting her friend, fighting her own private war as Europe was engaged in its fight against Hitler. The last section of *The Fiery Fountains*, entitled "War and our World," is a touching account of this period. "I had again become nothing," Anderson recalls, "because I could not face life without the presence of the symbol it had offered me—the symbol that Georgette represented—the perfect human being.... I had lived for twenty years in the presence of a 'saint of lyricism'; must I now enter the movement and mutter of a daily world?"

During the early days of the Occupation, Anderson, Leblanc, and their friend Monique went to live in Cannet near Cannes, and it was not until June 1942, eight months after Georgette's death, that Anderson sailed for New York. Ernest Hemingway, hearing of her penniless state, had sent her four hundred dollars to finance the trip. It was on the S. S. *Drottingholm* bound for New York that Anderson met Dorothy Caruso, the wife of Enrico Caruso and author of *Enrico Caruso: His Life and Death* and *Dorothy Caruso: A Personal History*. They began talking of the *Little Review* and then of Gurdjieff's philosophy. Caruso was to become a member of the Gurdjieff group and "the last great friendship" of Anderson's life.

In June 1948 they returned to France and to Gurdjieff, whom they saw almost continuously until his death in November 1949. Anderson eventually wrote *The Unknowable Gurdjieff* (1962) describing her years as Gurdjieff's disciple. It was inspired by reading Francois Mauriac's description of Katherine Mansfield's devotion to Gurdjieff at the end of her life. Anderson was determined to convince Mauriac of his error in dismissing Gurdjieff as a charlatan and an imposter. Her book is not so much an explanation of Gurdjieff's philosophy (Anderson maintained that he was essentially unknowable except to those who had worked directly with him) so much as it is an effusion of appreciation. Even so, it does not fully clarify Gurdjieff's tremendous appeal for her.

Anderson and Caruso stayed together until Caruso's death in 1955, when Anderson moved to Riderwood, Maryland. In May 1956 she returned to Le Cannet, where she lived a reclusive life with her friend Monique until the latter's death in June 1961. It was in that year that Anderson wrote the following as a conclusion to *The Strange Necessity* (1970), her book of reflections on art and friendship: "The blessings I wanted were love and music, books and great ideas and beauty of environment. I have had them all, and to a degree beyond my asking, even beyond my imagining."

At eighty-six Anderson died quietly in the night at Le Cannet on 18 October 1973, a self-confessed egoist, a woman who believed in "the unsubmissive, the unfaltering, the unassailable, the irresistible, the unbelievable—in other words, in an art of life." While *My Thirty Years' War*, her first of four autobiographical volumes, is today the most interesting of her productions, Margaret Anderson's major contribution was not as a writer herself but as one who recognized and published writers who

shattered the complacent literary attitudes of the twenties.

Other:

The Little Review Anthology, edited by Anderson (New York: Hermitage House, 1953).

References:

J. M. Edelstein, "Exuberance and Ecstasy," *New Republic*, 162 (13 June 1970): 19-22;
Janet Flanner, "Profiles: A Life on a Cloud," *New Yorker*, 50 (June 1974): 44-67.

SHERWOOD ANDERSON
(13 September 1876-8 March 1941)

SELECTED BOOKS: *Winesburg, Ohio* (New York: Huebsch, 1919; London: Cape, 1922);
Poor White (New York: Huebsch, 1920; London: Cape, 1921);
Many Marriages (New York: Huebsch, 1923);
A Story Teller's Story (New York: Huebsch, 1924; London: Cape, 1925);
Dark Laughter (New York: Boni & Liveright, 1925; London: Jarrolds, 1926);
Sherwood Anderson's Notebook (New York: Boni & Liveright, 1926);
Puzzled America (New York & London: Scribners, 1935);
Sherwood Anderson's Memoirs (New York: Harcourt, Brace, 1942);
France and Sherwood Anderson: Paris Notebook, 1921, ed. Michael Fanning (Baton Rouge: Louisiana State University Press, 1976).

Sherwood Anderson visited Paris twice during his life; once in 1921 and once in 1926-1927. Each trip lasted only a few months and, of the two, the first was by far the more important. Indeed, the second trip—which began in late December 1926 and ended in early March 1927—was more of a nightmare than a pleasure excursion. Writing to literary critic Paul Rosenfeld in January 1927, Anderson complained of his own ill health, ill-temperedness in other Americans, and a general lack of creative vitality in his work. The only thing that somewhat redeemed his second Paris visit was the opportunity to see a few old friends, the foremost of whom was Gertrude Stein. Other than that it was a trip best forgotten.

The Newberry Library

Sherwood Anderson, ca. 1921

The situation was quite different—personally and professionally—in 1921 when Anderson and his wife Tennessee visited Paris in the company of Paul Rosenfeld, who paid for the trip. If he was not a popular success in the best-seller sense, Anderson's literary reputation was nonetheless solid, and his work had earned him substantial respect in Europe as well as in America. With the winning of the *Dial* award for his contribution to American literature, which he accepted in October 1921 shortly after his return from Paris, there came an added measure of public acclaim. During the time of the 1921 Paris sojourn—from May through July—it is fair to say that Anderson was lionized; and for a man as self-conscious about his identity as an artist as Anderson, this kind of recognition was especially sweet.

It is also important to remember that Anderson was forty-five years old at the time of his first Paris trip. If his response to the city was at times emotional—he wept at his first sight of the Louvre—it was in keeping with his character. (His response to New Orleans, where he lived from time to time beginning in 1922, was hardly less enthusiastic.) Though Anderson's career as a writer was certainly not over in 1921, he had already published his two greatest fictional works—*Winesburg, Ohio* (1919) and *Poor White* (1920). Thus Sherwood Anderson did not encounter Paris as a young or unknown writer, as did Ernest Hemingway. And perhaps more importantly, he did not consider himself an expatriate in any sense of the word.

Venturing out from his base at the Hotel Jacob where he and his wife stayed, Anderson encountered most of Paris's literati. In his letters and notebook entries, Anderson mentions meetings or conversations with Andre Gide, James Joyce, Sylvia Beach, Gertrude Stein, Leon Bazalgette, and others. Of these, Gertrude Stein was by far the most important personal and professional contact. After he had returned to America, Anderson occasionally called on Stein to receive or assist an artist, or sometimes simply a friend, who was on his way to Paris. The most notable of these cases was that of Ernest Hemingway, whom Anderson introduced in his letter of 3 December 1921 as "an American writer instinctively in touch with everything worthwhile going on here [in America]."

Some caution must be exercised in assessing the influence of the 1921 Paris trip on Anderson's professional life. The Paris experience does not represent a significant watershed in Anderson's career; and though he later acknowledged the stylistic influence of Joyce in the writing of *Dark Laughter* (1925), the influence stems from a literary source, not necessarily from personal contact. Further, the entries in Anderson's 1921 Paris notebook reveal a strengthening, rather than a modification or shifting, of previously held views. He expresses mistrust of literary groups and movements, of writers who talk rather than write,

and for Anderson the wholesome attitude of the French people toward work—which he compares to that of the American Negro—underscores the drudgery and sterility of the white American work ethic.

The two most important by-products of the Paris interlude were the writing of *A Story Teller's Story* (1924) and, of course, the beginning of his lifelong friendship with Gertrude Stein. Just how much of an inspiration and source the Paris trip may have been for *A Story Teller's Story* is debatable; it is nonetheless true that several of Anderson's experiences in Paris figure in the autobiographical narrative, some of them prominently. The early influence of Stein on his own work is acknowledged, and his reaction to the cathedral at Chartres is one of the chief climactic episodes in the book. Michael Fanning has argued that the Paris influence on *A Story Teller's Story* is even more pervasive than the material Anderson took from his 1921 Paris notebook. Anderson seized on "the confrontation between fancy and fact" and made this confrontation the central theme of his work. *A Story Teller's Story* was praised highly in some circles, and it was reviewed enthusiastically by Hemingway and Stein in *Ex Libris* in 1925.

Anderson obviously knew of Stein's work long before he made his first Paris trip, though in good Anderson fashion he gives differing accounts as to how he first encountered the work. It was the expression of his admiration for and understanding of her work that formed the basis of the friendship, which involved a mutual respect between Anderson and Stein. Shortly after Anderson left Paris, he wrote a preface for her *Geography and Plays* (1922). In the preface Anderson points to *Tender Buttons* (1914) as a work that encouraged him to experiment with his writing, and he ends by giving Stein credit for "rebuilding . . . the city of words." Also in 1922 Anderson wrote in praise of Stein's work in a *New Republic* article entitled "Four American Impressions: Gertrude Stein, Paul Rosenfeld, Ring Lardner, Sinclair Lewis." Anderson's last article on Stein was published in 1934 in the *American Spectator*, and was written in response to B. F. Skinner's criticism of Stein's "automatic writing" in the January 1934 issue of the *Atlantic Monthly*. In all of these pieces Anderson developed the general theme that Stein's work was important, misunderstood, and underrated. For her part, Stein—after Anderson had written the preface to *Geography and Plays*—published an appreciation of Anderson in the Spring 1923 issue of the *Little Review* called "Idem the Same: A Valentine to

Paris.   May 23

One of the mistakes being made by the French is that they seem to take it for granted that all the rest of us, who come so gladly to France and Paris come to see and admire them.

To all the rest of us, Americans, English, South Americans, Germans, our own country and people are more attractive, more understandable. What attracts us to this place is old France. The streets here are haunted by memories. To stand far on home in the great open space facing the building of the Louvre is worth the trip across the Atlantic. The walk thru all these streets haunted by the ghosts of great artists of the past and the present day race of Frenchmen seem as far removed from these men as ourselves.

. . . .

There is something in the air of present day France, a kind of death. Before the war one felt something growing here. Now there is a kind of bitterness. I am sure it is affecting, will deeply affect French artists. Men who before the war were searching, longing, striving, have fallen to scolding. The men I have so far met give me no sense of something growing. For example it does not seem to me that present day France could now produce a figure as naive, honest, sweet in his outlook on life as our Sandburg.

. . . . Sandburg

In France the art movement just naturally into groups. One wonders if there is strength in that. Perhaps the time marone for all these group movements is past. The individual artist being doubtful or afraid gives himself to a group hoping to gain strength there.

Anderson's 1921 Paris notebook

12

Sherwood Anderson." This was followed by her 1925 review of *A Story Teller's Story*. Stein subsequently wrote of Anderson in *The Autobiography of Alice B. Toklas* (1933) and *Everybody's Autobiography* (1938); and she reviewed *Puzzled America* (1935) for the 4 May 1935 issue of the *Chicago Daily Tribune*. Her last piece on Anderson—"Sherwood's Sweetness"—appeared after his death in a 1941 memorial issue of *Story*. In her published criticism of Anderson's work, Stein pictured him as the chief exponent of an American tradition in literary craftsmanship which she traced from Cooper, Howells, and Twain. In her letters to Anderson, however, her criticisms were more searching and sometimes quite perceptive. Her comments on *Many Marriages* (1923) pointed to Anderson's tendency in his longer works to write "a beginning an ending an ending and an ending" rather than a beginning, a middle, and an ending.

Despite his brief European visits, his long literary and personal friendship with Gertrude Stein, and his avowed respect for certain European authors, Sherwood Anderson never had any doubts about his identity as an American artist. And that may go a long way toward explaining the durability of his relationship with Stein. As he saw Stein as a wanderer rather than an expatriate, as an American writer "attempting to do something for the writers of . . . English speech," and as a chef who "cares for the handmade goodies and who scorns the factory-made foods," so he consistently pictured himself.

—*Leland H. Cox, Jr.*

Other:

Gertrude Stein, *Geography and Plays*, includes "The Work of Gertrude Stein" by Anderson (Boston: Four Seas, 1922);

Sherwood Anderson Gertrude Stein: Correspondence and Personal Essays, ed. Ray Lewis White (Chapel Hill: University of North Carolina Press, 1972).

Periodical Publications:

"Four American Impressions: Gertrude Stein, Paul Rosenfeld, Ring Lardner, Sinclair Lewis," *New Republic*, 32 (11 October 1922): 171-173;

"Gertrude Stein," *American Spectator*, 2 (April 1934): 3.

Letters:

Letters of Sherwood Anderson, ed. Howard Mumford Jones and Walter B. Rideout (Boston: Little, Brown, 1953).

References:

Sylvia Beach, *Shakespeare and Company* (New York: Harcourt, Brace, 1959), pp. 30-32, 42, 72;

Lewis Galantiere, "French Reminiscence," *Story*, 19 (September-October 1941): 64-67;

Gertrude Stein, "Idem the Same: A Valentine to Sherwood Anderson," *Little Review*, 9 (Spring 1923): 5-9;

Stein, "A Stitch in Time Saves Nine. Birds of a Feather Flock Together. Chickens Come Home to Roost," review of *A Story Teller's Story*, *Ex Libris*, 2 (March 1925): 177;

Stein, *The Autobiography of Alice B. Toklas* (New York: Harcourt, Brace, 1933), pp. 241-242, 265-268, 302-304;

Stein, review of *Puzzled America*, *Chicago Daily Tribune*, 4 May 1935, p. 14;

Stein, *Everybody's Autobiography* (New York: Random House, 1937), pp. 222-223, 256-257, 270-272;

Stein, "Sherwood's Sweetness," *Story*, 19 (September-October 1941): 63.

NATHAN ASCH
(10 July 1902-23 December 1964)

BOOKS: *The Office* (New York: Harcourt, Brace, 1925; London: Holden, 1926);
Love in Chartres (New York: A. & C. Boni, 1927; London: Holden, 1927);
Pay Day (New York: Brewer & Warren, 1930; London: Payson & Clarke, 1930);
The Valley (New York: Macmillan, 1935);
The Road in Search of America (New York: Norton, 1937).

Nathan Asch's writing career began with the publication of his short stories in the Paris-based *transatlantic review*. The oldest child of the great Yiddish writer Sholem Asch and his wife Mathilda Spira Asch, he was born in Warsaw, Poland. When Asch was ten, the family moved to Paris; three years later, after brief stays in Germany and Switzerland, they immigrated to the United States. Settling with his family in rural Staten Island, New York, Asch completed his secondary education in the New York City public schools and attended Syracuse and Columbia universities.

In the early twenties he returned to Paris. Although Asch had had two stories accepted by the *Nation* before he left for Paris "to write and to find himself," his career as a writer was launched with the 1924 publication of the stories he submitted to the *transatlantic review*: "Gertrude Donovan," "Marc Kranz," and "The Voice of the Office," all of which were later incorporated into his first novel, *The Office* (1925). ("Gertrude Donovan" was also included in *The Best Short Stories of 1925*.) In the 18 January 1925 Paris *Tribune* (the European edition of the *Chicago Tribune*) Eugene Jolas quoted Pierre Loving as saying, "In the work of Ernest Hemingway and in that of Nathan Asch, Mr. Ford introduced two interesting young writers to the public."

The Office, which one reviewer compared favorably with John Dos Passos's *Manhattan Transfer* (1925), consists of seventeen chapters. The first and third chapters, "Wall Street" and "The Office," respectively, provide in terse language the background for the fourteen narrative sketches which characterize the employees, from porter to president, of a firm which goes bankrupt. As one reviewer said, the second chapter, "The Voice of the Office," employs "savagely staccato language" through a "sensational accumulation of words . . . like a list of irregular verbs" to mirror the mood of the office on the day that it failed. The remaining chapters are written in a "bald and hard, acidly economical, at times hot, but never warm hearted" style, and narrate the employees' "pallid, unimaginative, disheartened efforts at amusement" after they learn of the crash.

As a result of his association with the *transatlantic review*, Asch gained entree into the expatriate colony in Paris. Among his friends were Josephine Herbst, John Herrmann, Ivan Bede, Morley Callaghan, Evan Shipman, and Malcolm Cowley. Of course, he also knew Ford Madox Ford, who was instrumental in helping him get *The Office* published, and Ernest Hemingway; however, Asch felt that both alternated between "patronizing and snubbing him." About twenty-five years later, his reminiscences about those days were published in the *Paris Review* (Summer 1954) as "The 1920's: An Interior." This piece, an excerpt from an unpublished novel, "Paris Was Home," was, according to Malcolm Cowley, a "sensitive lyrical" description of a day at the Dome Cafe. Hemingway, though objecting to parts of the novel, also found the sketch "first rate."

While in Paris Asch met and married an American girl, Liesl. Although by the time his second novel, *Love in Chartres*, was published in 1927, Asch and his wife had returned to the United States, it chronicles their love affair in France. In this work the unnamed, sensitively drawn, young American novelist, recognizing that in order to devote himself to his art he must renounce marriage, leaves the girl and Chartres and returns to Paris to write. One reviewer described it as "spiritually allied to the Hemingway School" in its "absolute freedom from sentimentality and . . . disciplined compression." Another saw in its faithful and convincing rendition of "that mystical and exalted state of sexual attraction" a close resemblance to Sherwood Anderson's *Dark Laughter* (1925). The novel ironically foreshadowed Asch's divorce three years later in 1930.

When the Aschs and their son returned to America in 1926, they lived for a year in Preston, Connecticut, in a "frozen farmhouse" near John Herrmann and his wife Josephine Herbst (who had returned from Paris in the fall of 1924); next, along with Hart Crane, they stayed in a boardinghouse near Patterson, New Jersey; and then they moved to Sherman, Connecticut, in 1928. During this time Asch wrote *Pay Day* (1930), a novel set against the background of the Sacco-Vanzetti execution. It appeared simultaneously in the United States and Germany, and a year later it was published in Yiddish in Warsaw. Despite the book's apparently wide market, Asch and some of the other less successful former expatriates living near New York felt rejected by the New York publishing world. Thirty years later Asch commented: "I do think it's a crazy situation that the elimination was so brutal, that of all the writers in Paris then, Hem is holding the world by the handle and everybody else is either obscure or dead. But you can't blame Hem." If Asch felt rejected by the New York publishers, he was pleased by the reception his work received in Germany, where both *The Office* (*Als Die Firma Verkrachte*, 1929) and *Pay Day* (*Der 22. August*, 1930), and quite a few of his short stories continued to be sold until the rise of Hitler, who banned them because Asch was a Jew.

During the thirties Asch resided in various parts of the United States including Hollywood, where he was a scriptwriter for Paramount, and Washington, D.C., where he worked for the educational wing of the Works Progress Administration. In this period, Asch published two more novels: *The Valley* (1935) and *The Road in Search of America* (1937). Both resemble *The Office* in form and style in that they are composed of tales and sketches. The tales in *The Valley* reflect the tragedies of rural men whose soil has become a wasteland much in the same way as the sketches in *The Office* detail the tragedies of their urban counterparts, although the portraits in this later novel are drawn with greater sympathy and insight. These same qualities are carried even further, to the point of sentimentality and melodrama according to some reviewers, in *The Road in Search of America*. Others continued to see the influence of Dos Passos and Sherwood Anderson in this work, which Asch dedicated to his friend Josephine Herbst. Between 1931 and 1939 Asch also reviewed books regularly for the *New Republic*. The approximately three dozen reviews reveal his thorough knowledge of American and European culture and a sympathetic understanding of the human condition.

In 1939 Asch married Caroline Tasher Miles of Philadelphia, and they moved to Saratoga Springs, New York, where they stayed until both enlisted in the armed forces during World War II. After their discharges they moved to Mill Valley, California, where Asch wrote and published short stories and conducted writing workshops for interested students in his home. Most of his stories appeared in the *New Yorker*, but a few were published in such magazines as *Commentary*, *Forum*, and the *Virginia Quarterly Review*. All reveal a keen sense of place and a sensitive awareness of people. He died of lung cancer in 1964. According to Malcolm Cowley, as many as five of Asch's novels remain unpublished, but the location of the manuscripts is unknown.

—*Eva B. Mills*

Periodical Publications:

"The Voice of the Office," *transatlantic review*, 1 (June 1924): 414-420;

"Marc Kranz," *transatlantic review*, 2 (August 1924): 144-153;

"Gertrude Donovan," *transatlantic review*, 2 (December 1924): 608-622; reprinted in *The Best Short Stories of 1925*, ed. Edward O'Brien (Boston: Small, Maynard, 1926).

Papers:

Asch's letters to Malcolm Cowley are with the Cowley papers at the Newberry Library in Chicago.

WAMBLY BALD
(1902-   )

Wambly Bald was well-known on the Left Bank of Paris as the writer of the weekly column "La Vie de Boheme (As Lived on the Left Bank)," which appeared in the Paris *Tribune* (the European edition of the *Chicago Tribune*) from October 1929 to July 1933. A native of Chicago, Bald graduated from the University of Chicago in 1924, and according to an autobiographical note in Peter Neagoe's *Americans Abroad* (1932), he "spent several years knocking about over the country with brief lapses of itinerate journalism." Arriving in France in 1929, Bald took a proofreading job at the Paris *Tribune* and soon began writing his weekly column. Despite repeated offers of promotion to full time on the editorial staff, he chose to remain a proofreader. He returned to the United States in 1934 after the *Tribune* was merged with the Paris *Herald* (the European edition of the *New York Herald*).

Bald's column captured the mood of Left Bank life. The opening paragraph in his first column on 14 October 1929, the only one not bearing his name, sets the tone for all that follow:

> Occasionally the force of the summer tidal wave springs a leak in the Left Bank, and a few are listed among the missing. Perhaps, the influx of summer tourists creates an atmosphere of nostalgia. Some of the Old Faithful leave every summer, but very few fail to return. "They come back" is an axiom in the Latin Quarter. Which reminds us that Jennings Perry, author of *The Windy Hill* is expected back from Tampa, Fla. early in December.

The column goes on to discuss popular British novelist Michael Arlen, the painter Henry C. Lee, and Shorty Lasar, who, according to Bald, introduced baseball to France with the assistance of Jack Dallin. Finally, Bald reveals that Colonel Charles Wellington kept his youthful appearance by "sprinting to the summit of the Jungfrau and down again in something like two hours, fifty-nine minutes."

Bald's 16 December 1929 column reports that F. Scott Fitzgerald has a plan to help needy writers through proceeds from the sale of famous authors' autographs: "His idea is to refer the autograph hunters who are more interested in signatures than literature to the Authors' League who will supply that demand for $2. The money will then go to the fund for indigent authors." Bald goes on to say that Fitzgerald plans to finish his fourth novel the

Wambly Bald in Paris

following spring and that the book "will be an 'atonement' for *This Side of Paradise*" in which "all of the old bromides will prove felicitous instead of superfluous."

Although Bald often wrote about the more illustrious members of Paris society, he was not reluctant to write about the unknown, the new, or the exotic. On 13 January 1931, for example, he described a dance by Helba Huara at Princess Desiree's soiree, and later that year, on 24 November, he wrote about her dancing at Princess Leven's house: "When Helba Huara dances I can hear the pleading of my soul's lost empires and I kneel to the pageant of reconstructed images while my nerves lunch from a cornucopia." On that occasion she was accompanied on the piano by her husband, Gonzalo More. These two performers are major characters in the second volume of Anais Nin's *Diary*, and she transformed them into Zora and Rango, the major characters in her third novel, *The Four-Chambered Heart* (1950).

Bald's most famous column is probably the one of 14 October 1931, a portrait of Henry Miller, his friend and fellow proofreader at the *Tribune*. Miller occasionally wrote Bald's column for him, and he may have written this one. But regardless of who wrote it, the column stands as the first published notice of Miller, and it captures his personality: "Miller is not a son of badinage. He is a legitimate child of Montparnasse, the salt of the Quarter. He represents its classic color that has not faded since Murger and other optimists. A good word is *esprit*." In Miller's first book, *Tropic of Cancer* (1934), the character Van Norden is based on Bald. Others whose names appear frequently in Bald's column are such Left Bank characters as the Montparnasse artists' model Kiki (Alice Prin), James Charters (Jimmie the Barman who worked at a series of Left Bank bars), artist and bar owner Hilaire Hiler, the actress Gwen Le Gallienne, and artist Louise Bryant.

In addition to dealing in literary gossip and giving valuable character sketches, Bald also became involved in literary issues. He was, for example, an early champion of the *New Review*, Samuel Putnam's little magazine, which published Bald's own fiction in three of its five issues. On 4 November 1930, two months before the first number was to appear, Bald wrote: "Shoulder to shoulder, Samuel Putnam, its editor and publisher, and the jovial Voice from Rapallo [Ezra Pound], will march toward an 'honesty' in literature. Together, they will fight the 'corpse-raisers, pretenders and cheap miracle men of the past decades.'" He recommended it again on 23 December, and he wrote a review of the first issue on 27 January 1931. Time and again he commented on that journal, and usually favorably. Alfred Perles has suggested that Bald acted as Putnam's unofficial press agent.

There is an irrepressible spirit about Bald's columns that makes them eminently readable today. According to Samuel Putnam:

> Probably no columnist was ever more avidly read than he. He employed a sphinxlike idiom which was wholly unintelligible to the place de l'Opera tourist and to those aristocratic Americans who dwelt in the neighborhood of the place de l'Etoile, but which we of the Rive Gauche understood perfectly, as a rule, and appreciated to the full. Not always, however. Of necessity, he would often merely hint at things and we would then have to run them down for ourselves. He had a style that was somewhere in between *Gentlemen Prefer Blondes* and *The New Yorker*, with a dash now and again of James Joyce or the Surrealists. It was a truly uncanny amalgam of prose, the like of which was never seen before or since.

Putnam also made the most memorable comment about Bald: he "was in the habit of wandering in and out of the Quarter like a slightly alcoholic ghost, seeing nothing, hearing nothing, and telling all."

In addition to writing about the literary lives of others, both in his *Tribune* column and sometimes for the *Boulevardier*, and publishing his fiction in the *New Review*, Bald contributed to two of the period's important anthologies. In 1931 his story "Flow Gently" appeared in Bob Brown's *Readies for Bob Brown's Machine*. Brown was the inventor of the Reading Machine, which the reader operated by turning a crank so that words on a strip of paper moved past his eyes, and he had asked for contributions as different from conventional prose as sound motion pictures were from stage plays. Bald's Surrealistic story employs visual effects and unconventional syntax to contribute a sense of motion to the tale of a train ride that ends in death:

> Doubleup))) Arms high and Joan quick to shove poor Lefty backwards horror and back drop down ;; ;; :: Joan shoves male clear he drops to hell- -Joan grips iron rail and looks down death below is water flowing gently.

"Dreary," Bald's contribution to Peter Neagoe's *Americans Abroad An Anthology* (1932), first appeared in the August-September-October 1931 issue of the *New Review*. Bald captures the sexual maneuverings of Left Bank cafe life in the story of a discontented lesbian's suicide. This story, as well as Bald's column, suggests that Bald's true gifts were his keen observation of Bohemian Paris and his ability to capture its essence in a unique prose idiom.
—*Benjamin Franklin V*

Periodical Publications:

"From Work in Static," *New Review*, 1 (January-February 1931): 55-56;

"New Garters for Apollo," *New Review*, 1 (May-June-July 1931): 146-148;

"Dreary," *New Review*, 1 (August-September-October 1931); republished in *Americans Abroad An Anthology*, ed. Peter Neagoe (The Hague: Servire, 1932), pp. 7-18.

Other:

"Flow Gently," in *Readies for Bob Brown's Machine*, ed. Bob Brown (Cagnes-sur-Mer: Roving Eye Press, 1931), pp. 60-61.

References:

Alfred Perles, *My Friend Henry Miller* (London: Spearman, 1955), pp. 21-22, 30;

Samuel Putnam, *Paris Was Our Mistress Memoirs of a Lost and Found Generation* (New York: Viking, 1947), pp. 106-107, 150-151.

Djuna Barnes

Louis F. Kannenstine
New York, New York

BIRTH: Cornwall-on-Hudson, New York, 12 June 1892, to Elizabeth Chappell and Henry Budington Barnes (her father later changed his name to Wald Barnes).

SELECTED BOOKS: *The Book of Repulsive Women 8 Rhythms and 5 Drawings* (New York: Bruno Chap Books, 1915);
A Book (New York: Boni & Liveright, 1923; London: Faber & Faber, 1958);
Ladies Almanack (Paris: Privately printed, 1928; New York: Harper & Row, 1972);
Ryder (New York: Liveright, 1928);
A Night Among Horses (New York: Liveright, 1929);
Nightwood (London: Faber & Faber, 1936; New York: Harcourt, Brace, 1937);
The Antiphon (New York: Farrar, Straus & Cudahy, 1958; London: Faber & Faber, 1958);
Spillway (London: Faber & Faber, 1962; New York: Harper & Row, 1972);
Selected Works of Djuna Barnes Spillway / The Antiphon / Nightwood (New York: Farrar, Straus & Cudahy, 1962).

Djuna Barnes is known primarily for her poetic novel *Nightwood*, first published in England in 1936. Few works so intensely distill the anguish of the American abroad in Paris in the twenties and thirties, cut off from his native roots in a culture that has lost its own sense of history and tradition. *Nightwood* also appears to stand as an exceptional summation of the literary climate of the period, a high point in its formal and stylistic experimentation. Perhaps because of its singular reputation, many readers think of Barnes as a "one-book" novelist.

Her literary career, however, has been highly prismatic. She has been at various times a novelist

Djuna Barnes in Paris, 1928

and short story writer, a poet, a playwright, a journalist and theatrical columnist, as well as a portrait painter and illustrator of her own books. This diversity has given her work a unique quality in twentieth-century literature.

Once regarded as an obscure avant-garde writer, Barnes has recently been reevaluated as one of the last classicists whose work, like that of James Joyce and T. S. Eliot which had strongly influenced her, sustains the finest literary traditions of our culture. Her effect upon later generations of experimental writers now appears to be significant. Anaïs Nin, for instance, has repeatedly claimed that her formative roots are in the work of Djuna Barnes, while John Hawkes has noted the impact of her "extreme fictive detachment," her "pure and immoral" creation, upon his own work.

Barnes's literary reputation must ultimately rest upon a relatively small body of work. Since the early thirties, she has become reclusive, "a form of Trappist" by her own definition, and has chosen to publish infrequently. As she is rarely accessible to interviewers and critics, many details of her life and career remain obscure.

In her early years, however, Barnes was publicly active. Following her private education at home, largely by her father and paternal grandmother, the Barnes family moved from Cornwall-on-Hudson to Long Island. At the age of twenty, Barnes was in New York City studying art at Pratt Institute and the Art Students League. In 1913, she began to contribute illustrated feature articles and stories to the *Brooklyn Eagle*, starting a career in magazine and newspaper journalism which would continue, off and on, into the early thirties.

It was apparently Barnes's primary ambition at this early time to become a poet. Her first poems were published in 1911 in *Harper's Weekly*. Then in 1915, Guido Bruno, who had exhibited her Beardsleyesque drawings and pastels in his Greenwich Village garret, published her first collection, a slim illustrated chapbook called *The Book of Repulsive Women*. This volume not only mirrored the fin de siecle decadence characteristic of Village bohemianism of the period, but also showed a fascination with the grotesque which would color much of the author's later work.

It was in this decade that Barnes began to be known as a playwright as well. Three of her one-act plays were staged at the Provincetown Playhouse in 1919 and 1920, while others frequently appeared along with numerous poems and stories in many of the notable literary and popular magazines of the day, the *Little Review* and the *Dial* on the one hand, *Charm* and *Smart Set* on the other.

Barnes arrived in Paris in the early twenties, where, shortly after *Ulysses* appeared in 1922, she had the occasion to interview James Joyce for *Vanity Fair*. The effect of Joyce's work on her would become evident later in her first novel, *Ryder* (1928). At the time, however, she is supposed to have said, "I shall never write another line. . . . Who has the nerve to after that?" Yet in 1923, *A Book* was published, her first collection consisting of three one-act plays, twelve short stories, eleven lyrical poems, and six

drawings, uncaptioned line portraits of women remarkably evocative of those portrayed in her prose and verse.

The stories were all of this work that Barnes eventually cared to preserve. In 1929 *A Book* was republished as *A Night Among the Horses*; this collection omitted only the illustrations from the previous volume and included three new stories. And ten of the same stories were collected again in further revised form in *Spillway* (1962). The Paris experience is the immediate inspiration for several of these stories. The young girls in "Cassation" and "The Grande Malade," for instance, were modeled upon two precocious sisters from Holland, Bronja and Tylia, familiar figures in the Parisian cafe scene of the twenties. And the latter of these stories is said to be based upon the death of the poet Raymond Radiguet at the age of twenty.

The young girls, like all of the characters in these stories, are rootless, estranged from society and themselves. At home nowhere, they can do nothing but move on in the vacuum of contemporary civilization. In essence, they are representative victims of the "internationalism" of the twenties. The milieu of the short story "Spillway" is a twentieth-century purgatory in which all historical and spiritual connections have been severed, leaving only a terrible restlessness. The groom in "A Night Among the Horses," for example, finds himself to be a part of neither the natural world of his past nor the aristocratic world of his cruel lover-mistress. He is caught in the middle, reduced to "a *thing*, half standing, half crouching, like those figures under the roofs of historic buildings, the halt position of the damned." In all of Barnes's work, damnation is the terrible state of perpetual suspension between the unattainable dualities of existence.

The novel *Ryder* (1928) sustains this theme but involves a new experiment in style. Whereas the prose of the stories is economic and tersely poetic, that of *Ryder* is lavishly ornamented and copious. Ostensibly a family chronicle, the novel tells the story of several generations of Ryders and particularly Wendell, whose polygamous and freethinking ways bring pain and submission upon the women in his life. Its fifty chapters bring into play nearly every literary mode or tradition since the holy scriptures, creating the impression of an enormous stylistic display case. The influence of Joyce's experiments with language and craft are apparent here. Also, chronological plot development is deliberately ignored, leaving many chapters to stand as individual vignettes playing upon archaic modes of narrative. In the end, the author's parodic treatment of epic, fable, and scripture only points up the absurdity of modern man's attempt to resuscitate them. In Barnes's world, the convictions and patterns of existence once available in church and society have vanished, leaving a waste land not unlike T. S. Eliot's.

Ladies Almanack is equally satirical in concept but much smaller in scope. While *Ryder* became a brief bestseller in America, *Ladies Almanack* was privately printed in a limited edition in 1928. Although Edward Titus originally planned to publish the book and printed an announcement which bore a facsimile of the title page with his Black Manikin imprint on it, he and Barnes quarreled over money, and he withdrew his support. Robert McAlmon paid the printing costs, and the book appeared with the lines "EDWARD W. TITUS, 4 RUE DELAMBRE / at the sign of the Black Manikin" crossed out in some copies. The first American trade edition did not appear until 1972. In contrast to *Ryder*'s stylistic medley, a fairly uniform Elizabethan style prevails here, accompanied by illustrations in the manner of ancient chapbooks and broadsheets. *Ladies Almanack* concerns a society of lesbians, a cultural aristocracy of women with its rituals and credos, its chic and erotic intrigues. Virtually plotless, the narrative records the mock sainthood of its heroine, Evangeline Musset, throughout the twelve months of the almanack year. Sometimes the book reads as a Sapphic manifesto, arguing the prerogatives of women in the social, patriarchal world from which they are excluded. At other times it appears to delight in verbal wit and frivolity for their own sake. Amid much laughter, however, there is lamentation, for the condition of these women is the human condition of "Loneliness estranged."

Dame Musset's circle of women has been identified as a satirical portrait of Natalie Clifford Barney's celebrated salon in the rue Jacob. Djuna Barnes had become acquainted with this noteworthy circle of intellectual lesbians, with its crusaders and aesthetes alike. A chapter in Barney's *Aventures de l'esprit* (1929), in fact, first introduced Barnes's work to a French audience. The parody is loose, however, and far from malicious. The primary intention of *Ladies Almanack* is to confront the anomaly of sexual identity, a theme which recurs in the major novel *Nightwood*.

Implicit in *Ryder* and *Ladies Almanack* is the vision of a lost Eden and a confused present. Barnes seems to presume an hermaphroditic Adam before "the Earth sucked down her Generations." Since the sunderance of Eve, the pain in the world has been

A page from Ladies Almanack

rooted in sexual difference. Despite the irrevocable separation of the sexes, all human beings necessarily partake of androgyny. Thus Wendell Ryder is described as "much mixed . . . of woman and man" despite his aggressive patriarchal role. And the ladies of the almanack, not wholly woman but mixed of man, eternally pitted against the other sex, suffer the enigma of being neither one thing entirely nor the other. In the broadest sense, this paradox becomes what Doctor O'Connor in *Nightwood* calls the "middle condition."

Nightwood, first published in England in 1936, is generally considered to be Djuna Barnes's masterpiece. Certainly it exceeds all previous work in organizational perfection, intensity of conception, and power of phrasing. It also stands as the author's major "Paris novel," summing up the residual despair of the expatriate experience.

It would be more appropriate to speak of *Nightwood*'s situation than its plot. What actually "happens" in the book can be summarized briefly. The narrative concerns the effect of a woman, Robin Vote, upon the lives of four people who meet in Paris in the twenties. After marrying Felix Volkbein, a Baron with a falsified pedigree, and bearing his child, Robin leaves him for Nora Flood, an American journalist in Europe. Nora eventually loses Robin to the despicable lesbian, Jenny

Petherbridge. Abandoned, Nora turns to Matthew O'Connor in her agony. O'Connor's failure to mitigate her suffering in his role of father-confessor brings about his own spiritual collapse. Felix reappears briefly, still cast adrift but devoted to the spiritual custody of his pathetic son. At the end of the novel, Robin returns to confront Nora at a chapel on her American estate, an inarticulate encounter that only amplifies their estrangement.

Nightwood, like Barnes's novels of 1928, is a revolt against traditional linear plot development in time. It is divided into eight sections which are discontinuous in time and place, each seeming to initiate a new movement. The novel begins deceptively enough in historical time with Felix's birth in 1880 and the account of his ancestry. Exact chronology ends, however, in 1920 with his arrival in Paris and becomes progressively more difficult to determine as the novel moves ahead. A sense of clock time is lost altogether when the characters become involved in the realm of night and sleeping where rational perceptions end and timelessness begins.

The concern with dreams and the racial unconscious is a new element in Barnes's work. It appears to reflect the timely investigations into the Jungian-inspired subject in the pages of Eugene Jolas's magazine, *transition*, to which she herself had contributed and in which James Joyce's *Work in Progress* was appearing. An interest in those states of mind where the rigid dualisms of logic and arbitrary distinctions of the waking mind (such as human time) dissolved, was inevitable for an author with a view of life as being essentially tentative and unstable.

The section of the novel in which Robin Vote first appears is titled "La Somnambule," and indeed her movement throughout the novel and through others' lives is unvaryingly somnambulistic and elusive. Paradoxically, there is something tangibly unreal about Robin. She is described as living in two worlds, as a girl who resembles a boy, as "newly ancient," as innocent and depraved, and metaphorically as a beast turning human. Her allure is in her unresolved condition, her incessant act of becoming. It is finally the mystery and flux in Robin that irresistibly fascinates others.

Felix's attraction to Robin is understandable. He too "seems to be everywhere from nowhere," a Wandering Jew figure, forever homeless. He pays incessant homage to nobility, yet his title is a sham. Matthew O'Connor recognizes that there is something both missing and whole about him. Thus he complements Robin in his unstable being. Nora's life is a wandering, too. Guided by her Puritan ethic,

her pursuit of Robin is a quest for stability. Drawn to perversity and abandoned, Nora sinks into the world of sleep and the unconscious.

Matthew O'Connor is like Robin in being a paradox on all levels, an embodiment of the mystery of intermediate being. This same character had appeared briefly in *Ryder*, but in *Nightwood* he is given the central choral and prophetic role. O'Connor was fashioned by Barnes after an actual Irish doctor from San Francisco named Dan Mahoney, a well-known figure of the period. John Glassco has described Mahoney in his *Memoirs of Montparnasse* (1970) as "the most quoted homosexual in Paris, a man who combined the professions of pathic, abortionist, professional boxer and quasi-confessor to literary women." It would seem that Barnes went beyond fact only in the profundity with which she endowed the doctor.

O'Connor articulates a central theme of *Nightwood*: "Man was born damned and innocent from the start, and wretchedly—as he must—on these two themes—whistles his tune." In his oracular role, O'Connor is a figure similar to the immortal and androgynous prophet Tiresias in Eliot's *The Waste Land*. His brilliant, torrential, epigrammatic harangues dominate much of the novel, commenting upon and illuminating the predicament of the participants, which is his own as well. He too is caught in the "middle condition," between waking and dreaming, comic and tragic perception, good and evil, damnation and grace, and ultimately life and death.

Nightwood's style follows from the thematic breakdown of rigid distinctions. Early in the novel the forms of fiction begin to dissolve and the sensations commonly aroused by a poem, or a painting, or a drama, or a musical composition come into play. Various critics such as Joseph Frank and Wallace Fowlie have demonstrated that *Nightwood*'s structure is based upon poetic association, circular design or rococo arabesque patterns, dramatic structure, or musical configurations such as the fugue. All are correct: all of these function simultaneously. The novel is essentially transgeneric.

This work seems to relate to and derive inspiration from diverse literary types and periods as well. Its language and style have been related to the Old Testament, the Elizabethan and Jacobean periods, the metaphysical poets, early eighteenth-century novels, the nineteenth-century fin de siecle movement, Symbolism, and Surrealism. Transcending style and period as well as artistic genre, the novel becomes a kind of echo chamber, wherein faint and distant echoes of literary voices merge simultaneously and reverberate continuously. Ultimately, *Nightwood* is both rooted in and transcendent of the decade in which it was written.

In his introduction to the Americn edition of *Nightwood*, T. S. Eliot asserted that its appeal would be primarily to readers of poetry. Its brilliance of language and illuminating imagery suggest the truth of Eliot's statement, but its unique craft and complex view of history and the human condition should not be overlooked by any reader seeking the fullest sort of literary experience.

Barnes returned to New York by way of London in 1940, years before the 1958 appearance of *The Antiphon*. (An extensively revised version appeared in *Selected Works* in 1962.) This verse play begins at the end of the thirties when thousands were taking flight from the approach of war. Like T. S. Eliot's *The Family Reunion*, which may have inspired it, *The Antiphon* involves a return to an ancestral home and becomes a drama of sin and attempted expiation that reaches into the past. The action concerns the failed attempt at reconciliation between mother and daughter, estranged yet covictims of a cruel and sexually aggressive father. Like *Nightwood*, *The Antiphon* creates a state of seeming timelessness in which dualisms vanish and everything is interrelated and significant. Mother and daughter at least momentarily find their very strength in their mutual submission; united, they are able to draw a line at the threshold of masculine dominion. Because they are united, however, the fear of loss of identity asserts itself and hastens the final tragedy.

The Antiphon is Djuna Barnes's most complex work. Its blank verse, with its archaisms, obscure allusions, compact syntax, and compound metaphors, has bewildered some readers. As in all of her major work, an oblique approach to narration is taken and the themes are implied rather than explicitly stated. The response of critics to *The Antiphon* was typical of that to all Barnes's work. A few were quick to recognize the merits of each major work when it appeared, but a greater number were perplexed and prompted to dismiss her writing on the grounds of its obscurity. As a result, each book has suffered its measure of neglect. *Nightwood*, however, has remained steadily in print, attracting new readers and increasing scholarly interest.

There is no doubt that Djuna Barnes's most productive period was during the twenties and thirties. Despite the brilliance and intrinsic distinction of *The Antiphon*, *Nightwood* remains her single finest achievement and one of the representative books of the era. In recent years Djuna Barnes has remained silent, living in New York City and writing only poetry. Much of this work has yet to be published.

Periodical Publications:

"James Joyce," *Vanity Fair*, 18 (April 1922): 65;

"Vagaries Malicieux," *Double Dealer*, 3, no. 17 (May 1922): 249-260;

"Transfiguration," *London Bulletin*, first series, no. 3 (June 1938): 2;

"Lament for the Left Bank," *Town and Country*, 94 (December 1941): 92, 136-138, 148.

Bibliography:

Douglas Messerli, *Djuna Barnes: A Bibliography* (Rhinebeck, N.Y.: David Lewis, 1975).

References:

Kenneth Burke, "Version, Con-, Per-, and In-: Thoughts on Djuna Barnes' Novel, *Nightwood*," *Southern Review*, 2 (1966-1967): 329-346;

Suzanne C. Ferguson, "Djuna Barnes's Short Stories: An Estrangement of the Heart," *Southern Review*, 5 (January 1969): 26-41;

Wallace Fowlie, *Love in Literature: Studies in Symbolic Expression* (Bloomington: Indiana University Press / Midland Books, 1965);

Joseph Frank, *The Widening Gyre: Crisis and Mastery in Modern Literature* (New Brunswick, N.J.: Rutgers University Press, 1963);

Louis F. Kannenstine, *The Art of Djuna Barnes: Duality and Damnation* (New York: New York University Press, 1977);

James B. Scott, *Djuna Barnes* (Boston: Twayne, 1976);

Ulrich Weisstein, "Beast, Doll, and Woman: Djuna Barnes' Human Bestiary," *Renascence*, 15 (1962): 3-11;

Alan Williamson, "The Divided Image: The Quest for Identity in the Works of Djuna Barnes," *Critique: Studies in Modern Fiction*, 7 (Spring 1964): 58-74.

Papers:

Djuna Barnes's papers are in the McKeldin Library, University of Maryland.

Natalie Barney

George Wickes
University of Oregon

BIRTH: Dayton, Ohio, 31 October 1876, to Alice Pike and Albert Clifford Barney.

DEATH: Paris, France, 2 February 1972.

SELECTED BOOKS: *Quelques Portraits—Sonnets de Femmes* (Paris: Ollendorf, 1900);
Cinq petits Dialogues grecs (Paris: La Plume, 1901);
Actes et entr'actes (Paris: Sansot, 1910);
Pensees d'une Amazone (Paris: Emile Paul, 1920);
Aventures de l'esprit (Paris: Emile Paul, 1929);
Nouvelles Pensees de l'Amazone (Paris: Mercure de France, 1939);
Souvenirs indiscrets (Paris: Flammarion, 1960);
Traits et portraits (Paris: Mercure de France, 1963);
Selected Writings, edited with an introduction by Miron Grindea (London: Adam, 1963).

Natalie Clifford Barney, who lived most of her long life in Paris, was a legendary figure in France but almost completely unknown in her native land. She is the *Amazone* to whom Remy de Gourmont addressed his *Lettres a l'Amazone* (1914); she figures as a character in half-a-dozen works of fiction; and her name appears in scores of memoirs of the period ranging from the *belle epoque* almost to the present day. For sixty years her house at 20, rue Jacob was a Paris landmark, the setting of an international salon frequented by many of the leading writers and intellectuals of the century. Her own writings, chiefly in French, included verse, drama, fiction, essays, and epigrams, spanning the period from 1900 to 1963. But her reputation is due even more to the emancipated ideas by which she lived and to the personal magnetism which she exercised in her many love affairs. She was unquestionably the most candid, the most daring, and the most famous lesbian of her time.

Apart from her lesbianism, she was like a character out of Henry James, an attractive American heiress who might have married into the nobility of the Old World. She was in fact quite willing to be courted by several titled French and English men, partly to placate her father, who was anxious to see her married, but also because she enjoyed these flirtations and the cosmopolitan social life. Actually she belonged more to the world of Proust than to that of James, so much so that Proust once sought her out as a source of information.

Natalie Barney

Unlike most of the Americans who came to Paris, Natalie Barney was completely at home with the French language and temperament. In time she developed a wide acquaintance among French writers and established her own special place on the Paris literary scene. In was an altogether different place from the cafes of Montparnasse favored by other Americans. Remy de Gourmont's English translator, Richard Aldington, remarked: "I suppose Miss Barney has at some time been in a cafe, but she is not the kind of person you would think of inviting to such a place. Her world was that meeting place of society and literature which is better understood and organized in Paris than anywhere." Her salon in the heart of the Faubourg Saint-Germain became an institution, reaching its heyday in the twenties and thirties, when at one time or another such writers as Andre Gide, Jean Cocteau, Colette, Paul Valery,

Natalie Barney

Rainier Maria Rilke, Gabriele D'Annunzio, T. S. Eliot, Ezra Pound, Ford Madox Ford, James Joyce, Ernest Hemingway, F. Scott Fitzgerald, and Gertrude Stein could be found, and where some of them appeared quite regularly. Most of the Americans who came to Paris seldom or never met French writers. At Barney's Fridays they were offered a rare opportunity to meet the French writers who were the habitues of her salon. It was her proud boast that this was an *international* literary salon, and she did everything she could to bring the writers of her two countries together.

To her younger compatriots Natalie Barney had the look and demeanor of a wealthy, respectable society matron like Edith Wharton. But if they listened, they might be surprised by her witty and unconventional remarks, and if they knew something about her private life, they understood why Edith Wharton would never be seen at 20, rue Jacob. In her later years Natalie Barney bore an increasing resemblance to Queen Victoria, not only in her physical appearance but in her sense of decorum and in the dowdiness of her setting. Yet almost to the end of her days she continued to have love affairs and remained anything but Victorian in her thinking. Though born in the middle of Victoria's reign, she had decided early in life to live as she pleased, regardless of the prohibitions and conventions of her day, and though no rebel, she was extremely strong-willed and independent. In this she resembled her lively and talented mother, Alice Pike Barney, while her sister Laura took after their stuffy father, Albert Clifford Barney.

Both parents had inherited considerable wealth, which left them free to lead a fashionable social life, chiefly in Cincinnati during Barney's first ten years, then in Washington, D.C., with summers in Bar Harbor and occasional visits to Europe. The two girls received their first education from a French governess and their first regular schooling at a boarding school in Fontainebleau for eighteen months, while their mother studied painting in Paris. Thus before she entered her teens, Barney became completely bilingual, able to express herself with equal ease in either language. Later she had German-speaking governesses, and after completing her formal education at Miss Ely's School for Girls in New York, she went on a European tour and spent seven months in Germany, taking lessons in fencing, dancing, and the violin (which she played quite proficiently). Thus by the age of eighteen she had finished a proper young lady's education.

During the next few years, the Barney girls lived in Paris off and on with their mother while she

Natalie Barney, ca. 1900

studied painting there—with Whistler, among other masters. Alice Pike Barney became quite an accomplished painter and a generous patroness of the arts; she also became increasingly indifferent to social propriety. As Natalie Barney grew older, she was more and more inclined to model her life after her mother's example. She had always loved this warm, outgoing mother, and in her old age she wrote a Proustian reminiscence of the anxious nights she spent as a little girl waiting for her mother to come home and kiss her goodnight. Her father, on the other hand, appears to have represented the repressive influence of social convention, until his early death in 1902 left her independently wealthy and free to live as she wished. She chose to spend the rest of her life in Paris, which she pronounced the only city where one could live and express oneself as one pleased.

But long before her father's death Natalie Barney was already emancipated and, despite his efforts to make her behave, already quite notorious. In 1901 her private life became very public when one of the great courtesans of the day, Liane de Pougy, published a thinly disguised autobiographical novel entitled *Idylle saphique*. The Sapphic idyll begins with the seduction of this worldly courtesan by a pretty young American girl named Flossie, who despite her youth is already a bold and experienced seductress of women. Like the other novelists who were to write about this female Don Juan, Liane de Pougy scarcely found it necessary to fictionalize. A similar character appears briefly as Miss Flossie in Colette's *Claudine s'en va* (1903), at a time when Colette knew Natalie Barney chiefly by reputation. A few years later they were to become good friends, and their friendship was to endure for life.

A third novel, *Une Femme m'apparut* (1904), describes another love affair, the passion of the author for the beautiful but cold Lorely. The author, Renee Vivien, though born of Anglo-American parents, had chosen to live in Paris and to write in French. She and Barney not only fell in love but studied French prosody and Greek together, in order to translate Sappho into French verse. In imitation of Sappho they talked of forming a circle of women poets and living on Lesbos. Renee Vivien, who took everything more seriously, went on to make a name for herself as a poet but wasted away to an early death, dying, many said, of unrequited love. Actually, though neither could forget the other, their love affair had ended some years earlier, and the rumors about the death of this pathetic, doomed figure merely show the force of Natalie Barney's legend.

As a writer herself, she was facile but undisciplined. She did not really care enough to dedicate herself to writing. Instead she believed in making her life a work of art and exercising her talents mainly to further personal ends. Her writings were the by-products of her life: her poems addressed to the women she loved, her dialogues expressing her Sapphic ideals, her plays designed as entertainments to be performed among friends. All of her early work is amateurish, interesting mainly for the feminist principles it occasionally articulates. Yet she was interested in writers and went out of her way to cultivate their acquaintance.

Her most famous conquest was not a woman but an old man who was so ugly that he came out only at night. Remy de Gourmont was one of the leading French men of letters of his time, but a disfiguring disease, lupus, had made him completely antisocial. Yet she sought him out and exercised all her charms to win him, succeeding so well that he fell in love with her—platonically of course—and for the remaining five years of his life wrote her fervent letters. These were published posthumously as *Lettres intimes a l'Amazone* (1926). The previously published *Lettres a l'Amazone* (1914) was a collection of essays based on their conversations although the essays were addressed to Barney as letters and were submitted for her approval. *Lettres a l'Amazone* appeared regularly in the influential literary fortnightly *Mercure de France* during 1912-1913, making Barney a famous literary personage almost overnight.

In 1909 she had moved to the house in the rue Jacob, where she was to launch her salon. Her friendship with Gourmont began in 1910. When World War I broke out in 1914, her family urged her to return to America, but she discovered that she could not bear to leave her adopted country for one which was no longer home. So she remained in Paris, even while it was being bombarded, ignoring the war as much as possible and even going so far as to organize pacifist meetings. *Pensees d'une Amazone* (1920) includes a section that might be read as her wartime notebook, with precisely rendered scenes of wartime France. The book also reflects her complete skepticism about politics and strategy, her refusal to succumb to propaganda or hysteria or to surrender everything she valued to a questionable military necessity. All through the war she continued to receive guests in her salon, among them the American poet Alan Seeger, just before he was killed in action in 1916, and the French writer Henri Barbusse, back from the trench warfare described in his bitter anti-war novel, *Le Feu* (1917). Several of her friends later remembered with gratitude those moments of respite from the anguish and anxiety outside. From their testimonials it could be argued that she kept alive the civilized values for which the war was supposed to be fought.

When the war was over, Natalie Barney and her salon had a clearly defined place in French literary life. It was then especially that she undertook to bring French and American writers together. But most of the young Americans who congregated in Paris in the twenties regarded the salon and its hostess as archaic survivals from another age, and few of them came more than once or twice. She appealed more to writers of a slightly older generation, such as T. S. Eliot and Ezra Pound, both of whom esteemed her as the friend of Remy de

Gourmont. With Pound she formed a lasting friendship and collaborated in his patronage of the arts, notably in a scheme called "Bel Esprit," whose purpose was to subsidize poets such as Eliot and Valery so that they could devote all their time to writing. Pound also prevailed upon her to support the young American composer George Antheil financially and otherwise, and thus it happened that Antheil premiered some of his loud experimental pieces in the normally staid salon.

As a rule the salon was merely a weekly gathering of invited guests and habitues who had a standing invitation. Whenever possible a new literary lion was introduced, and at times there was a planned program of poetry readings, dramatic recitation, or music. In 1927 there was a concerted effort to organize a series of meetings featuring women writers. This "Academie des Femmes" was evidently intended as a counterpart, perhaps even as a reproach, to the venerable and exclusively masculine Academie Francaise. Gertrude Stein was celebrated in one of these special programs, with an opening presentation by Mina Loy, readings from Stein's work, and a performance of several songs by Virgil Thomson composed on texts by Stein. To introduce the author's work to a predominantly French audience, Barney had translated passages from *The Making of Americans* (1925), no easy task. Clearly she had made a great effort to entice Stein into her salon.

Surprisingly enough, the friendship between the two literary Amazons did not begin until 1926, although both must have known about each other for many years and had many acquaintances in common. But they moved in different circles, and perhaps Stein was wary of lesbian notoriety or afraid of becoming a tame lion in a salon. Natalie Barney always took pains to cultivate people she wanted to know, and eventually she overcame Stein's reluctance. Gradually they became good friends, visiting back and forth and sharing friends they both appreciated: Ford Madox Ford, Carl Van Vechten, Sherwood Anderson, Thornton Wilder, Edith Sitwell, Romaine Brooks, the duchess de Clermont-Tonnerre, and Dolly Wilde. The last three were among Natalie Barney's lovers who remained her lifelong friends. Passion was brief, but friendship endured, especially with women of intelligence and character like these and other women who had not been her lovers, such as Gertrude Stein and Alice B. Toklas. Paradoxically she was as constant in friendship as she was inconstant in love and demonstrated throughout life a genius for friendship.

Not that she abandoned her love affairs or became more discreet as she grew older. *Pensees d'une Amazone* published for all the world to read her views on Sapphic love, and she came to be regarded as *"l'imperatrice des lesbiennes."* Two novels of the twenties clearly portray her in that role, one solemnly, the other satirically. Radclyffe Hall's *The Well of Loneliness* (1928) was one of the most controversial novels of its day, banned in England because its subject was taboo. In hopes of appeasing the censors, the author presented homosexuality as an abnormal state doomed to ostracism, anguish, and guilt. Yet in the scarcely fictionalized figure of Valerie Seymour she presents a noble portrait of one who not only rises above this tragic fate but inspires courage and serenity in others by her very presence. Djuna Barnes's *Ladies Almanack* (1928) deals with the same subject, but the treatment is altogether different. This satiric spoof pokes good-natured fun at some of the better-known lesbians of Paris, gathered around a heroine named Evangeline Musset. It is easy to imagine that much of the bawdy humor was bandied about in Natalie Barney's circle, which included Djuna Barnes, Janet Flanner, Solita Solano, Esther Murphy (the sister of Gerald Murphy), and others caricatured in the book.

Two of Natalie Barney's books of the twenties represent an improvement over her earlier work, if only because they coincide more closely with her particular bent. She took no more pains with her writing than before, prompting Ezra Pound to comment in print that she had published "with complete mental laziness a book of unfinished sentences and broken paragraphs, which is, on the whole, readable and is interesting as documentary evidence of a specimen of liberation." *Pensees d'une Amazone* is a collection of observations and epigrams, many of them no doubt written down after they occurred to her in conversation. Her opinions were liberated, as Pound pointed out, but the wit and quick intelligence with which she spoke were less impressive in print than on the spur of the moment. Unquestionably her greatest natural talent was for epigram, but she could not be bothered to polish and improve her witty remarks as the great epigrammatists have done. Pound was her schoolmaster in English verse, and with his editorial assistance some of her poems appeared in little magazines, but he was all too well acquainted with her indolent writing habits.

Most readable of all her writings are the three volumes of memoirs that document her literary friendships. The first of these, *Aventures de l'esprit* (1929), chronicles her encounters with writers,

Natalie Barney and Romaine Brooks, ca. 1915

beginning in infancy, when she literally ran into Oscar Wilde in a hotel lobby, and dealing with the writers she knew from her literary apprenticeship in Paris through the first twenty years of her salon: Pierre Louys, Anatole France, Gourmont, Proust, Rilke, D'Annunzio, Valery, Max Jacob, and a few others. A second section of the book gives some idea of the proceedings of the "Academie des Femmes," with brief descriptions that evidently served as introductory remarks for each speaker when these women writers read from their works.

Of all her books this was the one that was most widely read. But a later volume of memoirs, *Souvenirs indiscrets* (1960), deserves to be better known, for it succeeds best in combining her personal and literary lives and is the closest thing to autobiography that she ever published. After all, she was more important as a literary legend and as a friend of writers than as a writer herself. In this book she serves as an important witness of the literary history of her time in the intimate sketches of writers who played major roles in her life and legend: Renee

Vivien, Remy de Gourmont, the duchess de Clermont-Tonnerre, Colette, and Lucie Delarue-Mardrus, who had written about Natalie Barney—passionately in love poetry, critically in a novel, and affectionately in her memoirs. *Souvenirs indiscrets* gives a much more intimate view of these writers than of those who appeared in her final book, *Traits et portraits* (1963): Bernard Berenson, Gertrude Stein, D'Annunzio, Rabindranath Tagore, Jacob, Cocteau, and Gide. By then Natalie Barney was in her eighty-seventh year and, having outlived her era and all of these contemporaries, felt free to write about them. But most of the memories belong to the period between the wars and even earlier.

Though she lived on to an extraordinary old age and though she revived the salon after World War II, it was clearly an anachronism during the grim postwar years when the existentialists gathered around the corner at Saint-Germain-des-Pres, to say nothing of the days of May 1968 when students rioted in the neighborhood. World War II had marked the end of an era for Natalie Barney, as it had for the

American expatriates who had come to her salon or shunned it. When war broke out in 1939, she decided once again not to return to America. She would leave Paris for Florence and miss her nightly walks with Gertrude Stein, who had now become a near neighbor and close friend. But they had weathered one war and would stay through another, keeping in touch and comforting each other. For they were a special breed of Americans, the Americans of Europe. Even in the darkest days, when it seemed the war would never end, she wrote to Stein about *Paris France* (1940) and her own books, all safely preserved in the Bibliotheque Nationale as a lasting record of their life in Paris.

References:

Jean Chalon, *Portrait d'une seductrice* (Paris: Stock, 1976);

Paul Lorenz, *Sapho 1900: Renee Vivien* (Paris: Julliard, 1977);

Liane de Pougy, *Mes Cahiers bleus* (Paris: Plon, 1977);

Meryle Secrest, *Between Me and Life: A Biography of Romaine Brooks* (Garden City: Doubleday, 1974);

Renee Vivien, *A Woman Appeared to Me*, trans. Jeannette H. Foster with an introduction by Gayle Rubin (Reno, Nev.: Naiad Press, 1976);

George Wickes, *The Amazon of Letters: The Life and Loves of Natalie Barney* (New York: Putnam's, 1976).

Papers:

Natalie Barney's papers, consisting mostly of letters written to her, are at the Fonds Litteraire Jacques Doucet in Paris, which has published a catalogue, *Autour de Natalie Clifford Barney* (1976), compiled by Francois Chapon, Nicole Prevot, and Richard Sieburth. Some of her letters and other manuscript materials are in the Beinecke Rare Book and Manuscript Library at Yale University.

Sylvia Beach

Noel Riley Fitch
Point Loma College

BIRTH: Baltimore, Maryland, 14 March 1887, to Eleanor Orbison and Sylvester Woodbridge Beach.

AWARDS: French Legion of Honor, 1938; Denyse Clairouin Award, 1950; Honorary Doctor of Letters, University of Buffalo, 1959.

DEATH: Paris, France, 6 October 1962.

SELECTED BOOKS: *Catalogue of a Collection Containing Manuscripts and Rare Editions of James Joyce, Etc.* (Paris: Shakespeare and Company, 1935);

Shakespeare and Company (New York: Harcourt, Brace, 1959; London: Faber & Faber, 1960).

The fame of Sylvia Beach lies primarily in her bookshop and lending library, Shakespeare and Company, which she ran in Paris from 1919 through 1941. Most of the writers in this volume, and scores more, visited this bank, clubhouse, library, post office, publishing house, and center for Franco-Anglo-American literary exchange. The main single achievement of the bookshop was its publication in 1922 of the first complete edition of James Joyce's *Ulysses*. Beach remained Joyce's publisher for a decade. During this decade she published nine of the first eleven editions of *Ulysses*, as well as Joyce's *Pomes Penyeach* (1927) and *Our Exagmination Round His Factification for Incamination of Work in Progress* (1929).

Sylvia (Nancy) Woodbridge Beach was a product of, yet a rebel against, her Victorian upbringing. She was the second of three daughters born to Eleanor Orbison, the daughter of missionaries in India, and to Sylvester Woodbridge Beach, eighth of nine generations of Presbyterian ministers. Although poor health often kept Beach out of the Bridgeton, New Jersey, schools, she loved books and played the neighborhood wit. When Beach was fifteen, soon after she had changed her name from

Nancy to Sylvia, she went to Paris with her parents and two sisters, Holly and Eleanor (later Cyprian). From 1902 to 1905 the Reverend Mr. Beach served as associate pastor of the American Church of Paris, with special service to the students of the Left Bank. During these years, the family—especially Mrs. Beach, a painter and musician—fell in love with Paris. The children attended the Sunday evening church gatherings for students, where artists such as Pablo Casals performed.

Aside from the Bridgeton public schools, which she attended infrequently, Beach's only other formal education was a brief study at a private school in Switzerland, where she learned a little French grammar. Chafing at the reformatory-like regimen and ill with the migraine headaches which always plagued her, she returned to live at Bourre outside Paris with her friend Carlotta Briggs. Books, travel, the study of languages, and an insatiable curiosity about the world were the sources of her education. Like Ernest Hemingway, she observed, she was self-educated.

The family moved permanently to Princeton, New Jersey, in 1905, where Beach's father was pastor to a Presbyterian congregation that included the Woodrow Wilsons and the Grover Clevelands. The Beach women frequently traveled from Princeton to Europe. Cyprian Beach studied first opera and then acting in Paris from 1911 through 1922, where she became a well-known French movie actress. Holly Beach worked for the International Red Cross in Paris, Belgrade, and Florence from 1917 to 1922. And Sylvia Beach spent a year in Florence in 1907-1908, returned to Florence and Paris in 1911-1912, and lived in Spain from 1914 through 1916. Mrs. Beach, until her death in 1927, spent the major part of every year with her daughters in Europe and later in Pasadena, California, where Holly and Cyprian lived upon returning to the United States.

In midsummer of 1916 Sylvia Beach moved from Madrid to Paris, where she lived for the next forty-six years, the remainder of her life. Her first three years in Paris were war years. She sought shelter from the shelling of Big Bertha, attended poetry readings at the bookshop of Adrienne Monnier, read French literature at the Bibliotheque nationale, and wrote several essays on French painting, one of which was published in the *International Studio*. But the sounds of World War I called her to service. During August and September 1917, she worked as a volunteer farmhand in Touraine and the first seven months of 1919 with the Red Cross in Serbia. While E. E. Cummings, Ernest Hemingway, Harry Crosby, John Dos Passos, and others drove ambulances in

Sylvia Beach

Europe, she worked as a secretary in war-ravaged Belgrade.

Beach returned from Serbia to Paris in July 1919 full of urgency to open a bookshop like that of her friend Adrienne Monnier, who ran La Libraire A. Monnier (later La Maison des Amis des Livres) at 7, rue de l'Odeon, in one of the oldest sections of the Left Bank. Beach had thought first of a French bookshop in New York or perhaps in London. Because of problems with financing and a negative assessment of the literary climate in those cities, she decided to start the first English and American bookshop and lending library in Paris. The doors of Shakespeare and Company opened on 17 November 1919 at 8, rue Dupuytren, a very small shop around the corner from Monnier's sanctuary. A year and a half later she moved to her larger and permanent location at 12, rue de l'Odeon across from Monnier's shop at number 7. On Beach's signboard, Marie Monnier painted a likeness of William Shakespeare. To entice the passerby, a window display of books and magazines often featured a single writer such as Joyce or T. S. Eliot.

The chief function of the bookshop was the lending of books. The rows of books on every wall were both traditional and avant-garde. As she and Monnier had agreed before the shop opened, Beach carried only English-language books and Monnier carried only French. In the selection of books she followed her own tastes. Sales and borrowing also reflected her personal preferences. She favored William Blake, Herman Melville, James Joyce, Walt

Whitman, and T. S. Eliot. There was no formal system of lending and no catalogue or bookcards. She kept only a library card for each member. By paying a deposit fee for one, two, three, six or twelve months, a person received a small membership card. The fee varied with the number of books borrowed, and she charged a fine for overdue books. Any customer, or "bunny" as her sister Holly called them after the French word *abonne* (customer), could claim his deposit fee at the expiration of a subscription or sooner if he needed the money. Hemingway borrowed more than his deposit fee several times.

Beach's first customers were the French, in fact Monnier's friends: Andre Gide, Paul Valery, Valery Larbaud, Leon-Paul Fargue, and Jules Romains. Her American customers came a few months later: Stephen Vincent Benet, Gertrude Stein, Ezra Pound, Robert McAlmon, John Peale Bishop, Thornton Wilder, Sherwood Anderson, and Hemingway. Later more Americans came: Archibald MacLeish, John Dos Passos, William Carlos Williams, Janet Flanner, Mina Loy, Glenway Wescott, Lincoln Steffens, Djuna Barnes, Natalie Barney, and scores of others. Early patrons from England included Wyndham Lewis, T. S. Eliot, John Rodker, George Moore, and Bryher (Winifred Ellerman McAlmon). Because this was a time before mass market paperback publication of quality books, when books in English were expensive, most of her patrons borrowed, rather than bought, books. Thus the library cards, now with the Sylvia Beach Papers at Princeton, are a valuable index to the reading of several of her famous patrons. The cards reveal, for example, that Gertrude Stein read all of William Dean Howells's works, Simone de Beauvoir read many novels by Hemingway and William Faulkner, and Paul Valery checked out poems of Robert Frost and essays by Ralph Waldo Emerson. Hemingway's cards reveal that nearly a fifth of the books he borrowed were written by Ivan Turgenev.

Three days after he moved to Paris from Trieste, James Joyce met Sylvia Beach on 11 July 1920 at a party at the home of poet Andre Spire. Amused by both her name and the name of the bookshop, Joyce visited her there the following day and regularly thereafter. The literary collaboration of Joyce and Sylvia Beach began after Margaret Anderson and Jane Heap were indicted in New York in February 1921 on obscenity charges for publishing the Nausicaa (Gertie MacDowell) portion of *Ulysses* in their July-August 1920 issue of the *Little Review*. Because of popular sentiment and legal indictments against the manner and matter of the book, publication in England or the United States was now impossible. Joyce suggested, and Beach immediately agreed, that Shakespeare and Company could publish the novel when it was completed. On 1 April 1921 Joyce and Beach reached a final commitment for her publication of *Ulysses* in France, and she immediately arranged with Monnier's printer, Maurice Darantiere of Dijon, to print 1,000 copies. During the next ten months, until the first copies were delivered by Darantiere on 2 February 1922 (Joyce's fortieth birthday), the work of author and publisher was prodigious. Despite persistent glaucoma, Joyce finished writing *Ulysses*. Beach and Darantiere extended the publication date many times because Joyce was not content merely to correct the page proofs of his novel. He added phrases, lists of names, and whole paragraphs in the margins until he had expanded it by a third. *Ulysses*'s existence in its present form is due in part to Beach's insistence that more and more fresh proofs be given to Joyce. She also worked long hours collecting subscriptions so that she could have the money to pay the printers. She arranged for a series of typists to prepare the manuscript for the printers, planned Joyce's vacation travel, wrote his checks, answered most of his correspondence, and sent all his telegrams—in short, she was his banker, clerk, propagandist, errand girl, appointment secretary, and business manager. She promoted the book, solicited reviews, negotiated its numerous translations, and advanced Joyce money on each future edition. This work continued through a decade, until the eleventh edition was published in May 1930. Malcolm Cowley recalls: "Joyce accepted favors and demanded services as if he were not a person but a sanctified cause. It was, he seemed to be saying, a privilege to devote one's life to the cause, and those who paid his debts for him were sure to be rewarded in heaven. Miss Beach agreed with him."

When Shakespeare and Company moved to its permanent address at 12, rue de l'Odeon in July 1921, Beach moved in with Adrienne Monnier, and until 1937 they shared an apartment at 18, rue de l'Odeon. Although they were physical and temperamental opposites, they served literature with a single-minded devotion. The fame of these two bookshops radiated northwest to London, west to the United States, south to Rapallo, and east to Russia, where Sergei Eisenstein wrote for the latest American books. Together, Monnier and Beach planned the presentation of Joyce and *Ulysses* to the French literati by enlisting the aid of their friend Valery Larbaud, celebrated polyglot translator and critic. Enthusiastic about *Ulysses*, he wrote an introductory

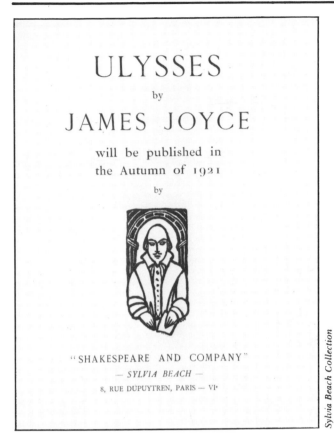

ULYSSES

by

JAMES JOYCE

will be published in
the Autumn of 1921

by

"SHAKESPEARE AND COMPANY"

— SYLVIA BEACH —

8, RUE DUPUYTREN, PARIS — VIᵉ

Sylvia Beach Collection

Ulysses *prospectus, front cover*

lecture for the Joyce reading at Monnier's library on 7 December 1921. Following his lecture, Larbaud read the passages from the Sirens and Penelope sections of the novel which had been translated into French by Jacques Benois-Mechin, and actor Jimmy Light read the passages in English.

Beach's only financial reward was the quickened business the bookshop realized when Shakespeare and Company became the Joyce center, attracting writers, students, and professors from around the world. The bookshop was the distribution center for little magazines such as *Poetry, Gargoyle, Exile, This Quarter, Criterion, Egoist, Broom, transition, Contact, Little Review,* and *transatlantic review.* Beach received writers' manuscripts and cajoled editors to publish them. Probably she and Pound, who founded or edited several of these publications, did more than any others to promote and sustain the little reviews of the twenties and thirties. Thus the bookshop was the center for current writing as well as for the traditional American literature on the shelves. Both avant-garde and traditional literature were available to the French for reading, translation, and criticism. She encouraged young American writers to write critical articles; influenced their reading; found them

printers and translators, rooms and protectors; received their mail; lent them money; collected money due them; and solicited funds for their support. Small expatriate publishers such as Robert McAlmon's Contact Publishing Company, William Bird's Three Mountains Press, Nancy Cunard's Hours Press, Edward Titus's Black Manikin Press, Gertrude Stein's Plain Editions, and Harry Crosby's Black Sun Press sold their books at Shakespeare and Company. McAlmon even used the Shakespeare and Company address for his mailing address, and Beach mailed publishing correspondence and manuscripts to him as he traveled from place to place.

Beach was Joyce's only publisher of *Ulysses* for ten years, except for several months in 1922-1923. While she was selling the first edition and trying to keep up the regular business of her bookshop, Harriet Weaver published two British reprints using the Darantiere plates. After Weaver's last (third) edition was destroyed at English customs, Beach resumed her publication, delivering to Joyce on Christmas eve of 1924 the first two copies of the fourth edition. She also plotted to get the novel to its subscribers in the United States. A newspaperman friend of Hemingway's smuggled forty copies from Windsor, Ontario, Canada, where he worked, to Detroit, where he lived, by carrying one copy at a time as he crossed from Windsor to Detroit on the ferry. From Detroit he mailed each book to its subscriber.

That same year she took under her protection fellow New Jerseyite George Antheil, who had come to Paris from Germany at the suggestion of Stravinsky. The twenty-three-year-old musician and composer soon flourished in this center of musical innovation. Beach introduced him to Pound, who championed his music and wrote a book about his theory of music, *Antheil and the Treatise on Harmony,* published by Three Mountains Press in 1924. With his wife Boski, Antheil moved into one of Beach's rooms above the shop, where he composed for a time without a piano. From funds which she and McAlmon collected for his support, Beach gave Antheil an allowance. And she loyally attended all his private recitals and public concerts. He, in turn, was devoted to her and brought fellow musicians, such as Virgil Thomson, Eric Satie, and Bravig Imbs, into her company. Other musicians who came later to the bookshop during visits to Paris included Paul Robeson, George Gershwin, and Aaron Copland.

Beach gave her assistance both to American and French literature. Most of her social hours were spent with French literati, especially Valery Larbaud,

Leon-Paul Fargue, Adrienne Monnier, Adrienne's sister Marie and her husband, Paul-Emile Becate. As Monnier's closest friend, Beach attended all the readings that Monnier sponsored and helped in all her publications. She devoted special energy to Monnier's *Navire d'argent*, a literary journal which appeared monthly from June 1925 through May 1926. The first issue carried a translation by Monnier and Beach of Eliot's *The Love Song of J. Alfred Prufrock* (1917), the first complete Eliot poem ever to be translated into French. When Beach could not persuade any periodical to publish portions of Joyce's *Work in Progress* without deletions, the *Navire* took his "Anna Livia Plurabelle" for the October 1925 issue. For the March 1926 issue Monnier and Beach, with Jean Prevost as assistant editor, prepared an all-American issue. For this issue Beach and Monnier translated "The Eighteenth Presidency" by Whitman, and Beach and Prevost translated a short story by McAlmon. Works by Hemingway, Cummings, and William Carlos Williams were also included for the first time in French.

She assisted a second distinguished French literary review. *Commerce* was founded during the Sunday gatherings of the rue de l'Odeon crowd at the Princesse de Bassiano's Villa Romaine at Versailles. Beach worked with Monnier, who published the first issue, and with her good friends Valery, Fargue, and Larbaud on the editorial board, and she assisted in the French translation of portions of *Ulysses* which appeared in *Commerce* in 1924. *Commerce*, which appeared quarterly from 1924 to 1932, enriched the literature of France and Europe, and Beach's involvement in both *Commerce* and *Navire* contributed to their international spirit.

From 21 April through 20 June 1926, Beach presented an important Whitman exhibition in her shop. She had always shared with Larbaud an enthusiasm for Whitman, whose *Leaves of Grass* was, after *Ulysses*, her most consistent seller. Her aunt, Agnes Orbison, had given her seven items of notes and verse scribbled on the back of envelopes that she had taken from Whitman's wastebasket with his approval, and Beach hung them, along with Whitman's picture, on the wall in her shop. It was these items which Joyce, who would later quote Whitman in *Finnegans Wake* (1939), first examined on his visit to the bookshop in 1920. Although the young American writers in Paris were less than excited about the exhibit, the French and Joyce were enthusiastic. "Only Joyce and the French and I were old-fashioned enough to get along with Whitman," she remembered. Pound and Hemingway came

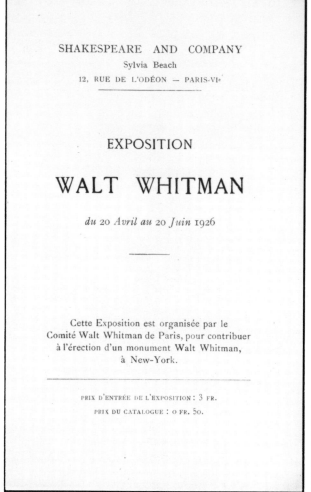

SHAKESPEARE AND COMPANY
Sylvia Beach
12, RUE DE L'ODÉON — PARIS-VIᵉ

EXPOSITION

WALT WHITMAN

du 20 Avril au 20 Juin 1926

Cette Exposition est organisée par le Comité Walt Whitman de Paris, pour contribuer à l'érection d'un monument Walt Whitman, à New-York.

PRIX D'ENTRÉE DE L'EXPOSITION : 3 FR.

PRIX DU CATALOGUE : 0 FR. 50.

Whitman Exposition booklet, front cover

opening night, but the largest group of names appearing in the guest book are those of the French writers. Joyce, on his way to the opening reception, declared to his English benefactress Harriet Weaver that he was going to "Stratford-on-Odeon."

For many months after the autumn of 1926, Beach was embroiled in the battle to suppress Samuel Roth's pirating of *Ulysses* in his *Two Worlds* magazine in New York. By writing hundreds of letters she collected prestigious signatures on two statements of protest which were sent to magazines and newspapers in several countries. The first protest, with sixty-eight signatures, was dated December 1926; the second, with 115, was dated February 1927, on the fifth birthday of *Ulysses*. But signatures and letters from most of the distinguished writers of the Western world did not stop the piracy of Joyce's work. A second and more serious blow to Joyce was the negative critical response to his new

Work in Progress, which would be published under the title *Finnegans Wake.* Responses to the portions published in *transition* had been bitterly negative. More important than these, however, was the loss of support from earlier Joyce enthusiasts such as Harriet Weaver and Ezra Pound, who did not like his experiment with language. Joyce was discouraged.

Beach, who loved and quoted *Ulysses,* accepted Joyce's new work uncritically because it was by the author of *Ulysses.* If she had doubts, she kept them to herself. She agreed to publish the work when it was complete. And she and her assistant, Myrsine Moschos, gave hours to research in foreign-language books for obscure names and allusions. But their support was not enough. Joyce became increasingly ill and discouraged, and he considered giving up writing. At his request Beach asked and received the agreement of James Stephens to collaborate with Joyce on completing the work, although eventually Joyce completed the work on his own. She also published his *Pomes Penyeach* in both France (1927) and the United States (1931). Although she never did publish *Finnegans Wake,* she collected early reviews of the work for a volume called *Our Exagmination Round His Factification for Incamination of Work in Progress* (1929). Beach wrote the introduction and Joyce wrote the title and probably the last two brief pieces by "G. V. L. Slingsby" and "Vladimir Dixon."

Meeting both the personal and professional needs of Joyce strained Beach's resources. During several of Joyce's serious glaucoma attacks and operations as well as major surgery for Nora Joyce, Beach drove them to clinics, looked for a larger apartment for them, handled their correspondence, and wrote all their checks. She had to borrow money from family and friends to cover their expenses, which were particularly high because of the mental illness of their daughter Lucia. Joyce could not live on book royalties and the interest on several legacies which had been placed in his name by Harriet Weaver. He chipped away at the capital and borrowed from friends. He also borrowed increasingly from the bookshop. Their mutual politeness averted a crisis in their relationship. She always addressed him as "Mr. Joyce." And though all others called her "Sylvia," Joyce always called her "Miss Beach."

The lives of the Americans, English, and Irish who lived permanently in Paris were markedly different from the lives American expatriates described in the popular histories of the twenties. Beach's closest friends were French. Her days were full of hard work; and her evenings frequently

Front wrapper

included quiet literary dinners, concerts, and readings. To this French literary world she introduced as many Americans as showed interest. William Carlos Williams, twice a visitor to Paris and one of the few French-speaking American visitors, met Valery Larbaud. F. Scott Fitzgerald met James Joyce and Andre Chamson over Adrienne Monnier's chicken dinner. But Montparnasse, whose transient inhabitants of the Dingo and the Dome saw Paris life superficially, was never more at variance with the literary world of Joyce and the rue de l'Odeon than in the closing months of the twenties. In Canadian Morley Callaghan's glowing account of 1929, *That Summer in Paris,* the Montparnasse life is at full tilt. Montparnasse cafes are full of Americans. The greatest concerns in Callaghan's Americans-in-Paris world are literary quarrels, parties, and Hemingway's boxing. It was not until February 1933 that the Paris *Herald* would announce that "Depression Hits Montparnasse." But those who lived in Paris had earlier faced a collapsing economy. Bookshop income decreased. Friends and patrons were beginning to return to America. Beach, whose grief over the sudden death of her mother months before had led her to drop the Roth piracy battle, began slowly to withdraw from the many demands of the Joyce family. And Joyce, suffering with his painful

Sylvia Beach and James Joyce at Shakespeare and Company

and debilitating glaucoma, worked valiantly on his last work, which would not be completed for another decade. The end of the twenties was marked by the Depression, the exodus of Americans, and the suspension of several literary reviews such as *transition*, which had been publishing portions of Joyce's *Work in Progress.*

With reduced capital and fewer Americans, the literary life of the bookshop continued. For example, one evening at Shakespeare and Company, with Gertrude Stein sitting prominently in the front row of the audience, Edith Sitwell read her poetry. And Monnier presented an evening reading to introduce Joyce's *Work in Progress* to her French literary patrons; Monnier, Beach, and Joyce hoped that the reading would stop resistance to this new work. But there were fewer public literary events. Literary exchange was reduced to chance meetings in the bookshops or private parties, such as Joyce's annual birthday party on 2 February. The 1931 celebration masked only temporarily the growing fears concerning Lucia Joyce's mental illness and the increasing tension between Joyce and Beach over his profes-

sional and economic demands. Within a month of the Joyce program in her bookshop, Monnier wrote Joyce a letter accusing him of excessive concern for money at the expense of Beach and Shakespeare and Company. The strain in the Joyce-Beach relationship reached a peak in 1932. Joyce was upset when Beach, whose primary concern was her bookshop and lending library, would not go to New York to fight Samuel Roth in court. And Monnier's letter deeply hurt Joyce. But the publication of *Ulysses* in America dealt the final blow. While Beach planned the printing of the twelfth edition of *Ulysses*, Joyce was negotiating with Bennett Cerf of Random House for a court test and a rival American publication. Padraic and Mary Colum, mutual friends of Joyce and Beach, warned her of Joyce's negotiations before the printing of the twelfth edition began. Surprised and hurt, she canceled the twelfth edition and renounced all claim to *Ulysses.* Judge Woolsey ruled in favor of *Ulysses* on 6 December 1933, and the novel was published in America the following February. Beach received nothing for her rights as publisher of *Ulysses.*

In the thirties, only the generosity of her friends kept the doors of the bookshop open. Finally, financial trouble forced Beach to offer for sale an array of manuscripts and first editions. Eventually and painfully she sold most of the manuscripts that Joyce had given her: the manuscripts of *Stephen Hero*, *Chamber Music*, *Dubliners*, and *Pomes Penyeach*. Fortunately for history, she did not sell everything; so the remaining manuscripts, first editions, letters, and library cards remain with her papers at Princeton University and the University of Buffalo. When Myrsine Moschos left the bookshop after nearly ten years to attend Lucia Joyce, Beach felt she had been abandoned by both Joyce and her assistant. Her resentment against Joyce's treatment was expressed only to her closest friends. Her praise of his work was unqualified.

Several of her early patrons, especially Hemingway, came to the shop when they were in Paris in the thirties. And once Joyce left, Gertrude Stein began to appear more often. Samuel Beckett came to borrow books and talk to Beach. Newcomers included Katherine Anne Porter, who first met Hemingway in the shop; Allen Tate, who remained a close friend; Thomas Wolfe; and Elizabeth Bishop. A group of young English writers who considered themselves heirs to the writers of the twenties were frequent visitors also: Stephen Spender, W. H. Auden, and Cyril Connolly. A new generation of French writers joined the two rue de l'Odeon libraries: Simone de Beauvoir joined Shakespeare and Company and Jean-Paul Sartre joined La Maison des Amis des Livres.

Shakespeare and Company literary activities of the middle and late thirties shifted back again to French literature almost exclusively. Beach helped Monnier compile a critical bibliography of Monnier's library of French literature and culture. She also served on the board of directors of *Mesures*, a French review owned by Henry and Barbara Church and administered by Monnier. It was published from 1935 to 1940 and had a strong international flavor. Beach was consulted often on English-language texts.

But the most important literary activities of the thirties were the readings by the Friends of Shakespeare and Company. In 1935 her French friends Gide, Valery, and Jean Schlumberger had drawn up a petition to the government for subsidy of Shakespeare and Company. When the petition failed for lack of funds, they organized the Friends. The organizing committee of the Friends also included George Duhamel, Luc Durtain, Louis Gillet, Andre Maurois, Paul Morand, Jean Paulhan, and Jules Romains. T. S. Eliot and Dorothy Richardson recruited members in England. The Friends guaranteed funds for the shop from membership fees. Extra income came from their readings, for which the public was charged entrance. The first two readings were by Gide and Valery during February 1936. Schlumberger read from his unpublished novel *Saint Saturin* in March 1936. Paulhan read in May, Eliot in June. Following a lengthy trip to America for surgery, Beach resumed the readings by the Friends in January 1937 with Romains and in April with Maurois. In May, after their return from the Spanish Civil War, Stephen Spender and Hemingway, who visited the bookshop often during 1937-1938, gave a joint reading at the bookshop. The readings helped pay outstanding bills but did not make an appreciable difference in daily business.

Beach's chief benefactor after the mid-thirties was Bryher, the former wife of Robert McAlmon and daughter of English shipping magnate Sir John Ellerman. Although Bryher did not come from her home in Switzerland for the readings, she sent a large donation for the bookshop. Through McAlmon, Bryher's money went to many literary causes including Joyce and the Contact Publishing Company. Through forty years of friendship and correspondence, Bryher gave generously to Beach. Beach sold Bryher's review, *Life and Letters Today*, at the bookshop from 1935 until the bookshop closed, and with Monnier in 1938 she translated Bryher's *Paris 1900*.

With the 1939 publication of *Finnegans Wake*, Joyce had written his last book. He died on 13 January 1941, just two months after Beach's father, and less than a year before Beach was forced to close Shakespeare and Company. Although most Americans had fled Paris before Hitler invaded in June 1940, Beach remained with the bookshop and a meager business. But when a Nazi officer threatened to confiscate her books after she refused to sell him her personal copy of *Finnegans Wake*, she called on friends to help her move every book, photograph, table, and chair upstairs. Within hours Shakespeare and Company was hidden. Twenty-two years after she had opened the shop 17 November 1919, Shakespeare and Company was closed.

After a six-month internment at Vittel, Beach returned to Paris to await its liberation, which was signaled on the rue de l'Odeon by Hemingway's arrival on 26 August 1944. Tired and without funds, she resisted the suggestions of Eliot and Spender, who wanted her to reopen the bookshop. But she continued to sell books from her apartment and to lend books to French friends and to new American friends such as Richard Wright. She gave interviews to students and Joyce scholars from around the world. And her translations continued with an English translation of Henri Michaux's *A Barbarian in Asia*, for which in 1950 she received the Denyse Clairouin Award.

Following the death of Monnier in 1955, Beach lived alone with history. As one of the few survivors of the twenties, she became a frequent spokesman for the twenties and James Joyce. She gave speeches and radio and television interviews. In 1959 she sold her Joyce collection to the University of Buffalo, which awarded her an honorary degree. But there were three major literary events of what she called her "official" period. The first was the great Twenties Exhibition of American writers in Paris, sponsored by the American Embassy in Paris in 1959. This display of hundreds of her photographs, books, and notes testified to the centrality of Shakespeare and Company in the twenties. At the opening of the exhibition, Thornton Wilder and Alice B. Toklas sat in front of a photo facade of the old Dingo cafe and reminisced, while in the background a pianola beat out Antheil's *Ballet mecanique*. That same year her memoirs, *Shakespeare and Company*, were published by Harcourt, Brace. And in 1962 she gave the dedication speech at the new James Joyce museum in the Martello Tower, outside Dublin, the setting for the opening passages of *Ulysses*. Several months later she was found dead in her apartment at 12, rue de l'Odeon.

Her memoirs are sketchy, self-effacing, and excessively protective of her friends—to the point of error. Well-versed in the diplomacy of good will, she is deliberately uncritical. Even Joyce, the only developed character in the book, is never criticized. She was much more discriminating in her tastes and friends than her book indicates. In fact, part of her genius was in knowing how to choose friends. These brief anecdotes about her friends only whet the desire for her full story. When it was published, she herself thought it too brief and "non-alcoholic." Beyond this volume the literary historian can find anecdotes about Sylvia Beach and Shakespeare and Company in hundreds of memoirs, biographies, and histories of the twenties and thirties. No full biography of Beach has been published.

The genius and gift of Shakespeare and Company was at least fourfold. First was its time and place. It opened on the eve of a period unmatched in its concentration of artists in one city. Writers, painters, and musicians from most of the countries of the Western world gravitated to Paris, where Shakespeare and Company was a warm and dependable place to meet, borrow books, leave messages, pick up mail, and cash checks—a place open nearly every day and evening. Second was the presence of Joyce. Shakespeare and Company was office and agent for one of the greatest writers of the twentieth century. When Beach agreed to be Joyce's publisher, the Shakespeare sign became home for many a young writer's voyage to Ithaca. Third was the presence across the street of Adrienne Monnier and her La Maison des Amis des Livres, a temple to contemporary French literature. Together, on either side of the rue de l'Odeon, they formed a gate through which a young writer entered the world of literature. And of all the spiritual and economic bonds uniting France and America, the bridges built by the artists remain the most enduring and appealing. Beach and Monnier were the architects. The fourth and cohesive factor in the genius of Shakespeare and Company was Beach herself. She had a gift for friendship and loyalty. Devoted to helping literary talent, she made no claims for herself as a writer or intellectual. Yet she was a voracious reader with a sense of the genuine in literature. She presided at the hub of American-Parisian literary activity, the one place where all groups, factions, and nationalities eventually met.

Other:

Our Exagmination Round His Factification for Incamination of Work in Progress, edited with an introduction by Beach (Paris: Shakespeare and Company, 1929);

Bryher, *Paris 1900*, translated into French by Beach and Adrienne Monnier (Paris: La Maison des Amis des Livres, 1938);

Henri A. Michaux, *A Barbarian in Asia*, translated by Beach (New York: New Directions, 1949);

Les annees vingt: les escrivains americains a Paris et leurs amis: 1920-1930 (Paris: Centre Culturel Americain, 1959).

Periodical Publications:

"A Musee Rodin in Paris," *International Studio*, 62 (July 1917): XLII-XLIV;

T. S. Eliot, "La Chanson d'Amour de J. Alfred Prufrock," translated into French by Beach and Adrienne Monnier, *Navire d'argent* (June 1925);

Robert McAlmon, "Agence de publicite," translated into French by Beach and Jean Prevost, *Navire d'argent* (March 1926);

Walt Whitman, "La Dix-Huitieme Presidence," translated into French by Beach and Adrienne Monnier, *Navire d'argent* (March 1926);

"La campagne autant que Paris," *Bravo: le magazine moderne*, 3 (October 1932): 18-19;

Dorothy Richardson, "De la ponctuation," translated into French by Beach and Adrienne Monnier, *Mesures*, 1 (15 January 1935);

Adrienne Monnier, "Joyce's *Ulysses* and the French Public," translated by Beach, *Kenyon Review*, 8 (Summer 1946): 430-444;

"Shakespeare and Co., Paris," *Listener*, 62 (2 July 1959): 27-28;

"Celtic Saga," *Saturday Review*, 43 (12 November 1960): 32;

"Allocution: Prononcee le 24 mai 1927 a l'institut radiophonique d'extension universitaire de la sorbonne," *Mercure de france*, 349 (August/September 1963): 91-94;

"Interned," *Mercure de france*, 349 (August/September 1963): 136-143.

References:

Richard Ellman, *James Joyce* (New York: Oxford University Press, 1965);

Noel Riley Fitch, "Ernest Hemingway—c/o Shakespeare and Company," *Fitzgerald/Hemingway Annual 1977* (Detroit: Bruccoli Clark / Gale Research, 1977), pp. 157-181;

Fitch, "Sylvia Beach's Shakespeare and Company: Port of Call for American Expatriates," *Research Studies*, 33 (December 1965): 197-207;

Fitch, "Voyage to Ithaca: William Carlos Williams in Paris," *Princeton University Library Chronicle*, 40 (Spring 1979): 193-214;

Hugh Ford, *Published in Paris American and British Writers, Printers, and Publishers in Paris, 1920-1939* (New York: Macmillan, 1975), pp. 3-33;

Richard McDougall, ed., *The Very Rich Hours of Adrienne Monnier* (New York: Scribners, 1976);

Jackson Mathews, "Conversation with Sylvia Beach and Company," *Kenyon Review*, 22 (Winter 1960): 137-150;

Mercure de france, Memorial Edition to Sylvia Beach, 349 (August/September 1963); reprinted as *Sylvia Beach (1887-1962)* (Paris: Mercure de france, 1963);

Adrienne Monnier, *Rue de l'Odeon* (Paris: Editions Albin Michel, 1960).

Papers:

Sylvia Beach's papers are at Princeton University. Her James Joyce Collection is at the State University of New York at Buffalo.

STEPHEN VINCENT BENET
(22 July 1898-13 March 1943)

SELECTED BOOKS: *Five Men and Pompey* (Boston: Four Seas, 1915);

The Beginning of Wisdom (New York: Holt, 1921; London & Sydney: Chapman & Dodd, 1922);

Jean Huguenot (New York: Holt, 1923; London: Methuen, 1925);

John Brown's Body (Garden City: Doubleday, Doran, 1928; London: Heinemann, 1928);

Western Star (New York & Toronto: Farrar & Rinehart, 1943; London: University Press, 1944).

Stephen Vincent Benet drew upon American themes for his work, but his best-known poem, *John Brown's Body* (1928), was written in Paris. Benet was born in Bethlehem, Pennsylvania, the son of a professional soldier with a deep interest in American history. This interest and the family's nomadic movement between widely separated American army bases had a decisive influence on Benet's choice and development of the American themes which are at the heart of his work.

At the age of fifteen he began to write seriously, and by the time he entered Yale two years later, he had published his first volume of poetry, *Five Men and Pompey* (1915). Following brief stints in the army and the State Department, he graduated from Yale in 1919 and earned a master of arts degree there a year later. He spent 1920-1921 on a Yale traveling fellowship to Paris, where he completed his first novel, *The Beginning of Wisdom* (1921). While in Paris, he associated with his Yale friend, composer

Douglas Moore, and the poet Edna St. Vincent Millay, and he spent time at Sylvia Beach's bookshop, Shakespeare and Company. On this first trip to Paris he also met Rosemary Carr, a reporter on the European edition of the *Chicago Tribune* (also known as the Paris *Tribune*). After a courtship there, they were married in Chicago in 1921. Following a honeymoon in France, they settled in New York, where Benet continued to write poetry, a number of short stories for popular magazines, and a second novel, *Jean Huguenot* (1923).

Benet was awarded a Guggenheim fellowship in 1926, and the Benets moved to Paris, where he planned to use this financially secure time to write a long poem inspired by his growing involvement in the exploration of American legends and history. That autumn he began work on *John Brown's Body* and completed it at the end of 1927. Although Benet called it a "cyclorama," it is generally regarded as an epic poem organized around sketches of fictional and historical characters through whom he depicts the vast conflict of the Civil War. Published in 1928, it won the Pulitzer Prize for Poetry the following year and ranks as his most important work. Its ambitious scale and intensely nationalistic, lyrical character appealed to a wide audience of readers.

The Benets remained in Paris until 1929. During that residence, Benet enjoyed a well-ordered and thoroughly domestic life while keeping alive his interest in the avant-garde literature of the era. Through friends like Archibald MacLeish and John Peale Bishop he stayed in touch with new artistic movements in the city. As a result of his relative freedom from financial worry during this brief period in his life, his physical remoteness from the United States, and his voracious reading in American history, he came to a new realization of the intensity of his feelings for his native country. It was that discovery in Paris which was to influence the course of his work for the rest of his life.

Benet died at the age of forty-four after years of ill health and recurrent financial worry. He had not only produced a prodigious body of poetry, short stories, and novels, but he had also been active as a lecturer, an editor, a book reviewer, and an opera librettist. Shortly before his death in 1943, he completed the opening portion of *Western Star*, intended to be an American epic larger in scale than *John Brown's Body*. This incomplete poem won a Pulitzer Prize in 1944. Benet's admiring readers rank him as the kind of mythical American poet Whitman had in mind. Less generous critics consider him a popularizer of our past. Measured by his exceptional grasp of American history, his anticipation of the

Stephen Vincent Benet

development of scholarly folk studies, and the scale and lyrical intensity of his affection for America, he is clearly a national poet. Much of that achievement is the consequence of Benet's years in Paris, which gave him the distance to see his country clearly.

—Seymour I. Toll

References:

Charles A. Fenton, ed., *Selected Letters of Stephen Vincent Benet* (New Haven: Yale University Press, 1960);

Fenton, *Stephen Vincent Benet: The Life and Times of a Man of Letters, 1893-1943* (New Haven: Yale University Press, 1958);

Gladys L. Maddocks, "Stephen Vincent Benet: A Bibliography," *Bulletin of Bibliography and Dramatic Index* (September 1951): 142-146; (April 1952): 158-160;

Parry Stroud, *Stephen Vincent Benet* (New York: Twayne, 1962).

Papers:

Benet's papers are in the Beinecke Library, Yale University.

WILLIAM BIRD
(1888-2 August 1963)

BOOK: *A Practical Guide to French Wines* (Paris: William Bird, 1922).

A journalist and the founder of his own wire service, the Consolidated Press, William Bird is best remembered for one of his hobbies—printing. Although his Three Mountains Press published books by Ezra Pound, Ford Madox Ford, William Carlos Williams, Ernest Hemingway, and Robert McAlmon, Bird always emphasized that he printed books for fun, in his spare time. In a 1956 letter to Robert Knoll he says, "I started the Three Mountains Press simply to have a hobby. Most of my friends were golfers, but sports never interested me greatly, whereas ever since my childhood I had had an interest in printing." Unlike his friend and associate Robert McAlmon, Bird had no literary aspirations. He published one book of his own, a small volume on his other hobby, French wines.

Nor did Bird ever have a wealthy backer for the Three Mountains Press. He wrote to Knoll in 1956, "I financed it myself. It did not cost much more than some men spend on golf." Bird's tendency to deemphasize his role in one of the most important literary movements of this century was in keeping with his personality. In the midst of the intrigues and jealousies of the Paris literary scene, Bird was universally liked. William Carlos Williams describes him best: "a tall, sharp-bearded American businessman who looked as though he'd been mellowed in Chambertin, gentle, kindly, and informal." Printing was his art, and according to Ford Madox Ford, Bird became "an almost hypersensitive dilettante" only when working at his hand printing press. Ford praises the appearance of Bird's books in contrast to McAlmon's Contact Editions, produced by the French printer Maurice Darantiere, which Ford calls "uglyish wads of printing."

Born in Buffalo in 1888, Bird graduated from Trinity College in Hartford, Connecticut, in 1912. With his longtime friend David Lawrence, he started the Consolidated Press Service in 1920 and went to France to take charge of the Paris office at 19, rue d'Antin. In *The Sun Also Rises*, Jake Barnes's job is based upon what Hemingway knew about Bird's career as European manager of the Consolidated Press.

After settling in Paris with his family, Bird's interest in printing was sparked when he met French journalist Roger Devigne, whose hobby was printing books on an eighteenth-century hand press.

William Bird, inscribed to Sylvia Beach

Sylvia Beach Collection

Bird promptly bought a full series of Caslon type and apprenticed himself to Devigne. At Devigne's shop on the Ile Saint-Louis Bird printed a few short manuscripts, including his book, *A Practical Guide to French Wines* (1922). When the shop next door at 29, Quai d'Anjou became vacant, Bird bought his own Mathieu hand press which was about 200 years old.

Bird got the idea for the name Three Mountains Press from D. B. Updike's *Printing Types: Their History, Form and Use*. Plate 117 in volume I reproduces the Vulgate text of Psalm 121 from a large-letter edition in the Vatican Library. He wrote to Carlos Baker in 1963 that he especially noticed the sentence "*Levavi oculos meos in montes*" ("I shall lift mine eyes unto the hills"), and, Baker adds, Bird realized that "The three mountains of Paris—Montmartre, Montparnasse, and St. Genevieve—could serve as a colophon, embodying Bird's initials. The triple peaks formed the W and the framework made the B."

Hugh Ford suggests that "Bird would have gone on indefinitely printing small books of no special value had he not met Hemingway who put him on to Pound." The two reporters met on the train as they were traveling to the Conferenza Internazionale Economica de Genova which opened in Genoa on 9 April 1922. Bird told Hemingway about his press, and Hemingway suggested that Ezra Pound might allow Bird to print part of a long poem he was writing. Bird went to see Pound, and Pound suggested instead that Bird publish a series of six books. As Bird wrote to Knoll in 1956, "He said the thing to do was to have a series of books that went together, and not just print things as they came along."

Bird promptly appointed Pound editor of Three Mountains Press, and they set about the task of bringing out the series which was announced as a "manifest of the present state of English prose" and was later called, in the final volume of the series, Hemingway's *in our time*, "The Inquest into the state of contemporary English prose." Bird's announcement of the series stressed that it would also be an "experiment in hand-printing" and that editions would be limited to 300 or fewer copies. Moreover, because there would be no second editions the books would be "rarities for collectors." The six books were *Indiscretions or, Une Revue de Deux Mondes* by Pound, *Women & Men* by Ford Madox Ford, *The Great American Novel* by William Carlos Williams, *Elimus: a story* by B. C. Windeler, *England* by B. M. G. Adams, and *in our time* by Ernest Hemingway. All but the last were published in 1923, and Hemingway's book was officially released in March 1924.

The first book, Pound's *Indiscretions*, the autobiography of the author's first sixteen years, appeared in March 1923. Bird felt that his first experiment with typography had fallen short of his ideal, and according to Hugh Ford, "he consoled himself by vowing that 'next time' he would approach it more closely, and that, anyway, selling books was of secondary importance." Ford Madox Ford's *Women & Men*, a collection of reminiscences exploring relationships between women and men, appeared the following month. But in order to keep up the one-book-a-month schedule, Bird had to turn to Herbert Clarke, an Englishman who had a printing shop in a courtyard off the rue Saint-Honore, for help with the third book. William Carlos Williams's *The Great American Novel* bears the note: "Finished printing in May, 1923, by Herbert Clarke and William Bird at Paris and in St. Louis' Island."

Also finished in May 1923 was *Elimus* by B. Cyril Windeler, an acquaintance of Pound's, whose story about a young immigrant in Canada adds little to the "inquest" into contemporary prose. The book does demonstrate Bird's increased expertise at innovative typography, however. His printing was successfully designed to complement woodcuts by Dorothy Shakespear and Robert Dill. The last book published in 1923 was *England* by B. M. G. Adams, another of Pound's friends. The most distinctive feature of this book is its appearance, especially the

in our time
by
ernest hemingway

A Girl in Chicago: Tell us about the French women, Hank. What are they like?
Bill Smith: How old are the French women, Hank?

LEVAVI OCVLOS
MEOS IN MONTES

paris:
printed at the three mountains press *and for sale at* shakespeare & company, *in the rue de l'odéon; london:* william jackson, *took's court, cursitor street, chancery lane.*

1924

Title page

cover pattern of birds and flowers designed by Bird.

The final book in Pound's inquest is also the most famous. The original announcement of the series simply lists Hemingway's name with the word "Blank" next to it. According to Bird, he was originally slated to be Hemingway's first publisher, but as Bird wrote to Knoll in 1956, "Hemingway got very impatient, as his book was the last on the list, and gave another ms. (Three Stories & Ten Poems) to Bob McAlmon, who thus got it out a few months before 'in our time.'"

Bird had suggested that if Hemingway could write a dozen more miniatures like the six he had recently published in the *Little Review* under the title "In Our Time," they would make a large enough volume. Hemingway complied and completed the manuscript before his departure for Canada in August 1923. Bird considered framing each sketch with a border of newsprint, suggesting both Hemingway's journalistic profession and the relationship of the sketches to current events, but he later discarded this idea. The title of the book was the same as the one used for the *Little Review* sketches, but Bird decided to set it in lower-case type, prompting Hemingway to write to Edmund Wilson: "Bird had put them in and as he was printing 'In Our Time' himself and that was all the fun he was getting out of it, I thought he could go ahead and be a damn fool in his own way if it pleased him. So long as he did not fool with the text." Bird shipped the first copies to Hemingway in November 1923. He had originally planned an edition of 300 copies, but some of the copies were spoiled, in Bird's judgment, because watermarked paper had been used in reproducing Henry Strater's woodcut portrait of Hemingway which served as frontispiece. The fifty copies sent to Hemingway as review copies were flawed in this way, and 170 perfect copies were officially released in March 1924.

A month after the release of this final volume in Pound's "*Inquest*" into the state of contemporary English prose," Bird published a collection of Pound's music criticism. Unlike earlier Three Mountains books, *Antheil and the Treatise on Harmony* (1924) largely consists of previously published material: a group of reviews which Pound wrote between 1917 and 1920 as music critic for the London magazine *New Age*; his treatise on harmony, most of which had been printed in the *transatlantic review*; and a short essay about his friend George Antheil. Although Bird published the book, it was printed by Maurice Darantiere in Dijon. The unusually large edition of 600 copies, including forty numbered copies on Arches paper, sold slowly.

Toward the end of 1923, Bird and Robert McAlmon decided to join together for purposes of distribution, and in early 1924, Bird printed a list headed "Contact Editions, including books printed at the Three Mountains Press." Bird later wrote to Knoll, "My idea was that the Three Mts was a printing office, and that Contact Editions was a publishing house. McAlmon, with his usual distaste for fine distinctions, never understood the arrangement and put both imprints on both [*sic*] his subsequent books." A printed label reading "CONTACT EDITIONS / 29 QUAI D'ANJOU, PARIS" was pasted over the "Paris / Three Mountains Press" imprint on Three Mountains books still in the publishers' possession.

Also in late 1923, Ford Madox Ford was making plans to start a new review and needed office space. Bird allowed him to use an "elevated gallery" at the rear of the Three Mountains shop as the magazine's headquarters. Bird may have been responsible for the lack of capitalization in the *transatlantic review*'s

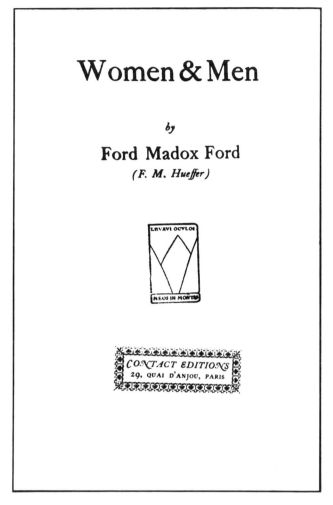

Title page, with pasted-on Contact Editions label

title. Bernard Poli quotes a 1961 letter from Bird in which he says that "the reason the review came out without capitals was not from any desire to be 'arty.' . . . the problem seemed to be to get the distinguishing word TRANSATLANTIC into the largest size possible. It turned out that that word would fit exactly provided it was not capitalized." Bird's practical innovation was later imitated by other avant-garde journals such as *transition*.

Because Bird and McAlmon retained no copyright privileges on the books they published, writers like Hemingway were free to seek other publishers for their Contact and Three Mountains books. Bird's not keeping the copyright on his books may have been motivated as much by principle as by generosity. In a letter to the editor which appeared in the March 1924 issue of the *transatlantic review*, Bird takes the position that copyright laws are undesirable. He argues that the copyright laws are only useful in preventing the pirating of money-making bestsellers and that if books with wide popular appeal could be freely reprinted, then publishers would be less concerned with making money and more interested in the literary reputations of their publishing houses. Under this plan, Bird says, writers would sell their manuscripts outright, rather than receiving royalties. He adds, "It would probably work out that each publisher would have a fixed scale of prices. So much for a novel, so much for a book of poems." He sees only one objection to his plan: it may be unjust to the good writer whose book becomes a popular success, but he concludes:

> No, it is not just to do this. It is not just to do this, and it is not just to close up a gambling-house from which a widow and her six children, unaware of the source, draw their living. It is not just to discharge a consumptive workman, on the ground that he may contaminate others. It is not just to take honey away from the bees, nor for express trains to run over grasshoppers. No, it is not just.

This idealistic and idiosyncratic proposal seems characteristic of the man who was more concerned with making beautiful books than with selling them.

While Bird was still printing *in our time*, Pound proposed another project which was also to ensure the fame of Bird's press. Pound wanted a special limited edition of sixteen of his cantos. He wrote to Kate Buss on 12 May 1923, "It is to be one of the real bits of printing; modern book to be jacked up to somewhere near level of medieval mss.... Not for the Vulgus." He and Bird planned an edition of ninety copies. Five copies on Imperial Japan paper, bound in leather, would sell for one hundred dollars; fifteen, on Whatman paper, bound in vellum, would be fifty dollars; and the regular edition of seventy copies on Roma paper would be twenty-five dollars. In November 1924 specimen pages went on display at Sylvia Beach's Shakespeare and Company, but a year after Pound's announcement of the book to Buss, it was still in production. Pound had become dissatisfied with the work of Henry Strater, who had been asked to draw the illustrations and the capital letters. On 17 April 1924, Pound wrote to Bird, "*Point* was to restrict Strater to *design*. Instead of staying in the design, he has wandered all over the page." Bird managed to revise the book's design to suit Pound, and when Pound received the finished book in January 1925, he called it "*Much* finer than I had expected." To advertise the book, Bird followed Pound's advice in a letter of 7 May 1924: "Do recall that the title of that book is '*A DRAFT* of 16 Cantos for a poem of some length.' If you will stick to that

you will produce something of gtr. val. to collectors. Also it ain't an epic. It's part of a long poem. Yr. best ad is the quiet statement that at auction recently a copy of Mr. P's *A Lume Spento* published in 1908 at $1.00 (one dollar) was sold for $52.50." Bird repeated Pound's words in the January 1925 issue of the *transatlantic review*.

The last book which Bird printed himself was Robert McAlmon's *Distinguished Air* (*Grim Fairy Tales*), also published in 1925. This book, which Robert Knoll calls McAlmon's finest, was favorably received by Pound, James Joyce, and Ernest Walsh. Although Krebs Friend's *The Herdboy* was published under the Three Mountains imprint in December 1926, Hugh Ford suggests that Maurice Lévy's printing of Friend's collection of poems was almost certainly subsidized by Friend's wife, Henrietta.

After printing *Distinguished Air* in 1925, Bird seems to have become more involved with his journalistic career. In 1926 he covered Admiral Richard Byrd's flight over the North Pole from Byrd's expedition base in Spitzbergen, and in 1928, as president of the Anglo-American Press Association, he helped to persuade the French government not to expel an American correspondent who had reported the terms of a secret Anglo-French naval agreement.

Also in 1928, Bird sold his press and some of his type to Nancy Cunard. The following year he sold the remaining stock of Three Mountains Press; as he wrote to Knoll in 1956: "About 1929 I moved my office and was wondering what to do with the hundreds of unsold books, when along came an American named Schwartz who offered me $100 for the lot (perhaps 400 or 500 volumes). I told him I did not need $100 but DID need $150, and the deal was made at that figure." Bird's career as a publisher ended as casually as it had begun, and true to his principles, he profited little from it.

After the Consolidated Press was dissolved in 1933, Bird became chief foreign correspondent for the New York *Sun*, and in the early part of World War II he was a war correspondent in Danzig. He later returned to France to cover the war in the West, and when the Germans took Paris in 1940, he went to Spain. In July 1940, he wrote a series of articles for the New York *Sun* warning that Hitler intended to continue the war "until first England and subsequently the United States are brought under subjection."

After the war, the Birds moved to Tangier, and Bird became editor of the *Tangier Gazette*, an English-language weekly newspaper. In 1948, he was appointed an American representative to the Legislative Assembly of the Tangier International Zone. When the Moroccan government closed his newspaper in 1960, Bird returned to France where he divided his time between his apartment in Paris and his country home, a converted mill near Chartres. He died in Paris in August 1963.

Bird's claim that he played at printing as other men played golf suggests his desire not to capitalize upon his acquaintance with men who were, or were later to become, well-known writers. But Bird's ability to work with writers of such different personalities as Pound, Hemingway, Ford, Williams, and McAlmon, as well as his genius for producing beautifully printed books of lasting literary value, belies his modesty. Ford Madox Ford credits Bird and Robert McAlmon with discovering many of the young writers whose work later appeared in the *transatlantic review*, and he recognizes Bird's contribution to literary history when he says that "the real germ of the Middle Western literary movement is to be found in the Three Mountains Press." —*Karen L. Rood*

Periodical Publication:

Letter to the editor, *transatlantic review*, 1 (March 1924): 82-85.

References:

Carlos Baker, *Ernest Hemingway A Life Story* (New York: Scribners, 1969), pp. 88-179;

Ford Madox Ford, *It Was the Nightingale* (Philadelphia: Lippincott, 1933), pp. 289ff.;

Hugh Ford, *Published in Paris American and British Writers, Printers, and Publishers in Paris, 1920-1939* (New York: Macmillan, 1975), pp. 95-116;

Robert E. Knoll, ed., *McAlmon and the Lost Generation A Self-Portrait* (Lincoln: University of Nebraska Press, 1962), pp. 182-382;

Robert McAlmon, *Being Geniuses Together 1920-1930*, revised edition with additional material by Kay Boyle (Garden City: Doubleday, 1968), pp. 180-183, 342-352;

Bernard J. Poli, *Ford Madox Ford and the* TRANSATLANTIC REVIEW (Syracuse: Syracuse University Press, 1967);

Ezra Pound, *The Letters of Ezra Pound*, ed. D. D. Paige (New York: Harcourt, Brace, 1950);

William Carlos Williams, *The Autobiography of William Carlos Williams* (New York: Random House, 1951).

Papers:

Bird's papers are in the Lilly Library at Indiana University.

JOHN PEALE BISHOP
(21 May 1892-4 April 1944)

SELECTED BOOKS: *Green Fruit* (Boston: Sherman, French, 1917);

The Undertaker's Garland, by Bishop and Edmund Wilson (New York: Knopf, 1922);

Many Thousands Gone (New York: Scribners, 1931);

Now With His Love (New York & London: Scribners, 1933);

Minute Particulars (New York: Alcestis, 1935);

Act of Darkness (New York: Scribners, 1935; London: Cape, 1935);

Selected Poems (New York: Scribners, 1941);

The Collected Poems, edited with an introduction by Allen Tate (New York & London: Scribners, 1948);

The Collected Essays, edited with an introduction by Edmund Wilson (New York & London: Scribners, 1948).

John Peale Bishop, essayist, fiction writer, critic, and poet, was never in Paris for longer than a year or so, but he spent nearly a quarter of his short life in fairly close proximity to the city, passing in and out of it and through it for about ten years. The experience of Paris had, seemingly, little influence on Bishop's work, but the French culture of which it was the capital meant much to him: it symbolized both contemporaneity and tradition.

Because of a protracted childhood illness, Bishop, a native of Charles Town, West Virginia, was twenty years old when he entered Princeton in 1913. At Princeton he quickly distinguished himself

John Peale Bishop

John Peale Bishop

among the minority of students concerned with writing and the serious study of literature; he also entered upon his lifelong friendships with Edmund Wilson and F. Scott Fitzgerald (who portrayed him as Thomas Parke D'Invilliers in *This Side of Paradise*). Upon graduation in 1917, he published a slim volume of verse, ironically titled *Green Fruit*, and he was commissioned a second lieutenant in the army. Bishop went overseas in the summer of 1918 and served there until September 1919, but he never saw action. His first experience of Paris was as an officer in the American Expeditionary Forces. This first encounter with Paris is refracted in a story, "Resurrection," which Bishop published just prior to his second departure for Europe in 1922. The story has to do with a young lieutenant's sense of "all the rotting desolation which filled the world," a feeling which comes upon him in the thronged streets of Paris as well as amidst the war-torn landscape of the battlefields. Ultimately, however, the young officer realizes that Paris is a city of life, that in Paris "whatever was left of life ran at the full."

"Resurrection" was included in *The Undertaker's Garland* (1922), a cynically nihilistic potpourri of poetry and prose which Bishop produced in collaboration with Edmund Wilson. The two young veterans had returned from the war

to become staff members of *Vanity Fair*, contenders in the New York literary scene, and two of Edna St. Vincent Millay's suitors. They remained friends, but their paths diverged after Bishop's marriage to Margaret Hutchins in 1922; her wealth made it possible for the couple to live abroad, and for the next ten years or so Wilson was to fret about Bishop's continued residence overseas. From 1922 to 1924, the Bishops traveled through Italy, Austria, and France, but they also spent much of their time in Paris. There, Bishop became well acquainted with Ezra Pound, E. E. Cummings, Archibald MacLeish, and Ernest Hemingway. He became a knowing connoisseur of the work of the painters and sculptors of the School of Paris; he sought out and visited with other young writers; and he did much to further the careers of fellow writers. (For example, he took charge of the preparation of a number of the little magazine *S4N* which featured the work of E. E. Cummings.) Something of the spirit of Paris in the twenties is conveyed in Bishop's "Homage to Hemingway": "I had just come abroad and, calling on Ezra Pound, had asked him about American writers of talent then in Paris. Pound's answer was a taxi, which carried us with decrepit rapidity across the Left Bank, through the steep streets rising toward Mont Saint-Genevieve, and brought us to the Rue du Cardinal Lemoine. There we climbed four flights of stairs to find Ernest Hemingway." And a glimpse of how Bishop fitted into the Parisian scene is provided in Donald Ogden Stewart's autobiography, *By a Stroke of Luck!* (1975). In the spring of 1923, Bishop urged Stewart in a letter to read *The Waste Land* and "to look up an interesting young writer in Paris named Hemingway." Stewart remembers being "extremely grateful" for the Eliot suggestion; he "was even more grateful to him for Hemingway."

During his two-year stay in Europe, Bishop appeared frequently in American publications and European-based little magazines; he continued to do so after his return to New York in 1924, but he was not able to find a publisher for the novel he had been projecting since the early twenties, a novel which he abandoned after Fitzgerald advanced the opinion, "It has occasional spurts . . . , but it is terribly tepid." Wilson believed that Bishop's unsuccessful resolution of the novel, which was to have dealt at length with the young hero's return to the United States after a sojourn in Europe, was linked to his distaste for the jazz-age America to which he himself had returned and which he judged to be, in Wilson's phrasing, "intolerable."

In 1926 Bishop sailed back to France, where he and his family were to reside until 1933. This time, however, after a brief stay in Paris, the Bishops purchased a centuries-old house in Orgeval, a village some thirty kilometers northeast of Paris. Bishop made occasional visits to the city, but for the most part he and his family lived apart and to themselves. Allen Tate, who visited the Bishops frequently during the latter part of their residence in Orgeval, concluded that Bishop "had not been happy in that charming isolation. More dependent upon a sympathetic literary society than most writers, he seemed in that period remote and without concentration, except at intervals when he produced, in a burst of energy, a group of poems or an occasional story."

Not until 1933, the year of his final return to America, would Bishop be able to assemble poems enough to make up the relatively slight volume, *Now With His Love*. Some of these poems are excellent, but many show too much of the influence of Pound and Eliot. Very few reflect anything of Bishop's sojourn in France, although it might be argued that three of the most successful—"Ode," "The Return," and "Perspectives are Precipices"— owe a good deal to the paintings he had viewed in the galleries and museums of Paris. The fiction Bishop was working at during these years was concerned with the remembered world of his Southern boyhood. The short-story cycle, *Many Thousands Gone*, was published in 1931, but the novel, *Act of Darkness*, would not be completed until 1935. Both of these genuinely distinguished books deal with the ambiguities of the Southern tradition. It seems likely that Bishop's sense of his Southern heritage was given an edge by his immersion in French culture. Looking back to the twenties, in 1941 he observed: "Nowhere was one more conscious of living in the present time than in France, and yet there the present was continuously enriched by the past."

When Bishop spoke these words, France had fallen to the Nazis, and he himself was in failing health, but he spoke with confidence and with a faith in the future. In the previous half-dozen years, he had completed and published *Act of Darkness*; he had finally realized, and demonstrated at length, his poetic talents (his elegy to Fitzgerald, "The Hours," is one of the finest of twentieth-century poems); and his wide-ranging taste and critical intelligence had found expression in a number of important essays. Bishop's contemporaries knew him as a critic as well

as a poet and novelist; it is unfortunate that today he is known, if at all, only as the author of one or two essays. As an essayist, Bishop never attempted to develop, or promote, a body of critical theory. He was never programmatic; in fact, he was not, essentially, a literary critic. Instead, his essays are, as Wilson noted, "a set of discourses on various aspects of civilization: literature, painting, moving pictures, architecture, manners, religion"—discourses which are utterances of a man capable of both scorn and sympathy, a man possessed of, and by, passionate intelligence. It may be that he had to come home to America before his gifts could be fully realized, but Bishop seems never to have regretted the years abroad, and he particularly relished his memories of Paris. For Bishop, as for many of his contemporaries, the central meaning of Paris was derived from its preeminence among those European centers of civilization where, "in each art, the tradition can best be acquired and with it an intenser consciousness of one's own time. . . . Twenty years ago there were many capitals in the world, but in only one was it possible to know the extreme moment of time. And that was Paris." —*Robert Lee White*

References:

William Arrowsmith, "An Artist's Estate," *Hudson Review*, 2 (1940): 118-127;

Jesse Bier, "A Critical Biography of John Peale Bishop," Ph.D. dissertation, Princeton University, 1956;

Joseph Frank, "The Achievement of John Peale Bishop," *Minnesota Review*, 2 (1962): 325-344;

J. Max Patrick and Robert W. Stallman, "John Peale Bishop: A Checklist," *Princeton University Library Chronicle*, 7 (1946): 62-79;

Simone Vauthier, "The Meaning of Structure: Toward a New Reading of John Peale Bishop's *Act of Darkness*," *Southern Literary Journal*, 7 (Spring 1975): 50-76;

Robert Lee White, *John Peale Bishop* (New York: Twayne, 1966).

Papers:

A collection of letters and documents relating to Bishop is in the Princeton University Library.

Kay Boyle

David V. Koch
Southern Illinois University

BIRTH: St. Paul, Minnesota, 19 February 1902, to Katherine Evans and Howard Peterson Boyle.

EDUCATION: Ohio Mechanics Institute, 1917-1919.

MARRIAGE: 24 June 1922 to Richard Brault, divorced; children: Sharon (by Ernest Walsh); 2 April 1932 to Laurence Vail, divorced; children: Apple-Joan, Kathe, Clover; 20 February 1943 to Baron Joseph von Franckenstein; children: Faith Carson, Ian Savin.

SELECTED BOOKS: *Short Stories* (Paris: Black Sun Press, 1929);
Wedding Day and Other Stories (New York: Cape & Smith, 1930; London: Pharos Editions, 1932);
Plagued by the Nightingale (New York: Cape & Smith, 1931; London: Cape, 1931);
Year Before Last (London: Faber & Faber, 1932; New York: Harrison Smith, 1932);
Gentlemen, I Address You Privately (New York: Smith & Haas, 1933; London: Faber & Faber, 1934);
My Next Bride (New York: Harcourt, Brace, 1934; London: Faber & Faber, 1935);
The White Horses of Vienna and Other Stories (New York: Harcourt, Brace, 1936; London: Faber & Faber, 1937);
Death of a Man (London: Faber & Faber, 1936; New York: Harcourt, Brace, 1936);
Monday Night (New York: Harcourt, Brace, 1938; London: Faber & Faber, 1938);
A Glad Day (Norfolk, Conn.: New Directions, 1938);
The Crazy Hunter (London: Faber & Faber, 1940; New York: Harcourt, Brace, 1940);
The Smoking Mountain Stories of Postwar Germany (New York, London & Toronto: McGraw-Hill, 1951; London: Faber & Faber, 1952).

Kay Boyle, 1931

One of the larger ironies of the renewed interest in the American expatriate movement of the twenties and thirties is the relative obscurity of one of the period's most important and prolific contributors: Kay Boyle. Boyle went to France in 1923 as the wife of a French citizen, intending to remain only long enough to meet her husband's family. But she stayed until World War II forced her to return to the United States in 1941, becoming a master of the short story and a protean member of the "Revolution of the Word" movement signaled by Eugene Jolas and the group of writers whose work appeared in Jolas's *transition* magazine. Perhaps her significance and greatness lie in the very fact that she has been so busy writing and acting upon her beliefs, already formed in the twenties, that she has had little time to cultivate a following. Indeed, seeking literary fame would be contrary to Boyle's beliefs, for she has consistently sought to speak for those who could not speak for themselves.

Boyle was born in 1902 into a publishing, if not necessarily a writing, family. Her grandfather Jesse Peyton Boyle was the founder of the West Publishing Company, publishers of legal texts and materials, in St. Paul, Minnesota. The family's affluence afforded her a liberal education which included little formal schooling but much traveling. She had an early educational encounter at Miss Shipley's school in Philadelphia and another at a private school in Cincinnati, plus violin classes at the Cincinnati Conservatory of Music. But early on the Boyle family traveled in Europe as well as the United States with extended stops in the Poconos, Atlantic City, Philadelphia, and Cincinnati.

Boyle's father, Howard Peterson Boyle, who had studied law at the University of Pennsylvania, was ineffectual if well-meaning, in contrast to her grandfather Boyle, whom she describes as domineering, willful, brilliant, and destructive. It was her mother, Katherine Evans Boyle, who, despite suffering from childhood with a severe curvature of the spine, was the dynamic force in the family's life. Indeed, the women in Boyle's family had a history of independence. Her maternal grandmother Eva Evans became one of the first women in federal civil service when she was appointed copyist for the Department of the Interior in 1874, and her aunt, Nina Evans Allender, painted the portrait of Susan B. Anthony which inspired the 1936 postage stamp honoring the suffragette.

Boyle's grandfather is the only family member consistently developed in her fiction, serving as the embodiment of those accepted values questioned and ultimately rejected by the narrators of several early short stories. But, in a positive sense, Boyle's mother was by far the most influential, instilling artistic and social values in her young daughter and remaining a confidante through the twenties and thirties. "Because of my mother, who gave me definitions, I knew what I was committed to in life; because of my father and grandfather, who offered statements instead of revelations, I knew what I was against," Boyle writes in one of the autobiographical chapters she added to her edition of Robert McAlmon's *Being Geniuses Together* in 1968. Her mother not only exposed her to art and literature, but taught her that they were an integral part of life. In *Being Geniuses Together* she tells of her mother's reading Gertrude Stein's *Tender Buttons* (1914) to a gathering of doctors in Philadelphia and early chapters of James Joyce's *Ulysses*, which were appearing in the *Little Review* in 1918-1920, to labor organizations in Cincinnati. Her mother also read Boyle's current teenage writings to the same audiences. Boyle's mother was also active in local politics and civic affairs, running for the Cincinnati school board on the Farmer-Labor ticket, assisting the Children's Crusade, and entertaining notable visitors such as writer and reformer Lincoln Steffens.

These activities, suffered in silence by Boyle's father and sternly and vociferously opposed by her grandfather, combined with the examples of her grandmother and aunt to give Boyle a sense of independence of her own. She was inspired to write some never published teenage poems with titles such as "Arise, Ye Women," and "The Working Girls' Prayer."

Not only did Boyle and her sister Joan write a great deal while they were young, but they produced books and magazines for members of their family. Boyle has mentioned that a handmade book or magazine was nearly an expected birthday or Christmas gift. Still extant are her preteen copybooks with neatly lettered poems and stories and illustrations laboriously drawn and colored. In the thirties when Boyle was married to Laurence Vail, this practice was carried over to the Vail children. As a family project, a single copy of the *Vail Modern Almanach* was "published" periodically. These included stories by the Vail children, houseguests, and Boyle herself. Prizes were given for the best contributions from the children. The covers were made by visiting artists. One cover is a collage by Peggy Guggenheim.

Boyle studied architecture at the Ohio Mechanics Institute in Cincinnati from 1917 to 1919 and then worked in her father's office and attended secretarial school at night when the family fell on hard times. Boyle's first contribution to a national publication was a letter to the editor, which appeared in Harriet Monroe's *Poetry: A Magazine of Verse* in 1921. Only nineteen and still in Cincinnati at the time, Boyle wrote in support of the idea that American poetry and art in 1921 were far more liberated and innovative than musical composition, presenting her argument with a certain amount of presumption as well as persuasion. Among the others who were contributing to *Poetry* at this particular time were William Carlos Williams, Ernest Walsh, Robert McAlmon, Emanuel Carnevali, and Laurence Vail—all individuals who were to affect Boyle's personal and professional life in the twenties and thirties.

In 1922 Boyle followed her sister Joan, a fashion designer with *Vogue*, to New York. Kay Boyle was soon working with Lola Ridge, the New York editor of *Broom*, whose chief editor Harold Loeb published the magazine first from Rome and later from Berlin. She also attended writing classes at Columbia University. In June 1922 Boyle married Robert Brault, a Frenchman she had met while he was an engineering student at the University of Cincinnati.

July 1916

The Working Girls' Prayer.

My heart is sad —
And yet the sky is blue,
— at least I think so
By what's pinched thru
That window over there.
The needle is so heavy
And my hands so slow. —
I'll ask her when she comes
If I may go
And get some air —
And yet it is so far to over there.
How wonderful 't would be
To feel the breezes
As they used to blow from off the sea
And hear the purring of the waves
Upon the jagged shore.
Ah, they would drown out
All this sickening roar.
If I could only crawl
To what wee square of blue —
There must be air there
Where the light peeps thru.
Oh, for some water! —
Not at that greased, grimy sink
But from the spring
Where the soft deer used to drink.

A page from Kay Boyle's copybook

While working for Ridge, Boyle met a number of writers and literary figures including Marianne Moore, John Dos Passos, Glenway Wescott, Monroe Wheeler, and most importantly, William Carlos Williams. Boyle and Williams remained lifelong friends and supporters of one another although Williams always thought of Boyle as a poet, not as a novelist or short-story writer.

Boyle's eighteen-year expatriation began as merely a summer's trip to her husband's family in the north of France. She and Brault sailed for France in June 1923, and she was not to return to the United States again until August 1941. After spending the summer with her husband's family in St. Malo, Boyle and her husband went to Paris to seek employment. There Harold Loeb introduced her to Robert McAlmon, whose work she had admired since she was in her late teens. McAlmon would become something of an elder brother and mentor. After his death, Boyle would champion his work, reediting and publishing his autobiography in 1968 and writing the afterword for the 1977 republication of McAlmon's short-story collection *A Hasty Bunch* (1922) by the Southern Illinois University Press.

Brault found a job in Le Havre, where late in 1923 Boyle finished her first novel, begun the summer before in St. Malo. Based upon her Cincinnati years, the manuscript was lost in 1928 when *transition* editor Robert Sage sent it to a publisher in Chicago. Also in the fall of 1923 Boyle began corresponding with Italian poet Emanuel Carnevali, although they did not meet until 1933 when Boyle traveled through Italy to Bazzano where Carnevali lay dying of encephalitis. In that year Boyle committed herself to seeing that his autobiography, consisting of bits and pieces sent to her through the years, be published. But it was not until 1967 that *The Autobiography of Emanuel Carnevali* finally was published.

In the spring of 1924 Boyle and Brault moved to the nearby village of Harfleur, where she worked on the novel which would later be published as *Plagued by the Nightingale* (1931). When she was only half finished, however, she abandoned it to start a third novel because "all the details of Le Havre and the sea, and Harfleur and the land, were clamoring in my mind. I did not want to have wiped from my memory the things I had borne witness to, and the things I had learned in this unhappy town." It was published in 1933 as *Gentlemen, I Address You Privately*.

Sometime in 1925 Ernest Walsh, who had been given her address by Carnevali, wrote to Boyle inviting her to contribute to the first issue of his new review, *This Quarter*. And in January or February of 1926, after Boyle had been suffering with severe bronchitis which was suspected to be tuberculosis, Walsh insisted that she join him and Ethel Moorhead at Grasse in the south of France. She became deeply involved with the editing and publishing of *This Quarter*, which published her work in the first three issues. Her first published pieces had been poems in *Poetry, Broom, Forum,* and *Contact*. In *This Quarter* short stories and the first version of *Plagued by the Nightingale*, which she began working on again in Grasse, appear beside the long poems "Summer" and "For an American." Boyle's poems, short stories, and novels have always been closely intertwined: her short stories emerged from poems; her novels usually contain segments which can stand easily on their own. In *This Quarter*, for the first time, Boyle's prose becomes as expressive as her poetry. After Walsh's death in 1926, Boyle remained in the south of France until after she gave birth to Walsh's daughter, Sharon, in March 1927. Her experiences with Walsh and Moorhead served as the basis for her novel *Year Before Last* (1932). In 1934 Boyle was instrumental in arranging for the posthumous publication of Walsh's *Poems and Sonnets* by her new American publisher, Harcourt, Brace.

In April 1927 Robert McAlmon gave Boyle money to join her husband in England, where he had been transferred by his company. During this year, she finished *Plagued by the Nightingale* and returned to work on *Gentlemen, I Address You Privately*. In October 1926 Eugene Jolas had written to Boyle asking for contributions to his new magazine, *transition*, and in April 1927 the first issue appeared. Boyle's review of William Carlos Williams's *In the American Grain* (1925) and her short story "Theme" appeared alongside the work of such writers as James Joyce, Gertrude Stein, Hart Crane, Archibald MacLeish, Philippe Soupault, and Robert Desnos. In *Being Geniuses Together* Boyle remembers the seriousness with which she and some other *transition* contributors viewed their experiments with style:

> It may appear to have been a time without much humor in the *avant-garde* literary movement, but it must be remembered that it was a time of the gravest crisis in letters, of furious schism and revolution in the arts, and it is not the way of revolutionaries in any uprising to go lightly to the block to lose their heads. And, it being a time of peril, gravity was demanded of writers who fought against

the sentence of death, of oblivion, passed on their work by critics and publishers, and on the life term offered as alternative, to be served in the ancient strongholds of the established conventional forms. . . . This was a serious business, and if one laughed a good deal over cafe tables, one did not laugh very loudly on the printed page.

Until 1929 Boyle published almost exclusively in *transition.* Fifteen of the first twenty numbers contain her poems, stories, reviews, a translation, and the preliminary drafts of *Year Before Last.*

In the spring of 1928 Boyle and her daughter went to Paris, where the British poet Archibald Craig helped her to find a position ghostwriting the memoirs of his cousin the Dayang Muda of Sarawak, Gladys Palmer Brooke, heir to the Huntley and Palmer biscuit fortune. Through Jolas and others she met most of the Left Bank literary establishment, including James Joyce, Gertrude Stein, Sylvia Beach, and Archibald MacLeish. She was one of the few people who was able to maintain friendships with both the so-called *"transition* crowd" and writers such as McAlmon who were unsympathetic to *transition*'s "Revolution of the Word." Among the people to whom McAlmon introduced her at this time were William Bird and Harold Stearns, who later served as the model for the central character in her novel *Monday Night* (1938).

After working for the Dayang Muda for several months, Boyle, with her daughter, joined Raymond Duncan's colony in Neuilly. Boyle's novel *My Next Bride* (1934) is the story of her six-months' experience with this experiment in communal living. Boyle worked in one of the colony's Paris shops which sold articles reputedly made in the colony. Although she had been attracted by the ideas Duncan espoused as early as 1923, she soon came to believe that the colony labored more for Duncan's personal profit than for the good of its members. In her short story "Art Colony" (1932), a young American girl says: "when I joined we were going to work the hand press. We were going to print poetry, and revive the dramy [*sic*]. But nothing ever came of it. Sorrel got some money and bought a new car instead." With the help of McAlmon Boyle left the colony in December 1928 and went to stay briefly with Harry and Caresse Crosby, whom she had met the previous summer. A fictionalized account of her friendship with the Crosbys appears in *My Next Bride.*

In 1929 the Crosbys' Black Sun Press published Boyle's first book, unpretentiously titled *Short Stories,* in a limited edition of 185 copies. After Harry Crosby's suicide in 1929, Boyle and Caresse Crosby

became close friends until the latter's death in 1970. In addition to the *Short Stories,* Caresse Crosby's Black Sun Press also published Boyle's translations of the first part of Rene Crevel's *Babylone* as *Mr. Knife Miss Fork* (1931) and Raymond Radiguet's *The Devil in the Flesh* (1932). Caresse Crosby also republished *Year Before Last* in her paperback series, Crosby Continental Editions, and after World War II she included Boyle's stories and poems in the Black Sun Press *Portfolio* series. *Short Stories* was followed the next year by New York publication of *Wedding Day and Other Stories* (1930), which adds six stories to the seven in *Short Stories.* The added stories include the remarkable "Wedding Day" itself and "Episode in the Life of an Ancestor," a statement of the strength and will of a young woman in the open ranges of nineteenth-century Kansas, a figure not unlike Boyle's maternal grandmother Evans. The seven stories of Boyle's first book serve proper notice of Boyle's emerging short-story career. Four had appeared initially in *transition,* and a fifth in the London magazine *Calendar of Modern Letters.* The stories are indicative of Boyle's early experimentation with syntax, compacted imagery, personification, and narrative point of view, including a modified form of stream of consciousness. These are stories dealing with the conflicts between generations or the sexes. But mostly they speak of people's need for each other and the chasms humans place between themselves. Even when the Englishman communicates with the French girl in "Bitte Nehmen Sie die Blumen," he does so in German.

With the publication of these two books of short stories, Boyle's work began appearing regularly and frequently in American magazines. Her first appearance in the *New Yorker* came in 1930 with "Kroy Wen," beginning an association which was to span the decades. By the time Boyle returned to the United States in August 1941 her stories had won two O. Henry first place awards ("White Horses of Vienna" in 1935 and "Defeat" in 1941), plus three additional appearances in the O. Henry annual anthologies ("The First Lover," 1932; "Anschluss," 1939; and "Poor Monsieur Panalitus," 1940). No fewer than forty of her stories made Edward O'Brien's honor rolls in his *Best American Short Stories* annuals. During the same period she published six novels, three short-story collections, three translations, two ghostwritten volumes, a book of three short novels, a children's book, a poetry collection, and an anthology. She also wrote a seventh novel. In the midst of this period, in 1934, she received a Guggenheim fellowship to work on an

Morris Library

Front cover, Vail's Modern Almanach, *by Vail*

epic-length poem on flight (only partially published, and left unfinished). She had met Laurence Vail, then the husband of Peggy Guggenheim, in the summer of 1928; the two were married in 1932. They had three children of their own, and Boyle cared for Vail's two children by Peggy Guggenheim and her own daughter Sharon Walsh as well.

Even though Boyle spent the greater part of two decades away from America, she actually spent little of that time in Paris. Vail and Boyle lived in the south of France in Villefranche and on the Col-de-Villefranche until the summer of 1933, when they moved to Austria, living first in Vienna and then Kitzbuhel. They lived in England in Devon for a year between the summers of 1936 and 1937, and then returned to France, where they bought "Le Chalet de Cinq Enfants" in Megeve, Haute Savoie. In June 1941 the Vails and the children left for America, traveling by way of Spain and Lisbon.

Boyle's experiences of the twenties form the

backgrounds for her first four novels published in the thirties: *Plagued by the Nightingale, Year Before Last, Gentlemen, I Address You Privately,* and *My Next Bride.* In *Plagued by the Nightingale,* Bridget, a newly married, young American woman is thrust into the culture of her French husband's family. The novel is set in Brittany, where Bridget and her husband Nicholas are living with his closely knit and domineering family. In addition to the struggle between the old French traditions and Bridget's modern American upbringing, the novel deals with the family's pressure on Bridget and Nicholas to have a child even though a hereditary disease may be passed on to that child. Bridget feels more and more stifled by the family, but when Luc, a young doctor, offers her an escape she refuses, telling him that she and Nicholas are going to have a baby.

Year Before Last tells of the relationship between Hannah, a young woman, Martin, a dying poet, and Eve, an older woman who has been looking after Martin, her nephew. When Hannah and Martin are introduced and fall in love, Eve is left out, and her resentment and bitterness form the struggle of the novel. The conflict among the three, as Martin attempts to throw off Eve's dominance, is intensified by Martin's illness and approaching death. Eve leaves the two for a time but returns as Martin nears death. By the end, the women have reached an uneasy truce, each recognizing what the other has given Martin. Many critics consider *Year Before Last* the best of Boyle's thirties novels because of its sound structure and successful characterizations. The volume was translated into French in 1937.

Gentlemen, I Address You Privately is probably the most oblique of Boyle's novels, partly because of the subject matter—homosexuality—and partly because of Boyle's attempt to capture her impressions of the strange people she had encountered around Le Havre and Harfleur. The novel explores the possibility of meaningful relationships between individuals by examining the involvement of Munday, an ex-clergyman, with Ayton, a seaman who has deserted his ship. Once he discovers Ayton's unlawful flight, Munday helps him hide from the authorities. They spend much of their time on the farm of Quespelle and Leonie, who are illegally living on the land of Rochereau, an old newspaperman. When the couple is evicted, Ayton flees with three young Alsatian women, selling Munday's prized piano to obtain money for their escape. At the end of the novel Leonie is pregnant with what is hinted to be Ayton's child, a possibility Munday is not ready to believe or understand.

In *My Next Bride*, which is dedicated to Caresse Crosby, a young American woman, Victoria, comes to Paris seeking to make her way in a perplexing world. She falls under the spell of Sorrel, the charismatic leader of a utopian colony, but her idealism ultimately is dashed by Sorrel's human frailty. At the same time she is discovered and befriended by Antony, a sad, though glitteringly rich, self-exiled Bostonian, and his charming, talented, and self-assured wife Fontana. From her friendship with Antony and Fontana she learns of new facets of her humanity. Victoria's final lesson comes from Fontana when the news of Antony's suicide reaches them. The novel ends with Fontana addressing Victoria: " 'Don't cry. Antony said you never cried,' said Fontana, a small clear voice picking it up and putting it together and going on with it forever."

Also in 1934 Boyle embarked upon one of the more unusual publishing ventures of the expatriate thirties, the compilation of "Short Stories 1934." The idea was to gather 365 page-length stories to be a "comment in fiction form on the history of the year 1934," according to an advertisement for contributions in *Caravel*. Even though William Saroyan sent them 365 stories, 97 of the stories ultimately selected are by Boyle (and several more are written by her under pseudonyms). The anthology also includes contributions by Bessie Breuer, Bob and Rose Brown, Kathleen Cannell, Emanuel Carnevali, Nancy Cunard, Paul Engle, James T. Farrell, Charles Henri Ford, Hilaire Hiler, Langston Hughes, James Laughlin, Norman Macleod, William March, McAlmon, Henry Miller, Kerker Quinn, Sydney Salt, Saroyan, Evelyn Scott, John Thompson, Parker Tyler, and coeditors Laurence Vail and Nina Conarain. Today the volume is something of a collector's item, but at the time they had difficulty in finding a publisher; finally the book came out in 1936 in London and then America as *365 Days*. In retrospect the ideas which prompted this volume suggest the way Boyle compacts fiction upon time and reality. In all her novels Boyle never is very far from fact, but it is incorrect to assume any of her novels is merely autobiographical. Boyle reexamines fact through fictionalization and thus comes to understandings that were not necessarily evident in reality. In one sense Boyle questions what reality is, and may even be suggesting that the true reality is the fiction itself. One's reactions to events are more important than the events themselves. Fiction, then, gives meaning and form to fact because it allows for a controlling sensibility to be imposed upon otherwise random events. For Boyle,

Kay Boyle, 1932

this sensibility often translates into a concept of social responsibility—one's reaction to the world as it is. In later years she would say, simply, that her writing is—and always has been—"political."

In her novels Boyle works from her own life experiences, creating objective, "as is" worlds, peopling them with intense, subjective characters, and then seeming to watch as characters attempt to come to terms with settings. The fictional worlds of Boyle's novels become increasingly complex as Boyle's own experience broadened. In *Death of a Man* (1936), she creates the character of a young Austrian doctor, both enthralled with nazism and full of the idealism which characterizes the heroines of earlier novels. But ultimately the doctor sees there is nothing substantial at the head of the nazi idealism, nothing upon which to place one's faith or hope solidly. At one point in the novel he says, "It is not necessary to think, only to believe—to believe in youth and being young." But for Boyle's sensibilities this conclusion is unsatisfactory because one cannot believe without thinking. Man is faced with making choices, and unthinking belief is an abdication of the choice-making responsibility. Unthinking belief in anything is wrong, and it makes no difference if one is a disillusioned European who has seen his land trampled by war too often to fight any longer, or a native American who thinks everything should be right "just because." Blind belief is defeat. On the other hand man must be willing to act upon his thought-out beliefs, to accept the responsibility of making choices. For Boyle's characters the finest personal qualities are nothing unless they are accompanied by personal integrity.

In the same year that *Death of a Man* was published, Boyle also published an important collection of short stories, *The White Horses of Vienna and Other Stories*. The title story, which won the O. Henry short story award for 1935, deals not so much with the rise of nazism in Austria as it does with the void left by the collapse of established human values. The story creates an intricate balance between the political scene and the regal Lippizaner horses who no longer have royalty to bow to, while a puppet play about a grasshopper and a clown suggests the conflict between the new breed and the old. Also in the collection of eighteen stories are "White as Snow," a study of bigotry and a girl's own inability to cope with the color of her skin, and "Astronomer's Wife," a story, not without humor or double entendre, about a woman's chance to escape from the intellectual heights of her husband's world to the good, heady, real earth of the plumber who comes to do repairs.

In 1938 Boyle published *Monday Night*, which she considers to be her best novel of the period despite the critics' tendency to dismiss it as detective fiction with an unsatisfactory ending. One reason Boyle singles it out is that the protagonist is not a young American girl searching for meaning in a disrupted world. The book details the search of two men, one of them a writer, for a famed toxicologist, Sylvestre. The writer believes Sylvestre has been providing false testimony to convict innocent men at criminal trials in order to compensate for his own early failures in love and life. The quest to expose Sylvestre's deeds is suspenseful and sinister, and for a bit it looks as though the writer will finally get the one big story that will assure a successful and fulfilled career. But how does one measure fulfillment, ultimately? *Monday Night* has had a successful career of its own, being translated into French, and included in the New Directions New Classics reprint series.

In the late thirties Boyle met Joseph Franckenstein, an Austrian baron, mountain climber, skier, and scholar of classical languages and culture, who had been displaced from his homeland by the Nazis. He tutored the Vail children in Megeve, Haute Savoie, and when Boyle, Vail, and their children returned to the United States in August 1941, he also came at about the same time. In 1943, after Boyle's divorce from Vail, Franckenstein and Boyle were married. He became an American citizen that year, and as an OSS officer, parachuted into France to help the Resistance. Much of Boyle's World War II writing is inspired by Franckenstein's examples and friends. He and Boyle were in Germany during the occupation when Boyle turned out some of the finest postwar fiction for the *New Yorker* (collected in 1951 in *The Smoking Mountain*). He also was with her when she was accused of communist sympathies during the McCarthy era of the early fifties, and consequently lost his government job. Though the charges were fought and ultimately dismissed, the blacklisting and the time and resources required to fight the charges exacted immeasurable harm on their personal and professional lives. Shortly after moving to San Francisco, where Boyle had been appointed to the creative writing faculty of San Francisco State College in 1963, Franckenstein died of cancer. They had had two children.

The general concept with which Boyle grew up was that privilege demands social responsibility as well. She has never strayed from this belief, although her sense of social responsibility has not, at times, been that of the critics. Harry T. Moore, one of her most effective supporters, has argued convincingly that Boyle's relative obscurity today rests with her refusal to write what the critics of the Depression era were looking for. Many admired her freshness of style, precision of image, and economy of syntax, but felt she dwelled on small, individual manners and matters rather than on the struggle of the masses. Because her novels of the thirties tended to have young American heroines involved in European events, not unlike the events Kay Boyle herself was involved in, the critics were able to pass the books over as relatively inconsequential fictionalized autobiography, no matter how well-written. So what if a little American girl had trouble understanding her French husband's family? So what if a wild-eyed publisher died young, or a narcissistic dilettante took his own life? These things did not speak to the problems of the thirties, the critics contended. Most critics were unwilling to look behind the fine style at the sensibilities underlying the actions within the

Please return to Bob Brown,
170 Ocean Boulevard, Atlantic Highlands, N. J.

Kay Boyle
Villa Coustille
Col-de-Villefranche
Nice, A. M.

For Bob from
Kay

A COMEALLYE FOR ROBERT CARLTON BROWN

I

There was one man, and he was not an Irishman, but he might have been one with all his lying thieving ways. Nor was he a priest, but he might have been one because of his way of walking through the woods as if it were a church, murmuring, with a cross around his neck that he kept there for the shape of the thing. Gothic or Corinthian the pillars or the pine-trees might have been for all he knew the difference. But if a beast were sick, he could turn up its hoofs and nurse it like a mother.

George, and will ye be my bridegroom

was the refrain in the wind and in the mosses whose species he knew in the sole of his foot. He was busy following the soft secret track of a deer running and he could not very well reply.

And will ye be my bridegroom
And wear a crown of glory

In stomping your foot in that impatient way, he said, you stomped out the mark of the little deer running.

When he rolled back the sleeves of his shirt, there were his arms out bare like twists of taffy. One of them he put lovingly around the soft bowed neck of the ailing cow. The lady had lost her cud, it had dropped into one of her stomachs. A cud, he said, it is made of daisy hearts and dandilions. He held a bouquet of it flowering in his hand. Her rosy tongue hung through her teeth, her noble breath lolled on this couch of flesh, her cloven feet gave battle to a thousand blades of grass.

And will you be my bridegroom, George,
And wear a crown of glory
Will you take the dark for an evening cloak
And the Pleiades for planets
Can I have the moon for a looking-glass
Can I dance on the milky highroad -

And will you shut up for half a minute, said George, until I get this cud in her mouth can't you be quiet ?

He took care of the stock. He was a horse thief and a liar, it turned out. He was no good to anybody at all. Hours he

Morris Library

Typescript, ca. 1932

novels. From the vantage point of time one can see elements in Boyle's earlier writings which indeed were difficult for the Depression-ridden critics of the thirties to ascertain. And from the same vantage point it can be seen that the sensibilities which emerged in the short stories, poems, and novels of Kay Boyle's thirties are most certainly consistent with those concerns of a mature Kay Boyle writing after World War II, after McCarthy, and after Vietnam. In a 1968 interview she says, "I feel that in our times it is not the writer who must seek to be accepted by the world in which he finds himself, but it is the world which must be transformed to acceptibility by the higher standards of the individual...." The writer's deepest concern must be with "the dimension of what might within the infinite capacities of man be enabled to take place." Kay Boyle has been writing from these beliefs since she picked up her first pencil.

Other:

Gladys Palmer Brooke, *Relations & Complications Being the Recollections of H. H. the Dayang Muda of Sarawak*, ghostwritten by Boyle (London: Lane / Bodley Head, 1929);

Joseph Delteil, *Don Juan*, translated by Boyle (New York: Cape & Smith, 1931);

Rene Crevel, *Mr. Knife Miss Fork*, translated by Boyle (Paris: Black Sun Press, 1931);

Raymond Radiguet, *The Devil in the Flesh*, translated by Boyle (Paris: Crosby Continental Editions; New York: Harrison Smith, 1932; London: Grey Walls, 1949);

365 Days, edited with contributions by Boyle, Laurence Vail, and Nina Conarain (London: Cape, 1936; New York: Harcourt, Brace, 1936);

Bettina Bedwell, *Yellow Dusk*, ghostwritten by Boyle (London: Hurst & Blackett, 1937);

The Autobiography of Emanuel Carnevali, compiled with a preface by Boyle (New York: Horizon, 1967);

Robert McAlmon, *Being Geniuses Together 1920-1930*, revised edition with additional material by Boyle (Garden City: Doubleday, 1968; London: Joseph, 1970);

McAlmon, *A Hasty Bunch*, afterword by Boyle (Carbondale & Edwardsville: Southern Illinois University Press, 1977).

Periodical Publications:

"Morning," *Broom*, 4 (January 1923): 121-122;
"Summer," *This Quarter*, 1 (Spring 1925): 40-44;

"Passeres' Paris," *This Quarter*, 1 (Spring 1925): 140-142;

"Flight," *This Quarter*, 2 (Winter 1925-1926): 167-171;

"Theme," *transition*, no. 1 (April 1927): 31-35;

Review of *In the American Grain* by William Carlos Williams, *transition*, no. 1 (April 1927): 31-35;

"Complaint," *transition*, no. 2 (May 1927): 142;

"To America," *This Quarter*, 3 (Spring 1927): 108-110;

"For an American," *This Quarter*, 3 (Spring 1927): 111-115;

"O this is not spring . . . ," *This Quarter*, 3 (Spring 1927): 116;

"Carnival 1927," *This Quarter*, 3 (Spring 1927): 117;

"Comrade," *This Quarter*, 3 (Spring 1927): 118;

"Plagued by the Nightingale," *This Quarter*, 3 (Spring 1927): 165-203;

"Portrait," *transition*, no. 3 (June 1927): 29-31;

"And Winter," *transition*, no. 5 (August 1927): 114;

"Polar Bears And Others," *transition*, no. 6 (September 1927): 52-56;

"Bitte Nehmen Sie die Blumen," *transition*, no. 9 (December 1927): 88-93;

"A Sad Poem," *transition*, no. 10 (January 1928): 109;

"Mr. Crane and His Grandmother," review of *White Buildings* by Hart Crane, *transition*, no. 10 (January 1928): 135-138;

"Written for Royalty," *transition*, no. 13 (Summer 1928): 60-64;

"The United States," *transition*, no. 13 (Summer 1928): 186-187;

"Letter to Archibald Craig," *transition*, no. 13 (Summer 1928): 188-190;

"Why Do Americans Live in Europe?," by Boyle and others, *transition*, no. 14 (Fall 1928): 97-119;

"Vacation-Time," *transition*, no. 14 (Fall 1928): 143-145;

"Mr. Benet looks at the Civil War," review of *John Brown's Body* by Stephen Vincent Benet, *transition*, no. 15 (February 1929): 169-170;

"Revolution of the Word Proclamation," signed by Boyle and others, *transition*, no. 16/17 (June 1929): 13;

"On the Run," *transition*, no. 16/17 (June 1929): 83-85;

"Dedicated to Guy Urquhart," *transition*, no. 18 (November 1929): 85;

Rene Crevel, "Mr. Knife, Miss Fork," translated by Boyle, *transition*, no. 19/20 (June 1930): 221-222;

"The Only Bird that Sang," *transition*, no. 19/20 (June 1930): 261-263;

"Glad Day for L. V.," *transition*, no. 19/20 (June 1930): 157-158;

"A Complaint for M and M," *transition*, no. 27 (April/May 1938): 34-40.

Bibliography:

David V. Koch, *Kay Boyle: A Descriptive Bibliography* (Carbondale & Edwardsville: Southern Illinois University Press, forthcoming [1980]).

References:

Richard C. Carpenter, "Kay Boyle: The Figure in the Carpet," *Critique*, 7 (Winter 1964-1965): 65-78;

Charles Fracchia, "Kay Boyle: A Profile," *San Francisco Review of Books*, 1 (April 1976): 7-9;

Frank Gado, "Kay Boyle: From the Aesthetics of Exile to the Polemics of Return," Ph.D. dissertation, Duke University, 1969;

Byron K. Jackson, "The Achievement of Kay Boyle," Ph.D. dissertation, University of Florida, 1968;

"Kay Boyle," in *Talks with Authors*, ed. Charles F. Madden (Carbondale: Southern Illinois University Press, 1968), pp. 215-236;

Harry T. Moore, "Kay Boyle's Fiction," in his *The Age of the Modern and Other Essays* (Carbondale: Southern Illinois University Press, 1971), pp. 32-36;

Dan Tooker and Roger Hofheins, "Kay Boyle," in their *Fiction! Interviews With Northern California Novelists* (New York & Los Altos: Harcourt Brace Jovanovich / William Kaufman, 1976);

Edmund Wilson, "Kay Boyle and *The Saturday Evening Post*," in his *Classics and Commercials: A Literary Chronicle of the Forties* (New York: Farrar & Straus, 1950), pp. 128-132.

Papers:

Most of Kay Boyle's extant manuscripts and papers are at the Morris Library, Southern Illinois University, Carbondale.

WILLIAM ASPENWALL BRADLEY
(8 February 1878-10 January 1939)

SELECTED BOOKS: *William Cullen Bryant* (New York: Macmillan; London: Macmillan Ltd., 1905);

French Etchers of the Second Empire (Boston & New York: Houghton Mifflin, 1916);

Garlands and Wayfarings (Portland, Me.: T. B. Mosher, 1917);

Old Christmas and Other Kentucky Tales in Verse (Boston & New York: Houghton Mifflin, 1917);

Dutch Landscape Etchers of the Seventeenth Century (New Haven: Yale University Press, 1918; London: Milford & Oxford, 1919).

William Aspenwall Bradley, writer, translator, and editor, made his greatest contribution to French and American literature as the most successful American literary agent in Paris during the twenties and thirties.

Born in Hartford, Connecticut, Bradley moved to New York City as a boy. He studied at Columbia University, receiving a B.A. in 1899 and an M.A. in 1900. He worked as art director and literary adviser for the McClure Company from 1900 to 1908, and then until World War I he worked mainly as a writer and editor. He contributed articles to the *Boston Herald*, *American Magazine*, and the *Delineator* while writing and editing a number of books. His books include a biography of William Cullen Bryant for the English Men of Letters series (1905), two volumes of poetry, published in 1917, and volumes on the etchers of Second-Empire France (1916) and seventeenth-century Holland (1918). The broad range of his literary and artistic interests is also apparent in the books he edited: a collection of Samuel Johnson's prayers (1903), an anthology of garden poems (1910), an edition of Edward Everett Hale's *The Man Without a Country* (1910), and *The Correspondence of Philip Sidney and Hubert Languet* (1912). In 1917 Bradley went to France as a captain in the U.S. Army and remained after the war. In 1921 he married a Frenchwoman, Jenny Serruys, who became well-known in Paris for her literary salons. Bradley became a passionate champion of French literature in America, publishing his own translations of works by Remy

William Aspenwall Bradley, Paris, 1926

Courtesy of Mrs. W. A. Bradley

de Gourmont, Rene Lalou, Marie Leneru, and Louis Hemon during the twenties. He completed a translation of Paul Valery's essays, *Variety: Second Series*, in 1938 shortly before his death in January of the following year. He was also American agent for Gertrude Stein's friend Bernard Fay, who was undoubtedly the most distinguished scholar of American culture in France during the period between the two World Wars.

In 1926 Bradley was awarded the Legion d'Honneur by the French government for his promotion of French literature. The extent of his influence upon the selection of French writers Americans would read in translation is suggested by Janet Flanner's comments in her "Letter from Paris" in the *New Yorker* for 9 February 1929. She calls Bradley the "leading agent and prophet here on transatlantic affairs," and gives her readers Bradley's list of the French books they will be reading in 1929. Among the volumes of fiction on the list are Francois Mauriac's *La Chair et le Sang, Massif Central* and *Les Hommes de la Route* by Andre Chamson, Blaise Cendrar's *Little Negro Stories for White Children*, and *Leviathan* by Julien Green, an American who writes in French.

One of Bradley's most famous negotiations for an American client was the sale of Gertrude Stein's *The Autobiography of Alice B. Toklas* (1933), which

was Stein's first financial success. Bradley was excited about the book and not only sold it to Harcourt, Brace, but helped Stein to achieve her dream of publication in the conservative *Atlantic Monthly* by persuading the magazine to accept excerpts from the book for serial publication.

A somewhat less tranquil literary relationship was Bradley's representation of Henry Miller and Anais Nin. Bradley recognized the genius of Miller's *Tropic of Cancer* (1934), but he also saw the impossibility of finding an American publisher for the novel and told Miller that Jack Kahane's Obelisk Press in Paris was the only publishing house that would dare accept it. Even Kahane appears to have been hesitant. Although Bradley persuaded him to accept the novel in October 1932, it was not published until September 1934. Bradley later incurred Miller's anger at least briefly by suggesting that Nin should edit for publication the five-foot-high stack of diaries she had sent him. Miller thought all the journals should be published as they were and was infuriated when Bradley asked that they be cut drastically. Bradley returned the diaries to Nin but continued to serve as her agent, offering her advice on *The House of Incest* (1936). Although she sometimes found his suggestions gratuitous, she remained fond of Bradley, calling him "humorous, quick, and stubborn too."

Other Americans represented at various times by Bradley include Nathan Asch, Natalie Barney, Stephen Vincent Benet, Louis Bromfield, Caresse Crosby, John Dos Passos, James T. Farrell, Ramon Guthrie, Bravig Imbs, Eugene Jolas, Ludwig Lewisohn, Claude McKay, Peter Neagoe, Katherine Anne Porter, Ezra Pound, Samuel Putnam, Robert Sage, William Seabrook, George Seldes, William L. Shirer, Glenway Wescott, Edith Wharton, and Thornton Wilder. After Bradley's death in January 1939, Mrs. Bradley took over the operation of the agency and continues to run it. Bradley's willingness to champion the avant-garde at a time when American publishers were unappreciative of experimental writing and unwilling to take the financial risks of publishing it had a significant influence upon the shape of modern literature.

—*Karen L. Rood*

Other:

The Prayers of Doctor Samuel Johnson, edited by Bradley (New York: McClure, Phillips, 1903);
The Garden Muse Poems for Garden Lovers, edited with an introduction by Bradley (New York: Sturgis & Walton, 1910);

Edward Everett Hale, *The Man Without a Country*, edited with an introduction by Bradley (New York: Merrill, 1910);

The Correspondence of Philip Sidney and Hubert Languet, edited by Bradley (Boston: Merrymount Press, 1912);

Remy de Gourmont, *Decadence and Other Essays on the Culture of Ideas*, translated by Bradley (New York: Harcourt, Brace, 1921; London: Richards, 1922);

Marie Leneru, *Journal*, translated by Bradley (New York: Macmillan, 1923; London: Macmillan, 1924);

Louis Hemon, *My Fair Lady*, translated by Bradley (New York: Macmillan, 1923);

Hemon, *Journal*, translated by Bradley (New York: Macmillan, 1924);

Wanda Landowska, *Music of the Past*, translated by Bradley (New York: Knopf, 1924; London: Bles, 1926);

Rene Lalou, *Contemporary French Literature*, translated by Bradley (New York: Knopf, 1924; London: Cape, 1925);

Hemon, *Monsieur Ripois and Nemesis*, translated by Bradley (New York: Macmillan, 1925; London: Allen & Unwin, 1925);

Paul Valery, *Variety: Second Series*, translated by Bradley (New York: Harcourt, Brace, 1938).

References:

Hugh Ford, *Published in Paris American and British Writers, Printers, and Publishers in Paris, 1920-1939* (New York: Macmillan, 1975), pp. 235-384;

Donald Gallup, ed., *The Flowers of Friendship Letters Written to Gertrude Stein* (New York: Knopf, 1953), pp. 258-281;

Jay Martin, *Always Merry and Bright The Life of Henry Miller* (Santa Barbara, Cal.: Capra, 1978), pp. 262, 299;

James R. Mellow, *Charmed Circle Gertrude Stein & Company* (New York & Washington: Praeger, 1974), pp. 349-376.

LOUIS BROMFIELD
(27 December 1896-18 March 1956)

SELECTED BOOKS: *The Green Bay Tree* (New York: Stokes, 1924; London: Unwin, 1924);

Possession (New York: Stokes, 1925); republished as *Lilli Barr* (London: Unwin, 1926);

Early Autumn (New York: Stokes, 1926; London: Cape, 1926);

A Good Woman (New York: Stokes, 1927; London: Cape, 1927);

The Strange Case of Miss Annie Spragg (New York: Stokes, 1928; London: Cape, 1928);

The Farm (New York & London: Harper, 1933; London: Cassell, 1933);

The Rains Came (New York & London: Harper, 1937; London: Cassell, 1937);

Mrs. Parkington (New York: Harper, 1943; London: Cassell, 1944);

Pleasant Valley (New York & London: Harper, 1945; London: Cassell, 1946);

A Few Brass Tacks (New York & London: Harper, 1946);

Malabar Farm (New York & London: Harper, 1948; London: Cassell, 1949);

Out of the Earth (New York: Harper, 1950; London: Cassell, 1951);

A New Pattern for a Tired World (New York: Harper, 1954; London: Cassell, 1954);

From My Experience (New York: Harper, 1955; London: Cassell, 1956).

Louis Bromfield was one of the many writers of his generation for whom residence in France provided a clearer understanding of his American subject matter. A native of Mansfield, Ohio, Bromfield and his family moved to his grandfather's farm during his last year of high school, and Bromfield contemplated a career as a farmer. He studied agriculture briefly at Cornell, but abandoned it to study journalism at Columbia in 1916. Later that year he went to France, where he served as an ambulance driver for nearly two years until the war ended in 1918. The French government later awarded him the Croix de Guerre for his service

Louis Bromfield

during the war. He returned to the United States late in 1919 and held a variety of writing jobs including that of drama and music critic for the *Bookman*.

The publication in 1924 of his first novel, *The Green Bay Tree*, brought him instant acclaim. It was quickly followed by *Possession* (1925), *Early Autumn* (1926), and *A Good Woman* (1927). Bromfield conceived of these four books as panels treating different phases of American life and suggested that they might be considered one novel under the general title of *Escape*. While not closely interrelated, they do have some characters in common and are tied thematically in their presentation of the struggles of individuals against the materialism of the new industrial order. They enjoyed moderate critical success and wide popular success: *Early Autumn* was awarded the Pulitzer Prize for 1927.

Bromfield returned to France with his family for a vacation late in 1925. What was to have been a vacation, however, turned into a residence of thirteen years. The Bromfields became prominent expatriates, attending Natalie Barney's salon and visiting Sylvia Beach's Shakespeare and Company bookshop. Bromfield defended the American expatriates in an essay, "Expatriate—Vintage 1927," published in *Mirrors of the Year* (1927), where he argued that the experience of living in Europe gave him a sharper perspective on his native land and that American culture was no longer in danger of being swallowed by European culture.

The Bromfields soon abandoned Paris itself, however, and took up residence in an old *presbytere* in Senlis, thirty-five miles to the north. Here Bromfield entertained lavishly, cultivated his interest in gardening, and found peace to maintain his prolific writing. His interest in gardening led to friendships with Edith Wharton, who lived nearby, and with Gertrude Stein, whom Bromfield praised as an "experimenter with words" in his review of *The Autobiography of Alice B. Toklas* (1933). He produced books at the rate of nearly one a year, but his critical reputation did not keep pace with his books' popular appeal. During the thirties, however, he produced his two best books. *The Farm* (1933) is a fictionalized account of his own family's history and depicts the gradual decline of their agrarian life and its replacement by an industrial one. *The Rains Came* (1937) deals with the struggle of India to enter the modern world without succumbing totally to the forces of materialism that had engulfed the West.

Bromfield's critical reputation has suffered from both the great quantity of his work and his large readership. In fact he did write easily, and the commercial demand for his work led him to publish much that was inferior. He was charged with writing fiction with the prospect of lucrative film sales in mind. But he also came under fire for his political philosophy, a Jeffersonian individualism which posited a natural aristocracy. Such a position was particularly unpopular in the collectivist-conscious decade of the thirties.

With the knowledge that war was imminent and that he could not remain in his comfortable home north of Paris, Bromfield returned to the United States late in 1938. The following year he bought three adjoining farms in Richland County, Ohio, near his native Mansfield, and threw himself actively into the scientific farming he had abandoned at the outset of his career. Malabar Farm became famous and provided source material for many of Bromfield's later books. *Pleasant Valley* (1945), *Malabar Farm* (1948), *Out of the Earth* (1950), and *From My Experience* (1955) record the development of Bromfield's agricultural experiments and offer advice on scientific farming. Farming now took precedence over fiction in Bromfield's life. He lectured widely on agriculture and conservation and published two books espousing his political views: *A Few Brass Tacks* (1946) and *A New Pattern for a Tired World* (1954).

Louis Bromfield

At the end of his life Bromfield was nearly as well-known as a farmer as he was as a novelist. Nevertheless he retained a strong hold on the reading public so that even several of his Malabar Farm books were commercial successes. His Jeffersonian agrarianism was classically American, but it was also a philosophy rooted in eighteenth-century French influences. Bromfield's years of residence in Paris and Senlis did not have much direct influence on his fiction. Still, he was powerfully attracted to the French people and to the simple life still found in the French countryside. His French experiences could only reinforce the independent agrarian spirit which he inherited from his Midwestern ancestors and which he defended in some of his best fiction. It is this clear and forceful presentation of an agrarian point of view for which Louis Bromfield is best remembered. —*Philip B. Eppard*

Other:

"Expatriate—Vintage 1927," in *Mirrors of the Year*,
ed. Grant Overton (New York: Stokes, 1927), pp. 228-239;
Review of *The Autobiography of Alice B. Toklas* by Gertrude Stein, *New York Herald Tribune Books*, 3 September 1933, pp. 1-2.

References:

David D. Anderson, *Louis Bromfield* (New York: Twayne, 1964);

Morrison Brown, *Louis Bromfield and His Books* (Fair Lawn, N.J.: Essential Books, 1957);

Merle Derrenbacher, "Louis Bromfield: A Bibliography," *Bulletin of Bibliography*, 17 (September-December 1941): 112; (January-April 1942): 141-145;

Ellen Bromfield Geld, *The Heritage: A Daughter's Memories of Louis Bromfield* (New York: Harper, 1962).

BOB BROWN
(14 June 1886-7 August 1959)

SELECTED BOOKS: *What Happened to Mary?* (New York: Clode, 1913);
The Remarkable Adventures of Christopher Poe (Chicago: F. G. Browne, 1913);
My Marjonary (Boston: Luce, 1916);
1450-1950 (Paris: Black Sun Press, 1929; enlarged edition, New York: Jargon Books, 1959);
The Readies (Bad-Ems: Roving Eye Press, 1930);
Globe-Gliding (Diessen: Roving Eye Press, 1930);
Words (Paris: Hours Press, 1931);
Gems: A Censored Anthology (Cagnes-sur-Mer: Roving Eye Press, 1931);
Demonics (Cagnes-sur-Mer: Roving Eye Press, 1931);
Nomadness (New York: Dodd, Mead, 1931);
Let There Be Beer! (New York: Smith & Haas, 1932);
Can We Co-operate? (Pleasant Plains, Staten Island, New York: Roving Eye Press, 1940);
The Complete Book of Cheese (New York: Random House, 1955).

Bob Brown lived a colorful and varied life as journalist, poet, novelist, editor, publisher, rare book dealer, world traveler, and bon vivant. His interest in the avant-garde, especially in the visual aspects of words, took him to France in 1929, where he set up the Roving Eye Press to promote his invention, the Reading Machine, which was intended to change the way people read by moving the words past the reader's eye at a speed controlled by the individual.

Robert Carlton Brown was born in Chicago, Illinois, to Robert Carlton and Cora Bracket Brown, both of whom were interested in writing and books. His father was a book publisher and rare book collector. Brown graduated from Oak Park High School, later attended by Ernest Hemingway, and went to the University of Wisconsin. There seems to have been little doubt that Brown would follow a career in writing. Explaining his family background, Brown said, "I was almost a book myself." He started writing stories in Chicago, but by 1907, at age twenty-one, he moved to New York, where he began an extraordinary career as a freelance writer. The next year he went to London to get the English "slant." When he returned to New York, he married Rose Johnston. A son, Robert Carlton, was born to them in 1912. The following year Brown had a best-seller when he published *What Happened to Mary?* (1913), a novel based on his play and stories that had appeared in *Ladies' World*. *What Happened to Mary?* was made into one of the first successful motion pictures. Meanwhile, Brown was writing or team writing a vast amount of pulp fiction including another popular success, *The Remarkable Adventures of Christopher Poe* (1913), a book of detective stories. He published under a variety of names and earned as much as $15,000 a year at the trade. Brown had intended to be a wealthy man and sometimes was. He reported to H. L. Mencken that in 1915 he made a small fortune on Wall Street and quit writing—and also that in 1916 he lost a small fortune on Wall Street and so resumed writing.

But successful as he was with pulp fiction, Brown was also interested in writing serious poetry. In 1913 he was part of an informal poetry group, led by Walter Arensberg and Alfred Kreymborg, who first met in Grantwood, New Jersey, and then in Greenwich Village. Others in the group were William Carlos Williams, Maxwell Bodenheim, Orrick Johns, Malcolm Cowley, Marcel Duchamp, and Man Ray. The group published *Glebe* (September 1913-November 1914), which printed the work of the Imagists, and later *Others*, which included poems by Marianne Moore, Ezra Pound, Wallace Stevens, T. S. Eliot, and others. John C. Thirwall calls Brown the Maecenas, or generous patron, of the group in Grantwood.

On his profits from pulp-fiction writing Brown spent part of 1913 in Spain. But after his return to the United States he found himself written out, and he felt that nothing worthwhile was being written in America. Two events renewed his enthusiasm for writing. At the Armory Show, held in New York City in late 1913, Brown, like most other Americans, had his first opportunity to see paintings by such artists as Matisse, Kandinsky, Brancusi, and Picasso. Brown was especially impressed by Marcel Duchamp's *Nude Descending a Staircase*. Duchamp's painting and subsequent meetings with Duchamp convinced Brown to write "optical" poems—pictures drawn in words. The second event was the 1914 publication in New York of Gertrude Stein's *Tender Buttons*. Brown was drawn to the visual aspects of her prose poems and described the book as "a case of champagne to me in a time of dire need." At age thirty he began to experiment with visual effects in his poetry, publishing a small collection of verse, *My Marjonary* (1916), with the help of H. L. Mencken.

It was inevitable that Brown would eventually make his way to Paris and into the company of those who frequented Stein's salon at 27, rue de Fleurus, but his journey to Paris was delayed by World War I and travel elsewhere. The *American Mercury* of September 1931 described Brown's activities during the war: "In 1917 he declined Mr. Wilson's invitation to make the world safe for U.S. Steel, but in 1918 he accepted a Committee of Public Information pastorate in Santiago de Chile, expounding the sacred myths about German atrocities to the benighted." In 1919 Brown and his wife founded in Rio de Janeiro the *Brazilian American* weekly magazine, which they published for a decade. The magazine inaugurated, as they testified in the dedication of *Amazing Amazon* (1942), "a whole generation of goodwill between the United States of Brazil and the United States of America." In 1929 the Browns left Rio de Janeiro to travel throughout the Orient, collecting jade, Japanese prints, and rare books. Eventually they settled in France, where Brown supported his family through dealing in rare books (the staple of his own reading) and began to write verse again.

From this new start in creative work emerged *1450-1950* (1929), the first indication of the ideas about innovative printing which Brown would expound upon at greater length in *The Readies* (1930). Brown's title, *1450-1950*, celebrates 500 years of movable type; it focuses on the "*isness*" of the word. Brown dedicated the book to "All monks who illuminated manuscripts—all early oriental artists—

Omar — Gutenberg — Caxton — Jimmy-the-Ink — Boccaccio — Rabelais — Shakespeare — Defoe — Goya — Blake — Sterne — Whitman — Crane — Stein—Joyce—Pagliacci—and myself." Brown illustrated his simple, earthy, humorous poems with his own drawings. He explained that in his optical poems he wanted to "recapture something of the healthy hieroglyphic." The book was first published in August 1929 by Harry and Caresse Crosby's Black Sun Press in a limited edition of 150 copies, and in 1959 a slightly enlarged edition was published in New York. Reviewing the 1959 edition in *Poetry* (April 1960), A. R. Ammons commented on Brown's desire to escape the tyranny of the printed word: "But Mr. Brown is right. *His* words alone are not worth a damn. His drawings alone, except for a savage and perhaps meaningful simplicity, also are not worth a damn. But his words and drawings together present a straightforward, brutal and innocent egotism and joy of life that no academician or other dull or bigoted soul should leave out of his response complex." Ammons judged *1450-1950* "a cool breeze from the Twenties for our hot, dry, thermonuclear times."

Indicative of the drive for newness in the Paris of that time was Brown's return to an idea that he had kept since he was eighteen and had read Stephen Crane's "Black Riders." Brown liked the look of the poem and saw the words as "black riders" across the page. He was convinced that people could read much faster than they did and that writers could learn to write in a new way if a reading machine were developed which allowed one's eyes to look straight ahead while the words moved by at a speed adjusted by the individual reader. Superfluous words such as "the" and "an" would become unnecessary, and punctuation could be reduced to a minimum. Brown explained his notion in "The Readies," which appeared in the June 1930 issue of *transition*. The title describes the new literature that would result from the invention of the Reading Machine, the designation "readies" a play on the "movies" and the "talkies." (The idea is already embodied in *1450-1950*, for one does not need to move the eye like a typewriter carriage to read that book.)

In 1930 Brown established the Roving Eye Press (a convenient imprint for a world traveler such as Brown) to publish his own books, which were intended to publicize his invention. His first publication, *The Readies*, contains examples of the streamlined poetry and prose to be read with the Reading Machine as well as an expanded version of the *transition* article. One of the poems says simply,

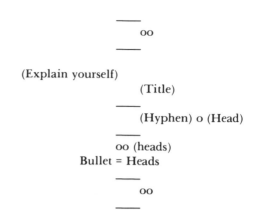

Brown's next publication was *Globe-Gliding*, a volume of free-verse description of various cities he had lived in or visited. At the artists' colony at Cagnes-sur-Mer, in the South of France, where the Browns established themselves, the American artists Hilaire Hiler and Ross Saunders made a crude working model of the Reading Machine for Brown, and Brown announced plans to publish an anthology of writings suited for his machine. He asked for contributions which would be as different from conventional books as sound motion pictures are from the stage. Some forty contributors wrote pieces in the new style for *Readies for Bob Brown's Machine* (1931), including Gertrude Stein, Ezra Pound, James T. Farrell, Kay Boyle, Paul Bowles, Alfred Kreymborg, Eugene Jolas, and Robert McAlmon. The fun of the experiment was enhanced by the inclusion in the middle of the book of "The Writies," a defense of the traditional printed page by Manuel Komroff. Brown provided an appendix on the history of the idea for his machine, and he touted the merits of his machine widely, attempting to proselytize writers other than those who contributed to the book, such as H. L. Mencken and William Carlos Williams.

Also in 1931 three books of Brown's own poetry appeared. Nancy Cunard's Hours Press brought out *Words*, intended to publicize the changes the Reading Machine would make in the printing industry, while Brown's own Roving Eye Press published *Demonics*, which Hugh Ford praises for containing some of Brown's best poems. Brown reached a larger audience with *Nomadness*, published by Dodd, Mead. The book is a collection of free verse rendering impressions from Brown's travels. Reviewing *Nomadness* in the *Saturday Review of Literature* (8 March 1931), William Rose Benet declared: "Mr. Brown is not a wit. He is a pleasantly acrid commentator who does not create

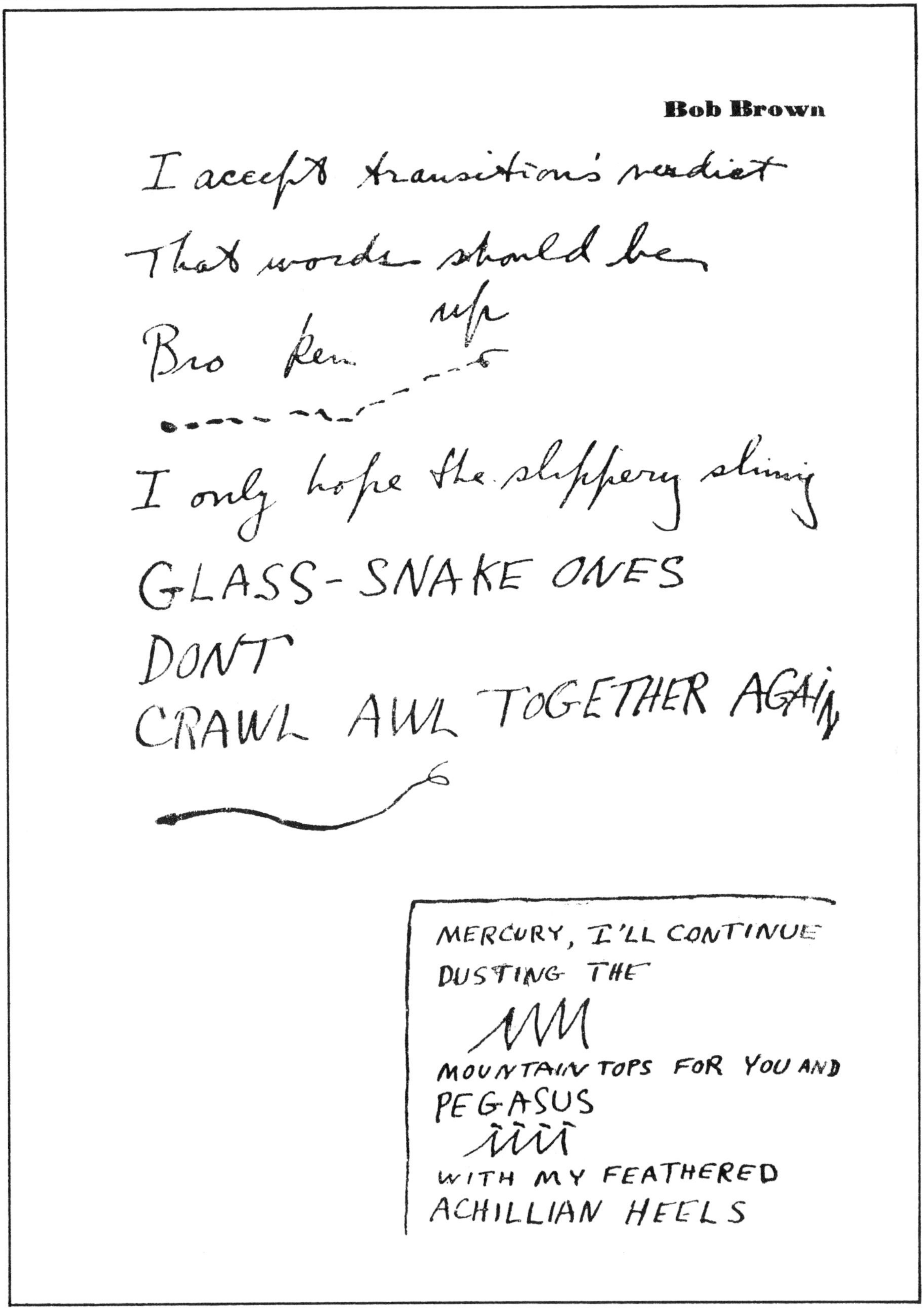

Bob Brown

I accept transition's verdict
That words should be
Broken up

I only hope the slippery slimy
GLASS-SNAKE ONES
DON'T
CRAWL AWL TOGETHER AGAIN

MERCURY, I'LL CONTINUE
DUSTING THE
/\/\/\
MOUNTAIN TOPS FOR YOU AND
PEGASUS
ũũũ
WITH MY FEATHERED
ACHILLIAN HEELS

"Experiment," transition, *no. 18 (November 1929)*

deathless lines and, indeed, sometimes proses quite blantantly, but for all that can, on occasion, be strikingly descriptive." Benet concluded, "If you intend to travel about this Spring to any of the 'Stops' that Mr. Brown made, you could do worse than secure his improvement on Baedecker, though you won't find a single statistic in it." Another project for 1931 was *Gems: A Censored Anthology*, which Ford calls "an insider's guide to the business of selling 'dirty' books to unwary customers who believe they are purchasing high-class pornography." Brown argues that censorship is a matter of taste and claims that it can make the most innocent literature seem pornographic. He illustrates his point by "censoring" a number of familiar poems and rhymes, such as:

> Old Mother Goose, when
> She wanted to * * *
> Would * * a fat goose
> Or a very fine gander.

Brown returned from Europe to live in New York City in late 1932, but he continued to write of the tastes he had cultivated in his European and other travels. Indicative of those tastes was his 1932 book *Let There Be Beer!*, a history of beer and great beer-drinking localities. A part of the book had appeared in Mencken's *American Mercury*, and Brown dedicated *Let There Be Beer!* to Mencken, who had published contributions from Brown while Brown was living in France as well as after his return to America. Brown later wrote a similar book dealing with cheese, *The Complete Book of Cheese* (1955). With his mother and wife, Brown wrote several books on cooking and food, including a book on wine. In 1942 Rose and Bob Brown collaborated on *Amazing Amazon*, a travel chronicle of a five-month trip up the Amazon. The book comments on the animals, flora, food, and people the Browns encountered on the journey, suggesting the verve that marked Brown's life.

As one of the moving spirits in Greenwich Village in the early years of the century, Brown was politically liberal, successful capitalist though he was. For the *American Mercury* he recounted those early days of the village and of *Masses*, of which Brown himself had been a contributing editor. He published poetry in *International Literature* and contributed to *New Masses*. In 1940 his own Roving Eye Press published *Can We Co-operate?*, one of his considerations of Communism.

Brown died after a brief illness in 1959, as the new edition of *1450-1950* was being prepared for publication. Brown wrote no great book, but his work arrests the imagination in its variety and serves as a history of an emerging modernism. Furthermore, Brown was a lively reporter on America, the expatriates, and the world.

—*Joseph M. Flora*

Other:

Readies for Bob Brown's Machine, edited with an appendix by Brown (Cagnes-sur-Mer: Roving Eye Press, 1931);

Amazing Amazon, by Brown and Rose Johnston Brown (New York: Modern Age, 1942).

Periodical Publications:

"I Am Aladdin," *Others*, 1 (August 1915): 28-30;

"Experiment," *transition*, no. 18 (November 1929): 208;

"Overseas Americans," *American Mercury*, 19 (January 1930): 22-29;

"The Readies," *transition*, no. 19/20 (June 1930): 167-173;

"National Festival: GW, 1732-1932," *American Mercury*, 24 (September 1931): 402-408;

"Sub-Tropical," *transition*, no. 21 (March 1932): 27-36;

"Pages from the Book of Beer," *American Mercury*, 26 (June 1932): 185-191;

"Drug-store in a Dry Town," *American Mercury*, 26 (August 1932): 405-411;

"Report of a Returned New Yorker," *American Mercury*, 27 (October 1932): 185-192;

"Swell Days for Literary Guys," *American Mercury*, 27 (December 1932): 480-485;

"Houdini," *Prairie Schooner*, 7 (Fall 1933): 156-158;

"Them Asses," *American Mercury*, 30 (December 1933): 403-411;

"Greenwich Village Gallops," *American Mercury*, 31 (January 1934): 103-111;

"The Bloody Beer Battle," *New Writings*, no. 3 (Spring 1937): 88-93.

References:

Hugh Ford, *Published in Paris American and British Writers, Printers, and Publishers in Paris, 1920-1939* (New York: Macmillan, 1975), pp. 302-311;

Bernard Harden Porter, *Robert Carlton Brown (Bob Brown)* (N.p.: Privately printed, 1956).

EDGAR CALMER
(16 July 1907-   )

SELECTED BOOKS: *Beyond the Street* (New York: Harcourt, Brace, 1934);
When Night Descends (New York: Farrar & Rinehart, 1936);
All the Summer Days (Boston: Little, Brown, 1961; London: Hodder & Stoughton, 1962).

Between 1927 and 1934 Edgar (Ned) Calmer served as a reporter first for the Paris *Tribune* (the European edition of the *Chicago Tribune*) and later for the Paris *Herald* (the European edition of the *New York Herald*). He traveled widely in Europe as a foreign correspondent from 1928 to 1934, but Paris remained his actual and spiritual focal point. In Paris during the late twenties and early thirties Calmer wrote his first novel, *Beyond the Street* (1934), published several short prose pieces and poems in *transition*, and moved in the company of many notable writers, including Henry Miller and Ernest Hemingway. His later novel, *All the Summer Days* (1961), is a fictionalized account of his experiences working for the Paris *Tribune* and living at the Hotel de Lisbonne, the Latin Quarter residence of nearly half the paper's staff.

Calmer was born in Chicago to Henry Edgar and May Regan Calmer and spent his childhood in Boston and later New York. He attended the University of Virginia in the mid-twenties before embarking for Paris without a degree. While in Paris in March 1929, Calmer married Priscilla A. Hatch. To be a reporter in Paris in the mid-twenties meant to experience a personal and artistic liberation from the moralistic purges of American society. As *All the Summer Days* indicates, the bohemian-artistic society of Paris in the twenties invited a frantic hedonism while at the same time offering the writing apprenticeship of newspaper work.

When his fellow *Tribune* staff members Eugene Jolas and Elliot Paul began editing *transition* in 1927, Calmer contributed a number of poems and prose pieces. Since the avowed purpose of *transition* was to be an "international magazine for creative experiment," much of the work it published, including Calmer's, showed the modeling influence of James Joyce and Gertrude Stein. "People from Across the Plains," a short story which appeared in the Fall 1928 issue of *transition*, depicts American society's attempts to ignore or suppress the unconscious as a source of creativity, a theme which is developed more fully in *Beyond the Street*. This first novel presents personal and sexual repression in

Edgar Calmer, 1934

a New York City high school as a metaphor for American society, and the restraints it describes contrast sharply to the freedom of Parisian life celebrated in *All the Summer Days*. Another member of the *Tribune*'s staff was proofreader Henry Miller. During the summer of 1931, Miller saved himself from starvation by inviting himself to lunch or dinner at the tables of various friends, among them Calmer.

A more significant friendship was initiated in November 1933 when Calmer met newspaperman turned fiction writer Ernest Hemingway. Because of their shared backgrounds and interests, the two liked each other immediately. Hemingway was horrified to learn that Calmer's two-year-old daughter Alden had not yet been christened and demanded that she be baptized without delay. After the ceremony, for which he stood as godfather, Hemingway took the Calmers to lunch. *Beyond the Street* was soon to be published in New York, but because Calmer did not have the ship fare, he resigned himself to missing the occasion. During their lunch, Hemingway learned of Calmer's plight and gave him "a check for $350, enough to pay the passage for the whole family," according to Hemingway biographer Carlos Baker.

Don Suca ~~reunited~~
Benny

22

Haines was in the luck all right! The feeling of his envy swept him like hunger. He had an image in his mind of days spent lying on beaches in the soft sun, nights in smart bars, mornings awakening in the luxury of hotel suites, with nothing to do, nothing to do!

Helen had come into the room again and shut the door quietly. "He promised me he'd lie down a while longer because I told him if he did the pain would go away," she said. "He has a little colic again, I guess. All this early heat. ~~I'm sorry I said that about Brace.~~ It's only because he's sensitive and easily frightened, Jack --. And it's a little hard for him -- Paris. The way we live."

"It's only because he's spoiled and sickly," Conway said. He turned and passed her, avoiding touching her as he went to the couch and threw himself down on his back with an arm across his eyes. He couldn't see her but he felt she was trying to smile, calmly, in the way she had that infuriated him. Then he felt her leaning over him, about to kiss him, and he jerked his head violently away.

"If you had the slightest vestige of pride," he said, "you couldn't do a thing like that."

She was silent for a moment and then she sat down on the edge of the couch and said: "I guess I don't have much pride. Where you're concerned, anyway. I think I know how it is with you. I don't really blame you, I guess. You want to be free to write, and you're not."

The soft patience in her voice irritated him all over again. "We won't go into that. We've been over all that."

Conway not revil!

Typescript from an early version of All the Summer Days

Hemingway also wrote a letter of recommendation on 9 December 1934, supporting Calmer's unsuccessful attempt for a Guggenheim Fellowship. In a later letter Hemingway confessed that no one he recommended ever received a Guggenheim.

Returning to the United States in 1934, Calmer remained in New York until 1939 and worked as a news editor of the Agence Havas, France, while he wrote his second novel, *When Night Descends* (1936). His dual role as journalist and fiction writer led him to CBS and to Hollywood in the early forties and then to London, to Supreme Headquarters in Paris, and to the front lines during World War II. He was married for a second time in August 1957 to Carol Church, and they had a son, Regan. Calmer continued to work as a news editor and broadcaster for CBS until 1967, when he retired to devote himself fulltime to writing fiction. In 1974 he married Gloria Hercik.

As his novel *All the Summer Days* attests, Calmer's experiences in Paris during the twenties and thirties proved essential to his future as a journalist and fiction writer. *All the Summer Days* offers a vivid, authentic portrait of American writers and journalists in Paris in the twenties. Paris itself becomes a pervasive symbol of freedom and imagination serving as a background for the personal dramas narrated by journalist Alex Gardner: the would-be novelist's drinking himself into downfall while his wife quickly learns to love Paris and another man who unfolds the city's beauty to her; the innocent poetess falling victim to romance's cruelties; and the American provincial becoming transformed into Parisian sophisticate. Paris is liberating and inspiring for those Americans with the maturity and self-discipline to shape the life of the city into art, but it is destructive to those who lack the ability to order their lives when free of societal rules. Adding to the realism of these lives are the actual news events of the day: Lindbergh's transatlantic flight, Babe Ruth's batting records, Isadora Duncan's dancing, and the Sacco-Vanzetti trial. In many respects Calmer's novel ranks with Dos Passos's *The Best Times* (1966) and with Hemingway's *A Moveable Feast* (1964) as an important record of American expatriates in Paris.

—*Ronald Baughman*

Periodical Publications:

"People from Across the Plains," *transition*, no. 14 (Fall 1928): 131-136;

"Self-Portrait," *transition*, no. 15 (February 1929): 137-138;

"Prayer," *transition*, no. 18 (November 1929): 86;

"Printed Opus," *transition*, no. 18 (November 1929): 87;

"The Letter," *transition*, no. 18 (November 1929): 88;

"The Watcher," *transition*, no. 19/20 (June 1930): 274-275;

"Paris Interlude," *Lost Generation Journal*, 3 (Winter 1975): 23-26.

References:

Ralph Jules Frantz, " 'I Tell it This Way,' " *Lost Generation Journal*, 2 (Spring-Summer 1974): 18-19;

Frantz, "The Chicatrib: 1917-34," *Lost Generation Journal*, 2 (Fall 1974): 2-4, 36.

KATHLEEN CANNELL
(6 March 1891-23 May 1974)

BOOK: *Jam Yesterday* (New York: Morrow, 1945).

Kathleen Biggar Eaton Cannell, sometimes called Kitty, is best known for her affair with Harold Loeb, which is satirized in Ernest Hemingway's *The Sun Also Rises* (1926). Hemingway depicts her as Frances Clyne, an ill-tempered, desperate woman, but the portrait is unjustified. For most of her life, she was a financially independent journalist, working as the Paris fashion editor for the *New York Times* from 1931 to 1941 and as the ballet critic for the *Christian Science Monitor* for many years thereafter. Although sometimes Cannell said that she was born in Utica, New York, her autobiography, *Jam Yesterday* (1945), says that she was born in the Fort George section of New York City. She later lived in Port Ontario, Canada, Philadelphia, and Paris, where she studied French at the Sorbonne. In 1921, she was in Paris awaiting a divorce from her husband, the poet Skipwith Cannell, when Alfred Kreymborg introduced her to Harold Loeb, who was about to launch *Broom*, an international magazine of the arts. She was soon sharing quarters with Loeb. Cannell's knowledge of French enabled her to publish a number of translations in Loeb's *Broom*, which he continued to edit until 1923.

Later in the decade, she made several contributions of her own writing to *transition*, edited by Eugene Jolas and Elliot Paul. Two of her contributions are short stories in which proper, well-to-do ladies are confronted with grotesque, repulsive women whose actions they cannot comprehend. "Miss Bliggins," which appeared in the July 1927 issue, is about a woman who is so ugly that for most of her life her only companion has been a tamed rat she has named Colin. To the surprise of the two women who employ her as a maid, she becomes pregnant by a young man who has seduced her while she sat with him in the dark beside his mother's corpse. She is immediately abandoned by the young man, and as she lies dying from complications of childbirth, she names her baby after the now deceased rodent, the only being that has ever returned her affection. "The Money," published in the May 1928 *transition*, also links ugliness and death. This third-person narrative recounts the events of the puzzling death of Mme. Lebosc from the perspective of Miss Fitch, who rents a cottage from her. Miss Fitch thinks she may have seen Mme. Lebosc, a repulsive, foul-tempered old woman, bury

Kathleen Cannell, 1940s

a considerable sum of money shortly before her death. Her nephew wants the money, and it is not clear whether Mme. Lebosc has died of natural causes or whether he has murdered her. The story ends without resolution of its ambiguities. Taking part in *transition*'s symposium on "Why Do Americans Live in Europe?" in the Fall 1928 issue, Cannell does not give the expected expatriate's response: she prefers the United States; she loves the twentieth century; she is concerned with reforming herself, not society; and she is in Europe merely because she can live there more cheaply. Her final contribution to *transition*, "The History of a Dream," appeared in a section of the Fall 1928 issue entitled "The Synthetist Universe: Dreams and the Chthonian Mind." In her article Cannell recounts one of her recent dreams and tells how she and someone she calls "R.V." have traced the origins of all its elements back to events which took place as recently as a few days before to as long as her third year of life. "R.V." was probably Roger Vitrac, one of the Surrealists, whom she had known for several years.

In 1932, Cannell contributed another short story, "Fantocci," to Peter Neagoe's anthology, *Americans Abroad*. A young American woman who manufactures marionettes decides to manipulate the behavior of two Roman beggars, as though they too are puppets, by favoring one over the other with her gifts. The beggars, who look like personifications of good and evil, grow to hate each other, and finally, the saintly looking one kills the other and is taken away by the police. The woman, who has shown signs of increasing derangement, still sees the two old men in their usual places and concludes, "So you were only old puppets, after all!" Although Cannell is not a major writer, she made a significant contribution to the intellectual life of the twenties, and she deserves to be remembered for the originality of her work rather than simply as the prototype for Frances Clyne in Hemingway's novel.

—*Bertram D. Sarason*

Other:

"Fantocci," in *Americans Abroad An Anthology*, ed.

Peter Neagoe (The Hague: Servire, 1932), pp. 64-72.

Periodical Publications:

"Miss Bliggins," *transition*, no. 4 (July 1927): 26-39;
"The Money," *transition*, no. 12 (March 1928): 92-106;
"Why Do Americans Live in Europe?," by Cannell and others, *transition*, no. 14 (Fall 1928): 97-119;
"The History of a Dream," *transition*, no. 18 (November 1929): 37-47.

References:

Harold Loeb, *The Way It Was* (New York: Criterion, 1959);
Bertram D. Sarason, *Hemingway and* The Sun *Set* (Washington, D.C.: Bruccoli Clark / NCR Microcard Editions, 1972).

ROBERT M. COATES
(6 April 1897-8 February 1973)

SELECTED BOOKS: *The Eater of Darkness* (Paris: Contact Editions, 1926; New York: Macaulay, 1929; New York: Capricorn / Putnam's, 1959—adds an introduction by Coates);
The Outlaw Years (New York: Macaulay, 1930);
Yesterday's Burdens (New York: Macaulay, 1933; Carbondale & Edwardsville: Southern Illinois University Press, 1975—adds an introduction by Malcolm Cowley);
The Bitter Season (New York: Harcourt, Brace, 1946; London: Gollancz, 1949);
Wisteria Cottage (New York: Harcourt, Brace, 1948; London: Gollancz, 1949);
The Farther Shore (New York: Harcourt, Brace, 1955; London: Gollancz, 1955);
The View from Here (New York: Harcourt, Brace, 1960).

Although Robert M. Coates spent most of his life working as an art critic for the *New Yorker*, his literary career began in Paris where his first novel, *The Eater of Darkness* (1926), was published by Robert McAlmon's Contact Editions. Coates was born in New Haven, Connecticut, in 1897, the only child of an itinerant inventor/designer and sometime goldminer who moved his family across the country and back again during Coates's youth. After growing up in such diverse places as New York City, Rochester, Buffalo, Cincinnati, Seattle, and Christmas Crossing, Colorado, Coates attended Yale and served as a naval aviation cadet during World War I, though the war was over before he could get his wings. He returned to Yale after the armistice, graduated in 1919, and sailed for Europe in 1921, steerage class. Once there, he traveled in Corsica, Italy, and France, settling and writing for a time in Giverny, a small town approximately fifty miles down the Seine from Paris, before living in Paris itself.

Like other American "exiles," Robert Coates did his share of mingling with writers and artists in cafes; but his five-year sojourn in Europe (financed mostly by his parents and by writing he sold to such little magazines as Harold Loeb's *Broom*) included less conventional diversions: the mountain climbing, camping, canoeing, and walking tours he catalogues in *The View from Here* (1960), a book of reminiscences of his youth. His recollections of Paris in that book are fondly nostalgic. He sees the twenties as a happy, hopeful, and confident era when young men could look forward to peace "timeless, unhurried, and indestructible"; he sees Paris as the "dream city . . . faraway, mystical, magical," where luminaries in the arts, such as Fernand Leger, Pablo Picasso, Erik Satie, Tristan Tzara, and Juan Gris, were accessible and congenial, even to novices like himself. He tells of wandering through the "workaday" neighborhoods of the city (Place d'Italie, Menilmontant, Pantin) with the same enthusiasm he uses to describe a party given by Ford Madox Ford.

Though Coates was never at the center of literary life in Paris, he did have connections with important figures—he boxed with Ernest Hemingway, and he was warmly encouraged by Gertrude Stein, for whom he always felt a grateful admiration. He later lamented that neither Ford nor Stein had received proper recognition for their tremendous influence on writers of the period; and he apparently felt a lasting bitterness toward Hemingway for what Coates saw as a disavowal of Stein. It was Stein who helped arrange for Coates's *The Eater of Darkness* to be published by McAlmon. The book, the story of a homicidal maniac who invents a sinister death machine and sets about a mass execution, has been called the first Dada novel in English, and it suggests much of the experimentation Coates would later tame and use to skillful ends in *Yesterday's Burdens* (1933), a novel Malcolm Cowley has called "essential."

Coates returned to America in 1926 to work for the *New Yorker*, where he was art critic for the next three decades. During that time he continued with his other writing, producing over a hundred short stories (many of them published in the *New Yorker*); several novels—*Yesterday's Burdens*, *The Bitter Season* (1946), *Wisteria Cottage* (1948), *The Farther Shore* (1955); and a history of land pirating on the Natchez Trace, *The Outlaw Years* (1930); as well as articles and book reviews.

From America, Coates contributed several pieces to Eugene Jolas's new Paris-based journal of the avant-garde, *transition*. They are all in the scrambled mode of *The Eater of Darkness*, odd conjunctions of lyric and advertisement, italics and parenthetical asides, lists and letters. One piece, "In Memoriam," is especially interesting because it contains several elements one has come to expect in most of Coates's major fiction: time fusion, a discontinuous plot, an elusive female character, violence and the threat of violence, the portrait of an exceptionally agitated mind, and an episode in which the central character trails someone only to discover or reveal an unsettling truth about himself.

In 1928 when Jolas asked his American editor Matthew Josephson for contributions from writers in New York for the special American number of *transition* (Summer 1928), Josephson gathered together a group of his friends, including Slater Brown, Kenneth Burke, Malcolm Cowley, and Coates, in a suite at the Hotel Chelsea, where they worked from 10:30 one morning to 6:45 the next to complete the "New York: 1928" section of the issue. The various pieces in the section are equally critical of the hypocrisy of life in the United States and of the expatriates who have stayed in France so long that they have lost touch with their native land. Josephson's "Open Letter to Mr. Ezra Pound, And the Other 'Exiles' " is especially critical of the writers he accuses of trying to ignore the existence of modern, industrialized America. Coates's contribution to the section, "Letter-Carrier," which follows a mailman on his rounds through New York City, is an example of how the avant-garde writer can use the very elements of modern city life, which supposedly suppress individuality and creativity, as images in a uniquely personal and original statement.

Though Coates was prolific, he never achieved the stature of those he called "the Titans" of Paris in the twenties—Gertrude Stein, James Joyce, and Ezra Pound—nor of Hemingway and F. Scott Fitzgerald, who have had such a strong appeal to the popular American imagination. Yet both *The Outlaw Years* and *Wisteria Cottage* were well-received when they were published; *The Eater of Darkness*, panned by early reviewers as "extravagantly difficult to follow" and "typographically, rhetorically, artistically . . . mad," attained an underground readership and was republished by Putnam's in 1959; *Yesterday's Burdens*, a superbly crafted novel, was reprinted in the Lost American Fiction Series in 1975. Coates has gained a reputation as a significant minor figure, and it is likely that his reputation will grow as critics begin to put into perspective the implications of his early experimentation for current fiction. Coates was a brilliant stylist, a master of the self-reflexive novel long before it became the fashionable enterprise it is today.

It was in Paris that Coates had contact with the great novelists of the twenties as well as the Dadaists and the Surrealists who put him onto his experimentation, and thus Paris must be considered one of the crucial influences on his literary life. Yet he makes little use of the Parisian setting in his fiction. The brief scenarios that frame the action of *The Eater of Darkness* are the most prominent overt acknowledgments he makes that he had ever moved in the "dream city." But the surreal short stories that deal with displacement and curious apprehensions of life, the novels that abruptly shift focus and mesh

phases of time, the sensitive reviews—all bespeak an intimate awareness of the energy and innovation of what he has called, with all respect, "a crazy time."
—*Constance Pierce*

Other:

Nathanael West, *Miss Lonelyhearts*, introduction by Coates (New York: New Directions, 1933).

Periodical Publications:

"Conversations, no 7," *transition*, no. 1 (April 1927): 83-84;

"In Memoriam," *transition*, no. 6 (September 1927): 47-51;

"Letter-Carrier," *transition*, no. 13 (Summer 1928): 90-93.

EMILY HOLMES COLEMAN
(22 January 1899-13 June 1974)

BOOK: *The Shutter of Snow* (London: Routledge, 1930; New York: Viking, 1930).

Emily Holmes Coleman, society editor of the Paris *Tribune* (the European edition of the *Chicago Tribune*), was part of the group of writers who contributed to *transition* magazine, edited by two of her fellow *Tribune* staff members, Eugene Jolas and Elliot Paul. A native of Oakland, California, she graduated from Wellesley College in 1920 and married Loyd Ring Coleman, a psychologist, in 1921. She arrived in Paris with her young son John in 1926.

Coleman's interest in the instinctive and the subconscious is in keeping with *transition*'s call for a "revolution of the word" and a renewal of language's roots in the depths of the collective unconscious. As she says in her response to the *transition* questionaire, "Why Do Americans Live In Europe?" (Fall 1928): "Great art in the past has existed only when a medium was being struggled with; great literature has come generally in the early development of a language. America has her language bought and paid for . . . when it was necessary to return to the primitive to find health and vigor." The source for much of Coleman's poetry and prose is her experience in childbirth and her subsequent stay in a mental hospital while suffering from postpuerperal insanity. Full of images of heat and cold, her work examines the paradoxical logic of madness. Most fully developed in her autobiographical novel, *The Shutter of Snow* (1930), the theme runs throughout her work in *transition*. In "The Liberator" (October 1927) heat and life are equated

Loyd Ring Coleman and Emily Holmes Coleman

with destruction and entrapment while coldness and death symbolize freedom. The speaker, an inmate in a mental hospital, says,

> i will break all their heads
> and lay them in neat rows
> and we shall wave high the keys
> and open wide the doors
> and all of us shall dance in the snow

and that poor woman in the spiral casket
   shall warm a wooden doll to her dress
      and lean her hair in the fire
the grating shall be taken from about the fire
and the woman and the keys shall go within
      all of us
         shall
            dance
               within

The desirable mean between the two extremes is cool, running water—ice warmed by sun, sun cooled by ice—as in "The Wren's Nest" (Summer 1928), where "His eyes were waterfalls over the rocks and from his chin went out assurances of desire. . . . Down the stream they had gone and their feet had chiselled its depth. They stood making rivulets through the dam and lay on the bank in the sun. . . ." But such a compromise between the two forces is only momentary. In *The Shutter of Snow*, the heroine remembers, "That had been in green summer and trees and fine-cooled water. . . . Stillness and summer rain. Christopher had been her love," but having come through the heat of passion and childbirth, she concludes, "I shall have snow on my glassy fingers she said, and a shutter of snow on my grave tonight." In Coleman's last poem to appear in *transition*, "The Shepherd's Vision," in the March 1932 issue, heat and cold, birth and death achieve mystical union:

> Now the hand clasps the knife
> And cuts secure, sliding through silken thread.
> The pattern perishes, the form anew is spread.

The shepherd wakes from his vision to feel ecstasy burning his body as "The foreign roofs mingle in the night, the turrets freeze / Into the darkness, sinking on his body burning." Later in 1932 "The Shepherd's Vision" was reprinted in Peter Neagoe's anthology, *Americans Abroad*.

Coleman spent one year in St. Tropez as secretary to Emma Goldman while Goldman was writing her autobiography, *Living My Life* (1931), and by late 1932 she was spending most of her time in Italy. In addition to her work for *transition*, she published poems in the *New Review*. A second novel, "The Tygon," along with numerous poems, stories, and plays, remains unpublished. She expressed her lack of concern about publication in a letter to Virgil Geddes:

> I don't care anything about recognition yet—I suppose I need it for confidence, but I have so much without it! I am certain it will come—I don't care if it is after I am dead. I want chiefly to grow—I am starved for growth. I am like

Melville's Egyptian seed, which was taken out of a coffin where it had been for three thousand years, and planted. Your talent is all you actually possess. My God, I do not want more than that!

Her later years were spent in Italy, writing mostly poetry. At the age of forty-five, she was converted to Catholicism. She returned to the United States and died in Tivoli, New York, on 13 June 1974, where she had lived at The Farm, cared for by Catholic nuns.

In the opinion of Virgil Geddes, Emily Coleman was more a catalyst during the twenties in Paris than an exemplary writer. She circulated extensively among writers and exerted influence by her personality rather than by her aesthetics. In his obituary for the *Catholic Worker* Joseph Gerci wrote:

> Emily had a barbarous personality for someone so civilized. She was intense and passionate, sometimes to the point of mania. She was remarkable, reasonable and quite simply the most important influence on the lives of those who knew her.

> *—Minna Besser Geddes*

Periodical Publications:

"Invocation," *transition*, no. 5 (August 1927): 110;

"Paris Roofs," *transition*, no. 5 (August 1927): 111;

"Thunderstorm Brooding," *transition*, no. 5 (August 1927): 112;

"Young Orchard in Spring," *transition*, no. 5 (August 1927): 113;

"The Liberator," *transition*, no. 7 (October 1927): 124-125;

"Interlude," *transition*, no. 8 (November 1927): 89-94;

"Grave Song," *transition*, no. 10 (January 1928): 92;

"love of the silent twilight," *transition*, no. 10 (January 1928): 93;

"The Wren's Nest," *transition*, no. 13 (Summer 1928): 215-218;

"Why Do Americans Live in Europe?," by Coleman and others, *transition*, no. 14 (Fall 1928): 97-119;

"Dry Leaves," *transition*, no. 15 (February 1929): 135-136;

"The Wasted Earth," *transition*, no. 18 (November 1929): 92-95;

"The Shepherd's Vision," *transition*, no. 21 (March 1932): 159-162; reprinted in *Americans Abroad An Anthology*, ed. Peter Neagoe (The Hague: Servire, 1932).

Malcolm Cowley

Donald G. Parker
Orange County Community College, State University of New York

BIRTH: Belsano, Pennsylvania, 24 August 1898.

EDUCATION: A.B., Harvard University, 1920; Diploma of French Studies, Universite de Montpellier, France, 1922.

MARRIAGE: 12 August 1919 to Marguerite Frances Baird, divorced. 18 June 1932 to Muriel Maurer; children: Robert.

AWARDS: American Field Service Fellowship, 1921-1923; Helen Haire Levinson Prize, *Poetry* magazine, 1927; John Peale Bishop Memorial Prize, 1946; National Institute of Arts and Letters Award in Literature, 1946; Senior Fellowship, National Endowment for the Arts, 1967; Signet Medal, 1976; National Magazine Award, 1979.

SELECTED BOOKS: *Racine* (Paris: Union, 1923);
Blue Juniata (New York: Cape & Smith, 1929; London: Cape, 1929; expanded edition, New York: Viking, 1968);
Exile's Return (New York: Norton, 1934; London: Cape, 1935; revised edition, New York: Viking, 1951; London: Bodley Head, 1961);
The Dry Season (Norfolk, Conn.: New Directions, 1941);
The Literary Situation (New York: Viking, 1954; London: Deutsch, 1955);
Think Back on Us . . . A Contemporary Chronicle of the 1930's, ed. Henry Dan Piper (Carbondale & Edwardsville: Southern Illinois University Press, 1967);
A Many-Windowed House Collected Essays on American Writers and American Writing, ed. Henry Dan Piper (Carbondale & Edwardsville: Southern Illinois University Press, 1970);
A Second Flowering Works and Days of the Lost Generation (New York: Viking, 1973; London: Deutsch, 1973);
—And I Worked At the Writer's Trade (New York: Viking, 1978).

Malcolm Cowley, poet, critic, editor, cultural commentator, translator—in the exact professional sense, literary historian—is best known for painting in *Exile's Return* (1934, revised 1951) the accepted picture of the "lost generation" of writers that matured during and after World War I. *Exile's*

Malcolm Cowley, 1930

Return chronicles his French experiences in the early twenties and delineates the importance of Paris to American writers of the period who, "feeling like aliens in the commercial world, sailed for Europe as soon as they had money to pay for their steamer tickets." As a young writer in France from June 1921 to August 1923, Cowley met or was influenced by the important writers of his generation. That experience and his formal study, while there, of French history and literature provided a sound base for his developing critical aesthetic and, later, for his eclectic, cosmopolitan literary interests.

Born on 24 August 1898 in a farmhouse near Belsano, Pennsylvania, Cowley attended Peabody High in Pittsburgh, where with his friend Kenneth Burke he began writing for school publications. At Harvard he edited the *Advocate* and, while an undergraduate, began to publish reviews in the *Dial* and the *New Republic*. He left the university during his sophomore year in 1917, intending to serve with other young writers in an American ambulance unit in France, but soon found himself driving munitions trucks for the French military transport. Cowley said later in *Exile's Return* that being a volunteer was in many ways "ideal"—"good food, a congenial occupation, furloughs to Paris"—and it provided a means of observing "the once-in-a-lifetime spectacle of the Western Front," seeing firsthand, gaining valuable experience. Cowley compares the activity to a college-extension course:

> A few miles north of us the guns were booming. Here was death among the flowers, danger in spring, the sweet wine of sentiment neither spiced with paradox nor yet insipid, the death being real, the danger near at hand.

Besides nurturing "a spectatorial attitude," the war enormously benefitted future writers, for it "revivified the subjects that had seemed forbidden because they were soiled by many hands and robbed of meaning; danger made it possible to write once more about love, adventure, death." But foreign soil and the war experience exacted an expense of spirit from the expatriate: after the armistice he discovered that "the country of his boyhood was gone and he was attached to no other." On the other hand, Cowley had developed the beginnings of his intense interest in French literature and civilization.

Returning from Europe in the fall of 1917, Cowley served briefly in the U. S. Army and then completed his A.B. degree at Harvard during 1919-1920 after marrying his first wife, Marguerite Frances Baird. They lived among "the proletariat of the arts" in Greenwich Village while Cowley supported them by writing reviews. Cowley describes the Village life of 1920-1921 in *Exile's Return*. In that intellectual current one idea seemed to float more securely and confidently than any other: the idea of "salvation by exile." A young, talented, postwar generation found the American experience to be closed to imaginative or artistic endeavor—philistine. In Europe, as Harold Stearns had just pointed out in *Civilization in the United States* (1921), people seemed to know how to live. Exile to Montparnasse was deemed more and more desirable, even necessary.

In 1921, encouraged by an American Field Service Fellowship of 12,000 francs (then about $1,000) for study at a French university, Cowley returned to France with his wife to attend the Universite de Montpellier, where he received a Diploma of French Studies. When the fellowship was renewed for a second year, he lived in Giverny

and continued his study of French history and literature. In a 17 January 1979 letter Cowley describes his arrival in Paris:

> I never *lived* in Paris, though I often stayed at the Grand Hotel de Bretagne, 10, rue Cassette, in the Quarter. . . . But I had advantages: six months with the French Army in 1917; a wife, nee Peggy Baird, who knew everyone from Greenwich Village; and introductions to the Dada group. When we reached Paris in 1921, we went straight to the Dome (after registering at the hotel) and found friends on the terrace.

Among the Greenwich Village people were Arthur Moss and his wife Florence Gilliam, who had arrived in France shortly before the Cowleys. In August 1921 Moss and Gilliam launched *Gargoyle*, the first English-language little magazine to appear in Continental Europe during the period between the two World Wars. Cowley was among the Americans who contributed to this short-lived magazine (August 1921-October 1922?), which he describes in *Exile's Return* as "Greenwich Village in Montparnasse."

He also contributed to *Secession*, edited by Gorham B. Munson and Matthew Josephson. In fact during their travels through Europe in the summer of 1922, the Cowleys carried the material for the magazine's third issue, which Munson and Josephson had assembled in Paris, to Vienna, where the magazine was printed. After Vienna the Cowleys went to the Austrian Tyrol, where they heard that Josephson had accepted a position as associate editor of *Broom*, which was moving its main headquarters from Rome to Berlin. *Broom* had been founded in November 1921 by Harold Loeb, whom Cowley had known in New York, and two poems by Cowley had already been published in that magazine. Now with his friend Josephson serving as associate editor, Cowley became involved in decisions about *Broom*'s editorial policy, corresponding with both Josephson and Loeb.

After their summer tour, the Cowleys returned to France, where "Jim Butler, son of Monet's stepson-in-law, the painter Theodore Butler, found us a place in Giverny, over the former blacksmith shop." Remembering his American friends in France, Cowley writes in his 1979 letter:

> You might say that I met "everybody" during those two years. My closest American friends, besides Jim Butler, were Robert M. Coates and his first wife Elsa (they took our apartment when we sailed home), Laurence Vail and his lovely sister Clothilde (with

whom I was almost in love), Kathleen Cannell the fashion writer (at first she was living with Harold Loeb), and who else? Anyhow I saw them all.

Cowley also made several visits to Ezra Pound in Paris, and in the summer of 1923 Pound introduced him to Ernest Hemingway.

Also in 1923, Cowley had a brief interview with James Joyce. But during his second year in France, Cowley saw more of the Dadaists to whom Josephson had introduced him in Paris in June 1922:

> I spent more time with French-speaking friends, Louis Aragon, Tristan Tzara (who was Rumanian)—those two especially, but also Breton, Roger Vitrac, Robert Desnos, and Jacques Rigaut, who came to New York in 1923 and later committed suicide there. I became widely known as a result of that silly gesture at the Rotonde in 1923, which was written up in a lot of American papers and was the subject of an editorial in the NY *Times*.

His "silly gesture at the Rotonde," which he discusses in *Exile's Return*, occurred in the summer of 1923 when Cowley struck its notoriously disagreeable proprietor in a moment of Dadaist abandonment.

The relationship of France, and Europe in general, to Cowley's literary career is detailed in *Exile's Return*, published in 1934 and revised in 1951. In 1921 the American exiles, like their Russian counterparts in the middle of the nineteenth century, came to France to escape provincialism and to be at the center of artistic sophistication and tradition. For some the trek to Paris was a religious pilgrimage. As Cowley explains,

> France was the birthplace of our creed. It was in France that poets had labored for days over a single stanza . . . ; in France that novelists like Gourmont had lived as anchorites . . . ; in France that Flaubert had described "the quaint mania of passing one's life wearing oneself out over words," and had transformed the mania into a religion. Everything admirable in literature began in France, was developed in France; and though we knew that the great French writers quarreled among themselves, . . . we were eager to admire them all.

In America Cowley had had close friends with whom to exchange literary repartee; Paris, however, offered what amounted to a network of talented writers—American and European. There he read the work of his great expatriate and French contemporaries, Eliot, Proust, Valery, Hemingway, Pound, and Joyce, and met many of them, including the French writer Pierre MacOrlan, whose work he later translated.

Importantly, Paris was congenial to experimentation, and the French even seemed to understand what was important in the American literary past. Their admiration for Poe and Whitman, for example, pointed American expatriate writers toward a viable literary tradition. "Our poets," stated Cowley in a review for the New York *Evening Post* in 1922, "reclaimed Poe and Whitman from the French only a dozen years ago. This reclamation is the basis of our contemporary poetry." In an essay entitled "This Youngest Generation," begun six weeks after arriving in France, Cowley summed up why the exiles were there:

> Form, simplification, strangeness, respect for literature as an art with traditions, abstractions . . . these are the catchwords repeated most often among the younger writers. They represent ideas that have characterized French literature hitherto, rather than English or American. They are the nearest approach to articulate doctrine of a generation without a school and without a manifesto.

The academic experience at the Universite de Montpellier and social and literary contacts in Paris were crucial to the early development of Cowley's critical thought: he was drawn to the idea of becoming a man of letters in the great French tradition. He greatly admired French classicism, with its insistence on form, clarity, and intelligence, but he was nevertheless wooed by the tenets of Dada, which appealed to his skepticism and youthful rebelliousness. Ironically, concentration on Racine at Montpellier (his pamphlet *Racine* was printed in Paris in 1923) provided him with a stance from which to consider Dada, whereas his personal relationship with Dadaists Tristan Tzara and Louis Aragon provided an understanding of the strengths and limits of classicism.

In Paris and Giverny Cowley socialized with the leading proponents of Dada, which had been transported to the banks of the Seine when Tzara came to Paris in 1920. Feeling that the movement was at that point the "very essence of Paris . . . , young and adventurous, and human," he was even moved to sign one of its manifestoes, though he never considered himself one with—or of—the group. The description in *Exile's Return*, in fact, overemphasizes the influence Dada had on Cowley. For example, George Wickes, commenting on American expatriates of this period, notes in *Americans in Paris*: "Chiefly they felt the all-pervasive classical spirit of France, even in an iconoclastic age. Under this influence, they became more conscious of form, style, language or medium than any previous generation of Americans." The epigraph from Gide that Cowley chose for his study of Racine suggests clearly the tenor of his sympathy: "L'art est toujours le resultat d'une contrainte." While Dada cavorted and mocked and challenged, classicism offered to make life and literature manageable.

Nevertheless, the figure that influenced Cowley most during his years in France was a Dadaist, Louis Aragon. His admiration for the French writer made of him a veritable disciple. He wrote frankly of the experience, confessing that "for the first and last time in my life I admitted to having a master." Aragon, he explained, "has read everything and mastered it, . . . lives literature," and "judges a writer largely by his moral qualities, such as courage, vigor of feeling, the refusal to compromise."

According to *Exile's Return*, the beginning of the end of the expatriates' adventure in France came when they "rediscovered" America: when the country they had left in disillusionment came, from a distance, to seem more complex and exciting. Harold Loeb, defending American literary exiles in France, felt that postwar experience there had influenced such pilgrims in two main ways: first, it resulted in a meticulous attention to form; second, and more important, it ended in a reevaluation of America.

In the third stanza of "Three Hills," written during this period, Cowley rebels against exposure to too much "meticulous attention to form," summing up quite directly a mood based on a desire to return to "my own country":

> my stomach turns against
> geometry and rows of plum trees,
> wanting a country where briars rout
> under the non-Euclidean gum trees.
> An unprecise, untutored country
> with gardens growing inside out.

France had provided Cowley with what Stein called a writer's second country, one "romantic" and "separate" which helps him to understand his first country, the one where he belongs.

Cowley discovered, as others did, a new perspective. He realized that America, surprisingly enough, held out the possibility of new material for artists; there was potential in the country's very

monstrousness, in its machinery, its dynamic energy. In a letter to Kenneth Burke in 1923 Cowley wrote:

> America shares an inferiority complex with Germany. . . . The only excuse for living two years in France is to remove this feeling of inferiority and to find, for example, that Tristan Tzara, who resembles you in features like two drops of water, talks a shade less intelligently. To discover that the Dada crowd has more fun than the Secession crowd because the former, strangely, had more American pep. . . . The only salvation for American literature is to BORROW A LITTLE PUNCH AND CONFIDENCE FROM AMERICAN BUSINESS.

Clearly, two years in France afforded Cowley the opportunity to broaden his intellectual scope dramatically, enabling him to contemplate his literary future with assurance and insight. In a letter to Burke dated 5 July 1923, his last from Normandy, Cowley wrote that his French sojourn had helped him to arrive at a personal philosophy or "a collection of beliefs": (1) that a man of letters is "one who adopts the whole of literature as his province," (2) that such a man must "concern himself with every department of human activity," (3) that since "more writers were ruined by early success than by the lack of it," he could accept being considered foolish "in order to avoid being successful," (4) that it was fallacious for a writer to speak of conserving his energy, for "the mind of a poet resembles Fortunatus's purse: the more spent, the more it supplies," and (5) that "the work of expanding the human mind to its extremest limits of thought and feeling . . . is the aim of literature." This sense of the writer's social responsibility appears in his work as early as his prose piece "Young Mr. Elkins," published in the December 1922 issue of *Broom*.

Armed with such beliefs, amounting to a personal manifesto, Cowley felt prepared for what lay ahead, even to the extent of assuming leadership in a "crusade." Thus did he return to New York City just before his twenty-fifth birthday with new ideas, definite values, and much enthusiasm. Paris had been the ideal place to begin to come to terms with his role and his goals in the literary world; he had been able to encourage and explore in complex ways his developing aesthetic sense. His later literary values would evolve, essentially, from those he had experienced and pondered in France, though not in a simplistically derivative fashion. As he wrote to Waldo Frank in 1924, he considered himself one of those "Americans who go to Paris, meet many people of many schools, take the best of each, and

Malcolm Cowley

4

PROLOGUE: THE LOST GENERATION

SO IT WAS to be the Lost Generation. . . . Gertrude Stein made a
famous remark to Ernest Hemingway, and Hemingway used it as the inscription for a novel, and the novel was good and became a craze--
young men tried to get as imperturbably drunk as the hero, young women
of good family cultivated the heroine's nymphomania, and the name was
fixed. It was a boast at first, like telling what a hangover one had
after
xx/a party to which someone else wasn't invited. Afterwards it was
used apologetically, it even became ridiculous; and yet in the beginning, as applied to writers born at the turn of the century, it was as
accurate as any tag could be.

They were, in the first place, a generation, and probably the f
real one in the history of American letters. They came to maturity
during a period of violent change, when the influence of time seemed
temporarily more important than that of class or locality. Everywhere
after the War people were fumbling for a word to express their feeling
that youth had a different outlook. The word wouldn't be found for
many years; but long before Gertrude Stein made her famous remark, the
young men to whom she was referring already had undergone the similar
experiences and developed the similar attitude that made it possible
to describe them as a literary generation.

In this respect, as in their attitude itself, they were sharply
different from their predecessors. Sectional and local influences were
relatively unchanging during the years before 1900, and were therefore
more important than they later became. Two New England writers born
twenty years apart might bear more resemblance to each other than

Typescript

retain the conviction to write about their own surroundings in their own manner."

The remainder of *Exile's Return* chronicles the problems Cowley and others faced in New York City at the end of their exile, not only in reference to earning a living but in trying to fulfill their French experience by remaking the New York cultural scene. Eventually they adjusted or escaped the city to farms in Connecticut or New Jersey, finally realizing that their "real exile was from society itself." Isolated on "private islands," their true "homecoming" would not occur until the social and political activities of the next decade claimed all their energy and attention. Adjustment would, however, prove to be impossible for some American expatriates, notably Harry Crosby and Hart Crane. In *Exile's Return* Cowley examines the lives and eventual suicides of these two poets in the context of the successful careers of others, among them Cummings, Dos Passos, Hemingway, Fitzgerald, and Pound.

After returning to New York City in August 1923, Cowley worked for *Sweet's Architectural Catalogue*, preparing copy, while in his spare time pursuing his writing career and serving as an associate editor of *Broom*, then being edited in New York City with Matthew Josephson as managing editor. The last issue was published in January 1924.

In 1926 the Cowleys moved to the Connecticut countryside, where Cowley worked as a free-lance writer contributing to various periodicals and doing translations from the French. He had begun to publish essays on contemporary French literature as early as 1922; over several years, a series appeared in the *Bookman*, including an assessment of recent French poetry and evaluations of Barbusse, Vildrac, Proust, and others. In the last half of the decade he translated many full-length French works, among them Pierre MacOrlan's *On Board the Morning Star* (1924), Paul Valery's *Variety* (1927), Raymond Rodiguet's *The Count's Ball* (1928), and Maurice Barres's *The Sacred Hill* (1929). Part of his translation of *On Board the Morning Star* had appeared first in the August 1923 issue of *Broom*. *Poetry* awarded him the Guarantors Prize of $100 in 1927, part of which became the down payment on a farmhouse.

Indicative of Cowley's growing belief in the writer's social responsibilities is a project he undertook in January 1928 with Josephson, Kenneth Burke, Slater Brown, and Robert Coates. The editor of the Paris-based magazine *transition*, Eugene Jolas, had asked Josephson, a contributing editor, to prepare a statement about literary trends in America for an American number of *transition*. Josephson

brought his friends together in a suite at the Broadway Central Hotel in New York City, and they spent the day writing a collection of poetry and prose, which Jolas published under the section title "New York: 1928." The section begins with parodies of American advertisements and press releases, but more significant is the second part in which Josephson, in particular, criticizes the American expatriates who remain abroad rather than coming home and concerning themselves with social justice. Cowley's poem with satiric endnotes, "Tar Babies," is critical of the "art for art's sake" attitude of many of *transition*'s contributors, pointing out the emptiness of experiment for its own sake. As he says in one of the notes to the poem:

> Evidently to write a poem about the stockyards is to write a modern poem. Or to write a poem the grammar of which is arbitrarily bad. Or to make drawings without perspective. To distort is modern. To be obscure is modern. To omit punctuation and connectives is the white shirt-front of modernism.

The aesthetic attitude with which Cowley first approached France in 1921 has been transformed to that which he would express in *Exile's Return*.

Blue Juniata (1929), his first volume of poems, captures Cowley's French experience differently from *Exile's Return*. The sections of the book are arranged in an autobiographical sequence and the poems chronicle, in a measured, meditative way, the same years Cowley describes five years later in prose. Although he had established himself by the end of the twenties as a writer of critical prose, the reviewers' consensus at that point was that he had most distinguished himself as a poet. "It is in poetry," wrote Allen Tate in the *New Republic*, "at least for the present, that Mr. Cowley may be seen at his best." He praised the poems in *Blue Juniata* for their "exact feelings and images; and overall, a subtle vision of the startling qualities of common things." John Chamberlain aptly characterized them, in the *New York Times*, as being "of an intellectual order, wholly disciplined," but with an "indigenous flavor." The volume, despite being well received by critics, sold fewer than a thousand copies.

Morton Dauwen Zabel, in an enthusiastic review for the *Nation*, characterized *Blue Juniata* as a "self-confessed logbook of literary youth in America during the ten years which followed the war." Books I and II explore the heritage of Cowley's boyhood and adolescence in western Pennsylvania and the first years in New York City. Book III, containing poems he wrote in France from 1921-1923, is called "Valuta," a reference to "a new race of tourists, the *Valutaschweine*, the profiteers of the exchange, who wandered . . . in search of the lowest prices and the most picturesque upheavals of society." The note that prefaces the section vividly sets the scene of exile:

> I saw a chaotic Europe that was feverishly seeking the future of art and economics. I saw the picturesque rather than the enduring. And I wrote poems from day to day, sometimes in a great chilly hotel-room in Tyrol, sometimes in a French pension, sometimes in Berlin crouching beside a porcelain stove and listening to the roars outside that came, perhaps, from a mob.

Such a statement evokes the mood of the poems Cowley wrote abroad: a sense of remorse felt by a wanderer, who searches for "that rarer ether which is breathed by mortal lips, by mortal lungs, ah never." Kenneth Burke remarked that the characteristic overall note of the volume is regret; in Book III such a mood is manifested in poignant moments haunted by the nuances and rhythms of Eliot and the irony of Laforgue, but dominated by Cowley's control and wit. Books IV and V chart his life after returning from France.

Also in 1929, encouraged by Edmund Wilson, he joined the staff of the *New Republic* as an associate editor. For the next eleven years he oversaw the magazine's literary section, becoming a powerful literary voice by the mid-thirties. In *Starting Out in the Thirties* (1965), Alfred Kazin remembers:

> The lead review in the *New Republic*, a single page usually written by Cowley himself, brought the week to focus for people to whom this page, breathing intellectual fight in its sharp black title and solid double columned lines of argument, represented the most dramatically satisfying confrontation of a new book by a gifted, uncompromising critical intelligence.

In the thirties and early forties most of Cowley's critical writing appeared in the *New Republic* in the form of essays and book reviews. Some of these pieces were later collected in *Think Back on Us . . . A Contemporary Chronicle of the 1930's* (1967). Divorced in 1931, Cowley married Muriel Maurer the following year. During this personally and politically tumultuous period, he placed his social conscience in the foreground alongside his aesthetic concerns and became involved with Communist and Popular Front groups in the protest movement.

Though he did not discard his earlier ambition of becoming an American man of letters, he did subordinate it to his editorial responsibilities and political activities. His "Red Romance," as he called it, continued until 1940, when he resigned from the League of American Writers, a left-wing organization he had helped found five years earlier after the publication of *Exile's Return* in 1934.

In the first edition of *Exile's Return* Cowley did not tightly restrict his attention to his ostensible subject, an evaluation and depiction of the aesthetic milieu of the twenties. The rhetoric of his left-wing political perspective and the subjective outrage directed toward conservative groups blurred the book's focus, and it was in many cases judged on political, rather than literary, grounds. Lewis Garnett, in the *New York Herald Tribune*, found it "very charming, very readable, sometimes penetrating, often witty, and . . . basically empty." In the New York *Post* Hershell Brickell felt the writing to be "a good deal better than the thinking." Edmund Wilson agreed, telling Cowley that he was "much better when . . . conveying impressions and depicting scenes than when you were handling ideas—when you get into trouble is with generalizations." Cowley later agreed that he should have concentrated on one or the other.

However, with its revision in 1951, *Exile's Return* was revealed as central to the study of modern American literature: the definitive account of the maturing of Cowley's generation written as an evocative autobiographical historical narrative guided by a lyric persona. The revision was much less subjectively political in tone and subject matter. Three chapters were excluded: a study of the exploitation of the proletariat, a discussion of the politics of his contemporaries from 1924 to 1930, and the epilogue, which outlined political measures that should replace the aesthetic values of the twenties. Additions included chapters on Hart Crane and Sacco and Vanzetti. The original subtitle, *A Narrative of Ideas*, was changed to *A Literary Odyssey of the 1920s*.

The critical reception in 1951 was overwhelmingly favorable. It was hailed as "unique" by Van Wyck Brooks, who called it "the irreplaceable account of the most dramatic episode in American literary history." Lloyd Morris stated in the *New York Herald Tribune* that "Mr. Cowley has painted the classic picture [of that era] and it is not likely to be surpassed in authenticity, eloquence or beauty." To Arthur Mizener *Exile's Return* was "far and away the best book about the generation of the 1920's by a participant, . . . a generation that was crucial not only for American literature, but for the whole of American culture."

In 1937 Cowley and Marxist critic Bernard Smith edited *After the Genteel Tradition*, an anthology of essays that evaluated authors after 1910 who shattered the gentility of the previous age. This effort began a long series of collections edited by Cowley, including *Books That Changed Our Minds* (1939) and popular editions of selected works by Hemingway, Faulkner, Hawthorne, Whitman, and Fitzgerald. His attention to such writers was in most cases instrumental in augmenting or establishing their reputations as major figures. Robert Penn Warren, for example, noted that Cowley's edition of the *Portable Faulkner* "marked the great turning point in Faulkner's reputation in the United States."

Cowley wrote little poetry during the thirties, as is suggested by the title and the slimness of *The Dry Season* (1941), his second volume of poems. In 1944 he resigned from the *New Republic*. Since the mid-forties Cowley has pursued his writing career in a singularly eclectic fashion. However, the publication in 1968 of an expanded edition of *Blue Juniata*, which added only nineteen uncollected poems to selections from his two earlier volumes, stressed that over his long career he has developed primarily as a writer of prose. In that capacity he has firmly established himself as one of America's leading literary critics and literary historians. The titles of his major works of this period reveal the extent of his range: *The Literary Situation* (1954); *Writers at Work The Paris Review Interviews* (1958), which he edited; *The Faulkner-Cowley File Letters and Memories, 1944-1962* (1966); *A Many-Windowed House Collected Essays on American Writers and American Writing* (1970); *A Second Flowering Works and Days of the Lost Generation* (1973); and *—And I Worked At the Writer's Trade* (1978). In the midst of such a distinguished career he has served as president of the National Institute of Arts and Letters from 1956 to 1959 and 1962 to 1965 and as Chancellor of the American Academy of Arts and Letters for ten years from 1966 to 1976. From time to time he has been a visiting professor of English at leading universities and has lectured extensively.

Certain themes dominate Cowley's prolific writings. A key concept has been the nature of literary generations—the idea that memorable writers appear, not individually or at random, but in clusters or constellations at regular, almost predictable intervals. He has also tended to support the neglected and has tried to direct the public's attention to gifted but forgotten literary figures. His defense of the underdog is related to his more general interest in the structure of society, to his concern for the individual, and to his insistence on a humanistic approach to life and art. His social concerns have usually been expressed in terms of a liberal sympathy for the disadvantaged and the oppressed.

Cowley has made use of the past and of traditions in order to comment more effectively on the present, especially as he continues to amplify and update his contemporary history of American letters, which, as he remarks in *—And I Worked At the Writer's Trade*, is his "proper field of interest." For Cowley, literature involves both human thought and human actions, aesthetic principle and social consideration, dimensions that cannot be separated without a serious erosion of value and accuracy. What really matters, Cowley tells his readers, is literature as part of history, and he also stresses that without ethical stances works of literature will reflect their author's strictly intellectual or impersonal view of the world. Such an abdication of moral will and responsibility is never acceptable in the world Malcolm Cowley has perceived, written about, and helped create.

Other:

Pierre MacOrlan, *On Board the Morning Star*, translated by Cowley (New York: A. & C. Boni, 1924);

Joseph Delteil, *Joan of Arc*, translated by Cowley (New York: Minton, Balch, 1926; London: Allen & Unwin, 1927);

Paul Valery, *Variety*, translated with an introduction by Cowley (New York: Harcourt, Brace, 1927);

Marthe Bibesco, *Catherine-Paris*, translated by Cowley (New York: Harcourt, Brace, 1928);

Raymond Radiguet, *The Count's Ball*, translated by Cowley (New York: Norton, 1929);

Bibesco, *The Green Parrot*, translated by Cowley (New York: Harcourt, Brace, 1929; London: Selwyn & Blount, 1929);

Maurice Barres, *The Sacred Hill*, translated with an introduction by Cowley (New York: Macaulay, 1929);

After the Genteel Tradition, edited with contributions by Cowley (New York: Norton, 1937; revised edition, Carbondale: Southern Illinois University Press, 1964);

Books That Changed Our Minds, edited by Cowley and Bernard Smith (New York: Doubleday, Doran, 1939);

Andre Gide, *Imaginary Interviews*, translated with an introduction by Cowley (New York: Knopf, 1944);

The Viking Portable Library Hemingway, edited with an introduction by Cowley (New York: Viking, 1944);

Aragon Poet of the French Resistance, edited by Cowley and Hannah Josephson (New York: Duell, Sloan & Pearce, 1945); republished as *Aragon Poet of Resurgent France* (London: Pilot, 1946);

The Portable Faulkner, edited with an introduction by Cowley (New York: Viking, 1946; London: Macmillan, 1961; revised, enlarged edition, New York: Viking, 1967); republished as *The Essential Faulkner* (London: Chatto & Windus, 1967);

The Stories of F. Scott Fitzgerald, edited with an introduction by Cowley (New York: Scribners, 1951);

F. Scott Fitzgerald, *Tender Is the Night A Romance . . . With the Author's Final Revisions*, preface by Cowley (New York: Scribners, 1951);

Three Novels of F. Scott Fitzgerald The Great Gatsby Tender Is the Night (With the Author's Final Revisions) The Last Tycoon, edited with introductions by Cowley and Edmund Wilson (New York: Scribners, 1953);

Writers at Work The Paris Review Interviews (New York: Viking, 1958; London: Secker & Warburg, 1958);

Three Novels of Ernest Hemingway, introduction to *The Sun Also Rises* by Cowley (New York: Scribners, 1962);

The Faulkner-Cowley File Letters and Memories, 1944-1962 (New York: Viking, 1966; London: Chatto & Windus, 1966);

Fitzgerald and the Jazz Age, compiled by Cowley and Robert Cowley (New York: Scribners, 1966);

Susan Jenkins Brown, *Robber Rocks Letters and Memories of Hart Crane, 1923-1932*, includes a note by Cowley (Middletown, Conn.: Wesleyan University Press, 1968);

Paul Valery, *Leonardo Poe Mallarme*, translated by Cowley and James R. Lawler (Princeton: Princeton University Press, 1972; London: Routledge, Paul, 1972).

Periodical Publications:

"This Youngest Generation," New York *Evening Post, Literary Review*, 15 October 1921, pp. 81-82;

"Chateau de Soupir: 1917," *Broom*, 1 (January 1922): 226;

"Mountain Farm," *Broom*, 2 (May 1922): 134;

"Day Coach," *Secession*, 1 (Spring 1922): 1-3;

"Play it for Me Again . . . ," *Secession*, 2 (July 1922): 5;

"One morning during carnival," *Secession*, 2 (July 1922): 6;

"Mediterranean Beach," *Gargoyle*, 3 (August 1922): 12;

"Meanwhile, I observed him . . . ," *Secession*, 3 (August 1922): 13;

"Young Man With Spectacles," *Broom*, 3 (October 1922): 199-203;

"Valuta," *Broom*, 3 (November 1922): 250-251;

"Young Mr. Elkins," *Broom*, 4 (December 1922): 52-56;

"Pascin's America," *Broom*, 4 (January 1923): 136-137;

"Mortuary," *Broom*, 4 (February 1923): 170;

"Portrait by Leyendecker," *Broom*, 4 (March 1923): 240-247;

"Love and Death, I," *Secession*, 5 (July 1923): 18;

"They Carry Him Off in a One-Horse Hack . . . ," *Secession*, 5 (July 1923): 19; republished as "Memphis Johnny," *Broom*, 5 (September 1923): 97-98;

"Snapshot of a Young Lady," *Broom*, 5 (August 1923): 3-10;

Pierre MacOrlan, "On Board the Morning Star," translated by Cowley, *Broom*, 5 (August 1923): 17-28;

"Into That Rarer Ether . . . ," *Secession*, 6 (September 1923): 5-6;

Louis Aragon, "The Extra," translated by Cowley, *Broom*, 5 (November 1923): 211-216;

"Towards a More Passionate Apprehension of Life," *Broom*, 5 (November 1923): 217;

Roger Vitrac, "Poison," translated by Cowley, *Broom*, 5 (November 1923): 226-228;

Philippe Soupault, "My Dear Jean," translated by Cowley, *Broom*, 6 (January 1924): 6-9;

"Comment: Open Letter To the Dial," by Cowley and Slater Brown, *Broom*, 6 (January 1924): 30-31;

"The Hill above the Mine," *transition*, no. 10 (January 1928): 90-91;

"Seven O'Clock," *transition*, no. 13 (Summer 1928): 54;

"Tar Babies," *transition*, no. 13 (Summer 1928): 96-97;

"In Memory of Florence Mills," *transition*, no. 15 (February 1929): 121;

"Inquiry about the Malady of Language," by Cowley and others, *transition*, no. 23 (July 1935): 148;

"Inquiry into the Spirit and Language of Night," by Cowley and others, *transition*, no. 27 (April-May 1938): 233-245.

Bibliography:

Diane U. Eisenberg, *Malcolm Cowley A Checklist of His Writings, 1916-1973* (Carbondale & Edwardsville: Southern Illinois University Press, 1975).

References:

Daniel Aaron, *Writers on the Left Episodes in Literary Communism* (New York: Harcourt, Brace & World, 1961);
R. P. Blackmur, "The Dangers of Authorship," in his *The Double Agent Essays in Craft and Elucidation* (New York: Arrow Editions, 1935), pp. 172-183;
Eleanor Bulkin, *Malcolm Cowley: A Study of His Literary, Social, and Political Thought to 1940*, Ph.D. dissertation, New York University, 1973;
Matthew Josephson, *Life Among the Surrealists* (New York: Rinehart, 1962);
Harold Loeb, *The Way It Was* (New York: Criterion, 1959);
Gorham B. Munson, "The Fledgling Years, 1916-1924," *Sewanee Review*, 40 (January-March 1932): 24-54;
Munson, "A Comedy of Exiles," *Literary Review*, 12 (Autumn 1968): 41-75.

Papers:

Malcolm Cowley's papers are at the Newberry Library, Chicago.

HART CRANE
(21 July 1899-27 April 1932)

SELECTED BOOKS: *White Buildings*, with a foreword by Allen Tate (New York: Boni & Liveright, 1926);
The Bridge (Paris: Black Sun Press, 1930; New York: Liveright, 1930);
The Complete Poems and Selected Letters and Prose of Hart Crane, ed. Brom Weber (Garden City: Doubleday, 1966; New York: Liveright, 1966; London: Oxford University Press, 1968).

Like many other American writers of the twenties Hart Crane visited France. Crane's stay, which lasted from early January to mid-July 1929, was briefer than most. The poet had hoped that France would be a place where he could work on his epic *The Bridge* (1930), free from interruptions by family and friends. Having published one book of poems, *White Buildings*, in 1926 as well as numerous poems in little magazines, Crane was anxious to finish what he considered to be his most important work and the one on which his reputation would be made.

Crane was born "with his little toe in the last century," as he put it, on 21 July 1899 in Garrettsville, Ohio. His parents' married life was one of considerable strain, which was reflected in their relations with their only son. In December 1916, when his parents were filing for a divorce, Crane moved to New York to begin his career as a writer. Before going to France in 1929, Crane lived in New York City, Cleveland, upstate New York, Los Angeles, and Cuba.

Even after his parents' divorce Crane found himself caught in their tug-of-war for his affections. It was perhaps these strains that contributed to the poet's reliance on alcohol, which he contended enhanced his artistic abilities, and to his homosexuality. His life can be regarded as a series of flights from those around him who knew of the intimate details of his experiences: from his mother, to whom he confided his homosexuality in the spring of 1928; from his father and acquaintances in Cleveland, who he feared would soon learn; and from his friends in New York to whom his drinking and sexual exploits had become legendary. Aided by a legacy from his maternal grandparents, Crane set sail for Europe on the Cunard Lines' *Tuscania* on 8

December 1928. After spending Christmas in London with Laura Riding and Robert Graves, Crane left for Paris on 6 January 1929.

The first person Crane visited after his arrival in Paris was Eugene Jolas. Jolas, who had corresponded with Crane since 1927, had translated Crane's poem "O Carib Isle" into French for his *Anthologie de la Nouvelle Poesie Americaine* (1928) and had published several others in his little magazine *transition*. Jolas introduced Crane to a small circle of artists and writers including Eva Gautier, Philippe Soupault, Laurence Vail, Kay Boyle, and most importantly, Harry and Caresse Crosby. Within days of his arrival Crane wrote on a postcard to a friend in New York, "Dinners, soirees, poets, erratic millionaires, painters, translations, lobsters, absinthe, music, promenades, oysters, sherry, asprin, pictures, Sapphic heiresses, editors, sailors, *And How!*" His enthusiasm for his new environment had a positive effect on his writing.

No doubt Crane had the Crosbys in mind when he wrote of "erratic millionaires" on his postcard. The Crosbys, who owned the Black Sun Press, were enthusiastic about *The Bridge* and made arrangements to publish the first edition. Crane also showed the Crosbys the manuscript for his friend Malcolm Cowley's *Blue Juniata* (1929), and the Crosbys considered publishing it until Crane received word from Cowley that the book had been accepted for publication in New York. Though Harry Crosby possessed a self-destructive nature that often has been compared to Crane's, he initially served as a positive force by providing the poet with the isolation they both felt was necessary to finish his great work. In February 1929 Crosby gave Crane the use of the Moulin du Soleil, his country retreat at Ermenonville outside Paris. The several weeks he spent at Ermenonville marked the first time in more than a year that Crane had been able to concentrate on his poetry, and he went back to work on *The Bridge*. By the end of the month, after several weeks of reading and note-taking, he had roughed out a draft of the "Cape Hatteras" section, the only significant poetry he wrote in France and one of the most important sections of his epic.

In March, however, Crosby enticed Crane to a chaotic round of parties and social engagements, and his work on the poem ceased. Between visits to the Crosbys, Crane met Gertrude Stein, saw his friends Allen Tate and Caroline Gordon, and gradually extended his circle of friends to include a group of young French and American artists and writers, of which Eugene MacCown, Allen Tanner and his sister Florence were a part. The pace in Paris was too much even for Crane, so in April and May he visited Collioure and Marseilles in the South of France. He was not without remorse over the brevity of his creative period and wrote friends in America: "I've been . . . hoping . . . that I'd have more 'progress' to report than the usual preoccupations of a typical American booze-hound in Paris. . . . However, as regards creative writing—I can't say that I'm finding Europe extremely stimulating. . . ." Crane did some work in Marseilles, though. It was there that he wrote the gloss that accompanies *The Bridge* and helps to bind the poem together.

Crane returned to Paris in late June 1929. "Hart C. back from Marseilles where he slept with his thirty sailors and he began again to drink Cutty Sark . . ." Harry Crosby somewhat dramatically recorded in his diary. The entry marks the beginning of Crane's final and most spectacular binge in Paris. After a fight in the Cafe Select, Crane was arrested, beaten by the Paris police, and incarcerated in La Sante for a week until Crosby paid Crane's fine and advanced him money for the passage home. On 18 July 1929, six and a half months after his arrival, and four days before his thirtieth birthday, Crane embarked on the S. S. *Homeric* for New York. His first and only trip to Europe was at an end.

Crane's association with the Crosbys did not end when the poet left Paris. Indeed, he was with Caresse Crosby on 10 December 1929, when she learned of her husband's suicide, and Caresse Crosby oversaw the publication of the Black Sun Press edition of *The Bridge* in early 1930. After the book's publication they drifted apart. "To the Cloud Juggler," Crane's poem in memory of Harry Crosby, appeared in the June 1930 issue of *transition*.

Until his death by suicide in 1932, Crane lived in various places including New York City, Ohio, and Mexico, where he went on a Guggenheim fellowship in 1931. There he became increasingly frustrated at his inability to complete poems that he considered first rate, drank himself into madness, and often found himself in trouble with the Mexican authorities. On his return to New York City in April 1932 Crane jumped from the stern of his steamship and drowned.

Surely one of the most difficult sections in what many consider as an altogether difficult poem, "Cape Hatteras" stands with "Cutty Sark" as the pivotal point of *The Bridge*. Several recent critics, including R. W. B. Lewis and Robert L. Combs, regard it as containing some of the most remarkable lines Crane wrote, but earlier critics like Yvor Winters and Allen Tate felt that the poet had overly sentimentalized Walt Whitman's *Passage to India*.

Whatever the critical reception, most agree that "Cape Hatteras" grasps for the experience of space and the transcendence of old values: "Thou hast there in thy wrist a Sanskrit charge / To conjugate infinity's dim marge— / Anew . . . !" The poem, like others he wrote, affirms the ability of the human spirit to renew itself. The tone alternates between pessimism and optimism. While acknowledging man's technological triumphs, Crane questions the purposes to which they have been put. "Cape Hatteras" ends in affirmation as the poet envisions himself moving in the tradition of Whitman, celebrating the engineers and traveling "onward and without halt" toward the future. In this way "Cape Hatteras" may be interpreted as reflecting the state of Crane's mind in Paris, when—if only briefly—he made a new beginning and renewed his spirit.

—*Thomas S. W. Lewis*

Other:

"O Ile des Antilles!," in *Anthologie de la Nouvelle Poesie Americaine*, trans. Eugene Jolas (Paris: Kra, 1928), pp. 46-47.

Periodical Publications:

"O Carib Isle!," *transition*, no. 1 (April 1927): 101-102;

"Cutty Sark," *transition*, no. 3 (June 1927): 116-119;

"The Harbor Dawn," *transition*, no. 3 (June 1927): 120-121;

"Van Winkle," *transition*, no. 7 (October 1927): 128-129;

"East of Yucatan," *transition*, no. 9 (December 1927): 132-136;

"Moment Fuge," *transition*, no. 15 (February 1929): 102;

"The Mango Tree," *transition*, no. 18 (November 1929): 95;

"To the Cloud Juggler," *transition*, no. 19/20 (June 1930): 223.

Letters:

The Letters of Hart Crane 1916-1932, ed. Brom Weber (New York: Hermitage House, 1952);

Robber Rocks Letters and Memories of Hart Crane, 1923-1932, ed. Susan Jenkins Brown (Middletown, Conn.: Wesleyan University Press, 1969);

The Letters of Hart Crane and His Family, ed. Thomas S. W. Lewis (New York & London: Columbia University Press, 1974);

Hart Crane and Yvor Winters Their Literary Correspondence, ed. Thomas Parkinson (Berkeley, Los Angeles & London: University of California Press, 1978).

Bibliographies:

Kenneth A. Lohf, *The Literary Manuscripts of Hart Crane* (Columbus: Ohio State University Press, 1967);

Joseph Schwartz, *Hart Crane An Annotated Critical Bibliography* (New York: Lewis, 1970);

Schwartz and Robert C. Schweik, *Hart Crane A Descriptive Bibliography* (Pittsburgh: University of Pittsburgh Press, 1972).

Biographies:

John Unterecker, *Voyager A Life of Hart Crane* (New York: Farrar, Straus & Giroux, 1969);

Brom Weber, *Hart Crane A Biographical and Critical Study* (New York: Bodley Press, 1948).

References:

R. W. Butterfield, *The Broken Arc: A Study of Hart Crane* (Edinburgh: Oliver & Boyd, 1969);

Robert Combs, *Vision of the Voyage: Hart Crane and the Psychology of Romanticism* (Memphis: Memphis State University Press, 1978);

L. S. Dembo, *Hart Crane's Sanskrit Charge: A Study of* The Bridge (Ithaca: Cornell University Press, 1960);

Samuel Hazo, *Hart Crane An Introduction and Interpretation* (New York: Barnes & Noble, 1963);

Hilton Landry and Elaine Landry, *A Concordance to the Poems of Hart Crane* (Metuchen, N.J.: Scarecrow Press, 1973);

Herbert Leibowitz, *Hart Crane An Introduction to the Poetry* (New York & London: Columbia University Press, 1968);

R. W. B. Lewis, *The Poetry of Hart Crane A Critical Study* (Princeton: Princeton University Press, 1967);

Dougald McMillan, transition *The History of a Literary Era 1927-1938* (New York: Braziller, 1976), pp. 125-147;

Sherman Paul, *Hart's Bridge* (Urbana, Chicago & London: University of Illinois Press, 1972);

Vincent Quinn, *Hart Crane* (New York: Twayne, 1963);

Margaret D. Uroff, *Hart Crane: the Patterns of His Poetry* (Urbana, Chicago & London: University of Illinois Press, 1974).

Harry and Caresse Crosby

Sy M. Kahn
University of the Pacific
Karen L. Rood
Columbia, South Carolina

Morris Library

Harry and Caresse Crosby by Bradford Johnson, Paris, 1923

Harry Crosby

BIRTH: Boston, Massachusetts, 4 June 1898, to Henrietta Marion Grew and Stephen Van Rensselaer Crosby.

EDUCATION: B.A., *honoris causa*, Harvard University, 1921.

MARRIAGE: 9 September 1922 to Mary Phelps Jacob Peabody (who later changed her name to Caresse).

DEATH: New York, New York, 10 December 1929.

BOOKS: *Sonnets for Caresse* (Paris: Privately printed, 1925; enlarged edition, Paris: Privately printed, 1926; new enlarged edition, Paris: Privately printed, 1926; revised edition, Paris: Editions Narcisse, 1927);

Red Skeletons (Paris: Editions Narcisse, 1927);

Chariot of the Sun (Paris: At the Sign of the Sundial / Cour Du Soleil D'Or, 1928);

Shadows of the Sun (Paris: Black Sun Press, 1928);

Transit of Venus (Paris: Black Sun Press, 1928; enlarged edition, Paris: Black Sun Press, 1929);

Mad Queen (Paris: Black Sun Press / Editions Narcisse, 1929);

Shadows of the Sun, second series (Paris: Black Sun Press, 1929);

The Sun (Paris: Black Sun Press, 1929);

Sleeping Together (Paris: Black Sun Press, 1929);

Shadows of the Sun, third series (Paris: Black Sun Press, 1930);

Aphrodite in Flight (Paris: Black Sun Press, 1930);

Torchbearer (Paris: Black Sun Press, 1931);

War Letters (Paris: Black Sun Press, 1932);

Shadows of the Sun The Diaries of Harry Crosby, edited with an introduction by Edward Germain (Santa Barbara, Cal.: Black Sparrow Press, 1977).

Caresse Crosby

BIRTH: New York, New York, 20 April 1892, to Mary Phelps and William Jacob.

MARRIAGE: January 1915 to Richard Rogers Peabody, divorced; children: William Jacob, Polly. 9 September 1922 to Henry Grew Crosby. 24 March 1937 to Selbert Young, divorced.

DEATH: Rome, Italy, 24 January 1970.

BOOKS: *Crosses of Gold* (Paris: Privately printed, 1925; enlarged edition, Paris: Messein, 1925);
Graven Images (Boston & New York: Houghton Mifflin, 1926);
Painted Shores (Paris: Editions Narcisse, 1927);
The Stranger (Paris: Editions Narcisse, 1928);
Impossible Melodies (Paris: Editions Narcisse, 1928);
Poems for Harry Crosby (Paris: Black Sun Press, 1931);
The Passionate Years (New York: Dial, 1953; enlarged edition, London: Redman, 1955).

Of all the Americans who lived in Paris during the twenties few were more vociferous than Harry Crosby in his rebellion against American puritanism, particularly as it was manifested in Boston society. By deed and by word Crosby railed against Boston, emblem of all that was awry in American life. Harry and Caresse Crosby went to Paris in 1922, not to seek an atmosphere congenial to creativity, but to escape the hostility of upper-class Boston, outraged at Harry Crosby's marriage to a divorced woman six years his senior. After their arrival in Paris, however, the Crosbys became part of its literary and artistic life, and Harry Crosby became one of the most flamboyant and extravagant of all the American expatriates until his notorious suicide in December 1929. During the seven years the Crosbys spent mostly in Paris, both of them wrote and published their own books of poetry, first under the imprint Editions Narcisse and then under that of the Black Sun Press. It was a press born "of Necessity out of Desire." As Caresse Crosby notes in her autobiography *The Passionate Years* (1953), "we knew that some day we must see our poems in print," and "the simplest way to get a poem into a book was to print the book!" Not only did they print their own

books, however, but they went on to publish the work of such contemporaries as D. H. Lawrence, Archibald MacLeish, Kay Boyle, James Joyce, Hart Crane, and Ezra Pound. The Black Sun books were to achieve a reputation not only for the excellence of their contents but also for their physical appearance. Consequently the Crosbys have been remembered not so much as poets, but as publishers of books by some of the most accomplished writers of their time.

Harry Crosby was born Henry Sturgis Crosby, but soon after his birth his parents changed his middle name to Grew. His father was descended from the wealthy Van Rensselaers of the Hudson River Valley area of New York State near Albany as well as from Alexander Hamilton; Revolutionary War general Philip Schuyler; and William Floyd, a signer of the Declaration of Independence. Harry Crosby's maternal grandfather, Henry Sturgis Grew, added the blood of a third patrician family to the Sturgis and Grew lines by marrying a Wigglesworth, and Harry Crosby's maternal aunt married John Pierpont Morgan, Jr.

Crosby attended St. Mark's School in Southborough, Massachusetts, from 1911 until his graduation at the age of nineteen in June 1917. A month later he sailed to France as a volunteer in the American Field Service Ambulance Corps, and by August he carried his first wounded soldier at the Somme. His motives for volunteering were not unlike those of other young Americans, such as Ernest Hemingway, John Dos Passos, and E. E. Cummings, who returned to France as writers in the twenties. Galvanized into action by the patriotism of the time, they did not want to miss "the big show" and the chance for personal glory. But no one was more anxious for heroism than Crosby, who hoped for a medal with the avidity of a knight seeking the Holy Grail. His 1917-1918 letters to his family, published as *War Letters* by the Black Sun Press in 1932, juxtapose his expressions of youthful idealism and patriotism with clinical descriptions of the wounded and the dead. In the late summer of 1917 the American Field Service ambulance sections were absorbed by the United States Army, and in September Crosby enlisted in the army as a private and continued to serve as an ambulance driver. On 3 November he arrived at the Battle of Verdun, where three weeks later, on 22 November, a shell destroyed his ambulance. A friend commented that Crosby was sitting in the only part of the vehicle that remained untouched. Crosby was physically unharmed, but his biographer Geoffrey Wolff calls the experience "the trial whose anniversary he would never neglect to note, the most important day of his life, his first death-day." On 22 November 1927 he wrote to his mother from Paris:

> Ten years ago today on the hills of Verdun and the red sun setting back of the hills and the River Meuse and the black shells spouting up in columns and the roar of the barrage and Spud was wounded and the ride down and the metamorphose from boy into man on November 22, 1917 I shall never forget. . . .

But, as Malcolm Cowley suggests, the metamorphosis was "not from boy into man: rather it was from life into death." It is probably too simple to draw a straight line between Verdun and Crosby's 1929 suicide. Yet there is little in his life to suggest that he was entranced by death before the war. After his brush with death in 1917, beginning in the *War Letters* and later in poems and diary entries, the theme of death is interwoven with the themes of love, sex, religion, sacrifice, and salvation. The letters detail the increasing violence Crosby encountered and display an increasing morbidity in clinical descriptions of the wounded. Yet the prevailing tone is boyishly exuberant, and these letters to his family suggest that he was essentially untarnished by the war. With a sincerity that seems altogether authentic he writes that he cannot wait to return to the joys and peace of Boston. Although Crosby was already drinking heavily, one would not easily guess that he would soon find himself unable and unwilling to conform to the expectations of proper Bostonian society. Moreover, while still serving in France, he achieved his goal of winning a medal for heroism and wired home: "Saturday, March 1, 1919. Won oh Boy !!!!!!! THE CROIX DE GUERRE. Thank God." Crosby's final goal would later become not a medal for valorous survival but a valorous death.

Soon afterward Crosby returned to Boston and matriculated at Harvard, and in June 1921 he was awarded a "war degree," a privilege granted to returned veterans that allowed them to graduate early. During those postwar years, Crosby met and subsequently fell in love with Mary Phelps Jacob Peabody, then called Polly, later known as Caresse.

Polly Jacob was born in New York City to a family that could trace its ancestry back a thousand years to the Isle of Wight, and her maternal great-great-great-great grandfather was William Bradford, the first governor of Massachusetts, who had come to America on the *Mayflower*. She was also descended from Robert Fulton, the inventor of the steamboat, and her grandfather was General Walter Phelps, leader of "The Iron Brigade" in the Battle of Antietam during the Civil War. As for the women of the family, they were, as she judges in her memoirs, "Despots, darlings, sorcerers, ladies of steel." In her youth, while attending various private schools in and around New York, Polly Jacob wrote and "published" a small newspaper containing local-color pieces and poetry. Like Fulton, she was an inventor. She worked on a perpetual motion machine, but she had more success in inventing and patenting the wireless brassiere when she was in her twenties, later selling the patent for $1,500. Many of her obituaries in 1970 emphasized this fact, ironically ignoring her considerable accomplishments as a publisher. When she was twenty-two she married Richard Rogers Peabody, son of a wealthy and prominent Boston family, and later bore him two children. Peabody served in World War I, and after his return the marriage foundered because of his increasingly severe alcoholism and because Polly Peabody had fallen in love with Harry Crosby.

Despite a troubled courtship that outraged three prominent families—the Crosbys, the Peabodys, and the Jacobs—Polly Peabody and Harry Crosby found more than sufficient attraction in each other to overcome Boston society's contempt and ridicule. Doubtless Crosby took pleasure in their defiance of convention. Since his return from the war his drinking and generally outrageous behavior seemed to be part of an active campaign to recant all the mores to which his family wholeheartedly subscribed. His courtship of a married woman, six years his senior with two young children, did little to repair or improve the opinion of society.

Polly Peabody's divorce became final in December 1921, but she and Crosby were not married right away. Hoping to discourage the union, Crosby's mother persuaded her brother-in-law, J. P. Morgan, to give her son a position for one year at his Paris bank, Morgan, Harjes et Cie. Crosby arrived in Paris on 1 May 1922 and was joined almost immediately by his fiancee, who stayed until the end of July. In September Crosby returned to New York City, married Polly Peabody on 9 September, and forty-eight hours later he left again for Paris with his new wife and two stepchildren.

In late November 1923 Harry Crosby resigned his position in the Paris bank, and he and Polly Crosby embarked on a concentrated program of eclectic reading and studying, and of writing, editing, and publishing. These activities eventually gained them entrance into Parisian cultural life, and their residences became gathering points for members of the expatriate literary community. Because of their energy and good looks and Harry Crosby's flamboyant—even bizarre—dress and behavior, they drew attention to themselves. During the Crosbys' seven years together in Paris and the nearby Moulin du Soleil, the country house they had created from an old mill in Ermenonville, they entertained writers, artists, royalty, and many other new-found friends. They traveled, went regularly to the races, where they won and lost extravagant sums, and eventually even owned their own racehorses and racing dogs. At Ermenonville they kept a string of burros for racing and playing polo. There were many parties, and there were numerous affairs. But in the midst of all this social activity, both Crosbys found time for writing and publishing. Harry Crosby wrote and published nine books of his own poetry, kept a diary that was published in three volumes, and worked as a publisher. Though Harry Crosby published more of his own poetry than Caresse Crosby did during their Paris years, she was more active in the everyday business of the Black Sun Press. Her life is of interest to literary scholars because of her marriage to an eccentric poet, but she also deserves attention for her own accomplishments as poet, patron of the arts, and cofounder of the Black Sun Press.

The Crosbys' interest in publishing first showed itself in 1924 when Harry Crosby edited and had printed a collection of his favorite poems. Called *Anthology*, the book had a preface by Crosby's Boston friend Ellery Sedgewick and was printed in Dijon by the printer Maurice Darantiere. The book is an eccentric collection of poems by American, British, and French poets ranging from Chaucer and Shakespeare to Robert Service and Caresse Crosby.

Although she later remembered that she changed her name to Caresse when she was working on the proofs for the first edition of *Crosses of Gold* (1925), all Mrs. Crosby's poems in *Anthology* appear under the name Caresse Crosby. While her sense of chronology is faulty, her memory of how the name was chosen may be correct. According to her memoirs, she and Harry Crosby "were sitting up side by side in bed, books piled up all around us, Huysmans, Poe, Rimbaud, Mallarme, Flaubert. Harry was engrossed in Poe's magic formulas and I was working on the proof sheets for my first poems *Crosses of Gold. . . .*" She could not decide whether her pen name should be "Polly Crosby, which sounded unpoetic," or "Mary Crosby, which sounded bluestocking." Her husband suggested a new name that would "begin with a C to go with Crosby and it must form a cross with mine." They finally settled upon "Caresse," which they joined to "Harry" to form the "Crosby Cross":

```
        C
        A
H A R R Y
        E
        S
        S
        E
```

This symbol first appeared in *Crosses of Gold* and later in other books by both of the Crosbys.

Crosses of Gold was privately printed in an edition of 100 copies, and it contains twenty-two poems, illustrated with Caresse Crosby's own watercolors. That same year an augmented edition was published by Albert Messein, chosen by the Crosbys because Messein had published Rimbaud. This edition omits three poems included in the first and adds thirty-three new poems, but it contains only one of the watercolors. Both editions begin with the poem "Harry," and indeed many of the poems are either in praise of Harry Crosby or in celebration of their love. In "Harry" the first letter of each line spells out his name:

> Heaven has given thee strength, wit, integrity,
> Angels, Beloved, might envy thy soul,
> Rich is thy spirit in fairness and charity,
> Rare charm is there and a clearness untold,
> Youthful and passionate. Heart of pure gold.

While some poems are gentle or wistful, others are passionate. "Etreinte" ends with the lines: "And exultantly I cling, embrace you— / Limb to limb, / Our flaming bodies wed." The poems are written in a variety of forms, although with the exception of one or two prose poems, all have regular meter and rhyme schemes. Besides love poems, the book contains observations about people and the natural world, reactions to works of art, and aphoristic comments about life in general. Although the poems are charming, they in no way indicate that Caresse Crosby will become a poet of great originality, nor did she.

Caresse Crosby's second book of poems, *Graven Images*, published by Houghton Mifflin in 1926, was the only book of poems by either Crosby not to be published first at their own expense. Harry Crosby's cousin Walter Berry, a close friend of Edith Wharton and Marcel Proust, had urged her to submit her manuscript to Houghton Mifflin in Boston. In *The Passionate Years* Crosby quotes him as saying, "they have just lost Amy Lowell." While she protested that she was not in Lowell's class, Crosby submitted her manuscript. It was immediately accepted, although the poems, as she remarked, were "still rhyming love with dove." In *Crosses of Gold* and *Graven Images*, as well as in the later *Painted Shores* (1927) and *Impossible Melodies* (1928), Caresse Crosby hewed to tradition. Although she admired and published the avant-garde work of others, as a poet she chose to present her world in her own conventional manner.

Also in 1925 Harry Crosby had privately printed his first book of poems, *Sonnets for Caresse*. The first edition, printed by Herbert Clarke, was limited to 17 copies and contains thirty poems. The following year Clarke printed another edition of 27 copies which includes thirty-seven sonnets, while the third edition of 108 copies, published by Albert Messein later in 1926, contains forty-eight poems. For the 1927 fourth edition of 44 copies, which bears the Crosbys' own Editions Narcisse imprint, Crosby included twenty-four poems. While each edition contains some new poems, old poems are also included under new names.

Like Caresse Crosby's *Crosses of Gold*, *Sonnets for Caresse* contains poems about the Crosbys' relationship, but the title is more dedication than subject—an appropriate dedication because Caresse Crosby had taught her husband how to use the sonnet form. Within its strictures, he examines what Wolff calls a "potpourri of odds and ends" that have been on his mind since the end of the war. Full of mythological characters, the collection contains poems about memories of childhood and war and poems that criticize sexual conventions. Wolff says the tone of the book is that of "lamentation, heavy as oatmeal, elegiac," with frequent references to the poet's early death or suicide. Even the love poems, such as "Desaccord," are about the torture of the loved one's neglect when she gazes at the poet "With cold disdainful eyes," but does not "deign / To smile or talk or even set me free." Like Caresse Crosby's poems, these sonnets echo poetic conventions of nineteenth-century Romantic poetry, but Harry Crosby's poems also show the influence of Baudelaire and the Symbolists' favorite American poet, Poe. Harry Crosby's later work was more experimental in form and more responsive to the current influences of Dadaism and Surrealism. Even in these early poems Crosby's vision is darker than his wife's.

When the Crosbys decided to establish their own press they set out to find a printer, taking with them three books whose typography they admired. As Caresse Crosby remembers in *The Passionate Years*, they wanted a printer "who would follow our dictates, not we his. The three books that we chose as

models were especially lovely editions: *Heloise and Abelard*, Brussels; *The Boussole des Amants*, Paris, and the Bodley Head edition of John Donne's poems." The printer they found was Roger Lescaret, whose shop was in the rue Cardinale, not far from their apartment. Although his specialty was printing marriage, christening, and death announcements, and although he had never printed books before, the Crosbys were so pleased with his work that he continued to be their printer for all the Editions Narcisse and Black Sun books. Caresse Crosby explains their publishing house's division of labor in *The Passionate Years*: "Lescaret remained the master printer—it should have been master copyist, but the results were as good as the models copied, and if it was I who set the margins and planned the pages and Harry who chose the material, it was Lescaret and [his assistant] who worked the press." They chose the imprint "Editions Narcisse" in honor of their black whippet, Narcisse Noir, and Caresse Crosby designed their first colophon: Narcissus gazing into a pool. During 1927 they published four of their own books, *Red Skeletons* and the fourth edition of *Sonnets for Caresse* by Harry Crosby and Caresse Crosby's *Painted Shores* and *The Stranger*.

Red Skeletons contains ten new poems and twenty-four poems that had appeared in the first three editions of *Sonnets for Caresse*, including some which would appear again in the fourth edition published later the same year. The edition of 370 copies is illustrated with the drawings of the Crosbys' friend Alastair, the Hungarian artist whose real name was Baron Hans Henning von Voight.

The republished poems combine with the new poems to create a unified mood of despair. Wolff calls the book "a decadent imitation of Baudelaire," but Hugh Ford says it is "far more than an adolescent exercise in the macabre," calling it "a litmus paper of his life, past and present." One republished poem is a sonnet celebrating Baudelaire, apostrophizing his "phantom fevered brain, with subtle maze / Of decomposed loves, remorse, dismays / And all the gnawing of a world's despair."

In Crosby's diaries there are references to Rimbaud, Baudelaire (particularly *Les Fleurs du Mal*), Verlaine, Mallarme, and Huysmans, and their influence can be seen in the themes and metaphors of *Sonnets for Caresse* and *Red Skeletons*. But as Ford points out, "the passion that filled the war poems" in *Red Skeletons* "came directly from his own past. . . ." The death he saw in the war haunted Crosby until his own death, creating a feeling of

Morris Library

The Crosbys and Narcisse Noir, ca. 1927

"deadness" inside him that he seemed to nurture even while he opposed to it his system of sun worship, which he explains in "Uncoffined," a poem Ford calls the best one in *Red Skeletons*. In this sonnet the speaker catalogues his regrets about his past and concludes:

> And as I sought to find excuse I came
> Upon the fatal words of wise Voltaire:
> Tout est dangereux et tout est necessaire—
> They whirled like autumn leaves within my
> brain,
> Until I sought the Sun to disentomb
> This long-dead foetus from my strangled
> womb!

Ford goes on to explain the basic contradiction between the seeming opposites of sun and death: "since it was the sun that lay at the center of Crosby's

sun-worshiping system, and since at the center there was emptiness and death, and since the ultimate experience toward which he moved was union with the 'Red-Gold (night) of the Sun,' the system itself only served to propel him faster toward self-destruction."

Red Skeletons completed Crosby's exercise in the sonnet as well as his apprenticeship to the Decadent school and its characteristic expression of the macabre, of futility, of derangement, and of dissolution and evil. Later, discontented with *Red Skeletons*, Crosby destroyed the eighty-four remaining copies. *Red Skeletons*, he wrote to his mother later that year, was his "swan song to the decadent." Although *Red Skeletons* is also a farewell to Oscar Wilde, a disciple of Baudelaire whose novel *The Picture of Dorian Gray* (1891) Crosby had read several times, Wolff points out that Crosby's love of

Baudelaire continued. Now however, rather than following the line that led from Baudelaire to Wilde, Crosby discovered the links among Baudelaire, Rimbaud, and T. S. Eliot.

Caresse Crosby's *Painted Shores* (1927), published in an edition of 246 copies, is similar in style and subject matter to *Crosses of Gold*. More interesting is her epic poem *The Stranger* (1927), which was published in an edition of 47 copies but later reprinted in the November 1929 issue of *transition*. The poem borrows some of Harry Crosby's imagery: in a chariot drawn first by a silver bird and then by one of gold, the poem's speaker approaches the Stranger, who waits behind the sun. She addresses the three important men in her life individually. She sees her husband standing in front of the sun:

> Against the sun
> O my lover you stand
> And I
> against the sun and the hills
> and the world.

But the two are drawn back to earth again where "We must yield to the rain," and she wonders if the Stranger still waits behind the sun. Before another attempt she addresses her son:

> I have bartered with youth
> For a cycle of fears
> O my son
> You are young
> You are young without years.

She advises him, "Put your feet in the fields / Give your strength to your play / I am free—I am through." But despite her attempts, her quest fails. She knows no more than when she started and is "tortured with flame." In *The Passionate Years* Crosby remembers the poem especially for its lines about her father, a man long afflicted with asthma, who as a consequence of his affliction was forced to live in Texas away from the family for several years until his death in 1908. In her autobiography she attributes to him her "indestructible idealism," and she says that he died before she really knew him. Characteristically inaccurate about facts—she was sixteen in 1908—Crosby remembers, "Up until the time I was eight years old he was my world, but from eight to fourteen living away from home . . . separated us and temporarily obscured his importance to me." A few months before his death, her father visited her at school, bringing a wicker basket of grapes. Twenty years later she was finally able to put the meeting into words:

> No more O Father
> from your hands
> The Gift of Love.
> Once only and forever all of love
> Was given
> Crimson ribbons, damson grapes,
> with tears above.

In her memoirs she adds, "Taking the basket into my neophyte hands, I knew I had accepted a gift more precious than sapphires, more ancient than wisdom." Although she admits that her poetry was "flagrantly *demodee*" and calls herself a "user of easeful cliche and well-worn rhyme," she claims that *The Stranger* captures at least some of the innovative spirit called for in *transition*.

With the death of Walter Berry on 12 October 1927, his cousin Harry Crosby became the executor of his estate. In his will Berry left Crosby "All the rest of the books in my appartement (except those bequeathed by Articles First and Second above, and those books which Edith Wharton may desire to take, as provided by Article Third above). . . ." Crosby later felt that Wharton was interpreting her provision too liberally and asked her to return at least half of the books. Wharton, who had never been fond of Crosby, wrote him what he described to his father as "an exceedingly cold letter," but in the end she took only seventy-three books and sets of books, which, according to Wolff, were valued at about what she had spent for Berry's funeral. When the remaining collection of nearly eight thousand volumes was delivered to the Crosbys on 8 May 1928, it nearly filled several rooms of their apartment, and Crosby feared that the floors would collapse. The library included such things as a leaf from the Gutenberg Bible, a first edition of DeQuincey's *Opium Eater*, illuminated copies of the Koran and the Psalms, the works of writers such as Casanova, Bacon, Henry James, and de Maupassant, or as Crosby described the collection to his mother, "every kind of book imaginable from the oldest Incunabula down to the most recent number of Transition. . . ."

Also in 1927 and in 1928 Harry Crosby met a number of his contemporaries who were to have an influence upon his poetic style and upon his career as a publisher. Early in 1927 he listed his favorite living poets as T. S. Eliot, Archibald MacLeish, and E. E. Cummings. He had read Eliot's *The Waste Land* soon after its publication in 1922, and he included MacLeish's early poem "Hands" in his *Anthology*. In 1926 his interest in MacLeish was renewed when he read MacLeish's more experimental verse in the recently published *Streets in the Moon*. E. E. Cummings was a more recent discovery, and Crosby also admired the work of Ezra Pound. Although he never cared much for reading novels, he idolized James Joyce, whose *Ulysses* (1922) he had read in the early twenties, and he expressed interest in Andre Gide and Gertrude Stein.

The Crosbys met the MacLeishes and Hemingway in Switzerland shortly after Christmas of 1926, and Crosby was often in the company of both writers thereafter in Paris. The Black Sun Press was later to publish two books by MacLeish, who sometimes advised Crosby about his poetry. Crosby's relationship with Hemingway was more purely social; they both went to Pamplona for the running of the bulls in 1927, but MacLeish remembers Hemingway's comment about Crosby's poetry: "he has a great, great gift. He has a wonderful gift of carelessness."

In the fall of 1927 Harry Crosby, who had recently discovered Eugene Jolas's avant-garde magazine *transition*, offered to send Jolas $100 anonymously for the poet "who in your judgment has written the best poem in the first twelve numbers of *Transition*. But for God's sake, don't make a prize out of it." The letter led to a friendship between the two men and Harry Crosby's subsequent involvement with *transition*, first as a contributor and later as an advisory editor. Although the change would not be readily apparent in Crosby's next book of poetry, *Chariot of the Sun* (1928), his involvement with Jolas and *transition* marked the beginning of his using for literary models the twentieth-century writers he had been reading.

Beginning in 1928 the Crosbys published books by others as well as their own. The first book suggests a link between Crosby's earlier interests and his developing modernist tastes. The Crosbys' 307-copy edition of Edgar Allan Poe's *The Fall of the House of Usher*, illustrated by Alastair, includes an introduction by Arthur Symons, the author of *The Symbolist Movement in Literature* (1899), the book that introduced French Symbolism to English readers and had seminal importance for the work of such poets as William Butler Yeats and T. S. Eliot. Not long after the appearance of this relatively large edition, the Crosbys published Caresse Crosby's fourth book, *Impossible Melodies*, a collection of thirty-eight poems in an edition of 48 copies. They also published the poems of a close friend, Lord Gerald Lymington, entitled *Git Le Coeur*, in an edition of 200 copies; and later in the year they produced English and French editions of Oscar Wilde's *The Birthday of the Infanta* (113 copies in English and 110 in French), mainly as a vehicle for the illustrations of their artist-friend Alastair.

Crosby wrote the foreword for the Wilde book. Despite their increasing involvement in literary circles, the Crosbys' press remained a vehicle for pleasing themselves and their friends.

From 26 January to 24 March 1928 the Crosbys and his mother traveled through Egypt, Jerusalem, Turkey, and Yugoslavia. During this time Crosby wrote many of the poems that would be published in *Chariot of the Sun*, and in Egypt on 1 February he began reading D. H. Lawrence's *The Plumed Serpent* (1926). Crosby had read and admired Lawrence's work as early as 1923, but in *The Plumed Serpent* he found a fellow sun worshipper. According to Wolff, Crosby was profoundly influenced by Lawrence's symbolic romance of a Mexico "rife with pagan gods and ancient rituals of blood sacrifice." Although Lawrence's system of sun worship was far more coherent than Crosby's, as Wolff points out, Crosby identified with Kate in *The Plumed Serpent*; he "felt himself pulled toward the source, toward the life-impulses centered in the sun."

Crosby's increasing obsession with the sun is apparent in *Chariot of the Sun*, which was published with a unique imprint: At The Sign of the Sundial Cour Du Soleil d'Or. Even titles such as "Quatrains To The Sun," "Cinquains To The Sun," "Sun Rhapsody," "Whippets to the Sun," "Angels of the Sun," "Pharmacie Du Soleil," "Sundrench and Sons," "Suns in Distress," and a number of others suggest his fixation with the sun as a multifaceted and ambiguous image. Life-giving and life-destroying, it is at once a cleansing force and a fiery, destructive destination. The literary models for this volume are the Symbolists rather than Baudelaire and Poe. Like the earlier poems, however, the dominant theme is death—but death as violent, quick, and liberating.

While still in Egypt, Crosby had begun corresponding with Lawrence and sending him copies of the poems that would appear in *Chariot of the Sun*. At Crosby's invitation Lawrence wrote an introduction to the book, which expresses honestly his ambivalence about Crosby's poetry. He calls the book "a sheet of flimsies," adding that the tone of the poems is jarringly uneven and that the use of imagery is clumsy. Moreover, "There is no colored thread of an idea; and no subtle ebbing of a theme into consciousness. . . . There is only a repetition of sun, sun, sun, not really as a glowing symbol, more as a bewilderment and a narcotic." Still, says Lawrence, the book "has something to say": "It is a glimpse of chaos not reduced to order. But the chaos *alive*, not the chaos of matter. A glimpse of the living, untamed chaos. . . . From it we draw our breath of life. If we shut ourselves off from it, we stifle." Thus, he concludes, "What does it matter if half the time the poet fails in his effort at expression! The failures make it real. . . . Failure is part of the living chaos." That Crosby's life was itself chaotic is made apparent by the next book published by the Crosbys, the first volume of Harry Crosby's diaries.

Shadows of the Sun is the first book to bear the Black Sun imprint, itself a symbol of the contradictions in Crosby's system of sun worship. As Wolff explains, Crosby took the symbol from medieval alchemy in which *Sol niger* is primal matter, or by modern thinking "the unconscious in its unworked, base state." In premodern astronomical theories the sun crosses the heavens hidden at night so that it may rise again at the East at dawn, and Wolff points out that in the *Rig-Veda*, an early Indian religious text that describes the creation of the universe, the sun, which is an all-pervading force, is "at its most magical and portentous" in its night crossing of the heavens. Moreover, just as the sun is resurrected at every dawn, Crosby believed that "he should persist again, in and like the sun, beyond his own sun-fall." Thus, the title Crosby chose for his diaries combines with the new name for the press to suggest the magical power of the sun as a symbol of life and death, creation and destruction. If death is a return to the unconscious, the source of all creative impulse, then suicide is not self-destruction but the ultimate act of creativity.

Crosby had shown his diaries to Jolas and *transition*'s associate editor Elliot Paul in late 1927, and *transition* asked to publish parts of it. Although Crosby was reluctant at first to make public any of the diaries, in 1928 he published the first volume, an edited version of his diaries for the years 1922-1926. The other two volumes, which cover 1927-1928 and 1929, appeared in 1929 and 1930. All three volumes of *Shadows of the Sun* were published in editions of forty-four copies; Edward Germain's 1977 edition of the diaries not only makes them more readily available, but restores many omitted passages from the original manuscripts.

Crosby's diaries provide insights into a restless mind, by turns exuberant and morbid. They also provide a record of his reading and the experiences, observations, and speculations that were the matrix for his poems. Moreover, they reveal Crosby's tendency to mythologize the events of his life. He calls Caresse Crosby the Cramoisy Queen and gives his lovers names such as the Mad Queen, the Queen of Pekin, the Youngest Princess, and the Dark Princess. He records the discoveries about ancient sun worship that went into his religion of the sun and makes himself a sun god. Like his poems, the diaries are full of references to the sun as both life giver and destroyer. Wolff calls the style of *Shadows of the Sun* a crude approximation of the syntactical reflexes in Joyce's *Ulysses*, but not discounting Crosby's conscious desire to imitate the novelist he most admired, the increasing breakdown of syntax in the diaries may be accounted for in part by Crosby's increasing mental derangement accompanied by his growing dependence upon drugs such as hashish and opium.

One result of the Crosbys' trip to Egypt was their publication in the fall of 1928 of an ancient erotic manuscript they claimed to have found in Damascus. The small book, published in a limited edition of twenty copies, is illustrated with twenty-two miniature drawings, which are purported to show the twenty-two positions for lovemaking, but, as Hugh Ford says, the drawings carry "minuteness to the brink of invisibility."

A far more significant result of the Crosbys' trip is their publication of D. H. Lawrence's *Sun* (1928). Writing to Lawrence from Egypt, Harry Crosby had asked to publish a story about the sun. Lawrence responded by sending his short story "Sun," which had previously been abridged for publication. The October 1928 Black Sun Press edition of 165 copies, with a drawing by Lawrence, is the first unexpurgated edition of the story. In September 1929 the Black Sun Press published another of Lawrence's stories, *The Escaped Cock*, in an edition of 500 copies, with illustrations by Lawrence. Although Lawrence commended *Lady Chatterly's Lover* (1928) to Crosby, Crosby found that novel "disgusting."

Another 1928 Black Sun publication is the *Letters of Henry James to Walter Berry* in an edition of 116 copies. These letters had been part of the library left to Crosby by his cousin, as were the letters from Marcel Proust, which the Crosbys published in English and French as *47 Unpublished Letters from Marcel Proust to Walter Berry* in 1929. Although Harry and Caresse Crosby are listed as the translators, Wolff gives credit for the translation to American poet Richard Thoma. In *The Passionate Years*, however, Caresse Crosby says that because Thoma failed to complete the job satisfactorily, she took over the work of translating the letters.

The last Black Sun book for 1928 was Harry Crosby's *Transit of Venus*. Published in an edition of 44 copies, it was followed in the summer of 1929 by a second edition of 200 copies, to which are added ten new poems. The book's title comes from an astronomical term describing the passage of Venus between the earth and the sun during which Venus appears to travel across the sun's face. While *Transit of Venus* is dedicated to Caresse Crosby, the Venus to Harry Crosby's Sun was Josephine Rotch, a beautiful young Boston woman whom Crosby met in the summer of 1928 while she was in Europe to buy her trousseau for her marriage to Albert Bigelow. While Caresse Crosby claimed never to believe that her husband was totally serious in his proposals that the two of them should die together by their own hands, Josephine Rotch was perhaps even more enthusiastic about the idea of the joint suicide of lovers than Harry Crosby. The love poems of *Transit of Venus* are inextricably linked with death; in one the lover wishes he were a cat so that he could go to the loved one while she slept "And suck your breath / Slowly and surely / Into death." The dominance of the sun in *Chariot of the Sun* has given way to a fixation upon murder and suicide.

As Wolff points out, this is the first of Crosby's books to show the influence of Dada and Surrealism: "The poet's voice is icy rather than frenzied, and every trace of the Decadent influence upon him has been expunged." The poems are written in short, dramatically elliptical lines, in which sentences do not run over from one line to the next. Wolff calls this style "one of ellipsis, arrest, stuttering hesitation and diverted utterance." A good example of the sense of energy created by such a style is "Kiss":

> This blessed fruit, this,
> This goodly red,
> This fire, this O, this This the last of
> This kiss.

Archibald MacLeish wrote Crosby a letter of qualified praise. MacLeish was not completely convinced that the incompleted phrases of Crosby's poems were effective, but, he added, "you hit upon a kind of true brevity. . . . And that brevity is signed with your name." In his preface to the 1931 posthumous edition of *Transit of Venus*, T. S. Eliot also commented upon the poems' brevity, calling Crosby "a young man in a hurry." But Eliot acknowledges that Crosby was moving in a new direction with his poetry even if he was unsure about the exact significance of his goal, adding that Crosby "was in a hurry, I think, because he was aware of a direction, and ignorant of the destination, only conscious that time was short and the terminus a long way off." Kay Boyle, whom the Crosbys had met in the spring or summer of 1928, was also ambivalent about the merits of *Transit of Venus*. She wrote to Crosby that the poems were better than any she had seen in print recently, but she called for "stronger

and harder" poems and found "the conviction and despair of originality" only in Crosby's "testament to the sun."

Harry Crosby had been contributing to *transition* since the Fall 1928 issue, which included his response to *transition*'s questionnaire, "Why Do Americans Live in Europe?" and "Hail: Death!," one of the prose pieces he called "tirades," which was included in his next book, *Mad Queen*, as "Sun Death." Among his reasons for living in Europe, Crosby lists his desire not "to devote myself to perpetual hypocrisy," and he adds that "outside America there is nothing to remind me of my childhood." Moreover, he says, "I prefer transitional orgasms to atlantic monthlies," and "the Rivers of Suicide are more inviting than the Prairies of Prosperity." His conclusion echoes a phrase from T. S. Eliot's *The Hollow Men* (1925) that runs throughout his later work: "I prefer explosions to whimperings." The poet must choose a sudden and violent death. Crosby continued to contribute poems, prose, and photographs until his death in December 1929. In the spring of 1929 he paid for the printing of an entire issue of *transition*, and in the June and November 1929 issues, he is listed as one of the advisory editors.

In June 1929 both Crosbys were among the signers of *transition*'s "Revolution of the Word Proclamation," which announced the death of traditional literary forms and said, among other things, that "PURE POETRY IS A LYRICAL ABSOLUTE THAT SEEKS AN A PRIORI REALITY WITHIN OURSELVES ALONE." Such poetry can be written "ONLY THROUGH THE RHYTHMIC 'HALLUCINATION OF THE WORD'. (Rimbaud)." As Dougald McMillan points out, Rimbaud writes in *Une Saison en Enfer* (1873) about "how he had become intoxicated with words until he achieved a state of revelation." McMillan adds that Jolas did not mean that a writer should "lose control of his sense when writing," only that he should become "attuned to the incantatory power of words. . . ." Harry Crosby does not always seem to have made the same distinction.

Some of the poems and prose pieces in Crosby's next book, published in an edition of 141 copies, had appeared first in *transition*. He divided the prose in *Mad Queen* (1929) into two categories: tirades and dreams. The latter type suggests the influence of Jolas's interest in dream psychology. The title comes from one of Crosby's names for Josephine Rotch Bigelow, and references to the Mad Queen run throughout the volume. In "Heliograph" Crosby portrays himself as "Too rigid to crumple but not too strong to fracture" and goes on to catalogue her power over him:

> The Mad Queen, The violent state of fusion. Her Sun tattooed on my back. Multiplication of Madness. Anarchism. I lay Siege to the Sun. . . .

In "Sun Death," one of the tirades, he begins with a long catalogue of famous suicides and goes on to state the necessity of enjoying "an orgasm with the sombre Slave-Girl of Death, in order to be reborn..." or even to become nothing: "for it is stronger to founder in the Black Sea of Nothingness, like a ship going down with flags, than to crawl like a Maldoror into the malodorous whore-house of evil and old age. Let not this be said of those who founder or those who, like red arrows, wing chaste and unafraid into the redgold of the Sun." He quotes the last four lines of Eliot's *The Hollow Men* and concludes that "Eliot is right . . . as regards the stupid Philistines, whose lives have always been a whimper. . . ." The poet, however, must seek for a more heroic death:

> But for the Seekers after Fire and the Seers and Prophets (hail to you O men of transition!) and the Worshipers [sic] of the Sun, life ends not with a whimper, but with a Bang. . . . Let them devourdung, let their maggot fingers swarm over the red cloth, while we, having set fire to the powder-house of our souls, explode (suns within suns and cataracts of gold) into the frenzied fury of the Sun, into the madness of the Sun into the hot gold arms and hot gold eyes of the Goddess of the Sun!

The longest poem in the volume is "Assassin," set in Constantinople. Wolff says that this poem is based upon Crosby's experience during his 1928 trip to that city when he had eaten hashish and taken opium pills. Although the chronology follows actual events, Crosby has transformed that experience into a Surrealistic, dreamlike vision of himself as the assassin. The poem begins with the statement that the Mad Queen has commanded him to "Murder the sterility and hypocrisy of the world . . . in order that a new strong world shall arise to worship the Mad Queen, Goddess of the Sun." After describing the setting, the speaker continues with a vision of himself as destroyer and creator of chaos. All representatives of law and order, of learning and tradition, are subject to his murderous hatred as Crosby's original rejection of Boston's social codes and outmoded traditions is extended to its farthest extremes. All must be destroyed in order to create the "New Sun World," so that the speaker may "bring

the Seed of a / New Copulation / I proclaim the Mad Queen." Not only does he "resurrect madness" and "murder the world," but the speaker ends with a promise:

> I the Assassin chosen by the Mad Queen I the Murderer of the World shall in my fury murder myself. I shall cut out my heart take it into my joined hands and walk towards the Sun without stopping until I fall down dead.

It is difficult not to read "Assassin" as an announcement of Crosby's impending suicide. As Wolff says, " 'Assassin' is less a poem than a testament and its art is almost overwhelmed by its pathology."

During the last years of his life, Crosby was more involved in literary pursuits and experiencing more success than ever before. Not only was his work appearing in *transition*, which he was helping to edit, but his poems were also being published in the American little magazines *Blues*, *Pagany*, and *Morada*. Moreover, the Crosbys' press was publishing the books that would earn it a place in literary history. In March 1929 the Black Sun Press published Kay Boyle's first book, *Short Stories*, a collection of six stories in an edition of 165 copies. They also published *Einstein*, a long poem by another of their friends, Archibald MacLeish, in an edition of 150 copies. In 1930 Caresse Crosby published MacLeish's *New Found Land*, a collection of fourteen poems, in a limited edition of 135 copies, and the Black Sun Press printed the trade edition of 500 copies for Houghton Mifflin in that same year.

Books by two other notable American expatriates were published by the Black Sun Press in 1929. *1450-1950* by Bob Brown appeared in an edition of 150 copies. It is a history of innovative printing that calls for the restructuring of printed language and foreshadows Brown's invention of the Reading Machine, which was supposed to revolutionize the way people read by moving the words past the reader's eye at an individually controlled speed rather than forcing the reader to move his eyes back and forth across the page. Eugene Jolas's *Secession In Astropolis*, published by the Black Sun Press in an edition of 135 copies, is an illustration of the points set forth in the "Revolution of the Word Proclamation," a collection of dreams and parables illustrating Jolas's mythic theories, which influenced Crosby's own attempts to record his dreams in *Sleeping Together*.

In January 1929 Jolas introduced the Crosbys to Hart Crane. Crane was newly arrived in Paris, but

Jola had been an admirer of his work for some time, publishing it in *transition* from the very first issue in 1927. Harry Crosby read Crane's first book, *White Buildings* (1926), and was soon negotiating to publish Crane's still-unfinished epic poem, *The Bridge*. Crane agreed to have the Black Sun Press publish his poem and also showed Crosby the manuscript of his friend Malcolm Cowley's *Blue Juniata* (1929), which he hoped the Crosbys would also publish. Before any final decisions were made, however, Crane received word that Cowley's book had been accepted for publication by Cape and Smith in New York.

Later Crane gave the Crosbys the manuscript of his poem "O Carib Isle!," which had appeared in *transition*. In a June 1929 *transition* article, Harry Crosby quotes this poem and calls Crane "dynamic energy, concentration, fresh vision, a migratory crane flying above the worn-out forest of the poetic phrase. . . ." He adds that Crane's poetic ancestors are "Marlowe and Coleridge and Whitman and Rimbaud." The Crosbys allowed Crane to spend time writing at the Moulin du Soleil, where he completed the "Cape Hatteras" section of the poem. But a combination of the Crosbys' active social life and Crane's own problematic work habits prevented him from finishing *The Bridge*. In July 1929 Crane became involved in a fight at the Cafe Select in Paris and spent several days in La Sante prison until friends got word to Harry Crosby, who paid Crane's fine and advanced him the money for his passage home. *The Bridge* was still unfinished and was not published until January 1930, after Harry Crosby's December 1929 suicide. Crane had originally hoped that Joseph Stella's painting of the Brooklyn Bridge could illustrate his poem, but although he managed to interest both the Crosbys and Jolas in Stella's work, plans for using the painting for the frontispiece did not work out. Instead the edition of 275 copies contains three photographs by Crane's friend Walker Evans.

Undoubtedly the most exciting event of 1929 for Crosby was his meeting with James Joyce and the Black Sun Press's subsequent publication of *Tales Told of Shem and Shaun*, three fragments of Joyce's *Work in Progress* (published in book form in 1939 as *Finnegans Wake*) that had previously appeared in *transition*. Crosby was first introduced briefly to Joyce by Ernest Hemingway at a concert given by Ada MacLeish in the spring of 1928. A far more significant meeting took place on 4 March 1929, however, when fellow *transition* editor Stuart Gilbert took both Crosbys to Joyce's apartment. On that occasion Harry Crosby presented Joyce with the

Harry Crosby

Sylvia Beach Collection

large *Book of the Dead* that had been part of Walter Berry's library and received a promise that Joyce would give the Black Sun Press something to publish. A month later Sylvia Beach, who had Joyce's power of attorney, drew up a contract for the Crosbys to publish the three fragments: "The Mookse and the Gripes," "The Muddest Thick That Was Ever Heard Dump," and "The Ondt and the Gracehoper." As Beach had done before them, the Crosbys allowed Joyce to rewrite when the book was in galleys with the result that the proofs came back looking "like a bookie's score card." As Caresse Crosby remembers in *The Passionate Years*, a final crisis came when their printer Roger Lescaret discovered that there would be only two lines of type on the last page. Lescaret asked her "if I wouldn't beg Mr. Joyce to add another eight lines to help us out." She responded that one did not ask a great writer "to inflate a masterpiece to help out the printer," but Lescaret took matters into his own hands and went to Joyce himself. Joyce added the lines cheerfully. As the printer told Caresse Crosby, "he told me he had been wanting to add more, but he was too frightened of you, Madame, to do so." *Tales Told of Shem and Shaun* was published in June 1929 in an edition of 400 copies with an abstract portrait of Joyce by Brancusi. In 1936 Caresse Crosby published *Collected Poems of James Joyce* in an edition of 800 copies under the Black Sun imprint in New York.

Other 1929 publications of the Black Sun Press include a 400-copy edition of Laurence Sterne's *Sentimental Journey*, with illustrations by the Crosbys' friend Polia Chentoff; *Spring Song of Iscariot*, another book of poems by the Crosbys' friend Lord Gerald Lymington, in an edition of 125 copies; two volumes of *Les Liaisons Dangereuses* by Choderlos De Laclos, illustrated by their friend Alastair, in editions of 1020 copies; and two miniature books: *The Sun* by Harry Crosby, with drawings by Caresse Crosby (100 copies) and *The Rubaiyat of Omar Khayyam* (number of copies unknown). The Crosbys' interest in miniature books began with their 1928 publication of the erotic Hindu manuscript they had found in Damascus; in that same year they also published *The News Letter of the LXIVMOS* for a society of miniature book collectors headquartered in Brookline, Massachusetts.

Harry Crosby's last publication before his death was *Sleeping Together*, which appeared in November 1929 in an edition of seventy-seven copies. The dreams recorded in this book, together with earlier ones described in contributions to *transition*, demonstrate the influence of Eugene Jolas's interest in dreams as the source of the mystical unity lacking in modern life. The dream descriptions are interesting, but they lack the mad vitality of Crosby's poetry. Wolff suggests that Crosby "first read Freud and Jung, and then created conundrums for their theories to solve." Several of the dreams record his recent passion for flying. (He began flying lessons in August 1929 and flew alone for the first time on 11 November 1929 shortly before sailing for the United States.) One description, which he calls "White Slipper," combines the images of airplane and sun, as he addresses his wife:

> A white aeroplane whiter than the word Yes falls like a slipper from the sky. You come dancing over the silver thorns of the lawn and by holding up the corners of your rose-and-white skirt you catch the white slipper which I kick down to you from the sun.

Crosby's increasing desire for death is apparent throughout the record of his dreams as well.

The Crosbys arrived in the United States for a visit on 22 November 1929, and on 10 December 1929 Harry Crosby and Josephine Rotch Bigelow were found dead in the studio of a friend, apparently the victims of a suicide pact. Hart Crane was with Caresse Crosby and her mother-in-law when they received the news of Harry Crosby's death, and at Caresse Crosby's request Archibald MacLeish kept a watch over his body in the morgue. Although the newspapers emphasized the sensational aspects of Crosby's death, others chose to remember him as a poet and man of letters. Norman Macleod, who had published Crosby's poetry earlier, prepared a special Harry Crosby issue of *Morada*, and *transition* included tributes by Kay Boyle, Hart Crane, Stuart Gilbert, Eugene Jolas, Archibald MacLeish, and Philippe Soupault. While Gilbert, Jolas, and Soupault wrote personal reminiscences, and Crane and MacLeish contributed poems ("To the Cloud Juggler" and "Cinema of a Man," respectively), Boyle alone wrote of Crosby as a poet:

> To be living now, to be living, alive and full of the thing, to believe in the sun, the moon, or the stars, or in whatever is your belief, and to write of these things with an alertness sharp as a blade and as relentless, is a challenge that is a solemn privelege [*sic*] of the young. In any generation there are but few grave enough to acknowledge this responsibility. In ours, Harry Crosby stands singularly alone.

She credited Crosby with taking "his time and his contemporaries to heart" and added that with "the courage of his determination to make his life a testament of stern and uncompromising beauty, he wrote his diary in words that never faltered in their pursuit of his own amenable soul."

Stuart Gilbert's "Harry Crosby A personal note," which was later used as the introduction to the 1931 edition of *Sleeping Together*, suggests that Crosby would have been most at home in the age of knighthood. In the modern age, "There remains, of course, vast unexplored territories of mind, dream-cities to visit, cloud-capped palaces to explore; but the high-priests of madness and modernity have blocked the way with their dopes and denials—*No Thoroughfare: Sens (le bon sens) Interdit*—till only one virgin adventure . . . seems left, the final, futile plunge 'down the Valley of the Shadow' to

> *the undiscovered country from whose bourn no traveller returns . . . "*

Eugene Jolas acknowledged Crosby's support of *transition* and praised "his keen understanding and fervor for *transition's* aims," calling him "a mystic of the sun-mythos" whose "spirit was still fermenting at the time of his death." Philippe Soupault, who had met Crosby only once, said that Crosby's mistake lay in his accepting the role of victim too easily; the world was "a ball he set revolving. But he, too, revolved around that ball." Finally, "Friendship, love, poetry became words. Death remained the only reality."

After Harry Crosby's death, Caresse Crosby continued to run the Black Sun Press and to publish her husband's work. In 1930 she published the third volume of *Shadows of the Sun* and *Aphrodite in Flight,* a slim volume with the subtitle "Some Observations On The Aerodynamics of Love," published in an edition of 27 copies. The following year she published the Collected Poems of Harry Crosby in four volumes, each in an edition of 570 copies. The first, *Chariot of the Sun,* contains the preface Harry Crosby had solicited from D. H. Lawrence while the third volume, *Sleeping Together,* is prefaced by Stuart Gilbert's tribute from *transition.* For *Transit of Venus* Caresse Crosby obtained a preface from T. S. Eliot, and the fourth volume, *Torchbearer,* contains "Notes" by Ezra Pound.

Torchbearer, the only previously unpublished book in the Collected Poems, contains thirty-nine poems and short prose poems, written in a style which Wolff calls close to automatic writing. Pound calls his preface "Notes" because only a "blighted pedagogue subsidized to collect Washlists and obstruct the onrush of letters" would try "to concoct a preface" to Crosby's "magnificent finale," and he asserts that Crosby's "life was a religious manifestation" and that his suicide was "a comprehensible emotional act, that is to say if you separate five minutes from all conditioning circumstance and refuse to consider anything Crosby has ever written. A death from excess vitality. A vote of confidence in the cosmos." Thus, Pound says, Crosby's life is more important than his poetry because of his religious concern for his relationship to the universe.

In 1932 the Black Sun Press published a final volume by Crosby, *War Letters,* in an edition of 125 copies. This collection of letters written during World War I contains a preface by Crosby's mother. Full of patriotic fervor and expressions of conventional piety, the letters in no way suggest that the same young man could write a poem like "Assassin."

Even in a decade when obscurity was sometimes unjustly admired as experimentation, Crosby's work was recognized as second-rate. As it was for his contemporaries, including those who wrote the

prefaces to his books, his poetry is interesting for its revelations about the workings of a brilliant and insane mind. As Wolff points out, the development of Crosby's style between 1925 and 1929 is remarkable in itself: "during five working years Harry duplicated a century of complicated aesthetic traditions. If it is true that the literary topography of a certain age is best read in the contour maps left by its minor writers, Harry mapped the interior territories of several cultural epochs." From the conventional late nineteenth-century Romanticism of his early sonnets, Crosby followed the development of several literary generations from Decadent to Symbolist to Surrealist and ended with a fascination for subconscious and automatic writing. Unconsciously, he explicated the linkages in an important segment of literary history.

Caresse Crosby's work shows no such development. Her final book of poetry, *Poems for Harry Crosby* (1931), is much the same as her first, although, as Wolff suggests, it expresses "sentiments beyond the artifice of grief and memorial convention." If the poems do express her love and anger honestly, however, her literary gifts are still limited. Published in an edition of 522 copies, the book contains a preface by Stuart Gilbert that praises Harry Crosby while saying little about Caresse Crosby's poems.

Besides overseeing the publication of Hart Crane's *The Bridge,* Proust's letters to Walter Berry, and MacLeish's *New Found Land,* Caresse Crosby published four more books under the Black Sun imprint in Paris. Probably the most significant are Ezra Pound's *Imaginary Letters* (1930), which had first appeared in the *Little Review* in 1917, published in an edition of 375 copies, and *Mr. Knife Miss Fork* (1931), a fragment of Rene Crevel's novel *Babylon,* translated by Kay Boyle with illustrations by Max Ernst and published in an edition of 250 copies. The other two books were *New York 1929* (1930), a 10-copy edition of photographs by the Crosbys' friends Gretchen and Peter Powel, and Lewis Carroll's *Alice In Wonderland,* illustrated by Marie Laurencin, published in 1930 in an edition of 790 copies.

In 1931 Crosby and Jacques Porel originated Crosby Continental Editions in imitation of the Tauchnitz company whose inexpensive reprints of English classics and some modern works were the only ones available on the Continent at that time. Crosby and Porel hoped that their reprints of avant-garde literature would sell as well. Ezra Pound offered a number of suggestions, most of which were ignored, and Crosby decided to ask Ernest Hemingway for a book to launch the series, hoping that his name would help to publicize her new venture. Hemingway offered to let her reprint either *The Torrents of Spring* (1926) or *The Sun Also Rises* (1926), and Crosby made the mistake of deciding upon *The Torrents of Spring* because *The Sun Also Rises* had been republished so often that it had probably "lost its interest." She apparently had not read *The Torrents of Spring*, and she was later distressed to discover its satiric treatment of Sherwood Anderson. This first volume of the series was published in December 1931, and nine more books appeared in 1932: Ramond Radiguet's *Devil in the Flesh*, translated by Kay Boyle; *Sanctuary* by William Faulkner; Laurence Vail's translation of *Bubu of Montparnasse* by Charles-Louis Philippe; Dorothy Parker's *Laments for the Living*; Hemingway's *In Our Time*; Antoine de Saint-Exupery's *Night-Flight*, translated by Stuart Gilbert; Boyle's novel *Year Before Last*; Francoise Delisle's translation of *Big Meaulnes* by Alain-Fournier, and *Indefinite Huntress and other stories* by Robert McAlmon. Only McAlmon's book was previously unpublished and was included in the series at the suggestion of both Boyle and Pound. The translations of *Night-Flight* and *Big Meaulnes* were done especially for the series, however. After the first six months of operation, Crosby Continental Editions had made only about twelve hundred dollars. Crosby traveled to New York in late 1932 hoping to interest American publishers in paper-covered books, but the era of mass-market paperbacks had not yet come to America.

In the mid-thirties Crosby returned to the United States and continued to publish books sporadically under both the Black Sun and the Crosby Continental Editions imprints. At the end of 1936 she bought Hampton Manor, a plantation about twenty-five miles from Fredericksburg, and set about restoring the house, which had been designed by Thomas Jefferson. She married Selbert Young in March 1937, and the couple lived in Virginia until their divorce in the early forties.

After her divorce, Crosby moved to Washington, D.C., where she ran the Crosby Gallery of Modern Art. One of the gallery's exhibitions was a one-man show of Henry Miller's paintings. At the end of World War II she inaugurated *Portfolio An Intercontinental Review*. During the next three years, she published six issues under the Black Sun imprint from Washington, Paris, Rome, and Greece. The first issue lists Caresse Crosby as editor; Harry T. Moore as associate editor; and Henry Miller, Selden Rodman, and Sam Rosenberg as editorial advisers. As *Portfolio*'s title suggests, it contained

Caresse Crosby

Sylvia Beach Collection

experimental poems, prose, and art work printed on loose sheets of paper. Besides its editorial advisers, the contributors were Kay Boyle, Karl Shapiro, Gwendolyn Brooks, Henry Moore, Eleanor Clark, Matisse, Paul Eluard, Robert Lowell, Picasso, Jean-Paul Sartre, Stephen Spender, Jean Genet, Anais Nin, Emanuel Carnevali, Max Ernst, and Man Ray. *Portfolio* also republished poems, diary entries, and photographs by Harry Crosby.

In the early fifties Crosby purchased the castle of Rocca Sinibalda, about fifty miles north of Rome. The 500-year-old structure was to remain her home, though she continued to travel widely until the end of her life. During the fifties and sixties she invited various writers and artists to come and work at the castle. She also headed two international organizations during these years: Women Against War and Citizens of the World. In 1953 she published her memoirs *The Passionate Years*, which deals mainly with her life with Harry Crosby in Paris. Despite the strain caused by Crosby's jealousy of her children, his numerous love affairs, and his erratic behavior, she insists that she always loved him:

"Immaturity of mind and spirit were the forces that warred within him. He combined the naiveness of youth with the wisdom of the ages. He seemed like one who had taken on burdens from many former lives and discarded many along the way." Although her memory of chronology and events is unreliable, the book remains an important source of information about the Crosbys' part in Paris literary life. To Malcolm Cowley, who advised her about the book and urged her to check her facts more carefully, she wrote, "As for ideas underlying the actions of the 20s, I haven't the foggiest notion. As you say, I am not introspective, not [*sic*] do I judge motives only actions. I am 100% extrovert (or was); if I had been otherwise I doubt it I could have weathered the 20's. I don't suppose I ever have a thought unrelated to action—and I can't describe our ideas, only what we did."

During the sixties Crosby published, under the imprint Castle Continental Editions, books by poets Sy Kahn and Bill Barker. Also in this period she bought property in Delphi, Greece, and later a mountaintop in Cyprus with the idea of establishing a world meeting center for political leaders and artists. For the property in Cyprus, her friend Buckminster Fuller was to design a geodesic dome. However, her death in January 1970 ended these plans. The final passage of *The Passionate Years* applies not only to her Paris years, but to her entire life:

> I have learned that personal life is the individual's only means of expression in a cosmos forever mysterious. It is the right to this life itself that must be made secure for the unborn citizens of a challenging universe. Like Harry, I believed there could be no compromise. The answer to the challenge is always *"Yes."*

Wolff describes her as remaining "to the end ebullient, an odd mixture of shrewdness and goofiness, courageous in the extreme, and proud."

The Crosbys have often been remembered for their eccentricities rather than for their actual accomplishments, and perhaps, as Wolff suggests, the true interest of Harry Crosby's career to scholars lies in its unconscious charting of an important segment of literary history. In *Exile's Return* Malcolm Cowley, who met the Crosbys at a party given by Hart Crane a few days before Harry Crosby's death, sees the progress of his involvement with avant-garde literary movements and finds him in some ways typical of the young Americans who sought exile: "the separation from home, the effects of service in the ambulance corps, the exile in France, then other themes, bohemianism, the religion of art, the escape from society, the effort to defend one's individuality even at the cost of sterility and madness, then the final period of demoralization when the whole philosophical structure crumbled ·from within . . . —all this is suggested in Harry Crosby's life and is rendered fairly explicit in his diary." While Wolff emphasizes Crosby's differences from the other American writers in France, both critics agree upon Crosby's final assumption of the persona of the mad poet, not simply as a literary role, which can be taken off and on at will, but as his own personality. As Cowley says,

> He was not more talented than his associates, but he was more single-minded, more literal, and was not held back by fear of death or ridicule from carrying his principles to their extremes. As a result, his life had the quality of a logical structure. His suicide was the last term of a syllogism; it was like the signature to a second-rate but honest and exciting poem.

Harry Crosby's poetry will always be read for clues to the sources of his monomania rather than for its artistic merits, and the brilliant madness of his life in Paris will undoubtedly continue to overshadow the Crosbys' accomplishments as publishers.

Other:

Anthology, edited by Harry Crosby with contributions by Caresse Crosby (Paris: Privately printed, 1924);

Oscar Wilde, *The Birthday of the Infanta*, foreword by Harry Crosby (Paris: Black Sun Press/Editions Narcisse, 1928);

47 Unpublished Letters from Marcel Proust to Walter Berry, edited and translated by Harry Crosby and Caresse Crosby; republished in French as *47 Lettres Inedites de Marcel Proust a Walter Berry*, edited by Harry ·Crosby and Caresse Crosby (Paris: Black Sun Press, 1930);

Ernest Hemingway, *The Torrents of Spring*, includes "Open Letter to Ernest Hemingway" by Caresse Crosby (Paris: Crosby Continental Editions, 1963);

Sy M. Kahn, *Our Separate Darkness and Other Poems*, introduction by Caresse Crosby (Rocca Sinibalda, Italy: Castle Continental Editions, 1963).

Periodical Publications:

"Why Do Americans Live in Europe?," by Harry Crosby and others, *transition*, no. 14 (Fall 1928): 97-119;

"Hail: Death," by Harry Crosby, *transition*, no. 14 (Fall 1928): 169-170;

"Suite: Aeronautics; The Sun," by Harry Crosby, *transition*, no. 15 (February 1929): 19-24;

"Revolution of the Word Proclamation," signed by Harry Crosby, Caresse Crosby, and others, *transition*, no. 16/17 (June 1929): 13;

"The New Word," by Harry Crosby, *transition*, no. 16/17 (June 1929): 30;

"Head: 1929," photograph by Harry Crosby, *transition*, no. 16/17 (June 1929): following 156;

"Observation-Post," by Harry Crosby, *transition*, no. 16/17 (June 1929): 197-206;

"Dreams 1928-1929," by Harry Crosby, *transition*, no. 18 (November 1929): 32-36;

"For a protection," by Harry Crosby, *transition*, no. 18 (November 1929): 47;

"The Stranger," by Caresse Crosby, *transition*, no. 18 (November 1929): 96-101;

"Short Introduction to Words," by Harry Crosby, *transition*, no. 18 (November 1929): 206-207;

"Apparition" and "Aerotics," photographs by Harry Crosby, *transition*, no. 18 (November 1929): following 252;

"Illustrations of Madness," by Harry Crosby, *transition*, no. 18 (November 1929): 102-103;

"Sleeping Together," by Harry Crosby, *transition*, no. 19/20 (June 1930): 233-238.

Bibliography:

George Robert Minkoff, *A Bibliography of* The Black Sun Press, introduction by Caresse Crosby (Great Neck, N.Y.: Minkoff, 1970).

Biography:

Geoffrey Wolff, *Black Sun The Brief Transit and Violent Eclipse of Harry Crosby* (New York: Random House, 1976).

References:

Jane Baltzell, "The Answer Was Always 'Yes'!," *Brumonia* (January 1955): 5-9;

Millicent Bell, "The Black Sun Press to the Present," *Books at Brown*, 17 (January 1955): 2-24;

The Black Sun Press, Exhibition catalogue (Carbondale: Morris Library, Southern Illinois University, 1977);

Kay Boyle, "The Crosbys An Afterword," *ICarbS*, 3 (Spring-Summer 1977): 117-125;

Malcolm Cowley, *Exile's Return*, revised edition (New York: Viking, 1951), pp. 246-288;

Hugh Ford, *Published in Paris American and British Writers, Printers, and Publishers in Paris, 1920-1939* (New York: Macmillan, 1975), pp. 168-230;

Edward B. Germain, "Harry Crosby His Death His Diaries," *ICarbS*, 3 (Spring-Summer 1977): 103-110;

"In Memoriam: Harry Crosby," memorials by Kay Boyle, Hart Crane, Stuart Gilbert, Eugene Jolas, Archibald MacLeish, and Philippe Soupault, *transition*, no. 19/20 (June 1930): 221-232;

Sy M. Kahn, "Hart Crane and Harry Crosby: A Transit of Poets," *Journal of Modern Literature*, 1 (1970): 45-56;

Kahn, "No Armistice for Harry Crosby," *Lost Generation Journal*, 5 (Winter 1977-1978): 6-8, 20-21;

Kahn, "The Slender Fire of Harry Crosby," in *The Twenties: Poetry and Prose*, ed. Richard Langford and William E. Taylor (DeLand, Fla.: Everett/Edwards, 1966), pp. 1-6;

Robert McAlmon, *Being Geniuses Together 1920-1930*, revised edition with additional material by Kay Boyle (Garden City: Doubleday, 1968);

Dougald McMillan, transition *The History of a Literary Era 1927-1938* (New York: Braziller, 1976);

Harry T. Moore, "The Later Caresse Crosby Her Answer Remained 'Yes,' " *ICarbS*, 3 (Spring-Summer 1977): 127-134;

Sasha Newborn, "Harry Crosby's Sun Code," *ICarbS*, 3 (Spring-Summer 1977): 111-116.

Papers:

The Black Sun Press archives, including unpublished notes and diary entries by Harry Crosby, are at the Morris Library, Southern Illinois University at Carbondale.

HOMER CROY
(11 March 1883-24 May 1965)

SELECTED BOOKS: *When to Lock the Stable* (Indianapolis: Bobbs-Merrill, 1914);
West of the Water Tower (New York & London: Harper, 1923);
They Had to See Paris (New York & London: Harper, 1926);
Country Cured (New York & London: Harper, 1943);
Jesse James Was My Neighbor (New York: Duell, Sloan & Pearce, 1949);
He Hanged Them High (New York: Duell, Sloan & Pearce, 1952);
Our Will Rogers (New York: Duell, Sloan & Pearce, 1953).

Although he visited France and wrote a novel, *They Had to See Paris* (1926), about his experiences there, Homer Croy, a Midwestern novelist and humorist, never associated with the other American writers in Paris. Croy was born and raised on a farm near Maryville, Missouri; after graduating from high school, he began his writing career by working as a cub reporter for the *St. Joseph Gazette* and the *St. Joseph Press*. He attended the University of Missouri, supporting himself in part as a correspondent for the *Kansas City Star*, and went on to work for the *St. Louis Post-Dispatch* before moving to New York. In New York, Croy worked under Theodore Dreiser, then an editor at Butterick Publications, and also wrote his first novel, *When to Lock the Stable* (1914), which was a modest critical and financial success. The outbreak of World War I found him in India preparing newsreels and travel pictures for the Universal Film Company. On his return to the United States, Croy married Mae Belle Savell on 7 February 1915. During World War I, Croy worked with the YMCA as a liaison man with the Signal Corps; he also continued his writing career as a humorist. His first major success, however, came with *West of the Water Tower* (1923), which was first published anonymously because its "serious" tone conflicted with Croy's public image. A thoughtful treatment of small-town sexual standards, the novel, now generally considered to be Croy's most significant work of fiction, was well-received by its first reviewers, who praised its authenticity and compared it to Edgar Wilson Howe's *The Story of a Country Town* (1883) and Sinclair Lewis's *Main Street* (1920). The novel was sold to Paramount Pictures for $25,000, and Croy used the proceeds to finance an extended trip to Europe.

Homer Croy, ca. 1926

Though Croy met such public figures as Walter Lippmann, Frank Harris, and Lord Alfred Douglas in his twenty-two months in Paris and on the Riviera, he apparently formed no close friendships there and was never part of any literary circle. In his autobiography, *Country Cured* (1943), he writes of his experiences in Paris with a curious mixture of confusion and contempt. For him, Paris "was disappointing. It was odd and strange and . . . certainly not wonderful. . . . The people seemed to be slightly on the demented side. . . . The French seemed aloof and artificial, sometimes on the verge of childishness." After the serious novel he wrote in Paris was rejected by his publishers, Croy returned home to America.

Out of these experiences came Croy's *They Had to See Paris* (1926). Ostensibly based on the activities of a disgruntled American businessman Croy had met in Paris, who had come to France to "parley voo 'em," the novel also reflects Croy's dissatisfaction with his months in Paris. Pike Peters, a garage owner in Clearwater, Oklahoma, suddenly becomes a wealthy oil well owner and, upon the urgings of his socially ambitious wife, travels with his family to Paris. Once there, he cannot comprehend the manners and mores of the French. The Peterses leave Europe after Pike Peters refuses to pay a substantial dowry to an impoverished marquis who has proposed to his daughter. The novel was well-received on its appearance, surely in part because it reflected the misgivings many Americans felt at the time toward the European experience. In 1929, *They Had to See Paris* was made into a motion picture directed by Frank Borzage and starring Will Rogers

in his first talking role. Released under the same title as the book, it was a major success for Fox and Rogers's first real success in the movies.

Croy continued to work as a novelist and continued to sell properties to the motion pictures, but none of his later fiction duplicated the success of his early work. Relatively late in life, however, he turned to biography. *Jesse James Was My Neighbor* (1949), *He Hanged Them High* (1952), the life of Judge Isaac C. Parker, and *Our Will Rogers* (1953) now appear to be among the most lasting of his books. —*Creath S. Thorne*

COUNTEE CULLEN
(30 May 1903-9 January 1946)

SELECTED BOOKS: *Color* (New York & London: Harper, 1925);
Copper Sun (New York & London: Harper, 1927);
The Ballad of the Brown Girl An Old Ballad Retold (New York & London: Harper, 1927);
The Black Christ and Other Poems (New York & London: Harper, 1929);
The Medea and Some Other Poems (New York & London: Harper, 1935);
On These I Stand An Anthology of the Best Poems of Countee Cullen (New York & London: Harper, 1947).

Born Countee Leroy Porter on 30 May 1903, Countee Cullen was orphaned while still a child and subsequently adopted, though the relationship was never made legal, by Frederick Asbury Cullen. While an air of mystery—apparently maintained by the poet himself—surrounds the earliest years of Cullen's life, the facts of his biography following adoption by the Reverend Mr. Cullen are well-documented. Study at DeWitt Clinton High School in New York City where Cullen first began to write poetry, was followed by attendance at New York University, from which he graduated in 1925. In the fall of 1925 Cullen enrolled for graduate work at Harvard and finished an M.A. in literature the following summer, having already published his first book, *Color* (1925). After a brief episode as an

assistant editor of *Opportunity*, Cullen received a Guggenheim fellowship in 1928 for a year of study and writing in Paris, and his lifelong fascination with French language and culture began. By 1934 Cullen's career as a writer had declined, and he took a position teaching French in Frederick Douglass High School in New York, which he held until his death in 1946.

France appears to have been a special place for Countee Cullen as evidenced both in the few poems he wrote about Paris and in the fact that he chose to finish out his life as a teacher of the French language. A recurring idea in Cullen's work is his determination that he be regarded primarily as a poet, not as a black poet. In his language, themes, and forms, he sought to base his work upon the major traditions of European literature, and he bitterly resented the parochialism which encouraged Negro poets to limit their interests to subjects reflecting black experience. In France, Cullen sought the freedom to be just a poet. As he wrote in his poem "To France,"

> I have sought in you that alchemy
> That knits my bones and turns me to the sun;
> And found across a continent of foam
> What was denied my hungry heart at home.

Unfortunately for Cullen, France did not have the positive effect on his work he had hoped for. Before leaving for his Guggenheim year in Paris, he had married Yolande DuBois, daughter of W. E. B. DuBois, who joined him there. Yolande discovered that the marriage was a "tragic mistake," and returning home, she sued for divorce, which was granted in 1929. Perhaps as a result of this disaster, the love poems in *The Black Christ and Other Poems* (1929), the work Cullen completed in Paris, reflect bitterness and anguish that seem more self-indulgent than tragic. Even the title poem, which draws an analogy between a lynching and the Crucifixion, lacks the poignance of Cullen's strongest racially oriented work.

While in Paris, Cullen was associated with a group of black artists and writers whose focal point was the studio of the sculptress Augusta Savage. Prominent among this group, in addition to Cullen and Savage, were painters Palmer Hayden and Hale Woodruff, and the Jamaican novelist Eric Walrond. He was also close to Steve and Sophie Green, an American couple who generously provided him a quiet place to work in their home on the rue du Dounaier near Montsouris Park. In addition to his writing, he continued at the Sorbonne the study of French literature he had begun at New York University.

With the publication of *The Black Christ*, Cullen's life as a poet was essentially finished. *The Medea and Some Other Poems* (1935), also partially written in Paris and containing two of his translations from Baudelaire as well as "To France," did little to enhance his declining reputation. France, however, continued to occupy a central place in his consciousness, and he returned each year until 1939 when World War II ended his visits to the land where he once dreamed of finding, in old age, a place "among a fair and kindly folk," where he might

> breathe my latest days,
> With those rich accents falling on my ear
> That most have made me feel that freedom's rays

> Still have a shrine where they may leap and
> sear,
> Though I were palsied there, or halt, or blind,
> So I were there, I think I should not mind.

—William E. Grant

Other:

Caroling Dusk, edited by Cullen (New York & London: Harper, 1927);

The Lost Zoo (A Rhyme for the Young, But Not Too Young), by Cullen and Christopher Cat (New York & London: Harper, 1940).

References:

Houston A. Baker, Jr., *A Many-Colored Coat of Dreams The Poetry of Countee Cullen* (Detroit: Broadside Press, 1974);

Blanch E. Ferguson, *Countee Cullen and the Negro Renaissance* (New York: Dodd, Mead, 1966);

Blyden Jackson, "Largo for Adonais," in his *The Waiting Years* (Baton Rouge: Louisiana State University Press, 1976), pp. 42-69;

Margaret Perry, *A Bio-Bibliography of Countee P. Cullen 1903-1946* (Westport, Conn.: Greenwood Press, 1971);

J. Saunders Redding, *To Make A Poet Black* (Chapel Hill: University of North Carolina Press, 1939), pp. 108-112;

Darwin T. Turner, *In a Minor Chord: Three Afro-American Writers and Their Search for Identity* (Carbondale: Southern Illinois University Press, 1971), pp. 66-88;

Jean Wagner, *Black Poets of the United States: from Paul Lawrence Dunbar to Langston Hughes*, trans. Kenneth Douglas (Urbana: University of Illinois Press, 1973).

E. E. Cummings

Robert K. Martin
Concordia University

BIRTH: Cambridge, Massachusetts, 14 October 1894, to Rebecca Clarke and Edward Cummings.

EDUCATION: B.A., 1915, M.A., 1916, Harvard University.

MARRIAGE: To Elaine Orr, divorced; children: Nancy. 1927 to Anne Barton, divorced. 1932 to Marion Morehouse.

AWARDS: *Dial* Award, 1925; Richard Aldington Poetry Award, 1931; Guggenheim Fellowship, 1933; Levinson Prize, 1939; Shelley Memorial Award, 1945; Academy of American Poets Fellowship, 1950; Harriet Monroe Poetry Award, 1950; Eunice Tietjens Prize, 1952; National Book Award for *Poems 1923-1954*, 1955; Bollingen Prize, 1958; Oscar Blumenthal Award, 1962.

DEATH: Silver Lake, New Hampshire, 3 September 1962.

SELECTED BOOKS: *The Enormous Room* (New York: Boni & Liveright, 1922; London: Cape, 1928);
Tulips and Chimneys (New York: Seltzer, 1923; enlarged edition, Mount Vernon, N.Y.: Golden Eagle Press, 1937);
& (New York: Privately printed, 1925);
XLI Poems (New York: Dial, 1925);
is 5 (New York: Boni & Liveright, 1926);
Him (New York: Boni & Liveright, 1927);
[No title] (New York: Covici Friede, 1930);
CIOPW (New York: Covici Friede, 1931);
ViVa (New York: Liveright, 1931);
Eimi (New York: Covici Friede, 1933);
no thanks (New York: Golden Eagle Press, 1935);
1/20 (London: Roughton, 1936);
Collected Poems (New York: Harcourt, Brace, 1938);
i: Six Nonlectures (Cambridge: Harvard University Press, 1953);
Poems 1923-1954 (New York: Harcourt, Brace, 1954).

Many of the Americans in Paris in the twenties may have had some occasion to encounter French law, and several even spent a few hours in jail. But few began their lives in France by being arrested and sent to detention camp, as E. E. Cummings did. For Cummings it was the source of his first book, *The Enormous Room* (1922), which recounts the

E. E. Cummings

experience and turns it into the source of one of Cummings's abiding themes, the victory of the innocent individual over a corrupt system. Despite his difficulties with French bureaucracy, Cummings maintained his love for France and continued to visit Paris during the twenties and thirties.

Edward Estlin Cummings was born in Cambridge, Massachusetts, . to Rebecca Clarke Cummings and Edward Cummings. Edward Cummings taught sociology and political science at Harvard, where he became friends with William James, until 1900 when he was ordained minister of South Congregational Church, Unitarian, in Boston. Raised in his family's Cambridge home, Cummings attended public schools and entered Harvard in 1911, where he majored in English and classics. During his undergraduate years he formed lasting friendships with John Dos Passos, Robert

Hillyer, Gilbert Seldes, and S. Foster Damon, later a distinguished Blake scholar, poet, and biographer of Amy Lowell. Among the significant literary influences of his years at Harvard, the most important are his discovery of Marlowe, his training in Greek and Latin poetry (Catullus and Sappho remain significant forces in his work), and his awareness of the new poetry movement, centered around Ezra Pound and *Poetry* magazine.

On 24 June 1915 Cummings received his B.A. magna cum laude and delivered a commencement address on "The New Art," in which he demonstrated his awareness of the trends in literature and painting that would be at the roots of experimental writing in Paris during the twenties. He defended Cubism and Futurism against the "rampant abuse" of contemporary critics and praised the music of Erik Satie, Igor Stravinsky, and Arnold Schoenberg before going on to discuss writing. Quoting poems by Amy Lowell and Donald Evans to illustrate "the literary parallel of sound-painting," he ended with a discussion of Gertrude Stein's *Tender Buttons* (1914): "Gertrude Stein is a Futurist who subordinates the meaning of words to the beauty of words themselves. Her art is the logic of literary sound-painting carried to its extreme." He concluded his speech by suggesting that it was too early to tell how much contemporary experimentation was art, but, he said, "The New Art, discredited though it be by fakirs and fanatics, will appear in its essential spirit to the unprejudiced critic as a courageous and genuine exploration of untrodden ways."

Cummings remained at Harvard to take his M.A., which he received in 1916. In the fall of 1915 he and several friends formed the Harvard Poetry Society. One offshoot of this group was the publication of some of the members' poems in *Eight Harvard Poets* (1917), where Cummings's work appears with poems by Damon, Dos Passos, Hillyer, R. Stewart Mitchell, William A. Norris, Dudley Poore, and Cuthbert Wright. Some of the eight poems by Cummings display the typographical innovations with which he later came to be identified. In subject these early poems are highly Romantic in the tradition of Keats.

After finishing his M.A., Cummings lived in New York City until early 1917, when he enlisted in the Norton-Harjes Ambulance Corps and sailed for France on the French Lines' *Touraine* in late April 1917. He later described his status as "neither warrior nor conscientious objector," adding, "It was an opportunity to do something useful and see France at the same time." After arriving in France,

Cummings and his friend William Slater Brown, whom he had met on the *Touraine*, became separated from the rest of their group and spent a month in Paris before being assigned to an ambulance section. Many years later in *i: Six Nonlectures* (1953), Cummings remembers his first visit to Paris:

> I participated in an actual marriage of material with immaterial things; I celebrated an immediate reconciling of spirit and flesh, forever and now, heaven and earth. Paris was for me precisely and complexly this homogeneous duality: This accepting transcendence; this living and dying more than death or life. Whereas—by the very act of becoming its improbably gigantic self—New York had reduced mankind to a tribe of pygmies, Paris (in each shape and gesture and avenue and cranny of her being) was continuously expressing the humanness of humanity. . . . While (at the hating touch of some madness called La Guerre) a once rising and striving world toppled into withering hideously smithereens, love rose in my heart like a sun and beauty blossomed in my life like a star. Now, finally and first, I was myself: a temporal citizen of eternity; one with all human beings born and unborn.

For Cummings Paris represented a spiritual place of rebirth where he felt himself freed from the spiritual heritage of Puritanism. Following the inclination to break with tradition that is already apparent in his commencement address on "The New Art," Cummings made Paris a city symbolic of love and beauty in his mythic universe. He expressed the call of Paris in terms of a religious conversion experience: Paris offered an "imperishable communion" that might revive the religious spirit dormant under the "stone-cold Unitarianism" of his forefathers.

After their month in Paris, Cummings and Brown were assigned to ambulance duty at Ham in the Noyon sector of the front. Three months later they were arrested, on the suspicion that they were not sufficiently supportive of the French war effort and harbored secret pro-German sympathies. The suspicions of the French censors had arisen because of comments Brown had made in letters home, and the case against Cummings would have been weak, if he had dissociated himself from Brown. Cummings not only insisted upon supporting Brown, however, but he refused to testify that he hated the Germans, saying simply that he loved the French very much. For these offenses Cummings and Brown were taken to a concentration camp, La Ferte Mace, where they were interrogated further. Largely because of his father's efforts, Cummings was released on 19 December 1917, and Brown was finally freed in February 1918.

Both Cummings and Brown returned to the United States as soon as they were released, and the two men shared quarters in New York City until Cummings was drafted in the summer of 1918 and sent to Camp Devens, Massachusetts, for training as an infantry soldier. After the Armistice Cummings and Brown settled again in New York, where Cummings worked on poems that would appear in *Tulips and Chimneys* (1923). By now Cummings's style was established. He used typography to indicate rhythm, timing, and emphasis. He saw words not merely as signifiers of meaning, but as objects having lives of their own. At the time many of Cummings's poems seemed like exercises in deliberate nonsense, but later critics have pointed out their source in Baroque poetry (such as the shaped poems of George Herbert) as well as in the *Calligrammes* (1918) of Apollinaire. (The latter source was denied by Cummings, but it offers at the least a very striking parallel.) Cummings was also working seriously at his painting and drawing. The drawings illustrate his love of vaudeville and musical entertainment. The striptease dancer, the clown, the jazz singer, and the prostitute all became inhabitants of Cummings's imaginative world. After two of Cummings's Harvard acquaintances, Scofield Thayer and James Sibley Watson, bought the *Dial* and Cummings's friend Stewart Mitchell became the managing editor, Cummings became a regular contributor starting with the January 1920 issue. While imprisoned in La Ferte Mace, Cummings had kept a notebook, and in September 1920 his father, who was still indignant about his son's treatment, convinced him to write the account of his experience that was published as *The Enormous Room*. A modern, ironic version of John Bunyan's *Pilgrim's Progress* (1678), the book covers Cummings's experiences from the time of his arrest until his release. Despite the prison's filth and the behavior to which the inmates were reduced in order to stay alive, the narrator discovers that everything good is not outside the prison, nor all the bad within. In prison he meets the "Delectable Mountains," individuals who are "cursed with a talent for thinking" when "great governments . . . demanded of their respective peoples the exact antithesis of thinking." He decides that treason is "any little annoying habits of independent thought or action which *en temps de guerre* are put into a hole and

covered over, with the somewhat naive idea that from their cadavers violets will grow. . . ." From this realization comes a sense of a redemptive alienation from the conventional. Caught up in a meaningless world, it is the individual's discovery of the self that enables him to transcend the experience and find true value in meaning. Paradoxically, society's imprisonment of the innocent individual (the Everyman of a Kafkaesque world) becomes a blessing. For it is precisely the isolation from the conventional world of unmeaning that permits him access to the timeless world of meaning. The camp is transformed into a metaphor for the human condition, in which adversity is changed into personal triumph. As the narrator concludes, "There is and can be no such thing as authentic art until the *bons trucs* (whereby we are taught to see and imitate on canvas and in stone and by words this so-called world) are entirely and thoroughly and perfectly annihilated by that vast and painful process of Unthinking which may result in a minute bit of purely personal Feeling. Which minute bit is Art."

Publication of *The Enormous Room* was greeted by most critics with general incomprehension, but with great praise from John Dos Passos in the *Dial*. Dos Passos compared Cummings's writing to that of Defoe, seeing in Cummings "a gusto, an intense sensitiveness to men and women and colors and stenches and anger and love." With the publication of *The Enormous Room*, declared Dos Passos, "it is time to take off your new straw hat and jump on it." Later critics saw *The Enormous Room* as an important contribution to the literature of its decade.

In *The Twenties American Writing in the Postwar Decade* (1962) Frederick J. Hoffman praises *The Enormous Room* for "its picture of a life from which all decorum and artifice have gone" and compares the book to Ernest Hemingway's *A Farewell to Arms* (1929):

> Hemingway described the psychological results of the battlefield; Cummings portrayed the terrors and pointed to the survivors of the concentration camp. In each case, there was a suspension of time and a modification of customary space; in each case, conditions governing life were reduced to the borderline of consciousness; in each case fundamental changes took place in the formation of the postwar attitude toward those who continued to live and to believe "conventionally." The two, more than any others, gave the 1920s the most complete rationalization of its postwar attitudes.

I

1

We had spent almost three four of our six months at the section
sanitaire, my friend and I, and at the Moment which subsequent
experience served to capitalize had just finished our job of
cleaning and greasing--nettoyer is the convenient French verb,--
the chef's own Flivver. Neither of us, as I recollect, were intensely thrilled by this form of service to France, which
owing to Jupiter pluvius and the tranquility of that section of
the French line wherewith our section was affiliated) our conates
and almost unique heroism in the service of France.
Of course if I wanted to I could write a thrilling enough dairy
of things that almost didnt fail to occur, inserting volumin-
eus accounts of hair-raising gas scares, trips by night with
wounded poilus along roads infested with thundering ravitaillemе
nt trains coming in the opposite direction--guns and groceries
are generally brought up by night to the trenches--occassional
ponderings on the ultimate location of certain merrily whistling
obus,etc.etc. But America is crammed at the present moment with
many conducteurs voluntaires of the ambulance service whose
experiences (according to themselves, who should certainly
somebody said, know best) far surpass my own
comparatively drowsy thrills, that I will not presume upon the
thrill-saturated readers in that particular. My tale is of othe
matters, and brgins, as I started to explain with the cleaning
of the chief's peculiar Fliv., said Fliv. being dirtier than
heroes like ourselves might have expected ran cold as we viewed
the spectacle before we got through.

I had washed up--do not forget this,reader, when you hear of
subsequent proceedings--and was strolling carelessly from the
cock wagon toward the tent which housed our huddling forms by
night, munching a historic morceau de chocolat, when a spick not
to say span gentleman in a suspiciously quiet uniform allowed
himself to be driven up to the bureau in a Renault whose painful cleanliness shamed my recent efforts.
Two French soldiers(as I assumed) in tin derbies formed the
stranger's retinue. This must be a general at least, I thought,
regretting the extremely undress character of my uniform at the
moment, which consisted of overalls and a cigarette.
The gentleman allighted, received a conventional welcome from
the chef and the French officer who accompainied our section for
translatory reasons, and betook myself with all haste to the

Typescript, The Enormous Room

In the spring of 1921 Cummings and Dos Passos traveled to Portugal and Spain, and after climbing in the Pyrenees, they arrived in Paris in May. Dos Passos went on to Persia, but Cummings remained in Paris where he soon found himself in the company of old friends Slater Brown and Scofield Thayer. In July Cummings met Ezra Pound, whom he described in a letter to his parents as "a gymnastic personality. Or in other words somebody, and intricate." Cummings remained in France until the autumn of 1923. During this period Cummings published poems in *Secession*, edited by Gorham Munson and Matthew Josephson and printed in Vienna. Through a New York friend, Alfred Kreymborg, Cummings had poems accepted for publication in *Broom*, then edited by Kreymborg and Harold Loeb in Rome, and he continued to contribute to the magazine after its subsequent moves to Berlin and New York. Not only did Cummings contribute poems to *Secession*, but in the contributors' notes on the inside front cover of the July 1922 issue, he attacked the conservative taste of anthologist Louis Untermeyer:

> E. E. Cummings. Candidate for the mayoralty of Paris, the present literary capital of America. Indorses *Secession*, campaign against Louis Untermeyer, an anthologist best known for the omission of William Carlos Williams and Marianne Moore from his *Modern American Poetry*.

Untermeyer later included poems by Williams, Moore, and Cummings in his 1925 edition. While in France, Cummings also spent time with John Peale Bishop, Archibald MacLeish, Malcolm Cowley, Lewis Galantiere, and Paul Morand, among others.

In October 1923, before Cummings left Paris, Pound recommended four of Cummings's poems for publication in Ford Madox Ford's new *transatlantic review*. They appeared in the first issue, published in January 1924. Back in New York City, he began writing for *Vanity Fair*, and his first book of poetry, *Tulips and Chimneys*, was published. John Dos Passos had given the manuscript to publisher Thomas Seltzer, who agreed to publish a shorter version. Poems cut from *Tulips and Chimneys* found their way into a number of later volumes. One of the eliminated poems, eventually published in *&* (1925), evokes the Paris of these years through the voices of prostitutes:

> (in the twilight of Paris
> Marie Louise with queenly
> legs cinq rue Henri
> Mounier a little love

> begs, Mimi with the body
> like une boite a joujoux, want nice sleep?

> toutes les petites femmes exactes
> qui dansent toujours in my
> head dis-donc, Paris

> ta gorge mysterieuse
> pourquoi se promene-t-elle, pourquoi
> eclate ta voix
> fragile couleur de pivoine?)

The peony-colored throat of Paris in the twilight represents the deep sensuality that the city evoked for Cummings. The language has some of the harshness and the frankness of the twenties, but the figure of the city as a mysterious dark lady has its sources in the poetry of the French Symbolists.

Besides *Tulips and Chimneys* and *&*, Cummings published two other books of poetry during the twenties: *XLI Poems* (1925) and *is 5* (1926). The critical response to his work was mixed. Although often praised for their technical innovations, the poems were also criticized by Edmund Wilson for their "immaturity." Other critics echoed the complaint. What had seemed appealing in the undergraduate poet was beginning to seem like a frozen mannerism. And Marianne Moore, in a perceptive early review, called attention to what she saw as a central weakness of Cummings's work, the absence of love except as "the devouring passion of master for slave." Moore's comment, however, may also be read as the Puritan response to Cummings's exuberant celebration of sexuality.

Cummings visited Paris again in 1924 and stayed with Lewis Galantiere, who introduced him to Dadaist Louis Aragon. (In 1933 Cummings published a translation of Aragon's *The Red Front*.) By now Cummings was in contact with the intellectual and artistic communities of Paris. He knew Picasso briefly but soon came to dislike the man and his art. He responded to Jean Cocteau with much greater enthusiasm, and the influence of Cocteau on Cummings's drawings is evident. Among the American writers he saw during this trip were Robert McAlmon, Ernest Hemingway, and Archibald MacLeish. MacLeish has recalled Cumming's extraordinary memory and ability to recite verse: "snatches of Heine alternating with Rimbaud, advertising catch-lines tied up with Catullus and Longfellow." The same lively juxtaposition of style and tone is familiar to readers of Cummings's verse. His poems rarely develop an idea or an image, but rather play off one line against another. They represent, in part, a literary adaptation of the collage.

Cummings continued to be an acute recorder of the sights and sounds of Paris life, but a sense of the changing political atmosphere can be detected in some of his poems, such as "16 heures," from *is 5*. The vision of the Prefect of Police is comic (and in fact seems drawn in part from a Chaplin comedy), but his confrontation with the Communists and their "bruised narrow questioning faces" seems an omen of other things to come. The policeman,

(a dapper derbied
creature, swaggers daintily
twiddling
his tiny cane
and, mazurkas about tweak-
ing his wing collar pecking at his im
-peccable cravat directing being
shooting his cuffs
saluted everywhere saluting
reviewing processions of minions
tappingpeopleontheback

"allezcirculez")

For Cummings, though, whatever happened to Paris, whatever idiocy might befall it, one could still discover there "the deep, extraordinary, luminous triumph of Life itself and of a city founded upon Life."

Another event of his 1924 sojourn in Paris was a visit to the restaurant Au Pere Tranquille, which became the setting for a scene in Cummings's first play, *Him*. Although part of the play was written in Paris, most of it was written in New York City, where it was completed not long before its 25 October 1927 publication date.

Although Cummings went to Paris again many times between 1926 and 1960, he had transferred his creative energy to New York. As Cummings's biographer Charles Norman says, Cummings visited Paris "again and again; but it was to New York that he returned to live." Sometimes he only stopped in Paris on the way elsewhere, as in 1931 when he made the visit to Russia that he wrote about in *Eimi* (1933). Nonetheless, he was still in touch with the expatriate community in Paris. His poems and line drawings appeared frequently in *This Quarter*, edited by Edward Titus. Titus was a great admirer of Cummings's work, and in 1931 Cummings was Titus's choice to receive *This Quarter*'s Richard Aldington Poetry Prize. Peter Neagoe's *Americans Abroad An Anthology* (1932) also included two poems by Cummings.

Questions about the significance of Cummings's contribution to American poetry are of two kinds. How seriously can we take his ideas, and is his form anything more than clever? Cummings relies upon an emotional appeal to a rather ill-defined spirit of goodness, and those critics who have argued that literature must acknowledge life's darknesses often consider Cummings's verse superficial. As R. P. Blackmur has put it, Cummings's poetry might survive if only it were lighthearted: "Taken for what it is, it is charming and even instructive. Taken solemnly, as it is meant to be, the distortion by which it exists is too much for it, and it seems a kind of baby-talk." For critics like Blackmur, Cummings has not really gone very far from his Unitarian and Transcendental heritage; he is still a preacher, offering a vision of a redeemed world. On the other hand Cummings's defenders praise his "passionate attention to the simultaneity of the living moment, a deep honesty toward experience."

The question of form is no easier to resolve. Cummings himself spoke of his "ineluctable preoccupation with The Verb." He saw his strength precisely in his ability to burrow under the language of ordinary speech to find lost meanings. But only a relatively few of Cummings's poems achieve that. In many others the dominant tone is hatred or sarcasm, and the voice is raised to a shout. At his best Cummings provides a brilliant satirical portrait of American life, fusing together the language of advertising and the rhetoric of American politics (as in "Poem, or Beauty Hurts Mr. Vinal") to provide a startling cacophony of experience bombarded by cant. But although such apparent linguistic playfulness may be useful in such a poem, it is doubtful whether it can be the foundation for a body of mature poetry.

Perhaps the most telling criticism of Cummings's work has been directed at its "almost complete failure to evolve." As G. S. Fraser said in 1955, "Mr. Cummings wrote in 1923 as well as he does now, and not very differently." Perhaps because of this singleness of method, Cummings seems fixed in the American experience of Paris in the twenties. It is hard to dissociate from him the image of the young American poet, not long out of Harvard, celebrating his discovery of personal freedom in a city unencumbered by American Puritanism.

Other:

Eight Harvard Poets, by Cummings and others (New York: Gomme, 1917);

"so standing, our eyes filled with the wind . . . ," in *Americans Abroad An Anthology*, ed. Peter Neagoe (The Hague: Servire, 1932), p. 123;

"Somewhere i have never travelled, gladly beyond,"
in *Americans Abroad An Anthology*, pp. 123-124;

Louis Aragon, *The Red Front*, translated by
Cummings (Chapel Hill, N.C.: Contempo
Publishers, 1933).

Periodical Publications:

"Three United States Sonnets" ["when you rang at
Dick Mid's place," "the Cambridge ladies who
live in furnished souls," "by god i want above
fourteenth"], *Broom*, 2 (May 1922): 146-147;

"Sunset," *Broom*, 2 (July 1922): 273;

"Three Portraits" ["Pianist," "Caritas," "Arthur
Wilson"], *Broom*, 2 (July 1922): 306-308;

"Four Poems" ["on the Madam's best april the,"
"(and i imagine," "life hurl my," "workingman
with hand so hairy-sturdy"], *Secession*, no. 2
(July 1922): 1-4;

"Four Poems" ["a man who had fallen among
thieves," "poets yeggs and thirsties," "the
season 'tis, my lovely lambs," "this evangelist"],
Secession, no. 5 (July 1922): 13-17;

"Five Americans" ["Liz," "Mame," "Gert," "Marj,"
"Fran"], *Broom*, 5 (October 1923): 134-136;

"Four Poems" ["when the spent day begins to frail,"
"my smallheaded pearshaped," "now that fierce
few," "the wind is a Lady with"], *Broom*, 6
(November 1923): 204-207;

"Four Poems" ["ohld song," "i'd think 'wonder,"
"if (you are i why certainly," "Will i ever forget
that precarious moment?"], *Broom*, 6 (January
1924): 1-5;

"Four Poems" ["impossibly," "voices to voices, lip
to lip," "death is more than," "weazened
Irrefutable unastonished"], *transatlantic
review*, 1 (January 1924): 1-5;

"Bal Negre" (drawing), *This Quarter*, 2 (July-
August-September 1929): 147;

"Two Poems" ["come a little further—why be
afraid—," "if there are heavens my mother will
(all by herself) have"], *This Quarter*, 3 (January-
February-March 1931): 473-474;

"Three Poems" ["When rain whom fear," "i met a
man under the moon," "you"], *This Quarter*, 3
(June 1931): 599-601;

"Three Poems" ["what time is it i wonder never
mind," "in a middle of a room," "i will cultivate
within"], *This Quarter*, 4 (July-August-
September 1931): 11-13;

"Two Poems" ["nothing is more exactly terrible
than," "Wing Wong, uninterred at twice"],

This Quarter, 4 (December 1931): 252-253;

"Three Poems" ["when hair falls off and eyes blur
And," "a clown's smirk in the skull of a
baboon," "touching you i say (it being
Spring"], *This Quarter*, 4 (March 1932): 458-461;

Drawing, *This Quarter*, 5 (December 1932): 319.

Letters:

Selected Letters of E. E. Cummings, ed. F. W. Dupee
and George Stade (New York: Harcourt, Brace &
World, 1969).

Bibliography:

George J. Firmage, *E. E. Cummings: A
Bibliography* (Middletown, Conn.: Wesleyan
University Press, 1960).

Biography:

Charles Norman, *E. E. Cummings The Magic-
Maker*, revised edition (New York: Duell, Sloan
& Pearce, 1964).

References:

S. V. Baum, ed., *EΣTI: eec E. E. Cummings and the
Critics* (East Lansing: Michigan State
University Press, 1962);

Bethany K. Dumas, *E. E. Cummings A
Remembrance of Miracles* (New York: Barnes &
Noble, 1974);

Norman Friedman, *E. E. Cummings The Art of His
Poetry* (Baltimore: Johns Hopkins University
Press, 1960);

Friedman, *E. E. Cummings The Growth of a Writer*
(Carbondale: Southern Illinois University
Press, 1964);

Frederick J. Hoffman, *The Twenties American
Writing in the Postwar Decade*, revised edition
(New York: Collier, 1962);

Barry Marks, *E. E. Cummings* (New York: Twayne,
1963);

Eve Triem, *E. E. Cummings* (Minneapolis:
University of Minnesota Press, 1969);

Robert E. Wegner, *The Poetry and Prose of E. E.
Cummings* (New York: Harcourt, Brace, 1965).

Papers:

The major collection of Cummings's manuscripts is
at the University of Texas.

Hilda Doolittle
(H. D.)

Melody M. Zajdel
Michigan State University

BIRTH: Bethlehem, Pennsylvania, 10 September 1886, to Helen Woole and Charles Leander Doolittle.

EDUCATION: Bryn Mawr College, 1904-1906.

MARRIAGE: October 1913 to Richard Aldington, divorced; children: Perdita.

AWARDS: Helen Haire Levinson Prize, *Poetry* magazine, 1938; Award of Merit Medal for Poetry, American Academy of Arts and Letters, 1960.

DEATH: Zurich, Switzerland, 28 September 1961.

SELECTED BOOKS: *Sea Garden* (London: Constable, 1916; Boston & New York: Houghton Mifflin, 1916);
Hymen (London: Egoist Press, 1921; New York: Holt, 1921);
Heliodora & Other Poems (Boston: Houghton Mifflin, 1924; London: Cape, 1924);
Collected Poems (New York: Boni & Liveright, 1925);
Palimpsest (Paris: Contact Editions, 1926; Boston: Houghton Mifflin, 1926);
Hippolytus Temporizes (Boston: Houghton Mifflin, 1927);
Hedylus (Boston: Houghton Mifflin, 1928; Oxford: Blackwell, 1928);
Borderline—A Pool Film with Paul Robeson (London: Mercury, 1930);
Red Roses for Bronze (London: Chattos & Windus, 1931; Boston & New York: Houghton Mifflin, 1931);
The Hedgehog (London: Brendin, 1936);
The Walls Do Not Fall (London & New York: Oxford University Press, 1944);
Tribute to the Angels (London & New York: Oxford University Press, 1945);
The Flowering of the Rod (London & New York: Oxford University Press, 1946);
By Avon River (New York: Macmillan, 1949);
Tribute to Freud (New York: Pantheon, 1956);
Selected Poems (New York: Grove, 1957);
Bid Me To Live (New York: Grove, 1960);
Helen in Egypt (New York: Grove, 1961);
Hermetic Definition (New York: New Directions, 1972).

Sylvia Beach Collection

Hilda Doolittle

Hilda Doolittle is best known as the "perfect" Imagist. Since the publication of three short poems in January 1913, under the name "H. D., Imagiste," she has been the model of Imagism, the 1913-1917 literary movement which marked the starting point of twentieth-century American poetry. H. D.'s poems are, indeed, excellent examples of Imagist form and theory, but a too limited and too facile adherence to this categorization has distorted her critical reputation. Although H. D. has written extensively in several genres, little critical attention has been paid to either her later, post-1925 writings, or to the shape of her career. This neglect is surprising since H. D.'s themes and techniques place her near the center, rather than at the periphery, of modern literary development. Peers such as Ezra Pound and Denise Levertov have acknowledged her power as a poet and her influence as an example. She was intimately involved in modernist forums: serving on the editorial staffs of the *Egoist* and *Close Up*, while maintaining friendly contacts with Harriet Monroe's *Poetry* and Robert McAlmon's Contact Publishing Company. She studied cinematic techniques, both as an observer and a participant, even acting with Paul Robeson in an avant-garde movie, *Borderline*. She was one of Sigmund Freud's analysands, a combination student and patient, in the thirties. She experimented with both fictional and poetic forms, helping to define the nature of free verse (as an Imagist) and to suggest the possibilities of stream-of-consciousness narration in her first novel. Her research into myths and the occult places her in the mainstream of intellectual inquiry during a period dominated by Sir James Fraser and Freud. Even though critics seemed to ignore her later works, H. D.'s significance continued to be acknowledged by her fellow artists. In 1960 the American Academy of Arts and Letters awarded her the Medal of Merit for Poetry.

Like many of her contemporaries, H. D.'s writings trace her personal quest to understand the world around her and the nature of her role as artist. Her quest is specifically a woman's search for self-identity, self-integration, and self-fulfillment. H. D. is one of the few modern writers whose characters speak directly to the problems, both personal and societal, faced by the woman artist. She is also one of the first and most successful twentieth-century women writers to seek a mythic past for all women.

One of H. D.'s primary themes is the recognition that both life and artistic creation are continual acts of synthesis. Believing in a holistic world in spite of the fragmentary nature of modern life, H. D.'s protagonists are engaged on personal, artistic, and mythic levels in fusing discrete elements of experience into a single, meaningful whole. Much of their search for personal completion is represented in the form of a quest for love. Often, particularly in her later works, this quest bears striking parallels to the myth of Isis and Osiris. Her women questers strive to unify the fragments of their lives and to find reality in the presence of a love which will require them to reconcile the conflicts of their pasts as well as crises in their presents. In H. D.'s vision a mysterious oneness lies at the center of reality. This mystery can be understood—in so far as understanding is possible—when, through love, the apparently conflicting elements of the world are accepted as compatible and meditated upon.

Another theme, closely linked to H. D.'s quest for unity, is the universality of experience. For H. D. and her personae, all experience, all history, form a single recurring moment; an individual thing, yet simultaneously a variation of a universal pattern. As one of her characters explains, "Somewhere, somehow, a pattern repeated itself, life advances in a spiral. . . ." H. D.'s own symbol for this theme became the palimpsest: the layering of various experiences and emotions, one atop the other, to demonstrate the unity of the past with the present. As a result of this theme, H. D. uses classical myths as objective correlatives for intensely personal experiences. Using mythological figures becomes a way for H. D. to universalize her ego. Her characters are true to her own psychic reality, rather than to their historical counterparts. Mythic patterns illuminate the important relationships and events of the individual life. In H. D.'s works memory becomes the meditative tool for exploring the present. H. D.'s career chronicles her evolution of a personal mythology and the prosodic means to convey it. In the end, as her posthumous volume of poems states, H. D. achieves her own "hermetic definition." Her final vision remains one of fusion, a fusion which is almost magical, alchemical, grounded in sound and poetic forms as much as the physical and rational world.

H. D.'s awareness of the dichotomies in her own life and her desire to somehow confirm her own identity started in her childhood. Her father was an astronomer, first at Lehigh University, then at the University of Pennsylvania. An aloof New Englander whose work occupied his attention, he dominated the Doolittle household. It was in his study that H. D. remembered first seeing the signs of the zodiac and the names of the constellations, first feeling that these magical names and stories which held her father's interest contained some special powers. The words themselves seemed "subconsciously potent," a repository of hidden knowledge which would explain the actions of the world. H. D.'s mother was a descendant of an early Moravian pioneer family. A pianist, she was the emotional and artistic center of the home. From her mother, H. D. claimed an inheritance including the penchant for mysticism and a love of artistic creation. Both parents, however, were busy, and H. D. perceived herself as essentially estranged from them. Her need to understand her relationship to each parent and to reconcile her two heritages (the New England intellectual and the Moravian mystical) became a focal point in her later analysis with Freud and was the first of many contradictions which she felt needed to be integrated before she could forge her own identity in either her life or her writing.

One of the earliest influences on H. D.'s artistic development was her friendship with Ezra Pound. H. D. met Pound in 1901 in Philadelphia; she was fifteen and he sixteen, a freshman at the University of Pennsylvania. They became close friends, sharing an interest in both literature and one another. They were briefly engaged, until H. D.'s father forbade the match. Pound encouraged H. D.'s studies of classical literature and her writing by bringing her "armfuls of books," both classical and modern, to read. H. D.'s schooling had already included a thorough grounding in Greek and Latin, and these early studies fostered her interest in comparative prosodic forms as well as ancient myths. By 1902 Pound had introduced H. D. to another student at the University of Pennsylvania, also interested in writing poetry: William Carlos Williams. When H. D. entered Bryn Mawr in 1904, the three friends continued to meet and discuss poetry, both their reading and some of their own writings. The friendships established among these three continued with varying degrees of affection and approval throughout their lives. They were actively involved in one another's careers, particularly when they first started publishing. Each helped the others to place their works (Pound through *Poetry,* H. D. through the *Egoist,* Williams through several small American magazines), and all felt free to criticize one another.

In 1906 H. D. withdrew from college because of ill health and started to apply herself seriously to a career in writing. Between 1906 and 1911 H. D. published articles and stories in newspapers and small journals. Most of her writing during this time consisted of Sunday school stories and articles on astronomy for children. For at least part of 1910 she lived in New York, where she wrote what she later called her first serious poems in free verse. During this period she continued working on translations, including some of Heine's short lyrics and works of the lyric Latin poets. Few of these poems were published, however, and most were destroyed.

In the summer of 1911, H. D. sailed for Europe, ostensibly for her vacation, although it may well have been to see Pound. She was twenty-six and would never return to the United States to live. After a brief tour of Italy and France, H. D. settled in London, renewing her acquaintance with Pound. Through him she met many of the literati of London: W. B. Yeats, Ford Madox Ford, May Sinclair, F. S. Flint, and Richard Aldington. By the winter of 1911-1912, H. D., Pound, Aldington, and Flint had begun to meet on a regular basis to exchange their verses and to discuss current poetic developments in England and France. Each contributed a special interest to the group: Flint provided knowledge of contemporary French poetry; H. D. and Aldington contributed their enthusiasm and appreciation of Greek and Latin lyricism; Pound contributed his eclectic readings in aesthetics and poetry. These four young poets, meeting informally, formed the nucleus of the Imagist Movement.

The notion of a movement was Pound's idea. He wanted to "get H. D.'s . . . poems a hearing without its being necessary for her to publish a whole book." The publication of "Hermes of the Ways," "Priapus," and "Epigram" in the fourth issue of *Poetry* (January 1913) initiated the Imagist Movement. In his capacity as overseas agent for *Poetry,* Pound had the means to launch this new movement. He praised H. D.'s poems to Harriet Monroe as "*modern* stuff by an American . . . the sort of American stuff that I can show here and in Paris without its being ridiculed." These earliest poems clearly exhibited the basic points all four of the young poets admired: concern for the outward form of verse, concern for a return to concrete, sensual, immediate images, and a belief in the image as a means of perception. This final point relied on the juxtaposition of images to produce understanding. These Imagists hoped for a sudden act of synthesis or "intuition" on the part of the reader, rather than a prolonged analysis by the poet.

With this first publication of her work, H. D.'s poetry was an almost unanimous critical success. Readers and reviewers praised her individual forms and her uncluttered images. They noticed her directness of style and meaning, her sparseness of language, her vivid visual presentation of the physical world, and her equally strong presentation of an emotional world, which were all in sharp contrast to the work of her Georgian predecessors.

The years 1913 to 1919 were among the most active and personally trying in H. D.'s life. In October 1913 she and Richard Aldington married. Although Aldington was several years her junior, the two shared a mutual interest in classical literature, a mutual contempt for middle-class hypocrisy, and a mutual dedication to careers in poetry. To observers, like John Cournos, they seemed the ideal artistic couple. Both H. D. and Aldington had begun publishing their poems, and both were major contributors to the first Imagist anthology, *Des Imagistes* (1914). When Pound left the Imagist Movement after this volume was printed, H. D. and

Aldington served as liaisons between Amy Lowell and the other original Imagists; they helped organize the publication of the succeeding three Imagist anthologies edited by Lowell. During the first years of World War I, the couple remained busy writing, publishing, and working on translations for a new monograph project at Egoist Press. For a brief time in 1915, they hoped (with Amy Lowell's support) to come to America to edit a new literary journal. But the arrangements fell through, and Aldington was drafted into military service.

H. D.'s activities increased in 1916. She replaced Aldington as the literary editor of the *Egoist*, after he was called to active duty. Her translation of *Choruses from Iphigenia in Aulis* (1916) was published by Egoist Press. Most significantly, her first volume of poetry, *Sea Garden* (1916), was published. The twenty-seven poems in *Sea Garden* solidified H. D.'s position as one of the most original and exciting poets of the period. These poems are short, free verse writings; many are set in Greece, or mention classic mythological settings or characters. Most of the poems, like "Storm" and "Hermes of the Ways," seek to present the timeless quality of experience. They strive for an immediacy of feeling rather than situation. H. D. shows the personae's passions and sorrows, forcing the reader to see and experience the same emotions. The book was well-received, with critics quick to acclaim the sensitivity of H. D.'s perceptions of nature and the diversity of her cadences.

In 1917 H. D. became acquainted with D. H. Lawrence. When he and his wife Freida were forced to leave the coastal area of Cornwall at the request of the security police, H. D. offered the couple her London flat. Throughout the fall, they boarded there while H. D. visited Aldington at camp. Lawrence filled a special place in H. D.'s life at the time. Aldington was most often away and, when he returned, he became embroiled in an affair with Dorothy Yorke. Lawrence came to symbolize what H. D. called the *gloire*, the intense passion and beauty which is the artist's natural domain. Although their friendship remained platonic, Lawrence would always represent for H. D. a prime example of the poet-as-priest, a theme she explored in her later works.

The war years were years of personal trauma. The war led to her estrangement from Aldington, the death of her brother in France, the death of her father from a stroke partially caused by the shock of the son's death, and her own emotional and physical breakdown. For H. D., as for many of the writers of her generation, the world seemed a shattered place after the war. The search for a lost beauty and security, the quest for a means to order the newly fragmented world, the loss of love, all arise as conflicts in H. D.'s writing after this time.

Throughout 1917 H. D. continued to be active in editing and writing. The emotional crises of 1917 and 1918, however, along with her declining health, began to slow her publishing slightly. In late 1918 she and Aldington formally separated. This, combined with her second pregnancy and a severe case of double pneumonia, left her physically and emotionally exhausted. (Her first pregnancy had ended in a miscarriage.) The single bright spot at this time was H. D.'s friendship with Bryher (Winifred Ellerman, the daughter of wealthy British shipping magnate Sir John Ellerman). Bryher's promise to take H. D. to Greece and her active concern over H. D.'s needs cemented a lifelong friendship. Even after Bryher's February 1921 marriage to Robert McAlmon, the two women continued to live together. Bryher said later that she married McAlmon to gain more freedom from the restrictions of her family and that from the start they had agreed to live separate lives apart from occasional visits to her family. They were divorced in 1926. Throughout their marriage, and after their divorce, Bryher contributed substantially to McAlmon's Contact Publishing Company, which published the work of both Bryher and H. D.

After the birth of her daughter in March 1919 and her own recovery, H. D. undertook an extended period of traveling and writing. In the summer of 1919, H. D. went with Bryher to the Scilly Isles. In Scilly she had the first of two important psychic experiences which she would later analyze with Freud. Her second experience occurred the following spring when the two women visited Greece. While sitting in a hotel room in Corfu, H. D. suddenly saw projected on the wall six successive pictures. The vision was confirmed by Bryher, who saw the last image. Both these experiences provided H. D. with images she would later incorporate into her poetic mythology. But she would wait until after her analysis to develop them. In between her travels H. D., her daughter, and Bryher all lived in London.

In 1921 H. D. published her second book of poems, *Hymen*. Like her first book, *Hymen* was critically acclaimed. The biggest change came in her increased use of personae. More of the poems had identifiable personae, and most were women: Hymen, Demeter, Circe, Leda. Many of the poems explored feelings of lost love and the passion to create. *Hymen* confirmed H. D.'s position as one of the best vers-librists in English.

H. D. continued her travels, visiting America in 1920-1921 and Egypt in 1923. In 1923 she settled in Switzerland, near Zurich. Throughout the twenties and thirties she also maintained an apartment in London, where she spent a portion of each year. Although she needed the quiet and solitude of her home in Switzerland to write, she made extended visits to London and Paris throughout the years between the wars.

The publication of *Heliodora & Other Poems* was the major event in H. D.'s life in 1924. This volume and the two preceding books were collected and published in 1925 as *Collected Poems*. With each new publication from 1913 to 1925, H. D.'s reputation had grown. Critics such as Mark Van Doren were calling her "the most perfect woman poet alive." It is on *Collected Poems* that critics have focused, to the exclusion of her other works. In many ways, this volume marks the popular high-water mark of H. D.'s career.

With each book, H. D. expanded the technical innovations of Imagism. Between 1913 and 1925, there is an increased complexity in her use of rhyme and rhythm. H. D. moved from predominantly visual imagery toward an increased reliance on phonetic and rhythmic effects to recreate moods and objects. More and more, the meaning of the poems is built upon the voice of the narrator. The persona and the persona's reaction to her experience had become the occasion for H. D.'s poems. The majority of H. D.'s narrators in *Collected Poems* are mythological characters who allow H. D. to present universal emotional states concretely. All the personae confirm H. D.'s growing belief that human problems and feelings change little from age to age. As the intuitions she wanted her readers to seize became more complex, H. D. needed to expand her poetry beyond static, single-image poems. After the publication of *Collected Poems*, she began to experiment in different genres and techniques. Between 1925 and 1932, she turned her attention to fiction, cinematography, and a new kind of poetry.

H. D.'s fiction is remarkably consistent in form and themes. As a single unit of her career, it clearly forms a bridge from her early poems to her post-World War II writings. Her first novel, *Palimpsest* (1926), first published by Robert McAlmon's Contact Publishing Company, is an excellent touchstone for understanding all her fiction. *Palimpsest* juxtaposes three separate stories which, by their similarity, reveal themselves to be essentially the same. Hence, the book's title. Each story focuses on the experience of a female protagonist, and jointly the stories form a triptych whose panels illuminate one another the longer they are meditated on. Not surprisingly, juxtaposition and compression are the major structural methods of the book. Each of the three sections is, in effect, a single complex image placed contrapuntally against the other two. The major themes become clear through comparison and contrast. As in her poetry, H. D. uses both visual and sonal repetition to emphasize themes and to unify the work. Colors, for example, are used to link objects or situations which at first seem unrelated. In "Hipparchia," the story of a Greek courtesan-writer, the story is infused with shades of yellow and gold, the bright colors of Hipparchia, who sees herself as the child of Helios. Yellow is both the saffron garb of a courtesan and the final color of Helios's "pure honey-white flame" of inspiration and Aphrodite's "pure gold" ideal love.

Not merely images, but words and phrases recur, serving as thematic evocations as well as refrains. H. D.'s use of language in *Palimpsest* is a turning point in her technical development. The prose verges on the incantational, the transformational. "Murex" has a particularly poignant merging of visual and auditory imagery. The marching "feet, feet, feet, feet," of soldiers are the echo of Raymonde's past, her experience in World War I London. She heard the sound of soldiers marching toward the troop train outside her hospital room, as she labored to deliver her stillborn child. It is both the sound of her soldier-husband Freddie going to war and the heartbeat of her child. The sound of feet is transformed into something more, however, as her associations shift from death, the war, and Freddie, to Freddie as a poet, herself (another poet), and her own poetic creation. To deal with the pain and loss (the first "feet, feet, feet, feet"), she must turn to Freddie's feet, to the metrical feet of her poetry. To create the poem she seeks, Raymonde must confront the past and transcend the personal in the eternal, for poetry/art is eternal.

In her fiction, H. D. worked on some of the areas critics had found limited in her poetry. The concrete details still abound, but the narrative voice has become even stronger. Flashbacks and stream-of-consciousness monologues develop her characters. Repetition is used more subtly and complexly. Finally, the themes are larger. *Palimpsest* is a repository for the themes H. D. would explore throughout the rest of her career. H. D.'s increased interest in flashbacks and in placing cultures in apposition to one another exemplifies her growing belief in the universality of experience and in the efficacy of juxtaposition to convey sudden moments of recognition. A second theme concerns the role of the artist. In both "Hipparchia" and "Murex" the artist is responsible for discerning and transmitting the universal patterns she sees. "Art was magic. . . . Poetry was to remember." A third major theme is the search for self-identity and self-integration. The chief characters work to fuse the contradictions they see in their own pasts. All three women sense a split between their intellects and their sexuality. All are expatriates, exploring the relationship of their homelands to their new selves. All are writers who perceive their careers as both necessary and painful, and who hope for some personal revelation which will indicate that their integration is complete. Finally, this search for identity leads to the search for completion on an interpersonal level: the search for love.

H. D.'s second novel, *Hedylus* (1928), is the story of a mother-son relationship and uses many of the themes and techniques which appear in *Palimpsest*. Part of this novel first appeared in McAlmon's *Contact Collection of Contemporary Writers* (1926). The main characters are Hedyle, the Greek mistress of Samos's king, and her illegitimate son, Hedylus, who wants to be a poet. The story revolves around the characters' need to break their mutually destructive dependence and to assert their independent identities. The appearance of Demetrius, one of Hedyle's former lovers, now an Athenian delegate on his way to Alexandria, precipitates the novel's action. The book focuses on two of H. D.'s favorite themes: the search for identity and the role of the artist. Both Hedylus and Hedyle recognize themselves as partial, rather than whole, personalities. Both need to understand their heritage better. Both want to be committed to something or someone. Both find a way to answer these problems as artists. Hedyle creates a world of beauty and culture in Douris's palace; Hedylus leaves to create new poetry.

"Narthex" (1928) continues H. D.'s fictional study of personality integration and the role of the artist. A new element is added, however. For the first time, H. D. explores overtly the question of the compatibility of a life of love and a life of art for women. The novella is more a character study than a story. Raymonde Ransom, the female writer, is trying to understand her last affair; she has rejected a lover whose socially determined expectations for women would interfere with Raymonde's work as a poet. What becomes significant is the character's recognition that her role as artist is of primary importance both to herself and to her culture. The poet is the reader of linguistic hieroglyphs; she understands the search for the substratum of meaning in the world. Raymonde asserts her self and herself as artist.

H. D.'s fiction met with little critical enthusiasm. Most critics found the works obscure and disjointed. They failed to see the purpose of all H. D.'s word-play, feeling that plot was being sacrificed to linguistic games. As a result, H. D. was perceived as falling away from her past poetic power. As she was writing fiction, H. D. was also working in cinematography. For four years, 1927-1931, H. D. wrote for *Close Up*, an avant-garde cinema journal edited by her friends Bryher and Kenneth MacPherson. H. D. perceived movies as images, "a universal language, a universal art open alike to the pleb and the initiate." Like the hieroglyphs she was beginning to mention in her poems, movies had "subtlety, that feeling of something within something, of something beyond something." Her work with *Close Up* illustrates H. D.'s involvement in new artistic trends. Although living primarily in Switzerland, she was very much a part of the artistic and expatriate circles of Paris and London.

In 1931 H. D. returned to poetry, publishing *Red Roses for Bronze*. These twenty-three verses were the least effective of H. D.'s poetry. She continued to touch on her major themes: the function of art and the artist, the belief in a "mystery" at the center of reality, and the commonality of experience. But the book has serious flaws. H. D.'s casual use of stream-of-consciousness monologues resulted in loss of rhythm and sloppy images, and sonal qualities seemed mere ornamentation. Her too extreme movement toward the personal undercut her concrete imagery, always one of her greatest strengths. The volume marked the end of H. D.'s popularity with the public. The difficult techniques of the novels and the mediocre quality of *Red Roses for Bronze* left her audience confused and disappointed.

From 1932 to 1942, H. D. published little. The H. D. who emerged at the end of World War II was very different from the author of *Red Roses for Bronze*. One of the major reasons for the change is H. D.'s increased interest in psychoanalysis and her personal encounter with Sigmund Freud. H. D.'s first sessions with Freud started in March 1933, and lasted between three and four months. She returned to Vienna in October 1934 for an additional five weeks. H. D.'s experience with Freud is recounted in her book *Tribute to Freud*, written during World War II and published in 1956. She gave several reasons for going to Freud. First, she wanted help in understanding and interpreting the two psychic visions she had in 1919 and 1920. Secondly, her previous experience with war led her to hope that studying with Freud would teach her how to cope with the trauma of future wars. Behind these two reasons was an implicit third: the need to articulate her own identity. H. D. wanted to take stock of herself and her emotional resources.

Freud confirmed for H. D. the idea of universality and the power of myths. More importantly, he provided her with a means of linking myths with her personal visions: "One day, he said to me, 'You discovered for yourself what I discovered for the race.' " What both realized was "man, meeting in the universal understanding of the unconscious or subconscious, would forego barriers of time and space. . . ." What was most real, most important, most enduring were the mythic patterns behind common actions. In analysis, H. D. came to see her own writing as the hieroglyph which could give permanent form to universal truths.

Between 1934 and the outbreak of war in 1939, H. D. published two book-length works: *The Hedgehog* (1936), a children's story, and a translation of Euripides's *Ion* (1937). Both works displayed the themes that H. D.'s analysis had confirmed, but neither was widely read. During this period of relative quiet, two important things happened to H. D.: in 1938 she and Aldington were divorced, and she received the Levinson prize for poetry. At the outbreak of World War II H. D. returned to London to live. Here, she says, "outer threat and constant reminder of death drove me inward," and she experienced a new outpouring of poetry. The result was her war trilogy: *The Walls Do Not Fall* (1944), *Tribute to the Angels* (1945), and *The Flowering of the Rod* (1946). The three form a major statement of H. D.'s belief in art and mankind.

The Walls Do Not Fall is concerned with the identity and function of the poet. The poem is "a vindication of the writer" against critics who saw him as "non-utilitarian." H. D. proclaimed the poet the intermediary between the eternal and the immediate, writing poems which are magic runes leading the reader to wisdom. The poem is a chronicle of spiritual regeneration leading to the realization that "through our desolation, / thoughts stir, inspiration stalks us / through the gloom . . ." The poem asserts that there is a benevolent presence, or Oneness, behind the world which we know only in parts.

Tribute to the Angels posits even more explicitly the faith which awaits the revelation of the divine pattern. War is personified as only one of the seven Angels who surround God. *Tribute to the Angels* explores the method of double sight which allows a person to see "spiritual realities," the flowering of the rod behind the burnt apple tree. If war exists, so does beauty, which becomes personified in the image of "Our Lady." At the center of the mystery stands a woman, the symbol of man's desire for and effort to achieve transcendence. Whether in the form of Santa Sophia, the Virgin, Psyche, or Astarte, she is "beauty incarnate," whose spirit is the counterweight to death and evil.

The Flowering of the Rod (1946) recounts a moment of transcendence. It shows the actual fusion of experiences which lead to spiritual regeneration and a reconciliation of opposites into mystical oneness. Kaspar, one of the Magi, strives to understand what he has seen in his past and in his dreams of the future. His understanding comes "transmuted . . . through spiral upon spiral of the shell / of memory that yet connects us."

Until their 1973 publication in one volume, these three poems were little known in America. Small wartime editions of the first two volumes appeared, but *The Flowering of the Rod* was never published in the United States. Of the three, *The Walls Do Not Fall* was the best-received, praised as an example of good civilian war poetry. The other two volumes were generally considered too mystical and too vague in both form and theosophy. Poets, however, have been attracted to her remarkable use of language for enchantment and incantation.

During the war, H. D. was also busy writing prose. Most of her fiction, however, has never been published, although some of it still remains in manuscript form. While in London, H. D. drafted *Tribute to Freud* and started work on her novel *Bid Me To Live*. But the war was a severe physical and emotional strain for H. D. In 1945 she again suffered a breakdown. With the help of Bryher and other friends, she returned to Switzerland to recuperate.

After her recovery, H. D. published *By Avon River* (1949), which consists of a poem, "Good Frend," and an essay, "The Guest." Both pieces were like her war trilogy in their focus on the regenerative spirit of man. Claribel, in "Good Frend," represents the person fulfilled by love. She is the Lady figure acknowledged in *Tribute to the Angels*, the regenerated spirit who knows "Love is God, . . . Love is strong."

In Switzerland H. D. slowly regained her health. The flurry of writing at the end of the forties receded. In 1956 she broke her hip, which left her essentially bedridden. During the same year *Tribute to Freud* was published, and in 1957 *Selected Poems* provided a sampling of H. D.'s poetry from her early Imagism to her war trilogy. For many readers it was the first complete overview of H. D.'s career. Although it went through more than one printing, it received relatively little critical notice.

The last two works published in H. D.'s lifetime, *Bid Me To Live* (1960) and *Helen in Egypt* (1961), contain similar themes and strengths. Both books resolve conflicts that H. D. had confronted in earlier works. More importantly, each provides strong, questing, female protagonists. Both are extremely personal works, fusing the experience of H. D. the poet with those of Hilda Doolittle Aldington, the twentieth-century woman. *Bid Me To Live* is H. D.'s roman a clef, the story of her World War I experience and the breakup of her marriage to Richard Aldington. A story of destruction and the quest for regeneration, it revolves around a woman who has been rejected in love and who must forge a new, autonomous identity. Julia Ashton is an American poet whose marriage to Rafe, a fellow artist, is destroyed by the war. Traumatic personal experiences (a miscarriage for Julia, trench warfare for Rafe) complicate their relationship until neither is capable of understanding or meeting the other's needs. Rafe leaves Julia; Julia's platonic lover withdraws from her; and Julia is left to piece together the remains of her life. Her solution is a dedication to her life as an artist and an affirmation of her identity as a creator and poet. The novel is the mature fictional statement of H. D.'s belief in the poet as synthesizer, the key to spiritual regeneration. Critical response found the book an interesting footnote to the biographies of Lawrence, Aldington, H. D., and their artist-friends.

Helen in Egypt is the culmination of H. D.'s work in both philosophy and prosody. H. D. starts with the traditional legend of Helen of Troy, but reshapes it, using a fifty-line fragment from Stesichorus of Sicily's *Pallinode*, into a modern epic. It succeeds as both a personal quest and as the mythic quest of all women. According to Stesichorus, Helen never went to Troy; she was conveyed by the gods to Egypt. The Trojan war was fought over a phantom, or illusion. The poem is Helen's quest to understand the reality of her life. To do so, she must reexamine her past, question the gods' plan for her, separate illusion from reality, and find the means to express her new-found identity. As an initiate in Egyptian hermeticism, Helen is both an artist who can read the universal hieroglyph of experience and a woman who is striving for self-actualization. Her identification with other women (Thetis the mother, Clytemnestra the wife, Iphigenia the child and sacrifice, and Cassandra the prophetess) leads to the integration of all the facets of her personality. She becomes both herself and all women. Her relived past with men (Theseus the godlike father figure, Paris the child and seducer, and Achilles the Eternal Lover) leads her to the secret that is no secret, the knowledge that "there is no before and no after, / there is one finite moment." Helen realizes that integration and synthesis are the true reality and becomes whole when, in her quest for self-identity, she becomes an artist who can use the mythic method to explore all experience.

In 1960 H. D. traveled to America for the last time, to receive the Award of Merit Medal for Poetry. Upon her return to Switzerland, she lived in a nursing home at Kusnacht. Here she wrote the poems which would be printed posthumously as *Hermetic Definition* (1972). Her sense of imprisonment came through clearly—in "Sagesse," she identifies herself with a captive Scops owl, the symbol of wisdom. In June 1961 she suffered a stroke and was further frustrated by the resulting speech and memory problems. Ironically, the poet who saw in individual words the way to understanding could not produce the words she wanted and needed. On 28 September 1961, H. D. died.

Hermetic Definition contains three long poems: "Hermetic Definition," "Sagesse," and "Winter Love." The title poem and "Sagesse" recreate the story of artist as priest and trace variations on the theme of cyclic regeneration. Both illustrate H. D.'s ability to link the past and the present, the personal and the mythic, in her writings. "Winter Love" was written as a coda to *Helen in Egypt*. It continues Helen's story and exults Helen's role as creator (both as poet and as mother). It portrays Helen's final love affair, with Odysseus, and her questioning of "why endure when Love closes the door?" Helen's realization is H. D.'s final answer: one endures to create again. The poem ends with the birth of Helen's child, Esperance—hope.

Early critical writings on H. D. focused upon her as a model of Imagism, but since the publication of her last three books and her death in 1961, attention has shifted to her longer, mature works. Recent critical articles have focused on her use of personal myth and her strong feminine heroes. H. D. saw her poetry as a hieroglyph; contemporary critics are just beginning to learn how to read it.

Other:

"Epigram," in *Des Imagistes An Anthology*, ed. Ezra Pound (New York: A. & C. Boni, 1914), p. 30;

Hilda Doolittle (H. D.)

Euripides, *Choruses from Iphigenia in Aulis*, translated by Doolittle (London: Egoist Press, 1916; Cleveland: Clerk's Private Press, 1916);

"Hedylus," in *Contact Collection of Contemporary Writers*, ed. Robert McAlmon (Paris: Contact Editions, 1925), pp. 91-113;

Euripides, *Ion*, translated by Doolittle (London: Chatto & Windus, 1937; Boston: Houghton Mifflin, 1937).

Bibliography:

Jackson R. Bryer and Pamela Roblyer, "H. D.: A Preliminary Checklist," *Contemporary Literature*, 10 (Autumn 1969): 632-675.

References:

Stanley K. Coffman, *Imagism. A Chapter for the History of Modern Poetry* (Norman: University of Oklahoma Press, 1950), pp. 16-32, 145-149;

Contemporary Literature, Special Hilda Doolittle Issue, 10 (Autumn 1969);

Robert Duncan, "Two Chapters from *H. D.*," *Triquarterly*, 12 (Spring 1968): 67-98;

Susan Friedman, "Who Buried H. D.? A Poet, Her Critics, and Her Place in 'The Literary Tradition,' " *College English*, 36 (March 1975): 801-814;

Kathryn Gibbs Gibbons, "The Art of H. D.," *Mississippi Quarterly*, 15 (Fall 1962): 152-160;

Susan Gubar, "The Echoing Spell of H. D.'s *Trilogy*," *Contemporary Literature*, 19 (Spring 1978): 196-218;

Norman N. Holland, *Poems in Persons An Introduction to the Psychoanalysis of Literature* (New York: Norton, 1973);

Glenn Hughes, *Imagism and the Imagists* (New York: Humanities Press, 1931);

Denise Levertov, "H. D.: An Appreciation," *Poetry*, 100 (June 1962): 182-186;

Vincent Quinn, *Hilda Doolittle (H. D.)* (New York: Twayne, 1967);

Thomas B. Swann, *The Classical World of H. D.* (Lincoln: University of Nebraska Press, 1962).

Papers:

H. D.'s papers are at the Beinecke Library, Yale University.

JOHN DOS PASSOS
(14 January 1896-28 September 1970)

SELECTED BOOKS: *One Man's Initiation—1917* (London: Allen & Unwin, 1920; New York: Doran, 1922);

Three Soldiers (New York: Doran, 1921; London: Hurst & Blackett, 1922);

Manhattan Transfer (New York & London: Harper, 1925; London: Constable, 1927);

Orient Express (New York & London: Harper, 1927; London: Cape, 1928);

Facing the Chair (Boston: Sacco-Vanzetti Defense Committee, 1927);

The 42nd Parallel (New York & London: Harper, 1930; London: Constable, 1930);

1919 (New York: Harcourt, Brace, 1932; London: Constable, 1932);

The Big Money (New York: Harcourt, Brace, 1936; London: Constable, 1936);

U. S. A. (New York: Harcourt, Brace, 1938; London: Constable, 1938);

The Best Times (New York: New American Library, 1966; London: Deutsch, 1968).

John Roderigo Dos Passos, social and political chronicler, was born John Roderigo Madison in a Chicago hotel. His father, John Randolph Dos Passos, a prominent attorney, and his mother, Lucy Madison, a Maryland gentlewoman, were not married until 1910. Because of his parents' unconventional relationship, Dos Passos spent much of his childhood traveling abroad with his mother. This "hotel childhood," as he later described it, established his lifelong penchant for travel and his love of Europe.

Dos Passos's association with France began when he was very young, and his knowledge of the language was quite thorough. He especially loved Paris and often worked and partied there, but he

John Dos Passos

121

remembers in *The Best Times* (1966) that he dreaded the "huddle of literary expatriates round Montparnasse." He explains further, "Of course Hemingway was an exception, just as Cummings was an exception. In the private universe I was arranging for myself, literary people generally, and particularly Greenwich Village and Paris exiles, were among the excommunicated categories. Their attitude toward life made me want to throw up. But as soon as I got to be friends with one of them he or she became the exception, unique and unassailable." An addicted traveler and a serious critic of the United States, Dos Passos never viewed himself as an expatriate or an exile.

Having completed Choate School at the age of fifteen, Dos Passos entered Harvard University in 1912. In that same year his last name changed from Madison to Dos Passos. While at Harvard, he developed a close, long-lasting friendship with E. E. Cummings. After his graduation in 1916, Dos Passos made his first long visit to Spain, a country which held a fascination for him all of his life. With the death of his father in 1917, he joined the Norton-Harjes Ambulance Group and sailed for France. During his tour of duty in France as an ambulance driver, Dos Passos collaborated with a friend, Robert Hillyer, on alternate chapters of a novel. Dos Passos's chapters later became, after much revision, *One Man's Initiation—1917* (1920). Later in 1917 Dos Passos transferred to the American Red Cross Ambulance Corps in Italy, where in 1918 he had his first brief encounter with Ernest Hemingway.

Dos Passos was discharged dishonorably from the American Red Cross in 1918 because of antiwar comments he had written in personal letters. He was sent back to the United States, but his determination to return to France was rewarded, and he was accepted in the Medical Corps. After a short time in the army, he was released in 1919 to attend classes at the Sorbonne. By the time he returned to France, Dos Passos had completed his first novel, *One Man's Initiation—1917*, based largely on his own wartime experiences in France and Italy. The manuscript was finally published in England after he agreed to guarantee part of the publication costs. Because of the novel's realistic presentation of military language, the publishers demanded several revisions and omissions. The novel appeared in October 1920, and it sold only sixty-three copies in the first six months.

In 1920 Dos Passos finished his second novel, *Three Soldiers*, which received fourteen rejections before Doran accepted it. Arguments over its frank language again ensued, but despite some outraged critics the novel was a success in America when it was published in September 1921. It was the first significant war novel to emerge from the generation of writers who served in World War I. The bitterness, rage, and disillusionment Dos Passos felt during the war are reflected in the novel. Although the central character is clearly the artist figure, John Andrews, the three soldiers, from different social backgrounds, combine into one composite soldier, representative of the American enlisted man in World War I. Much of *Three Soldiers* is set in France, and John Andrews's fascination with the French reflects Dos Passos's own. French critics returned the compliment by praising *Three Soldiers* and ranking it with the work of the French novelists Georges Duhamel and Henri Barbusse. Thus began Dos Passos's long popularity and influence with the French intellectual avant-garde. He was never well-known with the average French reader, but because of the homage paid him by the French literati he became known as a writer's writer. Not surprisingly, Dos Passos's social and political ideas had been influenced by the French writers who impressed him: Henri Barbusse, Romain Rolland, and Arthur Rimbaud.

After the publication of *Three Soldiers*, Dos Passos spent most of 1921 traveling, stopping often in Paris and joining the Near East Relief. He spent 1922 primarily in New York, where he formed friendships with several young authors: Zelda and F. Scott Fitzgerald, John Peale Bishop, and Edmund Wilson. By 1924 he was working intently on a new novel, and during his summer trip to Paris he renewed his acquaintance with Hemingway. At Hemingway's suggestion, Ford Madox Ford asked Dos Passos to write a story for the *transatlantic review*. Dos Passos greatly admired Ford and was flattered to be asked. His story, "July," a sketch from his work in progress describing Jimmy Herf, later the central character in *Manhattan Transfer*, was published in the *transatlantic review* in August 1924 while Hemingway was acting editor.

During the summer of 1924, Dos Passos and Hemingway met Gerald and Sara Murphy, wealthy expatriate Americans known for their lavish entertaining both in Paris and later at their Villa America in Cap D'Antibes. Parties at the Villa America frequently included the Fitzgeralds, Archibald and Ada MacLeish, the Hemingways, Donald Ogden Stewart, Dos Passos, and Picasso. As always, Dos Passos was often traveling all over Europe, using Paris as a stopping place. Malcolm Cowley, writing in *Exile's Return* (1951), describes Dos Passos as "the greatest traveler in a generation of

The Correlation to Three Soldiers

A man who's trying to write of our times and who wants what he writes to make sense and to have some historical reality, writes under one great disability. Society has become so rigidly organized that the very fact of writing, of being a writer, classifies the writer and makes it hard for him to get any contacts except with other writers

Introduction to the 1934 publication of Three Soldiers

123

ambulant writers. When he appeared in Paris he was always on his way to Spain or Russia or Istanbul or the Syrian desert."

In 1925 Harper published *Manhattan Transfer*, a city novel in which Dos Passos first began to use the experimental techniques he would develop more fully in his major contribution to American fiction, the *U. S. A.* trilogy. His characters are again representations of several American social orders, and the themes of the novel are typical of Dos Passos's work: alienation, loneliness, frustration, and loss of individuality. His cinematic technique, his sensuous details of the urban scene, and his kaleidoscopic portrayal of New York in the first two decades of the twentieth century make it memorable.

Borrowing from Flaubert, Zola, Balzac, James Joyce, and T. S. Eliot, Dos Passos created in *Manhattan Transfer* a truly experimental American novel. Though *Manhattan Transfer* is emphatically American in language and content, Dos Passos found many of his technical and artistic ideas in early twentieth-century French literature. He adapted such art forms as Cubism, Futurism, and Unanimism to his own aesthetic vision. He saw Paris as the center of modernism and turned to the French poets Blaise Cendrars and Guillaume Apollinaire for techniques to reproduce the sights, sounds, and movements of modern city life. Apollinaire's conversation-poems and Cendrars's telegram-poems were models for Dos Passos's prose-poems in *Manhattan Transfer*. Dos Passos's use of popular songs, images piled upon images, and scenes following scenes with little or no transition suggests the influence of the collage. Like Guy de Maupassant and Prosper Merimee, Dos Passos attempted an objective novel, with little authorial intrusion. Behind all the apparent objectivity, however, is a careful focus on the irrationality and dehumanization involved in pursuing the American dream of success. *Manhattan Transfer* was generally well-received by American critics, and when a translation into French appeared in 1928 French critics responded favorably to Dos Passos's techniques. They praised the novel's cinematic effect, its objectivity, and its break with old traditions. *Manhattan Transfer* established Dos Passos as an important, innovative American author.

In 1927 Dos Passos published *Orient Express*, a travel book in which he explains his admiration for Blaise Cendrars, calling him a "medicineman" and a "son of Homer." In the same year he also published *Facing the Chair: Story of the Americanization of Two Foreignborn Workmen*, an attempt to free

Sacco and Vanzetti. In August 1927 Sacco and Vanzetti were executed, and Dos Passos was filled with disgust and bitterness toward the American government. He became even more active in politics, and though he did not join the Communist party, he was sympathetic to many of its views.

In 1929 Dos Passos married Katharine Smith, one of Hemingway's boyhood friends, whom he met while visiting Hemingway at Key West. Shortly after their marriage they went to Paris, where they spent most of their time sightseeing, skiing, and enjoying French cuisine. They visited the Fitzgeralds, Pauline and Ernest Hemingway, Fernand and Jeanne Leger, the Murphys, and Dorothy Parker; and they spent a week with Cendrars in Montpazier. Dos Passos writes in *The Best Times* that he was "much smitten" with Cendrars's poetry at the time, but that he "was getting further away from the *vie litteraire* with every passing year." On the return trip to the United States, Dos Passos amused himself by translating into English Cendrars's *Le Panama et Mes Sept Oncles*, published in 1931 as *Panama, or the Adventures of My Seven Uncles*.

Early in 1930 *The 42nd Parallel*, the first volume of Dos Passos's *U. S. A.* trilogy, was published. The novel is set in pre-World War I America and explores the first stirrings of the social discontent which arose in the Midwest and eventually spread to all parts of the United States. *The 42nd Parallel*, with Chicago as its backdrop, was followed in 1932 by *1919*, in which Paris is the main focal point. This setting allows Dos Passos to continue the history of the United States by reporting the disasters, hypocrisies, and disappointments brought by World War I, relying on his own wartime Paris experiences as material. The third volume of the trilogy, *The Big Money* (1936), centered in New York, delineates the moral bankruptcy of the majority of the American people as they enjoy the prosperity which follows the war. This last volume ends on the eve of the Great Depression. Originally, Dos Passos planned *U. S. A.* as a single novel, but it outgrew his expectations, and he spent roughly a decade working on the three volumes. The trilogy was published as one volume in 1938.

Dos Passos's debt to French art and poetry is even greater in *U. S. A.* than in his earlier works. His borrowings from Cubism and the collage poem can be seen in his three new technical devices: the "Newsreel," the "Camera Eye," and the biographical sketch. Using these innovative techniques, Dos Passos is able to present a juxtaposed perspective that presents the reader with a multidimensional view of the first thirty years of

American life in the twentieth century. The trilogy is divided into fifty-two narrative sections, and with the inclusion of the three auxiliary technical devices *U. S. A.* recounts the social, political, and economic history of the nation, as well as the private history of the author.

The "Newsreel" employs actual clippings from newspapers of the era interwoven with popular songs of the period. In *1919* Dos Passos uses the clippings from the European edition of the *New York Herald Tribune* (popularly known as the Paris *Herald*), which include American news, local news, and French commentary. "The Camera Eye" is an impressionistic recounting of the author's experiences as a boy and as a young man in France during the war. The heavily biased biographical sketches present histories of representative men in the nation's history. Some of the most vigorous writing in the trilogy can be found in these sketches. Both American and French critics praised *U. S. A.* for its original techniques, and French intellectuals began writing of Dos Passos as one of the most influential American writers of the century.

In 1934 Dos Passos became openly dissatisfied with the Communist party and abandoned his position as leftist spokesman, and in 1937 he published "Farewell to Europe" in *Common Sense,* an essay that renounced his ties with Europe and declared his preference for American democracy. After 1940 Dos Passos continued to travel, as a war correspondent and as a tourist, to write social and political analyses, to publish fiction, and to become involved in historical research. Eventually, critical opinion viewed him as an arch conservative, a traitor to his earlier liberal ideals. He always insisted that his main focus remained a concern for individual freedom.

John Dos Passos ranks among the important American writers of this century. Critically, however, he is appreciated more in France than he is in America. He is not, perhaps, as Jean-Paul Sartre declared in 1938, "the greatest writer of our time," but as political novelist and chronicler of American civilization from 1900 to the Great Depression Dos Passos has an established place in American literary history. His reputation as a technical innovator has not diminished, and his art is inextricably interwoven with his view of American history.

—*Ruth L. Strickland*

Other:

Blaise Cendrars, *Panama, or The Adventures of My Seven Uncles,* translated by Dos Passos (New York: Harper, 1931).

Periodical Publication:

"July," *transatlantic review,* 2 (August 1924): 154-179.

Letters:

The Fourteenth Chronicle, ed. Townsend Ludington (Boston: Gambit, 1973).

References:

Allen Belkind, ed., *Dos Passos, the Critics, and the Writer's Intention* (Carbondale: Southern Illinois University Press, 1971);

John D. Brantley, *The Fiction of John Dos Passos* (The Hague: Mouton, 1968);

Malcolm Cowley, *Exile's Return,* revised edition (New York: Viking, 1951);

Anne Freudenberg and Elizabeth Fake, *John Dos Passos: Writer and Artist 1896-1970 A Guide to the Exhibition at the University of Virginia Library* (Charlottesville: University of Virginia Library, 1975);

Melvin Landsberg, *Dos Passos' Path to U. S. A.* (Boulder: Colorado Associated University Press, 1972);

John H. Wrenn, *John Dos Passos* (New York: Twayne, 1961).

Papers:

John Dos Passos's papers are at the University of Virginia Library.

RALPH CHEEVER DUNNING
(1878-1930)

BOOKS: *Hyllus* (London: John Lane / Bodley Head, 1910);
Rococo (Paris: Black Manikin Press, 1926);
Windfalls (Paris: Black Manikin Press, 1929).

Ralph Cheever Dunning

Ralph Cheever Dunning's brief reknown in Paris during the twenties was perhaps more a result of his mysterious personality and preoccupations than of his poetry. Although his work was the subject of a heated debate in 1926 on the Left Bank, it was the man himself who was most scrutinized. A native of Detroit, Dunning arrived in Paris around 1905. By 1910 his first volume of poetry, *Hyllus*, had been published in London by John Lane, despite the poet's noted apathy toward publication. Little more of his work appeared until the early twenties when, under Ezra Pound's influence, Dunning was persuaded to release his manuscript "The Four Winds" to *Poetry* and the *transatlantic review*, each of which published large portions of it in 1924 and 1925. The event delighted Pound but stirred his friend and protege little. (In 1929 the poems were published as *Windfalls* by Edward Titus's Black Manikin Press.)

It was enough for Dunning that he should write poetry, and he lived for nothing else. Markedly detached from people and things, he spent most of his life laboring slowly over a small group of poems in his room on rue Notre Dame des Champs, which Paris *Tribune* columnist Wambly Bald called "virtually a wooden box," furnished only with a cot, a stove, a bookcase, and a single chair. Occasionally he emerged from his "shelter" to frequent, oddly, the noisiest, most crowded cafes. There he would sit perfectly still, gripping a glass of hot milk (his principal nourishment) and a book—"an apparition," in Samuel Putnam's words, "weirdly out of place there." Dunning was said to have spoken only a few sentences throughout his twenty-odd years in Paris, and few besides Pound, Putnam, and Sisley Huddleston ever managed to converse with him. These friends did their best to take care of him, but he usually refused their offerings, having developed, thought Huddleston, "a definite dislike of eating." Huddleston deemed him, nevertheless, the most likeable man he had ever met.

Putnam defined Dunning's nature as Oriental, by which he surely meant more than the poet's addiction to opium, but the habit may have intensified his obsession with terror and death—an obsession which permeates his writings. His verse communicates a feeling of impermanency and sadness—a regret expressed, perhaps, at seeing awe inspired not by the permanent but by the transitory. Steadily his work progressed from lamenting the uselessness and meaninglessness of most elements in life, to proclaiming no permanency but in death. Above all his poetry reflects his own profound death wish.

Obviously influenced by the generation of English poets writing during his youth, Dunning adopted the styles, dialect, and regular verse forms associated with the eighteen-nineties and the Victorians. When in 1925 he received *Poetry*'s Helen Haire Nevinson Prize, and shortly thereafter had his long poem *Rococo* chosen by Edward Titus to appear as the Black Manikin Press's maiden volume in 1926, a number of his contemporaries voiced their dismay. *Rococo*, a twenty-two-page classic love story written in faultless terza rima, was, decreed modernist critic Elliot Paul, "hopelessly antiquated" by its language, form, and "laughable philosophy." Pierre Loving's response in the Paris *Times* was that Dunning's "outworn and rather conventional language" enhanced "the beauty of the achievement." Pound, meanwhile, dubbed Dunning "one of the four or five poets of our time" and railed against the "hyper-modernists" and free-versifiers whose rabid insistence upon "certain properties of *one* kind of good poetry" blinded them to the beauty and musicality of Dunning's verse. The most caustic remarks appeared in *This Quarter* from Ernest Walsh, who accused Dunning of having "the soul of Dowson and Swinburne and Keats and Shelley as well as their petty agonies and florid importance of expression," and vehemently contended that Pound had mistakenly praised what he had not read but only surveyed. To this Pound suggested that "anyone who cannot feel the beauty of [Dunning's] melody had better confine his criticism to prose and leave the discussion of verse to those who know something about it." Although *Rococo* is neither as good nor as bad as the arguments imply, Dunning remained for some time a whetstone on which others sharpened their critical powers. None of the comments, however, seemed to make the least impression on the man whom Ford Madox Ford called "the living Buddha of Montparnasse."

Ralph Cheever Dunning's unsought fame quickly diminished after his death in 1930. Hemingway's terse diagnosis was that the man "forgot to eat"; others believed he had spent forty years of contemplation preparing for a death which he finally accomplished when at the age of fifty-two, weak from tuberculosis, he simply refused to eat. It was the ideal poet's death, declared Samuel Putnam: utterly sincere, without vulgarity or showmanship. In *Paris Was Our Mistress* (1947) Putnam referred to him as, simply, "a poet of the old school whose name is wholly forgotten now." This rapid and final obscurity was, perhaps, just what Dunning would have wished for. —*JoAnn Balingit*

Periodical Publications:

"The Homecoming," *Poetry*, 7 (January 1916): 179-181;

"Falling Leaves," *Poetry*, 24 (July 1924): 182-185;

"Twelve Poems," *transatlantic review*, 2 (November 1924): 478-489;

"The Four Winds," *Poetry*, 26 (April 1925): 1-13;

Ralph Cheever Dunning, by Polia Chentoff

"Threnody in Sapphics," *Exile*, no. 2 (August 1927): 31-34;

"Tony," *Exile*, no. 3 (1928): 43-52;

"Poems from The Four Winds," *Exile*, no. 3 (1928): 61-68;

"Sonnet," *This Quarter*, 2 (July-September 1929): 149;

"The Rose and the Thistle," *This Quarter*, 2 (January-March 1930): 489-490;

"The Lady in the Cellar," *This Quarter*, 3 (July-September 1930): 117-120.

JAMES T. FARRELL
(27 February 1904-22 August 1979)

SELECTED BOOKS: *Young Lonigan A Boyhood in Chicago Streets* (New York: Vanguard, 1932; London: Panther, 1959);

Gas-House McGinty (New York: Vanguard, 1933);

The Young Manhood of Studs Lonigan (New York: Vanguard, 1934; London: Panther, 1959);

Calico Shoes and Other Stories (New York: Vanguard, 1934; London: Panther, 1959);

Judgment Day (New York: Vanguard, 1935; London: Panther, 1959);

Guillotine Party and Other Stories (New York: Vanguard, 1935);

Studs Lonigan: A Trilogy (New York: Vanguard, 1935; London: Constable, 1936);

Can All This Grandeur Perish? and Other Stories (New York: Vanguard, 1937);

The Short Stories of James T. Farrell (New York: Vanguard, 1937);

$1,000 a Week and Other Stories (New York: Vanguard, 1942);

When Boyhood Dreams Come True (New York: Vanguard, 1946);

The Life Adventurous and Other Stories (New York: Vanguard, 1947);

An American Dream Girl (New York: Vanguard, 1950);

French Girls Are Vicious and Other Stories (New York: Vanguard, 1955; London: Hamilton, 1958);

An Omnibus of Short Stories (New York: Vanguard, 1956);

A Dangerous Woman and Other Stories (New York: Vanguard, 1957; London: Panther, 1959);

Side Street and Other Stories (New York: Paperback Library, 1961);

Sound of a City (New York: Paperback Library, 1962);

Childhood Is Not Forever (Garden City: Doubleday, 1969);

Judith and Other Stories (Garden City: Doubleday, 1973).

James Thomas Farrell, American novelist and short-story writer, was born on Chicago's South Side, the son and grandson of Irish-Catholic laborers. The young Farrell attended neighborhood parochial schools, and after graduating from high school he worked almost two years as an express company clerk. In 1925 he began four years of intense study and wide reading at the University of Chicago, taking time out during several months in 1927-1928

James T. Farrell

University of Pennsylvania

while he unsuccessfully tried to make his way as a writer in New York City. The following year he published his first short story, and by the end of the decade he had amassed manuscripts of many other tales and most of the first two Studs Lonigan novels. A half century later, the huge body of Farrell's realistic fiction numbered forty-two volumes.

In April 1931 with $65 between them, Farrell and his bride Dorothy Butler arrived in Paris to begin a year's residence. To the young couple, who lived in a succession of inexpensive lodgings in Sceaux-Robinson and on the Left Bank, it was to be a year of poverty and personal tragedy but also one of signal literary success and happiness. Ineligible for a work permit, Farrell managed to earn some $700 during the year by writing, a sum supplemented at irregular intervals by gifts and loans from family and friends. His story "Soap" portrays the financial hardships he and his wife endured in Paris. In December they sustained the death of their five-day-old son, and the year was further saddened for Farrell by the deaths of Julia Daly, the grandmother in whose home he had been brought up, and Paul Caron, a close Chicago friend of the twenties. "In

Paris," Farrell has written, "my youth really ended." There too he first distinctly emerged as an important writer of realistic fiction.

Samuel Putnam, then living in Fontenay-aux-Roses, a suburb of Paris, was the earliest effective champion of that fiction. Late in 1930 Putnam was responsible for publishing "Studs" in *This Quarter*, going behind the back of the magazine's editor, Edward Titus. One year later he accepted Farrell's "Jewboy" for his own magazine, the *New Review*, and assigned its author two book reviews. His enthusiasm about Farrell spilled over in a letter directed to Ezra Pound in Rapallo and accompanied by a batch of Farrell's stories. Pound's response was immediate and decisive: the stories should be published; a new writer had arrived, he asserted, who answered several questions raised by the fiction of Henry James. Farrell and Pound met in May 1931 in a Paris restaurant, and Pound tried to find a publisher for a small book of four Chicago tales that he particularly liked: "The Scarecrow," "Looking 'Em Over," "Meet the Girls," and "Honey, We'll Be Brave." However, Desmond Harmsworth, the interested English publisher, and Jacob Schwartz of London, a few months later, both felt that Farrell's material was ill-suited for an English audience.

Nevertheless, Farrell did succeed in placing some stories while in Paris. Whit Burnett took "A Casual Incident" and "Spring Evening" for *Story*; Edward Titus purchased "The Merry Clouters" for *This Quarter*; and—as Farrell learned upon his return to New York City—H. L. Mencken selected "Helen, I Love You!" for the *American Mercury*. Peter Neagoe, who became a good friend of the Farrells in Paris, accepted "Soap" for his anthology *Americans Abroad* (1932). Bob Brown, writing urgently from Cagnes-sur-Mer, drew heavily on Farrell for his *Readies for Bob Brown's Machine* (1931), a collection which includes Farrell's "Jeff" and "Sylvester McGullick" as well as two Farrell collaborations. (Farrell "readified" "One of the Many" by his brother John A. Farrell and "adapted" Lloyd Stern's story "Percentage.")

In June 1931 James Henle of the Vanguard Press accepted Farrell's first novel, *Young Lonigan* (1932), and thereby initiated a long and fruitful association between author and publisher. At Henle's suggestion, Farrell added a new first chapter to *Young Lonigan* in order to introduce more effectively the central character Studs, and he deleted the gang-shag scene with Iris (published in 1957 as "Boys and Girls"), which was deemed vulnerable to censorship litigation. Henle's complete confidence in Farrell's talent was tangibly demonstrated during the Paris year by three advances on his work. This confidence and support were crucially important in Farrell's career, for *Young Lonigan* launched Farrell's most famous work: *Studs Lonigan: A Trilogy* (1935), which also includes *The Young Manhood of Studs Lonigan* (1934) and *Judgment Day* (1935). This massive work carefully chronicles the relentless drift of the title character Studs toward a premature death. Through the lens of Studs's consciousness, Farrell pictures an urban milieu densely populated with well-defined characters, many of whom, like the weak-willed Studs, are victimized by the illusions and spiritual poverty of their culture. The trilogy is a powerful and unified realistic narrative tragic in its emotional force and trenchant in its implicit social criticism.

With the manuscript of *Young Lonigan* in hand, Henle quickly contracted for Farrell's second novel, the as yet unwritten *Gas-House McGinty* (1933). Thus encouraged, Farrell put in long days and nights to produce the first draft of *Gas-House McGinty* in three weeks. Like *Young Lonigan*, this novel looks back to the author's Chicago past. It employs a richly idiomatic language to dramatize the effect of occupation—here a mindless commercial routine—upon the lives of Ambrose McGinty and his coworkers in the wagon call department of the express company. The company office, hectic in its rhythms and raucous in atmosphere, emerges as a central presence dominating the consciousness of all the characters. Their frustrations, passions, and sheer survival tactics in a corporate world are exposed with clarity and understanding. Farrell's intense imaginative involvement with the express company material kept him writing at his desk long after *Gas-House McGinty* was complete. From the manuscript that piled up came many tales published later, including "Omar James," "A Jazz-Age Clerk," "Lunch Hour: 1923," "Memento Mori," "Heinie Mueller," and the Willie Collins stories.

The impact made by Paris upon Farrell's mind and art derives in part from his wide reading at the time—in Trotsky, Proust, Upton Sinclair, William Faulkner, Thomas Wolfe, Lewis Carroll, James Joyce, D. H. Lawrence, Dashiell Hammett, Henry James, Spinoza, and Djuna Barnes, among others. It is suggested by the extraordinary number of friends and acquaintances he made there: Kay Boyle, Adam Fischer, Pierre Jean Robert (who translated *Young Lonigan* for the French edition), Christine Stead, Kathleen Coyle, Henri Poulaille, Emma Goldman, Robert McAlmon, Nancy Cunard, George Seldes, Nathan Klein, Eve Adams, Kenneth Knobloch,

James T. Farrell

It is now over thirty years, since I first conceived the idea of writing a novel with a hero or chief protagonist whose name would be Studs Lonigan. This occurred on a sunny afternoon of June, 1929. I was twenty five years old.

I began writing this intended novel immediately. My original intentions and plans kept changing, and evolving, and finally this work of fiction grew into the trilogy, Young Lonigan, the Young Manhood of Studs Lonigan, and Judgment Day. On February 14, 1935, I finally completed the third and final draft of Judgment Day. I was twenty seven days short of being thirty one years of age

Farrell's recollections of Lonigan *composition*

Meyer J. Handler, Ramon Fernandez, Lawrence Drake, and A. Lincoln Gillespie, to name only some. The Paris he knew in 1931-1932 is reflected in thirteen published stories ("Sorel," "An American Student in Paris," "Edna's Husband," "Guillotine Party," "Soap," "Mendel and His Wife," "After the Sun Has Risen," "Counting the Waves," "The Girls at the Sphinx," "Love Affair in Paris," "Fritz," "Paris Scene 1931," and "Scrambled Eggs and Toast") and in an unfinished manuscript of novel length. Farrell's Paris stories also include nine other tales drawing on his later experiences of that city, which he regularly revisits. Taken together, they form an important "panel" in the huge work he mapped out early in his career, one that now includes the Studs Lonigan, Danny O'Neill, and Bernard Carr series of novels, many volumes of short stories, and the ongoing cycle "A Universe of Time."

Assisted by Traveller's Aid, the Farrells, broke but resolute, returned to a Depression-ridden New York City in April 1932. Of his return Farrell has written: "I was not lacking in confidence. When I had come to Paris, I thought that I knew what I was doing, and after about a year, I was returning, with more, not less, confidence. . . . A good and productive year had ended. A sad year had ended. And I could no longer consider myself a youth."

After 1932 Farrell lived and worked in New York. There in the mid-thirties he became a leader in the anti-Stalinist literary-cultural Left in America. In particular he spoke out for integrity in criticism and for the artist's right to freedom of thought and expression from all forms of oppression. Still respected as a social and literary critic, he exerted an even stronger influence through his fiction—upon younger writers and the public at large. He remained a leading practitioner of twentieth-century critical Realism. Among his strengths are his sympathetic understanding of ordinary Americans, particularly Irish-Americans; his ability to create convincing major characters and entire communities of lesser characters deeply rooted in their urban environments; his architectural skill in building massive fictional structures; and the enduring soundness of the humanistic values dramatized in his fiction. —*Edgar M. Branch*

Other:

"Sylvester McGullick," in *Readies for Bob Brown's Machine*, ed. Bob Brown (Cagnes-sur-Mer: Roving Eye Press, 1931), pp. 16-25;

"Jeff," in *Readies for Bob Brown's Machine*, pp. 25-30;

"Soap," in *Americans Abroad An Anthology*, ed. Peter Neagoe (The Hague: Servire, 1932), pp. 143-148.

Periodical Publications:

"Studs," *This Quarter*, 3 (July-August-September 1930): 187-195;

"Jewboy," *New Review*, 1 (August-September-October 1931): 21-26;

"A Casual Incident," *Story*, 1 (September-October 1931): 54-60;

"Spring Evening," *Story*, 1 (March-April 1932): 43-54;

"Helen, I Love You!," *American Mercury*, 26 (July 1932): 267-271;

"The Merry Clouters," *This Quarter*, 5 (December 1932): 373-389;

"Children of the Twilight" ["The Scarecrow"], *New Masses*, 11 (29 May 1934): 13-16;

"Guillotine Party," *Partisan Review*, 2 (October-November 1935): 44-51;

"A Jazz-Age Clerk," *New Frontier*, 1 (July 1936): 9-11;

"Scrambled Eggs and Toast," *Briarcliff Quarterly*, 2 (July 1945): 106-110;

"Lunch Hour: 1923," *View*, 3 (October 1945): 9, 20, 22;

"Willie Collins," *Chicago Review*, 1 (Winter 1946): 5-19;

"The Nothingness of Milt Cogswell" ["Memento Mori"], *Swank*, 3 (February 1956): 60-65;

"Scene at the Coupole," *Bachelor*, 3 (September 1961): 8-9, 70, 72;

"Afternoon in Paris," *Thought*, 14 (18 April 1964): 11-12;

"An American Student in Paris," *Southern Review*, 3, new series 4 (October 1967): 958-989.

References:

Edgar M. Branch, *A Bibliography of James T. Farrell's Writings, 1921-1957* (Philadelphia: University of Pennsylvania Press, 1959)—see also the supplements in *American Book Collector*, 11 (Summer 1961): 42-48; 17 (May 1967): 9-19; 21 (March-April 1971): 13-18; 26 (January-February 1976): 17-22;

Branch, *James T. Farrell* (New York: Twayne, 1971);

Henry Hopper Dyer, "James T. Farrell's Studs Lonigan and Danny O'Neill Novels," Ph.D. dissertation, University of Pennsylvania, 1965;

Irene Morris Reiter, "A Study of James T. Farrell's Short Stories and Their Relation to His Longer Fiction," Ph.D. dissertation, University of Pennsylvania, 1964;

Jack Salzman, "James T. Farrell: An Essay in Bibliography," *Resources for American Literary Study*, 6 (Autumn 1976): 131-163;

Twentieth Century Literature, Farrell number, 22 (February 1976);

Alan Wald, *James T. Farrell: The Revolutionary Socialist Years* (New York: New York University Press, 1978).

Papers:

The Farrell Archives at the Charles Patterson Van Pelt Library of the University of Pennsylvania contain Farrell's manuscripts, letters, publications, and other relevant materials.

F. Scott Fitzgerald

W. R. Anderson
Huntingdon College

BIRTH: St. Paul, Minnesota, 24 September 1896, to Mary McQuillan and Edward Fitzgerald.

EDUCATION: Princeton University, 1913-1917.

MARRIAGE: 3 April 1920 to Zelda Sayre; children: Frances Scott.

DEATH: Hollywood, California, 21 December 1940.

SELECTED BOOKS: *This Side of Paradise* (New York: Scribners, 1920; London: Collins, 1921);

Flappers and Philosophers (New York: Scribners, 1920; London: Collins, 1922);

The Beautiful and Damned (New York: Scribners, 1922; London: Collins, 1922);

Tales of the Jazz Age (New York: Scribners, 1922; London: Collins, 1923);

The Vegetable (New York: Scribners, 1923);

The Great Gatsby (New York: Scribners, 1925; London: Chatto & Windus, 1926);

All the Sad Young Men (New York: Scribners, 1926);

Tender Is the Night (New York: Scribners, 1934; London: Chatto & Windus, 1934); revised edition, ed. Malcolm Cowley (New York: Scribners, 1951; London: Grey Walls, 1953);

Taps at Reveille (New York: Scribners, 1935);

The Last Tycoon (New York: Scribners, 1941; London: Grey Walls, 1949);

The Crack-Up, ed. Edmund Wilson (New York: New Directions, 1945; London: Falcon Press, 1947);

The Stories of F. Scott Fitzgerald, ed. Malcolm Cowley (New York: Scribners, 1951);

Afternoon of an Author A Selection of Uncollected Stories and Essays, ed. Arthur Mizener (Princeton: Princeton University Library, 1957; London: Bodley Head, 1958);

The Pat Hobby Stories, ed. Arnold Gingrich (New York: Scribners, 1962; Harmondsworth, England: Penguin, 1967);

The Basil and Josephine Stories, ed. Jackson R. Bryer and John Kuehl (New York: Scribners, 1973);

F. Scott Fitzgerald's Ledger, ed. Matthew J. Bruccoli (Washington, D.C.: Bruccoli Clark / NCR Microcard Editions, 1973);

Bits of Paradise, ed. Scottie Fitzgerald Smith and Bruccoli (London: Bodley Head, 1973; New York: Scribners, 1974);

The Notebooks of F. Scott Fitzgerald, ed. Bruccoli (New York & London: Harcourt Brace Jovanovich / Bruccoli Clark, 1978);

The Price Was High The Last Uncollected Stories of F. Scott Fitzgerald, ed. Bruccoli (New York & London: Harcourt Brace Jovanovich / Bruccoli Clark, 1979).

Zelda Sayre Fitzgerald

Save Me the Waltz (New York: Scribners, 1932; London: Grey Walls, 1953).

An air of transience pervades the biographies of F. Scott Fitzgerald and Zelda Sayre Fitzgerald and slips into their writing. This lack of permanence is a key to understanding their relationship with Paris and France. Unlike such contemporary American writers as John Dos Passos, John Peale Bishop, or Ernest Hemingway, Fitzgerald was never truly at home in Europe, despite the fact that he spent a total of six and a half years there—about a third of his professional lifetime, and almost half of the period (1920-1934) during which he was most productive. As his biographer Andrew Turnbull has observed, Fitzgerald was always an *American* in France, frequenting the Right Bank hotels and bars popular with American tourists rather than the Left Bank literary circles with which Hemingway was far more familiar. Nevertheless France for the Fitzgeralds was a strong influence on both life and art. Although much of the writing Fitzgerald produced while living in France was not about France, the experiences, events, and settings of Paris and the Riviera color a number of his best stories and are at the center of his novel *Tender Is the Night* (1934), as well as Zelda Fitzgerald's novel, *Save Me the Waltz* (1932).

The Fitzgeralds' first contact with France was unabashedly a tourist jaunt. On 3 April 1920, having just published his first novel, *This Side of Paradise*, Fitzgerald married Zelda Sayre at the rectory of Saint Patrick's Cathedral in New York City. For the next year, flushed with the success of that novel, the

Fitzgeralds threw themselves upon New York, establishing a pattern of life with which they would become identified, and by which they would be haunted, during the rest of the decade. Despite their hectic social life, Fitzgerald dedicated himself to the composition of a second novel. Early in the spring of 1921 Zelda Fitzgerald found she was pregnant, and they decided to make a tour of Europe before the baby's birth. Fitzgerald completed the serial version of *The Beautiful and Damned* (1922) in late spring, and on 3 May 1921 they boarded the *Aquitania* for their voyage to England, France, and Italy. They visited London briefly, went on to the Continent, then returned to England. During their first stay in London they visited the Irish writer Shane Leslie, and their second sojourn in the British capital was highlighted by dinner with novelist John Galsworthy, then at the height of his success. The Fitzgeralds were less impressed with France and Italy. "God damn the continent of Europe," Fitzgerald wrote his friend Edmund Wilson. "It is of merely antiquarian interest." In more understated tones he wrote his literary agent, Harold Ober, "Our trip has been rather a dissapointment."

The first months back in the United States were rewarding. Their daughter, Frances Scott, whom they called Scottie, was born on 26 October 1921 in St. Paul, Minnesota, where Fitzgerald revised *The Beautiful and Damned*. In October 1922, following the March 1922 publication of the novel and the September 1922 publication of a collection of stories, *Tales of the Jazz Age*, they returned to New York, settling in Great Neck, Long Island. Although his second novel did not achieve either the popular acclaim or the high sales figures of *This Side of Paradise*, Fitzgerald was now an established literary success and earned about $25,000 in 1922, principally from sales of magazine stories—relative affluence in the twenties. Nevertheless the Fitzgeralds had already become caught in their lifelong pattern of living beyond their means. Despite his generally increasing income over the next ten years, he remained burdened by debt, constantly seeking advances and loans from his publisher, Scribners, and from Harold Ober, his agent. They were never able to live moderately, even economically; yet ironically, they rarely seemed to live comfortably either.

Their increasingly frenetic social lives necessitated more and more effort to produce remunerative short stories, principally for the *Saturday Evening Post*. Fitzgerald wrote an unsuccessful play, *The Vegetable* (1923), but found considerable difficulty in settling down to his next novel. Finally the Fitzgeralds decided to go to France: "We were going to the Old World to find a new rhythm for our lives, with a true conviction that we had left our old selves behind forever—and with a capital of just over seven thousand dollars," Fitzgerald says in "How to Live on Practically Nothing a Year" (1924). The underlying emphasis on economics betrays the real motivation for their move to France. They were convinced that the favorable rate of exchange would permit them to live in their accustomed style and still reduce their debts. It would prove a self-deluding conviction.

The pattern of life they established upon arriving in Paris in May 1924 is significant. The Fitzgeralds never really became part of the community of experimental artists and writers who made up the Anglo-American expatriate community gathered upon the Left Bank of the Seine, although they came to know many of its members. They arrived in France with Fitzgerald's success and popularity well established. Although he had not achieved an artistic success, he had become a symbol of a new wave of writing. Even critics who did not entirely like his first two novels had discerned flashes of genius in them which promised substantial achievement. The Fitzgeralds, already popular symbols of what he had named the Jazz Age, would lodge in expensive hotels, eat at the best restaurants, and frequent the fashionable cafes of the Right Bank at least as much as they appeared in the more modest cafes and bars of Montparnasse and the university quarter.

The Fitzgeralds were in Paris only briefly before going to the Riviera at the end of May for most of the rest of 1924. They stopped at Grimm's Park Hotel in Hyeres, fifty miles southeast of Marseilles, before moving to the Villa Marie at nearby Valescure, St. Raphael, in June. Sometime after their arrival in France, probably after their move to St. Raphael, the Fitzgeralds met Gerald and Sara Murphy. The Murphys had arrived from New York three years earlier, seeking to live an attractive and stylish existence while Gerald Murphy studied first landscape architecture, then painting. The Murphys had quickly established friendships with a number of European and American painters, musicians, and writers. They wintered in or near Paris, and, through Gerald Murphy's Yale friend Cole Porter, discovered the neglected charm of the off-season summer Riviera. Names associated with the Murphys eventually included those of painters Pablo Picasso, Georges Braque, Fernand Leger; ballet impressario Serge Diaghilev and through him the composer Igor Stravinsky; writers Archibald MacLeish, Philip

The Fitzgeralds in Rome, winter 1924

Barry, John Dos Passos, and Ernest Hemingway, as well as the Fitzgeralds.

The Murphys' villa was at Cap d'Antibes, between Cannes and Nice, and although the Fitzgeralds socialized with them that summer, they tried to live quietly. Once they were established, Fitzgerald settled in for a summer of serious writing. By 25 August he had completed the first draft of his third novel and was able to promise Maxwell Perkins at Scribners a revised typescript by October. Despite Fitzgerald's successful work on his novel, there occurred that summer a crisis which, if relatively minor at the time, would subsequently loom larger and larger in the Fitzgeralds' lives and writings. Their relatively controlled social activities that summer had included friendships with several young French naval officers stationed nearby at Frejus. For Zelda Fitzgerald, isolated from friends and shut out of Fitzgerald's life by his writing, one of them, Edouard Jozan, became more than a casual acquaintance. Jozan, who subsequently would become a war hero and vice-admiral, later insisted that the relationship was no more than an extended flirtation. Nevertheless Fitzgerald, whose amusement at his wife's effect on male acquaintances did not extend to tolerance when she reciprocated their affections, felt threatened and betrayed and took steps to end the relationship on 13

July. The Fitzgeralds successfully concealed the crisis for the remainder of the summer from visitors such as the critic Gilbert Seldes and his wife and their friends Ellis and Ring Lardner. But in September they frightened the Murphys when Fitzgerald sought their aid one night because Zelda Fitzgerald had taken an overdose of sleeping tablets. Although Fitzgerald went on with his work successfully, neither Fitzgerald was able to forget the impact of the Jozan affair. It was fictionalized in both *Save Me the Waltz* and *Tender Is the Night*.

Fitzgerald had come to France with an already established plan for his third novel, tracing the decay of American idealism through the shattered romance between a rich girl and a poor boy who achieves financial success. Although it was written in France, it is a quintessentially American novel, gently and sympathetically examining the myth of material success that had been central to American culture since Benjamin Franklin. One of the central images of Fitzgerald's life, cherished (and dreaded) since adolescence, was that of the poor boy whose beloved is taken from him by a rich and powerful rival, but the tragedy of Jay Gatsby, and the impression that tragedy makes on the sensitive observer-narrator Nick Carraway, may have been strengthened by the events of the summer of 1924.

Financial necessity made Fitzgerald pause in his

work on the novel to write a brief piece for a humor magazine and to produce the only partly facetious "How to Live on Practically Nothing a Year" for the *Saturday Evening Post*. The piece, a companion to his earlier "How to Live on $36,000 a Year" (1924), mocks their inability to live cheaply in France and demonstrates the financial necessity for writing such pieces—the *Saturday Evening Post* paid Fitzgerald $1200 for it, more than he received that year in total royalties from his books. As soon as the revised typescript of the novel—tentatively entitled *The Great Gatsby*, though Fitzgerald would also suggest "Gold-Hatted Gatsby," "Trimalchio in West Egg," and "The High-Bouncing Lover"—could be put in the mail on 27 October 1924, the Fitzgeralds went to Rome. While still revising *The Great Gatsby*, Fitzgerald had written to Perkins on 25 August recommending that he read the serialization of Gertrude Stein's *The Making of Americans* in the *transatlantic review*, and in early October he gave Perkins an even heartier recommendation for Ernest Hemingway, whom he called "the real thing." Fitzgerald had not yet met either writer, although Edmund Wilson may have urged Fitzgerald to meet with Hemingway while he was in France. By the time Fitzgerald wrote to Perkins, he had at least read Hemingway's *in our time* (1924).

The winter in Italy was desultory. Although he sent Perkins a stream of corrections for *The Great Gatsby*, Fitzgerald worked little. From the Hotel des Princes near the Piazza di Spagna, the Fitzgeralds explored Rome's night life and made friends among the film crew for *Ben-Hur*. Fitzgerald began a pattern of drunken dissipation which would more or less characterize his social life for the rest of his experience in Europe, getting in fights with cab drivers and alarming, if not insulting, friends. He would look back on that cheerless winter in Rome as the beginning of a slide toward deterioration and would use some of its events with telling effect in his next novel.

Somehow he found time to complete three stories, two of which had European backgrounds. "Love in the Night" is a formula story—boy meets, loses, wins girl—with a happy ending, but its setting in Cannes, its theme of Russian aristocrats dispossessed by the Revolution, and its undertones of the difficulty of achieving true romance are the beginnings of material that would find its way into *Tender Is the Night*. Perhaps this work stirred him to think of beginning a new novel. The Fitzgeralds moved on to the Hotel Tiberio in Capri, arriving on 18 February 1925. There Fitzgerald fretted over the reception *The Great Gatsby* might receive, and Zelda

Fitzgerald, seeking an artistic identity of her own, took up painting. Fitzgerald spent an evening with the English novelist Compton MacKenzie, once his idol. Zelda Fitzgerald contracted colitis, from which she suffered the next year. Fitzgerald revised "Not in the Guidebook," a story with a Paris setting, which he had written in Rome. His revisions did not salvage its slightness, but its concern with treachery in love and war almost offset its trick ending, and *Woman's Home Companion* paid him $1750, which was an increase in his story price.

The Great Gatsby was published on 10 April 1925. On the way back to Paris the Fitzgeralds' car broke down in Lyons. By 12 May, after a brief stay in the Hotel Florida, they had moved into an apartment at 14, rue de Tilsitt near the Place de l'Etoile. A fashionable address, it was nevertheless stuffy and uncomfortable, and Fitzgerald was already writing Wilson that he would like to return to the United States, provided he could come back with money. He was depending on the sales of *The Great Gatsby*, but he was soon disappointed. There were two printings, totaling approximately 23,870 copies, in 1925, indicating a respectable, but not overwhelming, popularity. Scribners would not reprint the book during Fitzgerald's lifetime, though a British edition appeared in 1926, and a small Modern Library printing was published in 1934. Fitzgerald's 1925 revenues from *The Great Gatsby* were less than $2000 after his advances had been paid back. On the other hand, the critical reception greatly encouraged Fitzgerald. Intelligent readers appreciated the novel's sophisticated handling of the first-person narrative perspective, its taut control, and its carefully balanced structure. The poetic evocativeness of his prose and his ability to balance moral judgment with appreciation for the subjects of his criticism came fully into their own in *The Great Gatsby*. Gilbert Seldes termed it a masterpiece, and Fitzgerald received highly appreciative notices or personal letters from Alexander Woollcott, George Jean Nathan, James Branch Cabell, Paul Rosenfeld, and most rewardingly, T. S. Eliot, Edith Wharton, and Gertrude Stein.

Shortly after the Fitzgeralds arrived in Paris in late April 1925, Fitzgerald met Ernest Hemingway in the Dingo Bar on the rue Delambre in Montparnasse. By the time they met, Perkins, who had had difficulty finding a copy of *in our time*, had finally written Hemingway in February 1925, but he did not have the correct address. When he met Fitzgerald, Hemingway had already signed a contract with Boni & Liveright. Fitzgerald is often said to have aided Hemingway in his efforts to break his contract with

Boni & Liveright, but when Hemingway sent them *The Torrents of Spring* (1926), a parody of one of the firm's best-selling writers, Sherwood Anderson, which they would almost certainly reject, Fitzgerald actually wrote a letter to Horace Liveright and editor T. R. Smith urging Boni & Liveright to publish the book. As Matthew J. Bruccoli points out in his discussion of the matter in *Scott and Ernest* (1978), Fitzgerald continued to praise Hemingway to Perkins, however, and was pleased when Hemingway was able to sign a contract with Scribners.

At the time of their first meeting Fitzgerald was a well-established novelist whose best work to date had just been published. Hemingway was still a struggling writer whose long, carefully planned apprenticeship was just beginning to pay off. From the beginning their relationship was almost the opposite of what one might expect. Fitzgerald had always been a hero worshipper who regretted his failure to become a football hero and his lack of battlefield experience in World War I. He was drawn to Hemingway's masculinity, self-sufficiency, and self-confidence, and he was deeply impressed by Hemingway's reputation for athletic prowess and his war record. He came to respect immensely Hemingway's discipline as a writer, as well as his extraordinary talent and craftsmanship. From the beginning the successful author was in awe of the newcomer, whom he would later characterize as "my artistic conscience" against whom he measured his literary successes and failures. Hemingway in turn came to admire Fitzgerald's talent, although he believed that it was never fully applied, and he welcomed Fitzgerald's help in his campaign to develop his career.

Fitzgerald's inability to handle alcohol and his diffidence and self-doubt were weaknesses, however, that Hemingway noted at the beginning of their relationship and which he was never able to overlook in his assessment of Fitzgerald. Soon after they met, Hemingway and Fitzgerald went to Lyons to recover the Fitzgeralds' abandoned car. In *A Moveable Feast* (1964) Hemingway describes the trip as a series of disasters during which Fitzgerald proved himself to be a hypochondriac and a drunk, but Fitzgerald lists it in his *Notebooks* as one of his "Most Pleasant Trips," and in June 1925 he wrote to Gertrude Stein about how enjoyable the trip had been. As Bruccoli points out, Hemingway's account of his friendship with Fitzgerald has factual errors. *A Moveable Feast* was written between 1957 and 1960, decades after the events it records, and as Hemingway warns in the book's preface: "If the reader prefers, this book may be regarded as fiction."

Hemingway took Fitzgerald to meet Gertrude Stein some time in the late spring or the early summer. Fitzgerald and Stein were not to meet frequently over the next decade, but their friendship was a sustained one, reflected in mutual respect and in an infrequent but warm correspondence. Stein had already read *This Side of Paradise* and *The Great Gatsby*, and in a 22 May 1925 letter to Fitzgerald she wrote, "You write naturally in sentences and one can read all of them and that among other things is a comfort. You are creating the contemporary world much as Thackeray did his *Pendennis* and *Vanity Fair.* . . ." She repeated this praise in *The Autobiography of Alice B. Toklas* (1933) and added that "Fitzgerald will be read when many of his well known contemporaries are forgotten." In December 1934, during a visit to the United States, she spent a day in Baltimore with the Fitzgeralds. In turn Fitzgerald was enthusiastic about her experimental writing and continued to urge Scribners to publish *The Making of Americans* (1925). While she did not influence his writing, her opinions may have influenced Fitzgerald's judgment of the French Surrealist writer Rene Crevel, whose work Fitzgerald recommended to Perkins.

Edith Wharton had responded to Fitzgerald's sending her a copy of *The Great Gatsby* by writing him a letter that combined praise with intelligent criticism. When Fitzgerald went to visit her at her country estate, the Pavillon Colombe, in mid-June, his characteristic awe of established writers caused him to stop several times along the way to fortify his courage with alcohol. Although there are several versions of what happened at the meeting, Fitzgerald told what he considered to be a "rough story" which seems to have embarrassed him far more than it shocked Wharton.

In his *Ledger* Fitzgerald describes the summer of 1925 as one of "1000 parties and no work," but he was actually hard at work on "The Rich Boy," one of his best short stories, which occupied much of his attention during the spring and summer of 1925. Its anatomy of the decline of Anson Hunter continued one of Gatsby's themes: the debilitating effect of great wealth on those who lack sufficient moral resources to withstand the special pressures it creates. The story's sophisticated narrative technique and elegiac tone also united it with *The Great Gatsby*, but its violence, heavy irony, and unhappy ending made it unsuitable for *Saturday Evening Post*, and it went instead to *Red Book* magazine, which paid him $3500. In July Fitzgerald took time off to write a more representative *Post* story, "A Penny Spent." It is a typical love story: impoverished but formerly wealthy boy wins rich girl from pompous, self-righteous rival through his heroics in a suspenseful ending. The cosmopolitan American hero introduces a naive but likable newly rich American family to his Europe. In his handling of setting—the Paris of the Ritz bar and hotel, Brussels (where Fitzgerald had visited that summer), and Capri with its Blue Grotto—and in his striking imagery, Fitzgerald made highly effective use of his experience. The dialogue and narrative prove the craftsmanship which Fitzgerald could, and frequently did, apply to his magazine fiction, too often summarily dismissed as hackwork. Fitzgerald himself undervalued much of his short fiction and established an unfortunate precedent still too easily followed by unperceptive readers. He received his new *Post* price of $2000 for the story.

The Fitzgeralds spent the month of August 1925 at Cap d'Antibes, where Gerald and Sara Murphy, at their Villa America, were having one of their most socially successful summers, full of surface brilliance and hidden feverishness noted in Fitzgerald's consciousness for subsequent use in *Tender Is the Night*. He wrote to John Peale Bishop in September: "There was no one at Antibes this summer except me, Zelda, the Valentinos, the Murphys, Mistinguet, Rex Ingram, Dos Passos, Alice Terry, the MacLeishes, Charlie Brackett, Maude Kahn, Esther Murphy, Marguerite Namara, E. Phillips Oppenheim, Mannes the violinist, Floyd Dell, Max and Chrystal Eastman, ex-premier Orlando, Etienne de Beaumont." The Murphys' relaxed, friendly, casual yet ordered lives were occasionally interrupted by the Fitzgeralds' erratic behavior. Yet there was also opportunity for a growing mutual affection among the Fitzgeralds and Murphys. The fall of 1925 continued the social patterns the summer had established. Back in Paris, the Fitzgeralds spent much time with the Murphys, who, although they were rich in comparison to the Fitzgeralds, were not as wealthy as their lifestyle suggested. Nevertheless Fitzgerald persisted in associating Murphy with great wealth.

That fall Fitzgerald toured the Verdun battlefields, storing up materials for *Tender Is the Night*. He was also seeing a great deal of Hemingway, and through him he met other members of the Left Bank literary colony such as the publisher and writer Robert McAlmon, whom he immediately disliked. His own writing was not going well. Since the previous spring he had been dropping hints to Perkins and Ober that he was following *The Great Gatsby*'s success by plunging immediately into another novel, tentatively entitled "Our Type," but there is little evidence that he went much beyond his initial vague idea of developing a

plot around the sensational murder, by her sensitive son, of an American woman traveling in Europe. Most of his writing energy went instead into the composition of short stories, needed for income. Between November 1925 and February 1926 he wrote four stories—"Presumption," "The Adolescent

F. Scott Fitzgerald at the time of The Great Gatsby

Marriage," "The Dance," and "Your Way and Mine"—none of which represented his best work and none of which reflected his life in Europe. The best of them, "The Dance," is a mystery story set in a southern town much like the Montgomery, Alabama, where he had met Zelda. Ironically the least successful, "Your Way and Mine" is the most heartfelt, reflecting his growing concern with the price in misunderstood intentions and nervous energy one must pay for success. He was paid a total of $8750 for the four stories.

He would complete no more fiction during 1926. Instead the Fitzgeralds would be enabled to continue to live in France through substantial revenues derived from stage and film rights to *The Great Gatsby*. Fitzgerald's total income for 1926 exceeded $25,000, most of it from those indirect proceeds from the novel. Once the economic pressure to write was eased, he found it more and more difficult to discipline himself to writing, though he continued to struggle with the matricide novel, which, he wrote to Perkins at the end of 1925, was wonderful, though far from its end. He planned to come home when it was finished.

From mid-January until 1 March 1926 the Fitzgeralds withdrew to the Hotel Bellevue, Salies-de-Bearn, in the French Pyrenees, where Zelda Fitzgerald took the cure for colitis and Fitzgerald finished "Your Way and Mine." Scribners published his third volume of stories, *All the Sad Young Men*, on 26 February. By the beginning of March the Fitzgeralds were living in the Villa Paquita at Juan-les-Pins on the Riviera. Except for two weeks in Paris when Zelda Fitzgerald had an appendectomy in June, the Fitzgeralds spent the rest of 1926 on the Riviera. There Fitzgerald applied himself more energetically to the new novel, alternative titles for which became first "The World's Fair," later "The Melarkey Case," and "The Boy Who Killed His Mother." He drew on his fascination with the Leopold-Loeb murder of 1924 and the Dorothy Ellingson matricide of January 1925; on his friendship with the Murphys; on his acquaintance with the composer Theodore Chanler, who during the summer of 1925 had told Fitzgerald he had to break away from the enchantment of the Murphys' circle to protect his artistic studies; and on his observations of the tendency toward dissipation in his own life and that of his college friend Walker Ellis, under the influence of France's charm. He was struggling with these disparate materials to fashion a story of a sensitive but weak young man, Francis Melarkey, traveling in Europe with his domineering mother, who comes under the sway of a brilliant circle centered upon a couple whose names changed frequently during the successive drafts: Seth and Dinah Roreback or Rorebeck or Piper. Melarkey was to become increasingly distracted and dissipated until his incipient violence and willfulness led him to kill his mother. Fitzgerald would continue to work on the novel, more or less on those lines, but in many stages, abandoned concepts, and fresh starts, for the rest of the decade, feeling more and more frustrated by his compulsion to make of these bare bones a masterpiece which would go beyond the achievement of *The Great Gatsby*. Hemingway came to ridicule him for that self-conscious struggle with his own reputation and to blame reviewers of *The Great Gatsby*, especially Gilbert Seldes, for making Fitzgerald unable simply to write well instead of attempting to live up to their predictions for him.

In April, however, Fitzgerald seemed enthusiastic about the matricide novel, writing Ober that it was "about one fourth done." He planned twelve chapters, totaling 75,000 words. In May he expressed the same enthusiasm to Perkins. He also eagerly pressed upon Perkins the case for Hemingway. Through Fitzgerald *Scribner's Magazine* had agreed in January 1926 to consider Hemingway's story "Fifty Grand," ultimately published in the July 1927 issue of the *Atlantic*. Hemingway somehow came secretly to resent Fitzgerald's editorial advice and some of the Scribners editors' suggestions, although at the time his resentment was unexpressed. During the fall of 1925, Fitzgerald had also found time to write an extremely enthusiastic review of Hemingway's *In Our Time* (1925), entitled "How to Waste Material: A Note on My Generation," which belatedly appeared in the May 1926 issue of the *Bookman*.

Hemingway had also been working since the previous summer on the novel which would become *The Sun Also Rises* (1926). During their occasional contacts in 1925 and early 1926 the two writers had discussed their novels in progress, and in May Hemingway brought a carbon of his revised typescript to Juan-les-Pins to show it to Fitzgerald. The Hemingways had come to know the Murphys through the Fitzgeralds and stayed at first in the guesthouse of the Murphy's Villa America at Antibes. In mid-May the Fitzgeralds turned over the Villa Paquita to the Hemingways and moved to the larger Villa St. Louis nearby. Fitzgerald took seriously the task of reading Hemingway's manuscript and produced a list of suggested revisions. The most important of them concerned the opening of the novel. Fitzgerald found its first fifteen pages of exposition clumsy and pretentious, full of "elephantine facetiousness"—an astonishing description of the famous Hemingway style—and suggested it be cut. Hemingway followed his suggestion, strengthening the manuscript, although he later undervalued Fitzgerald's suggestions. Fitzgerald would provide similar advice on Hemingway's second novel, and their later correspondence was sometimes filled with serious debates about how to write, but neither author ever exhibited any significant influence upon the other's material or style.

The Fitzgeralds' behavior became increasingly destructive and bizarre, and it is difficult to see how Fitzgerald could have accomplished much writing that summer. Their response to their difficulties—personal and professional—was to return to the

United States. They left the Riviera at the end of October, spent a few weeks in Paris preparing for their return home, and on 10 December were in Genoa to embark on the Italian vessel *Conte Biancamano*. They came home with little money, with little progress made on the matricide novel, and with sadly deteriorated morale. They went almost immediately to Hollywood, where Fitzgerald worked on a film script. They found little order for their lives there, but Fitzgerald met and became fascinated with the young actress Lois Moran, who would later influence his portrait of Rosemary Hoyt in *Tender Is the Night*. By March 1927 they had signed a two-year lease for Ellerslie, a mansion near Wilmington, Delaware. Oddly Scott almost immediately became nostalgic for France, which he remembered primarily as Paris, though more of their time had been passed in the South of France and Italy. He wrote: "The best of America drifts to Paris, to find intelligence and good manners."

The settled life at Ellerslie did not do much to restore calm or order to the Fitzgeralds' existence. Increasingly dissatisfied with the lack of accomplishment she felt in her life, Zelda Fitzgerald began to study ballet in Philadelphia. At twenty-seven she was too old, but she threw herself enthusiastically into the effort to create an artistic existence of her own. Fitzgerald did little writing during the next year and a half. The matricide novel eluded his sporadic efforts. He wrote five short pieces in 1927, none of which made more than slight references to Europe. They brought in a comfortable income: the *Saturday Evening Post* had increased his price to $3500 per story. Although he did not have much of the novel ready for publication, he had already arranged for its serialization in *Liberty* and received a $5700 advance. The growing weight of his inability to finish the novel, and of the troubles the Fitzgeralds were experiencing, found subtle expression in the themes of his stories, which were increasingly concerned with professional, personal, and romantic disappointment and failure.

In the spring of 1928 the Fitzgeralds decided to spend the summer in Paris. They sailed in April, and by 2 May they had rented another elegant but cheerless apartment—their first on the Left Bank—at 58, rue de Vaugirard near the Luxembourg Gardens and the Paris residence of the Murphys. Despite their concern over the Fitzgeralds' sometimes disruptive social conduct, the Murphys were pleased to see the Fitzgeralds. Gerald Murphy arranged for Zelda Fitzgerald to study under the prestigious tutelage of Madame Lubov Egorova, instructor with Diaghilev's Ballet Russe and former prima ballerina.

Fitzgerald did little work on the novel that summer, instead taking refuge—financially and psychologically—in a series of stories about Midwestern boyhood which he had begun that spring in Delaware. He completed two of these Basil Duke Lee stories during the summer.

Hemingway was not in Paris, but Fitzgerald renewed other old acquaintances and made new ones in the literary community. At some time or other, every American writer in Paris during the twenties visited Sylvia Beach's Shakespeare and Company bookshop at 12, rue de L'Odeon, which sold English-language books. Partly because of Beach's generous lending-library policy and partly because of her fame as the publisher of James Joyce's *Ulysses* (1922), Shakespeare and Company had become a center for the expatriate colony and for literate Americans visiting Paris. When the Fitzgeralds first came to know Sylvia Beach and her friend Adrienne Monnier, who ran La Maison des Amis des Livres, a bookshop specializing in contemporary French writing at 7, rue de l'Odeon, is unclear, though Beach identifies Fitzgerald as "one of our great pals" in her memoirs, *Shakespeare and Company* (1959). Certainly the close proximity of the bookshop to rue Vaugirard made it a regular stop that summer, and it was through Beach that Fitzgerald finally met James Joyce, for whom he had long had a deep admiration. Their meeting at a dinner party arranged by Monnier and Beach is memorialized in an inscription and caricature Fitzgerald placed in Beach's copy of *The Great Gatsby*: Joyce is depicted as a faceless pair of glasses dignified with a halo, Fitzgerald as a worshipper kneeling in veneration. The drawing is captioned *"Festival of St. James."* Fitzgerald's characteristic awe of other writers of achievement turned to embarrassing self-abasement at a second meeting, when Fitzgerald threatened to throw himself from the window as a gesture of respect for Joyce. Taken aback by Fitzgerald's wildness, Joyce nevertheless recovered sufficiently to send him a gracious note and an inscribed copy of *Portrait of the Artist as a Young Man* (1916).

Other guests at the "Festival of St. James" included a young French writer, Andre Chamson, and his wife. Beach thought a great deal of Chamson's recent novel, *Les hommes de la route* (1927), published in English as *The Road* (1929), which had been in candidacy for the prestigious Prix Goncourt. Fitzgerald came to share her enthusiasm, and he attempted to arrange for film production of the novel with his friend the director King Vidor. Although the project fell through abruptly, Fitzgerald and Chamson formed a lasting friendship. Typically Fitzgerald championed Chamson to Perkins, and Scribners subsequently became Chamson's English-language publisher. The relationship with Chamson was the only one Fitzgerald ever formed with a French writer, and it seems to have been based more upon friendship than on any abiding interest in the culture or art of the nation in which he lived so long without ever really feeling at home.

The Fitzgeralds returned to Ellerslie in September, where visitors found their lives more and more disordered. Fitzgerald was drinking heavily, and he was having severe difficulty making himself work. Hemingway visited Ellerslie in November 1928. It was the first meeting in more than two years, although the two had shared a pleasant, joking correspondence. Shortly thereafter, when Hemingway's father died suddenly, Fitzgerald met Hemingway in Philadelphia with an emergency loan—one of the last gestures of aid he would be able to extend. Fitzgerald's literary activities for the next six months consisted of three more Basil stories and the eloquent but despairing "The Last of the Belles." Zelda Fitzgerald's interest in ballet was beginning to border on obsession, and Fitzgerald became sufficiently, if belatedly, concerned to attempt to introduce her to a new artistic outlet. The magazine *College Humor* had approached him to write a series of slight but remunerative sketches about various types of modern girls. Unwilling to waste his limited resources, he turned the project over to Zelda Fitzgerald, who was eager to earn money so that she could pay for her ballet lessons and assert her financial independence. For commercial appeal, his name appeared with hers in the by-lines, and he occasionally helped her with ideas and revision, but the project—if not the credit—was essentially hers. The first one, "The Original Follies Girl," drew superficially upon their Paris background. The Fitzgeralds were already planning another trip to France when their lease expired in March 1929. Fitzgerald promised Perkins he would finish the novel there.

The sea voyage to Genoa was unpleasant. The weather was bad, and their sense of new beginnings evaporated in the storm. Stopping briefly on the Riviera, they arrived in Paris in early April, taking a flat on the Right Bank at 10, rue Pergolese, near the Bois de Boulogne. Fitzgerald settled down immediately to write a very fine short story from their shipboard experience: "The Rough Crossing." It is always a mistake to read Fitzgerald's work as autobiography, but examination of the story casts light on some of the concerns in their lives. Its tight, well-controlled plot traces the relationship between playwright Adrian Smith and his wife Eva as they depart New York with their children to take up a new life in Europe. The mood of the opening is one of escape: they are abandoning a past which hints of a slipping literary reputation and marital friction. As the ship approaches a hurricane, relationships between the Smiths become stormier. Adrian becomes embroiled in a romance with an admiring and attractive girl who feeds his flagging ego, and Eva, always impatient with people who are interested in her only as an appurtenance of her husband, retaliates by making a drunken scene, then beginning a flirtation of her own, also with a much younger man. The climax occurs when they are reconciled, during the height of the hurricane, and the resolution sees both natural and metaphorical storms pass from their lives. Nevertheless the sense of escape from the past is no longer there, leaving Adrian and Eva aware that they must concentrate on retaining the strong relationship with which their marriage had begun. The story's strength is in its consideration for and awareness of human frailty. There is neither the nostalgia nor the self-pity which had begun to creep into some of Fitzgerald's other stories.

Fitzgerald's pleasure at returning was marred by a new turn in his relationship with Hemingway. Hemingway was in Paris with his second wife, Pauline, intent on revising the manuscript of his second novel, *A Farewell to Arms* (1929). Worried that Fitzgerald would interfere with his work, he kept his address a secret and tried to avoid the Fitzgeralds as much as possible. The snubs hurt Fitzgerald, but he continued to find pleasure in Hemingway's company and showed him the manuscript of his novel. Hemingway liked what he had written and urged him to buckle down and complete it, forgetting about competition with the reputation of *The Great Gatsby* and simply writing as well as he could. At Fitzgerald's insistence Hemingway showed him the typescript of *A Farewell to Arms*, occasioning a not entirely welcome but detailed set of suggestions for revision. As with *The Sun Also Rises*, Hemingway did accept some of Fitzgerald's advice, markedly strengthening the famous closing passage of the novel, which Fitzgerald found overwritten and lame. Again, as with *The Sun Also Rises*, Hemingway later denied that Fitzgerald had helped him and secretly resented the suggestions. By 1929 Hemingway's reputation was well on the rise, and Fitzgerald's was in decline. Their friendship could never quite be what it had been earlier.

To worsen matters the notorious boxing episode took place that June. Morley Callaghan, another young Scribners author, was in Paris and spent time with both Fitzgerald and Hemingway. Callaghan and Hemingway shared an enjoyment of boxing and agreed, one June afternoon, to allow Fitzgerald to accompany them to the gym. Fitzgerald was delighted to be timekeeper but got so absorbed that he let one round run long, during which Callaghan knocked Hemingway down. When Fitzgerald admitted his error, Hemingway lashed out angrily at him. Although the episode seemed quickly forgotten, it became much more complicated later in the year after Callaghan's return to the United States, when a garbled newspaper version damaged Hemingway's pride. He blamed first Fitzgerald, then Callaghan, and by the time the entire incident had been laid to rest, after much transatlantic correspondence, another indelible scar had formed on the Fitzgerald-Hemingway friendship.

Another complication in their already difficult friendship occurred in the fall of 1929 when the two writers visited Gertrude Stein. She was delighted to see Fitzgerald again and declared him the most talented writer of his generation, saying that his "flame" was stronger than Hemingway's. The remark upset Fitzgerald more than it did Hemingway but added strain to their friendship. They continued to see each other during the fall of 1929, but after Hemingway returned to Key West at the end of the year, they would meet rarely during the rest of Fitzgerald's life.

The Fitzgeralds went to Cannes for the summer of 1929, living from June through September in the Villa Fleur des Bois. They were pleased to be back with the Murphys on the Riviera, but the atmosphere seemed changed. Relations were strained by Zelda Fitzgerald's eccentric conduct and by Fitzgerald's avowed intention to use the Murphys as models for characters in his novel, studying them like laboratory specimens. Fitzgerald had determined to make a fresh start on his novel that summer and was beginning to draw upon the Murphys for material. Abandoning the Francis Melarkey plot line, he incorporated some of the material he had created in "The Rough Crossing" to formulate a fragmentary new beginning in which film director Lew Kelly and his wife Nicole, tired of life in Hollywood, set out for an extended vacation in

The Fitzgeralds on the Riviera, 1929

Europe. On board ship they encounter an attractive young starlet, Rosemary, who attempts to impress Lew with her freshness. The fragment indicates no further plot, but Fitzgerald probably intended to adapt the Melarkey-matricide material at least thematically to trace the moral deterioration of Lew Kelly under the influence of the life and atmosphere of France.

The fresh start made him enthusiastic about writing—he promised Perkins he was "writing day and night," though some of the effort was expended on stories for the *Saturday Evening Post*—he was now being paid $4000, the highest price he would receive during his career. Before leaving Paris he had written two competent stories in his old society romance vein, "Majesty" and "At Your Age." In Cannes he turned to European material for "The Swimmers," one of his more underrated achievements. Its complex but controlled plot of infidelity and marital betrayal, involving an American expatriate and his unfaithful French wife, is played out against a background of Paris, the French coast, and Virginia's beaches. The story contrasts imagery of the cleansing value of water and physical activity with imagery of decay and death. Its themes involve pride in his protagonist's American heritage, psychological trauma, and a vision of Europe as decadent and worn-out: "France was a land, England was a people, but America, having about it still that quality of the idea, was harder to utter—it was the graves at Shiloh and the tired, drawn, nervous faces of its great men, and the country boys dying in the Argonne for a phrase that was empty before their bodies withered. It was a willingness of the heart." Although it had no direct relationship to his novel at this stage, its components are the germ of ideas his artistic consciousness was beginning to pull together out of the long struggle with his manuscript and his experiences.

Zelda Fitzgerald was also writing. She had finished another of the "Girl" sketches in Paris in April, and during the summer and fall in Cannes she wrote three more. She took her work seriously, as she had her painting and ballet, and the sketches became more sophisticated as she progressed. In the fourth and fifth of this series, "The Girl the Prince Liked" and "The Girl with Talent," she incorporated Paris settings. Characterization was not her strength, but she was beginning to learn the intricacies of plotting and narrative technique, and her descriptive imagery was crisp and striking. But she was still intensely unhappy. One night, as they drove along the Grande Corniche road, high above the Mediterranean, Zelda suddenly grabbed the wheel and tried to force the car over the cliff. (Fitzgerald later worked this episode into *Tender Is the Night*.)

Putting aside writing, they returned to Paris at the end of October. They spent the night of the New York Stock Market Crash in the Hotel Beau Rivage in St. Raphael. It seemed part of an uneventful trip, but Fitzgerald's propensity for identifying himself with the spirit of his times led him to make it one of the symbolic dates in his life, tied to that summer full of things winding down and breaking up. Another significant event involved Zelda Fitzgerald. Her long, hard hours of dancing exercise had led to an offer to perform with the San Carlo Opera Ballet Company in Naples. As desperately as she wanted to find meaningful achievement, the decision to stay with her family was psychologically costly, and the spirit of it was caught in Fitzgerald's story "Two Wrongs," completed in Paris in November. Not among his better efforts, it traces a theme of broken marital trust through the lives of a Broadway producer whose infidelity is balanced by his wife's decision to put her long-postponed career as a ballerina ahead of his health and the marriage.

American poet Allen Tate got to know the Fitzgeralds in Paris that winter. Although it was one of their most trying periods, Zelda Fitzgerald suffering heartbreak over her dancing and Fitzgerald drinking dangerously and asking his embarrassingly personal questions, he remembers also the warmth and charm. Fitzgerald had, he recalls, "a curious combination of naivety and cunning." Fitzgerald's other social contacts that fall included John Peale Bishop, Robert Penn Warren, and Sinclair Lewis.

With the new year Fitzgerald began a new series of stories about adolescence, this time featuring a tough but vulnerable girl named Josephine. He was only to complete one of them, however, before Zelda Fitzgerald's nervous disappointment over the lack of success of her dancing became acute. She had hoped to work her way into the Diaghilev troupe but had only received exploitive offers to dance in the Folies Bergere. In February 1930 they tried a vacation in Algiers, but the trip provided little relief. On their return both threw themselves into writing. Fitzgerald completed another of the Josephine stories, then returned to a Paris setting, and to an old theme of the poor boy who loses his girl to wealth and power, in "The Bridal Party." This time, however, there was a new twist. The story became a study of contrast between failure and success, as the resourceful and self-confident Hamilton Rutherford succeeds in holding Caroline Dandy despite a twist in fortune by which he loses his wealth. The weaker protagonist, Michael Curly, finds at the end that his sorrow and self-pity evaporate in admiration for Rutherford's American strength of will. The mood and tone of the story reflect both the atmosphere of lost dreams Fitzgerald associated with the end of the decade and a view of France as decadent and exhausted, in contrast with the vitality of the United States. Zelda Fitzgerald's last "Girl" story, "A Millionaire's Girl," a study of romantic disillusionment, showed such an improvement in narrative development that Harold Ober thought Fitzgerald had written it. It appeared with his by-line alone, increasing Zelda Fitzgerald's subsequent determination to break free from what she had come to view as Fitzgerald's domination of her creative ability.

On 23 April 1930 she suffered a breakdown. On the assumption that she was suffering primarily physical strain, Fitzgerald at first registered her in a clinic in the Paris suburb of Malmaison, but on 22 May, aware that it was much more serious, he arranged for transfer to a clinic at Valmont, on Lake Geneva near Montreux, Switzerland. He moved to the Hotel de la Paix in nearby Lausanne. It was the end of their French residence, though they left their daughter and her governess in Paris, where she was enrolled in school. Zelda Fitzgerald's illness was soon diagnosed as a severe psychological disorder. On 4 June 1930 she was transferred to Les Rives de Prangins sanitarium, also on Lake Geneva, near Nyon, and placed under the care of Dr. Oscar Forel, an eminent psychiatrist. Dr. Forel diagnosed her illness as an extreme psychosis, probably schizophrenia, and subsequently called on the assistance of Dr. Eugen Bleuler, Europe's foremost authority on that disorder. All through the rest of 1930, the struggle to help her was an arduous and doubtful one, and it became a time of reassessment for both Fitzgeralds. Fitzgerald's income for 1929 had been nearly $33,000, and it would remain at that level for the next two years. However, he recognized that his wife's treatment would be extraordinarily expensive. Partly to offset those expenses, and partly for occupation, he concentrated on writing short stories for the rest of the year.

To be near his wife, Fitzgerald continued his residence in Switzerland. In addition to staying in Lausanne, he also lived for a time at a hotel in Geneva, about fifty miles from Prangins. Between June 1930 and February 1931 he wrote six stories and two light nonfiction pieces. Two of the stories were continuations of the Josephine series, nostalgic, but introducing a new note of the price one pays for past indiscretions. Two more, "The Hotel Child" and "Indecision," have settings in Switzerland. The first,

written in November, is a melodrama contrasting a pretty, rich, and naive American teenager, Fifi Schwartz, with a cast of disreputable Europeans, snobbish and clannish, who have drifted toward Switzerland to pull their lives together. Fifi's innocent honesty triumphs over their corruption and triviality in a manner reminiscent of Henry James. "Indecision," written in early 1931, is set in a ski resort much like the ones which the Fitzgeralds visited that winter as Zelda Fitzgerald began to recover. Like "The Hotel Child," "Indecision" presents Fitzgerald's view of Switzerland as sick and corrupt, but it is less sentimental and mawkish than the earlier story. It is a competent but uninspired story of the struggle the egotistical Tommy McLane goes through in choosing between two women: Emily Elliott, a divorcee with two children, and the eighteen-year-old Rosemary Meriwether. After some formula complications, he opts for youth, but the story ends with a hint of indecision.

Two other efforts deal more effectively with the meaning of the Fitzgeralds' experiences in Europe. In August Fitzgerald wrote "One Trip Abroad." In it Fitzgerald struggled with the meaning of his wife's breakdown and their troubled love. It incorporates background from their Algerian trip, as well as Paris and the Riviera, as it traces the lives in Europe of Nicole and Nelson Kelly, young Americans of artistic temperament, from fresh optimism through marital infidelity and a series of increasingly decadent parties, to physical and emotional exhaustion in a Switzerland where "misery . . . has dragged itself . . . from every corner of Europe" to find "Weariness to recuperate and death to die." The Kellys' lives periodically cross those of two other couples, the older, more worldly wise Mileses, and an unidentified pair of *doppelganger* whose deterioration, Nicole and Nelson come to realize, mirrors their own. Fitzgerald's moral honesty does not preclude an ending of qualified optimism, reflecting the new start he hoped he and Zelda could make of their mutually supportive love. "One Trip Abroad" is strongly related in atmosphere and theme to the earlier "Rough Crossing." More important, it was the beginning of the novel that would become *Tender Is the Night*.

The major achievement of this period was "Babylon Revisited," one of Fitzgerald's best stories and his strongest effort to that time to explore the meaning of his European experiences, which had come to be thoroughly identified with the personal crises he and Zelda Fitzgerald had faced. Completed in December 1930, it traces the relationship between Charles Wales and his daughter, Honoria, as they

Scottie and F. Scott Fitzgerald in Switzerland, 1930-1931

find mutual trust and support in the wake of a series of disasters. These include financial ruin in the 1929 stock market collapse, Charlie's background of careless dissipation in the frenetic life of Paris in the twenties, and the accidental death of his wife and her mother—which Charlie feels resulted partially from his indifference and neglect during a drunken spree. Charlie is struggling to make a fresh start, but the past haunts him in the form of drunken friends who disrupt his campaign to win the approval of his sister-in-law and consequent custody of Honoria. In its controlled, understated conclusion, Charlie realizes that he has lost nearly everything of value during the glittering twenties, figuratively "selling short" in the emotional marketplace for which the crash is symbolic. However, the reader senses his defeat is temporary. Fitzgerald drew upon themes of unintentional marital irresponsibility explored in earlier stories, on his frequent weekend visits to his daughter in Paris, and on his growing recognition that his life had somehow become identified with the burst bubble of the twenties. At the close of the story Charlie's memories of the decade of the twenties serve as an eloquent judgment of its misspent energies and hopes:

> Again the memory of those days swept over him like a nightmare—the people they had met travelling; then people who couldn't add a row of figures or speak a coherent sentence. The little man Helen had consented to dance with at the ship's party, who had insulted her ten feet from the table; the women and girls carried screaming with drink or drugs out of public places—
>
> —The men who locked their wives out in the snow, because the snow of twenty-nine wasn't real snow. If you didn't want it to be snow, you just paid some money.

Fitzgerald's emotional control, elegiac eloquence, and the tenderness with which he creates scenes between father and daughter attest to his craftsmanship and talent, even in the most arduous of circumstances.

His restricted social life did not preclude renewed relationships with the Murphys, who, because of the debilitating illness of their youngest son, had moved to Switzerland even before the Fitzgeralds, settling at Montana-Vermala in the Alps. Fitzgerald saw them there several times. At the end of the summer of 1930 he and Gerald Murphy had a long, serious conversation about acceptance of personal tragedy, which may have helped shape Charlie Wales's strength and determination. Fitzgerald also visited that summer with the young novelist Thomas Wolfe, whom he had met before leaving Paris. Wolfe was also a protege of Perkins, who had brought them together at least partially in an effort to support Fitzgerald and spur his writing.

In January 1931 Fitzgerald's father died. He returned to the United States, attended the funeral in Maryland, and briefly visited Zelda Fitzgerald's parents in Montgomery. The death of his father, from whom, Fitzgerald realized, he had learned valuable lessons in gentility and dignity, was yet another of the losses of which his life had become composed, and he incorporated his realization into his novel.

There was a hiatus in Fitzgerald's professional activities in the spring of 1931, but as his wife became stronger, he began another spurt of short-story activity, completing seven pieces between April and September. One was a final Josephine story, "Emotional Bankruptcy," in which he enunciated a theory of limited moral and emotional resources that he would examine throughout much of his remaining writing. Another, "A New Leaf," continued to explore themes of alcoholic dissolution, the evanescence of surface charm, and the inability to escape the past, but its maudlin sentimentality mars it. Its Paris setting was Fitzgerald's last use of European materials for a while. Probably at the insistence of *Saturday Evening Post* editors, he returned to American settings, attempting not very successfully to make happy formula stories from the Depression conditions he had observed during his January trip to the United States. Occasionally, as in "Six of One—," his mood turned to bitter hostility toward wealth and privilege. Perhaps for that reason, the *Saturday Evening Post* rejected the story—the first rejection in four years. One theme that he pursued through most of these stories was the superiority of strength of character and willingness to work over mere breeding and education.

As she began to recover, Zelda Fitzgerald had also returned to writing, and her husband encouraged her. In the summer of 1930 she wrote three stories, for which Fitzgerald asked Perkins and Ober to find a publisher. Perkins praised her imagistic skill, but the stories were never sold and have been lost. In the fall she was more successful. Her story "Miss Ella" appeared in the December issue of *Scribner's Magazine,* after she had heavily revised it, with Fitzgerald's assistance, to bring her abstract metaphorical passages and lush imagery into sharper focus. "Miss Ella" is an exercise in Southern Gothic suspense with Faulknerian overtones set in the Alabama of Zelda's youth.

Structurally it evidences a continuity with the "Girl" series, focusing through a peripheral observer-narrator upon the strong character of a spinster whose mysterious past is redolent of tragic love and hidden violence. In this story Zelda Fitzgerald advanced her skills in plot development and characterization while exploring the complexities of a feminine psyche struggling unsuccessfully for mature fulfillment.

During the spring and summer her advanced recovery permitted several expeditions into the outside world, during which the Fitzgeralds drew closer together than they had been for years. They visited the Murphys, now living in the Austrian Tyrol. By the end of the summer Dr. Forel felt she was ready for release. In September the Fitzgeralds visited Paris for the final time, staying in the Hotel Majestic. Their return to America aboard the *Aquitania* was the final turning away from the Europe which had seemed to promise so much, but it also led toward two novels in which they would seek to come to terms with France and their European existence.

They first settled in Montgomery, Alabama. Fitzgerald went on to Hollywood alone for another attempt at screenwriting. In Montgomery Zelda Fitzgerald wrote another story, "A Couple of Nuts," in which she explored subject matter Fitzgerald had used so often in the past few years. A talented young American couple, Larry and Lola, move through marriage, and along the Paris-Cannes axis, from a kind of tough romantic innocence to dissipation and dissolution. Their ruin is brought about through a charming but corrupt master of social ease and coordination, Jeff Daugherty. As in "Miss Ella," the story is told by a detached observer, but the plot is handled more effectively, and the control of imagery sustains an ominous tone of loss and destruction. This story demonstrated that Zelda Fitzgerald was capable of writing well and showed promise for her next project: a novel, which she began in January 1932. The strain of the work, coupled with grief over the death of her father in November 1931, brought on another breakdown, and Fitzgerald took her to Baltimore for psychiatric observation. She would never again be free of the shadow of mental illness.

In the Phipps Clinic, which she entered on 12 February 1932, she continued to work on her novel. Fitzgerald was hard at work on his own novel and was afraid that she was preempting what he regarded as his material—a concern increased by the theme of "A Couple of Nuts." Partly because she was afraid he would make her change any portion that seemed too much like his book and partly to assert her

independence, Zelda Fitzgerald sent the manuscript to Perkins without her husband's knowledge. Despite Fitzgerald's initial anger, he helped her with revisions and handled publication arrangements with Scribners. *Save Me the Waltz* is a valuable literary document of the twenties, but it also deserves appreciation on its merits as a story, tracing the struggle of a talented but undisciplined woman to become an artist in the face of conflicting loyalties. Alabama Beggs, the protagonist, must overcome her self-indulgent southern past, her dominance by a stern father and a self-absorbed artist-husband, David Knight, and the commitment to David and her daughter Bonnie. The conflicting pressures of love and marriage, on the one hand, and her search for excellence as a ballerina on the other, finally destroy her hopes. But in the process Zelda Fitzgerald wrote movingly and beautifully about the complicated existence of a free feminine spirit in a modern world.

The novel's lush but sometimes baffling style is full of flashes of impressionistic color and sensuous metaphor. At first encounter the imagery seems primarily decorative, but as the novel progresses it begins to form a more organized pattern, providing a haunting, nightmarish framework for the novel's exploration of an increasingly tormented psyche struggling against physical and mental dissolution by concentrating on her art. The settings move from the provincial American South to New York, then on to Paris and the Riviera. Alabama's life is principally explored through a series of parties which grow less innocent and more destructive until she is threatened with spiritual suffocation, a threat complicated by her subordinate existence as wife and mother. She fights back by concentrating on dance and actually achieves a position with a company in Naples, but disaster strikes when her foot becomes permanently injured. Physical exhaustion and dashed hopes lead to a psychological collapse, and the novel's bittersweet ending finds Alabama and David reconciled but faced with recognition of a life compromised by lost opportunity and hope, and Alabama withdraws into musings about the evanescence of form, shape, and meaning in life.

Zelda Fitzgerald was only moderately successful at achieving the note of tragic dignity she presumably sought, and most of her characterization is shadowy. However, there is considerable beauty in her eccentric and intensely original imagery, and strength in the honesty and courage of her relentless and straightforward exploration of Alabama's doomed struggle. *Save Me the Waltz* was a commercial failure, but Fitzgerald came to appreciate its effort, cautioning Perkins not to speak

The Fitzgeralds at the time of Tender Is the Night

of it to Hemingway, who had always disliked Zelda Fitzgerald and who saw all other writers as rivals. Fitzgerald also recognized in the novel a workmanlike and honest use of experience he grudgingly conceded was not entirely his material.

Meanwhile Fitzgerald had also begun to come to literary terms with the meaning of that material. In April 1930 he had attempted a partial redraft of the Melarkey-matricide approach, but his wife's illness and the financially necessary short fiction prevented him from returning to the novel until they returned to the United States. Zelda Fitzgerald's second collapse and his involvement with *Save Me the Waltz* interfered, but by 15 January 1932 he had hit upon a whole new approach, and not long afterward he drew up a detailed outline. In May, after he had settled at La Paix, a house he rented in Maryland to be near his wife's clinic in Baltimore, he began a burst of work which occupied him for the next two years. By September 1933 he had completed a draft, which Perkins accepted on 18 October 1933, for serialization in *Scribner's Magazine* and spring publication. After considering "The Drunkard's Holiday," "Dr. Diver's Holiday," and a simple "Richard Diver" (his favorite), he reluctantly settled on the more evocative *Tender Is the Night* as a title. The novel appeared in book form on 12 April 1934, nine years after the publication of *The Great Gatsby*.

Fitzgerald had abandoned the matricide approach and the abortive Lew and Nicole version of 1929, but much hard work had gone into the earlier materials, and he salvaged themes, ideas, episodes, and passages for the new version. He also drew upon some of his short fiction of the past nine years. In a very real sense *Tender Is the Night* had been written during the entire course of the Fitzgeralds' lives in Europe. The new approach depicts an attractive but ultimately corrupt France, reflecting Fitzgerald's final feelings about the land to which the Fitzgeralds had fled in 1924. Its principal characters, Seth and Dinah Piper, later Dick and Nicole Diver, are avatars of the Kellys as well as the couples he had followed through "The Rough Crossing," "One Trip Abroad," and other stories, but they are also much fuller and more deeply realized, reflecting his observations about the Murphys and about himself and Zelda Fitzgerald, filtered through the lens of his imaginative creativity. The novel essentially tells two different but interrelated stories. One is that of a sensitive and idealistic American, Richard Diver, who comes to Europe to study medicine and psychiatry, and who is slowly ruined by a combination of his own failure of character and the seductive but destructive charm and beauty of life in the expatriate American colonies of Paris and on the Riviera during the middle and late twenties. The seeds of the Melarkey version are buried in it. The second story line more directly reflects significant events in the lives of the Fitzgeralds as well as in recent American and European history. Its central focuses are Dick's career as a psychiatrist; his marriage to the beautiful but disturbed Nicole Warren, daughter of a wealthy Chicago businessman; and the decay of the bright promise of the postwar decade, leading up to the economic (and in Fitzgerald's view, moral) collapse represented by the Stock Market Crash of 1929.

In combining the two stories Fitzgerald developed a plot which traces Dick and Nicole Diver's lives together from their first meeting, when Dick is a young physician with a brilliant future in psychiatric medicine and Nicole is a patient in a Swiss clinic; through their marriage, in which Dick sacrifices his professional aspirations in order to devote himself to making Nicole whole and strong; to the dissolution of that union and Dick's repudiation of both the European life and his career, to disappear into the obscurity of small-town practice in upstate New York.

Thematically the novel also has a dual identity. On the level of the characters' lives, it explores a theme sufficiently similar to that of *Save Me the*

Waltz to demonstrate that Fitzgerald had reason to worry that Zelda was using up his material. It is an almost clinical examination of emotional and marital disorder and of the price a craftsman—be he novelist or physician—might pay in terms of professional achievement if he is not strong or ruthless enough to protect his career. To do so, one must resist the attractions and demands of glamorous life, self-indulgence, and—most sadly—romantic love. *Tender Is the Night* is a romantic novel in several senses, not the least of which is its moving and tragic love story. Dick undergoes progressive moral and emotional deterioration, having reduced his idealism to the smaller scale of involvement in curing Nicole from childhood sexual trauma. He creates a tasteful, beautiful, but essentially hollow world for them in a France full of details drawn from the experiences of the Fitzgeralds and the Murphys. He succeeds in making Nicole whole and strong, removing her from obsessive dependence on the strength and charm of his personality and character, but only through irreparable damage to those attributes. Worse, the Divers find that their relationship turned on Nicole's psychological dependence. With subtle but devastating irony, Fitzgerald permits Nicole's recovery only at the cost of the Divers' marriage, which dissolves in a liaison between the now strong and self-sufficient Nicole and the equally tough Tommy Barban. Dick has achieved the goal he chose at the beginning of their relationship, but in the process he has used himself up. His steady decline is crossed by the rising path of Nicole's recovery of the hard self-sufficiency to which she was born as a Warren.

Unlike *Save Me the Waltz*, however, the story of Dick's deterioration is not one of pathetic victimization. Fitzgerald is careful to ensure that Dick is responsible for his own fate—he chooses it, and the wreckage of his life is at least as much his own doing as it is that of Nicole's. The Dick Diver who delivers a priestlike benediction to the Mediterranean before disappearing into the novel's dying-fall conclusion is a truly tragic figure, not simply a victim of others' self-absorption and the blows of fate. The novel carefully follows his decay through a series of more and more sordid debaucheries, involving drunkenness, fistfights, and adultery, all of which mitigate the view that Nicole is merely a heartless and destructive user.

To prevent this rake's progression from undermining reader sympathy, Fitzgerald developed a sophisticated and effective narrative perspective, related in part to the observer-narrator structure of *The Great Gatsby*. The novel is not developed in straight chronology. Early establishment of Dick's admirable capacity for selflessness, his great personal charm, is crucial, both so that one can watch him devour himself in the pursuit of his own and others' happiness, and so that he can be perceived as genuinely sympathetic. Therefore, Fitzgerald introduces the Divers at the height of their glamorous marriage, on the Riviera during the summer of 1925, and then goes back to the beginning of their relationship in 1917, brings the narrative back up to 1925, and follows the decline of their relationship until 1929. Thus the novel moves both backward and forward from a central high point. Furthermore, though the point of view is always third person, the Divers are first seen from the perspective of an uncritical, admiring outsider: Rosemary Hoyt, a very young Hollywood actress traveling with her mother. She falls in love with Dick but eventually outgrows him. Rosemary's initial roseate view of the Divers, especially Dick, subtly colors and softens the novel's harshness and corruption.

The structure of subtle revelation also leads the reader to an awareness that this examination of personal failure is developed within and intricately linked with a second, much broader theme: the decay of American—perhaps occidental—idealism, innocence, and moral value in the decade following World War I. Dick, Nicole, Rosemary, and Tommy are never merely symbolic figures: Fitzgerald knew that a novel's first responsibility is to create plausible, complex individuals. Nevertheless, their lives become intentional reflections of the loss of value, the materialism, the preoccupation with sensation and self-gratification, which lay close beneath the surface of wealth, glamor, and power of the postwar decade. If it is a theme Fitzgerald had already explored, it is nonetheless treated with fresh dramatic power and the sad wisdom of a maturity the author had gained at considerable personal expense. *Tender Is the Night* is, in one sense, a tragic fulfillment of a prophecy sounded in *The Great Gatsby*: the dark decline and final demise of American innocence. Fitzgerald took pains to make the parallels between the Divers' story and the events of its setting plain and integral. He peopled the novel with minor characters who seem at first colorful and glamorous, but are revealed as corrupt, perverse, decadent—from the homosexual Campion to the self-destructive Abe North. The festive atmosphere of the opening grows successively cloying and decaying as the various parties, dinners, and sorties to night spots merge into one nightmarish excess. In the end Dick's blessing of the beach is not so much a gesture of personal resignation as a fitting ritual for the irrecoverably lost promise of American innocence. His farewell at his father's graveside—"Good-by, my father—good-by, all my fathers"—is certainly a recognition that more than family history has become the dead past.

Beginning with *Our Type* in 1925, the work that finally became *Tender Is the Night* had encompassed some 3500 pages of manuscript and typescript and various stages of printer's proof; it had gone through seventeen distinct stages of drafts and represented three different versions of the novel. The original matricidal youth had somehow grown into aspects of both Rosemary Hoyt and Dick Diver, and the theme of destructive dissipation had taken on tragic implications. In the process the novel had become not only the principal professional activity of F. Scott Fitzgerald's European sojourns—and thus their primary literary legacy—but also the repository for and reflection of most of the experiences, events, and friendships of that period.

Also, *Tender Is the Night* embodies three major qualities of Fitzgerald's talent. First, his haunting, evocative style, so much appreciated by Gertrude Stein, makes even its most violent and perverse episodes aesthetically palatable. Second, perhaps more than any other of his novels, it represents his capacity for realizing in his own life and experience an identification with substantive events of his time, and for transposing them into art. Third, and most importantly, it represents his essential nature as a moralist. The quality of objective moral judgment thematically incorporated into the book is the product of what critics term his "double vision"— the capacity to step outside of and assess the very events and experiences with which he feels so strongly identified. Hence one essential and lasting quality of Fitzgerald's work is his ability to treat his subject matter both lovingly and critically so that his readers are involved with and receptive to the people and events and can form a larger judgmental vision of the characters and the culture and times they represent. That quality is more fully present in *Tender Is the Night* than in any other of Fitzgerald's works, even *The Great Gatsby*.

Because of the adverse conditions under which it was completed, *Tender Is the Night* does not have the tautness, control, and balanced structure of *The Great Gatsby*. Its complex chronology and many-fibered plot deserved more careful revision than they received. Consequently the novel had a disappointing reception. Few reviewers treated it unfavorably, but there was confusion over its chronology and some feeling that as a novel about the rich it was outdated in the Depression of the thirties. A criticism that hurt Fitzgerald more was that Diver's deterioration was not clearly motivated. Only 13,000 copies were sold during the next two years, but many other readers must have seen the novel as serialized in *Scribner's*. The reasons for its relative lack of success are uncertain, although it should be remembered that, except for *This Side of Paradise*, Fitzgerald's novels had never sold well. Fitzgerald came to believe the chronology was the problem and even worked out a straightforward narrative plan which was later adopted in Malcolm Cowley's revised edition (1951), but most readers agree that his original version is the better one.

At any rate the novel's seeming failure, taking with it so much life, energy, and effort, greatly discouraged Fitzgerald. The rest of his life was a painful struggle with financial problems, Zelda Fitzgerald's illness, and his own alcoholism. A few nonfiction pieces, such as Zelda Fitzgerald's " 'Show Mr. and Mrs. F. to Number—' " and "Auction—Model 1934," describe elements of their nomadic lives. In late 1934 and 1935 Fitzgerald wrote a series of slight historical adventure stories about a medieval French nobleman whose character reflected aspects of the personality of Ernest Hemingway. For the most part, however, he was content to forget France after he had dealt with his European experiences in *Tender Is the Night*. His final novel, *The Last Tycoon* (1941), incomplete at the time of his death, is set in Hollywood, where he had gone to work as a screenwriter in 1937. Ultimately France was more than anything a place through which the Fitzgeralds passed, a background against which to measure the value and worth of Americans and America.

Letters:

The Letters of F. Scott Fitzgerald, ed. Andrew Turnbull (New York: Scribners, 1963; London: Bodley Head, 1964);

Dear Scott/Dear Max The Fitzgerald-Perkins Correspondence, ed. John Kuehl and Jackson R. Bryer (New York: Scribners, 1971; London: Cassell, 1973);

As Ever Scott Fitz—Letters Between F. Scott Fitzgerald and His Literary Agent Harold Ober, ed. Matthew J. Bruccoli and Jennifer Atkinson (New York & Philadelphia: Lippincott, 1972; London: Woburn Press, 1973).

F. Scott Fitzgerald

Bibliographies:

Matthew J. Bruccoli, *F. Scott Fitzgerald A Descriptive Bibliography* (Pittsburgh: University of Pittsburgh Press, 1972; supplement, Pittsburgh: University of Pittsburgh Press, forthcoming 1980);

Jackson R. Bryer, *The Critical Reception of F. Scott Fitzgerald A Bibliographical Study* (Hamden, Conn.: Archon Books, 1967).

Biographies:

Matthew J. Bruccoli, *Scott and Ernest The Authority of Failure and the Authority of Success* (New York: Random House, 1978);

Bruccoli, Scottie Fitzgerald Smith, and Joan P. Kerr, eds., *The Romantic Egoists* (New York: Scribners, 1974);

Nancy Milford, *Zelda A Biography* (New York: Harper & Row, 1970);

Arthur Mizener, *The Far Side of Paradise A Biography of F. Scott Fitzgerald*, revised edition (Boston: Houghton Mifflin, 1965);

Andrew Turnbull, *Scott Fitzgerald* (New York: Scribners, 1962).

References:

Sylvia Beach, *Shakespeare and Company* (New York: Harcourt, Brace, 1959), pp. 116-119;

Matthew J. Bruccoli, *The Composition of* Tender Is the Night *A Study of the Manuscripts* (Pittsburgh: University of Pittsburgh Press, 1963);

Bruccoli, ed., *Fitzgerald Newsletter* (Washington, D.C.: NCR Microcard Editions, 1969);

Jackson R. Bryer, ed., *F. Scott Fitzgerald The Critical Reception* (New York: Burt Franklin, 1978);

Morley Callaghan, *That Summer in Paris* (New York: Coward-McCann, 1963), pp. 149-255;

Andre Chamson, "The Paris Conference: Remarks by Andre Chamson," *Fitzgerald/Hemingway Annual 1973* (Washington, D.C.: Microcard Editions Books, 1974), pp. 69-76;

Malcolm Cowley, *A Second Flowering Works and Days of the Lost Generation* (New York: Viking, 1973), pp. 19-47;

Kenneth Eble, *F. Scott Fitzgerald*, revised edition (Boston: Twayne, 1977);

Fitzgerald/Hemingway Annual 1969-;

William Goldhurst, *F. Scott Fitzgerald and His Contemporaries* (Cleveland & New York: World, 1963);

Ernest Hemingway, *A Moveable Feast* (New York: Scribners, 1964), pp. 147-186;

John A. Higgins, *F. Scott Fitzgerald A Study of the Stories* (New York: St. John's University Press, 1971);

Andre Le Vot, "Fitzgerald in Paris," *Fitzgerald/Hemingway Annual 1973*, pp. 49-68;

James E. Miller, *F. Scott Fitzgerald His Art and His Technique*, revised edition (New York: New York University Press, 1964);

Sergio Perosa, *The Art of F. Scott Fitzgerald*, trans. Perosa and Charles Matz (Ann Arbor: University of Michigan Press, 1965);

Henry Dan Piper, *F. Scott Fitzgerald A Critical Portrait* (New York: Holt, Rinehart & Winston, 1965);

Robert Sklar, *F. Scott Fitzgerald The Last Laocoon* (New York: Oxford University Press, 1967);

Calvin Tomkins, *Living Well is the Best Revenge* (New York: Viking, 1971).

Papers:

Fitzgerald papers are in the Firestone Library at Princeton University.

Janet Flanner

Karen L. Rood
Columbia, South Carolina

BIRTH: Indianapolis, Indiana, 13 March 1892, to Mary-Ellen Hockett and William Francis Flanner.

EDUCATION: University of Chicago, 1912-1914.

MARRIAGE: 1920, divorced.

AWARDS: Legion d'Honneur, member of the National Institute of Arts and Letters, National Book Award for *Paris Journal 1944-1965*, 1966.

DEATH: New York, New York, 7 November 1978.

BOOKS: *The Cubical City* (New York & London: Putnam's, 1926; reprinted, Carbondale & Edwardsville: Southern Illinois University Press, 1974—adds an afterword by Flanner);
An American in Paris, Profile of an Interlude Between Two Wars (New York: Simon & Schuster, 1940; London: Hamilton, 1940);
Petain The Old Man of France (New York: Simon & Schuster, 1944);
Men and Monuments (New York: Harper, 1957; London: Hamilton, 1957);
Paris Journal 1944-1965, ed. William Shawn (New York: Atheneum, 1965; London: Gollancz, 1966);
Paris Journal Volume II 1965-1971, ed. William Shawn (New York: Atheneum, 1971);
Paris Was Yesterday 1925-1939, ed. Irving Drutman (New York: Viking, 1972; London: Angus & Robertson, 1973);
London Was Yesterday 1934-1939, ed. Irving Drutman (New York: Studio Book / Viking, 1975; London: Joseph, 1975).

Janet Flanner's fortnightly "Letter from Paris," which appeared in the *New Yorker* from 10 October 1925 to 29 September 1975, provides a comprehensive picture of life in the city that drew so many young Americans to it during the twenties and thirties. Her more than seven hundred columns cover not only cultural events and trends in modern literature but fashion, sporting events, nightlife, fascinating trivia, bizarre crimes, and the activities of history-making individuals. Her many *New Yorker* profiles display a similar range. From major cultural figures to politicians to French couturiers to socialites and royalty, she applied her acute powers of observation and her incisive style to an analysis of culture in its broadest sense. Once an aspiring novelist herself and a friend to most of the major American writers, editors, and publishers in Paris during the twenties and thirties, her reports are notable for her early recognition of literary excellence in the work of her American and French contemporaries. As her *New Yorker* obituary points out, "Her estimates of people and events, her perceptions and illuminations, were rarely embarrassed by time. . . . She caught history as it raced by and before others knew that it was history."

The daughters of a prosperous Indianapolis businessman, Flanner and her two sisters gained an interest in the arts from their mother, an Indiana Quaker who, Flanner says, "had, oddly enough, barnstormed one season as Little Eva in a post-Civil War Tom show" and who continued to be involved in little theatre groups. Flanner's older sister, Maria Flanner, became a musician and composer while their younger sister, Hildegard, is a poet.

Flanner attended public schools in Indianapolis until the sixth grade, when her father enrolled her in a new private school, Tudor Hall, which had just opened in that city. At Tudor Hall she developed a love for diagramming sentences. As she wrote in her afterword to the 1974 reprint of her novel, *The Cubical City* (1926): "Diagrammed sentences looked like beautiful architectural drawings of horizontal, vertical, and angled lines on which the sentences' words roosted like birds perched on various lengths of wire." Her realization that the diagrammed sentence shows "the relations of all its words in a linear system of visible grammatical logic," had a lasting influence on her writing style. Her balanced, systematically constructed sentences, combined with her vivid, visual metaphors, later earned the admiration of the *New Yorker's* founder and editor, Harold Ross, who was not only a strict grammarian but a lover of unusual words.

After her graduation from Tudor Hall, Flanner and her family spent a year in Germany, where Maria Flanner studied music. On their return to the United States in 1912 Flanner entered the University of Chicago, where she studied under Robert Morss Lovett, who was later an editor for the *New Republic*. In *Current Biography* for 1943, Flanner is quoted as calling Lovett "the only man in western colleges who actually taught writing. . . ." Other influences at that time were "men whom I did not know . . . Henry James and Walter Pater. And Kipling." After two years at the University of Chicago, she "was requested to leave Green Hall Dormitory as 'a rebellious influence.' "

Flanner returned to Indianapolis, and in 1916-1917 she became "the first cinema critic ever invented" for the *Indianapolis Star*. While in Indianapolis she also made speeches favoring women's suffrage. Then her interest in crime, which proved to be lifelong, led her to take a job at a girls' reformatory in Pennsylvania.

At the end of World War I Flanner moved to New York City, where she tried "unsuccessfully . . . to learn to be the writer I had for twenty-five years already wished to be. . . ." An early attempt, a conventional short story about a young boy's first experience with girls and long pants, which was published in the October 1920 issue of *Century* magazine, displays none of the characteristics of her later style. Among Flanner's friends during this period were Alexander Woollcott, artist Neysa McMein, Harold Ross, his future wife Jane Grant, and journalist Solita Solano. With Grant, Flanner helped to found the Lucy Stone League, an early feminist organization, and in 1920 she married an Indianapolis banker whose name she never took for her own nor disclosed publicly. She and her husband were divorced in 1922, but earlier, in 1921, she and Solano had left on a tour of Greece, Crete, Turkey, and Vienna, finally arriving in Paris, where they settled in 1922, both intending to devote their time to writing.

The suicide of Flanner's father when she was in her late twenties had left her with a small income that enabled her to live in the relatively inexpensive Hotel Saint-Germaine-des-Pres in the rue Bonaparte on the Left Bank, the section of Paris favored by young Americans who were "richer·than most in creative ambition and rather modest in purse." As she explains in her 1972 *New Yorker* article "That was Paris," later expanded as the introduction for *Paris Was Yesterday* (1972), her hotel was near the Place Saint-Germaine-des-Pres with its cafe, Les Deux Magots, a favorite gathering place of Left Bank Americans, and "Though unacquainted with each other, as compatriots we soon discovered our chance similarity. We were a literary lot."

In her preface to *An American in Paris* (1940) Flanner describes the European political situation that allowed her generation to devote their time to literary pursuits: "In 1920 France began invisibly to recover from the habit of remembered hostilities. In 1921 the surface of French life suddenly began to look normal, that is to say France began reliving as if peace were natural, indigenous, and permanent to European man. This notion of existence lasted until the summer of 1938 or just long enough to produce a new generation old enough to bear arms, in the autumn of 1939, in proof of the falsehood." Although Flanner, like most of her friends, was aware of and interested in current political events and movements, she suggests that during the twenties, at least, "the names which most moved the intelligent Parisian mind and eye read today not like part of an important hidden chapter of European political history, but like a mere open esthetic footnote, recalling the cultivated readers' attention to four great artists named Picasso, Stravinsky, Proust, and James Joyce."

The young Americans came to a city that was already an international cultural center, and as Flanner points out,

> Whether these traveling Americans stayed for years or for a fortnight in France, it was a period of peculiar expatriation for as long as it lasted. Those for whom it lasted longest were, oddly, men who were shortly to become our most American writers and who, with their special analytical sentience knew what they needed—something foreign. Gertrude Stein had long since preceded them, but Ernest Hemingway, John Dos Passos, Scott Fitzgerald, E. E. Cummings, Stephen Vincent Benet, Archibald MacLeish, Louis Bromfield,

among others, did their French period like a form of international service for young men of letters.

Although Flanner was never to join the ranks of the writers she so admired, her fortnightly report of Paris cultural life remains a valuable record of the milieu in which they practiced their craft.

One of Flanner's earliest discoveries in Paris was Sylvia Beach's Shakespeare and Company bookshop, and in her book, *Shakespeare and Company* (1959), Beach remembers Flanner as "one of my earliest American friends." When Flanner arrived in Paris, Beach was in the process of publishing James Joyce's *Ulysses* (1922). Flanner later called it "the most exciting, important, historic single event of the early Paris expatriate literary colony," and she believed that Joyce had never been sufficiently grateful to Beach for her bravery in publishing the controversial novel.

Flanner and Solano also found their way to the salon of Natalie Barney, an American expatriate of an earlier generation and a well-known lesbian. Although others remember Flanner as a regular member of Barney's circle, Flanner told George Wickes in an 8 June 1972 interview, "I never felt that I knew her at all well, really. I rarely saw her alone. I used to breeze in and breeze out." At Barney's Flanner met the French novelist Colette, and in 1929 and 1930 she translated two of Colette's novels into English. Perhaps more important than her acquaintance with either Barney or Colette was Flanner's friendship with another frequenter of Barney's Friday gatherings, Djuna Barnes. As Flanner told Wickes, "Djuna was one of the strongest personalities around Natalie and one of the most devoted, one of the most appreciative." Barnes's devotion to Barney, as well as to a number of other friends, did not deter her from publishing *Ladies Almanack* (1928), a good-natured satire about Barney and her friends. Barney appeared as Dame Musset, and according to Flanner, "I was one of a pair of journalists called Nip and Tuck." (The other may have been Solano.)

In 1972 Flanner called Barnes "the most important woman writer we had in Paris." Barnes once showed Flanner a play she had already shown T. S. Eliot, who had told her "that it contained the most splendid archaic language he had ever had the pleasure of reading, but that, frankly, he couldn't make head or tail of its drama." Flanner also admired the play's language, but she admitted that she "did not understand jot or tittle of what it was saying." Barnes replied scornfully, "I never expected to find that you were as stupid as Tom Eliot."

Flanner thanked her for the compliment.

Gertrude Stein was another early acquaintance. In an October 1969 conversation, quoted in *Charmed Circle* (1974), Flanner told James R. Mellow that she met Stein "not the first minute I arrived in Paris, but shortly thereafter." Mellow says that Flanner "was never to become a great admirer of Gertrude's hermetic style of writing, but she remained loyal in her appreciation of Gertrude's personality and the integrity of her literary ambitions." In Flanner's Paris letters for the *New Yorker*, her references to Stein are more often confined to praise of Stein's vision as an art collector. When Stein moved from the rue de Fleurus to the rue Christine in 1938, Flanner helped her by making an inventory of her paintings.

Even when she wrote the foreword to Stein's *Two: Gertrude Stein and Her Brother and Other Early Portraits [1908-12]* (1951), the first volume of the Yale Edition of the Unpublished Writings of Gertrude Stein, Flanner continued to reserve her own judgments about Stein's writing on the grounds that Stein believed "other people's writings about writing did her more harm than her own writing." Instead Flanner recorded Stein's own conversations about her work as they had been recollected and respoken by Stein's companion, Alice B. Toklas. The result was an informative, admiring essay about Stein's work that never revealed Flanner's own personal opinions.

Another early friendship was with Margaret Anderson, whom Flanner met soon after Anderson's arrival in France early in 1923. Flanner, Anderson, and Stein sometimes had Sunday lunch at the home of a mutual friend in Orgeval, outside Paris. According to Flanner these lunches usually became "small verbal wars," which delighted Anderson. If Flanner was entranced by Anderson's talent for argument, she seems to have been less enthusiastic about the devotion Anderson, her close friend Georgette Leblanc, and Solano shared for the Russo-Greek mystic George Gurdjieff, who ran a retreat in a chateau at Fontainebleau-Avon. Flanner's friendship with Anderson and Leblanc endured despite their occasional differences of opinion, however. Flanner's translation of Leblanc's book about her years as Maurice Maeterlinck's mistress was published in 1932, and, after Anderson's death in 1973, Flanner wrote an admiring profile of her for the *New Yorker*.

Many of Flanner's early friendships became important sources of cultural information when she began writing for the *New Yorker*. One friend, who gave her access to one of the rival Surrealist groups in

Paris, was Nancy Cunard, later the founder of the Hours Press. According to Solano, she and Flanner met Cunard in the autumn of 1923, and they soon "became a fixed triangle, we survived all spring quarrels and the sea changes of forty-two years of modern female fidelity . . . ," ending only with Cunard's death in March 1965. In a memoir of Cunard, Iris Tree remembers Cunard's circle during the early twenties as including Louis Aragon, Andre Breton, Blaise Cendrars, Rene Crevel, Tristan Tzara, Marc Allegret, Ernest Hemingway, and Flanner.

Perhaps Flanner's closest literary friendship was with Hemingway. According to Hemingway biographer Carlos Baker, the two met in 1924, and Hemingway visited her frequently at her rue Bonaparte hotel to talk about writing. Even after he no longer lived in Paris, Hemingway remained friends with Flanner and Solano and visited them whenever he was passing through the city. One of Flanner and Hemingway's discussions may have been about the so-called lost generation. In *The Cubical City* Flanner includes her own ideas about the theme that also informs *The Sun Also Rises*, published in October 1926, the same month as Flanner's novel. At one point the heroine of *The Cubical City*, Delia Poole, decides: "There had always been a void between every generation and its offspring, of course, but certainly it seemed uniquely broad now. Broad enough, for the European war to have come between, killing a few of the younger American generation and setting all the rest free." Later, however, her mother says, "Each generation thinks itself unique. But they're all alike, I believe." Delia's eventual discovery that she is neither as free nor as different as she had thought demonstrates the truth of her mother's words.

Some time later in the twenties F. Scott Fitzgerald also became a visitor to Flanner's hotel. As she recalls in her 1972 memoir, "When Scott was in Paris he had an eccentric friendly habit of coming to my hotel to discuss literature at two o'clock in the morning, either with me or with Margaret Anderson, if she happened to be stopping there at the time." Flanner calls him the "most rarified of any of the young literary figures" in Paris, and says that "he seemed always to be suffering under the strain of his own genius. . . ." She also remembers him as "the only one of my writer friends who ever gave me the mutual identification of my having any literary sensibilities."

Other Americans Flanner mentions in her introduction to *Paris Was Yesterday* include Archibald and Ada MacLeish, John Dos Passos, E. E. Cummings, Glenway Wescott, Monroe Wheeler, Hart Crane, whom she met only briefly, and Kay Boyle, "with her variegated brood of children, who was for a writer a rare domestic center. . . ."

Despite her literary ambitions, Flanner wrote only one novel, *The Cubical City*. As she says in her afterword to the 1974 reprinting of the novel, "Like most authors of a first novel, in mine I fell back upon the people I knew best, my family, as my characters. I recall having noted that Colette always wrote only what she knew about, including the characters in her novels. . . . This left her free to utilize her literary gift for perfecting her style of writing rather than in creating imaginary human beings." Not only do Flanner's mother, father, and grandmother appear in the novel, but her choice of the Philippines as a suitably remote place to send her heroine's lover may be based upon the fact that Solano spent time in the Philippines before becoming a journalist in New York.

Flanner uses her novel as a vehicle to criticize American sexual puritanism, specifically the double standard of sexual conduct for men and women. Delia Poole, a young woman from the Midwest, is a successful designer of stage sets in New York City, and her sense of financial freedom contributes to a feeling of independence in her relationships with men. She is described as glamorous, physical, primitive, and unerringly natural: "For Delia had, set even in the midst of a mechanical civilization, some of that primitive archaic allure marked in ancient females who in small select numbers had received in absèntia, grain, prayers, milk, worship or hyacinth buds placed on credulous rural shrines." As she tells a friend who criticizes her, "I didn't leave home to have lovers. But I left home to be free. And I won't give that up—until I have to. . . . Passion is natural. . . . The world has always had lovers. And yet as near as I can observe, for thousands of years the concentrated aim of society has been to cut down kissing. With that same amount of energy . . . society could have stopped war, established liberty, given everybody a free education, free bathtubs, free music, free pianos and changed the human mind to boot. . . ." At the beginning of the novel Delia, who is the veteran of a number of affairs, discovers herself to be truly in love for the first time. But she fears the loss of freedom that marriage to Paul would bring, especially since he is about to leave for two years of work in the Philippines. Rather than marrying him and going with him, Delia chooses to remain with her job. While he is away, she nearly has an affair with an unprincipled, wealthy playboy, Compton Keith, who wants to sleep with her because he has heard so much about her sex life from other men, but who tells her frankly that he would "never marry a woman if I had been her lover." Delia realizes for the

Sylvia Beach Collection

Janet Flanner

first time that her reputation must have spread all the way to Keith's home state of California, and she realizes that her idealistic belief in her ability to live independently is an illusion: "Many young women in America led their own lives—yet virginity as a theory was apparently still well mixed with the republican civilization of the twentieth century. . . . Yes, a woman's reputation still counted. . . ." She feels "as if she had lost something. Her youth and her belief in herself." When Paul returns from the

Philippines a year ahead of schedule, she agrees to marry him, although she still fears the limits that marriage will place upon her freedom, because she realizes that both their families, and society, expect them to marry.

Two patterns of imagery in *The Cubical City* reinforce the sense that Delia's concept of personal freedom is largely illusory and that society's restrictions run counter to nature and represent a form of entrapment. Delia may be symbolically descended from a long line of nature goddesses, but the flowers which surround her are either from the hothouse, forced unnaturally into bloom before their seasons, or artificial, as those woven into the carpets and tapestries of Delia's studio. Moreover, the style of her modern city life cuts her off from nature in another way. All the important scenes of the novel take place either within the confines of a single room or outside in darkness, and night in the city is never truly natural when city lights obscure the stars and city trees always seem "worn from having stayed up late at night and from being there early each morning." As the novel's title suggests, city dwellings are restrictive. Moreover, they provide no privacy or protection for the individual. Delia believes that she creates her own environment, but she discovers that most of her antiques are fakes just as the stage sets she designs present only an illusion of space and the life she leads gives her a false sense of independence. The sense of stifling enclosure that pervades the novel culminates in Delia's realization, toward the end of the novel, that she has no place to be alone: "Three rooms, kitchen and bath: all modern comforts except that of privacy. Where in the compressed pyramided dwellings of New York did rent-payers go when their hearts were breaking?" A few pages later, having agreed to marry Paul, Delia realizes that her physical confinement is paralleled by her spiritual confinement: "Driven by circumstances and devotion, led by lack of privacy and the exhaustion of suffering, she was closing in on a question that would deprive her of all she wanted except Paul."

Although these patterns of imagery enhance the themes of *The Cubical City*, Flanner's artfully constructed descriptive passages finally overpower the characters. Dialogues are so often broken up by long narrative intrusions that they are singularly undramatic. The reader is told about the characters' personalities; he does not deduce their personalities from their actions. Indeed, the talent for elaborately structured rhetoric that contributes to the excellence of Flanner's nonfiction is the main flaw in her intelligent, strongly argued, and well-constructed novel. *The Cubical City* is full of passages in which the narrator indulges in digressions from the events only to return adroitly to the concerns of the characters. Finally, however, the narrator becomes the only vivid, three-dimensional personality in the novel.

Flanner's novel was widely, if briefly, reviewed. The most positive review came from her former teacher Robert Morss Lovett in the *New Republic* (1 December 1926). Lovett praises Flanner's "sensitiveness to the confused phenomena of modern life, and in her ability to discriminate sharply her impressions," but the characters are "pale sketches," and finally, "The background is Miss Flanner's best character." A brief item in the New Books section of the *Saturday Review of Literature* (27 November 1926) also focuses on the way in which the novel's style obscures the plot, calling Flanner "an obviously talented writer attempting to work out for herself an original and individual stylistic idiom," but adding that "she has not yet solved the problem." Unsigned reviews in the *New York Times Book Review* (31 October 1926) and the *Independent* (25 December 1926) focus on the more sensational aspects of the plot. The *Times* calls Delia Poole a variety of the "new woman" and comments on the "altered relations of hero and heroine in fiction" but concludes that "the 'new woman' is not so different from the old woman." The reviewer for the more conservative *Independent* is offended: "We can stand a certain amount of sex in the novels of this day and generation, can even find it typical and healthy. But when every phrase is clogged with consciousness of sex, when every simile has a sexual connotation, when sexual urgings are attributed to 'primordial instincts' which completely submerge the normal and decent reticences, the reader becomes threatened with spiritual nausea." He admits that the novel is not "purely salacious" but insists that it "betrays a number of unhealthy symptoms in the author." Flanner herself was not entirely pleased with her novel and tended to dismiss it in later years, calling it "a character sketch and not a novel at all." In her 1972 reminiscences she speaks of *The Cubical City* more fondly, however, and remembers that "Virgil Thomson had roundly declared that I should cease being apologetic about my book."

Even before the publication of her novel, Flanner had found what would be the most effective outlet for her gifts as a prose writer. Ever since Jane Grant's summer 1923 visit to Paris, Flanner had written to her occasionally to tell her about Paris theatre and opera. Grant showed some of these letters to her husband Harold Ross, and when she wrote to Flanner in the summer of 1925 to announce Ross's founding of the *New Yorker*, she suggested that Flanner write a fortnightly Paris letter for the new magazine. In her introduction to Grant's *Ross, The New Yorker and Me* (1968) Flanner recalls that she "sent two sample 'Letters from Paris,' which were . . . not good, especially after Ross condensed them into one. . . ." He seems to have put the beginning of the second letter first, for Flanner's very first column, in the 10 October 1925 issue, starts with the comment: "Paris has not chosen to alter much in the last two weeks. . . ." Flanner was surprised to discover that the column had been signed "Genet," a nom de plume chosen for her by Ross because "it seemed like a Frenchification of Janet."

The only instruction Ross ever gave Flanner about her letter was "I don't want to know what *you* think about what goes on in Paris. I want to know what the French think." Flanner seems to have interpreted his directive to mean that while he did not want her to talk about herself, she was free to include her own point of view about the events she reported. In 1972 she remembered that her style, like that of the *New Yorker* itself, took a while to develop, but she "instinctively leaned toward comments with a critical edge, indeed a double edge, if possible. Criticism, to be valid, in my opinion, demanded a certain personal aspect or slant of the writer's mind. . . . All I really knew about what Ross wished me to write, and what I wished for me to write, was that it must be precisely accurate, highly personal, colorful, and ocularly descriptive; and that for sentence style, Gibbon was as good a model as I could bring to mind, he having been the master of antithesis, at once both enriching and economical through his use of opposites."

Along with following her own natural interests and those of her friends, Flanner relied on the eight secular Parisian daily newspapers and the theatrical newspaper, *Comoedia*, for news of events that would interest her readers. Although her later columns tend to concentrate on one or two subjects rather than reporting a number of items, Flanner's first column sets the format for the letters of the twenties and early thirties. In it she reports that "the famous de Goncourt Diary (which, they say, roasts every famous person in France now over seventy years of age) is not going to be printed after all," that Sir Arthur Conan Doyle is lecturing in Paris, that more than ten million people have attended the Exhibition of Decorative Arts in Paris, and that the chic Paris nightclub is now the Florida. She goes on to explain that the "Caveau Caucassian still features Russian grand dukes as waiters and cooks. . . . Some of the waiters and grand dukes have been employed there so long that they are beginning to pick up a little Russian." She also talks about the weather, a recent bank clerks' strike, and the latest styles, concluding that scarfs as the rage are "quite dead," and "Big furs are their successors and I and the animals regret it."

Once she has covered what she thinks people expect to hear from Paris she goes on to talk about the activities of her friends: "Glenway Wescott, author of that excellent 'Apple of the Eye,' has written a ballet called 'Roulette' "; *Ulysses*, published by the bookshop Shakespeare and Company, is in its sixth printing; and Tristan Tzara, "founder of the Dada movement which most people think has something to do with bad taste in modern pictures or furniture, has just married a wealthy Swedish industrial. Or his daughter, rather." She goes on to explain that "Tzara is probably the greatest, most sensitive and original French poet to-day . . . , a great man of small stature and with a monocle." She ends the letter by reporting on the various socially prominent Americans passing through Paris.

Although she never wrote about herself, Flanner often included her literary friends and fellow Americans in the column. Before Djuna Barnes's reputation extended much beyond small literary circles in Paris and New York, she wrote in a humorous aside: "Djuna Barnes the well known author, and the Queen of Spain the well known English mother, have both left town after a short stay; one to finish a novel in Majorca, and the other to visit old family friends, the King and Queen of England, in London" (21 November 1925). Two years later in her letter for the 24 December 1927 issue, she announced the appearance of the first chapter of Barnes's novel *Ryder* (1928) in *transition* and the novel's impending publication in New York.

One of the most memorable cultural events of the twenties for artistically inclined Americans in Paris was the 19 June 1926 premiere of American composer George Antheil's *Ballet Mecanique*. Flanner, who probably met Antheil through their mutual friend Sylvia Beach, seems to have heard at least part of Antheil's composition earlier, and she provided advance publicity for the *Ballet*, originally scored for eight pianos, a player piano, and assorted percussion, in her letter for 24 October 1925:

> It is really very wonderful. It sounds like three people: one pounding on an old boiler, one grinding a model 1890 coffee grinder, and one blowing the usual seven o'clock factory whistle and ringing the bell that starts the New York Fire department going in the morning. It's good but awful.

The central cultural event of the twenties for Flanner, however, would always remain Sylvia Beach's publication of *Ulysses* in 1922, and she not only praised the novel in her Paris letters but supported Beach's efforts on its behalf. Flanner's frequent mentions of *Ulysses* constituted a subtle defense of the novel to an audience in the United States, where it was banned as obscene. In 1927 Beach was faced with a major legal battle when Samuel Roth, without any royalty agreement with Joyce or Beach, began to serialize *Ulysses* in his New York magazine, the *Two Worlds Quarterly*. In her 19 March 1927 letter Flanner joins the "protest against Samuel Roth's pirating of [Beach's] unprotected bookrights in America." She announces a petition already signed by "over two hundred of the most important intellectual names of Europe, England and sometimes the United States," and she asserts: "One day this protest, with annexed signatures, will be a bibliophiles' item. Today it is a grand gesture to Joyce and Miss Beach and to the writing craft's spirited solidarity."

Another important literary event recorded in Flanner's column was the October 1926 publication of Hemingway's *The Sun Also Rises*, whose characters are based upon some of Hemingway's Paris acquaintances. In her 18 December 1926 letter Flanner gives the novel ample coverage, naming some characters and hinting at the identity of others:

> The titled British declassee and her Scottish friend, the American *Frances* and her unlucky *Robert Cohn* with his art magazine which like a new broom, was to sweep esthetics clean— all these personages are, it is maintained, to be seen just where Hemingway so often placed them at the Select. Not being amorously identified with the tale, it should be safe to say that Donald Ogden Stewart is taken to be the Stuffed-bird-loving *Bill.* Under the flimsy disguise of *Braddocks,* certainly Ford Madox Ford is visible as the Briton who gives as Mr. Ford does, dancing parties in the *bal musette* behind the Pantheon.

As Flanner hints, Harold Loeb, formerly the editor of the little magazine *Broom,* is the model for Robert Cohn, and his mistress, writer and journalist Kathleen (Kitty) Cannell, is the model for Frances. The titled British woman and her Scottish fiance, called Lady Brett Ashley and Mike Campbell in the novel, are based upon two well-known denizens of Left Bank bars, Lady Duff Twysden and Pat Guthrie. Bill Gorton is usually considered to combine characteristics of Stewart and Hemingway's friend Bill Smith.

Flanner predicts the literary impact of *The Autobiography of Alice B. Toklas* (1933) when she announces the book's forthcoming New York publication in her letter for the 4 March 1933 issue,

calling it "a complete memoir of that exciting period when Cubism was being invented in paint and a new manner of writing being patented in words. . . ." She goes on to say that the only quarrels about the book's merits are "about which of its hundreds of merits is most meritorious: the Picasso part, or the analyses of Hemingway, the long, marvelous description of the cranky old picture merchant Vollard, the piece about William James in Harvard, or about Johns Hopkins." She also hints at the deceptive nature of the title: "the book is written simply—not in the manner of *The Making of Americans,* but, rather, completely in Miss St—that is to say, Miss Toklas's first, or easiest, literary manner." In her 15 February 1936 letter Flanner discusses Stein's forthcoming *Geography and Plays* by using the same method she employs later in her preface to *Two: Gertrude Stein and Her Brother*: she quotes Stein's own explanation of the book's subject.

Flanner was interested in the many expatriate publishers who published English-language books in France during the twenties and thirties, and she mentions them often in her column. Aside from her frequent references to Beach and *Ulysses,* Flanner probably gave the most space to Nancy Cunard's Hours Press, which always received high praise, but not all expatriate publications received Flanner's approval. One of her earliest mentions of an American book published in Paris is her announcement of Ralph Cheever Dunning's *Rococo* (1926), published by Edward Titus's Black Manikin Press, an occasion which affords her the opportunity to pan with a pun: "It still takes sixteen Dunnings to make a Pound" (6 November 1926). She is more impressed by, but not entirely uncritical of, Robert M. Coates's *The Eater of Darkness* (1926), published in Paris by Robert McAlmon's Contact Publishing Company. She admires Coates's stylistic parodies of successful modern writers even though she thinks they are sometimes only imitations (20 November 1926).

Flanner liked the appearance of *The Eater of Darkness,* whose "unorthodox typography . . . was set up quite correctly by orthodox French printers in Dijon," but she was not impressed by the Black Sun Press's edition of Lewis Carroll's *Alice in Wonderland* (1930), illustrated by Marie Laurencin: "the Rabbit wears a little pink Marie Laurencin hat and looks like a French poodle . . . ," while both Alice and the Red Queen look like Laurencin herself (21 February 1931). Her letters also mention the publications of Carrefour, run by Walter Lowenfels and Michael Fraenkel, whose theory of anonymous publication she praises in her letter for the 7 March

1931 issue. In her 3 December 1932 letter she devotes a great deal of space to Glenway Wescott's *Calendar of Saints for Unbelievers* (1932), published by Harrison of Paris, and the *Typographical Commonplace-Book* (1932) by Monroe Wheeler, one of the firm's partners.

Flanner was also an avid reader of Paris little magazines, many of them edited by her friends and containing contributions by other friends. In her 5 February 1927 letter she announces the plans for *transition*, a "new American review" to be edited by Elliot Paul and Eugene Jolas, literary editors for the Paris *Tribune*: "Outside of *Andy Gump*, Paul and Jolas are the most intelligent critical figures to be found in any of the three American dailies printing here" (5 February 1927). She is far less impressed by the second issue of Erskine Gwynne's *Boulevardier*, which "unfortunately resembles the first" (30 April 1927). In her 27 July 1929 letter Flanner mentions the final, May 1929 issue of the *Little Review*, edited by Margaret Anderson and Jane Heap, saying that "like any other mythical American, this Middle-Western radical finally went to heaven in Paris. . . ." Although she does not mention it in her letter, Flanner contributed to the final issue in answer to a questionnaire that Anderson had sent to a number of writers in order to construct a "non-literary" issue. Flanner's most revealing response was her answer to the first question, "What should you most like to do, to know, to be? (In case you are not satisfied)." Flanner's answer tells more about her tastes and personality than any of her letters for the *New Yorker*:

> 1. *a*) I should like to have been a writer—to have been Sterne or any of the Brontes. I should like to be a writer—to be even Hemingway since he is better at being Hemingway than any of the other Hemingways. *b*) I should like to know everything. Once it was simply God, now it has become departmental. It is therefore still beyond one brain. *c*) I should like to be a traveller proper to this century: a knapsack and diary is no longer enough. A voyage suitable to the 20th century is like no exploration into visible space ever taken before, must be conducted with elaborate knowledge, scientific data, vaccinations and most particularly, the superb modern mechanics which only a millionaire can rent.

Despite her ambitions to be a novelist, Flanner was clearly working hard at perfecting her style as a journalistic essayist. Her profiles for the *New Yorker* during the twenties and early thirties are further

proof of the seriousness with which she viewed her craft. Her first profile, which appeared in the *New Yorker* for 1 January 1927, deals with one of the most visible American expatriates in Paris, Isadora Duncan. She praises Duncan's innovative dance techniques, saying, "A decade ago her art, animated by her extraordinary public personality, came as close to founding an esthetic renaissance as American morality would allow. . . ." And she concludes that Duncan's "ideals of human liberty are not unsimilar to those of Plato, to those of Shelley, to those of Lord Byron which led him to die dramatically in Greece. All they gained for Isadora was the loss of her passport and the presence of the constabulary on the stage of the Indianapolis Opera House where the chief of police watched for sedition in the movement of Isadora's knees."

Another early profile is Flanner's article on Edith Wharton (2 March 1929), a tongue-in-cheek portrait of the woman whose "corpuscles were Holland burghers, colonial colonels, and provincial gentry who with the passage of time had become Avenue patricians . . ." of New York City. Flanner, like many of her literary contemporaries, was somewhat unsympathetic to the work of this member of an earlier generation of expatriates. She credits Wharton with documenting the decay of traditional values in American society, but she adds:

> Though the first to utilize the breakup of the American mold, Mrs. Wharton was still the last to understand it; she saw the plot but never the point. Born for ethics, she ignored the senses. Thus even her most famous character, Lily Bart, though a drug fiend did not have her heart in her work.

Flanner acknowledges Wharton's contribution to American letters, however, and attempts to dispel Wharton's reputation for coldness.

The full force of Flanner's caustic humor is reserved for people such as socialite Elsa Maxwell, whom she clearly considers a socially useless individual, saying "The only difference between the plump sociable Elsa of ten and the plump, social Elsa of middle age is the flight of time. Her growth consisted of not changing" (25 November 1933). No matter how seemingly trivial the subject, Flanner brought to bear upon it her own analytic, acerbic point of view, making no secret of her own prejudices. (Her many profiles of French couturiers betray her own taste in clothing.) During the thirties she also wrote profiles of Lily Pons (16 January 1932), Igor Stravinsky (5 January 1935), Queen Mary of England (4-11 May 1935), Adolf Hitler (29

February-14 March 1936), Lady Mendl (15 January 1938), the recently appointed American ambassador to France, William Christian Bullitt (10-17 December 1938), and Pablo Picasso (9 December 1939).

In the spring of 1934 Ross asked Flanner to take on the task of writing the *New Yorker*'s "Letter from London" in addition to the one from Paris, and Flanner began dividing her time between Paris and London. In fact she began writing *New Yorker* letters from wherever she happened to be on the Continent or in the British Isles, including Brussels, Berlin, Salzburg, Bayreuth, Vienna, Glasgow, Switzerland, and Spain. One result of her agreeing to write the "Letter from London" was Ross's assigning her a profile of the Queen Mother, Mary. Flanner never met Queen Mary, but with her own research plus the help of friends, including Louis Bromfield, who knew the queen's son the Duke of Kent, she produced a portrait that won the admiration of members of the Queen's own family.

Flanner's profile of Adolf Hitler, who had become Chancellor of Germany on 30 January 1933, was written in the autumn of 1935. In *An American in Paris* she explains that when she submitted her work, "there were justified editorial doubts as to whether Herr Hitler was worth ten thousand words of space to readers . . . ," and even after the article appeared as a three-part profile in the *New Yorker*, many readers considered him "not to be regarded seriously as a permanent or important European figure." As she explains, "it was still general to consider Hitler as a fool or an abnormal freak at best, a garrulous superenergetic comic pawn of the dour Reichwehr which would soon put him in his place. . . ." The profile was finally published in three parts from 29 February to 14 March 1936. Like most humane, rational people, Flanner underestimates the enormity of Hitler's threat to the Jews. Even though she was repelled by his anti-Semitism and criticized his racist policies in her "Letter from Paris" as early as 1933, she reasons that, while the "Jewish problem Hitler has raised is a vast one in emotional importance, both in and outside of Germany; numerically, from the German point of view, it is a small one. In 1934 there were less than six hundred thousand Jews in all Germany for the twelve million Nazi Party members to accuse of dominating the sixty-five million German Gentiles. . . ." As Flanner herself writes, however, Hitler's "brain is instinctive, not logical," and he "belongs to the dangerous, small class of subliminators from which fanatics are frequently drawn."

Although she continued to write about literary and cultural events, Flanner's letters were more and more often concerned with politics and threats of war. Even while she documented the omens of war, however, she hoped for peace. On 26 August 1939 she cabled in her "Letter from Paris" for the 2 September 1939 issue that despite repeated rumors of general mobilization, "there is today a faint hope for peace. . . ." By 30 September, however, she was cabling her "Letter from France" for the 7 October issue from Bordeaux as she waited to embark for the United States. Her final letter before her departure, sent on 4 October for the 14 October issue, ends with one of Flanner's typical rhetorical understatements: "it is really a commonplace war, since it is simply a fight for liberty. It is only because of its potential size that it may, alas, prove to be civilization's ruin."

An American in Paris, a selection of updated *New Yorker* profiles and a series on French crime that she had written for *Vanity Fair*, was published in the spring of 1940 to general acclaim. *Time* called each sketch "a mosaic of tidbits culled from hundreds of informants, each sleek with refined comedy . . . , a valuable dossier on the very highest life of the past 20 years." The reviewer goes on to say that Flanner's profile of Adolf Hitler is "extraordinarily prescient," but he does not believe that she captures the personalities of Stravinsky and Picasso.

During the war she wrote articles and spoke about France. *The New Yorker Book of War Pieces* (1947) contains three pieces by Flanner, including a fascinating account of an unnamed American woman's escape from Occupied France. Among the profiles she wrote for the *New Yorker* were an article on Thomas Mann (13-20 December 1941), which she had worked on for two years, and a four-part profile of the nominal head of the French Vichy government, Henri Philippe Petain (12 February-4 March 1944), which was published in book form later that year. She also wrote a guide to France for the American invasion forces. (Her chapter on the dangers of venereal disease was considered weak.) But after the book was in print she was told she could not see it because it was top secret.

In 1943 Flanner was quoted in *Current Biography* as saying that she no longer had any ties in the United States and that she planned to return to France as soon as she could. She was true to her word. Paris was liberated in late August 1944, and Flanner returned that autumn. Sylvia Beach considered it appropriate that a *Life* photographer photographed Flanner and Hemingway standing in front of Shakespeare and Company. Flanner's first postliberation "Letter from Paris" appeared in the 23 December 1944 issue of the *New Yorker*, and she continued to write Paris letters until 29 September 1975. Despite occasional mention of, and finally memorials to, old friends such as Sylvia Beach and Gertrude Stein, the names in her postwar letters are more exclusively French than in the twenties and thirties. Paris was no longer an American city.

Men and Monuments, a collection of Flanner's postwar *New Yorker* profiles, appeared in 1957, and her first collection of postwar Paris letters, *Paris Journal 1944-1965* (1965), which won a National Book Award in 1966, was followed by *Paris Journal Volume II 1965-1971* (1971). Excerpts from pre-World War II Paris and London letters were published as *Paris Was Yesterday 1925-1939* and *London Was Yesterday 1934-1939* (1975). In 1975 Flanner returned to the United States, where she made her home in New York City with her friend and literary agent, Natalia Murray, until her death on 7 November 1978.

Other:

Colette, *Cheri*, translated by Flanner (New York: A. & C. Boni, 1929; London: Gollancz, 1930);

Colette and Willy, *Claudine at School*, translated by Flanner (New York: A. & C. Boni, 1930; London: Gollancz, 1930);

Georgette Leblanc, *Souvenirs My Life With Maeterlinck* (New York: Dutton, 1932); republished as *Maeterlinck and I* (London: Methuen, 1932);

The New Yorker Book of War Pieces, includes contributions by Flanner (New York: Reynal & Hitchcock, 1947);

Gertrude Stein, *Two: Gertrude Stein and Her Brother and Other Early Portraits [1908-12]*, foreword by Flanner (New Haven: Yale University Press; London: Geoffrey Cumberlege / Oxford University Press, 1951);

Jane Grant, *Ross, The New Yorker and Me*, introduction by Flanner (New York: Reynal / Morrow, 1968);

Margaret Crosland, *Colette The Difficulty of Loving*, introduction by Flanner (Indianapolis & New York: Bobbs-Merrill, 1973);

Hugh Ford, *Published in Paris American and British Writers, Printers, and Publishers in Paris, 1920-1939*, foreword by Flanner (New York: Macmillan, 1975).

Periodical Publications:

"In Transit and Return," *Century*, 100, new series 78 (October 1920): 801-813;

"Letter from Paris," *New Yorker*, 1 (10 October 1925)-51 (29 September 1975);

"Isadora," [Isadora Duncan], *New Yorker*, 2 (1 January 1927): 17-19;

"The Egotist" [Paul Poiret], *New Yorker*, 3 (29 October 1927): 23-25;

"Dearest Edith" [Edith Wharton], *New Yorker*, 5 (2 March 1929): 26-28;

Answer to Questionnaire, *Little Review*, 12 (May 1929): 32-33;

"Perfume and Politics" [Francois Coty], *New Yorker*, 6 (3 May 1930): 22-25;

"Rue Cambon" [Gabrielle Chanel], *New Yorker*, 7 (14 March 1931): 25-28;

"The French Lily" [Lily Pons], *New Yorker*, 7 (16 January 1932): 20-23;

"Comet" [Elsa Schiaparelli], *New Yorker*, 8 (18 June 1932): 19-23;

"Come as Someone Else" [Elsa Maxwell], *New Yorker*, 9 (25 November 1933): 24-27;

"Those Were the Days" [Worth et Cie], *New Yorker*, 9 (20 January 1934): 17-20;

"Letter from London," *New Yorker*, 10 (16 June 1934)-15 (24 June 1939);

"Russian Firebird" [Igor Stravinsky], *New Yorker*, 10 (5 January 1935): 23-28;

"Her Majesty, the Queen" [Mary, Queen of England], *New Yorker*, 11 (4 May 1935): 20-24; 11 (11 May 1935): 28-32;

"Fuhrer" [Adolf Hitler], *New Yorker*, 12 (29 February 1936): 20-24; 12 (7 March 1936): 27-31; 12 (14 March 1936): 22-26;

"Handsprings Across the Sea" [Lady Mendl (Elsie de Wolfe)], *New Yorker*, 13 (15 January 1938): 25-29;

"Mr. Ambassador" [William Christian Bullitt], *New Yorker*, 14 (10 December 1938): 32-35; 14 (17 December 1938): 22-27;

"One-man Group" [Pablo Picasso], *New Yorker*, 15 (9 December 1939): 28-33;

"Pioneer" [Main Bocher], *New Yorker*, 15 (13 January 1940): 24-28;

"La France et Le Vieux" [Henri Philippe Petain], *New Yorker*, 19 (12 February 1944): 27-40; 20 (19 February 1944): 27-43; 20 (26 February 1944): 28-41; 20 (4 March 1944): 27-41;

"A Life On a Cloud" [Margaret Anderson], *New Yorker*, 50 (3 June 1974): 44-67.

Papers:

Flanner and Solano's papers are at the Library of Congress.

JOHN GOULD FLETCHER
(3 January 1886-10 April 1950)

SELECTED BOOKS: *Irradiations Sand and Spray*
(Boston & New York: Houghton Mifflin, 1915);
Goblins and · Pagodas (Boston & New York:
Houghton Mifflin, 1916);
Preludes and Symphonies (Boston & New York:
Houghton Mifflin, 1922);
Parables (London: Paul, Trench, Trubner, 1925);
Branches of Adam (London: Faber & Gwyer, 1926);
The Black Rock (London: Faber & Gwyer, 1928; New
York: Macmillan, 1928);
XXIV Elegies (Sante Fe, N.M.: Writers' Editions,
1935);
*Life Is My Song The Autobiography of John Gould
Fletcher* (New York & Toronto: Farrar &
Rinehart, 1937);
Selected Poems (New York & Toronto: Farrar &
Rinehart, 1938);
South Star (New York: Macmillan, 1941);
The Burning Mountain (New York: Dutton, 1946);
Arkansas (Chapel Hill: University of North
Carolina Press, 1947; London: Oxford
University Press, 1947).

Alderman Library

Nijinsky's ballet, Stravinsky's music, and the
city of Paris all helped create John Gould Fletcher's
"first period of full poetic inspiration." The *Sacre de
Printemps* (1913) confirmed his determination to
become a modern poet, rebelling against saccharine
prettiness and attempting to fuse painting, poetry,
and music in his work. Born in Little Rock,
Arkansas, Fletcher was the son of a banker and
cotton broker. He was educated privately and at
Harvard (1903-1907), from which he resigned in his
senior year. In 1908, after having inherited a sizeable
income upon the death of his father, he traveled to
Italy and then settled in London, which remained
his home until 1933.

In 1913 Fletcher spent seven weeks in Paris,
enjoying Postimpressionist art, opera, and theatre.
He met Ezra Pound with whom he shared an interest
in the French Symbolists, and Pound persuaded him
to lend financial support to Harriet Weaver's little
magazine the *Egoist*, for which Pound had agreed to
serve as literary editor. Other expatriate friends
included the artists John D. Ferguson and Anne Rice
and the poets Horace Holley and Skipwith Cannell.
Cannell became Fletcher's disciple, abandoning
rhyme and meter for vers libre. Pound later
introduced Fletcher to Amy Lowell, and as foreign
correspondent for *Poetry: A Magazine of Verse*,

Pound sent Fletcher's work to its editor Harriet
Monroe.

Before going to Paris, Fletcher had begun a
series of poems he named "Irradiations." Intoxicated
by Parisian life, he now forged his own style, writing
a poem a day. Attempting to "follow the inner
rhythm of [his] moods," and discarding precedent,
he soon completed the series. To him Stravinsky's
music had revealed that great art is Dionysiac,
ecstatic; "Irradiations" reflects this insight. In 1915,
upon the appearance of his work in the first volume
of Amy Lowell's anthology *Some Imagist Poets*, and
the publication of *Irradiations Sand and Spray*,
Fletcher won acclaim as an Imagist and innovator.
Though he soon left the Imagist movement, his
work is often mistakenly considered only in the
context of that movement.

In 1923 Fletcher returned to Paris, where James
Joyce was the idol of the postwar expatriates.
Though Fletcher had seen Joyce only once, he had
read *Ulysses* (1922) and considered the book as the
manifestation of a breakdown of values following
World War I. Fletcher admired Joyce's courage and
honesty, but he believed that *Ulysses* portrayed
mankind as "merely animal, grovelling in a sty."
Fletcher found the life-force not in Stephen Dedalus,

but instead in the unsavory Leopold Bloom, and therefore he concluded that the novel showed idealism to be a failure. As a counterblast to *Ulysses*, which he believed to be a portrayal of man motivated by lust and greed, Fletcher wrote *Parables* (1925) and *Branches of Adam* (1926), which upheld man's search for God as the theme of all great poetry. Despite this difference in philosophy from Joyce, Fletcher had some influence upon postwar poets, most notably Conrad Aiken and Hart Crane.

In contrast to his frequent appearance in the *Egoist*, T. S. Eliot's *Criterion*, and many American little magazines, Fletcher wrote little for the postwar publications in Europe. In 1922 his poems appeared in two issues of *Broom*, edited by Harold Loeb in Rome, and later in the decade he published one poem in the May 1927 issue of Eugene Jolas's Paris-based *transition*. Another Paris little magazine, *This Quarter*, edited by Edward Titus, published a poem and an article about French painting by Fletcher in 1930.

Though Fletcher returned to Paris again in 1925 and 1930, the experience was disheartening. To him Paris was "a mob of barbarians": no longer a cultural center but "a seething chaos." Perhaps partly in reaction he turned to Agrarianism, writing his "regional" books *XXIV Elegies* (1935), *South Star* (1941), and *The Burning Mountain* (1946), all of which express his love of nature and the primitive, and his despair over a mechanized civilization. Fletcher had suffered a nervous breakdown in 1932, and as Edmund S. de Chasca says an "atmosphere of defeat surrounds his later career," although his 1939 Pulitzer Prize for *Selected Poems* (1938) enhanced his reputation as an established poet. In 1950 he drowned himself in Little Rock, Arkansas.

—*Edna B. Stephens*

Periodical Publications:

"The Death of England," *Broom*, 1 (January 1922): 207;

"In the Gallery of Skulls," *Broom*, 1 (January 1922): 207-208;

"The Secret of Mars," *Broom*, 1 (January 1922): 208-209;

"The New World," *Broom*, 1 (January 1922): 209;

"The Way of Dust," *Broom*, 1 (January 1922): 210;

"Last Wishes," *Broom*, 1 (January 1922): 288;

"To a Starving Man," *Broom*, 2 (April 1922): 1;

"The Ballad of the Last Emperor," *transition*, no. 2 (May 1927): 119-124;

"Marine Eden," *This Quarter*, 3 (July-August-September 1930): 178-180;

"Some Thoughts on French Painting," *This Quarter*, 3 (October-November-December 1930): 356-360.

References:

Stanley K. Coffman, Jr., *Imagism A Chapter For the History of Modern Poetry* (Norman: University of Oklahoma Press, 1951);

Donald Davidson, "In Memory of John Gould Fletcher," *Poetry*, 77 (December 1950): 154-161;

Edmund S. de Chasca, *John Gould Fletcher and Imagism* (Columbia & London: University of Missouri Press, 1978);

Ben Kimpel, "John Gould Fletcher in Retrospect," *Poetry*, 84 (August 1954): 284-296;

Alfred Kreymborg, "A Poet's Story," *New Republic*, 93 (November 1937): 53-54;

William Robert Osbourne, "The Poetry of John Gould Fletcher, A Critical Analysis," Ph.D. dissertation, George Peabody College, 1955;

Charlie May Simon, *Johnswood* (New York: Dutton, 1953);

Edna B. Stephens, *John Gould Fletcher* (New York: Twayne, 1967);

Stephens, "The Oriental Influence in John Gould Fletcher's Poetry," Ph.D. dissertation, University of Arkansas, 1961;

Bernard Zur, "John Gould Fletcher, Poet: Theory and Practice," Ph.D. dissertation, Northwestern University, 1958.

CHARLES HENRI FORD
(10 February 1913-   )

BOOKS: *The Young and Evil,* by Ford and Parker
  Tyler (Paris: Obelisk Press, 1933; New York:
  Arno Press, 1975);
A Pamphlet of Sonnets (Majorca: Caravel Press,
  1936);
The Garden of Disorder (London: Europa Press,
  1938; Norfolk, Conn.: New Directions, 1938);
ABC's (Prairie City, Ill.: James A. Drecker, 1940);
The Overturned Lake (Cincinnati: Little Man Press,
  1941);
Poems for Painters (New York: View Editions, 1945);
The Half-Thoughts, the Distances of Pain (New
  York: Prospero Pamphlet, 1947);
Sleep in a Nest of Flames (Norfolk, Conn.: New
  Directions, 1949);
Spare Parts (New York: Horizon Press, 1966);
Silver Flower Coo (New York: Kulchur Press, 1968);
Flag of Ecstasy Selected Poems, ed. Edward B.
  Germain (Los Angeles: Black Sparrow Press,
  1972);
7 Poems (Kathmandu, Nepal: Bardo Matrix, 1974);
Om Krishna I (Cherry Valley, N.Y.: Cherry Valley
  Editions, 1979).

Charles Henri Ford was born in Brookhaven,
Mississippi, to native Mississippians Charles Lloyd
and Gertrude Cato Ford. He began his literary career
in Columbus, Mississippi, as the founder of *Blues: A
Magazine of New Rhythms,* which he edited with the
assistance of Parker Tyler and Kathleen Tankersley
Young. Although they published only nine issues,
the magazine's contributors included William
Carlos Williams, Ezra Pound, Gertrude Stein, E. E.
Cummings, and Kay Boyle as well as Bravig Imbs,
Edgar Calmer, Harold Salemson, John Herrmann,
and Alfred Kreymborg. Although the magazine was
not well-received in the United States, it was viewed
favorably on the Continent, and the contacts Ford
made through this publication assured his welcome
in the literary communities of Montparnasse and
Saint-Germain-des-Pres when he arrived in Paris in
1931. In *The Autobiography of Alice B. Toklas*
(1933), Gertrude Stein praised both Ford and his
magazine: "Of all the little magazines which as
Gertrude Stein loves to quote, have died to make
verse free, the youngest and freshest was the Blues. Its
editor Charles Henri Ford . . . is as young and fresh as
his Blues and also honest which also is a pleasure."
Ford was in Paris intermittently from 1931 until
1934, during which time he contributed to such
avant-garde magazines as Eugene Jolas's *transition,*

Charles Henri Ford,
carte d'identite photo, Paris, 1939

Samuel Putnam's *New Review,* Harold Salemson's
Tambour—all published in Paris—and *Front,*
printed in The Hague. From 1934 to 1936 he
contributed to and helped to edit *Caravel,* which was
published in Majorca, Spain. Two of the three
poems and the short prose piece that appeared in
transition both before and after his arrival in Paris
suggest Ford's interest in experimentation, and the
prose contribution, "Piece" (June 1930) foreshadows
his first novel, *The Young and Evil* (1933) in both
subject matter and style.
  During his early days in Paris, Ford also
contributed to two anthologies. A poetic prose piece,
"Letter from the Provinces," appeared in *Readies for
Bob Brown's Machine* (1931). Its editor, Bob Brown,
had asked for contributions suited for use with his
Reading Machine, which allowed the reader to move
words, printed on reels of paper, past his eyes by
turning a crank. Brown asked for streamlined
sentences as different from conventional books as
sound motion pictures are from the stage, and Ford
responded by eliminating punctuation and capital

letters. Ford also contributed four previously unpublished poems to *Americans Abroad An Anthology* (1932), edited by Peter Neagoe, the associate editor of the *New Review*.

After about a year in Paris, the young poet spent a short time in Morocco, after becoming intrigued by Paul Bowles's description of that country. While there he lived with Djuna Barnes, for whom he typed the manuscript of her best-known novel, *Nightwood* (1936). Upon his return to Paris later in 1932, Ford met the Russian neoromantic painter Pavel Tchelitchew at Gertrude Stein's. Through him Ford met Jean Cocteau, Max Ernst, and Cecil Beaton. Tchelitchew returned with Ford to the United States in 1934, where they lived together, with occasional trips abroad, for the next eighteen years before moving to Italy for the last five years of the painter's life.

Much of Ford's work during his Paris years testifies to his fascination with words and his eagerness to put words together in new ways. This tendency is especially evident in *The Young and Evil*, his first full-length novel, written in collaboration with his close friend Parker Tyler, who had remained in New York. This work, a narrative about a group of artists living in Greenwich Village, was published in Paris by Obelisk Press in 1933 and was banned in the United States and England. It was not published in the United States until 1975 when Arno Press included the book in its series Homosexuality: Lesbians and Gay Men in Society, History, and Literature. At the time of its first publication it was praised by Gertrude Stein, Djuna Barnes, Kay Boyle, and others, but it was condemned by Waverly Root of the Paris *Tribune* as "patching together incoherently all the well-known [homosexual] tags" and being "very dull dirt." Nevertheless, in its use of the stream-of-consciousness technique, in its intentional repetitive dullness of homosexual slang, and in its games with letters and words, it confirms Ford's interest in experimentation. Of interest also is his defense of Gertrude Stein:

> Theodosia was reading. Julian was lying on his back and heard her voice: Wyndham Lewis says that a page of a servant-girl novel smashed up equals a page of Gertrude Stein.
>
> What Julian said Mr. Lewis means is that he thinks Miss Stein is purely negative, but he has no better word for the behavior of the organism than negative; Miss Stein is writing or walking. In one way these are the same. In neither case is she smashing the pages of a servant-girl novel.

The years between 1935 and 1947 were probably the most productive of Ford's literary career. Possibly stimulated by his correspondence and association with such well-known writers and artists as Gertrude Stein, Edith Sitwell, Jean Cocteau, Cecil Beaton, and E. E. Cummings, he published several volumes of poetry. Some of the poems he wrote during his Paris years, including several sonnets dedicated to Djuna Barnes, reappeared in *A Pamphlet of Sonnets* (1936), illustrated by Tchelitchew. Also in 1936 three short prose pieces appeared in *365 Days*, edited by Kay Boyle, Laurence Vail, and Nina Conarain.

Ford's next volume of poetry, *The Garden of Disorder* (1938), contains an introduction by William Carlos Williams, who comments that the verses "form a single, continuous accompaniment, well put together as to their words, to a life altogether unreal." Herbert Read's review echoes these sentiments: "There are few poets writing today whose work is at once so personal and so prophetic." This book was followed two years later by *ABC's* (1940), a series of quatrains arranged alphabetically in the manner of an old-fashioned primer. In the first issue of Ford's new magazine, *View*, Henry Treece called the poems metaphysical, despite some Surrealistic methods, because they "move me in the same strange way that Donne and Herbert do."

During the late thirties and early forties, Ford contributed poems to a variety of little magazines, including *Life and Letters Today*, *Poetry*, *Tiger's Eye*, *Seven*, *VVV*, and *Furioso*. He also edited *The Mirror of Baudelaire* (1942), a collection of Baudelaire's work that also contains one of Ford's best-known poems, "Ballad for Baudelaire." In 1945 he edited a volume of Surrealistic short stories, *A Night With Jupiter*.

In the early forties he founded and edited the little magazine *View* (1940-1947), which evaluated Surrealist poetry and painting. Single issues were devoted to Max Ernst, Pavel Tchelitchew, and Yves Tanguy. Besides poems and editorials by Ford, *View* published poems by Parker Tyler, William Carlos Williams, E. E. Cummings, and Randall Jarrell; and essays were contributed by Wallace Stevens, Kenneth Burke, and Lionel Abel. Four books of Ford's poems were published during the forties: *The Overturned Lake* (1941); *Poems for Painters* (1945), which combines poems dedicated to Marcel Duchamp, Leonor Fini, Yves Tanguy, Esteban Frances, and Pavel Tchelitchew with sixteen halftone reproductions of the five painters' work; *The Half-Thoughts, the Distances of Pain* (1947), illustrated by Dimitri Petrov; and *Sleep in a Nest of Flames*

(1949), which contains an introduction by Edith Sitwell, whom Ford considered one of his mentors from his Paris days.

For the past quarter of a century Ford has published poetry only occasionally in magazines and anthologies. During the sixties he published two books of collage poems, *Spare Parts* (1966) and *Silver Flower Coo* (1968), and in 1972 he produced and directed an underground art film, *Johnny Minotaur*. He has also had several exhibitions of paintings, lithographs, and photographs, among them "Thirty Images from Italy," which was shown in London (1955) and New York (1975). The exhibition "Having Wonderful Time—Wish You Were Here" (New York, 1976) was a collection of 109 postcards he had received over three decades from such friends as Gertrude Stein, H. D., Joseph Cornell, and Georgia O'Keeffe. Most recently, "The Kathmandu Experience" (New York, 1976) featured artifacts designed by Ford and executed by Nepalese craftsmen.

At the present time Ford is involved in a variety of projects. Most significantly, he is assembling and editing "Blues 10," the fiftieth anniversary issue of *Blues*, which will contain work by some of the original contributors, as well as work by new writers, and an introduction by Kay Boyle. He is also working on a tetralogy of poetry, *Om Krishna*, and has completed the first draft of a novel, "Mississippi."

There is no doubt that Ford was and continues to be an innovator. As editor, first of *Blues* and later of *View*, Ford has promoted and drawn public attention to many American and European avant-garde artists; and he deserves recognition as a versatile, talented artist. During the past fifteen years, Ford has lived in Nepal, Crete, and New York City, where he stays with his sister, the actress Ruth Ford. Though he still owns a studio in Paris, he rarely occupies it.

—*Eva B. Mills and Elizabeth Davidson*

Other:

"Letter from the Provinces," in *Readies for Bob Brown's Machine*, ed. Bob Brown (Cagnes-sur-Mer: Roving Eye Press, 1931), pp. 132-133;

"Displeasure In an Orchard," in *Americans Abroad An Anthology*, ed. Peter Neagoe (The Hague: Servire, 1932), p. 158;

"Color Cold On Your Lips," in *Americans Abroad An Anthology*, pp. 158-159;

"Morning," in *Americans Abroad An Anthology*, pp. 159-160;

"Sonnet," in *Americans Abroad An Anthology*, pp. 160-161;

Kay Boyle, Laurence Vail, and Nina Conarain, eds., *365 Days*, includes three contributions by Ford (London: Cape, 1936; New York: Harcourt, Brace, 1936);

The Mirror of Baudelaire, edited with a contribution by Ford (Norfolk, Conn.: New Directions, 1942);

A Night With Jupiter and Other Fantastic Stories, edited by Ford (New York: View Editions, 1945; London: Dobson, 1947).

Periodical Publications:

"Somewhat Monday," *transition*, no. 18 (November 1929): 108;

"Piece," *transition*, no. 19/20 (June 1930): 307;

"Digressive Announcement for Spring," *transition*, no. 19/20 (June 1930): 362;

"Spring," *transition*, no. 21 (March 1932): 163.

Reference:

Hugh Ford, *Published in Paris American and British Writers, Printers, and Publishers in Paris, 1920-1939* (New York: Macmillan, 1975), pp. 307-309, 320-322, 357-359.

MICHAEL FRAENKEL
(1896-22 May 1957)

BOOKS: *Anonymous: the Need for Anonymity*, by Fraenkel and Walter Lowenfels (Paris: Carrefour, 1930);
Werther's Younger Brother (New York & Paris: Carrefour, 1930);
Death in a Room, Poems 1927-1930 (Paris: Carrefour, 1936);
Bastard Death, The Autobiography of an Idea (Paris & New York: Carrefour, 1936);
Death Is Not Enough, Essays in Active Negation (London: Daniel, 1939);
Land of the Quetzal (Yonkers, N.Y.: Oscar Baradinsky, 1946);
The Day Face and The Night Face (New York: Irving Stettner, 1947).

Michael Fraenkel was born in Kopul, Lithuania, and immigrated with his parents to New York City in 1903 when he was eight years old. Among his relatives was the great Yiddish writer Mendele Mocher Seforim (Solomon Jacob Abramowitsch, 1836-1917). Fraenkel early in life decided to be a writer. After graduation from the City College of New York, he entered the book trade, selling encyclopedias and remaindered books. By 1926 he had attained enough financial security to go to Paris and write. During the next twelve years he spent considerable time in Paris, where his circle of friends included Henry Miller, Walter Lowenfels, Anais Nin, and Alfred Perles.

Although he and Walter Lowenfels met in 1928, they did not become close friends until 1929. By this time Fraenkel had written a draft of *Werther's Younger Brother* (1930), the first formulation of his ideas about death, and Lowenfels had completed *USA with Music* (1930), a play inspired by the killing of several striking miners in Herrin, Illinois. Both men wanted to see their books in print and agreed to form their own publishing company, Carrefour. The venture was financed by Fraenkel, who was rumored to have brought nearly $100,000 to Paris in 1926.

Their first publication, *Anonymous: the Need for Anonymity* (1930), was a joint manifesto that grew out of their discussions about literature and the role of the writer. They believed that economic competition had separated man from the spirituality of the natural world. Anonymous publication would allow the writer to unite his "creative consciousness into the total creative consciousness of the world," to

Michael Fraenkel

become one with all the writers who had ever tried to restore the ties between man and the universe. Anonymous publication could end the domination of commercial publishers who judged writers upon the saleability rather than the quality of their work and who therefore turned artists into businessmen. Freed from seeking after fame, an anonymous writer could be a force for good and social change. Finally they argued that the anonymous author would be immortal because in refusing to pander to his own ego, he is writing for posterity.

The theme of all Fraenkel's books is the spiritual death suffered by Western man. He believed that Western man would become increasingly alienated until he recognized his living death and found, after enduring its reality, a truly humane life beyond. Man should give up his illusion of being spiritually alive. No existing organization, no revolutionary change in society, could obviate the need for a singular, total, personal death to one's self. The destruction of the old man to bring on the new goes back beyond history, but earlier beliefs in rebirth posited a God-figure outside ordinary existence that could provide a new basis for one's being. But death was enough for Fraenkel; he would avail himself only of his loneliness, the tenacity of his intellect, and the certainty of his death.

Fraenkel's first book was *Werther's Younger Brother*, published in 1930 in an edition of 400 copies under the Carrefour imprint. It is a novel of a young man's discovery of his inner death. Fraenkel had developed his concept of death after reading Goethe's *The Sorrows of Young Werther* (1774, 1787) in 1916 as a college freshman. Fraenkel had fallen calamitously in love with his elder brother's sweetheart, and even twenty years later insisted to Anais Nin that this had been the transforming pain of his existence. Fraenkel's experience had coincided with the slaughter of World War I, which no doubt helped fix in his mind the idea that the preeminent experience of the twentieth century was death. Only by spiritual suicide, destruction of one's ego, can one transcend the fear of death and live on as part of an "external pattern." As Fraenkel says in a 22 January 1941 journal entry, published in *The Life of Fraenkel's Death* (1970), the suicide of Werther's younger brother in his book is not like that of Goethe's Werther: "The Werther suicide is an extreme act of the creative will, a last poem. The modern suicide hasn't the guts to shoot himself, so he kills himself inside and carries on otherwise by means of affairs. . . . and many of us have to answer to 'why are we still existent, when, for creative intents and purposes, we are quieter than the daisies and not so pretty?'" Reviewing *Werther's Younger Brother* for the *Nation*, Gerald Sykes called Fraenkel "a tidy dexterous stylist" and said that the book "shows understanding, as though by some age-old influence, of the inner meaning of things. . . ." In general, however, the book was ignored by American critics.

Werther's Younger Brother and Lowenfels's *USA with Music* were both published anonymously in keeping with the authors' manifesto. Their idea attracted the praise and interest of a number of writers, but Carrefour received no manuscripts from these admirers. The practice of anonymity was dropped when in 1932 Lowenfels sued George S. Kaufman and George Gershwin, charging that they had plagiarized the plot of *USA with Music* for their play *Of Thee I Sing*. The similarity between the two plays was not specific enough for Lowenfels to prove his charges. Although he dropped the suit, he had already identified himself as the author of *USA with Music*, and the two partners declared their experiment with anonymity at an end.

In 1931 Henry Miller moved into Fraenkel's apartment at 18, Villa Seurat for about a month. Lowenfels had introduced the two men, and all three writers shared the belief that the West was dead,

though they saw widely divergent paths out of the cemetery. They formed a "school of death" in Paris that endured most of the thirties. In Miller's *Tropic of Cancer* (1934) the character Boris is based upon Fraenkel.

By the end of 1932 Fraenkel had nearly exhausted the money he had brought to Paris. Perceiving an untapped market for books, he went to the Philippines, where he worked at bookselling until 1935, when he returned to Paris claiming to have $50,000, part of which he invested in Carrefour.

In 1936 he published *Death in a Room, Poems 1927-1930*, fifteen poems expressing his death theme poetically. Several of these poems had already appeared in *transition* during 1928 and 1929. His other book of 1936 was *Bastard Death, The Autobiography of an Idea*. Fraenkel addresses the book's introduction to Henry Miller, explaining that his concept of symbolic death is equivalent to the rebirth of a "new self which is dead, dead, of course, in life, which is bastard death, or, if you like, alive in death which is a bastard life."

In 1935 Fraenkel, Miller, and Alfred Perles began a correspondence about death. Miller suggested that they could write a one-thousand-page book that would be the "longest funeral sermon in history." After Perles complained that "death" was too abstract a topic, Miller suggested that they could examine the subject more concretely by discussing Shakespeare's *Hamlet*. Perles dropped out of the exchange of letters after a month, but Fraenkel and Miller corresponded until November 1938. The result of their exchange was *Hamlet*, two volumes of letters published in 1939 and 1941. The significance of Shakespeare's play for Fraenkel is expressed in his 23 July 1936 letter from the second volume:

> I have spoken of Hamlet as a mode of artistic redemption. . . . I do not envisage a new life to arise quite in the way of the Great Flood—by a complete and outright liquidation of all humankind. This is after all only a symbol for a process—even if one man remains, humanity is never completely wiped out. A new life begins where all life begins—as far from the fatal edge as possible. I would like to think that there are already men among us, right in our midst, who have the seed of the new life within them. . . . Inwardly, spiritually, they are quietly making their way back to an earlier beginning, shedding, cutting loose from a past which is death and suicide. This is the direction I counsel the artist to take who would realize and rediscover himself afresh as artist.

168

Fraenkel's first book published by a press other than his own, *Death Is Not Enough, Essays in Active Negation*, appeared in London in 1939. A series of essays on what Fraenkel called various aspects of "the psychic malaise of our time," some were written as early as 1932, but the book is unified by the essays' stress upon the dominance of a universal will. As Fraenkel explained the book later, "From an end in himself, self-sufficient and self-contained, symbol and image of nothing but himself, man is transformed into a means to an end, a tool or instrument in the service of Will; vital, living, meaningful activity is replaced by the volitional furor of activity for activity's sake."

Fraenkel left France in 1939 and published the first volume of *Hamlet* in Puerto Rico that same year. The second volume was published in 1941 from New York. He stayed in Mexico during World War II, keeping a journal that was published in part as *Land of the Quetzal* (1946) and *The Day Face and The Night Face* (1947). Two more excerpts from his journals appeared in the first issue of *Death* (Summer 1946), a literary quarterly dedicated to Fraenkel and edited by Harry Herschkowitz. The same issue also republished Fraenkel and Lowenfels's *Anonymous: the Need for Anonymity*. In 1947 Fraenkel's essay on Henry Miller, "The Genesis of the *Tropic of Cancer*," appeared in *The Happy Rock*, a collection of essays about Miller edited by Bern Porter.

Fraenkel died in 1957. Perhaps the clearest summary of his death philosophy appears in his 22 January 1941 journal entry: "Life is as real as the sense of death is, and the most intense, most vital moments in life are those in which we have come closest to death. . . . I am preoccupied with death not because I am interested in death, really. What I am interested in is life. Death, as you see, is only the red herring." —*Howard McCord*

Other:

Hamlet, by Fraenkel and Henry Miller, vol. 1 (Santurce, Puerto Rico: Carrefour, 1939; enlarged edition, New York: Carrefour, 1943); vol. 2 (New York: Carrefour, 1941); vols. 1 and 2 enlarged again as *The Michael Fraenkel—Henry Miller Correspondence Called Hamlet* (London: Edition du Laurier / Carrefour, 1962);

"The Genesis of the *Tropic of Cancer*," in *The Happy Rock*, ed. Bern Porter (Berkeley, Cal.: Porter, 1945).

Periodical Publications:

"Wind Drift," *transition*, no. 8 (November 1927): 124;

"Masks," *transition*, no. 8 (November 1927): 125;

"Wait A Round Century," *transition*, no. 8 (November 1927): 126-127;

"Later Wonder," *transition*, no. 8 (November 1927): 128;

"To Blanche," *transition*, no. 8 (November 1927): 129;

"Mounting Breath," *transition*, no. 16/17 (June 1929): 133-150.

References:

Hugh Ford, *Published in Paris American and British Writers, Printers, and Publishers in Paris, 1920-1939* (New York: Macmillan, 1975), pp. 290-302;

Walter Lowenfels and Howard McCord, *The Life of Fraenkel's Death A Biographical Inquest* (Pullman: Washington State University Press, 1970).

RALPH JULES FRANTZ
(1 November 1902-   )

Ralph Jules Frantz spent the late twenties and early thirties in Paris on the staff of the European edition of the *Chicago Tribune* (also known as the Paris *Tribune*), holding the position of managing editor from 1 December 1929 until the paper merged with the Paris *Herald* (the European edition of the *New York Herald Tribune*) on 30 November 1934.

Frantz began his newspaper career in 1919 as a reporter, and later sports editor, for the Springfield *Sun* while he was attending Wittenberg College. In 1922 he joined the staff of the *Cleveland Commercial* (later the Cleveland *Times*). Taking a leave of absence in the summer of 1925, Frantz traveled in Britain, Holland, Germany, and Belgium before he arrived in France in November. By December he was working for the Paris *Tribune*.

In an article for the *Lost Generation Journal* Frantz describes the paper's beginning on 4 July 1917 as the Army Edition of the *Chicago Tribune*. *Tribune* publisher Colonel Robert Rutherford McCormick planned the paper to provide the increasing number of American troops in Europe a truer picture of America than he felt the Paris *Herald* was doing. The paper's profits were turned over to the American Expeditionary Forces in January 1919, after which the paper became the "European Edition" and shifted its focus from the dwindling military population to the many new American tourists and expatriates. Frantz writes: "The *Chicatrib* [the paper's cable name] brash, lusty and breezy, appealed to many of these newcomers. Compared to it, the older, well-established *Paris Herald* sometimes seemed stodgy. Furthermore, the *Chicatrib* devoted far more attention to the growing colony of expatriates on the Left Bank than did its rival. The paper became noted for its erudite literary, art and music criticism."

On the staff when Frantz joined the *Tribune* were Eugene Jolas and Elliot Paul, who started *transition* in 1927, at which time Jolas left the paper. Robert Sage, another staff member, soon left to become associate editor of *transition*. In the early thirties, Henry Miller and his friend Alfred Perles were proofreaders for the paper along with columnist Wambly Bald and poet Richard Thoma. When Miller failed to appear at work for ten days with no explanation, Frantz hired a replacement. Later Miller returned and found his job filled. In *Tropic of Cancer* he described the incident somewhat bitterly; but one of Frantz's prized possessions is a copy of Miller's *Aller Retour New York* (1935) inscribed "To Jules Frantz who fired me for being a rotten newspaper man." Frantz had the last word in *Lost Generation Journal* (May 1973): "I still insist I did NOT fire Henry Miller—he just abandoned the job."

One of the most memorable events during Frantz's newspaper career in Paris was Lindbergh's landing at Le Bourget in May 1927. Bernhard Rayner, then managing editor of the Paris *Tribune*, sent Frantz and William L. Shirer to cover the event, saying that he wanted only one story and the reporter who returned first could write it. Shirer found a ride back to Paris and wrote the story; Frantz was not allowed to write even a follow-up. "The Lindbergh story," Frantz comments, "was the most underplayed story in the history of the Paris *Chicatrib*."

When the *Tribune* was bought by the Paris *Herald* in 1934, Frantz joined the New York office of the *Herald Tribune*, where he remained for thirty-one years. A colleague on the Paris paper, O. W. Riegel, paid this tribute to Frantz: "We recognize him for what he was, a fast, reliable, competent editor, unconcerned with politics, fair, without malice.... Jules preferred to stretch his legs under a convivial table with his friends, not grope for the ladder to executive heights." —*Jean W. Ross*

Periodical Publications:

"I Did Not Fire Henry Miller," *Lost Generation Journal*, 1 (May 1973): 6-7;

"I Tell it This Way," *Lost Generation Journal*, 2 (Spring-Summer 1974): 18-19;

"The Chicatrib: 1917-34," *Lost Generation Journal*, 2 (Fall 1974): 2-4, 36;

"Noted Author-Correspondent Waverley Root Is Legendary," *Lost Generation Journal*, 4 (Winter 1976): 16-21.

Other:

"Recollections," in *The Left Bank Revisited Selections from the Paris* Tribune *1917-1934*, ed. Hugh Ford (University Park & London: Pennsylvania State University Press, 1972), pp. 308-316.

References:

O. W. Riegel, "Jules Frantz One Boss Who Never

went Highhat," *Lost Generation Journal*, 2 (Fall 1974): 16-19;
William L. Shirer, *20th Century Journey a Memoir*

of a Life and the Times (The Start 1904-1930) (New York: Simon & Schuster, 1976), pp. 331, 337-338.

KREBS FRIEND
(1895?-1967?)

BOOKS: *The Herdboy* (Paris: Three Mountains Press, 1926);
It Was Wisdom (New York: Margent Press, 1937).

Harold Krebs Friend, who usually went by his middle name, wrote miscellaneous, often humorous, prose, published two volumes of poetry, and for a brief period in 1924-1925, owned the *transatlantic review*, edited by Ford Madox Ford. Friend met Ernest Hemingway at the end of 1920 when they were both on the staff of the *Cooperative Commonwealth*, a Chicago-based magazine published by the Cooperative Society of America, and Hemingway borrowed part of Friend's name for the character Harold Krebs in his short story "Soldier's Home" (1925). Friend, who was shell-shocked in World War I, arrived in Paris in 1924 married to an heiress named Henrietta who was forty years older than he. Hemingway convinced his newly wealthy friend to back Ford Madox Ford's financially troubled *transatlantic review*, and in August 1924, Friend was given the presidency of the magazine. But he and his wife were unable to prevent bankruptcy, and the *transatlantic review* ceased publication in January 1925.

Friend's only two contributions to the *transatlantic review* are both humorous short essays written in the form of letters. The first, in the September 1924 issue, appears in the regular column, "And From the United States." Although Friend and his wife were in Paris, the piece is a satire on life in the United States written in the form of a letter from a farm in Massachusetts reporting on conditions at home: the fifty-year-old cook has bobbed her hair and drinks moonshine; the visiting music critic has given up Massenet for the foxtrot; a young man who works for the *Little Review* and knows all about art has spent his weekend visit collecting snakes; and the writer and his wife are inundated by information about Hindu psychoanalysts, Christian Science, New Thought, and a variety of other religious cults. The second humorous letter, "The French Wild Boar," in the "Communications" section of the November 1924 issue, is the story of a wild boar hunt in the tiny French town of Flammaurons which ends when the intoxicated hunters shoot a crow. Friend had told this story to Hemingway, who used it for his article in the *Toronto Star Weekly* for 3 November 1923. While in Paris, Friend also published a volume of lyrical, free-verse love poems, *The Herdboy* (1926), in an edition of sixty copies. Although the book bears the imprint of William Bird's Three Mountains Press, it was actually printed by Maurice Levy, and its publication may have been subsidized by Friend's wife. The lyrics of his second book, *It Was Wisdom* (1937), are also free verse and deal mainly with love and memories of war.

Except for the information about Friend's brief association with Hemingway and Ford in the early twenties, little is known about his life. During World War II, he was a Seabee assigned to the 26th Naval Construction Battalion in Kodiak, Alaska, where he befriended Fred Bliss of CBS and regaled him with stories about Paris in the twenties. He received an early discharge from the army for reasons of emotional instability. By 1964 he was living in Brookfield Center, Connecticut, and he died during or before 1967. Friend's poems and prose pieces add little to the literature of his period, but his brief ownership of the *transatlantic review* has gained him a place in literary history. Unfortunately, his management of the review may have hastened its demise. —*Bertram D. Sarason*

Periodical Publications:

"And From the United States, Massachusetts: Autumn," *transatlantic review*, 2 (September 1924): 303-304;
"The French Wild Boar," *transatlantic review*, 2 (November 1924): 554-557.

References:

Bernard J. Poli, *Ford Madox Ford and the TRANSATLANTIC REVIEW* (Syracuse:

Syracuse University Press, 1967);

Bertram D. Sarason, "Krebs in Kodiak," *Fitzgerald / Hemingway Annual 1975* (Englewood, Col.: Microcard Editions Books, 1975), pp. 209-215.

VIRGIL GEDDES
(14 May 1897-   )

SELECTED BOOKS: *Forty Poems* (Paris: Editions des meilleurs livres, 1926);

Poems 41 to 70 (Paris: Editions des meilleurs livres, 1926);

The Frog A Play in Five Scenes (Paris: Black Manikin Press, 1926);

Beyond Tragedy Footnotes on the Drama (Seattle: University of Washington Book Store, 1930);

The Earth Between and Behind the Night (New York & Los Angeles: French; London: French Ltd., 1930);

Native Ground, a Cycle of Plays (New York & Los Angeles: French; London: French Ltd., 1932);

Pocahontas and the Elders (Chapel Hill, N.C.: Abernethy, 1933);

The American Theatre What Can Be Done? (Brookfield, Conn.: Brookfield Players, 1933);

Towards Revolution in the Theatre (Brookfield, Conn.: Brookfield Players, 1933);

The Theatre of Dreadful Nights (Brookfield, Conn.: Brookfield Players, 1934);

The Melodramadness of Eugene O'Neill (Brookfield, Conn.: Brookfield Players, 1934);

Left Turn for American Drama (Brookfield, Conn.: Brookfield Players, 1934);

Four Comedies from the Life of George Emery Blum (Brookfield, Conn.: Brookfield Players, 1934);

Country Postmaster (New York: Austin-Phelps, 1952);

The Collected Poems (Orono, Maine: National Poetry Foundation, 1978).

Virgil Geddes in Paris, 1924

Although Virgil Geddes was financial editor of the Paris *Tribune* (the European edition of the *Chicago Tribune*) from 1924 to 1928, he was already a published poet and later became known as a playwright. In Paris he was acquainted with such writers as Ezra Pound, Gertrude Stein, Ernest Hemingway, Horace Gregory, Padraic Colum, and E. E. Cummings. Among his friends on the staff of the *Tribune* were Elliot Paul and Eugene Jolas, the founders of *transition* magazine in 1927, as well as William L. Shirer and James Thurber.

Geddes was born on a farm in Dixon County, Nebraska. Although his formal schooling ended after the eighth grade, he read widely. He served in the United States Navy from 1918 to 1921, first in an officers' training school at Newport, Rhode Island, and then in the Naval Reserve. In the early twenties he held various newspaper and stage jobs in Boston and Chicago. Before going to work for the Paris *Tribune*, Geddes traded on his experience in burlesque to get his first job in Paris. Because he spoke English, he was hired by a French stagehand to assist Josephine Baker backstage at the Folies

Bergere, where, Geddes writes, she "was cavorting, clad only in a string of bananas fastened around her waist. My job was to clasp the bananas from behind her on two hooks before the stage curtain parted for her act out front." In France Geddes met Minna Besser, a dancer who worked with Isadora Duncan. They were married in 1927.

Geddes's own poems had appeared in *Poetry, Modern Review, Voices, Prairie, Caprice, Forum, Art Review,* and other magazines before they were collected in *Forty Poems* (1926) and *Poems 41 to 70* (1926). The first volume contains a preface by Elliot Paul, who provided Geddes a place to write at the Hotel du Caveau de la Terreur. Paul says of Geddes's poetry: "Geddes has many rare qualities, but none of them are acquired. . . . His art does not intrude itself upon the unwilling. Like the old Chinese philosopher, he fishes with a straight hook, so that the fish may remain in the water if they choose. . . . His greatest joy is to escape for a moment from his loneliness, to catch a reflection or response in another's soul which betrays that men are not destined to wander eternally alone." Geddes's sense of solitude is tempered by his hope for communication:

> Ideas exist
> As bleak, conceited hopes within the mind.
> The will to cast themselves
> Upon the outer visage of some form
> Gives way to talk of semblance,
> Or of friends.

Reviewing *Forty Poems* in the Paris *Tribune* for 7 May 1926, Paul Shinkman wrote: "Geddes, one suspects, from no more than a casual survey of his works, is a wanderer, one of those wanderers in the realm of fancy who senses poignantly the tremors of emotional experience, who now smiles faintly at its whirligigs and arabesques, now cries out at the rumblings of its divine tympani." Geddes later contributed several poems to the first issue of *transition* (April 1927) and another poem and three short stories to later issues. The stories, in contrast to the sensuous imagery of the poems, are written in simple, realistic prose. Brief in form, they contain little overt action, but examine the tangle of emotion and motivation in relationships between men and women. In his foreword to the 1978 collected edition of Geddes's poetry, Louis Untermeyer calls him: "Not a conventional or complacent poet. On the contrary, his lines are a continual challenge. Far from pretty, they quiver with problems, bristle with protests, luxuriate in complexities." Untermeyer concludes: "All of this resuscitated collection was

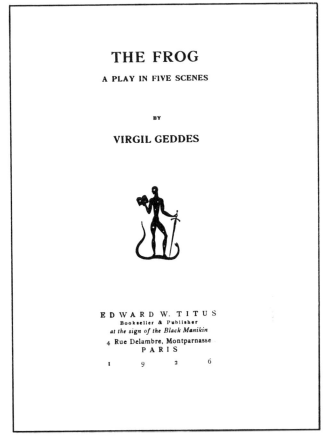

THE FROG

A PLAY IN FIVE SCENES

BY

VIRGIL GEDDES

EDWARD W. TITUS
Bookseller & Publisher
at the sign of the Black Manikin
4 Rue Delambre, Montparnasse
PARIS
1 9 2 6

Title page

written more than half a century ago. It is good to see that time has not silenced what Geddes had to say."

In 1926 Edward Titus's Black Manikin Press published *The Frog A Play in Five Scenes,* Geddes's first play, which was successfully produced in Boston in 1927 by the Boston Stage Society. The characters in *The Frog* are circus clowns. Hugo, a compliant clown, is led by the more persuasive Bob to assume the role of a frog. As the play progresses, Hugo takes on more froglike characteristics until he seems finally to have submerged his human personality completely in his new identity. Hugo and another clown, Glory, die as a result of Bob's manipulation and the jealousy of a fourth clown, Oscar. The play stresses the idea that true humor is based on sadness; in Scene I Oscar says: "Hugo makes them really laugh, deeply, because he makes them weep." Of further interest are the Freudian implications of the play: hypnotic suggestion, the death wish, and the power of the unconscious mind.

Barrett H. Clark, in *An Hour of American Drama,* quotes Geddes on playwriting: "My first effort in playwriting . . . came about in a rather curious manner. While riding on a bus with my friend Eliot [sic] Paul, I happened to say to him, 'There can't be anything to the notion that only people connected with the theater can write good plays.' 'No,' he answered. 'It is just the opposite.' And I immediately began writing my first play, *The Frog*." Subsequent plays made him a controversial dramatist in the United States. *The Earth Between*, Geddes's first play to open in New York, was produced by the Provincetown Players in 1929 and provided the vehicle for Bette Davis's first appearance on the New York stage. It dealt with the theme of incest from a Freudian point of view. *Native Ground* (1932) explored adultery as a theme and thus violated another taboo. Horace Gregory commented on this play: "Here are no experiments in verbal technique but the mature developments of a genuine style." Geddes said of his subject matter: "I took to writing plays because it seemed to me the most direct means of getting down in black and white the feelings and thoughts of . . . people. . . . Through my plays I have endeavored to present phases of American life not heretofore seen on the stage." The content and starkness of Geddes's plays continued to provoke controversy.

In 1932 Geddes founded The Brookfield Players in Brookfield, Connecticut, one of the earliest summer theatres. From 1935 to 1937 he was managing producer of Unit A of the New York City branch of the Federal Theatre. Also the author of several critical books on theatre, Geddes was an objective defender of Eugene O'Neill's work in such books as *Beyond Tragedy Footnotes on the Drama* (1930), *The American Theatre What Can Be Done?* (1933), and *The Melodramadness of Eugene O'Neill* (1934).

From 1941 until 1960 Geddes worked as postmaster of Brookfield. He recorded some of his experiences on the job in *Country Postmaster* (1952). Since 1964 the Geddeses have lived at Swans Island, Maine, where he continues to write.

—*C. F. Terrell and Jean W. Ross*

Periodical Publications:

"Ezra Pound Today," *Poetry*, 21 (November 1922): 95-100;

"To All the Men Under Tall Silk Hats; To the Women Under Soft, Pink Gowns," *transition*, no. 1 (April 1927): 109;

"I can recall . . . ," *transition*, no. 1 (April 1927): 108;

"To the Monks of Imperishable Song," *transition*, no. 1 (April 1927): 109;

"As women without names . . . ," *transition*, no. 1 (April 1927): 110;

"The Meddler," *transition*, no. 4 (July 1927): 88-89;

"The Stove," *transition*, no. 6 (September 1927): 79-81;

"Uncle James' Woman," *transition*, no. 10 (January 1928): 55-57;

"With the Passing of the Lesser Evil of the Two," *transition*, no. 10 (January 1928): 98;

"A Visit to Pound," *Paideuma*, 7 (Spring-Fall 1978): 95-100.

A. LINCOLN GILLESPIE, JR.
(11 June 1895-10 September 1950)

Abraham Lincoln Gillespie, Jr., known to his friends as "Linky" or "Link," was part of the group of revolutionary writers who contributed to the Paris-based literary magazine *transition* during the twenties and thirties. Although his work was far from the most significant to appear in *transition*, his experiments with language were so flamboyant that they were often singled out for ridicule by the magazine's critics. A native of Philadelphia, Gillespie received a B.S. from the University of Pennsylvania in 1918 and taught high school mathematics for several years until an automobile accident in 1922 left him with serious injuries from which he never fully recovered. Hoping that travel would improve his health, Gillespie and his wife went to Paris.

Even among the nonconformist Left Bank artists and writers, Gillespie was considered an eccentric, and a number of stories about him—some true and some apocryphal—began to circulate. The tales of Gillespie's exploits which have been verified are just as fantastic as those which have been disproved, and in many cases it is impossible to separate fact from fiction. Kay Boyle says that Gillespie decided to become a writer after someone told him he looked like James Joyce and that he once gave a lecture to the American Women's Club of Paris in which he explained that until after his accident, he did not understand Joyce and Gertrude Stein. Gillespie frequented the cafes of Montparnasse explaining his theories about writing to anyone who would listen, and in 1927, after he decided that he had perfected his style, he took his work to Elliot Paul, one of the *transition* editors. Dougald McMillan says that "Paul's acceptance of Gillespie's work was more an act of bravado than a serious assessment of its lasting literary worth and his pieces were generally considered a joke." Gillespie, however, evidently decided that publishing in *transition* made him an established writer. One anecdote about him which McMillan believes to be true is Samuel Putnam's claim that after Gillespie's first piece appeared, he separated from his wife because he no longer considered her his intellectual equal.

One of Gillespie's early enthusiasms was the polyphonic music of George Antheil, whom he had known in Philadelphia, and his 1927-1928 pieces in *transition* espouse similar innovations in the written word. As McMillan points out, Gillespie wanted writing to "contain indications of what the mind

had gone through in the process of forming an utterance." He believed that grammar, syntax, and vocabulary not only limit the writer's ability to express his ideas, but that they actually distort his thoughts by forcing them into conventional forms. Only by ignoring grammar, leaving out unnecessary words, and inventing new words can one truly communicate. "A PastDoggerel Growth of the Literary Vehicle: Language's Relapproach Music and Plastic" in the Fall 1928 issue of *transition* ends with a call to other writers: "TO WORK THEN, Gang, Miss Stein's & Mr. Joyce's peal clearly that the Vehicle is now The exrudimentablising CreateConcern, a now-yawning DisHibernial plasticklable at least. To furth-pursue Thought Context at neglexpense of VehiFormConcomitent will be ludisastrous." In June 1929 Gillespie was one of the signers of *transition*'s "Revolution of the Word Proclamation" which asserted, among other things, that "NARRATIVE IS NOT MERE ANECDOTE, BUT THE PROJECTION OF A METAMORPHOSIS OF REALITY" and that "THE LITERARY CREATOR HAS THE RIGHT TO DISINTEGRATE THE PRIMAL MATTER OF WORDS IMPOSED ON HIM BY TEXT-BOOKS AND DICTIONARIES." Some of the signers of the proclamation signed more out of friendship for the editor, Eugene Jolas, than because they subscribed to its contents, but Gillespie's writing follows its prescription quite closely.

Also in 1929, Gillespie joined a colony of expatriates at Cagnes-sur-Mer on the French Riviera; at various times, its residents included Kay Boyle, Laurence Vail, George Antheil, Hilaire Hiler, Peter Neagoe, Bob Brown, and briefly, Harry and Caresse Crosby. At Cagnes-sur-Mer, Gillespie came under the influence of Bob Brown, the inventor of the Reading Machine in which the reader turned a crank so that words moved past his eyes. Gillespie began to include visual effects in his writing, and in 1931 he contributed two pieces to Brown's anthology, *Readies for Bob Brown's Machine*. Brown had asked for contributions as different from conventional prose as sound motion pictures were from stage plays, and Gillespie's "Readie-Soundpiece" combines visual effects with musical cues in an attempt to evoke the atmosphere of a college campus in the fall. The poem was reprinted in Peter Neagoe's *Americans Abroad An Anthology* in 1932.

In early April 1932, Gillespie returned to the United States, where he frequented literary circles in Philadelphia and New York City's Greenwich Village. The injuries from his 1922 automobile accident continued to plague him, and he was hospitalized with tuberculosis for much of the time during the last few years of his life. He died in Philadelphia at the age of fifty-five. —*Edward Fisher*

Periodical Publications:

"Music Starts A Geometry," *transition*, no. 8 November 1927): 166-169;

"Textighter Eye-Ploy or Hothouse Bromidick?," *transition*, no. 12 (March 1928): 171-175;

"Antheil & Stravinski," *transition*, no. 13 (Summer 1928): 142-144;

"Why Do Americans Live in Europe?," by Gillespie and others, *transition*, no. 14 (Fall 1928): 97-119;

"A PastDoggerel Growth of the Literary Vehicle: Language's Relapproach Music and Plastic," *transition*, no. 14 (Fall 1928): 126-130;

"Revolution of the Word Proclamation," signed by Gillespie and others, *transition*, no. 16/17 (June 1929): 13;

"Amerikaka Ballet," *transition*, no. 16/17 (June 1929): 151-156;

"Monograph for Harold Weston's 'Evo-Love Series,' " *transition*, no. 19/20 (June 1930): 201-202;

"Voks," *transition*, no. 21 (March 1932): 321-322.

Other:

"Readie-Soundpiece," in *Readies for Bob Brown's Machine*, ed. Bob Brown (Cagnes-sur-Mer: Roving Eye Press, 1931), pp. 83-90; reprinted in *Americans Abroad An Anthology*, ed. Peter Neagoe (The Hague: Servire, 1932), pp. 167-174;

"Readievices," in *Readies for Bob Brown's Machine*, pp. 91-92.

References:

Dougald McMillan, transition *The History of a Literary Era 1927-1938* (New York: Braziller, 1976), pp. 48, 117-119;

Thomas A. Zaniello, "The Thirteenth Disciple of James Joyce: Abraham Lincoln Gillespie," *Journal of Modern Literature*, 7 (February 1979): 51-61.

Florence Gilliam in Paris, 1940

FLORENCE GILLIAM

BOOK: *France A Tribute by an American Woman* (New York: Dutton, 1945; London: William Earl, 1947).

Florence Gilliam, journalist and theatre critic, visited France in 1913 and again in 1919, but it was not until after she had left her high-school teaching job in Columbus, Ohio, and met editor Arthur Moss, whom she later married, that she decided to settle in Paris. Gilliam had spent her summers studying acting and attending the theatre in New York City before she moved there in the summer of 1920. She soon met Moss and went to work briefly for his Greenwich Village magazine the *Quill*. The September 1920 issue lists Gilliam as managing editor.

Early in 1921, Moss and Gilliam left Greenwich Village—and the *Quill*—for Europe, and they settled in Paris in February. They became involved in the intellectual atmosphere of the Left Bank, and in August 1921, they founded *Gargoyle*, the first

English-language review of arts and letters to appear in Continental Europe during the period between the two World Wars. Among the Americans who contributed to the magazine were Malcolm Cowley, Laurence Vail, Hart Crane, Edna St. Vincent Millay, Robert Coates, Matthew Josephson, Stephen Vincent Benet, Sinclair Lewis, Gorham Munson, John Reed, and Hilda Doolittle. *Gargoyle* lasted slightly more than a year, during which Gilliam covered theatre and musical events while Moss wrote book reviews and humorous essays.

The magazine never made money, and it had no outside financial backing, so Moss and Gilliam also worked as free-lance writers for various American publications. At one time, Gilliam was writing for all three American newspapers in Paris. She wrote "Round the Studios" and "Latin Quarter Notes" for the Paris *Herald* (the European edition of the *New York Herald Tribune*), a "window-shopping" column for the Paris *Times*, and feature articles for the Sunday edition of the Paris *Tribune* (the European edition of the *Chicago Tribune*). Besides working as one of the *Tribune*'s theatre critics and serving as Paris correspondent for the New York publications *Theatre Magazine* and *Theatre Arts*, she also edited a monthly bulletin for the American Women's Club in Paris until 1926 when she took an editorial job in the Paris office of Fairchild Publications. After Moss became editor for Erskine Gwynne's *Boulevardier*, Gilliam joined the staff as stage critic, writing the column "And So To the Theatre" until July 1931.

Gilliam and Moss were divorced in 1931. Gilliam remained in Paris until 1941, when, after living for eight months in German-occupied Paris, she returned to the United States. During World War II, she wrote *France A Tribute by an American Woman* (1945) in which she calls her adopted country "the stage as limited as a sonnet, on which the drama of Western Man is played out." After the war, Gilliam went back to France and worked with various relief organizations. In gratitude for her work as director of American Aid in Paris, the French made her a chevalier in the Legion of Honor and awarded her the Medaille de la Reconnaissance Francaise.

An admirer of all aspects of French culture, Gilliam praised the Paris of the twenties and thirties for providing the necessary environment in which influences from other countries could spark new creativity: "Once Diaghilev with Fokine and Bakst came smashing into [French] consciousness at the beginning of the twentieth century, Paris became the garden spot for the flowering of all the arts into a theatrical spectacle such as had never been seen." The ballet brought together writers, composers, painters, choreographers, and dancers of all nationalities working together to create a "transcendent type of theatre." For Gilliam, France provided both a link with tradition and a point from which she could observe human experience objectively, freed from the strictures of her native country. As she sailed into New York Harbor in 1941, she sensed the end of an era: "I felt something like the snapping of a continuity. Life had always seemed a chain . . . or quicksilver perhaps, which defies sharp beginnings and endings. Never was there a point at which to stop and look back, or peer ahead. That day, time seemed for once to stand still."

—*Karen L. Rood*

Periodical Publications:

"The Paris Conference: Remarks by Florence Gilliam," *Fitzgerald/Hemingway Annual 1973* (Washington, D.C.: Microcard Editions Books, 1974), pp. 43-48;

"My Years With Arthur Moss," *Lost Generation Journal*, 2 (Fall 1974): 10-13, 32-33; 3 (Winter 1975): 39-42.

CAROLINE GORDON
(6 October 1895-   )

SELECTED BOOKS: *Penhally* (New York: Scribners, 1931);

Aleck Maury, Sportsman (New York: Scribners, 1934); republished as *Pastimes of Aleck Maury The Life of a True Sportsman* (London: Dickson & Thompson, 1935);

The Strange Children (New York: Scribners, 1951; London: Routledge & Paul, 1952);

The Malefactors (New York: Harcourt, Brace, 1956);

How to Read a Novel (New York: Viking, 1957);

Old Red and Other Stories (New York: Scribners, 1963);

A Good Soldier: A Key to the Novels of Ford Madox Ford (Davis: University of California Library, 1963).

Caroline Gordon visited France twice during the twenties and thirties, in 1928-1929 and again in 1932-1933. She wrote much of her first two novels while living abroad, and she and her husband, poet Allen Tate, took an active part in the social and intellectual life of the American expatriate community in Paris. Unlike many other Americans living in Paris, however, Gordon, in her first novels, seems to have been affected little by Parisian life. Her early fiction is influenced more by her devotion to her native South, its history, and its people than by the avant-garde writers with whom she associated. It was not until much later in her career that she began to draw on events and characters from her stay in France.

Gordon was born in Todd County, Kentucky, to Nancy Meriwether and James Morris Gordon. She received her early education at a boys' school run by her father—she was the only female admitted—and later attended a public high school. In 1916 she was awarded a B.A. degree from Bethany College in West Virginia, and after teaching for several years, she decided to pursue a career in journalism. In 1920 she joined the staff of the *Chattanooga News*, for which she reviewed the works of the writers known as the Fugitives, a small group of students and professors at Vanderbilt University, and she met some of the members of this movement. In 1924 Robert Penn Warren introduced her to Allen Tate, another Fugitive, who was at the time visiting Warren in Kentucky.

In fall 1924 Gordon moved to New York, where she and Tate were married in November. She had already begun work on her first short stories, and in 1925, after the birth of their daughter Nancy, the

Caroline Gordon, by Rose Chavanne, early 1930s

Tates moved to a farmhouse near Patterson, New York, so that they could concentrate on their writing. When they learned of their friend Hart Crane's financial difficulties, the Tates invited him to live with them; he accepted, but none of the writers was able to devote full attention to writing, and they moved back to New York City in 1926. Soon after their return Gordon became secretary to Ford Madox Ford. She typed his manuscripts, and he in turn read her early stories and encouraged her to read works he believed would be of value to her writing. Gordon's subsequent study of Flaubert, James, and Ford influenced and improved her own fiction; her first short story, "Summer Dust," appeared in the November 1929 issue of *Gyroscope*, a West Coast literary magazine edited by Yvor Winters.

Ford was also partially responsible for Tate's 1928 Guggenheim Fellowship, which allowed Tate, Gordon, and their daughter to go abroad. They went first to England, where they met poet Leonie Adams; with Adams they traveled to Paris and moved into the Hotel de Fleurus, near the atelier of Gertrude Stein and Alice B. Toklas. Ford had written a letter of introduction to Stein, asking that she receive the

Tates at her Thursday night literary gatherings, and soon after their arrival Tate received a brief summons from Stein: "You and your wife will come to tea on Thursday at 27 rue de Fleurus. *Gertrude Stein.*" At Stein's Gordon was escorted by Toklas to the back of the salon, where the women were expected to talk to each other while Stein lectured to the men. Gordon disagreed with Stein's theories of fiction, resented being excluded from the literary discussions, and seems to have disliked the evenings spent with Stein. Other social and literary gatherings, such as those hosted by Ford on Saturday nights in his apartment in the rue de Vaugirard, were more enjoyable. At Ford's apartment, into which the Tates moved after his return to the United States, Gordon met poets Ralph Cheever Dunning and A. Lincoln Gillespie, and *transition* editor Eugene Jolas. Other Americans, including Hart Crane, and John Peale Bishop, who introduced her to F. Scott and Zelda Fitzgerald, she had known in New York. Tate met Ernest Hemingway at Sylvia Beach's bookshop, Shakespeare and Company, and Hemingway became a frequent visitor at the Tates'.

Although Gordon associated socially with some of the most innovative writers of the time, her writing was affected little if at all by her contemporaries' insistence on experimentation in fiction. Her first novel, *Penhally* (1931), much of which was written while Gordon was living in Paris, depends on traditional narrative technique to tell the story of the decline of an aristocratic Southern family. Gordon's earlier study of Flaubert and James was obviously more of an influence than was her association with writers of experimental fiction. Tate, too, rejected the more radical opinions of some expatriates—he refused to sign Eugene Jolas's "Revolution of the Word Proclamation," which appeared in *transition* (June 1929) and called for new innovative techniques in writing.

After a visit to Brittany, the Tates returned to the United States in January 1930 and settled at Benfolly Farm in Tennessee. They remained there until 1932, when Gordon was awarded a Guggenheim Fellowship and the Tates again sailed for France, arriving in July. Instead of going directly to Paris, the Tates went first to Cap Brun and moved into a house Ford had found for them near his own villa, where he was staying with Janice Biala. During an extravagant picnic at Cassis with Ford and other friends, Ford commented that the location for their picnic was probably similar to places at which Aeneas had rested on his journey. This remark influenced both Tate, who soon began work on his

poem "The Mediterranean," and Gordon, who was writing her second novel, *Aleck Maury, Sportsman* (1934). Aleck Maury, based on Gordon's father, is both an avid sportsman and a teacher of the classics, and allusions to the *Aeneid* recur throughout the novel.

The Tates moved to Paris near the end of the year. In February 1933 they returned to America and again settled at Benfolly, both Tate and Gordon becoming increasingly involved with the Agrarian movement. Two of Gordon's novels were published in 1937, and the following year she was appointed the first writer-in-residence at what was then the state women's college at Greensboro, North Carolina. She resigned that post when Tate accepted a teaching position at Princeton. Gordon continued to write, completing two more novels and a collection of short stories.

In 1951 *The Strange Children* was published, Gordon's first novel that draws directly on her personal experiences, including events and acquaintances from her Paris days and her conversion to Roman Catholicism in the late forties. *The Strange Children* is the story of writer Stephen Lewis and his wife Sarah, as seen through the eyes of their nine-year-old daughter, Lucy. The Lewises, once part of the literary and artistic community in Paris, have settled on a farm in Tennessee, where they are joined by old friends recently arrived in the United States from France. Lucy, childlike yet intuitive, is able to discern the rapid changes in her parents' personalities brought about by the visitors; she listens as the adults, the "strange children" of the title, become involved in intellectual discussions that only superficially disguise petty arguments. When one of the friends elopes with another friend's wife, Stephen Lewis, too, recognizes the self-centered nature of his associates and discovers within himself a need for spiritual guidance and meaning in life. Throughout the novel the rural, slow-paced life on the farm is contrasted with the frenetic pace of Paris, and the shallowness of the visitors from France is made all the more obvious when they are compared to the uneducated country folk who farm the Lewises' land.

The Strange Children was followed in 1956 by *The Malefactors*, in which Gordon again draws on her sojourn in France. The protagonist, Tom Claiborne, is a poet who attempts to deal with his discontent by intellectualizing his feelings. As does Stephen Lewis at the end of *The Strange Children*, Claiborne recognizes the emptiness of his life, which he tries to fill with an affair with his wife's cousin. He is brought to self-awareness and persuaded to return to his wife by Catherine Pollard, once noted for her promiscuity when she was part of the Paris literary community and now known for her philanthropy and devotion to the poor of New York City.

In *The Strange Children* and *The Malefactors*, the expatriate community in Paris is portrayed as unnatural, immoral, and destructive; the people who adopt that lifestyle quickly learn to express their emotions in intellectual terms, thereby hiding their true feelings. Their world is contrasted with the morality, spirituality, and honesty of agrarian life. Both Lewis and Claiborne find the value of rural life, however, only after realistic appraisals of their French experiences or confrontations with people who are still part of the intellectual community there.

Gordon's experiences in France also provided the source for "Emmanuele, Emmanuele!," collected in *Old Red and Other Stories* (1963). The story involves Guillaume Fay, a famous writer whose character Gordon based on a story she had heard about Andre Gide. Fay lives in an intellectual world he has created and is perceived by his secretary, Robert Heywood, as having attained the height of literary achievement. It is only when Heywood meets Fay's wife Emmanuele that he realizes Fay's famed love for his wife is really love for himself and the legend he has built.

Unlike Gordon's other fiction which draws on her visits in France, "The Olive Garden," published in the October-December 1945 issue of *Sewanee Review*, is almost nostalgic in tone. Set in Cap Brun, the story deals with Edward Dabney's return to the scene of some of his happiest memories. He finds people and places changed since the war, however, and realizes that the postwar generation is very different from his own.

In *How to Read a Novel* (1957) Gordon writes, "When I was a great deal younger than I am now, I sat in a corner of Gertrude Stein's vast studio on the rue Fleurus and listened—impatiently—while Miss Stein descanted on the nature of her own genius. She said that there had been only four American writers of any consequence—Hawthorne, Emerson, Whitman, and herself. . . . 'But the true American genius, the genius which is unique in being able to dispense with experience, comes to its flower in me,' she said." In contrast to Stein's theory, Gordon's fiction has consistently demonstrated her belief in the necessity of experience to good fiction. For Gordon Stein's aesthetic is empty; the only proper subject for fiction is the realistic portrayal of experience. She has stressed the importance of her personal experiences to her own novels in the many classes she has taught at universities throughout the country. Gordon and Tate were divorced in 1959. She now lives in Mexico and is at work on a new novel.

—*Cynthia H. Rogers*

Other:

"The Olive Garden," *Sewanee Review*, 53 (October-December 1945): 532-543;

The House of Fiction An Anthology of the Short Story, edited with commentary by Gordon and Allen Tate (New York: Scribners, 1950; revised edition, New York: Scribners, 1960).

References:

Frederick P. W. McDowell, *Caroline Gordon*, Pamphlets on American Writers #59 (Minneapolis: University of Minnesota Press, 1966);

William J. Stuckey, *Caroline Gordon* (New York: Twayne, 1972);

Allen Tate, *Memoirs and Opinions 1926-1974* (Chicago: Swallow Press, 1975), pp. 46-68.

Papers:

A collection of Gordon's papers is in the Princeton University Library.

JULIEN GREEN
(6 September 1900-   )

SELECTED BOOKS: *Mont-Cinere* (Paris: Plon, 1926); published in English as *Avarice House*, trans. Marshall A. Best (New York & London: Harper, 1927; London: Benn, 1928);
Adrienne Mesurat (Paris: Plon, 1927); published in English as *The Closed Garden*, trans. Henry Longan Stuart (New York & London: Harper, 1928; London: Heinemann, 1928);
Le Voyageur sur la Terre (Paris: Gallimard, 1927);
Leviathan (Paris: Plon, 1929); published in English as *The Dark Journey*, trans. Vyvyan Holland (New York & London: Harper, 1929; London: Heinemann, 1929);
Le Voyageur sur la Terre—Les Clefs de la Mort—Christine—Leviathan (Paris: Plon, 1930); published in English as *Christine and Other Stories*, trans. Courtney Bruerton (New York & London: Harper, 1930; London: Heinemann, 1931);
L'Autre sommeil (Paris: Gallimard, 1931);
Epaves (Paris: Plon, 1932); published in English as *The Strange River*, trans. Vyvyan Holland (New York & London: Harper, 1932; London: Heinemann, 1933);
Le Visionnaire (Paris: Plon, 1934); published in English as *The Dreamer*, trans. Vyvyan Holland (New York & London: Harper, 1934; London: Heinemann, 1934);
Minuit (Paris: Plon, 1936); published in English as *Midnight*, trans. Vyvyan Holland (New York & London: Harper, 1936; London: Heinemann, 1936);
Journal, I (1928-1934) (Paris: Plon, 1938); *Journal, II (1935-1939)* (Paris: Plon, 1939); published in English as *Personal Record (1928-1939)*, trans. Jocelyn Godefroi (New York & London: Harper, 1939);
Varouna (Paris: Plon, 1940); published in English as *Then Shall the Dust Return*, trans. James Whitall (New York & London: Harper, 1941);
Memories of Happy Days (New York & London: Harper, 1942; London: Dent, 1944);
Moira (Paris: Plon, 1950); published in English, trans. Denise Folliot (New York: Macmillan, 1951; London: Heinemann, 1951);
Sud (Paris: Plon, 1953);
Terre Lointaine (Paris: Grasset, 1966);
Memories of Evil Days, ed. Jean-Pierre J. Piriou (Charlottesville: University Press of Virginia, 1976).

Julien Green

Although Julien Green was born in Paris, has lived there almost all his life, and has written only one book in English, those Americans who know his best fiction—especially the books that are set in the American South—are eager to claim him as an American writer. The product of proud old families from Georgia and Virginia, Green has always been profoundly conscious of his Southern heritage. The family had moved to France in 1893 when Edward Moon Green was appointed European agent for the Southern Cotton Seed Oil Company. Educated in French schools until the age of eighteen, Green attended the University of Virginia at Charlottesville for three years and has been influenced by both the French and Anglo-American cultures. His favorite readings include not only Baudelaire, Victor Hugo, Pascal, and Peguy, but Keats, Hawthorne, Dickens, and the King James Version of the Bible.

Green is known primarily as a Catholic writer, but the era between the two World Wars was the period of his life in which he was least inclined to accept such a label. Returning to Paris from the University of Virginia in 1922, he found it impossible to pursue the monastic vocation to which he had aspired as an adolescent. He had gradually and painfully come to acknowledge his homosexuality, and that seemed in his own eyes to render him unworthy of calling himself a Christian. The nostalgia for monastic holiness is a persistent motif throughout his writings, and his fiction was to be a series of variations on the central thematic duality of spirit and flesh.

The family setting in which Julien Green grew up was the source not only of his unusual bicultural identity but also of the spiritually charged emotional atmosphere within which his fictional drama was born. His mother, Mary Hartridge Green, came from an old Savannah family with deep roots in the antebellum Georgia soil. Her severe Calvinism made Julien's struggle with homosexuality all the more devastating, and her nostalgic reverence for the Old South that she had left behind conjured up in young Green's mind a utopian dream of an exotic Southern scene that was to have a strong influence on the picture of the American South in Green's fiction. *Mont-Cinere* (1926) and *Le Voyageur sur la Terre* (1927) are examples of the emotional intensity with which Green has recast the South into his own imaginative world.

The decades between the World Wars were the time of Green's first literary productions, a time when he began to establish a reputation as a novelist and diarist. His early fiction—eight novels and four novellas—was referred to as "magic realism." The characterizations were drawn in conventional terms; the setting was described in an apparently realistic style; and yet there was always something a bit askew. Each character was haunted by some dark obsession that prompted critics to compare Green to the Bronte sisters and Nathaniel Hawthorne, and most plots culminated in a violent denouement: fires, murders, suicides, and madness. Green has said in his diary that he set out to write in an "invisible style," an unobtrusive, sober style that would not call attention to the person of the writer. And most of the protagonists in this period of his fiction are intentionally unautobiographical. Clearly the fictional realm was in great part a means of escape, and writing a therapeutic activity in which he could leave the all too painful situations of real life behind. *Adrienne Mesurat* (1927), his second full-length novel, is a typical example of this early period in Green's fiction. It was perhaps more widely read by the American public than any of his other novels, since it was a Book-of-the-Month Club selection.

It is indicative of the degree to which Green is—and always considered himself—a French rather than American literary figure that during the twenties and thirties he was apparently not much involved in the group of Anglo-American writers who were then living in Paris. Ernest Hemingway, John Dos Passos, James Joyce, F. Scott Fitzgerald, and the others are conspicuously absent from the diaries of this period, except for a few references to Hemingway's and Joyce's writings. The only notable exception was Gertrude Stein, who is mentioned several times in Green's autobiographical writings. A typically eccentric Gertrude Stein pronouncement is recorded in the 28 January 1932 entry of Green's diary: "She tells me that one day she opened a book of mine and saw that my sentences were really sentences; she adds that she read only one sentence!" Earlier, before embarking on his writing career, young Green had had an interest in becoming a painter, but when his father took him to see the Michael Steins' art collection, the sight of a Matisse portrait of a woman with a green face was enough to convince him that he could never paint successfully in the modern fashion.

Green's most important literary acquaintances of this period (and of his whole life) were Jacques Maritain and Andre Gide. He also saw Jean Cocteau and Francois Mauriac rather often. He was fond of Cocteau's engaging, playful wit, and Mauriac was able to share many of his spiritual insights. The meditations on art and morality in Mauriac's *God and Mammon* (1929) are, in fact, quite close to those one finds in Green's diary. However, Maritain was the strongest spiritual influence among Green's friends. His loyal friendship and deep understanding of the problems confronting the Christian artist were a lifelong support that Green has often acknowledged. Gide, on the other hand, seemed to represent the fiercely independent stance of *desengagement* and the full, explicit confession of homosexual love. The immense literary stature of Gide and his own characteristically Protestant passion for truth made his friendship an equally prized blessing in Green's estimation.

Green's inner struggle with spiritual and erotic forces (epitomized by Maritain and Gide) was especially violent in the thirties and is reflected in the novels of the period: *Leviathan* (1929), *L'Autre sommeil* (1931), *Epaves* (1932), *Le Visionnaire* (1934), *Minuit* (1936), and *Varouna* (1940). They all betray an obsession with escape and death and a new interest in Oriental mysticism. Though he had come to the point of not being able to pray, he did continue his spiritual quest. Not only was he involved in extensive readings on Buddhism, but he also began a study of Hebrew in order to read the Bible more profitably. Other significant resources during this searching period included Saint John of the Cross,

Saint Theresa of Avila, and Saint Thomas a Kempis. The culmination of the intense conflict was a spiritual rebirth in 1939 that brought him back to the Catholic faith.

During World War II, Green lived in the United States, where he performed duty for the Office of War Information, wrote, lectured, and taught creative writing at various colleges. His lectures in English have been gathered and edited under the title *Memories of Evil Days* (1976). In the early days of the war, he was afraid that he would never be able to return to France and pondered the difficult adjustment of having to write in English for the rest of his career. Actually, the years ahead held in store for him the prospect of publishing nearly twenty volumes of fiction, drama, and autobiography—all in French—but some of the greatest, ironically, were set in the American South. *Moira* (1950), *Sud* (1953), and *Terre Lointaine* (1966) are deeply personal evocations—both fictional and autobiographical—of the Georgia and Virginia scenes where the dramas of Green's youth were acted out with an emotional intensity that he could never forget.

When Green's candidacy was submitted to the French Academy, the requirement that members be French citizens appeared to threaten his chances. Since normally one of the requirements for French citizenship is to renounce one's previous nationality, it is a testimony to Green's loyalty to his American heritage that he refused to sacrifice his American citizenship. President Pompidou provided the more appropriate solution by declaring Green a French citizen, thanks to his military service in World War I and his contributions to French culture as a writer. He was thus elected to the Academy in 1971, filling the vacancy created by the death of his old friend Francois Mauriac.

A curious blend of French and American cultures, Julien Green has given us a profound insight into the human heart, suffering the conflicting claims of spirit and flesh. His autobiographical writings offer a penetrating study of what Leon Bloy called the only sadness—"the sadness of not being a saint." And the books set in the South are an intriguing personal statement on the bafflingly complex cultural identity of the American South. —*John M. Dunaway*

References:

Pierre Brodin, *Julien Green* (Paris: Editions Universitaires, 1957);

Glenn S. Burne, *Julian Green* (New York: Twayne, 1972);

John M. Dunaway, *The Metamorphoses of the Self: The Mystic, the Sensualist, and the Artist in the Works of Julien Green* (Lexington: University Press of Kentucky, 1978);

Jacques Petit, *Julien Green: "l'homme qui venait d'ailleurs"* (Paris: Desclee de Brouwer, 1969);

Robert de Saint-Jean, *Julien Green par lui-meme* (Paris: Editions du Seuil, 1967).

Ramon Guthrie, by Stella Bowen, 1928

Dartmouth College Museum and Galleries

RAMON GUTHRIE
(14 January 1896-22 November 1973)

BOOKS: *Trobar Clus* (Northampton, Mass.: S4N Society, 1923);

Marcabrun (New York: Doran, 1926);

A World Too Old (New York: Doran, 1927);

Parachute (New York: Harcourt, Brace, 1928; London: Howe, 1929);

The Legend of Ermengarde, as Homer Rignaut (Paris: Black Manikin Press, 1929);

Scherzo from a Poem To Be Entitled "The Proud City" (Hanover, N.H.: Arts Press, 1933);

Graffiti (New York: Macmillan, 1959);

Asbestos Phoenix (New York: Funk & Wagnalls, 1968);

Maximum Security Ward (New York: Farrar, Straus & Giroux, 1970; London: Sidgwick & Jackson, 1971).

Ramon Guthrie arrived in Paris within a few days of his twenty-first birthday and thereafter considered France a second, generally preferable, homeland. He lived in Paris and the south of France (visiting Paris often) from 1920 to 1923 and again from 1926 to 1929. From 1930 on he returned as frequently as war and his duties as professor of

French at Dartmouth permitted. Guthrie's France was a congenial place to write and —as a gifted amateur—to paint. But he also steeped himself in French culture, language, and literature. At the Sorbonne he studied Provencal and Old French while trying to support himself as poet, novelist, and translator. He married a Frenchwoman, Marguerite Maurey, in 1922 and took his only earned degrees, the *licence* and *doctorat en droit* degrees for foreigners, in 1921 and 1922 at the University of Toulouse. ("Privately tutored—by myself": he lacked even a high school diploma.)

In France he accumulated friends and experiences that gave him enduring poetic images:

> Montparnasse
> that I shall never see again, the Montparnasse
> of Joyce and Pound, Stein, Stella Bowen,
> little Zadkine, Giacometti . . . all gone in any
>   case,
> and would I might have died, been buried
>   there.

This passage from Guthrie's most important book, *Maximum Security Ward* (1970), is one of many passages in his mature poetry where Parisian memories from 1920-1939 loom decisively. The poetry he actually wrote during those years, however, is mainly apprentice work. He experimented with a variety of tones, attitudes, and styles derived in part from ancient and modern French tradition. The most successful early poems are his translations from the Provencal, which appeared in his first collection, *Trobar Clus* (1923), and were reprinted in his second, *A World Too Old* (1927). During 1920-1923, Guthrie also contributed poems to *Paris Review: The Illustrated American Magazine in France*, worked on an unpublished novel, "Philip," and mailed back poetry and criticism to the little magazine *S4N*, which Norman Fitts, Guthrie, Stephen Vincent Benet, Thornton Wilder, and others had founded in 1919. Economic necessity forced the Guthries back to America in 1923, and while teaching French at the University of Arizona, Guthrie wrote the novel *Marcabrun* (1926) and most of the poems in *A World Too Old*. Back in France in 1926, partly at the instigation of Sinclair Lewis, Guthrie translated Bernard Fay's *The Revolutionary Spirit in France and America* (1927). He then wrote a novel about aviators after the war, *Parachute* (1928), which had moderate critical success, and has confessed to writing the exuberantly indecent poem *The Legend of Ermengarde*, which Edward Titus's Black Manikin Press published in 1929. (Guthrie used an anagrammatic pseudonym, "Homer Rignaut," for this mock translation from the Provencal.) His only published poetry of the thirties, the little chapbook *Scherzo from a Poem To Be Entitled "The Proud City,"* reflects the ambience of Paris, and part of it may have been written there.

Guthrie published no more fiction after *Parachute*, explaining that once he had immersed himself in Proust for courses he taught at Dartmouth, he found it presumptuous to compete with the French master. Guthrie's finest poetry appeared in *Graffiti* (1959), *Asbestos Phoenix* (1968), and *Maximum Security Ward*, which is Guthrie's confrontation—at once comic and tragic—with his own devastating illness and despair. In these three books, the other artists and writers Guthrie knew, frequently intimately, in Paris over a period of fifty years are numbered among the people who keep the poet from damning life and a seemingly bloodthirsty human race. Thus one finds strikingly comic, poignant, or warm vignettes of such figures as Robert Desnos, Amedeo Modigliani, Alberto Giacometti, Ernest Hemingway ("Apple-cheeked manchild / right out of Satie's *Enfance de Pantagruel*"), Ezra Pound ("Whiffing centaurs' trails"), and the "erstwhile infant Pope of Unreason" Tristan Tzara, whom he wryly mourned in terms equally appropriate to himself:

Tzara, I don't like your being dead.
Somehow you seem less cut out for it
than almost any one I ever knew.

—*Sally Moore Gall*

Other:

Bernard Fay, *The Revolutionary Spirit in France and America*, translated by Guthrie (New York: Harcourt, Brace, 1927);

David Rousset, *The Other Kingdom*, translated by Guthrie (New York: Reynal & Hitchcock, 1947);

Prose and Poetry of Modern France, edited by Guthrie and George E. Diller (New York: Scribners, 1964).

References:

Diller, ed., *Ramon Guthrie Kaleidoscope* (Lunenburg, Vt.: Stinehour Press, 1963);

Sally M. Gall, "The Poetry of Ramon Guthrie," Ph.D. dissertation, New York University, 1976.

Papers:

Guthrie's papers, including manuscripts of unpublished poems, are deposited in Baker Library at Dartmouth College.

ERSKINE GWYNNE
(1898-5 May 1948)

BOOK: *Paris Pandemonium* (New York: R. Speller, 1936).

Erskine Gwynne was the wealthy publisher of the Paris *Boulevardier*, a magazine patterned after the *New Yorker*. The son of Edward Erskine and Helen Steele Gwynne and the great-nephew of Mrs. Cornelius Vanderbilt, Gwynne was educated in France, England, and the United States. In 1926, in Paris, he married Madeleine Armstrong, a great-niece of Jefferson Davis; the marriage ended in divorce in 1932.

Gwynne wrote articles in French for French magazines and contributed to little magazines in the United States and England, but he is best known as the publisher of the *Boulevardier*, an English-language magazine published in Paris from March 1927 until January 1932 under the editorship of Arthur Moss with Jed Kiley as assistant editor. *Boulevardier*'s tone was set by the editor's preface to the first issue (March 1927), which called the new venture the Anglo-American colony's "very own magazine" and said in part:

> Your Boulevardier . . . will not tell one tenth of what he really knows. He is a kindly soul and does not intend to hurt anybody.
>
> If on the other hand you think that he is not gossipy enough, write and tell us about it.

Subsequent issues featured stories by Michael Arlen, Noel Coward, Sinclair Lewis, Louis Bromfield, and Ernest Hemingway ("The Real Spaniard," October 1927). Gwynne contributed light articles such as "The Servant Problem" and "Throwing the Bulls." Irving Schwerke's column, "Words and Music," Arthur Moss's "Books and the Left Bank," and a column called "The Left-Over Bank," sometimes written by Wambly Bald, reported many of the artistic and literary happenings in Paris. Florence Gilliam's "And So To the Theatre" provided respectable stage criticism.

Unlike *transition* or the *transatlantic review*, however, *Boulevardier* was not a literary magazine. Its appeal was to the wealthy society people of the Right Bank. Travel, horse racing, golf, and yachting filled the recreation columns. The offerings for women readers included reports on shopping, fashion, and social events, often illustrated with drawings of prominent individuals. "Quelque Shows" provided a regular listing of current theatrical events and club entertainment. Gossip, sometimes bordering on the malicious, appeared regularly in "Ritz Alley," but also found its way into many other columns of *Boulevardier*.

In format, illustrations, and such features as "New York Letter" and "London Letter," *Boulevardier* attempted increasingly to become the *New Yorker* of Paris. The magazine's most blatant mimicry, however, was its editorial column "If Talk We Must. . ," which fell sadly short of its *New Yorker* model, "Talk of the Town."

Gwynne's only published book, the novel *Paris Pandemonium* (1936), is a light love story in which a young woman is taken to a round of bars and parties by a Right Bank roue. The plot seems merely an excuse for mentioning the names of socially prominent people such as Michael Arlen and Elsa Maxwell, but the book does capture the flavor of the society in which Gwynne traveled. In 1935, after his return to the United States, the car in which Gwynne was riding collided with a truck in Ridgefield, South Carolina. It is believed that the accident caused the attack of paralysis Gwynne suffered in 1938. He lived in New York City from 1940 until his death on 5 May 1948.

—*Jean W. Ross*

References:

Al Laney, *Paris Herald The Incredible Newspaper* (New York & London: Appleton-Century, 1947), p. 151;

Carol Weld, "Viva Ric!," *Lost Generation Journal*, 2 (Fall 1974): 30.

Ernest Hemingway

Nicholas Gerogiannis
Auburn University at Montgomery

BIRTH: Oak Park, Illinois, 21 July 1899, to Grace Hall and Clarence Edmonds Hemingway.

MARRIAGE: 3 September 1921 to Hadley Richardson, divorced; children: John Hadley Nicanor. 10 May 1927 to Pauline Pfeiffer, divorced; children: Patrick, Gregory. 21 November 1940 to Martha Gellhorn, divorced. 14 March 1946 to Mary Welsh.

AWARDS: Pulitzer Prize for *The Old Man and the Sea*, 1953; Nobel Prize, 1954; American Academy of Arts and Letters Award of Merit, 1954.

DEATH: Ketchum, Idaho, 2 July 1961.

SELECTED BOOKS: *Three Stories & Ten Poems* (Paris: Contact Editions, 1923);
in our time (Paris: Three Mountains Press, 1924);
In Our Time: Stories (New York: Boni & Liveright, 1925; London: Cape, 1926; revised edition, New York: Scribners, 1930);
The Torrents of Spring (New York: Scribners, 1926; Paris: Crosby Continental Editions, 1932; London: Cape, 1933);
The Sun Also Rises (New York: Scribners, 1926); republished as *Fiesta* (London: Cape, 1927);
Men Without Women (New York: Scribners, 1927; London: Cape, 1928);
A Farewell to Arms (New York: Scribners, 1929; London: Cape, 1929);
Death in the Afternoon (New York & London: Scribners, 1932; London: Cape, 1932);
Winner Take Nothing (New York & London: Scribners, 1933; London: Cape, 1934);
Green Hills of Africa (New York & London: Scribners, 1935; London: Cape, 1936);
To Have and Have Not (New York: Scribners, 1937; London: Cape, 1937);
The Spanish Earth (Cleveland: J. B. Savage, 1938);
The Fifth Column and the First Forty-Nine Stories (New York: Scribners, 1938; London: Cape, 1939);
For Whom the Bell Tolls (New York: Scribners, 1940; London: Cape, 1941);
Across the River and Into the Trees (New York: Scribners, 1950; London: Cape, 1964);
The Old Man and the Sea (New York: Scribners, 1952; London: Cape, 1952);
Hemingway: The Wild Years, ed. Gene Z. Hanrahan (New York: Dell, 1962);
A Moveable Feast (New York: Scribners, 1964; London: Cape, 1964);
By-Line: Ernest Hemingway: Selected Articles and Dispatches of Four Decades, ed. William White (New York: Scribners, 1967; London: Collins, 1968);
Islands in the Stream (New York: Scribners, 1970; London: Collins, 1970);
88 Poems, ed. Nicholas Gerogiannis (New York & London: Harcourt Brace Jovanovich / Bruccoli Clark, 1979).

Ernest Hemingway was twenty-two years old when he arrived in Paris in late December 1921. He had taken part in World War I as a volunteer ambulance driver, and after his experiences in Europe during the war he found life in the United States provincial and restrictive. He was part of a new generation of expatriates who did not have the cosmopolitan backgrounds of earlier expatriates such as Henry James and Edith Wharton. Like Hemingway, many of the young writers and artists who migrated to Paris in the twenties had been exposed to Europe during the war, and following the war a European economic recession, which caused the rate of exchange to favor the American dollar, brought many of these young Americans to France. However, for a young writer the economic enticement was secondary to the knowledge that some of the leading experimental writers of the day—James Joyce, Ezra Pound, and Gertrude Stein—were living and writing in Paris.

Hemingway went to Paris to be a writer, not an expatriate, but, although he was often derisive of them, his writing immortalizes the individuals whom he helped to characterize as the lost generation. He celebrated a place and time with a uniquely modern style, and at the same time he involved himself in feuds with other writers that still cause debates in literary circles. As a writer, at his best, he was governed by an absolute literary temperament and a sense for language that astonished his contemporaries.

Hemingway lived in Paris for a number of years during the twenties and returned to the city sporadically in the thirties. After 1925, when he experienced his first fame, he gradually became a victim of his youth and success; he was unfaithful first to his wife, then to his principles of life and art. By 1929, when he drifted away from Paris, he had published two highly praised, seminal volumes, *Three Stories & Ten Poems* (1923) and *in our time* (1924); two short-story collections, *In Our Time* (1925) and *Men Without Women* (1927); two major novels, *The Sun Also Rises* (1926) and *A Farewell to Arms* (1929); and the controversial parody, *The Torrents of Spring* (1926). Late in his life, when he rediscovered Paris by writing about it, he was inspired once again to create brilliant prose passages that evoked the sensations he had had in Paris when he was young and free to develop his craft.

Ernest Miller Hemingway was born in Oak Park, Illinois, an upper-middle-class suburb of Chicago. His father was a doctor, and his mother, Grace Hall Hemingway, had abandoned a promising career in music to marry and raise a family. Hemingway distinguished himself in high school by writing for the school newspaper and literary magazine. He never excelled in organized sports, but, like his father, he became a sportsman in the woods and lakes of northern Michigan, where the Hemingways had a summer cottage. Dr. Hemingway and his six children felt most at home at Walloon Lake while Mrs. Hemingway was more at home in Oak Park. Hemingway's summer experiences in Michigan and his relationships with his parents formed the basis of his later autobiographical fiction about his youth. He often displeased his mother, and her repressive influence on him, and on Dr. Hemingway, was an early source of pain for the sensitive young man. After graduating from high school he worked as a reporter for the *Kansas City Star* for seven months before enlisting as a Red Cross ambulance driver.

On 23 May 1918 Hemingway was on his way to Italy and the war. He saw Paris for the first time in early June 1918 when his company stopped there briefly on their way to Milan. Shortly after midnight on 8 July, near San Dona di Piave, Hemingway was severely wounded when an Austrian shell hit the forward listening post where he was passing out supplies to Italian troops. He carried another wounded man across an open area, but his right knee was hit by machine-gun fire before he reached the command post. A few weeks later he celebrated his nineteenth birthday in a hospital in Milan, and at about the same time the Chicago newspapers told the story of his being the first American wounded in Italy.

Ernest Hemingway at Shakespeare and Company

Hemingway had been seriously wounded; however, the event led to encounters during his recuperation that were crucial to his life and career. He became infatuated with Agnes von Kurowsky, an American nurse stationed in Milan who later became one of the models for his heroines. And he met Eric Edward (Chink) Dorman-Smith, an Irish officer, who became one of his first real-life heroes and his lifelong friend. The good companions made the rounds of the cafes and bars in Milan while Dorman-

Smith recounted his wartime adventures, some of which Hemingway later used in his fiction. During his nine-month recuperation Hemingway had the freedom to experience the peaceful side of life in northern Italy. After returning to the United States in January 1919, he felt homesick for Italy, and his mood was not lightened when Agnes von Kurowsky wrote in March to announce her engagement to an Italian lieutenant.

After several months in Oak Park, where he felt estranged from his family, he went to northern Michigan, where he began to write about his recent adventures. In January 1920 he went to Toronto and was soon working for the *Toronto Star*. He continued to write articles for the newspaper when he returned to the United States, first to spend the summer in northern Michigan and then to settle in Chicago, where he stayed in his friend Y. K. Smith's apartment. In October he met Hadley Richardson, who had come from St. Louis for a visit with Smith's sister. In December, desperately in need of a job, he went to work as an editor and writer for the *Cooperative Commonwealth*, a monthly magazine. He and Hadley Richardson were corresponding and visiting each other whenever they could. In some of his letters Hemingway included poems that he had typed on the typewriter she had given him for his twenty-second birthday. Seven years older than Hemingway, Hadley Richardson had lived under the close scrutiny of her invalid mother and a married sister. "The world's a jail and we're going to break it together," she wrote to Hemingway. On 3 September 1921 the two were married in Hortons Bay, Michigan. Immediately the couple began to make plans to leave for Italy. The problem, however, was money.

Hemingway had met Sherwood Anderson, one of the leading writers of the day, during a literary evening at Y. K. Smith's apartment the previous spring. After their marriage the Hemingways were invited to dinner at the Andersons', who had recently spent several months in Paris. Anderson told Hemingway that if he wanted to be a serious writer, he should go to Paris, but if he wanted to play, he should go to Italy. In Paris the Hemingways' meager resources—Hadley Hemingway's trust fund of two or three thousand dollars per year and Ernest Hemingway's earnings from articles he wrote for the *Toronto Star*—would sustain them because the rate of exchange made living there more economical. Anderson gave them the address of a hotel where they could live until they found an apartment, and he supplied Hemingway with letters of introduction: to the leader of the American expatriates, Gertrude Stein; to the owner of the English-language bookshop Shakespeare and Company, Sylvia Beach; to the writer whose novel Beach was about to publish, James Joyce; and to the influential poet, Ezra Pound. Anderson also mailed an introductory letter to Lewis Galantiere, one of his translators in France. In each of his notes Anderson lauded Hemingway's "extraordinary talent," which he believed would soon lead the young newspaperman beyond journalism.

The Hemingways sailed for Europe on 8 December 1921, arriving at Vigo, Spain, where Hemingway made notes on the tuna fishing in Vigo for a dispatch to the *Star*. The Hemingways proceeded to Paris by train, arriving a few days before Christmas. After Galantiere helped them settle into the Hotel Jacob, they began to explore their new city. Their exuberance gave way temporarily to feelings of displacement and sadness as they spent a lonely first Christmas in Paris, but the occasion was not lost on Hemingway; two years later he reminisced about these first few days in Paris in a seasonal article to the *Toronto Star Weekly*. "It is very beautiful in Paris and very lonely at Christmas time," he wrote, but he concluded with the prophesy that in time Paris would be different.

In January 1922, with the assistance of Galantiere, the Hemingways moved into a fourth-floor apartment at 74, rue du Cardinal Lemoine. It was next door to a *bal musette*, a workmen's dance hall, and around the corner from a squalid-looking place, the Cafe des Amateurs, but to Hemingway the neighborhood was "the best part of the Latin Quarter." Hemingway always tried to be like a native wherever he went. In Paris he adopted a Continental casualness of dress and wore a striped Breton fisherman's shirt to take his wife dancing at the working-class *bal musette*. He began to speak French—the argot of the street people—as easily as he had learned to speak Italian during the war, and he was more interested in talking to working-class Frenchmen than to other expatriates. He observed with irony the Parisians' reactions to the invading Americans. "Paris was always worth it," he wrote in *A Moveable Feast* (1964), "and you received return for what you brought to it." As Hemingway wandered over the city, he became a citizen of Paris; for many expatriates, Montparnasse was an English-speaking village within Paris. "But Paris was a very old city," he wrote in retrospect, "and we were very young and nothing was simple there. . . ."

He found a room where he could write; it was in the hotel where the poet Verlaine had died. He developed a routine: after an early breakfast, he would walk to his room and work until the afternoon, trying to write something in his notebooks every day. Sometimes the process was difficult, and he wondered whether he would ever be able to write: "I would stand and look out over the roofs of Paris and think, 'Do not worry. You have always written before and you will write now. All you have to do is write one true sentence. Write the truest sentence that you know.' So finally I would write one true sentence, and then go on from there."

From January to April 1922 Hemingway entered six "true sentences" in his notebook. They exemplify an important aspect of his ability: he could take things that others had told him, and through the power of his imagination and concentrated style he could make other people's anecdotes sound like his own experiences. His fourth "true sentence" presents a personal observation, however: "I have stood on the crowded back platform of a seven oclock Batignolles bus as it lurched along the wet lamp lit street while men who were going home to supper never looked up from their newspapers as we passed Notre Dame grey and dripping in the rain."

After completing the sentences he decided he "would write one story about each thing that I knew about." Perhaps his most successful form, ultimately, was the short story. He carried his notebook with him in the pocket of his coat, and whenever it was too cold to go to the room, he would find a warm cafe in which he could write. Possibly the first fiction he wrote in Paris was "Up in Michigan," a story set in Hortons Bay about a waitress's seduction by a brutish blacksmith. He discovered that distance could benefit his imagination; in Paris he "could write about Michigan." He also finished "My Old Man," a horse-racing story which reflected the interest in racing that he had first developed in Milan.

He tried to avoid the company of the dilettante writers who also frequented the cafes. In one of the first articles he sent to the *Toronto Star* (25 March 1922) he wrote with disdain about the bohemians of the Left Bank: "They have all striven so hard for a careless individuality of clothing that they have achieved a sort of uniformity of eccentricity.... They are nearly all loafers expending the energy that an artist puts into his creative work in talking about what they are going to do and condemning the work of all artists who have gained any degree of recognition. By talking about art they obtain the same satisfaction that the real artist does in his work."

Although Hemingway had Anderson's letters of

introduction, he was reluctant to use them. New in Paris and unsure of himself, he was in a rebellious mood and sat quietly when he and Hadley went to tea at Pound's studio early in 1922. A few days later he showed Galantiere a satire in which he characterized Pound's manners and dress as being pretentiously bohemian. He told the amazed Galantiere that he intended to submit it to Margaret Anderson and Jane Heap of the *Little Review*, who had asked him for some of his work. After Galantiere explained to him that Pound had served faithfully as that magazine's foreign editor for years, Hemingway decided to throw away the satire rather than ruin his opportunities with Anderson and Heap. Pound soon became Hemingway's adviser, advocate, and friend. "He's teaching me to write," Hemingway told Galantiere, "and I'm teaching him to box." Pound read some of the poetry that Hemingway had been writing over the past two years, and he submitted six of Hemingway's poems to the *Dial*, for which he served as a contributing editor. But an argument between the magazine's editor Scofield Thayer and Pound over T. S. Eliot's *The Waste Land*, which Pound had also submitted to the *Dial*, resulted in Thayer's dismissing Pound and rejecting Hemingway's poems. Pound also tentatively accepted one of Hemingway's stories for the *Little Review*, but, there too, the editors rejected the submission. Another of Pound's contacts, Harriet Monroe, the editor of the Chicago little magazine, *Poetry: A Magazine of Verse*, accepted six of Hemingway's poems, which appeared in the January 1923 issue under the general title "Wanderings." Hemingway also emulated his mentor by contributing expatriate community news to the magazine's notes. Hemingway's only previous publications in a little magazine were his fable, "A Divine Gesture," and a poem, "Ultimately," which had appeared in the New Orleans magazine, the *Double-Dealer*, in May and June 1922 respectively, probably through the influence of Sherwood Anderson.

Although Pound's editorial influence on Hemingway's work was not as great as it had been on Eliot's, he was centrally responsible for the promotion of Hemingway's reputation and helped to shape the course of his career. When John Peale Bishop arrived in Paris in 1922 and asked Pound about "American writers of talent" living in the city, Pound took Bishop to meet Hemingway. "He was instinctively intelligent, disinterested, and not given to talking nonsense," Bishop recalled. "Toward his craft, he was humble, and had, moreover, the most complete literary integrity it has ever been my lot to encounter." Pound summed up Hemingway's talent more simply: "The son of a bitch's *instincts* are right!" In *A Moveable Feast* Hemingway calls Pound "the most generous writer I have ever known and the most disinterested. He helped poets, painters, sculptors and prose writers that he believed in and he would help anyone whether he believed in them or not if they were in trouble."

It took Hemingway three months to develop the courage to call on Gertrude Stein. In March 1922 when he and Hadley Hemingway presented themselves at 27, rue de Fleurus, Stein's companion, Alice B. Toklas, performed her role (as she saw it) by taking Hadley off for a separate conversation while Stein and Hemingway sat by the fireplace and talked. He openly courted the attentions of this imposing and opinionated woman, and Stein seemed to like the rather "foreign-looking" young man with the "passionately interested" eyes. A few days later Stein and Toklas visited the Hemingways in their fourth-floor apartment at 74, rue du Cardinal Lemoine. Hemingway showed Stein his work: a portion of a youthful novel that was later lost, some short stories, and several poems. Stein liked the poems best; the novel contained too much description, "and not particularly good description." She told him to "Begin over again and concentrate." This advice, along with Pound's insistence upon a consciously austere language, corresponded with Hemingway's maturing artistic temperament. Stein told him that the heartless seduction scene in "Up in Michigan" made the story *inaccrochable*, or unpublishable—a judgment that nearly proved correct. She further advised him to give up journalism before it ruined him as a writer, but he was unable to take her advice right away. From the beginning their superficial roles as master and disciple were established by Stein. At first Hemingway was happy to tolerate Stein's idiosyncrasies, and until 1925 or 1926 their relationship was warm and mutually beneficial.

It was to Hemingway's benefit in Paris that he moved between opposing centers of influence. During his first months in Paris he also met James Joyce, whom Stein considered her rival. In March 1922 Hemingway wrote to Anderson that *Ulysses* was a "most god-damned wonderful book," an opinion that only grew stronger over the years. Toward Joyce, Hemingway was always respectful, and the Irishman admired the younger writer. Although they were never close friends, they were together occasionally in Paris, and during the thirties they corresponded. Hemingway wrote of Joyce in *Green Hills of Africa* (1935): "And when you saw him he would take up a conversation interrupted three years before. It was nice to see a great writer in our time." "He's a good writer, Hemingway," Joyce told a visitor in 1936. "He writes as he is. We like him. He's a big, powerful peasant, as strong as a buffalo. A sportsman. . . . But giants of this sort are truly modest; there is much more behind Hemingway's form than people know."

Hemingway's relationship with Joyce was formal, as was everyone's. He was far closer to the publisher of *Ulysses*, Sylvia Beach. As Beach says in her memoir, Joyce was the "most illustrious member" of Shakespeare and Company, and Hemingway was the bookshop's "best customer." Beach and Hemingway were friends from the first day he strolled into her bookshop. Paris was Hemingway's university; Shakespeare and Company was his library. He spent many days searching through the stacks for books he wanted to read and sitting behind the bookshelves reading contemporary poetry in the literary journals Beach ordered for her shop. His reading habits were eclectic: he preferred Russian fiction writers, particularly Ivan Turgenev and Fyodor Dostoevski; among English-language writers he selected works by Henry Fielding, W. B. Yeats, Joseph Conrad, D. H. Lawrence, and Joyce; among the French he liked Stendhal and Gustave Flaubert; and he greatly admired the German Thomas Mann. According to Beach, when copies of *Ulysses* were seized by the U.S. Customs in 1922, she appealed to Hemingway. He enlisted the aid of a friend who gradually smuggled forty copies from Windsor, Ontario, Canada, where he worked, to Detroit, where he lived. Once he got them into the country, he mailed them to American subscribers.

Both Beach and her friend Adrienne Monnier, who ran La Maison des Amis des Livres, the French bookshop near Beach's, were enthusiastic about Hemingway's fiction. "Hemingway has the true writer's temperament," Monnier said, and later she published a translation of his story "The Undefeated" in her journal *Navire d'Argent*. It was Hemingway's first publication in French, and it attracted a great deal of attention. In May 1937 Hemingway broke his personal rule against reading his work in public when he read his story "Fathers and Sons" during a benefit reading at Shakespeare and Company. He later wrote of Beach, "No one that I ever knew was nicer to me."

The Hemingways often went to the mountains to escape the periods of cold and rainy weather in Paris. Shortly after they were settled in Paris in the late winter of 1922, they left for a skiing vacation at

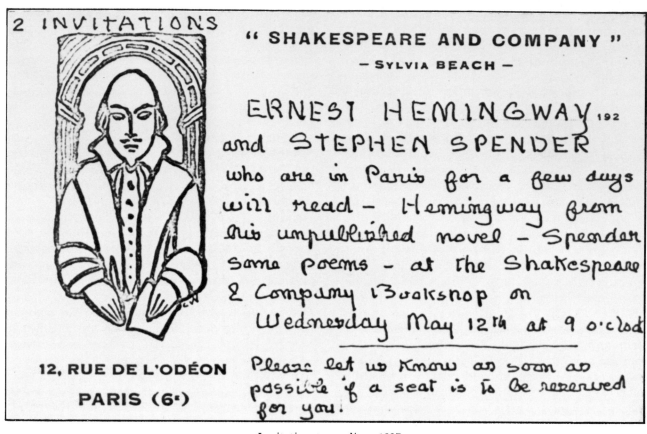

Invitation to reading, 1937

Chamby in the Swiss Alps. When Hemingway traveled, he often mixed business with pleasure. He helped pay for his vacation in the mountains by submitting color pieces to the *Toronto Star* and *Toronto Star Weekly* about the clientele at the hotels of Switzerland and about the winter sports there. He developed a unique journalistic voice while commenting on social life in Paris, and his keen assessments of French politics and German postwar problems formed the basis for the remarkable insights he displayed over the next two decades as he forecast Europe's slide into World War II. The datelines of his articles are a log of the places he visited during his first year in Europe when he journeyed more than 10,000 miles, often on assignment to cover events for the *Toronto Star*.

In April 1922 Hemingway covered the Genoa economic conference, where he met another American newspaperman, William Bird. Bird, whose hobby was printing on an eighteenth-century hand press, told Hemingway he was looking for publishable manuscripts, and Hemingway suggested he speak to Ezra Pound, beginning a sequence of events that eventually led to the

publication of Hemingway's second book, *in our time*. At Genoa Hemingway also met Lincoln Steffens, the muckraking journalist, and Max Eastman, an editor for the radical journal the *Masses*. Eastman read some of Hemingway's experimental sketches and sent them on to his magazine, but the work was rejected. Some of Hemingway's approximately fifteen articles from Genoa depicted the fascist-communist street clashes spawned by the conference, while others were short, cynical sketches of the delegates. These satisfied the needs of the *Toronto Star*, which, like most Canadian newspapers of the time, preferred color pieces and human interest stories to the American brand of objective journalism. Hemingway's articles were appearing in the *Toronto Star* at the rate of two a week.

In May 1922 with the money earned from the Genoa dispatches, the Hemingways, along with Dorman-Smith, hiked from Chamby, Switzerland, over the St. Bernard Pass into Italy. Hemingway had been anxious to show his wife the scenes of his wartime adventures, but on this occasion Italy was a disappointment; nothing was the same in the places

Hemingway had been to during the war. While they were in Milan, however, he interviewed Benito Mussolini, the rising fascist leader in Italy. Hemingway spent the next two months in Paris working on his fiction and entertaining friends from America. One visitor was John Dos Passos, a fellow Chicagoan, whom Hemingway had met briefly at Dolo, Italy, in 1918. Only three years older than Hemingway, Dos Passos had traveled extensively in Europe and the Middle East and had already published two novels. He was an enthusiastic man whose experiences and company Hemingway appreciated.

In August and September Hemingway mailed to the *Toronto Star* a series of articles on life in economically strained postwar Germany, based on observations made during an August trip to Germany. He was back in Paris from Germany for only a week before he was sent, in late September, to Turkey and Greece to cover the Greek evacuation of Asia Minor, where he witnessed the Greek civilian population marching through Adrianople in a "slow, ghastly procession" that taught him "what war was really all about."

In November 1922, shortly after he had returned from Greece, Pound asked Hemingway to contribute a short volume of his writings for a series of books he was editing for William Bird's Three Mountains Press. The series, which Pound called "*The Inquest* into the state of contemporary English prose," had been conceived when Bird followed Hemingway's advice and called on Pound. Although the eventual contents of the book would prove to be different, Hemingway's first reaction was to ask Harriet Monroe for permission to use the six poems that she had accepted for *Poetry*. He did not have an abundance of material to choose from for his volume. During this brief respite in which he could work on his "serious writing," Hemingway composed satiric sketches of people he knew in Paris, including Ernest Walsh, editor of *This Quarter*, and British novelist Ford Madox Ford, but literary exercises such as these would hardly have satisfied Pound's purpose for the series.

By the end of 1922 Hemingway had come full circle in his coverage of the Greco-Turkish War; he went to Lausanne in late November to cover the peace talks between Turkey and Greece, which were being orchestrated by England, France, Italy, and Russia. The conference was a frustrating affair; the only information newsmen could get came from official daily press releases. Finally there was some news when Mussolini arrived at the conference. Hemingway now saw the Italian dictator as "the

biggest bluff in Europe." "There is something wrong, even histrionically," Hemingway wrote, "with a man who wears white spats with a black shirt."

This remark exemplifies the strength of Hemingway's journalism: he exposed international problems through his characterizations of particular traits of both common people and statesmen. Whether his subject was a French-speaking Belgian lady's confrontation with a German French-hater on a German train or politicians like France's Clemenceau, Italy's Mussolini, Russia's Chicherin, Turkey's Ismet Pasha, or England's Lord Curzon, Hemingway portrayed them colorfully. In his articles he often displayed a natural cynicism that appealed to his Canadian readers who were suspicious of Europe. Even though Hemingway's work for the *Toronto Star* often took him away from his work on experimental fiction, his journalism helped him to mature as a prose writer. Because Hemingway was a journalist, he had to consider the world he lived in with a more observant eye than

Hadley and Ernest Hemingway at Chamby, Switzerland

many of his contemporaries; he learned how to see people and events as stories in the present. Furthermore, in his travels he picked up invaluable material for his fiction and poetry; the scope of his early experiences in Europe is reflected in the subject matter of his early work. Out of financial necessity Hemingway had to approach the writing of his journalism with a professional attitude: he developed the habits of working at his craft regularly rather than merely planning to write, which was the downfall for many of his contemporaries, and he learned to write in a compressed style that was direct and suggestive. Because he was a dedicated writer, he developed his craft in every type of writing that he worked at.

At Lausanne Hemingway saw a number of journalists he had met earlier in Paris and Genoa, including Lincoln Steffens, to whom he showed his short story, "My Old Man," and one of his dispatches from Greece. Steffens admired Hemingway's work, and he sent the story on to a friend at *Cosmopolitan* for possible publication. Soon thereafter, when Hadley Hemingway was leaving Paris for Lausanne to meet her husband and begin a Christmas holiday in Switzerland, the valise she was carrying, which contained most of Hemingway's manuscripts with the exception of "Up in Michigan" and "My Old Man," was stolen from her train compartment at the Gare de Lyon. Hemingway rushed back to Paris, where he learned the completeness of his loss; not only had his wife taken the original manuscripts and typescripts, but the carbons as well. He spent the following day with Stein, and, returning to Lausanne on the evening train, he wrote "They All Made Peace—What Is Peace?" a long free-verse poem satirizing the delegates at the conference, which imitated Stein's prose style. But despite the composition of this "joke," as he later called the poem, Hemingway was stunned by the loss of his manuscripts, and he felt for a time that he would never be able to write again.

He tried to forget about his setback, first in Switzerland, then at Rapallo, Italy, where in January 1923 he and his wife went to visit the Pounds, who had begun to spend more time there. The Pounds were gone when the Hemingways arrived in Rapallo, but while they awaited the Pounds' return, Hemingway met Edward O'Brien and Robert McAlmon. O'Brien read "My Old Man" and selected it for *Best Short Stories of 1923*, which he was then editing. Hemingway was surprised and delighted because it was customary to include only work that had appeared in American magazines during the year. McAlmon, an American expatriate and writer who had founded the Contact Publishing Company in Paris, was soon to become Hemingway's first publisher.

At Rapallo Hemingway began writing again by making some notes for a modest autobiographical story, "Cat in the Rain." The story concerns a young American couple staying in a provincial Italian hotel and is derived from the Hemingways' stay in the hotel in Rapallo while waiting for Pound. Hemingway later claimed, however, that the story was about a young couple he had met in Genoa. The story focuses on the ambiguous yearnings of the wife, while her husband spends the rainy afternoon in bed reading. The story implies that the woman wants something to care for, presumably a baby, while her husband is significantly passive about the entire matter.

After a walking tour with Pound through Pisa and Siena, the Hemingways went to Cortina d'Ampezzo, a mountain resort in the Dolomites in northern Italy. Invigorated by the setting at Cortina, Hemingway enjoyed a significant period of creativity. He began a series of six prose sketches, vignettes that were much like the "true sentences" he had written the previous year. The material came from different sources—stories that Dorman-Smith had told him about the fighting in Belgium during the war, a newspaper story about a political execution in Greece, accounts of Spain and bullfighting that he had heard from Stein and the artist Mike Strater; and he reworked into a fictional miniature the dispatch that Lincoln Steffens had admired about the caravan of Greek refugees at Adrianople.

His writing was interrupted in late March when he was called away from Cortina suddenly by the *Toronto Star*, whose editor wanted him to cover events in the Ruhr. The French had occupied the industrial Ruhr region on the grounds that Germany was remiss in its payments of war reparations. Passing through Paris on his way to Germany, Hemingway submitted his six new vignettes to Jane Heap for the Exiles Number of the *Little Review* (Spring 1923), to which she had invited him to contribute. From France and Germany he submitted ten articles on the tense economic and political stalemate between the two nations; despite his distaste for Germans and his love for France, Hemingway clearly placed the fault for the Ruhr conflict with the reactionary government of France's Premier Raymond Poincare. Hemingway's talent for political analysis is probably best displayed in this series of articles; his dispatches from Germany bore portentous signs of a new war in the making.

It was April before he rejoined his wife in

Cortina. Shortly after his return he went on a fishing trip that served as the basis for his short story "Out of Season." The Hotel Concordia employed an old reprobate as a guide, and the man took Hemingway fishing for trout out of season. After Hemingway complained to the hotel manager, the man was fired and hanged himself in the stables. Almost immediately Hemingway began to work this event into a story. "Out of Season" not only describes the incident between the guide and a young man, but also suggests a vague tension between the young

they understood." "Out of Season" represents some of Hemingway's best writing. He had expanded journalistic writing to the realm of art by charging the description of real events with a complexity of emotion—relating the truth of the situation. By traditional standards of plot and character development it was not a story at all. And in his delineation Hemingway had been critical of his own character.

Like the young couple in "Out of Season," the Hemingways were experiencing tension in their

Ernest Hemingway and Robert McAlmon in Spain, 1923

Sylvia Beach Collection

man and his wife. The third-person limited narration employed in this almost strictly autobiographical story is interesting for the fact that it presents the point of view of the guide rather than the young man. Hemingway wrote from experience rather than imagination, but it was the psychological and emotional impact of experience that mattered in his work rather than action by itself. This style was developed gradually, but with "Out of Season" Hemingway made a technical breakthrough that became central to his thinking about fiction, an idea later known as his "iceberg theory." In *A Moveable Feast* he says of the story: "I had omitted the real end of it which was that the old man hanged himself. This was omitted on my new theory that you could omit anything if you knew that you omitted and the omitted part would strengthen the story and make people feel something more than

marriage; Hadley Hemingway was pregnant and wanted their baby to be born in America. Hemingway felt that her pregnancy was an interference in their lives, both professionally and personally. He set out to squeeze in as much new experience and to write as much as he could before he had to leave Europe for what he hoped would be only a temporary absence. He had already written about a bullfight in one of his vignettes for the *Little Review*; now he wanted to see one. In May 1923 Hemingway journeyed to Spain to attend his first bullfights along with William Bird and Robert McAlmon. His relationship with McAlmon became strained during the trip when McAlmon was considerably less appreciative than he of the art of bullfighting, but shortly after they returned to Paris, McAlmon announced that his Contact Publishing Company would soon publish a volume by Ernest

Hemingway. Although Hemingway had already agreed to let Bird publish a volume of his work as the last book in Pound's series of six, he was growing impatient with the slow process of hand printing at Bird's Three Mountains Press and gave McAlmon nearly all the completed work he had. He collected his three finished stories, "Up in Michigan," "Out of Season," and "My Old Man." He added the six poems that had appeared in *Poetry*: "Mitrailliatrice" (French for machine-gun fire), a poem written in Chicago which employs military metaphors to describe the mechanical sound of his typing on the new Corona typewriter Hadley Richardson had given him for his birthday; "Oily Weather," which presents in heavy sexual images a ship on the rolling ocean; "Roosevelt," a remarkably insightful elegy on Theodore Roosevelt, which declares, "And all the legends that he started in his life / Live on and prosper, / Unhampered now by his existence."; "Riparto d'Assalto" and "Champs d'Honneur," two poems about dying in the war, which strip away all illusions of valor and glory; and "Chapter Heading," which reflects the spiritual unfaithfulness of the lost generation. To these he added four more poems from his stock: "Oklahoma," probably written in Petoskey or Chicago, sketches in raw images the Indians' way of life; "Captives" depicts a weary World War I prisoner-of-war march; "Montparnasse" ironically considers the fake suicides of the "people one knows" in Paris as compared to real suicides of anonymous Latin Quarter transients; and "Along With Youth" laments the unconscious passing away of boyhood. He was left with the problem of what to give to Bird. The vignettes that had appeared in the *Little Review* interested Bird; he suggested that if Hemingway wrote another dozen such pieces, they would make a respectable volume.

In early July the Hemingways, at Stein's suggestion, attended the Fiesta of San Fermin, held each July in Pamplona. Hemingway's final month in Paris before returning to Canada for the birth of his child was a productive and seminal period. He finished five vignettes based on his experiences in Spain, and he wrote six others from his memory of Kansas City and Chicago, the war, Italy, and his homecoming. Significantly, chapter 7 of *in our time* concerns the wounding of a soldier named Nick, who was to become Hemingway's autobiographical, youthful hero Nick Adams, and an Italian, Rinaldi, the name used for the Italian doctor in *A Farewell to Arms*. For the final vignette Hemingway borrowed from a colleague's account of an interview with the king of Greece. Before leaving France Hemingway

received a fifty-dollar advance when he delivered the manuscript for *in our time* to Bird, and on 5 August he received page proofs for *Three Stories & Ten Poems* from McAlmon. Thus Hemingway's first residency in Paris ended satisfactorily with tangible proofs of his accomplishment.

In mid-August 1923 the Hemingways returned to Toronto for the birth of their baby, and Hemingway went to work full time for the *Toronto Star*. The *Star*'s new editor was not impressed by Hemingway's journalistic credentials. He took away Hemingway's by-line and saw to it that he was in New York on a routine assignment when his son was born on 10 October. They named the boy John Hadley Nicanor Hemingway (Nicanor, after one of their favorite bullfighters), but they eventually came to call the boy Bumby. "I am getting very fond of him," Hemingway wrote to Stein. Hemingway's fiction writing was suffering because he lacked the time and energy to devote to it. Also that fall his first book, *Three Stories & Ten Poems*, was published. The American reviewers ignored it, although the critic Edmund Wilson and Hemingway's old friend Lewis Galantiere were promoting him as best they could. Wilson had given the issue of the *Little Review* containing the six vignettes to Burton Rascoe of the *New York Tribune*, and Galantiere had sent the powerful book reviewer a copy of *Three Stories & Ten Poems*, but in his column Rascoe only mentioned receiving the material and said that he had not gotten around to reading this "amusing stuff." Hemingway wrote to Wilson to thank him for his interest and included a copy of *Three Stories & Ten Poems*. Wilson sent a letter of qualified praise and offered to include a notice of the book in the *Dial*, but Hemingway suggested that he wait until he could announce *in our time* at the same time. Bird sent advance copies of the book in November, and Hemingway quickly mailed one to Wilson, but the book was not officially published until March 1924.

On 1 January 1924 Hemingway officially resigned from the *Toronto Star*, and by mid-January 1924 he and his family were on their way to Europe. Hemingway was back in Paris less than six months after he had left. They found an apartment on the rue Notre Dame des Champs, up the street from Pound's studio and close to the Luxembourg Gardens and Stein's apartment. Free from his responsibilities at the *Star* Hemingway now devoted more of his time to his fiction. His domestic duties were largely limited to the early mornings when he awoke and fed their son before sitting down at the dining room table to write. The Hemingways lived above a sawmill, but at that hour it was still quiet. After the saws started, he would go to a nearby cafe, the Closerie des Lilas, to work. Sometimes he was joined there by his friends, including the poet Archibald MacLeish, whom he met in late 1924. Later he would wander across Paris, visit friends, or go to the Musee du Luxembourg to see the Cezannes, Manets, and Monets. He wanted to accomplish in fiction what Cezanne had done in painting.

He was writing steadily but with difficulty. In "Indian Camp" his autobiographical character Nick Adams appeared for the first time in a short story. Nick, a young boy, accompanies his doctor father and his uncle to an Indian camp in the north Michigan woods. There Nick witnesses scenes of life (a cesarean birth performed with a jackknife) and death (the suicide by knife of the baby's father). Nick is aware that he has been exposed to some dark mystery of adult life, but he feels that he is exempt from such tragedy and pain and "that he would never die." Employing his technique of omitting essential material from a story, Hemingway deleted the first eight manuscript pages of "Indian Camp," which establish Nick's adolescent fear of being left alone in the woods. In the final version, rather than merely being the central character in a juvenile drama, Nick is a disinterested observer for whom the events are an initiation rite. Hemingway finished "The Doctor and the Doctor's Wife," a painfully insightful story about his parents, and "Soldier's Home," which captured the feelings he had had upon returning home from the war. Two related stories, "The End of Something" and "Three-Day Blow," expand upon Nick Adams's adventures in Michigan. In "The End of Something" Nick extracts himself from a youthful love affair, while the beginning of new interests for Nick is suggested in "Three-Day Blow" when Nick's wanderlust and a vague yearning for the literary life surface for the first time. Both stories take place against the autumnal setting of the Michigan woods. "Cross-Country Snow" brings Nick close to the present age of his creator by making him a writer in Europe who is soon to return to America with his pregnant wife. Hemingway also completed "Cat in the Rain," which he had begun in Rapallo the year before, and he wrote "Mr. and Mrs. Smith" (later changed to "Mr. and Mrs. Elliot") to satirize a middle-class American couple's sex life. "Big Two-Hearted River," his most ambitious story to date, was coming slowly, but the result satisfied him. "The story was about coming back from the war," Hemingway wrote in *A Moveable Feast*, "but there was no mention of the war in it." Hemingway had managed to take a daydream, the deliberate imaginings of

fishing that had occupied his waking hours while he was recovering from his war wounds, and turn it into realistic fiction. He was discovering the deliberate techniques by which he could characterize the psychological complexities of people on the verge of emotional breakdown.

Shortly after Hemingway returned to Paris, Pound involved him in the literary business of the day. The British novelist Ford Madox Ford had just published the first issue of his *transatlantic review*, and while Hemingway was still in Toronto, Pound had urged Ford to accept the young American as his assistant editor. The two were introduced at Pound's studio, where Pound told Ford, "He writes very good verse and he's the finest prose stylist in the world. . . . He's disciplined, too." Ford realized that Hemingway had great potential as a writer shortly after hiring him. In his memoir *It Was the Nightingale* (1933) Ford wrote of Hemingway: "I did not read more than six words of his before I decided to publish everything he sent me."

At first Hemingway's only duties at the *transatlantic review* were to read manuscripts. It wasn't long before he conceived the idea of serializing Stein's massive work *The Making of Americans* in the *transatlantic review*. According to his account in *A Moveable Feast*, Hemingway liked the first half of Stein's book very much, and he reasoned that Ford's review would not last long enough to publish the part that was repetitious and poorly written. He negotiated a deal between Ford and Stein, but a problem arose when Stein informed Hemingway that all she had on hand was a bound manuscript, which certainly could not serve as typesetter's copy. Hemingway was determined to see this project through so he volunteered to type the installments; he later read proof for Stein because she found this task distasteful. Hemingway already knew Stein's writings well, but the opportunity to work so closely with her manuscript allowed him to explore further her use of rhythm and language. Later he sometimes used her style for his more satiric passages, significantly in *The Torrents of Spring*. The April 1924 issue of the *transatlantic review* contained the first installment of *The Making of Americans*, an excerpt from Joyce's *Work in Progress* (published in 1939 as *Finnegans Wake*), the earliest reviews of *Three Stories & Ten Poems* and *in our time*, and Hemingway's story "Indian Camp," published here under the general title "Work in Progress."

When Ford had to go to New York in late May to try to raise more money for the review, he wrote an announcement for the July issue of the magazine that he was leaving the editorial duties to "Mr. Ernest Hemingway, whose tastes march more with our own than those of other men." Hemingway had been reluctant to accept the responsibility for the July and August 1924 issues. To the July issue he added an unsigned editorial called "And Out of America," which satirizes Tristan Tzara, Jean Cocteau, and Gilbert Seldes, all favorite targets of Hemingway in his satiric poetry. The August issue contains another installment of Stein's *The Making of Americans*, fiction by John Dos Passos and Nathan Asch, and nonfiction from Guy Hickok, an American journalist stationed in Paris. Hemingway had solicited material from people he knew so he could complete work on the issue in time to leave for Pamplona and the bullfights. His accounts of the previous summer's fiesta had encouraged several of his Paris friends to attend also. The company consisted of the Hemingways, Dorman-Smith, William and Sally Bird, Robert McAlmon, John Dos Passos, Donald Ogden Stewart, and George O'Neil, whom Hadley Hemingway had known in St. Louis. After the fiesta everyone except Stewart went fishing in Burguete, a Basque village in the Pyrenees foothills. The trip led Hemingway to declare that Spain was the only country in Europe that was untainted by modern events. When Ford returned to Paris and saw the contributors list for the August issue of the *transatlantic review*, he added a last-minute editorial note that was mildly critical of the issue because he thought that Hemingway had used the opportunity to publish his American friends' works. Hemingway felt he had worked hard for the review, at the expense of his own writing, and he considered Ford's criticism unfair. When Ford confessed that he had not been successful during his fund-raising trip, however, Hemingway suggested Krebs Friend, a Chicago acquaintance who had recently married an heiress, as a possible backer for the magazine. Friend subsequently agreed to underwrite the cost of publishing the review for six months. Hemingway soon vexed Ford again with his tribute to Joseph Conrad, who had died in August. His article for the October issue of the *transatlantic review* stated bluntly that if he could bring Conrad back to life "by grinding Mr. Eliot into a fine dry powder and sprinkling that powder over Conrad's grave in Canterbury" he would "leave for London early tomorrow morning with a sausage-grinder." Ford was left to apologize to his readers and to T. S. Eliot in the November issue.

The *transatlantic review* ceased publication in January 1925. During his association with the magazine Hemingway was never paid, but he was able to further his own literary reputation while he gained valuable experience from his position as Ford's subeditor. The *transatlantic review* had published Hemingway's short stories "Indian Camp," "The Doctor and the Doctor's Wife," and "Cross-Country Snow" as well as two editorials and two open letters. Although Hemingway gives the impression in *A Moveable Feast* that he disliked Ford from the beginning, Ford was a well-known writer with many friends, and association with him was beneficial to Hemingway.

Edmund Wilson's review of *Three Stories & Ten Poems* and *in our time* in the *Dial* (October 1924) was also important to Hemingway's career. Wilson wrote that "Miss Stein, Mr. Anderson, and Mr. Hemingway may now be said to form a school by themselves." He added, however, that Hemingway was "strikingly original, and in the dry compressed little vignettes in In Our Time has almost invented a form of his own." Wilson thought that Hemingway's poems were "not particularly important," but from early autumn 1924 through February 1925 *Der Querschnitt*, the German magazine of art and literature, published five more of Hemingway's poems; Hemingway claimed in *A Moveable Feast* that for a while after he returned to Paris, the meager payment he received for these poems was all he could earn from writing. However, the fiction that Hemingway had written after returning to Paris was beginning to appear regularly in journals; besides the three stories that Ford had accepted for the *transatlantic review*, "Mr. and Mrs. Elliot" appeared in the *Little Review* (Autumn/Winter 1924-1925), and in December he sold "Soldier's Home" to Robert McAlmon for his new anthology, *Contact Collection of Contemporary Writers* (1925).

In September 1924 Hemingway added the stories from *Three Stories & Ten Poems* to the nine stories he had completed since his return to Paris, recast chapters 10 and 11 from *in our time* into stories (entitled "A Very Short Story" and "The Revolutionist"), and sent this collection to Donald Ogden Stewart, who had offered to show Hemingway's work to his publisher in New York. John Dos Passos and Sherwood Anderson had also volunteered to help Hemingway find an American book publisher, as did Harold Loeb, a recent friend whose novel *Doodab* (1925) was being published by Boni and Liveright. When Liveright's literary scout Leon Fleischman came to Paris with the contract for *Doodab*, Loeb introduced him to Hemingway. Hemingway continued to work; in September he began writing "The Undefeated," and he completed the long story by 20 November. It demonstrated for the first time his dictum that "man can be destroyed but not defeated," as an old bullfighter named Manuel Garcia attempts a comeback against tremendous odds.

When the Hemingways realized that by subleasing their Paris apartment they could afford to spend the winter months in the mountains, they began to make plans to go to Schruns, Austria, for a skiing holiday. Before leaving Paris Hemingway had second thoughts about the ending of "Big Two-Hearted River" and wrote Stewart with instructions to delete the last nine pages because he felt the autobiographical interior monologue destroyed the effect of the story. Hemingway and his family arrived at the Hotel Taube on 20 December. While Hemingway waited for a good snowfall in Austria, his friends were circulating his story collection among New York publishers, and when Stewart failed to place the book with Doran, he sent Hemingway a personal check to boost his morale. In early February 1925 Hemingway returned to the hotel after a day on the slopes to find telegrams from both Stewart and Loeb informing him that Boni and Liveright had agreed to publish *In Our Time*.

There were a few problems. Horace Liveright objected to a passage in "Mr. and Mrs. Elliot" that he considered obscene, and he rejected "Up in Michigan" because of its portrayal of unsentimental sex. Hemingway toned down the questionable paragraphs in "Mr. and Mrs. Elliot," and he wrote "The Battler" to replace "Up in Michigan." In the new story his hero Nick Adams stumbles into a hobo camp after being bounced from a freight train and meets a former champion boxer who is dangerously simpleminded from having taken too many beatings in the ring and "crazy" from having lost his wife; interestingly, Hemingway maintains a fine distinction between physical and emotional injuries in his characterization of "the battler" Ad Francis. By merely showing without comment Nick's compassion for such people Hemingway suggests the temperamental qualities that make Nick an estranged young man.

While Hemingway was in Austria, Ernest Walsh sent a prospectus for his new magazine, *This Quarter*, the first issue of which was to be dedicated to Ezra Pound. After the demise of the *transatlantic review*, Hemingway needed a new outlet for his work, and he sent Walsh his short story "Big Two-Hearted River" and his tribute to Pound, "Homage to Ezra." Both appeared in the first issue (May 1925). After they returned to Paris, the Hemingways helped to prepare *This Quarter*'s first issue for the printer.

When the *Dial* rejected Hemingway's bullfight story "The Undefeated" as too realistic for American readers, Walsh purchased it for the second issue of *This Quarter* (Autumn-Winter 1925-1926).

On 5 March 1925, while still in Austria, Hemingway had wired his acceptance to Boni and Liveright's offer to publish *In Our Time*. In Paris, five days later, he picked up his mail at Shakespeare and Company and found a letter from Maxwell Perkins of Scribners. The editor had been urged to contact Hemingway by Scribners' author F. Scott Fitzgerald, who had seen the Paris edition of *in our time* and probably "Indian Camp" in the *transatlantic review*. Hemingway replied to Perkins that, regretfully, he had already signed a contract with Boni and Liveright, which also gave them options on his next three books. Until Boni and Liveright rejected one of his books he was bound to them.

Shortly after the Hemingways returned to Paris from Austria, Harold Loeb invited them to his home to celebrate the acceptance of *In Our Time*. There the Hemingways were introduced to Pauline Pfeiffer, a staff member for the Paris edition of *Vogue*, and her sister, Virginia. Pauline Pfeiffer began a friendship with Hadley Hemingway, but before long she had fallen in love with her friend's husband. When Hemingway became aware of Pauline Pfeiffer's feelings for him, he became increasingly intrigued by her.

In May 1925 Hemingway met Fitzgerald for the first time in the Dingo Bar. The letters the two wrote each other make plain that over the next eleven years Hemingway was a closer friend to Fitzgerald than he suggests in *A Moveable Feast*. Hemingway recognized the extraordinary natural talent that Fitzgerald had, but he also recognized Fitzgerald's lack of self-confidence and low tolerance for alcohol. Hemingway disliked Zelda Fitzgerald and claimed that Fitzgerald could have been the greatest of American writers if he had never married her. Hemingway looked with derision on the Fitzgeralds' self-indulgent way of life; he felt they represented the lack of seriousness of postwar American expatriate artists. Because Fitzgerald was three years older and never saw action during the war, Hemingway came to believe that Fitzgerald was steeped in the romanticism of the prewar past. However, Gertrude Stein, to whom Hemingway had introduced Fitzgerald in late spring or early summer of 1925, felt that the author of *This Side of Paradise* had "really created for the public the new generation," and her continuing praise for Fitzgerald became a source of tension in the two men's friendship. Despite Stein's compliments, Fitzgerald often felt Hemingway had a brighter future as a writer.

The Pamplona festival in July 1925 provided the setting and the material for Hemingway's first novel. Suddenly, Pamplona had been discovered by rich American tourists. Furthermore, the "completely worthless characters" who frequented the Dingo Bar in Paris—the striking Lady Duff Twysden and her crowd—followed the Hemingways to Pamplona that summer. Harold Loeb, who had been living with another woman, had just spent a week at St. Jean-de-Luz with Twysden. She was about to be divorced from her husband and had come to Paris with another man, Pat Guthrie, who was also part of the group in Pamplona. Into this imbroglio stepped Hemingway, who was drawn to Twysden. At Pamplona Hemingway, who had learned of Twysden and Loeb's affair before leaving Paris, nearly got into a fight with Loeb, but their mutual common sense stopped it. As much as Duff Twysden acted "crazy about" Hemingway, it was apparent to those around them that their relationship had not become sexual. Further bad feelings resulted when it became obvious that Twysden and her friends could not pay their bills at the hotel, and Stewart had to pay for them.

After the Pamplona festival the Hemingways went to the bullfights in Madrid where they saw the matador Cayetano Ordonez (Nino de la Palma), who dedicated two bulls to Hadley Hemingway. The recent events at Pamplona were arranging themselves in Hemingway's imagination, and while still in Madrid he began to write a novel that he called "Fiesta." He continued to work on the book as they traveled through Spain. In Paris, two months and seven notebooks later, he finished the first draft, dating it "Sept. 21-1925."

Hemingway was exhausted after the pace he had maintained in writing his first novel. He meant to set the manuscript aside until Christmas, when he would take it up again with a fresh perspective, but a few days later when he took his family to Chartres for a holiday, he carried the novel with him. He considered calling the novel "The Lost Generation" because of a conversation he had had with Stein while working on the novel and even wrote a foreword to explain the title. That previous summer Stein had been told by a garage owner that the young men who had served in World War I were a "generation perdue." As Hemingway tells the story in *A Moveable Feast*, Stein repeated the garage owner's story to him and added: "That's what you are. That's what you all are. . . . All of you young people who served in the war. You are a lost generation." The phrase intrigued Hemingway, but he did not agree with Stein and tried unsuccessfully to convince her she was wrong. On his way home he thought about the war experiences of those whom Stein had called "lost," and then, "I thought of Miss Stein and Sherwood Anderson and egotism and mental laziness versus discipline and I thought who is calling who a lost generation?" On 19 November 1926, shortly after the novel's publication, he wrote to Maxwell Perkins of Scribners that Stein's "lost generation" declaration was nothing but "splendid bombast," and that he did not take seriously her "assumption of prophetic roles."

While still at Chartres Hemingway decided to use Stein's comment as an epigraph, contrasting it with a second epigraph from which he took the novel's final title: *The Sun Also Rises*. The second epigraph is from Ecclesiastes:

> One generation passeth away, and another generation cometh; but the earth abideth forever . . . The sun also ariseth, and the sun goeth down, and hasteth to the place where he arose . . .

The title and the two epigraphs suggest the novel's complex form: its structure follows a pattern of opposing images, scenes, and characters.

In *The Sun Also Rises* Jake Barnes, Bill Gorton, Pedro Romero, and Montoya are aware of the earth's abiding values while Robert Cohn, Brett Ashley, and Mike Campbell have become lost in the abstractions of the age. The novel is as much about the significance of places as it is about people and their affairs. The book opens in Paris. The expatriate crowd moves frenetically from one Montparnasse nightclub to another. Jake Barnes, who suffers from an ambiguous war wound (suggested to be a missing phallus) tends to dissociate himself from the crowd until the appearance of Lady Brett Ashley, whom he had been in love with during the war. Brett's return to his life leads Jake to engage in the crowd's meaningless activities. Brett makes a new conquest in Robert Cohn, who has "a wonderful quality of bringing out the worst in anybody." Jake separates himself from the revelers, but later that night Brett arrives at his apartment while her entourage waits in the street. Jake's inability to consummate his love for Brett dramatizes the pathos of the war generation that carried its psychic and physical wounds into the twenties, and his pain is increased by his discovery that Brett and Cohn have had an affair. In the course of the novel, however, Jake gains control of his life by taking part in a succession of rituals: "Maybe if

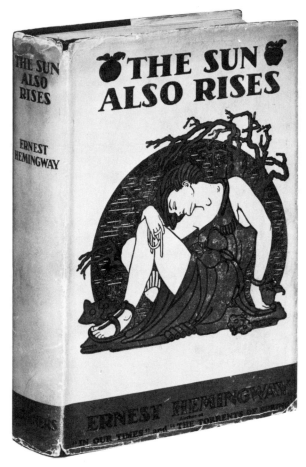

Dust jacket

you found out how to live it you learned from that what it was all about.''

The world of Montparnasse is diminished by the cold, clear air of the mountains around Burguete, Spain, where Jake and Bill Gorton go to fish. In this clear atmosphere pleasure takes on a different meaning. The pursuit of sanity through the enjoyment of nature, and of the men and women who live with nature, links Jake and Bill during a brief respite from the oppressing hedonism of their friends. Burguete is a place apart where Jake and Bill are men without women; where food, wine, warm beds on a cold night, and fishing in a clear stream are experienced in sensual appreciation.

The simplicity of Burguete becomes a frame of reference for what has preceded in Paris and what follows in Pamplona. Paris is pagan; Burguete is natural; Pamplona is religious, and the ritual is the bullfight. Against Catholic Spain and the mysticism of the bullfight world, Hemingway places Brett Ashley as a pagan goddess. Twice during the festivities she is deified as a Dionysian spirit in opposition to the traditional rituals going on

simultaneously in the town. All masculine jealousies, vanities, and melodramatic posturing revolve around Brett. The opposing worlds of the novel collide in Pamplona; Jake's relationship with the bullfight *aficionado* Montoya is threatened, and his own moral sense is jolted, when Brett and the jealous Cohn pull the young bullfighter Pedro Romero into their decadent affairs. Cohn, a college boxing champion, beats up Romero when he catches the bullfighter in Brett's room. But Cohn is morally defeated by Romero's stubbornness to yield to his superior strength and ability. As Cohn repeatedly knocks Romero to the floor, the scene becomes absurd and Cohn is "ruined." Romero's moral certitude protects him against Cohn's self-important posturings.

As though it were not painful enough for Jake to have seen Brett involved with Cohn, whom he despises, he allows himself to be used as the go-between for Brett and Romero, whom he admires. Furthermore, Jake suffers the censure of the Spaniards who witness his role in the temptation of their hero. Jake's final embarrassment comes when his friends cannot pay their hotel bill; in the eyes of Montoya he is damned by his associations. Following the tense atmosphere of Pamplona Jake escapes by himself back to France. He then travels to San Sebastian, where everything seems simple again and he can control his life, until he receives a cable from Brett, who is stranded in Madrid following her affair with Romero. Jake's musings well up inside him: "That was it. Send a girl off with one man. Introduce her to another to go off with him. Now go and bring her back. And sign the wire with love. That was it all right." Predictably he goes to help Brett. Hemingway's novel is so tightly structured that the final statement acts as a closing epigraph. Brett tells Jake that they "could have had such a good time together." His reply, "Isn't it pretty to think so," is a reminder of the futility of romantic illusions.

Even during a literary age when it was common practice to transcribe real people into fictional characters, in poetry as well as prose, *The Sun Also Rises* broke new ground by making legends of a group of generally banal people. The narrator, Jake Barnes, is based mainly upon Hemingway himself, although his job is much like that of William Bird, who, in addition to being a part-time publisher, ran his own news agency. Although Jake has significant faults, he is the only American or British character in the book with any sense of enduring values. Bill Gorton is drawn mostly from Hemingway's friend Bill Smith, with some characteristics of Donald

Ogden Stewart. Brett Ashley is a thinly disguised Duff Twysden, but some aspects of Hemingway's wartime romance with Agnes von Kurowsky are apparent in the history of Jake's love for Brett. Pat Guthrie, Twysden's inebriate companion, is the basis for Mike Campbell, while Harold Loeb is unflatteringly portrayed as the tormented and insufferable Robert Cohn. The hotel keeper Juanito Quintana is portrayed as the dignified *aficionado* Montoya, and the admirable bullfighter Pedro Romero is based on the bullfighter Cayetano Ordonez.

The Sun Also Rises is not just thinly veiled autobiography, however. Hemingway's first long sustained effort is remarkable for its style, deceptively simple and lacking any ornate musicality of language. It builds one image upon another into a representation that is true not to the confused world, but to the author's lucid perception of his world. Hemingway's dialogue achieves a realism of intent rather than a verisimilitude of speech patterns. Through the control of his language, Hemingway intended to construct fiction that would involve the reader through his senses. Although Hemingway admired many nineteenth-century writers, particularly the Russian novelists, he did not want to write novels like theirs, which contained explicit emotional and factual information.

While he was rewriting *The Sun Also Rises* Hemingway also wrote two new stories, "Ten Indians" and "Fifty Grand." In "Ten Indians" Nick Adams learns that he has been deceived by Prudence Mitchell, his Indian girlfriend. Nick's sense of loss is secondary to his hurt pride. Hemingway concluded his early draft with a midnight reunion between Nick and Prudie in the woods, but in the final version Nick wakes up the next morning and has almost forgotten that the night before he thought he was heartbroken. "Fifty Grand" is a boxing story in which, ironically, the underdog fighter, Jack Brennan, has an opportunity to claim a victory on a foul, but because he has bet "fifty grand" on the other fighter he continues with the contest long enough to lose the fight—on a foul. After Fitzgerald criticized the opening dialogue, which repeated a well-known anecdote about Benny Leonard and Jack Britton, the real-life models for the fighters, Hemingway deleted it, but he later regretted this decision. In the meantime Hemingway refused to let Fitzgerald read *The Sun Also Rises* until it was rewritten.

In October 1925 *In Our Time* was published. The reviewers for the *New York Evening Post*, the *Kansas City Star*, the *New Republic*, and the *Saturday Review of Literature* connected Hemingway to Sherwood Anderson. As early as 1923 Hemingway had told Edmund Wilson, the first critic to link Hemingway and Anderson in print, that he did not appreciate the comparisons of his work to Anderson's. The two best reviews appeared in Europe. Ernest Walsh wrote in *This Quarter* that the dust-jacket blurbs by Anderson, Ford, Dos Passos, and others missed the quality in Hemingway's prose that sets him apart: "His clarity of heart." Walsh added that Hemingway is blessed with extraordinary sensitivity which he uses "to face life rather than to avoid it." The insights of D. H. Lawrence, who also noticed the arrival of a new literary voice, complete the most serious assessment of Hemingway's early writing. In his review Lawrence recognized that although *In Our Time* is a book of stories, the single unifying sensibility of the author makes it a kind of novel. Lawrence also noted that like Hemingway's character Harold Krebs in "Soldier's Home," the characteristic of that voice of authority is that "he doesn't love anything," and his motto is "Don't get connected up." For Hemingway the time had come to break some connections, notably with Stein and Anderson.

Sometime after *The Making of Americans* began to appear in the *transatlantic review*, Stein and Hemingway's relationship changed. For a time after his return to Paris, their friendship had continued. Stein served as his son's godmother, a role that she (and Toklas) took seriously at first. The official break came in 1933 when Stein criticized Hemingway in *The Autobiography of Alice B. Toklas* and tried to reduce him to one of her and Anderson's creations. Hemingway's disaffection came earlier, however. In *A Moveable Feast* Hemingway describes the beginning of his estrangement from Stein in 1925 or 1926. He had been admitted to Stein's house by a servant, and while he was waiting to see her, he overheard an argument between Stein and Toklas in which Stein was groveling before the strong-willed Toklas. After that, he remembers, he went through the motions, but things were not the same. It was not the nature of the women's relationship that bothered him; it was the tone of the argument and what was said: "It was bad to hear and the answers were worse."

Hemingway reacted to suggestions that he was influenced by Sherwood Anderson with *The Torrents of Spring*, a parody of Anderson's most recent novel, *Dark Laughter*, published by Boni and Liveright in the same year that they published Hemingway's *In Our Time*. Hemingway borrowed

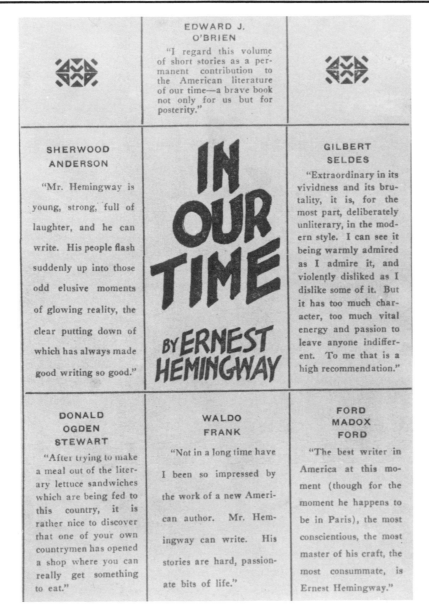

EDWARD J. O'BRIEN

"I regard this volume of short stories as a permanent contribution to the American literature of our time—a brave book not only for us but for posterity."

SHERWOOD ANDERSON

"Mr. Hemingway is young, strong, full of laughter, and he can write. His people flash suddenly up into those odd elusive moments of glowing reality, the clear putting down of which has always made good writing so good."

IN OUR TIME BY ERNEST HEMINGWAY

GILBERT SELDES

"Extraordinary in its vividness and its brutality, it is, for the most part, deliberately unliterary, in the modern style. I can see it being warmly admired as I admire it, and violently disliked as I dislike some of it. But it has too much character, too much vital energy and passion to leave anyone indifferent. To me that is a high recommendation."

DONALD OGDEN STEWART

"After trying to make a meal out of the literary lettuce sandwiches which are being fed to this country, it is rather nice to discover that one of your own countrymen has opened a shop where you can really get something to eat."

WALDO FRANK

"Not in a long time have I been so impressed by the work of a new American author. Mr. Hemingway can write. His stories are hard, passionate bits of life."

FORD MADOX FORD

"The best writer in America at this moment (though for the moment he happens to be in Paris), the most conscientious, the most master of his craft, the most consummate, is Ernest Hemingway."

Dust jacket

his title, *The Torrents of Spring,* from Turgenev and his epigraphs from Henry Fielding. The epigraph to part one suggests Hemingway's opinion of *Dark Laughter*: "The only source of the true Ridiculous (as it appears to me) is affectation." Hemingway parodies Anderson's use of self-conscious narrative intrusion. Hemingway's absurd linking of supposedly tragic themes and the provincial setting of Petoskey, Michigan, as well as his putting grand ideas and sophisticated speeches in the mouths of rustic characters, is an obvious parody of Anderson's tendency to ascribe mystical motives to simple acts. *The Torrents of Spring* also parodies Stein's extended syntax and deliberate repetitions, especially in part four, entitled "The Passing of a Great Race and the Making and Marring of Americans," which echoes Stein's *The Making of Americans.*

Stein was understandably angry not only because of the parody of her own work, but also because of the attack on a novelist who was "part of her apparatus." Dos Passos liked parts of the book and agreed with Hemingway's assessment of *Dark Laughter,* but he attempted to dissuade Hemingway from publishing it, at least at that time. Hadley Hemingway agreed with Dos Passos because she liked Anderson and "thought the whole idea detestable." Pauline Pfeiffer liked it, however, and urged Hemingway to submit it.

Hemingway believed—or wanted to believe—

that his attack on Anderson was not a personal one. "The parody is the last refuge of the frustrated writer," Hemingway told a friend in 1950. Before *The Torrents of Spring* was published, he wrote to Anderson explaining self-consciously that the book was "not personal," but merely a criticism of Anderson's bad writing. Although this letter seems to have affected Anderson more than the parody did, he accurately observed after seeing Hemingway in Paris in 1927 that the young author's "absorption in his ideas" had "affected his capacity for friendship." In 1938 Hemingway wrote an open apology to Anderson in "The Art of the Short Story," an essay that has never been published. "But writers have no business fingering another writer to outsiders while he is alive," Hemingway wrote. "I know you shouldn't do it because I did it once to Sherwood Anderson. I did it because I was righteous, which is the worst thing you can be, and I thought he was going to pot the way he was writing and that I could kid him out of it by showing him how awful it was. So I wrote The Torrents of Spring.... But then I was righteous and more loyal to writing than to my friend.... I'm sorry I threw at Anderson. It was cruel and I was a son of a bitch to do it. The only thing I can say is that I was as cruel to myself then. But that is no excuse."

Hemingway was dissatisfied with his association with Boni and Liveright, and he had continued a friendly correspondence with Maxwell Perkins of Scribners since the editor had first written to him. Hemingway sent his new novel to Horace Liveright. Although Fitzgerald had earlier tried to get Hemingway to sign a contract with Scribners, he now wrote a friendly letter to Horace Liveright and Boni and Liveright editor T. R. Smith, calling *The Torrents of Spring* "about the best comic book ever written by an American." Liveright disagreed; he cabled his rejection to Hemingway and urged him to submit *The Sun Also Rises*. Although it is uncertain how much influence Fitzgerald had on the final outcome, he wrote to Perkins with the news, reporting that Hemingway believed that Boni and Liveright's rejection freed him of his contract to them. Although neither Perkins nor Fitzgerald had seen *The Sun Also Rises*, Perkins had confidence in Fitzgerald's instincts and wired an offer to Hemingway. Finally, on 9 February 1926, Hemingway arrived in New York aboard the *Mauretania*; he had decided that matters were too important to be decided by mail from Schruns, Austria, where he had been skiing with his family and an assortment of friends. He visited Horace Liveright, and the two agreed to terminate their contract. On the following day he went to Scribners, where Perkins offered him a $1500 advance against fifteen percent royalties on *The Torrents of Spring* and *The Sun Also Rises*. A few weeks before he signed Hemingway as a Scribners' author, Perkins had written to Fitzgerald: "Hemingway would be better off in our hands because we are absolutely true to our authors and support them loyally in the face of losses for a long time, when we believe in their qualities and in them. It is that kind of publisher that Hemingway probably needs, because I hardly think he could come into a large public immediately." *The Sun Also Rises* was to prove Perkins wrong, but at the time he wrote to Fitzgerald, he had read only some of Hemingway's short fiction and *The Torrents of Spring*.

While the events surrounding Hemingway's switch to Scribners were going on, the Hemingways spent Christmas 1925 at Schruns, where they were joined by Pauline Pfeiffer. Also in Schruns were Hemingway's new friends Gerald and Sara Murphy, who praised *The Torrents of Spring* when he read it aloud to them. In late January Hemingway's wife and child remained in Austria while Hemingway left for New York to take care of his business with Liveright and Scribners, stopping in Paris to spend time with Pauline Pfeiffer on his way to and from New York. In *A Moveable Feast* he remembers his remorse as his train pulled into the station at Schruns, and he saw his wife and son waiting for him: "I wished I had died before I ever loved anyone but her. She was smiling, the sun on her lovely face tanned by the snow and sun, beautifully built, her hair red gold in the sun, growing out all winter awkwardly and beautifully, and Mr. Bumby standing with her, blond and chunky and with winter cheeks looking like a good Voralberg boy." In March 1926 the Murphys reappeared at Schruns with John Dos Passos, and they expressed their admiration for the chapters from *The Sun Also Rises* that Hemingway read them.

As his estrangement from his wife grew, Hemingway withdrew into his work. After returning to Paris that spring, he completed "An Alpine Idyll," a macabre story about an Austrian peasant who preserves his wife's corpse in a woodshed. During the long winter the peasant not only comes to ignore the corpse, but he begins to hang his lantern from his wife's jaw while he retrieves wood for his fireplace. Although the editors of *Scribner's Magazine* had recently returned "Fifty Grand," Hemingway mailed "An Alpine Idyll" to Perkins on 5 May. Perkins also rejected this story, calling it "too terrible." "Banal Story," another sketch about the bullfighter Maera, appeared in the *Little Review* (Summer 1926).

In mid-May Hemingway went to Madrid to attend the bullfights, but when the *corridas* were canceled due to an unseasonable snowfall, he spent much of his time revising and writing short stories. On Sunday, 16 May, he wrote the new ending for "Ten Indians," in which Nick awakes the following morning and forgets that his heart is broken by Prudie Mitchell's unfaithfulness, dramatizing once again that Hemingway's characters "don't love anybody." Hemingway then completed one of his finest short stories, "The Killers." In this story Nick Adams goes to warn Ole Andreson, a prize-fighter who "got mixed up in something in Chicago," that two professional gunmen have come to town to kill him. But the big man seems resigned to his fate. "After a while," he tells Nick, "I'll make up my mind to go out." Thus Ole becomes the archetype of the Hemingway character who stoically accepts that he cannot run away anymore. Hemingway's third production on that Sunday was the story "To-day is Friday," written in play form. The scene takes place after the crucifixion of Christ; three Roman soldiers, who talk like World War I infantrymen, are commenting that only Christ's women "stuck by him," while "his gang . . . faded out."

On 28 May, while Hemingway was still in Madrid, Scribners published *The Torrents of Spring*. Although the book did not sell well, it was more widely reviewed than *In Our Time*. Several reviewers used their praise of the book as a means for criticizing Anderson. Some reviewers noted that Hemingway's parody seemed to be aimed at the works of D. H. Lawrence, whom Anderson greatly admired. Allen Tate called the book "a small masterpiece of American fiction," and "the most deftly tempered ribaldry, and the most economically realized humor of disproportion that this reviewer has read in American prose." The wide attention the parody received set the stage for an even broader critical recognition of Hemingway's first novel.

In early June Hemingway joined his wife and child on the Riviera where they had gone to join the Murphys, the Fitzgeralds, and the MacLeishes. While there Hemingway showed Fitzgerald the typescript of *The Sun Also Rises* for the first time. Fitzgerald urged him to delete the first fifteen pages, two chapters describing the characters' backgrounds. Hemingway accepted Fitzgerald's suggestion and notified Perkins of the change. Pauline Pfeiffer joined the Hemingways in July, shortly before the Pamplona festival, which she attended with them and the Murphys. In August the Hemingways were back on the Riviera, visiting the Murphys and being introduced to Donald Ogden Stewart's new wife. It was the Hemingways' final journey together; when they arrived back in Paris, they set up separate residences. While correcting proofs of *The Sun Also Rises* at Murphy's studio in the rue Froidevaux, Hemingway dedicated the novel to his wife and son.

The Sun Also Rises was published on 22 October 1926. The novel was much discussed in Paris, where the expatriate community delighted in identifying the characters' living counterparts. The book sold well in the United States, and during the following months it received an extraordinary critical reception for a first novel. "The dialogue is brilliant," wrote Conrad Aiken in the *New York Herald Tribune*. "If there is better dialogue being written today I do not know where to find it. More than any other talk I can call to mind, it is alive with the rhythms and idioms, the pauses and suspensions and innuendoes and shorthands, of living speech." Burton Rascoe, the critic who had earlier ignored Hemingway's expatriate books, largely concurred: "Every sentence that he writes is fresh and alive." Allen Tate attached the "hard-boiled" label to Hemingway in his review in the *Nation*. The most disparaging note was sounded by Virginia Woolf in the *New York Herald Tribune*. Woolf did not consider Hemingway to be a modern writer, at least not by her definition, and she saw the characters in his novel as "flat" and "crude." However, no matter what the opinion, it was clear that Hemingway was suddenly at the center of the American literary scene. Furthermore, when Conrad Aiken began his review by repeating a rumor that Hemingway had once been a professional bullfighter in Spain, he contributed to the creation of Hemingway's legend.

Hadley Hemingway agreed to a divorce if Hemingway and Pauline Pfeiffer would separate for one hundred days to test the strength of their feelings for each other. Pfeiffer sailed for America on 24 September, and although Hadley Hemingway later revoked the separation requirement, she did not return to Paris until early January. Hemingway spent much time with the MacLeishes. He estranged himself from his old friend Donald Ogden Stewart in late October by reading his bitter poem "To a Tragic Poetess," which attacked Dorothy Parker, to a party at MacLeish's apartment. Stewart rebuked Hemingway, and Hemingway essentially ended their friendship.

In the fall of 1926 Edward O'Brien notified Hemingway that he wanted "The Undefeated" for the *Best Short Stories of 1926*, and *Scribner's Magazine* paid $200 for "The Killers," the first of his mature short stories to appear in an American periodical. A few weeks later he sold "A Canary for One" to *Scribner's Magazine* for $150, and in late November he mailed a new story called "In Another Country" to Perkins for the magazine. "A Canary for One" is a largely autobiographical account of the train ride from the Riviera back to Paris after the Hemingways had decided to separate. With "In Another Country" Hemingway began to reexplore his memories of the war, the material that would eventually be used in *A Farewell to Arms*. He wrote to Perkins that the period of his recuperation in Milan was beginning to seem very real. Again in this story the Hemingway persona is a sensitive observer. During a hospital therapy session a young American listens to an Italian major bitterly lament his sense of loss during the war: the crippling of his hand and his young wife's death of pneumonia. Stylistically the story is memorable for its remarkable opening paragraph. The story begins: "In the fall the war was always there, but we did not go to it any more." Fitzgerald called it "one of the most beautiful prose sentences I've ever read." "In Another Country" was a step toward a novel about the war.

In January 1927 Hemingway went skiing at Gstaad, Switzerland, with Pauline Pfeiffer, recently returned from the United States. They were there on 27 January when his divorce became final. By February 1927 *The Sun Also Rises* had sold over 12,000 copies. In the wake of this success Hemingway sold "An Alpine Idyll" to *American Caravan*, and the *Atlantic Monthly* bought "Fifty Grand" for $350, the most he had received to date for a short story. He had also completed two short stories in February. "A Pursuit Race" is a study of an alcoholic drug addict in the final stages of a nervous breakdown. "A Simple Enquiry" exposes the "corrupt" nature of an Italian major as he makes a homosexual advance toward his young orderly. In the middle of March Hemingway and Guy Hickock left for a trip through fascist Italy in Hickock's old Ford. Shortly after his return Hemingway set down his impressions of the journey and mailed the sketch he called "Italy, 1927" to Edmund Wilson for the *New Republic*, in which it appeared in May 1927.

In February Perkins had suggested that Hemingway follow his novel with a new collection of short stories, and by mid-May the contents for *Men Without Women* was set. Hemingway had suggested that "Up in Michigan," cut from *In Our Time* by Liveright, be included, but once again it was omitted and was not published in the United States until 1938 when Hemingway convinced Perkins to include it in *The Fifth Column and the First Forty-nine Stories.* "The Undefeated" and "In Another Country" were followed by the recently completed "Hills Like White Elephants," a story told almost entirely by enigmatic dialogue in which a self-conscious young man convinces his lover to have an abortion. The rest of the book was comprised of "The Killers," "Che Ti Dice La Patria?" (the new title for "Italy, 1927"), "Fifty Grand," "A Simple Enquiry," "Ten Indians," "A Canary for One," "An Alpine Idyll," "A Pursuit Race," "To-day is Friday," "Banal Story," and "Now I Lay Me," a new Nick Adams story. This recently completed story describes Nick's lying awake at night in a Milan hospital while he is recovering from his wounds. His waking dream about fishing, which he deliberately concocts to keep himself awake, recalls the earlier "Big Two-Hearted River." Since his wounding he has been afraid of falling asleep at night because he might die.

On 10 May 1927 in Paris Hemingway married Pauline Pfeiffer, who was three years his senior and a Catholic. Hemingway convinced the priest who performed the wedding ceremony that he had converted to Catholicism in a field hospital in 1918, and his first marriage was declared invalid, because it had not been performed in the Catholic Church. His new wife was the daughter of a wealthy family in Piggott, Arkansas. After their marriage her family's money, rather than his book royalties, were their primary means of support. Hemingway had acknowledged the importance of Hadley Hemingway's small inheritance during his early writing career, but he was not prepared for the long-term effect of the financial assistance that the Pfeiffer family lavished upon him.

Men Without Women was published on 14 October 1927, and over 15,000 copies were sold within three months. Virginia Woolf's review in the *New York Herald Tribune* irritated Hemingway. Woolf continued the comparative literary vein that she had used to review *The Sun Also Rises*; she found Hemingway's use of dialogue to be "excessive," and she concluded that "compared with his novel his stories are a little dry and sterile." One week later, in the same newspaper, Percy Hutchinson likened Hemingway to Lord Byron (one of many such comparisons over the years) and characterized Hemingway as "the supreme reporter." Dorothy Parker, writing in the *New Yorker*, clarified the label by adding that, unlike Sinclair Lewis, Hemingway goes beyond reporting and "stands as a genius" because he "has an unerring sense of selection." A key critical response came from Edmund Wilson, who wrote in the *New Republic* that Hemingway's

Ernest and Pauline Hemingway

reputation "has, in a very short time, reached such proportions that it has already become fashionable to disparage him." Wilson then reviewed some of the recent critical reactions to Hemingway's writings, notably the works of Joseph Wood Krutch (*Nation*) and Lee Wilson Dodd (*Saturday Review of Literature*). Hemingway expressed his own reactions to the critics in "Valentine," a blunt poem "For a Mr. Lee Wilson Dodd and Any of His Friends who Want it" in which he mocks Krutch's and Dodd's criticisms of his characters. In the *Dial* N. L. Rothman drew serious analogies between the works of Shakespeare and Hemingway's novel and stories as Hemingway himself later did. (He once referred to *A Farewell to Arms* as his *Romeo and Juliet*.)

Hemingway began work on a novel he called a "modern Tom Jones" in fall 1927, and by spring 1928 had reached 45,000 words, but he gradually abandoned this project. He attributed his loss of enthusiasm for the project to a series of accidents and illnesses. In March 1928 he received a bad cut across his forehead when a skylight fell on him in his apartment. This injury was the most severe of several mishaps that had befallen him in recent months.

The wire services picked up the story, and the reaction from Europe and America proved to Hemingway that he was now a writer with an international reputation.

Hemingway had been longing to return to America; he especially wanted to see Key West, Florida, after hearing about it from Dos Passos. His April 1928 to April 1929 visit to the United States, his longest stay in seven years, was an eventful year. Following a stay in Key West, the Hemingways visited her family in Piggott, Arkansas, and then went to Kansas City for the birth of their son, Patrick, by cesarean section on 28 June. They spent the late summer in Wyoming, and after returning to Arkansas they traveled to Chicago and down the East Coast, visiting the MacLeishes and the Fitzgeralds. In November they returned to Key West, where Pauline Hemingway's uncle bought them a house. On 6 December, while Hemingway was en route to New York to meet his older son, he received word that his ailing father had killed himself with a single shot to the head.

Throughout his travels and family crises that year Hemingway worked on *A Farewell to Arms*, which he had begun just before he left Paris. He finished the first draft of the novel at the end of August 1928 in Sheridan, Wyoming, and on 22 January 1929 he completed the revision in Key West, where Perkins joined him on 1 February and read the typescript. Perkins's admiration for the book was tempered only by a concern for the language which might, he feared, prevent it from being serialized in *Scribner's Magazine*. But the editors of the magazine did not object, and Hemingway was given $16,000 for first serial rights, the largest such payment that Scribners had made to date.

In April 1929 Hemingway took his family back to Paris. Unhappy with the conclusion of *A Farewell to Arms*, he spent ten days in May rewriting the ending in proofs until he was satisfied. The novel's heroine, Catherine Barkley, is based in part on Agnes von Kurowsky, the nurse whom Hemingway had been infatuated with in Milan. He had treated her in fiction before in "A Very Short Story" as well as in *The Sun Also Rises*, where he based Brett Ashley's wartime background on her nursing experiences. Some of Catherine Barkley's characteristics were also drawn from Hadley Hemingway, and Catherine's death from complications of childbirth reflect Pauline Hemingway's experiences during the birth of Patrick Hemingway. Hemingway is primarily interested, however, in creating fiction from his complex emotional involvement with von Kurowsky. His first treatment of her in "A Very Short Story" is neither romantic nor sympathetic; and when he began the story that became *A Farewell to Arms*, he intended to use Marlowe's lines, "but that was in another country, / and besides the wench is dead," for an epigraph. Catherine Barkley is portrayed early in the novel as being "crazy." Later she and Frederic Henry make love in a red hotel room that resembles a room in a brothel. Throughout the novel she remains strangely detached during their love scenes, and she treats Frederic Henry like a substitute for an earlier lover, killed in the war. Often Catherine controls the emotions of a scene. The one thing she cannot control is her fate—her death—which is symbolized throughout the novel by rain.

Because Frederic Henry is a first-person narrator, his reminiscences must necessarily reflect his rite of passage. The book contains a combination of adolescent and mature sensibilities. Hemingway's treatment of the war story is clear and magnificent, and the evolution of the characters involved in the war is realistic. Few war scenes in fiction can match the retreat in *A Farewell to Arms*. Following Frederic's escape from the Italian firing squad and his decision to make a "separate peace" by deserting from the Italian army, Catherine Barkley represents the pinnacle of secure sensuality that Frederic Henry acknowledges as his credo, and he says to himself that the war "was not my show any more." "I was not made to think. I was made to eat," he declares to himself. "Eat and drink and sleep with Catherine." Frederic and Catherine have declared their freedom from moral entrapments, but in Montreux Catherine and Frederic become victims of a biological trap. "And this was the price you paid for sleeping together," Frederic remarks at the scene of Catherine's death. "This was the end of the trap. This was what people got for loving each other."

Hemingway had returned to Europe for the summer bullfights. Paris no longer held any special significance for him. In 1929 the city merely served as a hub from which he traveled to Spain for the bullfights and to Berlin for the bicycle races. He was in Paris when *A Farewell to Arms* was published in September. A few weeks later Hemingway met Allen Tate for the first time at Shakespeare and Company. Tate had written favorable reviews of Hemingway's earlier books, and Hemingway was eager to hear Tate's assessment of the new novel. He delivered a copy of the novel to Tate's hotel and returned the following morning to hear Tate's opinion that the novel was a masterpiece. By November the book was at the top of the best-seller lists in America. Henry Hazlitt, in the *New York Sun*, called Hemingway "the greatest single influence on the American novel and short story." In the *New York Times Book Review*, Percy Hutchinson mistakenly attributed Frederic Henry's desertion to his love for Catherine Barkley. "The story of this attachment," wrote Hutchinson, "is poetic, idyllic, tragic." In this vein the word "sentimental" appeared frequently in the early criticism of *A Farewell to Arms*. Hemingway's friend Malcolm Cowley regarded the book as a lesser achievement than *The Sun Also Rises*, foreshadowing the later critical debate over the novel. Many readers regard *A Farewell to Arms* as Hemingway's finest book, however.

Hemingway closed the twenties in Paris in a preface he wrote for *Kiki's Memoirs* (1930), the reminiscences of Alice Prin, better known as Kiki of Montparnasse, a popular artists' model. He declared Kiki's era to be over; Montparnasse had become a gaudy tourist attraction and was no longer the haven for serious writers and artists that it had been in the early twenties. And Kiki had come to resemble "a monument to herself." He later summed up these feelings in "A Paris Letter," in *Esquire* (February 1934):

This year, at the same time, we are in Paris and it is a big mistake. . . . This old friend shot himself. That old friend took an overdose of something. That old friend went back to New York and jumped out, or rather fell from, a high window. That other old friend wrote her memoirs. All of the old friends have lost their money. All. of the old friends are very discouraged. Few of the old friends are healthy. Me, I like it better out on the ranch, or in Piggott, Arkansas, in the fall, or in Key West, and very much better, say, at the Dry Tortugas. . . . Montparnasse has been discovered by the French respectable bourgeoisie, just as Montmartre once was. So the big cafes do a pretty steady business. The only foreigners you see are Germans. The Dome is crowded with refugees from the Nazi terror and Nazis spying on the refugees. . . . Paris is very beautiful this fall. It was a fine place to be quite young in and it is a necessary part of a man's education. We all loved it once and we lie if we say we didn't. But she is like a mistress who does not grow old and she has other lovers now.

Hemingway never lived in Paris again after 1929 although he often passed through the city during the next thirty years. His most dramatic return came on 26 August 1944 when he returned to Paris with the first wave of Americans to enter the war-scarred city. He had an emotional reunion with Sylvia Beach before he went off "to liberate the cellar at the Ritz." Hemingway visited Paris for the last time in October 1959, but he spent most of his time nursing a cold in his room at the Ritz.

Hemingway's later fiction has often touched on his Paris years. Like "A Canary for One," "Homage to Switzerland" (1935) shows the effect of Hemingway's separation from Hadley Hemingway and his black mood that followed. *Green Hills of Africa* opens with a reminder of the good old days and recalls the preeminence of James Joyce in Paris during the twenties. Among his short stories, "The Snows of Kilimanjaro" (1936) is significant for its references to Paris and Schruns. The protagonist, Harry, is a spiritually corrupt writer who has sold out to a wealthy woman for security. Paris is mentioned like some distant Avalon in *Across the River and Into the Trees* (1950). However, in two posthumously published books, the years in Paris occupy a central place.

The publication of *A Moveable Feast* in 1964 began a popular interest in the twenties literary scene in Paris. Hemingway's memoir grew out of material that he found in 1956 in two old trunks that he had stored in the basement of the Ritz Hotel in 1928 before he left for America. Many of Hemingway's anecdotes in the book revived old quarrels. Hemingway remembered his meetings with Stein at her apartment, with Ford Madox Ford at the Closerie des Lilas, and with Ernest Walsh. Pound appears in passing, as does Joyce. Sylvia Beach occupies a central place. The anecdotes of Fitzgerald's drunkenness and insecurity caused the greatest reaction from his friends and admirers. Hemingway has often been compared to Byron, most notably by John Peale Bishop in his essay "Homage to Hemingway." Byron and Hemingway were men of action whose major literary strengths rested in their abilities to transform their experiences into literature. Both writers created archetypical heroes and suffered from the confused comparisons between their real selves and their myths. Hemingway, like Byron, became controversial because he wrote about his contemporaries. In short stories like "Mr. and Mrs. Elliot," in the first version of "The Snows of Kilimanjaro," and in *The Sun Also Rises*, he displayed a remarkable detachment from social relationships. In *A Moveable Feast* he pitted his view of himself as a poor young writer with a true artistic temperament against the corrupt pretensions of many, but not all, of his contemporaries in Paris in the twenties. However, the strength of *A Moveable Feast* is not in its portraits but in its evocation of Paris as a place where for Hemingway living, loving, learning, and writing were—for a brief time—all good. "To have come on all this new world of writing," he remembered in *A Moveable Feast*, "with time to read in a city like Paris where there was a way of living well and working, no matter how poor you were, was like having a great treasure given to you." During a walk across Paris Hadley Hemingway had told him: "We're too lucky," but Hemingway had wondered whether their elation over being in Paris wasn't caused by hunger. "There are many sorts of hunger," his wife replied; then she added prophetically, "Memory is hunger." And hunger for lost purity and happiness is the pervading sense in the book.

Much of the first section of *Islands in the Stream* (1970) deals with Hemingway's years in Paris. There are several anecdotes about Joyce and references to *Ulysses*. The central character, a painter named Thomas Hudson, lives on Bimini, where his three sons come to visit him. The oldest boy and his father reminisce about living in Paris when the boy was very young. The memory of those years, which separates the oldest boy from his brothers, who are uninitiated by Paris, is like a badge of superiority for the boy, while his father seems to live in a state of banishment from the happiness of those times.

In 1946 Hemingway began work on one of his longest projects, an unpublished novel he called "The Garden of Eden." There are two couples in the novel. David and Catherine Bourne live in the seaport village Le Grau-du-Roi, where Ernest and Pauline Hemingway spent their honeymoon. The circumstances of David's life parallel Hemingway's life in 1927. Nick and Barbara Sheldon live on the rue du Cardinal Lemoine, where Ernest and Hadley Hemingway first lived in Paris. In *A Farewell to Arms* and *For Whom the Bell Tolls* (1940) Hemingway was interested in creating a sense of oneness between the male and female lovers. This theme becomes more overtly sexual in "The Garden of Eden." Hemingway's heroes had sought sanctuary in relationships with women before, but the characters in this novel become androgynous. "The Garden of Eden" deals at length with the relationships that led to Hemingway's divorce from his first wife.

Carlos Baker has called Hemingway a "citizen of the world," placing him in a tradition of internationalist writers. As early as 1926, when his first marriage was coming to an end and his early literary relationships were breaking apart, Hemingway wrote to Max Perkins that "in several ways I have been long enough in Europe." Following his marriage to Pauline Pfeiffer, Key West and Africa became his new literary landscapes. It is unfair to identify Hemingway too closely with his fictional creations, but he seems to have been describing himself when he wrote of the writer Harry in "The Snows of Kilimanjaro": "He had had his life and it was over and he went on living it again with different people and more money, with the best of the same places, and some new ones." Like Harry, Hemingway "had seen the world change; not just the events; although he had seen many of them and had watched the people, but he had seen the subtler change and he could remember how people were at different times." Hemingway could have achieved his success as a writer only as an expatriate, free from the constraints of his homeland. In Paris he had the freedom to define himself and to create his original work outside of the distractions of the New York literary establishment. Hemingway's indifference to the American Protestant tradition was reflected in characters such as Nick Adams and Harold Krebs. He was a "born expatriate."

Some American literary critics have denigrated Hemingway's fiction. In his review of *Men Without Women* in the *Nation* Joseph Wood Krutch offered a reaction that is typical of the aversion to Hemingway's works that many critics have felt. "In his hands," Krutch wrote, "the subject matter of literature becomes sordid little catastrophes in the lives of very vulgar people. . . ." Critics have begrudged Hemingway his talent; some have tried to dismiss him; others have defended him, often on the basis of misguided interpretations; a few have attempted to remake him in their own images; Edmund Wilson, Malcolm Cowley, and Carlos Baker were the first to interpret his work in serious critical and historical analyses. The significant fact behind Hemingway's relationship with his critics is that however bad some of his books may have been, they have not been ignored. Since Hemingway was in his late twenties, critics have attempted to analyze the phenomenon of Hemingway himself, while often confusing the significance of his work. As early as 1929 Dorothy Parker addressed this issue when she wrote in the *New Yorker*: "Probably of no other living man has so much tripe been penned or spoken."

Archibald MacLeish has pointed out that, although Hemingway was not a literary writer, he was extraordinarily well read; what he read became part of his experience. From his first days in Paris he was interested in and conscious of his relationship to writers of the past. In Paris he developed and refined his historical sense. Paris offered Hemingway the wealth of Sylvia Beach's bookshop, the companionship of Ezra Pound with his sense of literary traditions, and the example of James Joyce's dedication to the art of writing. Although he was critical of self-consciously avant-garde writers, Hemingway was experimental in his creation of an undercurrent of complex psychological tension through a concentrated use of simple language. His contribution was a style that gained its naturalism from the northern Michigan woods, its sense of tragedy from Italy during World War I, and its sophistication from Paris. MacLeish summarized Hemingway's years best in his poem "Years of the Dog":

And what became of him? Fame became of
  him.
Veteran out of the wars before he was twenty:
Famous at twenty-five: Thirty a master—
Whittled a style for his time from a walnut
  stick
In a carpenter's loft in a street of that April
  city.

Bibliographies:

Audre Hanneman, *Ernest Hemingway A Comprehensive Bibliography* (Princeton: Princeton University Press, 1967; supplement, Princeton: Princeton University Press, 1975);

Philip Young and Charles W. Mann, *The Hemingway Manuscripts An Inventory* (University Park & London: Pennsylvania State University Press, 1969).

Biographies:

Carlos Baker, *Ernest Hemingway A Life Story* (New York: Scribners, 1969);

Matthew J. Bruccoli, *Scott and Ernest The Authority of Failure and the Authority of Success* (New York: Random House, 1978);

Alice Hunt Sokoloff, *Hadley The First Mrs. Hemingway* (New York: Dodd, Mead, 1973).

References:

Carlos Baker, *Hemingway The Writer as Artist*, fourth edition (Princeton: Princeton University Press, 1972);

Sylvia Beach, *Shakespeare and Company* (New York: Harcourt, Brace, 1959);

Charles A. Fenton, *The Apprenticeship of Ernest Hemingway* (New York: Farrar, Straus & Young, 1954);

Fitzgerald/Hemingway Annual 1969-;

Ford Madox Ford, *It Was the Nightingale* (Philadelphia: Lippincott, 1933);

Nicholas Joost, *Ernest Hemingway and the Little Magazines The Paris Years* (Barre, Mass.: Barre Publishers, 1968);

Harold Loeb, *The Way It Was* (New York: Criterion, 1959);

Robert McAlmon, *Being Geniuses Together 1920-1930*, revised with additional material by Kay Boyle (Garden City: Doubleday, 1968);

Bernard J. Poli, *Ford Madox Ford and the TRANSATLANTIC REVIEW* (Syracuse: Syracuse University Press, 1967);

Michael S. Reynolds, *Hemingway's First War The Making of* A Farewell to Arms (Princeton: Princeton University Press, 1976);

Earl Rovit, *Ernest Hemingway* (New York: Twayne, 1963);

Bertram D. Sarason, *Hemingway and* The Sun *Set* (Washington, D.C.: Bruccoli Clark / NCR Microcard Editions, 1972);

Robert O. Stephens, ed., *Ernest Hemingway The Critical Reception* (New York: Burt Franklin, 1977);

Linda Welshimer Wagner, *Ernest Hemingway A Reference Guide* (Boston: G. K. Hall, 1977);

George Wickes, *Americans in Paris* (Garden City: Doubleday, 1969), pp. 149-187;

Philip Young, *Ernest Hemingway A Reconsideration* (University Park & London: Pennsylvania State University Press, 1966).

JOHN HERRMANN
(9 November 1900-9 April 1959)

BOOKS: *What Happens* (Paris: Contact Editions, 1926);
Summer Is Ended (New York: Covici Friede, 1932);
The Salesman (New York: Simon & Schuster, 1939).

John Herrmann, a minor American author and an expatriate in Paris in 1924, was a native of Lansing, Michigan. He graduated from the University of Michigan and worked briefly as a salesman in his home state before going to Germany to study art history at the University of Munich. By 1924, having decided on writing as a career, he had moved to Paris where he mingled with the artists who inhabited the Left Bank, met Ezra Pound and James Joyce, and established friendships with Ernest Hemingway, William Carlos Williams, Robert McAlmon, and Josephine Herbst, who would become his first wife. While in Paris he became enthusiastic about the experimental prose of Gertrude Stein, but it was Hemingway's early work which seems to have influenced most the tone and style of his fiction.

In 1925 his prose piece "Work in Progress" was included in the anthology *Contact Collection of Contemporary Writers*, edited by Robert McAlmon. The following year McAlmon's Contact Editions also published *What Happens*, his first novel. Written in a simple, unadorned style and largely autobiographical in its external details, this story of the everyday experiences of a jewelry salesman in the Midwest provided a direct and authentic picture of a young man growing up in America during the Jazz Age. Though quite innocent, *What Happens*, like other books issued by expatriate presses, was believed to be obscene by customs officials and denied entry into the United States, even after the author protested with a petition signed by some noted writers.

After returning to America in the fall of 1924, Herrmann continued for a while to be affiliated with the literary world of Paris and published in several expatriate little. magazines. Among his contributions were "The New Multitudes" (*This Quarter*, Spring 1929), a short essay about superficial critical response to the work of the expatriates, and "Chasing the Absolute: Or Amnesia: A Novelized Scenario" (*transition*, February 1929), an experiment in Surrealism in the form of a collage of observations on such random topics as war, science, and religion.

With the onset of the Depression Herrmann's interests underwent a reorientation, for he became attracted by radical politics and got increasingly involved in Communist Party activities. His later work exposed the vulgarity and the failures of the middle class. In *Summer Is Ended* (1932), his second novel, he showed how a young woman's very ordinary aspirations were thwarted by her own shortsightedness and by the shallowness of the people around her, while in "The Big Short Trip," winner of *Scribner's Magazine* Prize Short Novel Contest in 1932, he gave an account of a salesman's travels through Depression America and tried to convey the idea that the country's socioeconomic system was moving inevitably toward disintegration. His last novel, *The Salesman* (1939), detailed the process by which an average citizen caught in the web of society lost his spirit and his identity. Herrmann died in Guadalajara, Mexico, in 1959.

Herrmann's most significant writings exploited the methods of conventional realistic fiction to study the limitations and the injustices of American life. They contained well-drawn characters and perceptive social insights but were marred by a lack of dramatic action and a certain flatness of style.

—*Winifred Farrant Bevilacqua*

Other:

Contact Collection of Contemporary Writers, by Herrmann and others (Paris: Contact Editions, 1925).

Periodical Publications:

"Chasing the Absolute: Or Amnesia: A Novelized Scenario," *transition*, no. 15 (February 1929): 27-31;
"The New Multitudes," *This Quarter*, 1 (Spring 1929): 252-255;
"The Big Short Trip," *Scribner's*, 92 (August 1932): 65-69, 113-128.

References:

Hugh Ford, *Published in Paris American and British Writers, Printers, and Publishers in Paris, 1920-1939* (New York: Macmillan, 1975), pp. 61-72;
Robert McAlmon, *Being Geniuses Together 1920-1930*, revised edition with additional material by Kay Boyle (Garden City: Doubleday, 1968), pp. 101-102, 283, 343.

LANGSTON HUGHES
(1 February 1902-22 May 1967)

SELECTED BOOKS: *The Weary Blues* (New York: Knopf, 1926; London: Knopf, 1926);

Fine Clothes to the Jew (New York: Knopf, 1927; London: Knopf, 1927);

Not Without Laughter (New York & London: Knopf, 1930; London: Allen & Unwin, 1930);

The Dream Keeper and Other Poems (New York: Knopf, 1932);

The Ways of White Folks (New York: Knopf, 1934; London: Allen & Unwin, 1934);

The Big Sea An Autobiography (New York & London: Knopf, 1940; London & Melbourne: Hutchinson, 1941);

I Wonder As I Wander An Autobiographical Journey (New York: Rinehart, 1956);

The Langston Hughes Reader (New York: Braziller, 1958);

The Selected Poems of Langston Hughes (New York: Knopf, 1959).

Langston Hughes

France held a special value for Langston Hughes even before he first visited Paris. "I will never forget the thrill of first understanding the French of de Maupassant," he writes in *The Big Sea* (1940). "I think it was de Maupassant who made me really want to be a writer and write stories about Negroes, so true that people in far away lands would read them—even after I was dead." Perhaps drawn by this spiritual bond, Hughes saw Paris as "a dream come true" when he first visited the city, and later he made it a personal symbol of civilization triumphant over the barbarous forces of fascism.

Following a decision to break with "everything unpleasant and miserable" out of his past, Hughes at twenty-one took a job as mess boy on an Africa-bound merchant ship, beginning a life of travel that would last until World War II ended his global experiences. Following six months along the coast of West Africa, he signed for a voyage to Holland, where, promptly on arrival in Rotterdam, he jumped ship and took the train to Paris. Arriving with seven dollars in his pocket in February 1924, Hughes began an exciting five-month stay among the black American exiles of Montmartre. This first visit, treated at some length in *The Big Sea*, essentially establishes Hughes's relationship to Paris; he would return to Paris briefly in 1937 and 1938 on his way to and from Spain to cover the Civil War for the *Baltimore Afro-American* and a second time in 1938 with Theodore Dreiser to represent the United States at the International Congress of Writers for the Defense of Culture.

Alone and almost broke, Hughes quickly learned that Paris offered little to an indigent black American in need of work. While jazz musicians and tap dancers might find employment in the Montmartre clubs, a poet had to scrape for a meager existence. Initially his salvation came through sharing the hardships with a stranded Russian ballerina who hustled drinks while Hughes sought work, but eventually a series of menial jobs as doorman, dishwasher, and waiter kept him going. A job at Le Grand Duc, a popular black nightclub, gave Hughes glimpses of the haut monde who supported Montmartre's night life, but more importantly it brought him into close contact with the black musicians and entertainers who gathered after hours for early morning jam sessions. While absorbing the richness of black culture in exile, he was amused to observe the absurdity of the American color bar as exposed by the club's singer, Florence Embry, who delighted in snubbing tourists "who wanted nothing in the world so much as to have her sit down with them." Among the many great black entertainers Hughes met at Le Grand Duc was

Florence Embry's replacement, Bricktop, who would take advantage of the atmosphere Paris offered blacks to rise in ten years from a penniless unknown to "the toast of Montmartre with dukes and princes at her table." Among the other patrons at Le Grand Duc was publisher and poet Nancy Cunard, who later included a number of Hughes's poems in her *Negro Anthology* (1934), a collection of literature, history, anthropology, and sociology by and about blacks. Although Hughes says in *I Wonder As I Wander* (1956), his second volume of memoirs, that he did not meet Cunard until he returned to Paris in 1937, the two began corresponding earlier.

To some extent, Hughes's Paris life was "right out of a book," as he describes it, "living in a garret, writing poems, and having champagne for breakfast." In the spring he fell in love with a beautiful English-African girl and shared with her the full romance of the city. Dr. Alain Locke sought out Hughes in Paris to solicit the poems that eventually would be included in the landmark anthology *The New Negro* (1925). Through Locke Hughes met art collector Paul Guillaume and was able to visit his magnificent collection of African art. Since Hughes's poetry is closely related to the rhythms of black music, meeting and hearing "the cream of the Negro musicians then in France, like Cricket Smith on the trumpet, Louis Jones on the violin, Palmer Jones at the piano, Frank Withers on the clarinet, and Buddy Gilmore at the drums" was a unique opportunity for the young poet.

But for all those happy memories of Paris, the champagne was left over, the girl's father broke up the romance, and the garret was more sordid than romantic. *The Big Sea* offers a unique picture of Paris in the twenties from one who, however briefly, shared the vibrant spirit of black Montmartre. Hughes's own struggle for existence, portraits of such characters as the one-eyed chef of Le Grand Duc, a wonderful sketch of a royal free-for-all in the club, and numerous glimpses of Paris low life combine to give these chapters of *The Big Sea* something of the flavor of George Orwell's *Down and Out in Paris and London* (1933).

Hughes left Paris in July 1924, traveled in Italy, and eventually signed on an American ship to work in return for his passage home. In 1937 Hughes passed through Paris again as he traveled to and from Spain to cover the Civil War there for a Baltimore newspaper. After a happy summer visit that year, on his way to Spain, he returned briefly at Christmas on his way home to find the city depressed by the mood of impending war. In his final description of Paris before World War II, Hughes seems subconsciously to return to the passage in de Maupassant which first inspired him to write. In that passage, "the soft snow was falling" through one of de Maupassant's stories which Hughes labored to understand. "Then all of a sudden one night the beauty and the meaning of the words in which he made the snow fall, came to me," Hughes says, and inspired his own literary ambitions. On this last visit to a Paris now shadowed by impending tragedy, Hughes writes,

> Slowly I walked through the lightly falling snow that had begun to sift down over the Paris rooftops in scattered indecisive flakes. The streets were very lonely as I passed the Galleries Lafayette and the Gare Saint Lazare and turned up the slight incline leading to Montmartre. Even the little clubs and bars along the way were quiet. Where could everybody be, I wondered. How still it was in this old, old city of Paris in the first hour of the New Year.

He goes on to wonder if, after Ethiopia and Spain, Hitler and Mussolini would "turn their planes on the rest of us? Would civilization be destroyed? Would the world really end?" In this final passage Paris becomes for Hughes a symbol of hope as "in the snowy night in the shadows of the old houses of Montmartre" he repeats to himself, "my world won't end." For Hughes there would always be a Paris, and the qualities of life and civilization represented by the city would survive even Europe's blackest hour.

—*William E. Grant*

Other:

Alain Locke, ed., *The New Negro*, includes poems by Hughes (New York: A. & C. Boni, 1925);

Nancy Cunard, ed., *Negro Anthology*, includes poems by Hughes (London: Wishart, 1934; New York: Negro Universities Press, 1969).

BRAVIG IMBS
(8 October 1904-June 1946)

SELECTED BOOKS: *Eden: Exit This Way and Other Poems* (Paris: Geoffrey Fraser, 1926);
The Professor's Wife (New York: Lincoln Mac-Veagh / Dial, 1928);
Confessions of Another Young Man (New York: Henkle-Yewdale House, 1936).

Bravig Wilbur Eugene Imbs is more often remembered for his chronicle of his Parisian literary friendships, *Confessions of Another Young Man* (1936), than for his own attempts at fiction and poetry. A worshipful regular at Gertrude Stein's salon, Imbs was also a friend and admirer of Elliot Paul, and he helped Paul and Eugene Jolas with some of the early issues of *transition*. Enamored with the idea of writing music as well, Imbs also studied composition for a time with George Antheil.

Imbs· was born in Milwaukee to Norwegian-American parents, but he was brought up in Chicago, where he found his family's fundamentalist religious ardor restrictive. For *Twentieth Century Authors*, Imbs wrote: "I was given such a dose of Bible study and hymn-singing in the United Brethren Church in my childhood that I had enough for the rest of my life. My only escape was music and I studied the violin assiduously. I also started writing poems as soon as I could write. . . ."

His musical talent was useful to him at Dartmouth, where he enrolled in the fall of 1923. He earned his way in part by playing his violin and by giving music lessons, and he also worked as a butler for a professor's family. These experiences later served as the basis for his novel, *The Professor's Wife* (1928), a satiric look at the cultural pretensions of the academic community.

In the summer of 1925, after two years at Dartmouth, Imbs and a friend took a cattle boat to Europe. Arriving in Paris with only five dollars and no job, Imbs decided to stay. Although he had never even been in a newspaper office before, Imbs went to the editor of the Paris *Tribune* (the European edition of the *Chicago Tribune*) and claimed to be an experienced reporter. He also said that he spoke fluent French even though at that time he did not know a word. He was given a job, but his incompetence was soon discovered, and he was fired. He found another job teaching in an American school, and after he had spent some time learning French, he was rehired by the *Tribune* to work in the advertising department. Later, in 1926, he also became the music critic for the Paris *Times*, but in

Bravig Imbs, by John Blomshield, 1926

January 1927, he was fired for writing too many negative reviews.

Imbs's first book, *Eden: Exit This Way* (1926), was published by his fellow *Tribune* employee Geoffrey Fraser, one of the few Englishmen to work for the paper. Another friend, John Blomshield, drew a portrait of Imbs for the frontispiece. The book consists mainly of poems he had written at Dartmouth, plus the title poem, written in Paris. In *Confessions of Another Young Man*, Imbs called "Eden: Exit This Way" "a 'modern' poem (shades of Vachel Lindsay!)," and he adds that the poem is "unimportant except that it marked the transition between the regular form of verse I had used up to then and the so-called free verse, which, after considerable struggle, I decided to adopt." The poem is dedicated to George Antheil, and it echoes Antheil's interest in mechanical sounds. The book was not widely noticed, although Imbs remembers that "it caused a proper ripple in Hanover." His friend Elliot Paul, novelist and *Tribune* reporter, wrote a good review, and the book was favorably noticed by Eugene Jolas, who was soon to launch his magazine *transition*.

After having been fired from the *Times*, Imbs convinced his father to support him for six months so that he could live at an inn he had discovered in Garnes and complete a life of Thomas Chatterton, which he had been struggling with for over a year. He made no progress on the book, but he did write some poems, and he spent many weekends in Paris helping Paul and Jolas with *transition*, which first appeared in April 1927.

In his memoirs, Imbs, who served mainly as a proofreader on *transition*, sides with Gertrude Stein in claiming that Paul was the true editorial genius behind *transition*. He admits, however, that his judgment may be affected by his personal feelings about Jolas. He says that he could never understand how Paul could like Jolas and that Jolas was amazed that Paul could be friends with him. He claims that Jolas resented him "not so much because my somewhat effeminate manner grated on his he-man brain, but because such an obviously supercilious person as myself should have the gift of writing poems that moved him." During the early years of *transition*, Jolas accepted a number of Imbs's poems. Imbs acknowledges Jolas's kindness and says that once his poems began appearing in *transition*, other magazines began printing his poems as well.

The most important event for Imbs during the first six months of 1927 was the writing of his first novel. According to his *Confessions*, one day in early March, he was telling Paul some stories about his life at Dartmouth when Paul interrupted him:

> "There you are," he said. "There's your first sentence 'The Ramson's place was called Otterby'—start your book there and continue. I have often thought a book could be written as a picture is painted, with a daub here and a daub there, a little work in one corner, a little work in the center, until it is all filled in."

Imbs returned to Garnes and followed Paul's advice, "bringing him the manuscript for correction, and never looking back at what I had done." Imbs finished *The Professor's Wife* before his father's six-month subsidy ran out; the final page is dated "Garnes, July 4, 1927."

The plotless, episodic structure fits Paul's prescription for "a daub here and a daub there." The rambling reminiscences of a young narrator who is butler and handyman for an English professor and his wife are based upon Imbs's own experiences. The focus is upon the social maneuvers of Mrs. Ramson, a kind, but pretentious, woman who thinks that "Barrie was greater than Shakespeare and that R. L.

S., despite certain youthful indiscretions, was one of the few real gentlemen who had ever lived and who was a great writer at the same time." Although Professor Ramson disagrees with his wife's admiration of Barrie and Robert Louis Stevenson, he shares her horror of the moderns. Through their censure of Sherwood Anderson, James Joyce, and Gertrude Stein, Imbs satirizes the narrow-minded priggishness of the arbiters of American taste.

Not only did Paul like Imbs's novel, but according to Imbs, it met with the approval of his other great literary mentor, Gertrude Stein, whom he had met in the spring of 1926. Indeed, in writing his book straight through without looking back, Imbs was following the advice she had given him earlier, which he quotes in his *Confessions*: "if you have something to say, the words are always there. And they are the exact words and the words that should be used. If the story does not come whole, **tant pis**, it has been spoiled. . . ." In general, Imbs's work is far more conventional than Stein's, however.

After completing his novel, Imbs returned to the United States, where he looked for work in Chicago and Detroit before settling in New York City. He met Allen Tate, John Herrmann, and Josephine Herbst, whose addresses had been sent him by Jolas, but he was unhappy in New York, and in January 1928, he returned to Paris. His first job was working with Kay Boyle in ghostwriting and typing the memoirs of the Dayang Muda of Sarawak, an Englishwoman who was the cousin of poet Archibald Craig and the niece of Oscar Wilde.

Imbs was not pleased with the job and kept it only because he was desperate for money. Consequently, he was delighted to meet Bernard Fay, who employed him to help with the English version of his new book about Benjamin Franklin. Imbs's translation was published by Little, Brown in 1929. When he met Fay in 1928, Imbs still had not found a publisher for *The Professor's Wife*, and William Aspenwall Bradley, the most successful American literary agent in Paris, had been unenthusiastic about it. Upon Fay's recommendation, however, Bradley placed it immediately; it was published by Lincoln MacVeagh / Dial Press in October 1928.

Imbs had less success with his next novel, "Parisian Interiors," which he completed in the summer of 1928. Although Stein praised it extravagantly, he was unable to find a publisher for it. He had a similar problem with his biography of Chatterton, which he finally completed in 1929. Fay recommended the book to Stein, who wrote a blurb for it, which Imbs quotes in his *Confessions*:

Bravig Imbs' life of Chatterton is a good book, it is a boy who is not a boy understood by a boy who is not a boy and written down with steady comprehension by a young man of a young man who never became a young man. A quite extraordinary piece of work, the whole history of the development of this boy who was not a boy in contact with those who were necessary to him could only have been done by a boy who was not a boy developing in contact with those who were necessary to him. It will be one of the important biographies.

Despite Stein's praise, Imbs failed to place the book with an English-language publisher. Fay introduced him to the Baronne J. Seilliere, who translated the book into French, and another friend of Fay's, the Comte A. de Luppe, serialized the translation in his magazine, the *Correspondant*, during May-July 1931.

Next, Imbs wrote another novel, "The Cats," which, he says, "few persons liked" except Paul and Stein: "Elliot enjoyed it and said that reading it was like looking at clouds: 'There was movement and nothing happened.' Gertrude wrote me: ' "The Cats" is a good book; the atmosphere is well sustained.' " But, Imbs continues, they were the only readers who liked it.

Despite Stein's praise, Imbs's friendship with her had been tenuous ever since 1928, when he had married Countess Valeska Balbarischky, whom he had met in Riga during a tour through Germany, Poland, Lithuania, and Latvia. He was in brief disfavor in late 1930 or early 1931, but the break was repaired after Imbs wrote Stein in January 1931 apologizing for whatever he may have done to offend her. The final break came in the spring of that year when on a visit to Stein, Imbs announced his plan to send his pregnant wife to spend the summer in the country near Stein and Alice B. Toklas and to join her later in the season. Stein and Toklas interpreted this idea as an imposition, and the next day Imbs received a telephone call in which Toklas said, "your pretension is unpardonable. You must not come to the house or write, for neither visit nor letter will be accepted. We want never to see you again." For Imbs, his break with Stein marked the end of the era. In *The Autobiography of Alice B. Toklas* (1933), Stein wrote, "We liked Bravig, even though as Gertrude Stein said, his aim was to please."

Some time after completing "Chatterton," Imbs had taken a job with an advertising agency in Paris, and he and his family remained until the beginning of World War II. During the war, he was a civilian attached to the army as a radio announcer for the United States Information Service. He set up the first free radio station in Cherbourg after its liberation in 1944, and according to *Time* magazine he became known for presenting "France's best recorded *jazz hot*." His career was ended in June 1946 when he was killed in an automobile accident. *Time* called him "an American more loved in France than known in the U. S."

Although Imbs's literary achievements are overshadowed by those of the writers to whom he paid adoring homage, his work deserves critical attention. Displaying a sharp sense of satire which occasionally approaches maliciousness, Imbs's writing is saved from becoming mere self-righteous gossip by his ability to laugh at himself. The Bravig Imbs of his *Confessions* and his fictionalized persona in *The Professor's Wife* are both as keenly aware of their own foibles as they are of others' shortcomings.

—*Karen L. Rood*

Other:

Bernard Fay, *Franklin the Apostle of Modern Times*, translated by Imbs (Boston: Little, Brown, 1929).

Periodical Publications:

"The Wind Was There," *transition*, no. 1 (April 1927): 116-117;

"Sleep," *transition*, no. 1 (April 1927): 118;

"no moth no leaf," *transition*, no. 2 (May 1927): 136;

"four seasons have passed . . . ," *transition*, no. 2 (May 1927): 137;

"Canticle," *transition*, no. 5 (August 1927): 102;

"Recitative," *transition*, no. 5 (August 1927): 103-104;

"Your Hands Are Not Hawthorn," *transition*, no. 5 (August 1927): 105;

"encircled lakes of light . . . ," *transition*, no. 6 (September 1927): 137;

"Eyes of a Dead Poet," *transition*, no. 10 (January 1928): 110;

"These Misted Eyes," *transition*, no. 10 (January 1928): 111;

"soggy festoons of mist . . . ," *This Quarter*, 1 (Spring 1929): 33;

"I have desired that the sun halt," *This Quarter*, 1 (Spring 1929): 34;

"Pavane," *This Quarter*, 1 (Spring 1929): 35;

"oval oasis of my orisons," *This Quarter*, 1 (Spring 1929): 36;

"Episode," *transition*, no. 18 (November 1929): 113;

"Doldrums," *transition*, no. 18 (November 1929): 113;

"Vie de Chatterton," trans. J. Seilliere, *Correspondant*, 323, new series 287 (10 May 1931): 338-362; (25 May 1931): 569-595; (25 June 1931): 878-898; 324, new series 288 (25 July 1931): 263-289.

References:

Donald Gallup, ed., *The Flowers of Friendship Letters Written to Gertrude Stein* (New York: Knopf, 1953), pp. 201, 212-213, 234-235, 247-248, 347-348, 369;

James R. Mellow, *Charmed Circle Gertrude Stein & Company* (New York & Washington: Praeger, 1974), pp. 325-345.

Eugene Jolas

Thomas E. Dasher
Georgia Southern College

BIRTH: Union-Hill, New Jersey, 26 October 1894.

MARRIAGE: January 1926 to Maria McDonald; children: Betsy, Tina.

DEATH: Paris, 26 May 1952.

BOOKS: *Cinema* (New York: Adelphi, 1926);

Secession in Astropolis (Paris: Black Sun Press, 1929);

Epivocables of 3 (Paris: Editions Vertigral, 1932);

Hypnolog des Scheitelauges (Paris: Editions Vertigral, 1932);

The Language of Night (The Hague: Servire, 1932);

Mots-deluge: Hypnologues (Paris: Editions des Cahiers Libres, 1933);

Vertigralist Pamphlet (Paris: Transition Press, 1938);

I Have Seen Monsters and Angels (Paris: Transition Press, 1938);

Planets and Angels (Mount Vernon, Iowa: English Club of Cornell College, 1940);

Vertical: A Yearbook for Romantic-Mystic Ascensions (New York: Gotham Bookmart Press, 1941);

Words from the Deluge (New York: Distributed by Gotham Bookmart, 1941);

Wanderpoem; or Angelic Mythamorphosis of the City of London (Paris: Transition Press, 1946).

For ten years, Eugene Jolas, poet and writer, was the editor of *transition*, one of the most important literary journals to appear in Paris during the twenties and thirties. Best known for its publication of segments from James Joyce's *Work in Progress*, *transition* also encouraged and published experimental writing of the period by such writers as Gertrude Stein, Hart Crane, Dylan Thomas, Franz Kafka, and Samuel Beckett. Even though Jolas originally coedited *transition* with Elliot Paul, it was most definitely *his* journal. Throughout the twenty-seven issues appearing from 1927 to 1939, Jolas developed a philosophy which stressed the unconscious as the source of literary creation and the need for a new language with which that creation might be expressed. Totally convinced that the poet's tapping of the unconscious resulted in a vision that transcended the sterile, mechanical world of the twentieth century, he opened the pages of *transition* to an international group of authors who contributed in quite different ways to what Jolas came to call the "revolution of the word." For Jolas and many of *transition*'s contributors, man had to break away from the prison in which modern society was enclosing him. They believed that *transition* and its guiding philosophy could be the liberating force. Often misinterpreted and reviled, *transition* consistently offered an exciting, challenging look into the work of contemporary writers and artists—both successful and foolish. At the center of this activity was always Jolas—encouraging, writing, and proselytizing.

Jolas was born in Union-Hill, New Jersey, on 26 October 1894 to immigrants from Lorraine. From his birth, with his mother's Rhenish German and his father's French, he was faced with linguistic and cultural conflicts which he spent his life trying to resolve. The Jolas family returned to Forbach, Lorraine, when young Jolas was two, and he did not see the country of his birth again until 1910. In Lorraine he "awoke to life in the mood of the thousand-year-old frontier scission." As he says in the preface to *I Have Seen Monsters and Angels* (1938):

> I did not see my native America again until I was almost seventeen years old, and I had to learn my native language paradoxically in the diaspora-wilderness of the legendary immigrant.
>
> Deep in my memory lies the spirit of the little European bordertown, where I lived before the World War, and where, at the beginning of the century, I heard the echoes of that other bloody conflict—the Franco-Prussian War—from the lips of those who had taken part in it, especially my French grandfather, whose stories of the battles of Metz, Mars-la-Tour, and St. Privat are indelibly imprinted on my mind.
>
> Twice, within half a century, my childhood-town has changed hands politically.
>
> The frontier-fear is a primordial emotion in the unconscious of my people.
>
> This history-haunted region . . . was, for many years, the source of many of my dreams.
>
> It followed me through the night-and-day-dreams that I had during my American migrations, struggling for my daily bread in the proletarian crucible of New York, vagabonding through the country, trying to conquer the mysteries of the English language.
>
> It followed me with its images of conflict, its Franconian patois, its blending of the Franco-German language sounds.

The strong sense of frontier, of a "Man from Babel," as he would call his unpublished autobiography, and his sense of being a displaced American, were combined with the strong religious background of his mother's devout Catholicism. Having returned to Lorraine in 1896, he spent 1908-1909 in a seminary at Montigny, near Metz, and considered becoming a

priest. However, by the age of sixteen he had rejected the priesthood, and his conflicting feelings about religion would later cause a temporary break with the church. Yet a concept of God, of some primal force in the universe, would permeate almost all of his writing. In fact, he would come to believe that through poetry and the mysteries of language man might find a new, and true, recognition of God.

Having never separated himself from his family's earlier experience in America, Jolas immigrated alone to New York with the help of a loan from an aunt in 1910. He took with him, as he said, not only dreams of his childhood in Lorraine, but also a dream of America engendered by his family's talk, American authors such as James Fenimore Cooper and Harriet Beecher Stowe, whom he had read as a child, and the promise of a new life in the new country. What he quickly found in America, though, was the "proletarian crucible" of New York. The large, exciting, vibrant city could also be threatening and destructive. He had trouble finding work and establishing a sense of belonging in the United States. Doubts began to replace dreams as he realized that what New York failed to offer symbolized what America itself denied most of its citizens. Industrial growth, burgeoning wealth, unlimited promises were only for the minority. The young immigrant began to formulate a young man's questions and an artist's quest.

Jolas worked as a delivery boy for a German grocery as he improved his English in the night schools of New York, but he gradually moved through several jobs until he became a newspaper reporter for the German language *Pittsburgh Volksblatt*, where he learned his trade. He then became "automobile reporter" for the *Pittsburgh Post*. At this time Jolas was also reading and beginning to write poetry, and some of his poems appeared in small literary journals such as the *Pagan*. The reporter was becoming the poet with all the apparent problems of such a transformation.

In 1916 Jolas was drafted into the army, served as secretary to an army psychiatrist, and edited an army newspaper in 1917-1918. Discharged in 1920, he became a reporter for the New York *Daily News*, a job which initially excited him. The newspaper reporters seemed to be at the heart of the modern age in America. But Jolas soon became dissatisfied. As he wrote in his autobiography, "we were simply echoing the epoch's anarchic individualism . . . of the mercantile philistine. . . . We were chiming the collective belief in unending progress and perfectibility, the triumph of the machine." For Jolas, this triumph was signaling man's demise. He quit the *Daily News* and worked for the Waterbury, Connecticut, *Republican*. Life at a quieter pace, though, proved no more satisfactory. He would also work in Chicago and Savannah at various times in his American journalistic career, but he would not recover the enthusiasm and excitement. Those feelings were being transferred to art, especially as he read more American poetry. He began to see that man's spiritual salvation, certainly his own salvation, lay not in contemporary society, but in the eternal, universal truths which the poet must first find for himself and then perhaps help other men to discover. Thus in 1923, temporarily disillusioned and somewhat disgusted, he decided to leave America and to return to his family in Forbach. Yet the quiet life with his family in provincial France, even though he was able to reread the German Romantics, especially Novalis, was no long-term solution. However tired he had become of America, he still knew that his identity was wrapped up in its contradictions.

In 1924 Jolas brought together forty-five of his poems, mainly dealing with his career as a journalist and showing the influence of his psychiatric work during the war. *Rhythmus*, a short-lived journal edited by Oscar Williams and Gene Derwood, devoted its entire May-June 1924 issue to these poems, collectively known as "Ink." At least eight of them appeared in *Cinema* (1926), Jolas's first published collection. These free verse poems are quite different technically from the poetry he would later write; they do, however, reveal much about the young man who would soon begin *transition*. For example, in "Ink" (the title poem renamed "News" in *Cinema*), the persona recoils from the "sinister vision of ink . . . swirling with evil things." The mechanical presses record the disintegration and deterioration of the human spirit; the natural world is clouded by the people who no longer function as individuals, who have become marionettes. The sordid desires, the hypocrisies of false love, the distorted Christ combine in the potential meaninglessness of life. Yet for the persona "life waits, tragic and beautiful, / a sculptured longing after God." The poet was determined to rise above the world of the reporter. Even though Jolas recorded the facts of life, the surface realities would finally mean nothing to him as he searched within himself—his dreams and his imagination—to discover an inner reality, an eternal truth. Moreover, the reporter's language, the jargon, the accepted descriptions, the cliches, would come to represent the sickness within the entire language. For the poet intent upon the inward journey, man's language, not man's spirit, had to be destroyed.

In 1924 Jolas accepted a position with the European edition of the *Chicago Tribune* (the Paris *Tribune*). He was discovering a comfortable role in Paris, where he was able to bridge the gap which existed between the European and the American experience, his own as well as the countries'. In a few months he became city editor, focusing upon intellectual and cultural developments. His predecessor had been Ford Madox Ford, and Jolas accepted the position with some hesitation; he began "Rambles Through Literary Paris," a series of articles for each Sunday edition. He also contributed articles on art, along with art critic B. J. Kospoth and Louis Gay, to the Sunday Magazine section, edited by Roscoe Ashworth. Besides the regular columns of Jolas and Elliot Paul, and H. L. Mencken's syndicated column, the magazine section included reviews, a listing of bestsellers in America, and literary letters from London and New York. Jolas was especially instrumental in introducing to Americans certain French writers, such as Jean Giraudoux, Andre Gide, Philippe Soupault, and Andre Breton, interviewing them and reviewing their work. He also discussed recent issues of French journals, notably *La Nouvelle Revue Francaise* and *La Revolution Surrealiste*, and works not yet published. On 19 October 1924 Jolas wrote a column in which he mentions now prominent American writers, such as Sherwood Anderson, Ezra Pound, and Eugene O'Neill, who were at the time unknown or misunderstood. He then comments: "It is so much more facile for them [European writers] to write about America, the cubes of its visionary skyscrapers, the roar of the Chicago pit, the sing song of Jazz. . . . The real America they do not know. They are ignorant of the groping psyche of the nation as manifested throughout its limitless spaces." Jolas was intent upon showing the "real America" not only to Europeans, but also to the world. Yet he was no jingoistic American: he was equally as interested in the Surrealists; the works of James Joyce; the activities of the various small literary magazines in America, England, and Europe; developments in music such as jazz; and the dominant Parisian figures such as Gertrude Stein, Natalie Clifford Barney, and Ernest Hemingway. He was equally fascinated by the personalities of the artists and the nonartists, both of whom helped to create the ambience and excitement of Paris.

Certainly working on the *Tribune* and being a part of the literary world in Paris in the mid-twenties was exciting. William Shirer records in *20th Century Journey* (1976) that on his first night at work in August 1925 he met not only Jolas, but also James Thurber, Elliot Paul, and Virgil Geddes, all of whom helped to initiate the young novice into the journalist's life in Paris. "We were," he writes, "young, anonymous, happy and perhaps hopeful." Jolas also knew the writers in Paris and what they were trying to do; he was never to be the detached, coolly cynical literary man. The late nights, the large amounts of alcohol, the philosophical cafe conversations—all blended with the works themselves to create the environment out of which *transition* grew.

In 1924 Jolas also met James Joyce, whose *Work in Progress* dominated the ten-year existence of *transition*. The meeting, as described by Jolas in 1941, however, gave little portent of the relationship which later developed between the two men. "It was at a rather dull banquet. . . . Joyce was beaming in the aureole of *Ulysses*, and in a happy mood, when I was introduced to him. He thanked me courteously for something I had written about the book. . . . We did not meet again until early in 1927." Jolas was already convinced of Joyce's greatness and permanent place as the major author writing in the twentieth century.

Jolas met his future wife, Maria McDonald, in 1925. Born in Louisville, Kentucky, she had gone to Berlin in 1913 to study voice and returned to New York during World War I. When the war ended, her voice teacher had returned to Paris, and McDonald followed. Much later, she commented: "There was no romanticism, no chestnut trees in bloom, no April in Paris, none of those things. It was just simply that I wanted to follow this singing teacher. And so I stayed with her until she died. And then I met Eugene Jolas and we got married and then I stayed on with him. I've never felt that I was an exile, an expatriate, and I've never had any of those feelings of being detached either from my own country or from [France]." She had first come to know Jolas through his *Tribune* column; she was attracted to "an American journalist for whom literature was the great adventure and who, in addition to his knowledge of English and American writers, was familiar with the new currents in Europe." His brother Jacques introduced them at a party in May 1925, and Jolas invited her to the annual meeting of the P. E. N. Club. The meeting itself failed to impress either of them, but talk of James Joyce and his work consumed much of their conversation when they met not long afterwards. They were both thrilled by the beauty of the language in a published fragment from *Work in Progress*. Jolas read aloud from it, and Maria, bewildered but fascinated, listened. She recognized Joyce's greatness and Jolas's passion; writing "was the exhilarating element in which he [Jolas] thrived." She wanted to share that passion, and they decided to marry.

Because the wedding was planned for January 1926 in New York, Jolas left his job with the *Tribune* and returned once again to America. It was not to be a long stay, but it helped to determine Jolas's decisions about his future. After their marriage in New York, the young couple moved to New Orleans, where Jolas became feature reporter for the *Item Tribune* and where they came to know the local writers and artists, especially Sherwood Anderson and the people associated with the *Double Dealer*, a small, important literary journal. However, Jolas quickly realized that he could not stay in New Orleans; he was not going to find a complete identity as either an American or a European. He was truly an international man, aware of America's raw strength and vitality, but also aware that the basis of that strength lay in Europe. Jolas could be excited about Anderson's praise for the "American ring" of his poems written during the early twenties. Yet Jolas was an American who could not accept the provinciality or the narrow-mindedness of most other Americans. He wanted to help America discover its base in Europe and provide the opportunity for Europeans to read the growing number of American authors who refused to be trapped by the anti-intellectual, antiliterary world of their native country. He wanted to edit an international literary journal and considered taking over the *Double Dealer*, but decided that he had to return to Paris, where the audience and atmosphere were more conducive to his ambitions. Thus the Jolases left for Paris in the spring of 1926, where Jolas again became city editor of the *Tribune*.

Not long after he left America, Jolas's volume of poems, *Cinema*, was published in New York with an introduction by Anderson. Anderson's son had introduced the two men in New Orleans, and Anderson thought Jolas was a kindred spirit. The sensitive young poet, "unsure of himself," yet "feeling his way," is "intent on expressing the age in which he lives and he believes America best expresses the present age." Anderson, perhaps not totally aware of Jolas's ambitions, proclaimed him "one of the few important new singers—here lifting up his voice to Americans." The poems in *Cinema*, in addition to those which had earlier appeared in *Rhythmus*, however, do not present a particularly optimistic view of the modern age, much less of America. Jolas proclaims that salvation comes from a transcendent vision, not from total involvement in American life. In "Hymn for the Lonely," for example, the speaker implores the "Dreamer of God" to "send certitudes to us lost in sinister darkness . . . / lead us into spaces beyond the fear of mysteries— / let us see visions silver as dawn thought . . . . . / O Dreamer of God, show us the Cinema of the Angels." For Jolas there had to be a world beyond that which continued to trap its inhabitants in empty lives of misery and sorrow. No earthly allegiances, no national nor familial bonds could answer man's longing. The persona in Jolas's *Cinema* is not a young man who will help to find a wholeness for the grotesques which he leaves behind. Instead, he is more concerned with the recognition of the universal need for transcendence which the poet can only evoke or plead for from some spiritual being or eternal truth. Jolas's plea is for help to make the poet's dream a reality. Ready to start his international literary journal, he was also ready to develop the philosophy and language which would capture that dream for the poet and whomever his audience chanced to be.

When Jolas returned to Paris, he was thirty-two, a published poet, respected journalist, and established figure in the Paris literary circles. He knew the German Expressionists, the Surrealists, and most of the American writers in Paris. In addition, he was a highly personable man—large, handsome, an excellent listener, as Kay Boyle noted—and a man who saw the need for a journal of courage, perhaps even revolution. The *Dial* and the *Little Review* offered little for English readers who were interested in the most recent literary innovations. Ford Madox Ford's *transatlantic review* had appeared for only a year, and in 1927 *This Quarter* had ended when Ernest Walsh died (although in 1929 it would be revived by Edward Titus). Thus Jolas, after Walsh's death, believed that he alone was left to carry on the struggle for the truly creative spirit in modern literature and began to set into motion the plans which he had been formulating for several years. He wanted more than an outlet for antirealistic, neoromantic literature, although he believed fervently in such writings; Jolas had "deep philosophical beliefs, approaching religious concern," as Dougald McMillan writes. "His dreams were particularly vivid and seemed portentous to him. At one time he had felt himself possessed and had actually had visions in which he had encountered the devil. These psychic experiences led him to seek new ways of expressing the unconscious with a fervour that made him unusually receptive to literary innovation in that direction."

In late fall of 1926 with Elliot Paul, a fellow literary editor at the *Tribune*, as coeditor, Jolas started work on the first issue of his magazine. They first worked in the Jolases' apartment but soon rented a room in the Hotel de la Gare des Invalides. Using the small "t" to provoke critics, they selected a name, *transition*, taken from Edwin Muir, who had published a collection of his essays on contemporary literature entitled *Transition* earlier in 1926. Muir's purpose had been to deal with "the things of the present," always aware that in a period of transition moving from established greatness of the past to the "raw potentiality" of the present, one must study and help reveal the artist in revolt, the writer struggling to express the spirit of his age. Jolas and Paul had a similar ambition for their magazine. In addition, the assurance of motion, the potential for growth, the excitement of change and stimulation contained within the word "transition" appealed to Jolas. Finally, he felt that the sense of established bases in Europe juxtaposed with the growing maturity of America was embodied in *transition*. Thus with coeditor, title, and a hotel-room office, Jolas set out to find worthy contributions for the first issue.

Jolas already had established contact with many French, German, and American writers throughout western Europe. Sofia Himmel, a young Russian woman living in Paris, suggested works by new Russian writers such as Alexander Blok and Serge Essenin, whom she translated. Paul had become one of Gertrude Stein's devotees, and she had urged him to join with Jolas because she wanted another outlet for her work. She chose "An Elucidation," which explained her method of writing in her own style, for *transition* 1 and "As a Wife Has a Cow A Love Story" for the third issue. Robert Desnos and Philippe Soupault, the Surrealists, and Georg Trakl, the German Expressionist, also appeared in the first issue. Kay Boyle contributed a story and a book review after Jolas had sent her a telegram announcing his plans for *transition* and asking for stories and poems. Jolas especially wanted to include something by Joyce, having read excerpts from his new work in the *Navire d'Argent* and *transatlantic review*. Through the help of Sylvia Beach, owner of Shakespeare and Company, the Jolases and Paul were invited to Joyce's apartment, where Joyce read from his work. They quickly agreed to publish the first part of *Work in Progress*, to republish fragments which had already appeared in other journals, and to continue the work serially. *Finnegans Wake* (1939) had found its public voice, and Joyce had made vitally important allies. Thus Jolas and Paul had the material for several issues, but the work proved more demanding and time-consuming than they had anticipated. Many of the works had to be translated, a task which fell primarily to Jolas. The editors had little money and high ideals, which they would not compromise, and *transition* would be supported only by their efforts and a few advertisements by publishers, bookstores, and other small journals. In addition, they would never have more than 4,000 copies of any issue printed, nor would they have any more than 1,000 paid subscriptions. Yet by early February 1927, they had the first issue ready.

Almost immediately they began to have problems. Before they could get the number to the printer, Archibald MacLeish wanted to withdraw his poem because he believed that it was not being given the prominence it deserved. After an exchange of telegrams, he relented. Then they discovered that "An Elucidation" had been incorrectly printed; Stein was furious and was mollified only after they promised to issue a special supplement to the first issue with the correct text of her entire piece. Finally, French officials held up the first issue because Jolas and Paul had failed to understand that only a French citizen could act as the responsible publisher of a work printed in France. Only after some negotiations did the first issue appear in April. The hard work and difficult problems proved to be worthwhile, though, for *transition* 1 was an immediate and controversial success. Orders for the first issue came from all over the world, and the impressive contents and quality of the editing elicited a large number of manuscripts. Jolas would never again have to struggle to fill an issue. He would be able to seek out contributions because of their content rather than to fill the necessary number of pages.

In December 1927 the Jolases had moved from Paris and rented a hunting lodge in Colombey-Les-Deux-Eglises in the Haute-Marne near Chaumont. The house later belonged to Charles de Gaulle. It became home for the Jolases, their young daughter Betsy, and Elliot Paul, who came to live with them even though they kept their hotel-room office in Paris. From *transition*'s beginning Maria Jolas had had her own important role in running the magazine. Eric Hawkins later gave her credit for having only the "talent for finding attractive places to live," but her husband depicted her significance more accurately. "I cannot forego mentioning the great debt we owed to my wife," he wrote in 1931, "who organized the technical side of *transition*, watched over the increasingly large bulk of correspondence, helped with reading proofs and with translations, and in general was a counselor without whose aid the magazine would have been impossible."

During the first year of *transition*, from April 1927 to March 1928, twelve issues appeared, all with the same format: about ten short prose selections, twelve to fifteen poems, reproductions of paintings, reviews, and a few essays—the last often by Jolas, Paul, or Robert Sage, who became an associate editor in September 1927 with the sixth number. More important than the essays, though, were the carefully chosen selections reflecting the editors' goals which they introduced in *transition* 1: "TRANSITION wishes to offer American writers an opportunity to express themselves freely, to experiment, if they are so minded, and to avail themselves of a ready, alert and critical audience. To the writers of all other countries, TRANSITION extends an invitation to appear, side by side, in a language Americans can read and understand. . . . No rigid artistic formulae will be applied in selecting the contents of TRANSITION. If the inspiration is genuine, the conception clear and the result artistically organized, in the judgement of the editors, a contribution will be accepted. Originality will be its best recommendation. Neither violence nor subtlety will repel us." Jolas and Paul wanted a truly international journal, aimed at Americans, but providing an outlet for any contemporary artist. In addition, they wanted the original, the experimental, even the bizarre to challenge and stimulate their audience. Thus Jolas could later describe the first year as an "Eclectic-Subversive Period." Jolas published ten fragments from *Work in Progress*; Gertrude Stein was represented in six issues. Hart Crane, Archibald MacLeish, Kay Boyle, Laura Riding, William Carlos Williams, Allen Tate, Yvor Winters, H. D., and Ernest Hemingway were some of the Americans for whom Jolas had great hopes.

Jolas, whose own work would appear increasingly, first published his own poems in the third number. One poem, "Frontier," seems particularly autobiographical as the speaker considers his youth in an "old-world town" from which he embarked on his quest for "miracles"—wandering now as a "lonely hoodlum in cities of the world." Also in the third issue was an important statement by the editors, "Suggestions for a New Magic."

> *transition* will attempt to present the quintessence of the modern spirit in evolution. . . . We believe in the ideology of revolt against all diluted and synthetic poetry, against all artistic efforts that fail to subvert the existing concepts of beauty. . . . We believe that there is no hope for poetry unless there be disintegration first. We need new words, new abstractions, new hieroglyphics, new symbols, new myths. . . . Perhaps we are seeking God. Perhaps not. It matters little one way or the other. What really matters is that we are on the quest. Piety or savagery have both the same bases. Without unrest we have stagnation and impotence.

This was essentially the guiding philosophy behind the entire run of *transition*. Jolas repeatedly denied that he or *transition* was committed to any certain political, ideological, or philosophical group. Instead, he insisted that the only guiding principle was creation through revolt. The poet could not merely build upon that which preceded him; he must first destroy it, then build in its place. For Jolas, the artist was the born enemy of any person or force which tried to limit his creative freedom, especially the philistine now more powerful than ever in the mechanical age.

Halfway through *transition*'s first year, Jolas

was thus intent upon drawing certain lines between his response and others' to the contemporary world. He had seen the serious problems of the modern age—industrial growth, mechanization, World War I, and nationalism, and had rejected the solutions with which some intellectuals and artists hoped to combat them. The Futurists with their machine as salvation, the new humanism, the spiritual renewal in Christianity, all disgusted Jolas. In "Enter the Imagination" in *transition* 7, he attacked Jacques Maritain's attempts to uphold a traditional dogmatism and supported the Comte de Lautreamont with his focus on the "evil functions of life." For Jolas, the artist who would sacrifice all for a liberation of the imagination was the genius of any age, not only the modern. Novalis, the German romantic philosopher, provided a guiding philosophy. In an unpublished essay, "Prolegomenon of White Romanticism and Mythos of Ascension," which McMillan describes, Jolas further explored how Novalis's theory reconciles the apparent duality of the world through a recognition of "the self as the manifestation of the creative spirit in which all being was unified. . . . man should cultivate any manifestations of his inner nature and try to bring the world into harmony with them." Novalis's poetry adds the dream to this theory as the main source of a possible unity transcending man's normal experience. Jolas, therefore, saw in the works he selected for *transition* a growing rebellion which manifested much of his own belief based upon his continued reading of the German Romantics.

However, as "The Pursuit of Happiness" in the eighth issue reveals, many people were not responding positively to what they believed *transition*'s rebellion supported. Reviewers in America and England began to attack the magazine and what they saw as its mindless, dangerous iconoclasm. Some issues were even being seized and destroyed. Wyndham Lewis in the *Enemy* was an especially virulent critic who proclaimed *transition* one of the destructive forces leveled against Western civilization. Concerned, but clearly delighted, Jolas tried to clarify *transition*'s mission in "On the Quest" in *transition* 9 (December 1927). He restates his opposition to realism and supports the "dual realism" which "has the two planes of the subconscious and the instinctive and the physical consciousness." He remains opposed to political revolt. "Poetry in itself is a revolt," where artistic vision can be achieved through the "re-creation of the word. . . . To capture the eternal values in the flux of the modern world, to create a cosmos, each in his own way, to find a new humanism in a marriage of reason and instinct—this, it seems, should be our universal goal."

Maria Jolas had, up to number 10, contributed only translations, but to reinforce her husband's call for a new simplicity, and for a renewal of the native elements in America such as William Carlos Williams was attempting in his poetry, she published "Black Thoughts," her only article to appear in a regular issue of *transition*. In it, she urges the Negro to fight the forces—political and literary—which had exploited him and to return to his people; Negroes should "sink their roots even deeper into the rich black loam that is their heritage, lest their inspiration be withered and destroyed by transplanting in soils which are either unfertile or entirely foreign to their genius." At this time the Jolases were translating and editing *Le Negre Qui Chante*, a collection of traditional Negro songs. He also began to emphasize his call for a new language, a focus on the word, in "The Revolution of Language and James Joyce," which appeared in *transition* 11 (February 1928). In a lengthy discussion of Joyce's linguistic innovations, Jolas once again stated that "modern life with its changed mythos and transmuted concepts of beauty makes it imperative that words be given a new composition and relationship." Thus he was ready, as the first year ended, to enter *transition*'s more revolutionary era as the magazine became a quarterly devoted to experimentation with new language to express the vision of the unconscious and the dream.

Elliot Paul, though, would no longer be his coeditor. According to Eric Hawkins in *Hawkins of the Paris Herald* (1963), Robert Sage, who became associate editor and assumed many of Paul's duties when Paul left, saw a problem of temperament and commitment between Paul and Jolas. "Paul was a facile worker and was in charge of the magazine's prose section. Poetry was in the hands of Jolas, who worked slowly and frequently changed his mind. Sage thought Jolas relied heavily on Paul's presence, since the latter never hesitated about anything. However, when work started on a new number, Paul would fix up the prose section in a few days and then hike out for the cafes of Paris or the company of a certain woman in nearby Troyes. Thus the evanescent Paul was almost never at Colombey when the Jolases wanted to consult him." Whatever the reasons, though, Jolas and Paul seemed to part amicably; Paul remained a contributing editor through the 16/17 number. In addition, *Transition Stories*, twenty-three stories taken from *transition* and edited by Jolas and Sage, was published in 1929 and dedicated to Paul. The Jolases later resented Gertrude Stein's assertion that Paul had been the guiding hand behind *transition*, but it was never clear if that resentment ever extended to Paul himself. After number 12, however, *transition* definitely reflected Jolas's taste and philosophy even more clearly.

Between March 1928 and June 1930, when Jolas temporarily ended *transition*, he edited six issues, two of which were double numbers, and coedited *Transition Stories*. Harry Crosby's Black Sun Press published *Secession in Astropolis* (1929), a small collection of Jolas's poems, and Jolas finally had published *Anthologie de la Nouvelle Poesie Americaine* (1928), which he had completed earlier in 1927. This important anthology, going through at least six printings, introduced, for the first time in translation, 126 contemporary American poets to the French. In his introduction, Jolas emphasized that he had undertaken this edition because he wanted the French to have a clearer understanding of the growing, exciting creative spirit in America since World War I; the brief biographical sketches and short selections indicated the diversity of the group. This anthology had also helped Jolas to establish contact with a great number of young American writers just as he was beginning *transition*.

In *transition* 12 (March 1928), which announced the magazine's change from monthly to quarterly, Jolas and Paul deplored the lack of American response to their call. While *transition* would continue "to reflect the chaos borne by our age" and would regard itself as a link between Europe and America, the emphasis in the future would "be placed on American contributions." They concluded with a renewed invitation "to all those who wish to express violently and sincerely their reaction to the age, who are interested in creative experiments, who revolt against the growing hegemony of philistinism and sterility." Thus number 13 was completely devoted to American authors, except for another segment from *Work in Progress*, and was called "The American Number." The format and size of the magazine changed, and a subtitle was added: "An International Quarterly for Creative Experiment." However, even though a number of minor writers appeared briefly, the major contributors, all Americans, remained primarily the same—Archibald MacLeish, Peter Neagoe, Gertrude Stein, Malcolm Cowley, William Carlos Williams, Kay Boyle, Stuart Gilbert, Jolas, Laura Riding, and Katherine Anne Porter. Two important group responses, though, did appear. One was from New York, signed by, among others, Kenneth Burke, Robert Coates, Cowley, and Matthew Josephson,

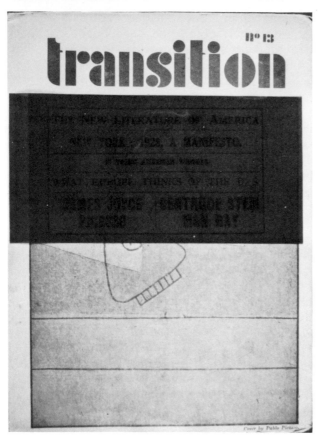

Front cover, transition, *no. 13 (Summer 1928)*

now a contributing editor to *transition*, who had convinced Jolas that a literary resurgence was indeed impending in America. This manifesto first attacked American advertising, then the American expatriates who had refused to return to America and to become political activists in the cause of social justice. The attack seemed directed at *transition*, and Jolas, of course, was disappointed. He saw the manifesto, as McMillan points out, as "an acquiescence (if not politically, at least artistically) in the status quo." The other group response was to *transition*'s "Inquiry among European Writers into the Spirit of America." The writers had been asked two questions: "How, in your opinion, are the influences of the United States manifesting themselves upon Europe and in Europe?" and "Are you for or against those influences?" Among those who answered were Tristan Tzara, Jules Romains, Philippe Soupault, and Bernard Fay. Twenty-four writers replied, some quite disturbed by American influence, others somewhat approving. Jolas himself provided an answer to both groups in a "Transatlantic Letter" in which he stated his opposition to physical revolt against the existing social structure and defended his decision to stay in Europe. "I am not anti-American

in the sense usually connected with that word, but I feel that America is intellectually in a deplorable state, that her civilization is a potentiality that for the moment is even doubtful, that she lives, not in the spirit, but in a false superficiality that abhors the deeper forces of life." He concluded by once again defining the revolution he advocated in poetry and language. "The wedding of reality with the automatic expressions of the subconscious, the intuitive, the somnambulist, the dream will lead us to a revolutionary mythos. . . . [The poet] must call for the barbaric catastrophe of the spirit and for an eternal anarchy."

Numbers 14 (Fall 1928) and 15 (February 1929) also reflected *transition*'s American focus although Jolas was already realizing that the revolution he had hoped for among American writers had not occurred nor had Americans rejected social realism. Similar to his inquiry among European writers was his inquiry among American expatriates about why they lived in Europe (*transition* 14). Among those who replied were again the familiar names often associated with *transition*: Gertrude Stein, Kay Boyle, Harry Crosby, George Antheil, and Lincoln Gillespie. The seventeen responses again varied, but they primarily agreed with Jolas's sentiments about the growth of industrialism and the state of revolutionary spirit expressed in various movements. Clearly the contributors and the philosophy of *transition* did not coincide with Matthew Josephson's call for the "industrial millenium," in which artists would become willing members of industrial society, and he no longer was associated with the magazine after number 15. Jolas once again asserted his opposition to any political involvement for the poet: "I should like to think that a hundred years hence, when capitalism and communism have finally merged, there will still be a place for the man who stands between the Greek ideal and that of Christ." And in a final plea for America to stand against collectivism before Jolas and *transition* looked back to Europe, he stated in number 15: "We must continue to oppose the present plutocratic materialism, fight for a new orientation of life based on the need for a universal humanity and on the idea of the American mythos in relation to the dynamic century, defend at all costs man's inalienable right to dream and rebel and create in himself the possibilities of the organic cosmos."

Jolas had already recognized, though, that *transition* could not be devoted only to America and American writers. Even in numbers 14 and 15, he had included substantial sections devoted to works by authors such as Robert Desnos, Italo Svevo, and, of course, Joyce. Thus in the next issue, the double number 16/17, he changed the format to emphasize the "Revolution of the Word Proclamation," a revolution advocated primarily in Europe by a few American, British, and European writers. This statement, which was signed by Jolas, Theo Rutra (Jolas's pseudonym), and fourteen of his supporters, was actually a personal manifesto which Jolas had drafted at his wife's urging; she believed that the ideas and philosophy which he had long been formulating needed concreteness and clarification. Among those who signed, Robert Sage, Elliot Paul, and Stuart Gilbert were *transition* editors; Whit Burnett, Leigh Hoffman, Douglas Rigsby, Harold J. Salemson, Kay Boyle, A. L. Gillespie, and Hart Crane were regular contributors; and Harry and Caresse Crosby had supported *transition* since their arrival in Paris. (Crosby had given Jolas one hundred dollars to send to the poet who had written the best poem in the first twelve issues; he had also paid for the printing of an entire issue at the end of 1928.) The proclamation accomplished its goal almost immediately; critics were outraged. Newspapers ridiculed both the twelve points and *transition*. Yet it also clarified what Jolas had been saying about form, language, the poet's role, and the relationship of writer to audience. None of the points were new, but they did signal that Jolas was drawing together many of the diverse strands from psychology, cultural anthropology, linguistics, and philosophy to form a coherent metaphysical position. He was clearly indebted to Janet, Freud, Jung, and Levy-Bruhl as he sought to redefine man, his subconscious, and his representative linguistic structures.

In *transition* 16/17 (June 1929) Jolas expressed much of his developing philosophy in "Logos." Innovations in language were his primary concern. "The magic idealism which is a means for destroying the mediocrity of the universe is translated into metaphysical terms. The poet acts in terms of the universal. He feels it to be his function to create the unity of an organism which is composed of elements by nature hostile to each other. Through the autonomy of his visionary operations, he proceeds to the synthesis which alone can satisfy him. He brings together realities far removed from each other, that seem without any organic relationships, that are even tending to mutual destruction. But his imagination demolishes the tyranny of the world by eliminating its customary analogies and substituting new ones." In number 18 (November 1929), as *transition* entered its third year, Jolas continued his analysis in "Notes on Reality": "the new creator is out to make the alliance

between the dionysian-dynamic and the nocturnal realities. He is out to discover the unity of life. Conquering the dualism between the 'it' and the 'I', he produces new myths." Jolas also published translations of Novalis, whom he proclaimed as a conscious creator of "a magical reality." Number 18's format emphasized the clarified focus; Jolas no longer identified authors by country. Instead, he stressed that all the writers in *transition* were working together in a conscious revolution which manifested his philosophy. The section titles, "The Synthetist Universe," "Explorations," "The Revolution of the Word," replaced the United States, Europe, and Great Britain. In addition, Jolas, Harry Crosby, Stuart Gilbert, and Robert Sage issued another proclamation, "The Novel is Dead Long Live the Novel," which stated in its twelve points that the contemporary novel was "an archaic form that no longer answers the needs of the modern psyche" while the novel of the future would form a new mythos and "express the magic reality in a language that is non-imitative and evolutionary."

Carl Einstein, a German art critic and author, whom Jolas had met earlier, moved to Paris in the summer of 1928 and became a contributing editor to *transition* in late 1929. Together with Hans Arp, Einstein and Jolas discussed the revolutionary and evolutionary trends in contemporary thought and their philosophical bases. Jolas reread Max Scheler, the German philosopher, whose emphasis upon the reintegration of fragmentary man melded nicely with Jolas's previous readings of Novalis and other romantics. Because the German Expressionists in Berlin were particularly in touch with these beliefs, Jolas visited Berlin in the winter of 1929-1930 to gather materials for *transition*. While in Berlin, largely through talks with Gottfried Benn, Jolas became even more convinced that *transition* should include more than artistic manifestations of the revolution; he would now deal more fully with the scientific as well as philosophical backgrounds of his thought. Especially important would be the studies of the unconscious. Although Freud was clearly an influence on this thought, Jolas found more to support his idealism in Jung. In May 1930 the Jolases were in Zurich to help Joyce and met Jung. They discussed Jolas's dreams, and Jolas urged Jung to contribute to *transition*. Thus when the Jolases returned to Paris, Jolas took one of Jung's essays, "Psychology and Poetry," to be published in number 19/20. The essay discusses the division of literature into "psychological" works and "visionary" works and calls the poet a seer, a concept of the artist which Jolas totally supported. Jolas believed that by mid-1930, he was indeed able to synthesize the different strands of his thoughts, now clearly worked out, through contributions, his own and others, to *transition*.

However, in number 19/20, Jolas announced that he was ceasing publication of *transition* because of the time and work which it required. In what he thought was the final issue, he published five additional essays and statements which express his views: "Literature and the New Man," "The Dream," "Towards New Forms?," "The King's English Is Dying: Long Live the Great American Language," and "The Machine and 'Mystic America.' " The death of the King's English was a continuation of the debate which *transition* had been having with the *Modern Quarterly*, whose Fall 1929 issue had been largely devoted to a discussion of their differences over the necessary extent of the revolution of the word. In "Literature and the New Man," Jolas summed up the ideas for which *transition* had stood: "the mythos and the dream, i.e. the evocation of the instinctive personal and collective universe; the attempt to define the new man in relation to his primàl consciousness; the revolution of the word. All of these are interdependent functions of the modern spirit." Thus as *transition* ended its first three years, Jolas believed that it had indeed accomplished even more than he had dared to hope for in 1926. Not only had it been a provocative voice which gave expression to many of the developing writers in modern society, but also it had developed a philosophy by which modern man might find a new wholeness and inspiration.

During the period between June 1930 and March 1932 when *transition* was resurrected, Jolas worked steadily on his own writing and published an important retrospective of his journal, "*Transition*: An Epilogue," in the May-August 1931 issue of the *American Mercury*. The Jolases moved back to Paris from Colombey in 1931, and Maria Jolas founded the Ecole Bilingue de Neuilly, a French-English school for boys and girls, which existed from 1932 to 1940. The school was housed in Paris with approximately sixty students. It was primarily a day school, but some students boarded. Later Joyce's grandson would be a pupil. Maria Jolas had a major role in determining *transition*'s editorial policy and had translated many of the French contributions. Yet her husband was clearly consumed by his work and his international friendships. Her bilingual school must have served as an outlet for her considerable energies at a time when her help was no longer needed on the

magazine. In addition, her school was compatible philosophically with both Jolases' views about the tremendous benefits of an international community where language might act as a bond, not as a barrier, to communication and understanding. In her own way, then, she could carry on the revolution which *transition* had begun.

Meanwhile, Jolas had translations, several small volumes of poems, and, most importantly, *The Language of Night* (1932) published. This small volume drew together the various strands of Jolas's philosophy and its background, which had been spread throughout three years of *transition*. Dedicated to Stuart Gilbert, the book establishes the context—the disintegration of society, spirit, and culture in the twentieth century—of the neoromantic movement in the modern age; it also examines the Romantic tradition out of which that movement grew. In a detailed discussion, Jolas traces the development of linguistic mutation through the centuries, ending with the "Revolution of the Word Proclamation," James Joyce, and Gertrude Stein. Then in "Depth and the Chthonian Image" he recounts much of the scientific, psychological, and philosophical background for the emergence of the irrational, the unconscious, and the dream as sources of man's magical, creative forces. "Art will be vertical instead of merely horizontal. The inner life will be again the center from which everything proceeds. A perpendicular movement from the nocturnal to stellar constellations will create a new emotion of wonder. Ecstatic immediacy!" He ends with a brief investigation of "vertical language" whereby the poet would be able to transcend surface realism. "And the poet in giving back to language its pre-logical function makes a spiritual revolution— the only revolution worth making today." That Jolas's revolution would again find a regular voice was announced on the back cover: the new *transition* "will be a laboratory for a modern metaphysics . . . will seek the eternal conception of the personality . . . will continue its war on linguistic orthodoxy and fight for the living word . . . will attempt to resurrect the mantic spirit in the twentieth century . . . will be an encyclopedia of the creative forces of the arc."

In late 1931 Carlus Verhulst of the Servire Press had approached Jolas about reviving *transition*. Verhulst wanted to present new works from many countries in translation and wanted Jolas to be the sole editor; in addition Servire was willing to underwrite the new *transition* totally. Jolas quickly agreed. Number 21 appeared in March 1932 with a new subtitle, "An International Workshop for Orphic Creation," and with a new emphasis on poetry. The prose texts included were called "Anamyths" and "Psychographs" and were by such authors as Franz Kafka, Peter Neagoe, and Gertrude Stein. The "Metanthropological Crisis" was a manifesto "regarding the evolution of individualism and metaphysics under a collectivistic regime"; again Stein was represented as well as Gottfried Benn, Martin Buber, Jung, Mencken, and Philippe Soupault. A more important manifesto, in terms of *transition*, was signed by Hans Arp, Samuel Beckett, Carl Einstein, Jolas, and four others: "Poetry is Vertical," which essentially listed in ten points the major concerns of *The Language of Night*. It proclaimed the poet as prophet, the primacy of dreams and the unconscious, and the romantic ideal of transcendent experience through the poetic vision. As McMillan notes, "It was clear now that *transition* was seeking God—if not an orthodox God, at least the God of theological existentialists like Martin Buber." The final section of number 21 fittingly presented a "Laboratory of the Word" ending in a dictionary which in later issues would define "anamyth" as "a fantastic narrative that reflects preconscious relationships" and "psychograph" as "a prose text that expresses hallucinations and phantoms." Especially significant, though, was the section which paid homage to James Joyce. More than anyone else, Joyce represented the quintessential modern spiritual revolutionary as defined by Jolas. His *Work in Progress* had not received adequate or perceptive responses; this section continued the series of articles which had started in the original *transition* intent upon reducing the neglect and misconceptions threatening the anticipated publication of what Jolas believed would be Joyce's greatest work. Joyce owed a great deal to Jolas and *transition*, but *transition* owed much to Joyce and his presence in seventeen issues.

Although number 22 did not appear until February 1933 and number 23 until much later in July 1935, these issues were quite similar to number 21. Jolas created a new term *vertigral* to replace vertical. McMillan explains that "Jolas believed a combination of negative and positive forces was necessary for an adequate view of life but, still true to Novalis, he also thought that the final resolution of forces should be in upward movement towards religious experience. Only through eternal quest could the positive movement be assured. The grail was the symbol of quest; by taking the German word *Graal* and dropping one 'a' he could include this concept in his key term. The new word also had overtones of 'integral' and thus also suggested the

universality which Jolas was seeking." In number 22 Jolas issued proclamations declaring, this time, the deaths of the horizontal age and of traditional grammar. The magazine also announced the abolition of the following words: novel, poetry, verse, poem, ballad, sonnet, short story, essay, and anthology. Thus writers, except for Joyce, now contributed vertigral documents and worked in the "Laboratory of the Mystic Logos." In number 23 Jolas continued the emphasis upon the primitive, the romantic-mystic, and the unconscious. He even included one of his young daughter's fantasies. Number 23 also contained another inquiry to which twenty-nine writers responded. Jolas asked two questions: "Do you believe that, in the present world crisis, the Revolution of Language is necessary in order to hasten the re-integration of human personality?" and "Do you envisage this possibility through a readaptation of existing words, or do you favour a revolutionary creation of new Words?" Most of the respondents, who included Gottfried Benn, Malcolm Cowley, Louis Untermeyer, and Laurence Vail, agreed that language was indeed in a period of crisis, but they disagreed about the necessary remedies. Only about half felt that Jolas's solution of introducing new words was desirable. The others felt that such a response would finally offer only a personal solution and would, therefore, have a very limited influence; however, Jolas clearly continued his focus on experimentation and innovation even though one of *transition*'s great experimenters had created a furor with her latest book, *The Autobiography of Alice B. Toklas* (1933). "Testimony Against Gertrude Stein," a supplement to number 23, attempted to rebut the inaccuracies in *The Autobiography of Alice B. Toklas*; Henri Matisse, Tristan Tzara, Maria Jolas, Georges Braque, Jolas, and Andre Salmon contributed. Jolas said of the *Autobiography*—"in its hollow, tinsel bohemianism and egocentric deformations, [it] may very well become one day the symbol of the decadence that hovers over contemporary literature." Maria Jolas primarily refuted Stein's claim that Elliot Paul had been the founder of *transition* and that Stein had been the most important contributor. The "Testimony" did little, of course, to counter the book's success, but it did clarify *transition*'s and Stein's positions; both had profitted from the association, and as in an unpleasant divorce, neither was willing to part company without vituperation.

In the fall of 1935, after *transition* 23 was published, Jolas decided to return to America and to work for the French news service, Havas. He had long recognized the many flaws in America, but *transition*'s early focus and Jolas's own background clearly indicated his continuing fascination with the country. At a time when Europe was already succumbing to the rise of fascism, and when his magazine was committed to the vertigral, Jolas must have seen America, with all its failures, as perhaps the final hope for a realizable idealism. Only in America did freedom for the artist still seem possible. However, Maria Jolas remained in Europe because of her commitment to her bilingual school. Their separation would last only a year, but the fact that they chose to separate suggests that Jolas considered his stay in America as initially experimental. The move necessitated a reorganization of *transition*; James Johnson Sweeney, a former contributor, now a resident of New York, became an associate editor. Together Jolas and Sweeney prepared the next three issues—24 (June 1936), 25 (Fall 1936), and 26 (May 1937)—and agreed to share any unpaid expenses after the Servire Press went bankrupt during the summer of 1936. The magazine itself underwent another change in format signaled by the change in subtitle from "An Orphic · Workshop" to. "A Quarterly Review." In place of the primary focus on poetry, *transition* now devoted regular sections to painting, music, architecture, the cinema, and documents supporting Jolas's philosophy, which did not change even though the format did. Fiction was still called "paramyths," and poetry remained vertigrally experimental. If the journal appeared slightly less revolutionary, it still published fine contributions: poems by Richard Eberhart, Samuel Beckett, James Agee, Dylan Thomas, and Randall Jarrell; paintings by Miro, Picasso, Calder, Arp, Matisse, and Mondrian; prose by Kafka, Dylan Thomas, and Joyce. Jolas himself continued to contribute his own works of prose and poetry but published almost no critical or philosophical pieces. By presenting a variety of material, he showed the success of the cultural revolution which was even more threatened by the growing crisis in Europe.

When Maria Jolas and their two daughters, Betsy and Tina, joined Jolas in the summer of 1936, she brought distressing news of the situation in Europe. By September they were back in Paris, where he alone edited the final, tenth anniversary issue of *transition*; they then returned to America. Although he announced that "*Transition* will continue to seek a pan-symbolic, panlinguistic synthesis in the conception of a four-dimensional universe" in his retrospective "Frontierless Decade," he realized that this issue would be the last. From the first issue, he had assiduously avoided allowing any political

involvement to intrude into his magazine. Now as he listened to Hitler's broadcasts, he knew that he could not remain politically inactive, and to turn *transition* into political propaganda, regardless of how noble the politics, would, to a great extent, compromise everything for which he and his journal had stood. Thus in number 27, he decided to end the magazine by illustrating the scope of *transition*'s decade and by showing how totally the artistic and literary forces were naturally aligned against any form of totalitarianism. He selected representative contributions from each of the groups and each of the innovations of the past ten years. The early Romanticism, Dadaism, German Expressionism, and Surrealism had been integral parts of *transition*'s development and were, therefore, given prominent places. He chose works by Joyce, Kay Boyle, Beckett, Andre Breton, Kafka, Anais Nin, Herbert Read, Henry Miller, and Philippe Soupault, among others. The final issue thus clearly reflected the impressive success for which the Jolases and their various associates had worked so hard.

By 1940, after the long-delayed final issue of *transition* appeared in 1939, the Jolases were back in New York, where they joined with other artists and writers as vocal opponents of fascism. In 1941 Jolas joined the United States Office of War Information; as he proudly declared in his own biographical sketch in *transition workshop*, which he edited in 1949, he "served with the American forces in both wars." He stayed in government service until 1950, but continued to work as a journalist and to write. He published several essays in the *Living Age* column "Poets and Poetry" during the early forties. In 1940 Clyde Tull announced in an introductory note to "Planets and Angels" that Jolas would soon be living in Mount Vernon, Iowa, where Cornell College was located. But the Jolases' other activities kept them in New York and Europe during and after the war, if indeed they ever seriously considered moving to Iowa.

After the war, Georges Duthuit, the French critic, edited *Transition Forty-Eight*, which Jolas helped as he could, but he never took an active role in its publication even though Maria Jolas did contribute several translations. They never seriously considered beginning a new journal or reviving the old *transition* again. The war had decimated what had remained of the Paris coteries even though a few writers, such as Beckett and the Jolases, did return. During the last two years of his life, Jolas continued to work on his autobiography and his translation of Novalis. On 26 May 1952, he died from acute nephritis. Maria Jolas still lives in Paris, occasionally writing short reminiscences of the writers she has known. Yet as Stuart Gilbert wrote in 1949, "Those *Transition* days linger with an unfaltering glow in the memories of all who shared in that great, perhaps Quixotic, enterprise. . . . The nucleus is dispersed . . . but there remains . . . this record of high, imaginative endeavor, a deflection of the trend of modern literature towards a visionary plane . . . and a contemporary recognition, wider than in those combative days we dared to hope for, of the plastic element in language as a means of expression transcending the scope of mere communication and sufficient to itself."

Other:

Anthologie de la Nouvelle Poesie Americaine, selected and translated into French by Jolas (Paris: Kra, 1928);

Le Negre Qui Chante, selected and translated into French by Eugene and Maria Jolas with an introduction by Eugene Jolas (Paris: Editions des Cahiers Libres, 1928);

Transition Stories, edited by Jolas and Robert Sage (New York: W. V. McKee, 1929);

Alfred Doblin, *Alexanderplatz, Berlin, the Story of Franz Biberkopf*, translated by Jolas (New York: Viking, 1931);

Gustav Theodor Fechner, *Life After Death*, translated by Jolas (New York: Pantheon, 1943);

Transition Workshop, edited by Jolas (New York: Vanguard, 1949);

"My Friend James Joyce," in *James Joyce: Two Decades of Criticism*, ed. Seon Givens (New York: Vanguard, 1963), pp. 19-26.

References:

Deirdre Bair, *Samuel Beckett* (New York: Harcourt Brace Jovanovich, 1978), pp. 77-391, 535-590;

Richard Ellmann, *James Joyce* (New York: Oxford University Press, 1959), pp. 600-816;

Eric Hawkins with Robert Sturdevant, *Hawkins of the Paris* Herald (New York: Simon & Schuster, 1963), pp. 149-152;

Frederick Hoffman, Charles Allen, and Carolyn F. Ulrich, *The Little Magazine: a History and a Bibliography* (Princeton: Princeton University Press, 1946), pp. 172-180;

Maria Jolas, "Joyce's Friend Jolas," in *A James Joyce Miscellany*, ed. Marvin Magalaner, first series (New York: James Joyce Society, 1957), pp. 62-74;

Maria Jolas, "A Bloomlein for Sam," in *Beckett at 60: A Festschrift* (London: Calder & Boyars, 1967), pp. 14-16;

Robert McAlmon, *Being Geniuses Together 1920-1930*, revised edition with additional material by Kay Boyle (Garden City: Doubleday, 1968), pp. 233-248;

Dougald McMillan, transition *The History of a Literary Era 1927-1938* (New York: Braziller, 1976);

Samuel Putnam, *Paris Was Our Mistress Memoirs of a Lost & Found Generation* (New York: Viking, 1947);

William L. Shirer, *20th Century Journey A Memoir of A Life and the Times* (New York: Simon & Schuster, 1976), pp. 217-233;

"Then and Now: The Expatriate Tradition," *Paris Review*, 9 (1965-1966): 158-170.

Matthew Josephson

David E. Shi
Davidson College

BIRTH: Brooklyn, New York, 15 February 1899, to Sarah Kasindorf and Julius Josephson.

EDUCATION: B.A., Columbia University, 1920.

MARRIAGE: 6 May 1920 to Hannah Geffen; children: Carl, Eric.

AWARDS: Guggenheim Fellowship, 1933; elected to the National Academy of Arts and Letters, 1948; Francis Parkman Prize for *Edison A Biography*, 1960; Van Wyck Brooks Award for *Al Smith: Hero of the Cities*, 1969.

DEATH: Santa Cruz, California, 13 March 1978.

SELECTED BOOKS: *Galimathias* (New York: Broom, 1923);
Zola and His Time The History of His Martial Career in Letters (New York: Macaulay, 1928; London: Gollancz, 1929);
Portrait of the Artist as American (New York: Harcourt, Brace, 1930);
Jean-Jacques Rousseau (New York: Harcourt, Brace, 1931; London: Gollancz, 1932);
The Robber Barons The Great American Capitalists 1861-1901 (New York: Harcourt, Brace, 1934; London: Eyre & Spottiswoode, 1962);
The Politicos 1865-1896 (New York: Harcourt, Brace, 1938);
Victor Hugo A Realistic Biography of the Great Romantic (Garden City: Doubleday, 1942);
Stendhal or the Pursuit of Happiness (Garden City: Doubleday, 1946);
Edison A Biography (New York: McGraw-Hill, 1959; London: Eyre & Spottiswoode, 1961);
Life Among the Surrealists A Memoir (New York: Holt, Rinehart & Winston, 1962);
Al Smith: Hero of the Cities, by Josephson and Hannah Josephson (Boston: Houghton Mifflin, 1969; London: Thames & Hudson, 1971).

During the brief periods between World Wars I and II that Matthew Josephson lived in Paris, he was one of the most colorful and involved American writers in Montparnasse. In the early twenties, as the controversial editor of *Secession* and *Broom*, Josephson became the high priest of American Dadaism, publishing the leading young writers among the avant-garde in the United States and France and championing from Europe an indigenous American art and literature reflecting the pace and tenor of the Machine Age. Several years later, after abandoning Dada and his Whitmanesque literary program, he returned to Paris to write what became a best-selling biography of Emile Zola. In the process his attitude toward literature and the role of the writer in society was dramatically transformed. Josephson would no longer lead the life of an apolitical aesthete pursuing art for art's sake; like Zola he would become a "writer turned public man" and make his mark among the literary Left in the United States.

Educated between 1916 and 1920 at Columbia University and in the bohemian cafes of Greenwich Village, Josephson began his literary career as an ardent experimentalist poet, espousing the use of free verse and other forms of technical innovation. Along with his friends Kenneth Burke, Malcolm Cowley, and Hart Crane, he emulated the intensity of the French Symbolists, discovering for himself a religion in art. He recalled that they were "young poetical and aesthetical rebels . . . [who] to the exclusion of almost everything else, gave ourselves to the pleasures of pure literature." In the years immediately following World War I (in which he did not participate), Josephson purposely ignored social and political issues. Psychological literature was everything to him, and his literary idols were European.

In October 1921, soon after graduating from Columbia, Josephson joined the migration of American writers headed for Paris. On arrival he found the literary activity in Montparnasse exhilarating. He wrote Burke that "the perfect ferment of activity around you is stimulating. . . . Paris seems the best place to starve in. . . . I suddenly got the conviction that I would be in Paris a long time." Josephson was quickly drawn to the madcap Dadaists, especially Louis Aragon, Philippe Soupault, Tristan Tzara, and Paul Eluard. He found them carefree, unpredictable, and totally without guile. They immersed themselves in literature and life and had no respect for their elders or entrenched literary conventions, qualities he found especially appealing. As he told Cowley at the time: "We have

Tristan Tzara and Matthew Josephson in the Tirol, 1922 (photo by Jean Arp)

decided to attach ourselves to the Dadaists, of whom thrills may be wrested at the lowest cost." Soon Josephson was a Dadaist himself, actively participating in the zany antics and boisterous demonstrations of his French friends. He also made for himself a place among the French editors of the Dadaist magazine *Aventure.*

Josephson firmly believed that underneath all the superficial nihilism which the Dadaists displayed there was a wealth of artistic talent. In December 1921, he tried to convince his American friends that this was the case. He stressed to Cowley that "these young men, when they break away from the rubbish of Dada will be the big writers of the next decade. They are working at more or less the same problems that we are, although they abjure technique." Not living in Paris, however, Cowley, Burke, and Crane found it difficult to appreciate the infectious effect which the Dadaists had upon Josephson.

Josephson learned to his surprise that many of the Dadaists were fascinated by modern American society and culture. Taking up where the Italian Futurists had left off, the more cosmopolitan Dadaists imitated in their writings the fast-paced tempo of urban industrial America. The French

fascination with life in the United States, gained largely through watching American films, stimulated Josephson to revise his own artistic attitudes. He related in his memoirs that he had come to France primarily to investigate the tradition of the Symbolists. "Instead," he recalled, "I was observing a young France that . . . was passionately concerned with the civilization of the U. S. A., and stood in fair way to be *Americanized.*" Earlier, in imitating the Symbolists, he had adopted a detached, exalted artistic perspective accompanied by a pose of fatigue and melancholy toward the everyday world about him. Now he discovered a completely new mood among the Dadaists, one that better fitted his personality. As he admitted to Burke, the "whole symbolist movement looks quite sterile . . . we, of course, are writing for *our* age."

In Paris Josephson began promoting an artistic attitude that would accept the reality of modern life and use the machine and the modern idiom to aesthetic advantage. He reflected the influence of Guillaume Apollinaire when he urged that literature "should not hesitate to keep abreast of the time, to adopt and even foreshadow the influence of the cinema, the avion, the phonograph, and the saxophone." To win over Americans to his ideas he decided in 1922, along with Gorham Munson, to publish a new review called *Secession*, to be printed in Vienna. As he explained to Burke, the new review would provide "an excellent chance to skirmish, to create a diversion, to make an opening sally. All the enemies of LITERATURE can be attacked as such. . . . Some headway can be won against the ill-informed snobbism of *The Little Review*, the eclecticism of *The Dial*, the barbarousness of the others." He and Munson solicited material from Burke, Cowley, William Carlos Williams, Marianne Moore, E. E. Cummings, and various French Dadaists.

In the magazine's first issue, printed in April 1922, Josephson surveyed the young Dadaist writers, praising inventive poets such as Louis Aragon, Andre Breton, and Philippe Soupault for "being bent frankly on unbounded adventures and experiments with modern phenomena." He urged American writers to follow the example set by the young French writers, to accept urban-industrial American society, and to integrate into their prose and poetry the inspiring dynamism of the modern Machine Age. American writers, he insisted, should quit criticizing their cultural heritage and modern environment and start creating a truly American art and literature amidst "their daily existence in the big cities, in the great industrial regions, athwart her marvelous and young mechanical forces." Josephson's rhetoric soared as he proclaimed that Americans "need play no subservient part in the movement. It is no occasion for aping European or Parisian tendencies. Quite the reverse, Europe is being Americanized." Years before, Emerson and Whitman had voiced similar sentiments, urging a national culture that would integrate contemporary life and subject matter into literature and art. But Josephson did not share their belief that literature should be dominated by a didactic, spiritual approach. His orientation was more superficial, more purely literary, concerned more with form and technique than with any mystical idealism.

Although many American readers criticized Josephson's Dadaist-inspired literary ideas, his Futuristic ideas gained momentum and support in Europe. Edith Sitwell, commenting on *Secession* in *New Age*, remarked that she would subscribe to the new magazine "for the purpose of watching the career of Mr. Matthew Josephson." In July 1922, Harold Loeb, the editor of *Broom*, invited Josephson to become an associate editor of his magazine. Josephson accepted, largely because of *Broom*'s larger circulation and more favorable financial position. With this decision Josephson's short stay

Front cover, by Jean Arp, August 1922

in Paris ended, and he soon moved to Berlin to take charge of *Broom*. He had found his calling. His duties as editor and critic suited perfectly his literary personality and his temperament. Eager to stimulate controversy and popularize his modernist views, he relished his mounting literary importance. His editorial prerogatives enabled him to take the offensive, to impose his own opinions and personality upon magazines and their reading public. Opinionated, quarrelsome, and fun loving, Matthew Josephson thrived on literary debate and contention, and he was effective. He slowly began to win over his skeptical American friends to his ideas. After meeting and living with the Dadaists in Paris, Malcolm Cowley admitted to Burke that "Matty is right about them. They are the most amazing people in Paris." Cowley decided to align himself with *Broom* and Josephson's editorial program. In August 1922, Hart Crane told Munson that Josephson had "developed a 'high hand' attitude in criticism that is . . . as effective as Pound's." In numerous articles and editorial comments in *Broom*, Josephson continued to criticize American writers for being preoccupied with social criticism instead of recognizing the cultural potential inherent in contemporary American life. He also continued to publish his Dadaist friends, such as Aragon, Soupault, Tzara, and Eluard.

In 1923 Josephson returned to New York and began publishing *Broom* in Manhattan, fully expecting to win over Americans to his new artistic ideas. In July he privately had printed *Galimathias*, a collection of his poems, many of which had already appeared in *Broom*. It was not received with enthusiasm among literary critics. The *Nation* commented that the volume "is magnificent—from the standpoint of the new non-intelligence; to sane people it is unimpressive raving." Such criticism did not dismay Josephson. The harsh realities of urban-industrial life in New York, however, soon dampened his naive enthusiasm. He discovered that machines, factories, skyscrapers, and automobiles tend to lose their inspiring and picturesque qualities when one is forced to live among them. Soon after his return to Manhattan he admitted that he needed "to get away from the noise of New York . . . in order to enjoy it." Moreover, American readers and post office censors failed to appreciate Josephson's new cultural ideas, and early in 1924 *Broom* collapsed.

Despite the unrealistic nature of Josephson's artistic program, he did recognize the importance of relating language and the plastic arts to the contemporary environment. He sought to rescue art from the romantic prejudice against modernity. In pursuing such a goal he assumed a leadership role in the revolution taking place in the arts during the early twenties. Moreover, through his editorship of *Broom*, he provided a forum for some of the most important experimental writing of the day. As Kenneth Rexroth has observed, *Broom* was "certainly the best of all the avant-garde magazines. It introduced to America the most exciting and innovative European literature of the time."

With *Broom*'s demise Josephson was temporarily forced out of his artistic existence, and he entered the stock market as a "customer's man." Within a little over a year, however, the frenetic pace and callousness of Wall Street activity began to take their toll. Early in 1926 he decided to resume his literary career. His Wall Street experience, however, had awakened in him a broader social vision, and he resolved to abandon pure literature. Writing in the *Little Review* in 1926 he attacked his former Dadaist companions for their antisocial and irrational tendencies. He now had no use for their abstruse literary works: "Of what value are these tedious and tepid dreams, these diffuse poems in prose, these wearisome manifestoes couched in a habitual

imagery and inverted syntax." He urged his European friends to involve themselves and their art in the pressing problems facing modern society rather than continue to retreat into esoteric irrelevance.

In a demonstration of his own changing perspective on literature, Josephson again sailed for France in the spring of 1927. This time, however, he was traveling to Paris to research and write his first serious historical work, a biography of Emile Zola, the exemplar of French Naturalism who only a few years before Josephson had so heartily condemned.

While writing *Zola and His Time* in Paris, Josephson occasionally saw his former Dadaist friends, but his relations with them were not the same. Andre Breton, he reported to Cowley, was "cool" to him. Josephson revealed the change that had taken place in his own thinking since his earlier stay in France when he wrote Burke that "as for the unconscious I find myself in a phase which reveres the conscious. At any rate I am convinced that Americans grow old more gracefully and fatalistically; the French grow absurd."

In Zola, Josephson found his permanent direction in life. Until then he had played the part of the assured aesthete oblivious to social or political concerns. But in reading about Zola he discovered that a writer is "heroic" if he takes up his pen for some great public cause. Indignant at the contemporary Sacco-Vanzetti affair, Josephson strongly identified with Zola's courageous role in the Dreyfus case. In *Zola and His Time* (1928), Josephson attacked those who focused narrowly on Zola as Naturalist. He stressed the romantic and poetic strain in the man who wrote *Germinal* (1885). The overriding theme of his study of Zola was that a writer is "heroic" if he emerges from the contemplation of pure art and confronts the reality of modern life, if he retains his individualism while at the same time committing himself to a great public cause. Malcolm Cowley characterized it as "vigorous, absorbing, hastily written, superbly documented, and rich, amazingly rich." Edward O'Neill has described the book as "one of the best literary biographies of modern times." Josephson had discovered his genre. Whereas he had no real genius for poetry, he felt at home with biography, making characters come alive and finding the unifying themes tying together a great life. Through biography, he believed, "I could communicate with my readers on a variety of ideas—on art and life, love and death, on human freedom and justice—and would feel myself in contact with a real public."

While he was working in Paris in 1927,

Josephson met Elliot Paul and Eugene Jolas, the editors of *transition*. Jolas, who was then under the spell of the Surrealists and the literature of the subconscious, found Josephson's stringent criticism of their esoteric life and literature interesting. He was also attracted by his optimism and strongly held opinions. After a second visit, he asked Josephson to serve as contributing editor to the review when he returned to the United States. After arriving in New York, Josephson organized his literary friends for a group writing project to be published in *transition*. He wanted to demonstrate to Europeans and Americans that there were writers who did not flee their country but stayed and attempted to cope with the Machine Age society. In January 1928, Kenneth Burke, Slater Brown, Malcolm Cowley, and Robert Coates joined Josephson in a suite at the old Broadway Central Hotel. They arrived at nine in the morning and worked all day, stopping only to laugh at what had been written or to argue some point.

The result of their efforts, "New York: 1928," a collection of poems, essays, and witticisms, was typically contentious, replete with ironic satire. Josephson and his friends savagely attacked American expatriates, even though he, Cowley, Brown, and Coates had once lived in Europe themselves. Now, however, they were determined to separate themselves from those American artists in Europe who still made a religion of art at the expense of society. In "An Open Letter to Mr. Ezra Pound," Josephson spoke of the innovative contributions of Pound, Eliot, Stein, and others. He then admitted that "for a time we went adventuring along the same trails, it was helpful to find your baggage a little everywhere. But in the end, we grow tired of our aesthetic wanderlust; we demand constants. . . . most of us who count on persisting are in search of an *active principle* for the artist." He and the other members of his group were no longer satisfied with art for art's sake. Josephson dismissed the "whole game of making words play with each other" as worthless, a waste of time and talent. Even though he described the United States as constituting a "cruel mistress," Josephson called on Pound and the others to return to their homeland and assume positions of responsibility in improving the lot of man and society.

After reading Josephson's essay, Ezra Pound grew indignant and wrote his close friend William Carlos Williams to find out more about Josephson and his group and why they were attacking him. Williams, a friend of Josephson and the others, tried to reassure Pound that their criticism of him was misguided: "What *transition*—per Josephson—

wants to say is that you are conservative. You are, what of it? It's just a class of radicals which wants to sell what it has high. . . ." Williams went on to say that, "As to the Hart Crane—Josephson group—to hell with them all. There is good there but it is not for me." But Josephson had accomplished his purpose. He had attracted Pound's attention and raised his ire. He also created a stir among the readers of *transition*. Jolas wrote him after the issue was published: "If you wanted to start something in Paris with your contribution, you did. . . . there is a powerful impression behind your articles, and a real fanatic conviction (which I do not share in the main outlines) which is expressed in strong accents." During the next year he continued to hammer away at the expatriates in essays he wrote for *transition*. Josephson had made his public break with the Symbolist and expatriate tradition. He was now ready to become the "writer turned public man."

During the thirties Josephson put his new artistic philosophy into practice. He became active on the literary Left, writing scores of essays in social and political criticism and choosing biographical and historical subjects that related directly to the social crisis at hand. He published a series of influential and best-selling popular histories from a Marxist perspective, including *The Robber Barons* (1934) and *The Politicos* (1938), which have had a significant impact upon the public's perception of American economic and political history after the Civil War. After completing his study of Zola, Josephson continued to distinguish himself as a biographer of French literary figures. His studies of Rousseau, Hugo, and Stendhal were widely acclaimed and read. In 1960 he won the Francis Parkman prize for his biography of Thomas Edison. John Erskine once referred to Josephson as one of the four or five best American biographers of this century. In 1962 Josephson recaptured the ambience of life in Paris in the twenties in his colorful memoirs, *Life Among the Surrealists*. Full of fascinating vignettes and incisive portraits, the book is one of the best sources for those interested in Paris literary life after World War I. Josephson died in 1978, secure in the belief that he had successfully assumed the role of the "writer turned public man," that he had served well both his craft and his conscience.

Other:

Guillaume Apollinaire, *The Poet Assassinated*, translated by Josephson (New York: Broom, 1923);

Lucien Romier, *Who Will Be Master Europe or America?*, translated by Josephson (New York: Macaulay, 1928);

Jean Marie Carre, *A Season in Hell The Life of Arthur Rimbaud*, translated by Josephson and Hannah Josephson (New York: Macaulay, 1931);

Stendhal, *Memoirs of Egotism*, translated by Josephson and Hannah Josephson with an introduction by Josephson (New York: Lear, 1949);

Hugh Ford, ed., *The Left Bank Revisited: Selections from the Paris* Tribune, *1917-1934*, foreword by Josephson (University Park & London: Pennsylvania State University Press, 1972).

Periodical Publications:

FICTION:

"The Oblate," *Secession*, 1 (July 1922): 21-29;

"Peep-Peep Parrish," *Secession*, 1 (August 1922): 6-11;

"Peripatetics VI and Vegetable Classic," *Broom*, 3 (August 1922): 41-42;

"Pursuit," *Broom*, 4 (January 1923): 105-107;

"The Brain at the Wheel," *Broom*, 5 (September 1923): 95-96.

NONFICTION:

"Apollinaire: Or Let Us Be Troubadours," *Secession*, 1 (April 1922): 9-13;

"Made in America," *Broom*, 2 (June 1922): 268-271;

"The Great American Billposter," *Broom*, 3 (November 1922): 304-312;

"Henry Ford," *Broom*, 5 (October 1923): 137-142;

"Letter to My Friends," *Little Review*, 12 (Spring-Summer 1926): 17-19;

"An Open Letter to Mr. Ezra Pound, And the Other 'Exiles,' " *transition*, no. 13 (Summer 1928): 98-102.

References:

Daniel Aaron, *Writers on the Left* (New York: Avon, 1961);

Malcolm Cowley, *Exile's Return*, revised edition (New York: Viking, 1951);

Harold Loeb, *The Way It Was* (New York: Criterion, 1959);

David E. Shi, "Matthew Josephson: The Evolution of a Historian," Ph.D. dissertation, University of Virginia, 1976;

Shi, "Munson vs. Josephson: Battle of the Aesthetes," *Lost Generation Journal*, 5 (Spring 1977): 18-22;

Marjorie Smelstor, "*Broom* and American Cultural Nationalism in the 1920's," Ph.D dissertation, University of Wisconsin, 1975;

Dickran Tashjian, *Skyscraper Primitives: Dada and the American Avant-Garde, 1910-1925* (Middletown, Conn.: Wesleyan University Press, 1975).

Papers:

Matthew and Hannah Josephson's papers are at the Beinecke Library at Yale University. Other relevant collections include the Malcolm Cowley papers at the Newberry Library in Chicago and the Harold Loeb papers at Princeton University.

JED KILEY
(10 June 1889-14 May 1962)

BOOK: *Hemingway An Old Friend Remembers* (New York: Hawthorn Books, 1965); republished as *Hemingway A Title Fight in Ten Rounds* (London: Methuen, 1965).

Jed Kiley, born John Gerald Kiley in Chicago, lived a varied life, working as a journalist, editor, nightclub owner, screenwriter, and free-lance writer. The chief source of information about Kiley is his own memoir of Ernest Hemingway, published in 1956 and 1957 as a series of articles in *Playboy*, and in book form as *Hemingway An Old Friend Remembers* (1965). According to the publisher's introduction to this book, Kiley attended St. Viator's in Bourbonnais, Illinois, and the University of Wisconsin before becoming a reporter for the Chicago *Examiner*. In 1916 he left his job to join the National Guard and serve in the punitive expedition against Pancho Villa in Mexico. Subsequently he worked for the *Chicago Tribune* for a short time before going to France as an ambulance driver for the American Field Service. When the United States entered World War I in 1917, he joined the army and was assigned duty with the Service of Supply in Paris. Discharged in 1918, he worked briefly for the Paris *Herald* (the European edition of the *New York Herald*) and made money arranging dances for the numerous American military personnel still in the city. After a short-lived career as a manufacturer of ice cream he became a highly successful nightclub owner, first with Kiley's and later with the College Inn, both in Montmartre. In addition to operating his nightclubs, Kiley was also a writer and assistant editor for the *Boulevardier*, a slick Right Bank imitation of the *New Yorker* published by Erskine Gwynne and edited by Arthur Moss. In 1929 one of Kiley's stories resulted in an invitation to come to Hollywood as a screenwriter, an invitation he accepted when the Stock Market Crash in New York forced many Americans home and thus caused the closing of his clubs.

During the time that he worked for the *Boulevardier*, from 1927 to 1929, Kiley was proud to have had a hand in publishing Sinclair Lewis, Louis Bromfield, and Ernest Hemingway. Kiley convinced Gwynne and Moss to publish Hemingway's "The Real Spaniard" (October 1927), a parody of Louis Bromfield's "The Real French," which had appeared in an earlier issue of the magazine. At Moss's instigation, Kiley added an ending to the

Jed Kiley, 1925

piece, an "improvement" that infuriated Hemingway.

Hemingway's ire, however, did not prevent Kiley from attempting to advise him about writing during the early days of their acquaintance. Although Hemingway ignored Kiley's literary advice, Kiley says in *Hemingway An Old Friend Remembers* that he did accept an invitation to spend an evening on the house at Kiley's Montmartre club. Concerned about the reputation of his club, Kiley was appalled at Hemingway's date: "Of all the females in the entire world there was only one barred permanently from my place." Hemingway had brought with him the notorious British remittance woman Lady Duff Twysden, the model for Lady Brett Ashley in *The Sun Also Rises* (1926). Later chapters of Kiley's book describe his meetings with Hemingway in New York, Key West, and Cuba during the thirties and forties.

Fond but not fawning, Kiley's recollections of Hemingway were published in book form partly at the instigation of his friend John Guenther, who wrote in a letter to the *Times Literary Supplement* that the original *Playboy* articles constituted an "unvarnished picture" of "the real Hemingway." The accuracy of Kiley's memoir, however, is open to question, as Archibald MacLeish demonstrated in a letter replying to Guenther's, in which he pointed out the spuriousness of an anecdote about F. Scott Fitzgerald's attempting to murder Hemingway. MacLeish was commenting only on an incident cited by Guenther, but other inaccuracies may be found in Kiley's record. The most damning criticism was from Hemingway himself. Kiley had sent Hemingway the original manuscript of the book in 1954, provoking an angry letter from Hemingway (17 December 1954), in which he calls Kiley's book "a long series of untruths, mis-statements and falsehoods" and says, "You were never a friend of mine in Paris nor anywhere else. . . ." Thus *Hemingway An Old Friend Remembers* is valuable only as an impression of a memorable personality, not as an accurate record of events.

Though he writes in a somewhat tiresome imitation of the Hemingway style, Kiley charms the reader by a willingness to laugh at his own attempts to patronize the young Hemingway. He even reports that Hemingway saw through his pretensions as a writer, advising him: "Make up your mind whether you want to be a writer or a saloon-keeper. If you want to run a saloon, keep talking. If you want to be a writer start slugging the typewriter." The reference to "slugging" is typical, for Kiley maintains that a literature-as-boxing metaphor dominated nearly all of their conversations. Though he repeatedly pretends not to have more than a vague idea of what is on the inside of Hemingway's books, his own is filled with understated allusions to them, which contribute to the backhanded compliment he intends to his friend.

In the years after his departure from Paris, Kiley lived and worked in Hollywood, Miami, and New York as a screenwriter and as a free-lance writer, occasionally bumping into Hemingway. In his last years he made trips to the Far East and to Paris. He died at the age of seventy-two at Lenox Hill Hospital in New York City. —*David Cowart*

References:

John Guenther, Letter to the editor, *Times Literary Supplement*, 9 July 1964, p. 613;

Ernest Hemingway, Letter to Kiley, 17 December 1954, in *F. Scott Fitzgerald and Ernest M. Hemingway in Paris* (Bloomfield Hills, Mich. & Columbia, S.C.: Bruccoli Clark, 1972), p. 16;

Archibald MacLeish, Letter to the editor, *Times Literary Supplement*, 3 September 1964, p. 803.

MANUEL KOMROFF
(7 September 1890-10 December 1974)

SELECTED BOOKS: *The Grace of Lambs* (New York: Boni & Liveright, 1925; London: Cape, 1926);

The Voice of Fire (Paris: Black Manikin Press, 1927);

Juggler's Kiss (New York: Boni & Liveright, 1927);

Coronet (New York: Coward-McCann, 1929; London: Harrap, 1930);

I, the Tiger (New York: Coward-McCann, 1933; London: Heinemann, 1934);

In the Years of Our Lord (New York & London: Harper, 1942; London: Chapman & Hall, 1943);

How to Write a Novel (New York: Simon & Schuster, 1950);

Big City, Little Boy (New York: Wyn, 1953).

Manuel Komroff was already established as a writer when he arrived in Paris in 1926. *The Grace of Lambs*, a collection of short stories, had been published in 1925 by Boni & Liveright, where Komroff was working as manufacturing manager and as an editor for the Modern Library series. He had also contributed a humorous short story, "A Union of Beggars," to the first issue of Harold Loeb's Rome-based little magazine, *Broom* (November 1921), and through his New York literary associations he had met many of the American writers he would see again in France. Komroff was born in New York City to businessman Samuel Komroff and Belle Komroff. In 1912 he left his engineering studies at Yale without a degree and became an art critic for the New York *Call*; he also wrote motion-picture scores during this period. Socialist sympathies led Komroff to Russia, probably sometime in 1917, where he became editor in chief of the English-language *Russian Daily News*. When the Bolsheviks came into power, he went to Shanghai and worked briefly for the *China Press* before his return to America and various writing jobs.

In Paris, where friends reported seeing him at work daily in a cafe near the Dome, Komroff was introduced to Edward Titus by Whitold Gordon, an artist who had designed the colophon for Titus's Black Manikin Press. The newly established press was already acquiring a reputation for publishing controversial books, and the anticlerical tone of the novelette Komroff was writing appealed to Titus. He published *The Voice of Fire*, handsomely illustrated with engravings by Polia Chentoff, in 1927. *The Voice of Fire* tells the story of a great cathedral in Paris whose priests order the finest organ money can

Front cover

buy. Andre Rivier, an orphan apprenticed to the master tinsmith Prudhon and working on the organ pipes, accidentally produces an awesome new sound which he names "Hell's Fire." Although this attraction helps to make the cathedral very wealthy, the priests never carry out their promise to pay Rivier for his invention. Later the pipes develop a "tin disease" and begin to emit an eerie laughing sound which gradually makes the once-proud cathedral a laughing stock in the community. The priests wrongly attribute this phenomenon to some scheme for revenge on Rivier's part and set out to ruin his life. Rivier finally discovers how to rid the organ of its monstrous laugh, but he refuses to do so, and the church's reputation in the community is destroyed.

Komroff's first full-length novel, *Juggler's Kiss*, was published in 1927. It was followed in 1929 by *Coronet*, a two-volume historical novel. The success of *Coronet* enabled Komroff to leave editorial work for full-time writing.

Asked to contribute to Bob Brown's *Readies for Bob Brown's Machine* (1931), Komroff sent an article entitled "The Writies," in which he satirized Brown's idea of compressed writing for a reading machine to be adjusted for speed by the individual. Komroff took the opportunity to comment on two of the leading literary figures of the day: "Joyce has done an Irish week-end that has no end and to me is very weak. Is this compression?" and "Gertie Stein made several attempts to write English before Tender Buttons but found she could not." Addressing his remarks to Brown, he continued:

> Therefore, if I wrote a piece for your Readies, it would be the same piece that I would do for the Writies, only with the ands and buts and ifs and thes left out. One might go a step further and leave out what one really wanted to say; but English (as it is used today) is a skilled device for hiding ones true thoughts and feelings. We might also leave out the questions and give the answers at once, but this might sound too much like a sermon. Or we could leave off the dots of the i or the little stroke off the T. . . . The truth is; I have no real objection to any device of this nature but after you have done it, I must ask; "What else have you got?"

Komroff wrote more than forty novels and numerous other books and articles. Much of his work reflected his interest in Christianity and in both European and Oriental history. In the forties he was active in the Authors' Guild, the Authors' League, and PEN, representing PEN International Writers at the United Nations in 1947. In 1974, at the age of eighty-four, Komroff died in Kingston, New York.

—*Jean W. Ross*

Other:

"The Writies," in *Readies for Bob Brown's Machine*, ed. Bob Brown (Cagnes-sur-Mer: Roving Eye Press, 1931), pp. 110-113.

Reference:

Hugh Ford, *Published in Paris ·American and British Writers, Printers, and Publishers in Paris, 1920-1939* (New York: Macmillan, 1975), pp. 128-130.

ALFRED KREYMBORG
(10 December 1883-14 August 1966)

SELECTED BOOKS: *Mushrooms* (New York: John
    Marshall, 1916);
Blood of Things (New York: N. L. Brown, 1920);
Plays for Merry Andrews (New York: Sunrise Turn,
    1920);
Puppet Plays (New York: Harcourt, Brace, 1923;
    London: Secker & Warburg, 1923);
Troubadour An Autobiography (New York:
    Liveright, 1925);
Funnybone Alley (New York: Macaulay, 1927);
The Planets, A Modern Allegory (New York: Farrar
    & Rinehart, 1938);
Selected Poems, 1912-1944 (New York: Dutton,
    1945).

Alfred Kreymborg, poet, dramatist, and former
editor of such influential small magazines as *Glebe*
(1913-1914) and *Others* (1915-1919), arrived in Paris
with his wife Dorothy and Harold Loeb in June
1921. They were en route to Rome to compile the
first issue of an international arts magazine, *Broom*
(1921-1924), which they intended to make a truly
catholic literary review by publishing the best of
American and European writing and art.
Kreymborg's first magazine, *Glebe*, had been active
in introducing to Americans the Imagist poetry of
Ezra Pound, Richard Aldington, and William
Carlos Williams. *Others*, his second effort, had
published poems by Williams, Aldington, Wallace
Stevens, Hilda Doolittle, T. S. Eliot, Amy Lowell,
John Gould Fletcher, Mina Loy, and Marianne
Moore. He was also a member of the Provincetown
Players, a group which at that time included Eugene
O'Neill, Djuna Barnes, George Cram Cook, Susan
Glaspell, and Floyd Dell. During his short stay in
Paris, Kreymborg met a number of artists, writers,
and musicians, many of whom were to contribute to
Broom.

His first contacts were with members of the
Dada group. He had known the artist Marcel
Duchamp in New York, and the artist and
photographer Man Ray had helped Kreymborg with
Glebe. Through these old acquaintances, including
the painter Albert Gleizes, Kreymborg met Jean
Cocteau, Francis Picabia, and Valery Larbaud.
Kreymborg was also approached by Tristan Tzara,
who introduced him to other Dadaists, including
Philippe Soupault, at the Cafe Michaud. As
Kreymborg writes in his autobiography,
Troubadour (1925), Tzara brought him "a pile of
documents appertaining to Dada—magazines,

Alfred Kreymborg

pamphlets, programs, posters and manifestoes in
every language, dead or alive." At the Cafe Michaud,
Kreymborg approached Erik Satie on behalf of
Edgar Varese, the founder of the International
Composers' Guild, which was soliciting
manuscripts. Kreymborg found Satie gracious and
sympathetic, but he "had no luck with the founder of
the Groupe des Sixes." At the same time Kreymborg
and Loeb were asking for contributions to *Broom*
from the Dadaists, they were also negotiating with
more established French writers, such as Paul
Claudel, Paul Fort, Jacques Riviere, and Andre
Gide—approached by Loeb's friend Leon
Bazalgette, the translator and biographer of
Whitman. As Kreymborg says, these discussions
caused "howls of derision from the Dada camp."
Also, Kreymborg's old friend Kathleen Cannell
introduced him to the sculptor Brancusi, who
became a *Broom* contributor.

Kreymborg met Ezra Pound, a longtime
correspondent and contributor to earlier Kreymborg
efforts, for the first time at the cafe Les Deux Magots.
In *Troubadour* Kreymborg describes Pound as "an
athletic figure in velveteens, wide-open collar and
flowing tie. . . . More Parisian than the Parisians,

with a shock of yellow hair tossed by the wind, and no hat on top of the hair. . . ." When Kreymborg showed Pound the list of contributors to *Broom*, Pound "pulled out a pencil and blue-penciled line after line, usually with some cutting remark, until only a few were left on the page. Then he drew up a short, sharp list of his own representing the men for whom he was now carrying the banner—Gaudier-Brzeska, James Joyce, T. S. Eliot, Wyndham Lewis, Jean Cocteau."

At Sylvia Beach's Shakespeare and Company bookshop Kreymborg ran into Robert McAlmon, who took him to meet Joyce at Joyce's apartment. Joyce, writes Kreymborg, "was so tired and the room in which the three men sat so dark and melancholy that the only distinguishable feature was his gently ironical voice." Kreymborg also went to visit Gertrude Stein and remembers that his praise of her work "meant a good deal to her. This was to be accounted for presently by the evidence that Miss Stein, outside the circles in which she moved, and a few devotees at home, had virtually no recognition, while quantities of her imitators, Dadas among them, were being graced with refreshing bouquets." Over Harold Loeb's objections, Kreymborg was able to publish one of Gertrude Stein's short narratives, "If You Had Three Husbands," in serial form in *Broom*.

In July of that year, Kreymborg and his wife moved on to Rome, where he and Loeb founded and edited *Broom*. The first issue appeared in November 1921. It included art work by Picasso, Juan Gris, Albert Gleizes, Jacques Lipchitz, and Man Ray; poems by Walter de la Mare, Amy Lowell, Louis Untermeyer, and Lola Ridge; an article by Conrad Aiken; and short stories by James Stephens, Manuel Komroff, and Haniel Long. The most notable contributors to the second issue (December 1921) were Sherwood Anderson, Wallace Stevens, Conrad Aiken, Joseph Stella, Henri Matisse, and Rockwell Kent. For this issue Kreymborg translated two poems by Aldo Palazzeschi. The January 1922 issue included poems by Marianne Moore, John Gould Fletcher, Malcolm Cowley, and Kreymborg, and the first installment of Stein's "If You Had Three Husbands." In the February 1922 issue Loeb announced Kreymborg's resignation, saying that ill health and the demands of his writing prevented him from continuing. A contributing factor, however, was a difference of opinion over the magazine's editorial policy. According to Kreymborg, "Harold inclined more and more toward Europe and established reputations, and Krimmie toward America and the future."

After a tour of the Continent and England, Kreymborg returned to New York, where he spent most of the next forty years. One of his most ambitious projects was a yearbook of American writing. The first volume, edited by Kreymborg, Paul Rosenfeld, Lewis Mumford, and Van Wyck Brooks, was published in 1927, and subsequent volumes, edited by Kreymborg, Mumford, and Rosenfeld, appeared in 1928, 1929, 1931, and 1936. Kreymborg also continued to write poetry, drama, and criticism until his death in 1966. In *Sixty American Poets 1896-1944*, Allen Tate calls Kreymborg's poetry unimpressive, but he adds that Kreymborg's efforts "in behalf of the 'new poetry' (now old) entitle him to consideration."

—*Stephen Thomas*

Other:

The American Caravan, edited by Kreymborg and others, published periodically (New York: Macaulay, 1927, 1928, 1929, 1931, 1936);
"A Good Story," in *Americans Abroad An Anthology*, ed. Peter Neagoe (The Hague: Servire, 1932), pp. 222-231.

References:

Harold Loeb, *The Way It Was* (New York: Criterion, 1959);
Allen Tate, ed., "Alfred Kreymborg," in his *Sixty American Poets 1896-1944*, revised edition (Washington, D.C.: Library of Congress, 1954), pp. 61-64.

AL LANEY
(1896-   )

SELECTED BOOK: *Paris Herald The Incredible Newspaper* (New York & London: Appleton-Century, 1947).

Al Laney, a native of Florida, was a reporter for the *Dallas Dispatch*, the *Minneapolis News*, and the New York *Evening Mail* before his move to Paris in 1924. There he spent most of the next decade on the staff of the Paris *Herald* (the European edition of the *New York Herald Tribune*), while at the same time covering golf and tennis championships for its parent paper in New York. On the Paris *Herald*

Laney was night editor, reporter, and rewrite man—"the all-round newsman," according to managing editor Eric Hawkins.

One of the many writers who frequented Sylvia Beach's bookshop, Shakespeare and Company, Laney was recruited there to type business letters for James Joyce and later to read to him. Speaking to a *Newsweek* reporter in 1960, Laney recalled that Joyce "talked about the sound of words and the sound one word makes on another and the sound of the silence between the words."

Laney's book *Paris Herald* (1947) provides an objective and lively account of the European edition of the *New York Herald* from its start in 1887 through the liberation of Paris at the end of World War II. He describes the paper's beginning as a plaything of the younger James Gordon Bennett, who by the time of his death in 1918 had spent much of his personal fortune to keep it going. Aided by increased American tourism and the growth of the American community in Paris, the paper began in 1924 the quick ascent that would double its circulation within two years and, Laney writes, make "this rather forlorn newspaper . . . blossom into a money-maker and a paper of prestige."

Laney's history of the *Herald* is enlivened with anecdotes about the eccentric Bennett and other members of the *Herald* staff, including Eric Hawkins, who was managing editor from 1924 until 1960. Hawkins provided a later account of the newspaper in *Hawkins of the Paris* Herald (1963). Another associate of Laney's was Sparrow Robertson, whom Laney describes as "the world's first, and by any comparison, the world's best gossip columnist and cafe society reporter." Robertson's column, "Sporting Gossip," Laney writes, "gave probably as true a picture of the life of Americans in Europe as can be found, and a far more interesting one than most."

As a result of Bennett's original policy of printing society news and filling columns with names of the well-to-do, the Paris *Herald* had become the chronicle of Right Bank Americans while its rival, the Paris *Tribune* (the European edition of the *Chicago Tribune*), reported the activities of the artists and adventurers of the Left Bank. The competition ended in November 1934 when the *Tribune*, a victim of the depression, was sold to the *Herald*. Laney writes: "This act of amalgamation brought a pitiful false hope to the Herald direction, but for Herald men and Americans generally, it was one of the saddest things that could have happened. For an epoch in the lives of Americans in Paris had ended and it was impossible any longer to ignore the fact."

Returning to New York in the mid-thirties, Laney joined the reporting staff of the *New York Herald Tribune* and remained in that capacity until the paper's demise in 1966. In 1977 Laney was honored by the Unites States Tennis Writers Association; in 1978 he received the Distinguished Service Award of the Metropolitan Golf Association, which praised his more than forty years of coverage as "a body of work that stands as a major contribution to the game of golf." —*Jean W. Ross*

Reference:

Eric Hawkins, with Robert N. Sturdevant, *Hawkins of the Paris* Herald (New York: Simon & Schuster, 1963).

EDWIN LANHAM
(11 October 1904-24 July 1979)

SELECTED BOOKS: *Sailors Don't Care* (Paris: Contact Editions, 1929; revised edition, New York: Cape & Smith, 1930);

The Wind Blew West (New York & Toronto: Longmans, Green, 1935; London & Toronto: Heinemann, 1936);

Banner at Daybreak (New York & Toronto: Longmans, Green, 1937; London & Toronto: Heinemann, 1937);

Another Ophelia (New York & Toronto: Longmans, Green, 1938; London & Toronto: Heinemann, 1938);

The Stricklands (Boston: Little, Brown, 1939; London & Toronto: Heinemann, 1939);

Thunder in the Earth (New York: Harcourt, Brace, 1941; London & Toronto: Heinemann, 1942);

The Iron Maiden (New York: Harcourt, Brace, 1954; London: Macmillan, 1954);

Monkey on a Chain (New York: Harcourt, Brace & World, 1963; London: Gollancz, 1964);

Speak Not Evil (New York: Farrar, Straus, 1964; London: Corgi, 1966);

The Paste-Pot Man (New York: Farrar, Straus & Giroux, 1967);

The Clock at 8:16 (Garden City: Doubleday, 1970).

Edwin Lanham began his writing career in Paris in 1928 when Robert McAlmon urged him to write about his sea voyages. Lanham's experiences preceding and during what he called his "Montparnasse Period" shaped much of his later work, which includes more than twenty novels and murder mysteries, as well as at least fifty short stories. In a 28 December 1978 interview Lanham said that he had always hoped to become a writer, but there was nothing literary in his upbringing. Much of his childhood was spent alternately in New York and Texas. His family had arrived in Texas as pioneers in the 1870s, and among its later members were a governor, several congressmen, and an appeals court judge. Edwin Moultrie Lanham was born in Weatherford, a town in the north central part of the state where the family had settled. His father, Edwin Moultrie Lanham, Sr., died when Lanham was four, and his mother, Elizabeth Stephens Lanham, remarried soon after and joined her husband in New York City. The boy journeyed back and forth between Texas and the East, living for a time in Fort Worth with his grandfather and attending preparatory school in Maryland and New York.

In 1922, having been forced to leave preparatory school because of an injury in athletics, the teenage Lanham studied art for a few months at the National Academy of Design until, in late spring, he shipped out on a freighter bound for around the world. Returning after eight months, he went to a tutoring school in order to enroll in Williams College in the fall of 1923, but dropped out after his junior year in 1926—because he was close to flunking out, he said—and studied art at the Connah Art School in New York for a time. Although Lanham said later that he was not serious about becoming an artist, painting provided him with "a good reason to go to Paris."

In Paris Lanham met Robert McAlmon, the owner of the Contact Publishing Company, which had already published books by Ernest Hemingway, William Carlos Williams, Gertrude Stein, and Hilda Doolittle, as well as McAlmon's own work. Lanham and McAlmon became friends, spending much of the summer of 1928 in Le Canadel, a Mediterranean village between Toulon and Saint Raphael, not far from the villa of Laurence Vail and his first wife, Peggy Guggenheim. Lanham's repertoire of sea stories interested McAlmon, and he offered to publish them if Lanham could write them as well as he told them. In the 1938 edition of *Being Geniuses Together*, McAlmon writes, "Mr. Lanham was not at the time having ambitions. He was as ready to let any form of work alone as man can be, and withal he was a companionable soul and did not care about the other man's work. I became wily and suggested that he write up his sea experiences. He started, thinking to please me by pretending to work, but once under way he found he liked writing." Shortly before his death Lanham departed from that account, saying that he had already bought a typewriter and started writing before he met McAlmon.

Lanham spent the summer of 1928 writing diligently. In the autumn he presented McAlmon with a sea yarn which related his experiences as a runaway working on a freight boat. The story was not entirely autobiographical. At a friend's suggestion Lanham ornamented the piece by adding a fictional account of a fierce storm at sea.

Impressed as he was with Lanham's writing, McAlmon was bothered by the title of the manuscript: "As We Sailed Down the Bay." It "didn't seem to have much zip." Author and publisher gave different accounts of how the book got its final title. According to McAlmon, Lanham was at the Select Bar in Paris when he heard a cry from a rowdy British naval officer—"Sailors don't care!"—and he had found a new title for his book. The author, however, later attributed the title to

McAlmon: "he heard a sailor singing 'Sailor, take care,' and got it wrong." *Sailors Don't Care* was published in March 1929. Lanham, like a few other writers published by Contact, paid some of the publishing expenses, but it was worth it: on the book's first day in print, he saw a copy of it "under the arm of a customer at the Dome." The customer identified himself as an American poet and novelist, Maxwell Bodenheim. Although Lanham never knew how *Sailors Don't Care* fared with Bodenheim, the novel was moderately successful in Paris. In America, however, customs agents burned at least one shipment of the book because they considered it obscene. Labeled "harmless" by McAlmon and "innocuous" by its author, *Sailors Don't Care* fell victim to the American customs officials' habitual suspicion of any book in English which came from France.

One reader who was particularly excited about *Sailors Don't Care* was William Rose Benet, who often disliked books published by Contact. His influence helped to get the novel published in the United States in expurgated and revised form. American publishers were ready for *Sailors Don't Care*, McAlmon says, only after they had persuaded Lanham to remove "the valid experiences which had given the book its quality as a document." The publishers, Jonathan Cape and Harrison Smith, also persuaded Lanham to rewrite *Sailors Don't Care* in the first person.

While he was still working on *Sailors Don't Care*, he met Kay Boyle's sister, Joan, who was a fashion designer for the London edition of *Vogue*. They were married in 1929. In early summer the Lanhams and her mother joined McAlmon in Theoule, a small fishing village near Cannes. The Lanhams rented a villa there, where he worked on a new novel, "Silver-Plated Wedding." The book, never published, concerns a covetous old man who discovers himself trapped in a marriage with a young woman. This novel is the first of several in which Lanham makes use of his experiences growing up in Texas. Even though "Silver-Plated Wedding" was never published, McAlmon remembers it vividly— and positively—in the 1938 edition of *Being Geniuses Together*. "That," he writes, "from a person with a critical faculty, is saying much for a book." As Kay Boyle and William Carlos Williams have observed, praise from McAlmon was a precious commodity for young writers. At the end of his life Lanham called the novel "entirely undistinguished." Before leaving France Lanham also published a short story in the Autumn 1929 issue of Edward Titus's *This Quarter*. In "The Temperance

Edwin Lanham in Theoule, 1929

Man" he describes a mayoral election in a fishing village faintly suggestive of Theoule. As the summer of 1929 drew to a close, the Lanhams left Theoule. After going to Paris, where Joan Lanham drew designs for a fashion show, they left for America.

Upon their arrival in New York in 1930, Edwin Lanham went to work as a reporter for the New York *Evening Post*. After nearly four years he was laid off because of the Depression and moved to the New York City News Association. In 1939 he began a five-year association with the *New York Herald Tribune*, working as a rewrite man. During the decade after his return from France, Lanham traveled frequently to the Southwest, gathering material for four more novels: *The Wind Blew West* (1935), *Banner at Daybreak* (1937), *Another Ophelia* (1938), and *The Stricklands* (1939).

Banner at Daybreak draws upon Lanham's memories of Paris. The novel concerns several American expatriates who leave their vagabond days in Montparnasse to return to New York and Texas. The central character, Clay Hall, is the rebel grandson of Amon Hall, a wealthy rancher whose family settled in western Texas in the 1870s. Clay is a painter endowed with a liberal grant from home and has been a familiar figure in Montparnasse. *Banner at Daybreak* tells of the readjustment Clay and his wife Hilda make upon their return to New York and, finally, to Texas.

Edwin and Joan Lanham were divorced in 1936, and he married Irene Stillman, a magazine editor, four years later. Financial necessity forced Lanham's shift into free-lance work, creating by his own admission a "confused career." "My freedom to work has been considerably hampered by the economics of existence," he writes. In 1940, on a Guggenheim Fellowship, Lanham wrote *Thunder in the Earth* (1941), for which he won the annual Award of the Texas Institute of Letters in 1942. His work was received favorably by critics, and he began to acquire a reputation for his novels, but they were not financially successful.

After 1944 Lanham contributed short stories to numerous publications, primarily *Collier's,* and serials to the *Saturday Evening Post*—murder mysteries later published in book form. In the early fifties he and his wife moved to Clinton, Connecticut, a town which celebrated its tricentennial in 1963, and the subject of Lanham's novel *Speak Not Evil* (1964).

While in Paris Lanham had become interested in psychoanalysis, which at that time was still controversial. That interest is reflected in one of his murder mysteries, *Monkey on a Chain* (1963), which tells of a young woman who seeks counsel in a therapy group after being accused of her husband's murder. The group works with her to solve the mystery and prove her innocence. The Freudian point of view is also an important feature of *The Paste-Pot Man* (1967), another novel that grew out of Lanham's experiences in France. In it two young men who grew up together in Texas go to Paris in the twenties. Frank Neal, a newspaperman, is exhilarated by the city's cabaret life, while Alan Shell, a deeply disturbed artist, is undergoing psychotherapy. The character Alan Shell is based on a young artist Lanham knew who committed suicide in 1927. Alternate chapters are excerpts from the artist's diary of that time and the reporter's reminiscences four decades later.

A visit to the city in the mid-sixties gave Lanham the inspiration to write *The Paste-Pot Man.* "I spent a lot of time roaming the streets," he remembered later. "Things had changed. All of the buildings had been sand-blasted (and were a golden sandstone instead of grimy gray) in the Fourteenth Arondissement, the district where Rousseau painted and where I lived. I found a few people that I knew, but it was a long time ago." In a similar fashion Frank Neal returns to visit the Left Bank some forty years after his expatriation there. Although Neal is not an autobiographical character, Neal's description of himself at the beginning of the book may reveal Lanham's attitude toward Paris: "I reckon myself an objective and contemporary man little given to sentiment or regrets, although as an American who knew the Montparnasse quarter of Paris in the Twenties I may be suspect as a relic of romanticism in a generation whose mission appears to be to extinguish all values of the past."

Lanham's most recent book is *The Clock at 8:16* (1970), and at his death in July 1979 he had a novel in progress. About Paris he said: "It's where I got my education," adding cautiously, "I was a very young man among some of those who were to become great." —*David Sours*

Other:

"The Temperance Man," *This Quarter,* 2 (Autumn 1929): 283-301.

References:

Hugh Ford, *Published in Paris American and British Writers, Printers, and Publishers in Paris, 1920-1939* (New York: Macmillan, 1975), pp. 80-87;

Robert McAlmon, *Being Geniuses Together An Autobiography* (London: Secker & Warburg, 1938); republished as *Being Geniuses Together 1920-1930,* revised edition with additional material by Kay Boyle (Garden City: Doubleday, 1968), pp. 350-361.

RICHARD LE GALLIENNE
(1866-1947)

SELECTED BOOKS: *Volumes in Folio* (London: Mathews, 1889);

The Quest of the Golden Girl (London & New York: Lane, 1896; New York: Fenno, 1903);

Little Dinners with the Sphinx and Other Prose Fancies (New York: Moffat, Yard, 1907; London: Lane, 1909);

A Jongleur Strayed Verses on Love and Other Matters Sacred and Profane (New York: Doubleday, Page, 1922);

The Romantic '90s (Garden City: Doubleday, Page, 1925; London: Putnam's, 1926);

From a Paris Garret (New York: Washburn, 1936; London: Richards, 1944);

From a Paris Scrapbook (New York: Washburn, 1938).

The relative obscurity of Richard Le Gallienne's literary reputation is perhaps due to his excess of romantic sensibility in an age of irony. By the time he got to Paris in 1927, Le Gallienne's heyday had passed.

Born Richard Thomas Gallienne at Liverpool in 1866, he was hailed by members of the Decadent Movement with the publication of *Volumes in Folio* (1889). Publishing prolifically not only in John Lane's controversial *Yellow Book*, whose editors included Aubrey Beardsley, but in a dozen other newspapers and magazines, he began, as he tells in *The Romantic '90s* (1925), to associate with such figures as Beardsley, Oscar Wilde, and William Butler Yeats. But Le Gallienne was not primarily of the Decadent spirit which he once called "limited thinking, often insane thinking." He was first and always the romantic author of *The Quest of the Golden Girl* (1896).

When he moved to the United States in 1903, Le Gallienne exclaimed: "An American writer! Yes! there was my new flag waving over the doorway—the flag under which henceforward . . . I am to write my books." Although he made his home in the United States until 1927, his relationship to America, and to the twentieth century, was ambivalent. Having no affinity with either, he clung to old world values which, though still marketable in fashionable publications such as *Cosmopolitan* or *Harper's*, were being left behind by writers disdainful of his sort of sentimental meditations upon daintily veiled sensuality. In 1922, the year of *The Waste Land*, the traditional lyrics of Le Gallienne's *A Jongleur Strayed* were criticized for evading the problems of modern life. After spending over twenty-three years in New York struggling to support himself at journalism, book publishing, and lecturing, Le Gallienne became disenchanted with his adopted home where he had expected to make his literary fortune. Growing tired of "this humdrum, half-baked, material country," he began to long for "that dear old, human, romantic world"—Paris.

Living in Paris from 1927 to 1935, Le Gallienne mingled with—but was not particularly interested in—the literary vanguard of Paris. He recognized that the Latin Quarter housed "the masters of modern thought and the representatives of modern dreams and modern art." But he did not care to ally himself with this society, preferring to avoid "all that modern nonsense which is as inseparable from 'modernity' nowadays as it was in the days of Abelard." He abhorred Samuel Putnam's *New Review* and what he called the "dirto-mania" of Joyce and his followers, but liked Joyce the man. He liked F. Scott Fitzgerald as well, but thought Ezra Pound affected and Ernest Hemingway insignificant. Modernism in general he found unpalatable and held to his own "not very 'modern' (thank God!) wares," as he called his work in a letter to American literary critic J. Donald Adams (25 August 1931).

In Paris Le Gallienne found a life style which he could transcribe into a weekly column for the New York *Sun* called "From a Paris Garret," selections of which were collected under the same title in 1936. For him Paris was a schizophrenic city: at once the modern, unimaginative bureaucracy which he rails against for its materialism and lack of imagination, and the historical, "Symbolic City of human experience" which allowed him to indulge his penchant for reflecting on the many layered romantic past of that much-lived-in city. The second collection of these articles, *From a Paris Scrapbook* (1938), his last book, won the Commissariat General du Tourisme prize for the best book about France by a foreigner. After 1935, when he moved to Menton, he wrote about Paris from a distance. He spent the years of World War II in neutral Monte Carlo, where his column became tinged with the modern problems he had so consistently evaded in his lyrics and novels of romance. At the age of eighty, having written almost ninety books and innumerable articles, Richard Le Gallienne died at Menton in 1947, survived by his third wife and two daughters, one of whom is the actress Eva Le Gallienne.

—*Richard Collins*

References:

Osbert Burdett, *The Beardsley Period* (London: Lane, 1925; New York: Boni & Liveright, 1925), pp. 186-190, 210-216;

Sisley Huddleston, *Bohemian Literary and Social Life in Paris* (London: Harrap, 1928);

Richard Whittington-Egan and Geoffrey Smerdon, *The Quest of The Golden Boy The Life and Letters of Richard Le Gallienne* (London: Unicorn, 1960).

LUDWIG LEWISOHN
(30 May 1882-31 December 1955)

SELECTED BOOKS: *The Modern Drama An Essay in Interpretation* (New York: Heubsch, 1915; London: Secker, 1916);

Up Stream An American Chronicle (New York: Liveright, 1922; London: Richards, 1923);

The Drama and the Stage (New York: Harcourt, Brace, 1922);

Don Juan (New York: Boni & Liveright, 1923);

Israel (New York: Boni & Liveright, 1925);

The Case of Mr. Crump (Paris: Black Manikin Press, 1926; New York: Henderson, 1930; London: Bodley Head, 1948);

The Defeated (London: Butterworth, 1927); republished as *The Island Within* (New York & London: Harper, 1928);

Mid-Channel An American Chronicle (New York & London: Harper, 1929; London: Butterworth, 1929);

The Romantic A Contemporary Legend (Paris: Black Manikin Press, 1931);

Expression in America (New York & London: Harper, 1932; London: Butterworth, 1932); republished as *The Story of American Literature* (New York: Random House / Modern Library, 1939);

The American Jew Character and Destiny (New York: Farrar, Straus, 1950).

Ludwig Lewisohn was an established writer, though a controversial figure socially and professionally, when he took up residence in Paris in the mid-twenties. Unlike the many writers then in Paris who sought to break from tradition, Lewisohn advocated a return to historical roots for "ultimate reality," but called for the reassessment of history in humanistic terms. In his autobiography *Mid-Channel* (1929) he wrote: "We . . . must somehow have values that we create to uphold within an order that gives them meaning." Much of his writing was shaped around this principle as he interpreted it from a Judaic point of view. Another major influence in his work was Freudian psychology. Although he had "except on the ground of mere human friendliness . . . little in common with the 'expatriates,' " he included among his friends and acquaintances publisher Edward Titus, British expatriate writer Sisley Huddleston, editor and translator Harold J. Salemson, critic Pierre Loving, and James Joyce. Theodore Dreiser, Sherwood Anderson, and Sinclair Lewis visited Lewisohn on their occasional trips to Paris. (Dreiser had appeared as the character Blaffka in Lewisohn's autobiographical novel *Don Juan* [1923].)

Lewisohn was born in Berlin to Jacques and Minna Eloesser Lewisohn, who were first cousins. When he was seven the family moved to the United States, and Lewisohn grew up in Charleston, South Carolina. Despite his Judaic background, he chose as a teenager, mainly through the influence of early teachers, to become a Methodist. Later he repudiated this choice vehemently, and his espousal of the Hebraic tradition colored much of his writing and led him to become active in the Zionist movement. As a boy Lewisohn read widely among the English writers; studied French, German, and Latin; and wrote poetry of his own as well as versions of Horace, one of which appeared in the *Charleston News-Courier* at the time of his graduation from high school. He majored in English literature at the College of Charleston, taking a B.A. in 1901, and went on to Columbia University, where he received an M.A. in 1903. In 1914 he was awarded a Litt.D. by the College of Charleston.

After graduation from Columbia, Lewisohn spent a year as an editor with Doubleday, Page and left to work as a free-lance writer for five years. In 1910 economic necessity forced him to take a position as German instructor at the University of Wisconsin. The next year he went to Ohio State

University as a professor of German language and literature. During his tenure there he became recognized for his work in literary and drama criticism and translations from French and German. His opposition to World War I, however, combined with his German background to make him the target of community pressure which brought about his resignation. In 1919 he became drama critic for the *Nation*, then a forum for the liberal movement in criticism of which Lewisohn was a part, and he was an associate editor from 1921 until 1924. Some of his drama reviews written for the *Nation* were collected in *The Drama and the Stage* (1922). In these, according to the assessment of Alfred Kazin, "Lewisohn's exciting contribution to the postwar renaissance is seen at its best."

Lewisohn's religious belief had for some years been shifting away from Christianity. A growing feeling of isolation, aggravated by academic racial discrimination and particularly his experience at Ohio State University, led him to believe that he could find roots only in the Jewish heritage he had been deprived of by his Southern Protestant boyhood. This spiritual loneliness was closely related to his disgust at what he felt to be America's provincialism toward art and morals. Lewisohn described these feelings in his autobiography *Up Stream* (1922). Although his viewpoint softened considerably after his years in Europe, his moral indignation gave him for several years an attitude of superiority that often weakened both his critical work and his fiction.

Domestic problems dealt the final blow that convinced Lewisohn to go abroad. Unable to obtain an immediate divorce from Mary Arnold, whom he had married in 1906, Lewisohn left the United States in 1924 with Thelma Bowman Spear, a singer and aspiring writer. After lengthy travel in Europe and the Near East and extended stays in Berlin and Vienna, Lewisohn and Spear settled in Paris. During their sixteen-year alliance, they had a son, James, who became the center of a custody dispute when Lewisohn married Edna Manley in 1940; the child was awarded to Spear in 1941. Lewisohn's marriage to Manley ended in divorce, and he subsequently married Louise Wolk, with whom he lived the rest of his life. The publicity resulting from Lewisohn's divorces and related legal disputes had a damaging effect on the general public reception of his work.

When he was settled in Paris, Lewisohn quickly wrote *The Case of Mr. Crump*, a tragedy about a young man who has been trapped into marriage by a scheming older woman and can extricate himself only by killing her. Because of certain similarities

between Lewisohn's first marriage and that described in the book, the manuscript was rejected by Liveright on legal advice that its publication would result in a libel suit against the firm. Lewisohn went to Titus, whose Black Manikin Press was just getting started, and Titus agreed to publish an edition of 500 copies. In the early winter of 1926 advance copies sent to Carl Van Doren, H. L. Mencken, Joseph Wood Krutch, and Sisley Huddleston were favorably received, and subscriptions began to come in; but the book was declared unmailable on grounds of obscenity by the United States Post Office. It was subsequently published in French, German, Dutch, Italian, Spanish, Swedish, and Dano-Norwegian. In 1931 Titus republished the book with a preface by Thomas Mann and a prefatory note reading in part: "The recent appearance in America of a pirated edition of the Case of Mr. Crump has induced the author and publisher to abandon their original intention not to reprint the book after the first edition of Five Hundred copies had been disposed of." The first authorized American edition did not appear until 1947.

Lewisohn's work appeared in the first two issues of *transition*, founded by Eugene Jolas and Elliot Paul. "The Defeated," described as "Opening Chapters of Work in Progress," was published in installments in the April 1927 and May 1927 issues. Reviewing the opening issue for the European edition of the *Chicago Tribune* (frequently called the Paris *Tribune*), Robert Sage described Lewisohn's prose as "conservative but richly woven." The work in progress had long been forming in Lewisohn's mind as a preliminary study toward a Jewish "epic narrative" he hoped to try. It became *The Island Within* (1928), a novel which follows several generations of a Jewish family from 1840 to the present and demonstrates Lewisohn's belief that the Jew cannot deny his heritage, either deliberately or through loyalty to his country, and remain spiritually whole. Critical reception of the book was generally very favorable. A skillful blending of history and fiction, *The Island Within* lacks the sermonlike quality that mars some of Lewisohn's work.

Lewisohn's "Introduction to a Projected History of American Literature" was published in *This Quarter* (July-August-September 1929), and subsequent issues contained essays from this work in progress on Melville, Whitman, and Henry James. The history, published in 1932 as *Expression in America*, had been inspired by a teacher Lewisohn had at Columbia. In a preface he explained his approach to the subject:

The book is not, in any hitherto accepted sense, a history of literature. Scholars who look in vain for a name, a date, a work, are asked to believe that these were not slighted but eliminated. For what is here attempted is a portrait of the American spirit seen and delineated, as the human spirit itself is best seen, in and through its mood of articulateness, of creative expression. To this end selection under the appropriate guiding principle was inevitable. It was equally inevitable that I use the organon or method of knowledge associated with the venerable name of Sigmund Freud.

Although the book later came to be criticized in some quarters for its narrow view, its initial reception was very good. It was republished in 1939 in a Modern Library edition as *The Story of American Literature.*

Lewisohn returned to the United States to live in 1934. With the rise of nazism he embraced the Zionist cause and became active in its leadership. From 1943 to 1948 he was editor of the *New Palestine,* a Zionist magazine. In his last years he taught English at Brandeis University and served as librarian there. Although personal publicity and changing critical values later adversely affected Lewisohn's literary reputation, his reassessment of the American literary tradition helped insure the public and critical acceptance of many of the American writers who worked in Paris during the twenties and thirties.

—*Jean W. Ross*

Periodical Publications:

"The Defeated," *transition,* no. 1 (April 1927): 85-97; no. 2 (May 1927): 74-89;

"The Pained Lady," *transition,* no. 13 (Summer 1928): 221-228;

"Introduction to a Projected History of American Literature," *This Quarter,* 2 (July-August-September 1929): 84-106;

"The Weakness of Herman Melville," *This Quarter,* 3 (April-May-June 1931): 610-617;

"Whitman," *This Quarter,* 4 (July-August-September 1931): 75-87;

"Where Henry James Never Entered," *This Quarter,* 4 (December 1931): 318-333;

"Johann Wolfgang von Goethe A Keepsake of Poems," translated by Lewisohn and others, *This Quarter,* 4 (June 1932): 571-591.

References:

Adolph Gillis, *Ludwig Lewisohn The Artist and His Message* (New York: Duffield & Green, 1933);

Alfred Kazin, *On Native Grounds An Interpretation of Modern American Prose* (New York: Reynal & Hitchcock, 1942), pp. 265-281;

David Singer, "Ludwig Lewisohn: The Making of an Anti-Communist," *American Quarterly,* 23 (December 1971): 738-748.

A. J. LIEBLING
(18 October 1904-28 December 1963)

SELECTED BOOKS: *Normandy Revisited* (New York: Simon & Schuster, 1958; London: Gollancz, 1959);

Between Meals (New York: Simon & Schuster, 1962; London: Longmans, Green, 1962).

Abbott Joseph Liebling's *Between Meals* (1962) is a singular reminiscence about his year as a student in Paris during the twenties. Born in New York City, Liebling paid his first visits to Paris as a child on European tours with his family, but it was not until 1926 that he was to enjoy an extended stay in the city, a year as a student at the Sorbonne. Shortly before his death, he drew upon this experience to write the group of *New Yorker* and *Vogue* pieces which constitute most of the text of *Between Meals.* He says of his visits to Paris: "if I had compared my life to a cake, the sojourns in Paris would have represented the chocolate filling. The intervening layers were plain sponge."

He attended Dartmouth College from 1920 until 1923, when he was expelled for repeated absences from chapel. Following graduation from the Columbia Graduate School of Journalism, he worked briefly for the *New York Times* before being fired, and then went to Providence, Rhode Island, where he served as a reporter on the *Providence Journal* and the *Evening Bulletin.*

In 1926 his father, a New York furrier, agreed to pay for a year of medieval studies at the Sorbonne, but Liebling only spent about two weeks there, attending a few classes. *Between Meals* is a portfolio of sketches about his post-Sorbonne experience that year, describing the Paris of student restaurants and young women in cafes, as well as cinema, popular theatre, and boxing arenas.

Liebling's account of "that soft Paris year"

displays his literary gifts at their brightest. Partial to the idiom of the big city, his terse, masterfully controlled prose style is embroidered with mock pedantry. By turns ironic and extravagant, he writes about the twenties in Paris with the same factual precision which earned him a reputation as one of the most talented World War II combat journalists to cover the American campaigns in North Africa and Europe. As in *Normandy Revisited* (1958), his middle-age reminiscence about the invasion of France and the road back to Paris, the nostalgic power of *Between Meals* results from Liebling's scrupulous avoidance of sentimentality for experiences which were among the most formative of his life.

When he returned to the United States from Paris in 1927, he worked as a newspaper reporter in Providence and later New York until 1935, when he joined the staff of the *New Yorker,* where he remained until his death in 1963. Liebling called himself a "chronic, incurable recidivist reporter," and his articles for the *New Yorker* department "The Wayward Press" earned him laurels as the gadfly of American journalism. Through his many books and magazine pieces runs the knowing tone of a humane skeptic. —*Seymour I. Toll*

HAROLD LOEB
(18 October 1891-20 January 1974)

SELECTED BOOKS: *Doodab* (New York: Boni & Liveright, 1925);

The Professors Like Vodka (New York: Boni & Liveright, 1927; reprinted, Carbondale & Edwardsville: Southern Illinois University Press, 1974—adds an afterword by Loeb);

Tumbling Mustard (New York: Liveright, 1929);

The Way It Was (New York: Criterion, 1959).

Harold Albert Loeb, now best-known as the prototype for the character Robert Cohn in Ernest Hemingway's *The Sun Also Rises* (1926), was recognized in his time for his talents as a writer and editor. The founder and chief editor of *Broom,* one of the earliest English-language reviews of the arts on the European continent between the two World Wars, he also had three novels published during the twenties.

Loeb was the descendant of two notable New York City families: the wealthy Guggenheims on his mother's side and the Loebs of Kuhn-Loeb and Company, investment bankers, on his father's. After receiving a Bachelor of Literature degree from Princeton University in 1913, Loeb went to Alberta, Canada, and settled in Empress, a new divisional point on the Canadian Pacific Railroad line, where, among other things, he went into the business of laying concrete foundations and may also have been involved in cattle ranching. He returned briefly to New York City early in 1914, married Marjorie Content in April, and took his new bride back to live in Empress. England's declaration of war on Germany on 4 August 1914, however, made it impossible for Loeb to continue successfully in his Canadian business enterprises. The Loebs returned

to New York City in September 1917, and he worked at various jobs for about a year and a half before going to work for the Guggenheims in California. There he was in charge of purchasing supplies for the San Francisco office and the Selby plant of the American Smelting and Lead Company.

Harold Loeb

Dissatisfaction with this job was the impetus for Loeb's growing interest in literature. Had he remained a businessman, he reflected later, he would have become like the humdrum character Doodab in his first novel.

When the United States entered World War I in 1917, Loeb enlisted in the army, and because of his poor eyesight, he was given a desk job in New York City. At the end of the war he bought a partnership in The Sunwise Turn, a bookshop in New York, in order to familiarize himself "with writers and writing," as he wrote in his private papers. Among the writers Loeb met because of his association with the bookshop were Alfred Kreymborg, Lola Ridge, Babette Deutsch, Malcolm Cowley, Harold Stearns, Laurence Vail, and F. Scott Fitzgerald. Although Loeb was later to work with Kreymborg, Ridge, and Cowley in the publication of *Broom*, his most important friendship initially was with Gilbert Cannan, a writer on the fringe of the D. H. Lawrence circle, whom Loeb met in 1920. He had read Cannan's novel *Ole Mole* when it was first published in 1914 and had admired the central character, a professor who escapes a restrictive environment

Back cover, Broom, *1 (November 1921)*

determined to live life fully. Loeb had attempted to emulate this character when he involved himself with literary people, and he later explored a similar theme in his first two novels.

In 1920 Cannan invited Loeb to go abroad with him. They arrived in Paris early that year and traveled through France, Italy, Ireland, and England before Loeb returned to New York in June. While abroad Loeb met a number of writers, including Romain Rolland, James Stephens, and AE (George Russell), establishing contacts that were to prove useful when he launched *Broom* in 1921. Even more important to Loeb's intellectual development was a comment Cannan made while they walked through the countryside near Dijon. Coming upon a factory in the midst of rural beauty, Loeb expressed his disgust at its ugliness, but Cannan answered simply, "It has its beauty too," and said nothing more. Loeb continued to think about Cannan's remark, and by the end of the day he was convinced that there was beauty in modern industrialism and that modern technology was beneficial because, as Loeb says in *The Way It Was* (1959), it would eventually "provide time for all men, instead of a privileged few, to look around and rejoice in what they saw." These ideas were to become an essential part of the editorial policy of *Broom*.

After Loeb's return to New York, he and Marjorie Loeb decided to separate; they were divorced in 1923. In February 1921, after selling his interest in The Sunwise Turn, Loeb decided to use his profits from the sale to start his own literary magazine. He asked Alfred Kreymborg, the former editor of *Glebe* and *Others*, to serve as his associate editor. They decided to publish the magazine in Rome, where the favorable rate of exchange would decrease production costs, and they sailed to France on the *Rotterdam* in June 1921. After a short time in Paris, where they met a number of writers and artists who would later contribute to their magazine, they went on to Rome to begin work on the first issue.

They called their magazine *Broom: An International Magazine of the Arts.* On the back cover of the first issue (November 1921) a colophon depicting a cartoon character with a broom gave the impression that this magazine intended, like the new broom of the adage, to sweep things clean. Also on the back cover, however, was a quotation from *Moby-Dick* that suggests a somewhat more ambiguous interpretation of *Broom*'s attitude toward traditional writing. Indeed, despite the further suggestion of defiance implied in Gordon Craig's cover drawing for the fourth issue—a grotesque figure thumbing his nose—*Broom* was

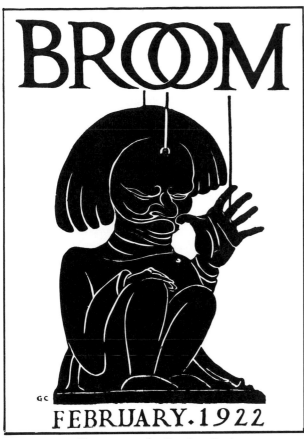

FEBRUARY · 1922

Front cover, by Gordon Craig

not a magazine of the avant-garde. The list of contributors for the early issues is notably eclectic. The first three issues contain photographs of art work by Pablo Picasso, Juan Gris, Joseph Stella, Andre Derain, Jacques Lipschitz, Man Ray, Henri Matisse, Rockwell Kent, Gordon Craig, Fernand Leger, and Raoul Dufy, among others. Contributors of poems, short stories, and criticism to these issues include James Stephens, Manuel Komroff, Conrad Aiken, Amy Lowell, Walter de la Mare, Sherwood Anderson, Leon Bazalgette, Aldo Palazzeschi, Wallace Stevens, Louis Untermeyer, Malcolm Cowley, John Gould Fletcher, Marianne Moore, Gertrude Stein, Elie Ehrenbourg, Waldo Frank, and Blaise Cendrars. In other words *Broom* published both young and old writers of a variety of nationalities whose work ranged from traditional to experimental, although the bulk of its literary contents tended toward the conservative.

In the fourth issue Loeb announced Kreymborg's resignation because of ill health and the demands of his own writing. The two editors had become divided over questions of finances and editorial policy. In *The Way It Was* Loeb accuses Kreymborg of incorrectly assuming that Loeb was wealthy and investing none of his own money in *Broom*. Kreymborg, in *Troubadour* (1925), claims somewhat unjustly that Loeb's taste was for the conservative and the European, while he was enthusiastic about modern and American art and literature. Edward Storer replaced Kreymborg, and Lola Ridge became the American editor, based in New York City.

Loeb's only plan for *Broom* had been to publish the best work by living writers and artists, but he began to believe that the magazine should have a more coherent editorial policy. His first attempt to define the kind of writing that *Broom* supported was a defense of the young American expatriates in France, "Foreign Exchange," which appeared in the May 1922 issue. Loeb argued that not only did French literature, especially that of Flaubert and his contemporaries, inspire young Americans to "a meticulous attention to form," but, more importantly, living in France gave them a valuable perspective from which they could view America objectively. At about this time *Broom* began to include more writing by the young Americans Loeb praised in his essay. Besides more work by Malcolm Cowley, Loeb began to publish poems and prose by John Dos Passos, Laurence Vail, E. E. Cummings, Gorham Munson, Robert Coates, and Matthew Josephson.

In "Foreign Exchange" Loeb had stated that the products of modern industry and technology in the United States were more original than the work of America's self-proclaimed artists, and he had asserted: "The influence of the cinema as well as that of other mechanical marvels of the age has scarcely begun to show any repercussion in literature, which lags far behind the other arts. . . ." In "The Mysticism of Money," written for the September 1922 issue, Loeb expanded upon this theme, proposing a new Machine Age aesthetic as the basis for American art. In part Loeb's article was intended as a response to the recently published *Civilization in the United States* (1922), edited by Harold Stearns. Stearns and his fellow contributors to the volume had characterized America as being crassly materialistic and destructive of creativity. In denying this thesis Loeb was also setting aside traditional standards for judging American culture. He argued that utilitarian objects—"Engines, forges, hearths, furnaces, turbines, kettles, motors, generators, dynamoes, automobiles, ships, aeroplanes"—are not disqualified from being works of art because they are designed to perform specific functions. Instead, because practicality is the designer's goal, "The result is simplification, elimination of inessentials, balance and beauty." Moreover, because these objects are created in order to make money, and the pursuit of wealth is religious in its fervor, materialism replaces traditional beliefs as the inspiration for great art.

In the following issue Loeb published an article by the Italian Futurist artist Enrico Prampolini called "The Aesthetic of the Machine and Mechanical Introspection in Art" (October 1922), which provided another enthusiastic perspective on the art of the machine. He also announced *Broom*'s move to Berlin, where he hoped to save money on the expenses of printing the magazine. Matthew Josephson, who at the time shared some of Loeb's idealistic beliefs about the salutary effect of modern industry on art, became the magazine's new associate editor.

Loeb continued to edit *Broom* from Berlin until March 1923, attracting such new American contributors as Kay Boyle, Jean Toomer, and Hart Crane, before lack of funds caused him to cease publication. *Broom* was revived in New York City from August 1923 to January 1924, but although Loeb was listed on the masthead as the editor, Josephson performed the actual editorial duties. Loeb moved from Berlin to Paris, where he devoted the next few years to writing fiction. His first novel, *Doodab* (1925), was published through the help of Harold Stearns, with whom Loeb had become friends in Paris.

Based on Loeb's own feelings of entrapment while he was working in California before World War I, the novel is the story of Henry Doodab, an ineffectual man who escapes from his failures in business and marriage by creating an imaginary dream world in which he has the power he lacks in real life. The novel is interspersed with Surrealistic dream episodes that prompted the anonymous reviewer for the *Saturday Review of Literature* to criticize "the self-conscious mental ramblings which constitute the bulk of the volume" (19 September 1925). Cowley, reviewing the book for the *New York Herald Tribune*, was more enthusiastic. Although he says there are "many pages of uninspired writing" in the novel, he also praises its "realistic passages written with a gusto, an excess of animal spirits, which make them something far better than realism." He exclaims over the "exact fancy shown in these Kapepulan descriptions" and credits Loeb with creating "living characters." Most reviewers were somewhat less enthusiastic, and the novel was not a commercial success.

In Loeb's next novel, *The Professors Like Vodka* (1927), he draws upon events in Paris during the fall of 1925. Two university professors, Mercado—a Jew, based on Loeb himself—and Halsey—based on Loeb's friend Bill Smith, who is also the prototype for Bill Gorton in *The Sun Also Rises*—are on vacation in Paris. At a cafe they meet two Russian bargirls, Cleopatre and Vera. Mercado is jolted out of his romantic fascination for Cleopatre when he discovers that she is a fanatical anti-Semite who claims that she helped kill Jews in Russia. Mercado gains revenge when, after seducing her, he horrifies her by revealing that he is a Jew. Meanwhile, Vera has convinced Halsey to marry her and take her back to the United States. The novel was not a great success in its day. An anonymous reviewer for the *New York Herald Tribune* accused Loeb of employing " 'Saturday Evening Post' sentimentality," but H. H. Brown, reviewing the book for both the *New York Evening Post* (23 April 1927) and the *Saturday Review* (21 May 1927), called the novel "a melodrama of the mind" and added that, like the Russian novelists, Loeb "has the gift of making melodrama convincing." Reviewing the 1974 republication, Cowley praised *The Professors Like Vodka* for revealing more of Paris life in the mid-twenties than most of the neglected novels of that era.

Loeb's third published novel, *Tumbling Mustard* (1929), was begun in France but finished in New York after his return in 1929. Set in an Alberta, Canada, frontier town much like Empress, it is the story of Dan Driggs, who comes to the town by chance, marries the pretty girl who works behind the hotel's cigar counter, and then finds himself unable to escape an intolerable marriage. The novel is a remarkable psychological study of the moody, unstable wife. A brief, unsigned review in the *New York Times* credits it with having "all the elements of strong drama: love, hate, fear and above all, suspense" (2 June 1929). For the most part, however, the novel has been unjustly ignored.

Loeb's unpublished novel, "The Arabs Come on Friday," written about 1929, is based in part on his experiences in Paris as well as a trip to present-day Israel. In this novel David Milhado, an American expatriate in Paris, and his mistress, Nicky, attend a party at which they meet Isadora Duncan and Berenkoff, a Zionist leader who inspires them to take a trip to Jerusalem. En route Nicky deserts David for an officer in the French Foreign Legion. After David reaches Israel, he falls in love with another woman, Ruth, and joins her on a kibbutz. One Friday she is killed by an Arab, and disconsolate, David returns to New York.

Loeb's trip to the Middle East inspired a number

of articles on Zionism which appeared in the *New Republic* and *Opinion* in the early thirties, but after 1929 he wrote no more fiction. For the next twenty-five years, until the end of World War II, he worked as an economist and government administrator, first for the Office of Price Administration and later for the War Production Board. Between 1933 and 1946 he published four books on economics.

Loeb's memoirs, *The Way It Was*, published in 1959, focus on his expatriate years, especially the publication of *Broom*, as well as Loeb's version of his experiences with Kathleen Cannell and Lady Duff Twysden, and with Hemingway and his friends at Pamplona—all of which Loeb felt Hemingway had misrepresented in *The Sun Also Rises*. He also wrote three articles about Hemingway and his contemporaries that appeared in the *Carleton Miscellany*, the *Connecticut Review*, and the *Southern Review* during the sixties.

Loeb had been married for a second time in 1928 in Paris to a woman whose name he never revealed; they were divorced in 1929. In 1933 he married Vera B. Currie, who died on 14 July 1961, and on 26 July 1963 he married Barbara McKenzie. He died in Marrakesh in 1974.

Although Loeb's novels are not without literary merit and his autobiography is a valuable source of information about the expatriates of the twenties, Loeb's most significant contribution to literature was *Broom*, judged by Kenneth Rexroth to have been the best literary magazine of the period.

—*Bertram D. Sarason*

Other:

The Broom Anthology, edited by Loeb (Pound Ridge, N.Y.: Milford House, 1969).

Periodical Publications:

"Foreign Exchange," *Broom*, 2 (May 1922): 176-181;
"The Mysticism of Money," *Broom*, 3 (September 1922): 115-130;
"Ford Madox Ford's *The Good Soldier*: A Critical Reminiscence," *Carleton Miscellany*, 6 (Spring 1965): 27-41;
"Hemingway's Bitterness," *Connecticut Review*, 1 (October 1967): 7-25;
Review of *Ernest Hemingway A Life Story* by Carlos Baker, *Southern Review*, 5 (Autumn 1969): 1214-1225.

References:

Alfred Kreymborg, *Troubadour* (New York: Liveright, 1925), pp. 359-381;
Bertram D. Sarason, *Hemingway and* The Sun Set (Washington, D.C.: Bruccoli Clark / NCR Microcard Editions, 1972).

WALTER LOWENFELS
(10 May 1897-7 July 1976)

SELECTED BOOKS: *Episodes & Epistles* (New York: Seltzer, 1925);
Finale of Seem (London: Heinemann, 1929);
Apollinaire: An Elegy (Paris: Hours Press, 1930);
Anonymous: the Need for Anonymity, by Lowenfels and Michael Fraenkel (Paris: Carrefour, 1930);
USA with Music (Paris: Carrefour, 1930);
Elegy in the Manner of a Requiem in Memory of D. H. Lawrence (Paris: Carrefour, 1932);
The Suicide (Paris: Carrefour, 1934);
Steel, 1937 (Atlantic City, N.J.: Unity Publishers, 1938);
The Prisoners Poems for Amnesty (Philadelphia: Whittier, 1954);
The Life of Fraenkel's Death A Biographical Inquest, by Lowenfels and Howard McCord (Pullman: Washington State University Press, 1970).

Walter Lowenfels, poet, journalist, and anthologist, was in the vanguard of nearly every liberal political and artistic movement from his early years in Paris until his death some forty years later. Two years after his arrival in Paris in 1926, he met Michael Fraenkel, with whom he founded the Carrefour Press in 1930, and by the time he returned to New York in 1934 his books has been published by both Carrefour and Nancy Cunard's Hours Press in Paris and Heinemann in London. What is more, his poetry had won him a reputation as one of the most promising young expatriate poets in Paris. Later a left-wing political activist, he was persecuted in the McCarthy era of the fifties but was admired as an avant-garde poet in the sixties. Although Lowenfels believed that art should inspire social change, his poetry cannot be construed as political propaganda; rather, it expresses his desire for a more humane society.

Following his graduation from a New York City preparatory school in 1914, Lowenfels submitted to his father's wish that he participate in the prosperous family butter business. Except for his World War I service in the army, during which he was not sent overseas, he continued to work at this job discontentedly until 1926. After the war Lowenfels began to write poems, some of which appeared in the local newspapers, and by 1924, when he met Lillian Apotheker, the daughter of a Yiddish scholar and humorist, he had written enough poems to produce, with her help, his first collection, *Episodes & Epistles* (1925).

By 1926 Lowenfels had saved enough money to go to France, where he could escape the butter business and devote his time to writing. After their arrival in Paris he and Apotheker were married on 19 June. In Paris Lowenfels found a place for his poems in such little magazines as *transition* and *This Quarter*. Many of these poems are groups of seemingly cryptic, alliterative words which are spaced on the page for visual impact, a mode made familiar by Gertrude Stein and in keeping with *transition*'s "Revolution of the Word" movement. Some of his work also appeared in periodicals in London, where his second book of poetry, *Finale of Seem* (1929), was published.

In Paris Lowenfels became friends with Nancy Cunard, proprietor of the Hours Press, who described him many years later as a "very sympathetic man . . . handsome and romantic looking . . . generous-spirited . . . of an ebullient, enthusiastic nature characterized by a zest that has never grown dim." Cunard also admired Lowenfels's poetry and published his *Apollinaire: An Elegy* in 1930. This long narrative poem imitates the style of the poet it eulogizes, as do many of Lowenfels's later poems about other poets. *Apollinaire* was the first in a series of books dealing with the subject of death, the philosophical obsession of his close friend Michael Fraenkel, whom he had first met in 1928.

Fraenkel believed that Western man was experiencing an increasing alienation from himself and the natural world that was leading to the moral death of civilization. In *The Life of Fraenkel's Death* (1970), which Lowenfels coauthored with Howard McCord, McCord explains that Fraenkel believed "Western man was doomed to increasing alienation and hurt until he recognized his wound as death, and gave himself up to it, lived in it, and found, after enduring the reality of it, a truly humane life beyond." Fraenkel pessimistically concluded that the world would never recognize its own decay; it was doomed to both moral and physical self-destruction. Lowenfels, on the other hand, felt that the world

Walter Lowenfels in France, 1930s

could be saved from moral death by replacing the dead social structure with a new type of socialistic humanism. In his poetry, the death of characters often symbolizes man's self-alienation and the moral decay of the world—the decay of humanism. Lowenfels had met Fraenkel in 1928 at a showing of the night paintings of De Hirsch Margulies held in Lowenfels's apartment on the rue Brezin, but they did not become close friends until 1929, when they began their discussions about death, later joined by Henry Miller. Fraenkel helped Lowenfels financially by getting him started as a real-estate agent, involving him in the leasing of apartments to such people as Marc Chagall, Archibald MacLeish, and Tristan Tzara.

In the course of their discussions Fraenkel and Lowenfels became excited by the idea of total anonymity in art, deciding to found their own press and publish unsigned books. In 1930 they began the Carrefour Press and published a thirty-two-page pamphlet, *Anonymous: the Need for Anonymity*, their manifesto for their new movement. They believed that gaining recognition in art was like competition in business—competition alienates man from the natural world and himself. The "anonymous" movement would allow the artist to merge his individual "creative consciousness into the total creative consciousness of the world." It was an idealistic goal which they hoped would unite artists everywhere in the task of "remodeling the world." To get their "anonymous" movement going, Lowenfels and Fraenkel each contributed work—Fraenkel his death-theme novel, *Werther's Younger Brother* (1930), and Lowenfels a play, *USA with Music* (1930). A number of writers, including Kay Boyle, F. Scott Fitzgerald, and Michael Arlen, expressed interest in the venture, but no manuscripts were forthcoming.

USA with Music was inspired by killings during a miners' strike in Herrin, Illinois. An absurd Brechtian tragicomedy, it was scheduled for production in Berlin, with music by Kurt Weill, but was canceled as being politically dangerous. Influenced by Fraenkel's philosophies, *USA with Music* has death as its theme—both the deaths of individuals and the spiritual death of America. A scathing satire of American values, it deals with the exploitation of a trapped miner by inhumane opportunists who see the public interest in the cave-in as a chance to make money. The theme is similar to that of the George S. Kaufman and George Gershwin musical hit *Of Thee I Sing*, which appeared soon after *USA with Music*. It seemed so similar to Lowenfels that in 1932 he sued for plagiarism but lost his case. The suit, however, forced Lowenfels to reveal himself as the play's creator, thus aborting the "anonymous" movement before it was able to gain momentum. The Carrefour Press continued to publish books, but it began crediting the author.

The next Carrefour publication, *Elegy in the Manner of a Requiem in Memory of D. H. Lawrence* (1932), credited Lowenfels as author. The typescript for the poem included voice markings and accents because Lowenfels meant it to be read aloud like a choral service. For Lowenfels Lawrence was a "symbol for creative vitality undergoing sacrificial death." According to Hugh Ford the poem is also an elegy for the "poet's own dead past," a past he killed when he left the family business in 1926. Verses from the D. H. Lawrence elegy which had earlier appeared in *This Quarter* won Lowenfels that magazine's Richard Aldington Poetry Prize, which he shared with E. E. Cummings in 1931. It was a small but prestigious monetary award then presented by the well-known novelist and poet Richard Aldington to the "ablest" young American poet to appear in *This Quarter*.

Also in 1931 Lowenfels met the novelist Henry Miller and persuaded Fraenkel to house him briefly at his Villa Seurat apartment building. Together they formed what Lowenfels later called the "death school" of poetry, with Fraenkel's death philosophy the constant subject of discussion. Lowenfels later withdrew from active participation in the exchange of ideas that was becoming an obsession for Fraenkel and Miller. The two exchanged hundreds of letters on the subject of death which they collected in *Hamlet* (1939, 1941), which Miller called "the longest funeral sermon in history." Fraenkel later appeared in Miller's writing as Boris in *The Tropic of Cancer* (1934); Lowenfels was the model for Jabberwhorl Cronstadt in *Black Spring* (1936). The name Jabberwhorl is a good description for the character, a bohemian poet/landlord who jabbers ceaselessly in a manic whirl of abstract non sequiturs.

Death—this time the death of Hart Crane—was the subject of Lowenfels's last publication before leaving Paris, *The Suicide* (1934). According to Hugh Ford, the poem "explores the three levels of experience remembered by the dying poet": fear, faith, and reason. The poet dies but is reborn through his works. It ends with the lines, "Only his song / pounds the Atlantic Highlands, / looking, America, for you." Lowenfels returned with his wife and three daughters to the United States in 1934. Living in New York, he resumed work in the wholesale butter business until 1938, when he moved to Philadelphia to become a reporter for the Pennsylvania edition of the *Daily Worker*. His poems dealing with a labor movement to organize steel workers, *Steel, 1937* (1938), originally appeared in the *Daily Worker*. Eventually he became managing editor, and as his involvement in leftist labor activism increased, his poetry writing ceased, not to resume again until after his arrest in 1953 for treason as defined by the Smith Act—conspiracy to teach and advocate the overthrow of the government by force. He spent several weeks in jail before his conviction was overturned on appeal. He began writing again while imprisoned, and the next year *The Prisoners Poems for Amnesty* (1954) was published.

Throughout the late fifties and the sixties Lowenfels worked as an anthologist, and although he edited several collections of poems by his favorite poet, Walt Whitman, he became best known as the major American anthologist of the avant-garde. He edited several volumes of social consciousness poetry: *Where Is Vietnam?* (1967), a collection of war protest poems; *In the Time of Revolution* (1969), civil-rights poems by black Americans; *From the Belly of the Shark* (1973), poems by native Americans—Chicanos, Eskimos, Hawaiians, and Indians; and *For Neruda, for Chile* (1975), poems eulogizing the Chilean poet Pablo Neruda and protesting U. S. involvement in the overthrow of Salvadore Allende's socialist regime. Lowenfels was also a leader of the oral poetry revival which began with the beat generation. He died of cancer in his seventy-ninth year.

Although his poetic style has caused him to be classified as an avant-garde poet ever since his first appearance in the pages of *transition* in the twenties, Lowenfels's themes have varied little since that time. Most of his later poems seem like new blocks on a foundation laid in the twenties, a foundation that uses existential death symbolism and an idealistic Marxist political ideology that includes a condemnation of the alienating effects of technology. Jonathan Cott describes Lowenfels's later poetry: "With a vocabulary derived from astronomy, geology and microbiology, Walter developed a style—influenced in part by William Carlos Williams—which he called 'scientific surrealism.' " But common to his early Parisian poetry and his sixties protest poetry is his preoccupation with death symbolism. In a letter printed in *The Life of Fraenkel's Death* (1970), Lowenfels wrote: "I never gave up my belief in death. Perhaps that's the essential continuity between my years as a poet in Paris, then as a reporter and editor of the *Daily Worker*, and thereafter my return to poems." —*Mark Fritz*

Other:

Walt Whitman's Civil War, edited by Lowenfels with the assistance of Nan Braymer (New York: Knopf, 1960);
Selections from Leaves of Grass, introduction by Lowenfels (New York: Crown, 1961);
Poets of Today: A New American Anthology, edited by Lowenfels (New York: International Publishers, 1964);
Where Is Vietnam?, edited by Lowenfels with the assistance of Braymer (Garden City: Anchor Books, 1967);

The Tenderest Lover: Walt Whitman's Love Poems, edited by Lowenfels (New York: Delacorte, 1970);
From the Belly of the Shark, edited by Lowenfels (New York: Vintage, 1973);
For Neruda, for Chile, edited by Lowenfels (Boston: Beacon, 1975).

Periodical Publications:

"In Kosciusko, Mississippi," *Double Dealer*, 6 (July 1924): 136;
"Epistle to C. S. Concerning Burial in Illinois," *Double Dealer*, 7 (April 1925): 149-150;
"Sonnet," *Double Dealer*, 8 (January 1926): 305;
"4 to the Rain," *Poetry*, 29 (March 1927): 306-309;
"Three Verses," *transition*, no. 8 (November 1927): 123;
"Creed," *transition*, no. 12 (March 1928): 119;
"Solstice," *transition*, no. 13 (Summer 1928): 59;
"Prometheus: A Chorus at 40 ALFRESCO," *transition*, no. 15 (February 1929): 76-78;
"Sonnet," *This Quarter*, 2 (July-August-September 1929): 136;
"Minuet," *This Quarter*, 3 (October-November-December 1930): 323;
"Lines for Lawrence," *This Quarter*, 3 (October-November-December 1930): 324;
"Mental Climate—Paris 1929," *Shenandoah*, 14 (Summer 1963): 47-53.

References:

Jonathan Cott, *Forever Young* (New York: Random House, 1977), pp. 120-144;
Nancy Cunard, *These Were the Hours* (Carbondale: Southern Illinois University Press, 1969), pp. 86-94;
Hugh Ford, *Published in Paris American and British Writers, Printers, and Publishers in Paris, 1920-1939* (New York: Macmillan, 1975), pp. 290-297;
Kenneth Rexroth, *American Poetry in the Twentieth Century* (New York: Herder & Herder, 1971), pp. 62-65.

MINA LOY
(27 December 1882-25 September 1966)

BOOKS: *Lunar Baedecker* (Paris: Contact Editions, 1923);
Lunar Baedeker & Time-Tables (Highlands, N.C.: Jargon, 1958).

The subtle interplay of the verbal and the visual in Mina Loy's poetry assured her place in experimental writing during the twenties. The younger generation of expatriate writers admired her involvement in avant-garde movements and her European sensibility. Born in London and trained as an artist in Munich and Paris at the turn of the century, she later went to New York, where she associated with the group of poets whose work appeared in Alfred Kreymborg's magazine *Others* during World War I. When she returned to Paris with her daughters in 1923, Robert McAlmon published *Lunar Baedecker*, a collection of her poems. (The misspelling of "Baedeker" was McAlmon's.) As the widow of poet-boxer Arthur Cravan, she had considerable contact with the Dadaists and Surrealists, who saw Cravan as a Dada hero. Her friendships with Marcel Duchamp, Gertrude Stein, and Djuna Barnes were long-standing; in Paris she came to know Joyce and Brancusi, about whose work she wrote poems reflecting her preoccupation with the nature of artistic creation.

By the twenties her writing was already familiar to readers of little magazines. Harold Loeb, the editor of *Broom*, considered her poetry respectably modern, in the same class as that of Marianne Moore, Joyce, and Eliot, and other contemporaries noted affinities with Laforgue and Apollinaire. From the start her writing was distinguished by a strong visual sense and a persistent concern with the nature of consciousness. Her earliest poetry, published when she was living in Florence, criticized the fin de siecle sensibility of her milieu and reflected her interest in the Futurists, who called for a renunciation of the past and for art that captures the images and rhythms of modern industrial society. "Costa San Giorgio" and "Parturition," for example, use indentation, a variable line, and the white spaces on the page to create visual and kinesthetic transcriptions of experience. "Love Songs," the frank yet dreamlike sequence that remains her best-known work, is an analysis of the course of a love affair. In the twenties Loy turned to more formal concerns with the creative process, the status of the artist, and the nature of the modern.

In "The Metaphysical Pattern of Aesthetics," an unpublished essay, she distinguishes between representational subject matter and the abstractions of modern art, which provide maps of the artist's mind rather than imitations of reality. Her poetry of the twenties can be read as a series of such maps: "Brancusi's Golden Bird," "Joyce's Ulysses," and " 'The Starry Sky' of Wyndham Lewis" mirror the formal qualities of their subject matter and probe artistic consciousness in the face of the public's insensibility. "Apology of Genius" serves as an introduction to her view of the modernist generation: artists are "lepers of the moon / all magically diseased" by the godlike gifts that have made them outcasts. Defending them against the uncomprehending bourgeois audience, she declares, "Our wills are formed / by curious disciplines / beyond your laws." An artistic credo follows:

> In the raw cavern of the Increate
> we forge the dusk of Chaos
> to that imperious jewelry of the Universe
> —the Beautiful—

In Loy's version of art as religion, the artist's splendid isolation testifies to the divine nature of creativity.

Reviewing *Lunar Baedecker* in 1926, Yvor Winters singled out "Apology of Genius" for special praise. He saw in the poem "a genius that rises from a level of emotion and attitude which is as nearly common human territory as one can ever expect to find in a poet." Winters speculated that of their generation, William Carlos Williams and Mina Loy had the most to offer the younger writers. However, what Winters called her "cerebral" quality gave Loy the reputation of one whose poetry was not accessible to the uninitiated. Her modernist contemporaries greatly admired "Brancusi's Golden Bird," published in the *Dial* opposite a picture of the sculpture. Loy imagines the artist as "some patient peasant God," whose activity is embodied in his work's "incandescent curve." She concludes with an analogy between poem and sculpture; both achieve completion in formal silence: "The immaculate / conception / of the inaudible bird / occurs / in gorgeous reticence." The artist recreates the world in the luminous abstractions of form.

Loy reaffirmed this notion in an essay on Gertrude Stein, published in the *transatlantic review*. The epigraph, her own poem, calls Stein the Madame Curie of language: "she crushed / the tonnage / of consciousness / congealed to phrases / to extract / a radium of the word." Loy had read *The Making of Americans* (1925) in manuscript and was impressed with its author's verbal designs. Praising her friend's efforts to "track intellection back to the embryo," she saw Stein's work as a kindred attempt to translate consciousness into artistic form. Although her essay was one of the best contemporary evaluations of Stein's writing, Loy did not continue in this vein. When Eugene Jolas interviewed her for the Paris *Tribune* (the European edition of the *Chicago Tribune*), he commented upon her "almost Stoic slowness" in composition. Loy replied that in her experience, "one must have lived ten years to write a poem."

Loy published little after *Lunar Baedecker*, with the exception of "Anglo-Mongrels and the Rose." The first two parts appeared in two issues of the *Little Review* in 1923, and a third long section was published in Robert McAlmon's *The Contact Collection of Contemporary Writers* (1925). This long verse sequence examines the psychic and social consequences of a Victorian upbringing: Ova, the heroine, is in some respects the embryonic consciousness traced back to its beginnings. The most successful sections evoke the family structure in which the child's aesthetic perceptions are met with antagonism. "Illumination," by contrast, enacts her transcendent awareness of self in relation to the universe:

> She is conscious
> not through her body   but through space
>
> This saint's prize
> this indissoluble bliss
> to be carried like a forgetfulness
>   into the long nightmare

Such visionary moments prefigure the bliss of artistic creation: both occur in opposition to a hostile society.

By the end of the twenties Loy was kept busy with the design and manufacture of lampshades for the shop that she opened with the backing of Peggy Guggenheim. She began a prose version of her autobiography, which remains unpublished. After her return to New York in 1936, little of her work was published, and she saw few friends from the Paris years. She became an American citizen in 1946 and entered a new phase of creative activity after moving to the Bowery in 1949. There she began to assemble a series of constructions made from found materials, frequently depicting neighborhood scenes. "Hot Cross Bum," a poem of this period, is their verbal equivalent: the bums are "blowsy angels," counterparts of the artists-outcasts, but they achieve transcendence only by means of their "infamous incense." Loy left New York in 1953 to live with her family in Aspen, Colorado, where she continued to

work on constructions. In 1958 much of her poetry was republished in *Lunar Baedeker & Time-Tables*. The following year she received the Copley Foundation award for her painting, and her constructions were exhibited in New York at the Bodley Gallery. She died in Aspen in 1966 after a short illness, having outlived most of her generation.

In 1944 Kenneth Rexroth argued that Mina Loy was an important American poet whose work deserved to be well-known and classed her with her modernist contemporaries. Rexroth conjectured that she had been forgotten because of her "extreme exceptionalism"—the lucidity of her love poetry and the intelligence of her approach. More recently Jerome Rothenberg observed that Loy "had a largeness of theme & an energy of sound & image that few in her generation could match."

—*Carolyn Burke*

Other:

"Anglo-Mongrels and the Rose," part 3, in *The Contact Collection of Contemporary Writers*, ed. Robert McAlmon (Paris: Contact Editions, 1925), pp. 137-194;

Hayden Carruth, ed., *The Voice that is Great Within Us*, contains poems by Loy (New York: Bantam, 1971);

Ann Stanford, ed., *The Women Poets in English*, contains poems by Loy (New York: Herder & Herder, 1972);

Louise Bernikow, ed., *The World Split Open*, contains poems by Loy (New York: Viking, 1974);

Jerome Rothenberg, ed., *Revolution of the Word*, contains poems by Loy (New York: Seabury, 1974).

Periodical Publications:

"Aphorisms on Futurism," *Camera Work*, 45 (January 1914): 13-15;

"The Pamperers," *Dial*, 69 (July 1920): 65-78;

"O Hell," *Contact*, 1 (December 1920): 7;

"Mexican Desert," *Dial*, 70 (June 1921): 672;

"Perlun," *Dial*, 71 (August 1921): 142;

"Brancusi's Golden Bird," *Dial*, 73 (November 1922): 506-508;

"Anglo-Mongrels and the Rose," parts 1 and 2, *Little Review*, 9 (Spring 1923): 10-18; 9 (Autumn-Winter 1923-1924): 41-51;

"Gertrude Stein," *transatlantic review*, 2 (October 1924): 305-309; 2 (November 1924): 427-430;

Answer to Questionaire, *Little Review*, 12 (May 1929): 46;

"Summer Night in a Florentine Slum," *Contact*, 1 (December 1929): 6-7;

"The Widow's Jazz," *Pagany*, 2 (April-June 1931): 68-70;

"Lady Laura in Bohemia," *Pagany*, 2 (July-September 1931): 125-127.

References:

Carolyn Burke, "Becoming Mina Loy," *Women's Studies*, 7 (forthcoming, 1980);

Kenneth Wayne Fields, "The Poetry of Mina Loy," *Southern Review*, new series, 3 (July 1967): 597-607;

Peggy Guggenheim, *Out of this Century* (New York: Dial, 1946), pp. 50, 73-87;

Virginia M. Kouidis, "The Cerebral Forager: An Introduction to the Poetry of Mina Loy," Ph.D. dissertation, University of Iowa, 1972;

Alfred Kreymborg, *A History of American Poetry: Our Singing Strength* (New York: Tudor, 1934), pp. 466, 482-490, 515;

Kreymborg, *Troubadour* (New York: Boni & Liveright, 1925), pp. 218-223, 235-236, 309-311;

Robert McAlmon, *Being Geniuses Together An Autobiography* (London: Secker & Warburg, 1938);

Samuel French Morse, "The Rediscovery of Mina Loy and the Avant Garde," *Wisconsin Studies in Contemporary Literature*, 2 (Spring-Summer 1961): 12-19;

Kenneth Rexroth, "Les Lauriers Sont Coupes: Mina Loy," *Circle*, 1, 4 (1944): 69-72;

Jonathan Williams, "Things are Very Far Away," *Nation*, 192 (27 May 1961): 461-462;

William Carlos Williams, *The Autobiography of William Carlos Williams* (New York: Random House, 1951);

Yvor Winters, "Mina Loy," *Dial*, 8 (June 1926): 496-499.

Papers:

Loy's papers are in the Beinecke Library at Yale University.

ARCHIBALD MACLEISH
(7 May 1892-   )

SELECTED BOOKS: *Tower of Ivory* (New Haven: Yale University Press, 1917; London: Milford, 1917);

The Happy Marriage and Other Poems (Boston & New York: Houghton Mifflin, 1924);

The Pot of Earth (Boston & New York: Houghton Mifflin, 1925);

Nobodaddy A Play (Cambridge, Mass.: Dunster House, 1926; London: Jackson, 1926);

Streets in the Moon (Boston & New York: Houghton Mifflin, 1926);

The Hamlet of A. MacLeish (Boston & New York: Houghton Mifflin, 1928);

Einstein (Paris: Black Sun Press, 1929);

New Found Land (Paris: Black Sun Press, 1930; Boston & New York: Houghton Mifflin, 1930);

Conquistador (Boston & New York: Houghton Mifflin, 1932; London: Gollancz, 1933);

Frescoes for Mr. Rockefeller's City (New York: John Day, 1933);

The Fall of the City A Verse Play for Radio (New York & Toronto: Farrar & Rinehart, 1937; London: Boriswood, 1937);

J. B. A Play in Verse (Boston: Houghton Mifflin, 1958; London: Secker & Warburg, 1959);

The Collected Poems of Archibald MacLeish (Boston: Houghton Mifflin, 1963);

New & Collected Poems 1917-1976 (Boston: Houghton Mifflin, 1976).

Unlike many members of the American expatriate community in France between the World Wars, Archibald MacLeish is best known not as an alienated modernist, but as the continuator of the nineteenth-century American tradition of the man of letters as a public man, even government official, and as the advocate of a "public poetry" that he feels has not yet been achieved in the contemporary world.

Even during the twenties in Paris MacLeish never thought of himself as an expatriate. Born in Glencoe, Illinois, he was a distinguished graduate of Harvard Law School, a teacher at Harvard College, and a successful lawyer in a traditional Boston firm before he decided to take his family abroad in 1923. Later he was to become Librarian of Congress (1939-1944) and Assistant Secretary of State (1944-1945) during the presidency of Franklin D. Roosevelt. Even the period between the summers of 1923 and 1928 that he spent largely in France developing his primary interest in poetry was interrupted by summers back in Conway, Massachusetts, and one five-month stay in Persia that provided imagery for some of his most highly regarded poems. The poetry that he wrote in France was at first in the tradition of the great modernists, W. B. Yeats, T. S. Eliot, and Ezra Pound; but this work proved finally to be quite apart from his most significant achievements as an artist—the Pulitzer-Prize winning *Conquistador* (1932), an epic poem about Cortez's expedition in Mexico; the masterfully ironic *Frescoes for Mr. Rockefeller's City* (1933); pioneering radio dramas, especially *The Fall of the City* (1937); and the Pulitzer-Prize winning play *J. B.* (1958), a modern-dress reconsideration of the biblical Book of Job.

MacLeish had already written the poems that a friend collected in *Tower of Ivory* (1917) before he rose from private to captain in the U.S. Army in France during World War I, and these highly formal, traditional, and emotionally detached verses suggest—as does the book's title—the unworldly isolation of New England intellectuals before the disillusioning impact of the war and the ensuing prohibition era. Finding that he "turned out to be fairly good at law," MacLeish survived the years of the early twenties brilliantly as success was conventionally measured, but, as he told Stanley Koehler during an interview in 1975, "It came over me on a long night walk home from Boston to Cambridge that I had reached the point at which I would either fish or cut bait." He and his wife Ada, a singer who had earlier spent a year in Paris, decided to go with their two children to the French capital, drawn there "for the most obvious reason: which is that others were there, things were happening there."

In Paris MacLeish at first devoted himself to learning to read Dante in the original Tuscan. Curiously he was intimate with few poets, except for E. E. Cummings and John Peale Bishop, whom MacLeish called "in some not unimportant ways . . . the most interesting of the lot." His warm friendship with French poet St. John Perse (Alexis Leger) did not begin until years later in the United States. The MacLeishes, however, were gregarious, and they did become close friends with several aspiring novelists, especially F. Scott Fitzgerald, John Dos Passos (who remained a "great friend" for many years despite their disagreements "about everything political"), and Ernest Hemingway, who "more or less lived" with the MacLeishes for months when his first marriage was breaking up.

Eventually the close relationship with Hemingway ended in a quarrel, as, MacLeish commented, "almost all of Ernest's" did. MacLeish also got to know James Joyce but saw him only occasionally. He never met Gertrude Stein, of whose

Archibald MacLeish, by Paul-Emile Becat, 1927

Sylvia Beach Collection

ideas he speaks rather skeptically. Also, of all the prominent painters in Paris at the time, he speaks of knowing only Andre Masson well. An important friendship was with minor poet and publisher Harry Crosby, who repeatedly spoke of MacLeish as one of the few great writers of the generation, along with Joyce, Eliot, and Perse.

MacLeish's *The Happy Marriage* was published in Boston in 1924, but this first collection of work to appear after his move to Paris is a formal sequence of tributes to his own marriage that clearly is the work of his Boston years. The first obvious product of his *Wanderjahren*, a blank-verse play called *Nobodaddy* after William Blake's derisive name for an orthodox God, did not appear until 1926, when a limited edition was published in Cambridge, Massachusetts. It is difficult to argue strongly for *Nobodaddy*'s artistic merits, because, as Grover Smith observes, "none of the four characters comprehends the meaning of [the] actions," so that there is no climactic recognition scene. As Signi Falk points out, however, the play is important as evidence of "a new point of view and an acquaintance with a new kind of poetry." It also foreshadows MacLeish's verse drama for radio performance, beginning in the thirties, and especially his commercially successful play *J. B.*

Nobodaddy's first two acts are set in the Garden of Eden. Although MacLeish cautions in his preface that he has "not assumed that the legend as a legend symbolizes the accident of human self-consciousness and the resultant human exclusion from nature, animal and inanimate," these are precisely the assumptions that underlie the central concern with the question of man's responsibility for his actions. The play explores the devastating consequences of the emergence of human self-consciousness, especially as it expresses itself in guilt feelings. Although God is much talked about in the play, he never appears or even manifests his power, so that he exists only as a projection of the infant human imagination.

In the first act the serpent tempts Adam with the possibility of his becoming a god in his own right. When Eve and Adam eat the forbidden fruit despite her forebodings, they experience a separation both from nature and from each other. In a drastic change from the biblical story, Adam, in the second act, inflicts the concept of sin upon himself as a form of guilt, and the tortured pair are not expelled from Eden by a heavenly emissary, but literally drive themselves out. Another drastic change occurs in the third act when, years later in the wasteland east of Eden, Cain kills Abel not in rage at the refusal of his sacrifice, but because he objects to the irrational bloodlust of Abel's executing an innocent ram. Cain revels in his separation from God and nature and tells a grieving Eve, "What [earth] gave / You as her children she refuses now. / No we are not her children. We are men, / Beggars for food—because we think as men." In the figure of Cain, self-conscious man emerges in *Nobodaddy* as triumphant over the ghost-haunted Adam, who has sunk into silence, and over Abel, whom MacLeish presents as a kind of prototype of D. H. Lawrence, seeking to lose his self-consciousness in a bloody ritual that will reunite him with purely instinctive nature.

Although published before *Nobodaddy*, *The Pot of Earth* (1925) was written later, after the death of MacLeish's son, one of the most affecting tragedies of his Paris years. This poem reinterprets and presents in modern terms an Adonis myth from Sir James Frazer's *The Golden Bough*. In the myth plants forced to grow too rapidly soon die, just as a modern young woman's early pregnancy leads to her death. The originality of the concept is overwhelmed, however, by echoes of T. S. Eliot's work in the dramatic structure, in the verse forms, and especially in the language. The influence of both *The Waste Land* and "Gerontion" is evident in

Letter from MacLeish, 28 February 1979

these final lines: "Come. / I will show you chestnut branches budding / Beyond a dusty pane and a little grass / Green in a window-box and silence stirred, / Settling and stirred and settling in an empty room—."

MacLeish might at the time have been placed in the same tradition as T. S. Eliot on the basis of the poems collected in *Streets in the Moon* (1926). Even the wry satire "Corporate Entity," written in 1916, has similarities to Eliot's poem "Mr. Eliot's Sunday Morning Service," published later. The collection contains also two of

MacLeish's most frequently anthologized poems— "Ars Poetica" and "The End of the World." "Ars Poetica," ending "A poem should not mean / But be," has come to be widely regarded as a manifesto for the whole modernist movement, first in poetry such as Eliot's and Wallace Stevens's and then in the American New Criticism that stressed "the heresy of paraphrase." According to this doctrine poetry is not a form of logical discourse, but a special kind of knowledge that can be apprehended—like modernist painting—not as a representational image translatable into some kind of equivalent terms, but as a presentation in a unique language. The poem does not really describe MacLeish's own subsequent practice, however, for most of his poems stray from the principle of "Ars Poetica" by making philosophical and satirical points that can be paraphrased. Characteristic of his sensibility, for example, is "The End of the World," a macabre sonnet, which presents the world as a circus (a metaphor MacLeish used later in *J. B.*) and arrives at the startling conclusion, recalling the antitheology of *Nobodaddy*, that when "the top blew off" "there overhead" was "in the sudden blackness the black pall / Of nothing, nothing, nothing— nothing at all."

The high point of MacLeish's work abroad was a long poem that still remains one of his most controversial, *The Hamlet of A. MacLeish* (1928). Using the structure of Shakespeare's play about a son's uncertain relationship to his father's ghost as a framework for exploring his own relationship to his human ancestry, "MacLeish goes up the / Stair built by the ancestors," glossing his monologue with references to the action of the play to keep readers apprised of the double movement. MacLeish later explained the "rather preposterous idea" behind the work to Stanley Koehler: "We all live through a Hamlet-like experience. It was an attempt to take the. small pieces of that experience that I, in my early thirties, had had of the world . . . to take the Hamlet situation and move it out of Denmark, out of the palace, out of the whole feel of that late medieval mystery that hangs over it, move it into *now*, and see if the form—not the formula but the form—would hold the meaning." Reviewing rapacious human history as a dumb show, MacLeish's poetic persona recalls that the tribes of men "go on, thousands and thousands, / Taking the lands, killing the male, consuming / The fat earth. They live in the land. They are lords there." Asking "What is it that we have to do?," he wonders if he must "play the strong boy, spit in the world's face, shout / Whore! Ghoul! Harpy! at her. Call her Jakes. / Call her corpse-

eating planet, worm's gut." But he reflects, apparently in reaction to the jaded sophistication of the twenties, "We have learned the answers, all the answers: / It is the question that we do not know. / We are not wise," and decides, "We know what our fathers were but not who we are." Then he concludes, as do the survivors of the carnage at the end of Shakespeare's play, "It is time we should accept. . . ."

After MacLeish returned to the United States in 1928, two of his books were published in Paris by Harry and Caresse Crosby's Black Sun Press. The Crosbys had met the MacLeishes with Hemingway at Gstaad, Switzerland, in December 1926. Harry Crosby had already read and admired the poems in *Streets in the Moon*, published earlier that year, and despite their markedly different temperaments, Crosby and MacLeish became good friends. Although MacLeish had no patience with Crosby's "phony mysticism," he was a kind and objective critic of Crosby's poetry, and after Crosby's suicide in December 1929, he kept a death watch over Crosby's body in the morgue, at the request of Caresse Crosby.

The first of MacLeish's books to be published by the Black Sun Press was the first separate edition of his poem *Einstein* (1929), which had originally been included in *Streets in the Moon*. Another meditation with marginal glosses in the manner of *The Hamlet of A. MacLeish*, it also expresses MacLeish's doubts about modern man's wisdom. Published in a limited edition of 100 copies, *Einstein* is a somewhat satirical portrayal of the scientist who "can revolve in orbits opposite / The orbit of the earth and so refuse / All planetary converse." Although "He can count / Ocean in atoms and weigh out the air / In multiples of one and subdivide / Light to its numbers" in order to "Solve them to unity," "still the dark denies him. Still withstands / The dust his penetration and flings back / Himself to answer him."

In 1930, after Harry Crosby's death, Caresse Crosby published MacLeish's collection *New Found Land* in a limited edition of 110 copies. The trade edition, published later that year by Houghton Mifflin in Boston, was printed from the Black Sun plates. A number of the poems in this book had previously appeared in Eugene Jolas's Paris-based *transition*, one of the most influential international little magazines. MacLeish had contributed to *transition* since its inaugural issue appeared in April 1927, and Harry Crosby, who met Jolas in 1928, became an even more enthusiastic contributor and finally an associate editor before his death in December 1929. Among the *transition* poems that were included in *New Found Land* are "Tourist

Death," dedicated to Sylvia Beach, the first publisher of *Ulysses* (1922) and the proprietor of the Shakespeare and Company bookshop, and "Cinema of a Man," a highly personal tribute to Harry Crosby, which first appeared in the "In Memoriam: Harry Crosby" section of the June 1930 issue of *transition*.

MacLeish's own ambiguous feelings upon leaving France for Massachusetts color another poem in *New Found Land*, "American Letter," which is dedicated to expatriate artist Gerald Murphy, Fitzgerald's model for Dick Diver in *Tender Is the Night* (1934). The speaker is "sick for home for the red roofs and the olives, / And the foreign words and the smell of the sea fall," especially since "America is neither a land nor a people." Yet at last he resolves that "This, this is our land, this is our people, / This that is neither a land nor a race," and "Here we will live our years till the earth blind us."

MacLeish's growing traditionalism and seeming acceptance of things as they are were not popular with contemporary critics, especially those of a Marxist persuasion; and *The Hamlet of A. MacLeish* was viciously parodied as muddleheaded in Edmund Wilson's "The Omelet of A. MacLeish." MacLeish's reputation was not strengthened, either, with prophets of the collectivist millenium when Henry Luce called him away from his turkey farming to become one of the roving reporters for the new magazine *Fortune*, designed as an opulent tribute to American business.

While capitalism has never fulfilled (any more than any other system) the ambitious hopes that MacLeish expressed for it in "To the Young Men of Wall Street" (*Saturday Review of Literature*, 1932), he has outlasted his belittlers both as an artist and a public servant. Not driven abroad by a need to escape American philistinism, but going to Paris as a result of what he calls "a streak of incredible luck," he managed to avoid years of a demoralizing collapse of values at home, while flourishing in an atmosphere of creative freedom. He came back to this country, "in every possible sense," as he put it to Stanley Koehler, prepared to serve his country during a period that urgently needed both his boundless energies and his caustic, clear vision of man's follies which he offered both in his poems and plays and in his public service. —*Warren French*

References:

Signi Lenea Falk, *Archibald MacLeish* (New York: Twayne, 1965);

Stanley Koehler, "Conversation with A. MacLeish," *Pembroke Magazine*, no. 7 (1976): 95-108;

Edward J. Mullaly, *Archibald MacLeish A Checklist* (Kent, Ohio: Kent State University Press, 1973);

Grover Smith, *Archibald MacLeish* (Minneapolis: University of Minnesota Press, 1971);

Sanford J. Smoller, "Escape from the Shadow of Hamlet: Archibald MacLeish's Social and Political Writings," *Pembroke Magazine*, no. 7 (1976): 11-27;

Geoffrey Wolff, *Black Sun The Brief Transit and Violent Eclipse of Harry Crosby* (New York: Random House, 1976).

Papers:

There are collections of MacLeish's papers at the Library of Congress, in the Houghton Library at Harvard University, and in the Beinecke Library at Yale University.

NORMAN MACLEOD
(1 October 1906-   )

BOOKS: *Horizons of Death* (New York: Parnassus, 1934);

Thanksgiving Before November (New York: Parnassus, 1936);

You Get What You Ask For (New York: Harrison-Hilton, 1939);

We Thank You All the Time (Prairie City, Ill.: Decker, 1941);

The Bitter Roots (New York: Smith & Durrell, 1941);

A Man in Midpassage (Columbus, Ohio: Cronos, 1947);

Pure As Nowhere (Columbus, Ohio: Golden Goose, 1952);

The Selected Poems of Norman Macleod (Boise, Idaho: Ahsahta, 1975);

The Distance: New and Selected Poems (1928-1977) (Pembroke, N.C.: Pembroke Paperbacks, 1977).

Norman Wicklund Macleod, college professor, editor of literary magazines, poet, and novelist, was born in Salem, Oregon, and was raised in the western United States. His poetry and fiction are influenced by the cultural traditions and history of the Spanish and American Indian civilizations, the natural beauty and rugged life of the western frontier, his perceptions of urban despair, and his left-wing political interests. His style ranges from the lyrical realism of early works to Surrealism later. Macleod founded and edited a number of literary magazines between 1928 and 1978, and although he was only in Paris for a few months, as editor of the literary magazine *Morada* founded in late 1929, he developed strong ties with the expatriate literary community in Paris, corresponding with Kay Boyle, Robert McAlmon, and *transition*'s editor Eugene Jolas, among others.

Macleod first published poetry at the age of twelve in the Missoula, Montana, *Daily Missoulian* and the Salt Lake City, Utah, *Salt Lake Tribune*. He brought out his first literary magazine, *jackass*, in 1927 while attending the University of New Mexico. Later, while he was custodian of the Petrified Forest National Monument in Arizona, he contributed to *New Masses* and Harold Salemson's Paris little magazine, *Tambour*. When he returned to complete his degree at the University of New Mexico, he founded *Morada* (1929-1930), which Ezra Pound said was destined to become the next *Little Review*, the well-known literary magazine edited by Margaret Anderson and Jane Heap that folded in 1929. *Morada* lasted for only five issues, however. First published in Albuquerque, New Mexico, the magazine's final issue (December 1930) was published in Lago Di Garda, Italy.

When he began editing *Morada* in Albuquerque, Macleod corresponded with Harry Crosby of the Black Sun Press in Paris and received complimentary books of Crosby's poetry. After Crosby's suicide in December 1929, Macleod made the second number of *Morada* a special Harry Crosby issue, containing work by and about Crosby. Another connection to the American expatriate community came in the summer or fall of 1930 when Robert McAlmon visited Macleod on his way from Mexico City to New York and Paris. This meeting began a friendship that lasted until McAlmon's death.

Because of his activity in publishing avant-garde literature, Macleod was named American editor of *Front* in 1930. This short-lived magazine, published in The Hague, included work in French, German, and English, and its European editor was Sonja Prins of Amsterdam. *Front* lasted for four

Norman Macleod

Letter from Norman Macleod, 12 March 1979

issues and contained contributions by Ezra Pound, John Dos Passos, Dudley Fitts, Kay Boyle, Eugene Jolas, Robert McAlmon, William Carlos Williams, and others.

In June 1930 three of Macleod's poems appeared in the "Dream and Mythos" section of *transition* 19/20. Surrealist poets Andre Breton and Rene Crevel had already sent him books of their poems, and this issue of *transition* increased his interest in Surrealism. Macleod said later, "I was tremendously influenced, in what ways I don't exactly know, by the issue of *transition* edited by Eugene Jolas, an issue in which some of my work was included, a number that came out during the summer of 1930. . . . Crevel felt that Surrealism was a new method, a new approach to writing, in terms of reliance on the subconscious and free association and knowledge of a kind that was available in terms of magic and psychoanalysis—and that issue of *transition* also included an article by Jung—so I was liberated, I suppose, as a writer, by Surrealism to a certain extent, but I never consciously became a Surrealist."

Before he went to Paris in the spring of 1932, Macleod's work had also been published in other Paris-based literary magazines such as *Nouvel Age, Mercure de France, Monde, This Quarter*, and the *New Review*. His first published prose, "Blood of a Body," had appeared in the July-August-September 1931 issue of *This Quarter*, and his correspondence with Samuel Putnam had led to the acceptance of his prose poem "Communication for C.S." (to Catherine Stuart Macleod, his first wife) for the April 1932 issue of Putnam's *New Review*. While in Paris he met Edward Titus, editor of *This Quarter*, in addition to Andre Breton, whom he considered the leader of the aesthetic group of the Surrealists, and Rene Crevel, whom he regarded as the leader of the Surrealists' Communist faction.

Not long after his arrival in Paris, Macleod became involved in a "foolish" altercation with the French gendarmerie, was beaten up, and had a vertebra in his neck broken by a rabbit punch. He was jailed in solitary confinement for two weeks in the Maison D'Arret de la Sante before he was released through the help of the American consul and ordered to leave France. He had to hide from French authorities until the French section of the International Union of Revolutionary Writers collected enough money for his passage to Holland. Once in Amsterdam he served as a delegate to the World Congress Against War and Fascism, meeting in that city, and returned to New York in the fall of 1932 to work briefly for Harper & Brothers. In 1933 Macleod went to the Soviet Union, where he worked in the cultural department of the *Moscow Daily News*, but within three months, discouraged by events there, he returned to New York to work again for Harper's.

Macleod's first book of poetry, *Horizons of Death*, was published in 1934 and was followed by a second collection of poetry, *Thanksgiving Before November*, in 1936. His poetry ranges in subject from Indian and western life, city life, and socialism, to the very personal themes of life, love, promise, and despair. During this period Macleod maintained his ties with the expatriates in France, contributing three one-page stories to *365 Days* (1936), an anthology edited in France by Kay Boyle, Laurence Vail, and Nina Conarain.

In 1936 Macleod received his master's degree from Columbia University, and in 1939 he became founder and director of the New York City Poetry Center of the Young Men's Hebrew Association. Also in that year his first novel, *You Get What You Ask For*, was published. In 1940 he edited *Calendar*, an anthology of poems selected from those read by poets in a series at the Poetry Center. A second novel, *The Bitter Roots*, and a third collection of poetry, *We Thank You All the Time*, were published in 1941.

While teaching at the University of Maryland, Macleod founded the *Maryland Quarterly* in 1944. In 1945, when he went to teach at Briarcliff Junior College, he took this literary magazine with him, and it was renamed the *Briarcliff Quarterly*. The quarterly soon became well-known, especially for such special issues as the William Carlos Williams issue.

In 1947 another book of poetry, *A Man in Midpassage*, was published. Alfred Kreymborg wrote that this poetry "is not for readers who yearn for an evening's escape from the turmoils of this age, but for tough-minded beings who seek some measure of truth in what they read." *Pure As Nowhere*, his fifth book of poetry, appeared in 1952, and William Carlos Williams wrote that "Macleod's poetry reminds me of the desperate seriousness of Baudelaire. . . ." In 1975 *The Selected Poems of Norman Macleod* was published and was followed by *The Distance: New and Selected Poems (1928-1977)* (1977). R. C. Kenedy, a British critic, called one poem in *The Distance* "lines which, in my opinion, can vie with any written during the century."

Macleod's final years of teaching before his retirement in 1978 were spent at Pembroke State University, a branch of the University of North Carolina, as a teacher of poetry and creative writing. In 1969 he founded and edited *Pembroke Magazine*, which published its eleventh annual issue in 1979. Macleod now lives in Bay Minette, Alabama.

—*Victor P. Dalmas, Jr.*

Other:

Kay Boyle, Laurence Vail, and Nina Conarain, eds., *365 Days*, includes contributions by Macleod (London: Cape, 1936; New York: Harcourt, Brace, 1936);

Calendar, edited by Macleod (New York & Prairie City, Ill.: Decker, 1940).

Periodical Publications:

"Dreams" ["Twelve Knives," "Revenge of the Three Brothers," "Cacked"], *transition*, no. 19/20 (Summer 1930): 59-60;

"Blood of a Body," *This Quarter*, 4 (July-August-September 1931): 101-103;

"Communication for C.S.," *New Review*, 2 (April 1932);

"I Never Left Anything in Istanbul," *Pembroke Magazine*, 4 (1973): 37-45; 5 (1974): 35-62; 6 (1975): 53-64; 7 (1976): 149-162; 8 (1977): 71-82.

References:

R. C. Kenedy, "Distinguished and Faith-Permeated Oeuvre," review of *The Distance, Pembroke Magazine*, 10 (1978): 135-142;

Sanford Smoller, "Norman Macleod—'An Unforgetting Heart,'" *Pembroke Magazine*, 12 (forthcoming 1980).

Papers:

Macleod's papers are in the Beinecke Library at Yale University.

SHERRY MANGAN
(27 June 1904-24 June 1961)

BOOKS: *Cinderella Married* (New York: A. & C. Boni, 1932);

No Apology for Poetrie and Other Poems Written 1922-1931 (Boston: Bruce Humphries, 1934);

Salutation to Valediction (Boston: Bruce Humphries, 1938).

John Joseph Sherry Mangan was born in Lynn, Massachusetts. Under the name Sherry Mangan he launched successive careers as a little magazine editor, a novelist, a poet, a short-story writer, and a book designer prior to 1938. His first literary associates were mainly American expatriates in Paris during the mid-twenties, and the cultural life of that city was the most persistent influence on his intellectual development ever afterward. A number of Mangan's experimental prose writings were partly inspired by the techniques of the French Surrealists, and Mangan was responsible for introducing work by several Paris-based writers to the American public.

Between 1938 and 1948 Mangan was an internationally known journalist for *Time*, *Life*, and *Fortune*, and he frequently reported on cultural and political events in Paris. He was also a dedicated Marxist and in the last twenty-five years of his life an adherent of Leon Trotsky's ideas; he served on the leading bodies of the Fourth International, which

Houghton Library

Sherry Mangan

was headquartered in Paris from 1938 to 1940 and from 1945 to 1958. After World War II he drifted into literary obscurity and died penniless and alone in Rome.

Mangan graduated from Harvard with an honors degree in classics and first lived in Paris from 1925 to 1926. Through his college friends Virgil Thomson and Maurice Grosser he developed literary relationships with Robert McAlmon, Georges Hugnet, and Gertrude Stein. When Mangan returned to the United States, he sustained these ties through several ventures with little magazines. From February 1927 to June 1928 he edited the little magazine *larus: The Celestial Visitor*, and between 1930 and 1933 he assisted Richard Johns with *Pagany: A Native Quarterly*. Mangan's expatriate connections énabled these journals to bring to the United States Robert McAlmon's "The Revolving Mirror," Gertrude Stein's "Five Words in a Line," and other works from Paris by Georges Hugnet, Mary Butts, and Bernard Fay. Mangan's own critical writings in *Pagany* prompted Ezra Pound to publish a statement in the magazine saying that "In choosing

WALK DO NOT RUN

In my mind lives a small clever gentleman
—ah there, M.ʳ Schmidt! Listening, M.ʳ Schmidt?
When I count from one to one hundred
M.ʳ Schmidt waits patiently, and between
sixty-two and sixty-three M.ʳ
Schmidt murmurs: "Seventy-one."
Ho ho, M.ʳ Schmidt! Not yet, M.ʳ Schmidt.

Still, it's a pleasure having you. Try
some more prolans? a nicely grilled testicle?
Might I suggest some Lagrima Prostatæ 1930?
But I shouldn't recommend the cervelle brulée: it's
full of adrenalin today. But, my dear sir,
pray make yourself comfortable: my house is yours.

A way out.

—Sherry Mangan

Manuscript

. . . a critical spokesman I don't see that *Pagany* cd. have done better than accepting Mr. Mangan."

Mangan's poetry and fiction exhibited a remarkable versatility, but his difficulty in communicating a philosophic vision caused Virgil Thomson to describe him as "a sterile virtuoso." His novel *Cinderella Married* (1932) is a highly mannered social satire, stylistically imitative of Ronald Firbank. His collection *No Apology for Poetrie and Other Poems Written 1922-1931* (1934) was praised by many reviewers for its sophisticated irony, which stemmed from a combination of wit, erudition, and weltschmerz. In *Esquire, London Mercury,* and *Atlantic Monthly* Mangan published a series of short stories about his hometown which were traditional in form and Chekhovian in theme and characterization. But his fictional contributions to *Pagany,· New Directions, Black Mountain*

Review, and Peter Neagoe's anthology *Americans Abroad* showed the impact of Surrealism. French influences are most evident in "Enter in Grey; or, Breton en Bretagne," which Mangan called a "polyglot ebullition . . . about Breton and *l'amour et l'inconscient* and what not." This obscure story of a mysterious figure on a beach contains a number of symbolic references to the French neo-Thomist philosopher Jacques Maritain.

When Mangan moved to Paris for a second time, in the spring of 1938, he was a convinced Marxist and regarded himself as a revolutionary poet. He was active in organizing the French section of the International Federation of Independent Revolutionary Art, which was inspired by a manifesto written by Trotsky, Andre Breton, and Diego Rivera. Under the name Sean Niall he wrote the "Paris Letter" for the left-wing journal *Partisan Review* in the United States. There he provided unusual information about the French publication of works by Benjamin Peret and Nicholas Calas, and in great detail he described the literary conflicts among radical writers in Paris. Paris fell to the Nazis in June 1940, and Mangan used his position as a journalist to remain in the city. He aided the French Trotskyist underground until the Germans expelled him from France in August. His description of the occupation, "Paris Under the Swastika," was published in the 16 September 1940 issue of *Life* and received much notoriety.

In his last decade Mangan was self-employed as an editor and translator. He published stories and poems in *Arizona Quarterly*, *Harper's*, and *Essence*. A revolutionary novel he had researched in Bolivia, about the struggles of the tin miners, was nearly completed at the time of his death in 1961.

—*Alan Wald*

Other:

"Enter in Grey; or, Breton en Bretagne," *Pagany*, 1 (October-December 1930): 24-30;

"Spot Dance," in *Americans Abroad An Anthology*, ed. Peter Neagoe (The Hague: Servire, 1932), pp. 263-269;

Frederick Lang, *Maritime*, edited by Mangan as Terence Phelan (New York: Pioneer, 1943);

Wolfgang Amadeus Mozart, *Idomeneum, King of Crete*, verse libretto translated by Mangan, New York, Juilliard Opera Company, 1955.

References:

Stephen Halpert and Richard Johns, eds., *A Return to Pagany* (Boston: Beacon, 1967);

Virgil Thomson, *Virgil Thomson* (New York: Knopf, 1966);

Alan Wald, "Introduction to 'Snow' by Sherry Mangan," *Michigan Quarterly Review*, 17 (Summer 1978): 273-277;

Wald, "The Pilgrimage of Sherry Mangan: From Aesthete to Revolutionary Socialist," *Pembroke Magazine*, no. 8 (1977): 85-99.

Papers:

The Houghton Library at Harvard University contains an extensive collection of Mangan's papers with an emphasis on his journalistic and political activities after 1940.

Robert McAlmon

Robert K. Martin
Concordia University
Ruth L. Strickland
University of South Carolina

BIRTH: Clifton, Kansas, 9 March 1896, to Bess Urquhart and John Alexander McAlmon.

EDUCATION: University of Minnesota, 1916; University of Southern California, 1917-1920.

MARRIAGE: 14 February 1921 to Annie Winifred Ellerman (Bryher), divorced.

DEATH: Hot Springs, California, 2 February 1956.

BOOKS: *Explorations* (London: Egoist Press, 1921);
A Hasty Bunch (Paris: Contact Editions, 1922; Carbondale & Edwardsville: Southern Illinois University Press, 1977);
A Companion Volume (Paris: Contact Editions, 1923);
Post-Adolescence (Paris: Contact Editions, 1923);
Village: as it happened through a fifteen year period (Paris: Contact Editions, 1924);
Distinguished Air (Grim Fairy Tales) (Paris: Three Mountains Press, 1925); enlarged as *There Was a Rustle of Black Silk Stockings* (New York: Belmont, 1963);
The Portrait of a Generation, Including the Revolving Mirror (Paris: Contact Editions, 1926);
North America Continent of Conjecture (Paris: Contact Editions, 1929);
Indefinite Huntress and Other Stories (Paris: Crosby Continental Editions, 1932);
Not Alone Lost (Norfolk, Conn.: New Directions, 1937);
Being Geniuses Together An Autobiography (London: Secker & Warburg, 1938); republished as *Being Geniuses Together 1920-1930*, revised with additional material by Kay Boyle (Garden City: Doubleday, 1968; London: Joseph, 1970);
McAlmon and the Lost Generation A Self-Portrait, ed. Robert E. Knoll (Lincoln: University of Nebraska Press, 1962).

In many ways Robert McAlmon was one of the best representatives of his time. He came to Paris in 1921 with little French and no particular interest in French culture; he spent most of his productive years in Paris, but he remained always an American writer, pursuing American themes, depicting American landscapes, and insisting on an American vernacular. While McAlmon's works have never received widespread critical or popular acclaim, his importance to the literary life of the twenties cannot be ignored. He was a writer, a publisher, and a friend to many writers and artists whose reputations have greatly eclipsed his. Not only was he a member and financial supporter of the "lost generation," but his life and works almost define the term.

Robert Menzies McAlmon was born in Clifton, Kansas, to the Reverend Mr. John Alexander McAlmon and Bess Urquhart McAlmon. McAlmon was the youngest of ten children, and his early years were nomadic and rather impoverished. His father was a Presbyterian minister who moved his family to a succession of small towns in South Dakota and later to Minneapolis. McAlmon was graduated from high school in 1912 at the age of sixteen; for the next four years he worked at a number of menial jobs from which he gained impressions and situations for his later short stories. In 1916 he attended the University of Minnesota for one semester but moved with his family to Los Angeles in January 1917 and enrolled at the University of Southern California, which he attended sporadically until the winter of 1920. In 1918 McAlmon joined the air force, but he only got as far as San Diego, where he helped edit a camp newspaper. After his return to Los Angeles, he edited a magazine about flying, the *Ace*, during the winter of 1918-1919. He was an indifferent, rebellious student, but by the time he left college he was writing prose and verse seriously. In March 1919 his first six poems, with his flying experiences as subject matter, appeared in Harriet Monroe's *Poetry*. He also began a correspondence with Emanuel Carnevali, a young Italian poet who served as associate editor for *Poetry* from October 1919 to March 1920. In 1920 McAlmon dropped out of college and left Los Angeles for Chicago. This move turned out to be the beginning of a lifetime journey in search of ever-elusive recognition.

While in Chicago McAlmon met Carnevali, who was at the time confined to a private sanatorium. Carnevali knew and admired Sherwood Anderson and Carl Sandburg; McAlmon did not share his admiration. Chicago was a disappointment to him, and he soon left for Greenwich Village. In New York McAlmon came in contact with many writers and artists who later influenced both his life and his work.

The most important friend he made in New York was William Carlos Williams, who became McAlmon's collaborator as well as his most faithful and generous friend and critic. Their close friendship lasted thirty years, and Williams always persisted in trying to find an audience and an American publisher for McAlmon. The painter Marsden Hartley had discovered McAlmon while McAlmon was working as a nude model for art classes at Cooper Union and had introduced him to Williams, Lola Ridge, Marianne Moore, Djuna Barnes, and H. D. (Hilda Doolittle). McAlmon later used these experiences and newfound friends in New York as the basis for his novel *Post-Adolescence* (1923).

Soon after their first meeting, Williams and McAlmon decided to establish a little magazine, called *Contact* because they aimed at "the essential contact between words and the locality that breeds them." This insistence on the American experience became characteristic of both men's work. Four issues of *Contact* appeared in 1920 and 1921; one last issue appeared in June 1923. Though it had a short life, *Contact* published poetry and criticism by several writers who became leaders on the American literary scene: Ezra Pound, Wallace Stevens, Marianne Moore, H. D., Kay Boyle, Glenway Wescott, and Marsden Hartley.

Another important person who entered McAlmon's life in 1920 was Winifred Ellerman, an English poet and novelist who wrote under the name Bryher. Bryher was the frequent companion of H. D. and the author of an autobiographical novel, *Development* (1920), with a foreword by Amy Lowell. Bryher was the daughter of Sir John Ellerman, a wealthy British shipping magnate. She and McAlmon were married within a few months of their first meeting. The reasons for the marriage, as well as its exact nature, remain uncertain. McAlmon's critics have claimed that he married her for her money; others have suggested it was a marriage of convenience to conceal homosexuality on the part of both partners. Bryher's recollection was that it was an arranged marriage which would enable her to escape from her oppressive family; she maintained that McAlmon fully understood that they were to lead separate lives. McAlmon, in his memoirs, wrote that he "had married a girl under her writing name" and had no knowledge of her wealth; in a 1921 letter to Williams, however, McAlmon described his marriage as a "proposition" made to

him by Bryher, a marriage that was "legal only, unromantic, and strictly an agreement." Whatever the reasons for the marriage, McAlmon and Bryher spent little time together except for brief visits to her family in England. The Ellerman money provided McAlmon an escape from the United States and the opportunity to travel. More importantly, the allowance at his disposal enabled him to publish his own work and the work of others who were unable to find publishers in America.

After a short visit with the Ellermans in London (and after arranging with Harriet Weaver for publication of a book of poems, *Explorations*),

Sylvia Beach Collection

Robert McAlmon
at Shakespeare and Company

McAlmon proceeded to Paris in the spring of 1921. He soon met Sylvia Beach, proprietor of the bookshop Shakespeare and Company, as well as James Joyce and Ezra Pound. He also renewed his Greenwich Village connections with Djuna Barnes, Alfred and Dorothy Kreymborg, and Harold Loeb, as well as his London friendship with Wyndham Lewis. At this time McAlmon collected the stories for his first volume of short stories, but an English printer was offended by the stories and refused to print them. Joyce, however, liked the stories, found the language racy, and thought them reminiscent in attitude of the stories in his own book *Dubliners* (1914). It was Joyce who provided the title, *A Hasty Bunch*, referring perhaps to the speed and haphazard quality with which they were written. Encouraged by Joyce's enthusiasm, McAlmon decided to go ahead with the volume and published it at his own expense. It was printed by Maurice Darantiere, the printer of *Ulysses* (1922), at Dijon. *A Hasty Bunch* probably came off the presses in early 1922. Although it bears no publisher's imprint, it is, in effect, the first publication of McAlmon's Contact Publishing Company, officially established in 1923.

One of the finest stories in the collection is "Sing the Baby to Sleep, Marietta," although it is not completely representative of McAlmon's work because, as Kay Boyle would later point out, it contains the "fancy writing" which McAlmon later abjured. He uses the landscape to create character and atmosphere in a Mexican-American town, located somewhere in the American Southwest. Marietta and Mathilde are drawn together in a combined bond of love and hate, linked by Marietta's husband Jose. After Mathilde is killed by her ex-husband, Jose "stood by the bedside, his heart cold with anguish, not because he had loved Mathilde but because her face, palely shining beneath his eyes, was freezing forever into his soul an image of what he wished she might have been." The sharp directness of focus and the pervasive sense of frustration and despair are characteristic of McAlmon's writing at its best.

Another important story in the volume is "A Boy's Discovery." Like stories by his contemporaries Anderson and Hemingway, this early story depicts a painful initiation. Harry, the "sissy," is "a frail slender-limbed lad" who is too delicate to take part in the games of other boys. His best friend is Harold, a boy who also appears delicate but who "was able to take care of himself." The closeness of the boys' names suggests that they are two aspects of the same person, and McAlmon writes that they are so close that they seem "brothers, perhaps twins." Harold is the more masculine of the two and more aware of the sexual life that surrounds them in the country. Harry's hope for lasting love ("You and I will have to be together always") is not reciprocated by Harold, for whom Harry is merely "somebody that needed to be taken care of." Harold introduces Harry to "the act of breeding" on the stud farm and later initiates sexual experiments with several girls. These experiences confirm Harold's passage into manhood. Harry, however, dies of lockjaw, his illness suggesting his sexual inadequacy. McAlmon seems to suggest a Freudian interpretation: Harry,

A Hasty Bunch

Robert Mc Almon

Title page

the child in latency, must die in order for Harold, his alter ego, to emerge as a man.

Other stories in the collection, such as "Backslider," draw upon McAlmon's past as the son of a minister. Dr. Johnson, a "wildfire evangelist," comes to Mervale and converts 1,400 out of the town's 5,000 inhabitants. Six months after he leaves, Jake Murray and Gert Northrup, two of the more difficult sinners, revert to their preconversion behavior. Another story, "Filling the Pulpit," depicts the pettiness of a small town congregation in choosing a minister. McAlmon's best writing emerges in these stories based largely on his own recollections of childhood and of the American Midwest. Less successful are the pensive, autobiographical stories, such as "Light Woven Into Wavespray" and "The Baby of the Family," in which the main character, while trying to be cynical, reveals his confusion about the meaning of life. McAlmon also drew from his experiences as an artists' model in his story of an "ineffective" artist, Ronald Wallace, in "From Maine" and in his portrait of the jaded Raymond in "The Futility of Energy." The last section of the volume is entitled "Momentary Essays" and consists of brief, self-conscious sketches of McAlmon's attitudes and concerns.

When *A Hasty Bunch* was published, it provoked a mixed reaction. Pound's review for the *Dial* noted that McAlmon showed "little skill" but praised him nonetheless for showing the American small town "in hard and just light." William Carlos Williams praised his "accuracy of observation," but added a significant warning: "do not remain in Europe so long that you will allow America to slip away from you." Highest praise came from Katherine Mansfield, who called the stories "quite extraordinarily good" and admired their "fresh and unspoiled" quality. It was a promising start, but it was a promise not to be fulfilled.

In the summer of 1921 McAlmon traveled from Paris to Berlin, where he saw Marsden Hartley, whom he used as the basis for several characters in his fiction. The Berlin of that summer is reflected in McAlmon's book of three stories, *Distinguished Air (Grim Fairy Tales)* (1925). During this time McAlmon had begun subsidizing Joyce with generous gifts of cash. This generosity was not unusual in McAlmon; he contributed financially to the support of several writers, artists, and musicians. In addition to his financial support of Joyce, McAlmon had earlier helped Joyce by typing the "Penelope" section of *Ulysses*; unfortunately he grew tired of trying to read Joyce's many insertions and began to revise the manuscript gratuitously, a service for which Joyce was not grateful. While McAlmon admired Joyce's erudition and wit, he was not impressed with the elaborate structure or abstract diction of *Ulysses*.

In 1922 McAlmon published only one poem, "Blackbird," which appeared in the February issue of *Bookman*. Instead of writing, he broadened his circle of acquaintances and led an increasingly active social life. He began to frequent the Boeuf sur le Toit, an avant-garde cabaret opened by Jean Cocteau and other artists, and to socialize with the French writer Ramon Radiguet. By the end of 1922 McAlmon was firmly established in the Paris expatriate world.

In 1923 McAlmon received a gift of $70,000 from Sir John Ellerman. This, an enormous sum at the time, permitted him to establish the Contact Publishing Company. This venture alone insures McAlmon a significant place in American literary history. During its first year of operation McAlmon's company published two of his own books, *A Companion Volume*, a group of short stories to follow *A Hasty Bunch*, and *Post-Adolescence*, his autobiographical novel based on his Greenwich

Village friends and experiences, as well as *Two Selves* by Bryher, *Lunar Baedecker* by Mina Loy, *Twenty-five Poems* by Marsden Hartley, *Spring and All* by William Carlos Williams, and *Three Stories & Ten Poems* by Ernest Hemingway.

McAlmon's two books of that year were the first to bear the Contact Publishing Company imprint. *A Companion Volume* was set largely in mid-America again, and the stories were full of the American raw reality that McAlmon saw as the neglected ingredient in American fiction. Like *A Hasty Bunch*, the volume contains stories that are largely autobiographical, based on McAlmon's youth. Some of the stories in this volume are superior to his earlier stories, but the lack of rewriting, sloppy diction, and inconsistency of quality found in all of McAlmon's work were present in this book also. One long story of the Midwest, "Putting a Town on the Map," deals with two young businessmen who find themselves caught in an ambivalent relationship with the townspeople. On the one hand they manipulate them in order to increase their profits, but on the other they must give the appearance of honesty to keep their customers satisfied. The story is handled with candor; McAlmon does not resort to caricature to make a point. The young businessmen are not villains, nor are the townspeople innocent victims. Perhaps the best story in the collection is "Evening on the Riviera," a story about Tootles, a rich sixty-year-old widow who is surrounded by decadent young men trying to exploit her. Tootles is pathetic, funny, and disgusting all at the same time. Most of the characters in these stories meander through life with no direction; they are presented as they are without glamour or romance.

Post-Adolescence was really the first book McAlmon wrote. It is the most autobiographical of his books. Peter, the central character, is clearly McAlmon. William Carlos Williams calls the book "a *journal intime*," and it is obviously written with youthful exuberance. Like McAlmon's other works, *Post-Adolescence* is essentially plotless, describing Peter's wanderings around Greenwich Village. The use of McAlmon's friends and acquaintances is quite clear; Edna St. Vincent Millay appears as Vere St. Vitus, Marianne Moore as Martha Wallus, and William Carlos Williams as Jim Boyle. Although the book could have been improved with revision, it still merits more critical attention than it has received.

McAlmon met Ernest Hemingway in February 1923 at Rapallo, where Ezra Pound was living. Hemingway and McAlmon shared a similar background and appreciation for realism in literature. At their first meeting they began a tentative friendship, and McAlmon agreed to publish Hemingway's stories and poems, though he found · "My Old Man" imitative of Sherwood Anderson's "I'm a Fool." Later that spring McAlmon and Hemingway went to Spain to see the bullfights, Hemingway's trip financed largely by McAlmon. During this trip the two men found their personalities incompatible. Hemingway saw McAlmon as lacking in manly qualities, and McAlmon doubted the sincerity of Hemingway's enthusiasm for bullfighting. In later years this fragile friendship turned to bitter enmity. Hemingway summed McAlmon up cruelly, but neatly: "Amusements and occupation drinking, night life and gossip. Writes. Travels about."

Contact Publishing Company announced in its first preview: "We will bring out books by various writers who seem not likely to be published by other publishers, for commercial or legislative reasons." Contact's first publications were chosen because "they are written" and because "we like them well enough to get them out." Three hundred copies of each book were printed, and most were sent to Sylvia Beach's Shakespeare and Company for distribution. This system was not satisfactory, however, and in late 1923 McAlmon went to William Bird, who had been printing books by hand for a year at his Three Mountains Press. McAlmon and Bird agreed to join forces for the purposes of distribution, and in 1924 they published a prospectus headed "Contact Editions, including books printed at the Three Mountains Press," which included the publications of both firms. This association lasted until 1926 when Bird sold his press to Nancy Cunard.

In the summer of 1924 McAlmon began sending his completed manuscript, *Village*, to American publishers. As he expected, it was rejected, and he decided to publish it himself in the fall. When *Village: as it happened through a fifteen year period* appeared in the late fall of 1924, it received a more favorable response than any other book McAlmon wrote. Ford Madox Ford printed a portion of the novel in *transatlantic review*, and Ethel Moorhead in *This Quarter* wrote admiringly of its form and language. Walter Yost of the *New York Evening Post* found the author's prose "unliterary and as direct as an invoice." Hemingway thought the book "absolutely first-rate," and even Gertrude Stein found it realistic and pleasing.

McAlmon's prose epic of the village of Wentworth is constructed around a series of portraits. This montage technique presents a small town in its relentless monotony, a sort of prison for its inhabitants. No one character dominates, the novel is again essentially plotless, and the scenes fade into one another. What holds it together is its sense of pervasive oppressiveness. It is more somber than McAlmon's earlier works, lacking humor and suffering from general disillusion. The youthful exuberance is gone. While *Village* may be McAlmon's most ambitious work, the sense of the characters' futility and the bleakness of the themes limit the novel's power. Again, the work could have benefited from revision.

In May 1923 McAlmon had met Gertrude Stein, with whom he was fairly unimpressed. He did, however, admire "Melanctha," the second section of her novel *Three Lives* (1909), and he agreed to publish her voluminous *The Making of Americans*. After differences over contracts, free copies, subscriptions, money, and distribution, the book came out in 1925 as a Contact Edition. The book did not sell well, and McAlmon asked for a compensatory payment from Stein. She refused, and he was left to pay a huge printing bill. This affair led to vilifying attacks on Stein by McAlmon for several years. In turn, she says in *The Autobiography of Alice B. Toklas* (1933) that she found his writing dull.

The year 1925 also saw the publication of McAlmon's three stories, *Distinguished Air (Grim Fairy Tales)*, by Three Mountains Press. Hand-printed by Bird, it was published in an edition of only 115 copies and is now rare. These stories emerged from McAlmon's nightlife experiences in Berlin. The first story, "Distinguished Air," McAlmon's favorite, deals with an evening spent in a nightclub which is patronized by male homosexuals. Foster Graham is a homosexual with an air of distinction, but even for him life has become too much. The second story, "Miss Knight," was admired by Joyce and Pound and was translated and published in French at Joyce's suggestion. Miss Knight is a male homosexual who possesses only female instincts. The third story, "The Lodging House," presents joyless heterosexual relationships, aided by cocaine and whiskey. All three stories present a world void of love and joy—a world of complete abandon where nothing permanent remains except despair.

Ernest Walsh, coeditor of *This Quarter*, reviewed McAlmon's *Distinguished Air* in the summer of 1925, saying that the stories are "about Lesbians male and female." He continues, "They ought to be disgusting to the average reader, but they remain comic. . . . McAlmon never writes disgusting books. . . . He doesn't exclude anything from his world and is like Walt Whitman in his completeness. . . ." Walsh goes on to write that McAlmon does not apologize or explain; he simply observes. His objectivity, according to Walsh, turns the stories into art. The characters and the world which they inhabit are sharp and clear. *Distinguished Air* may, in fact, be McAlmon's best book. His treatment of a subject often discussed but seldom presented with honesty best demonstrates his directness, his coolness, and his insistence on the real experience.

In the same year McAlmon brought out an anthology of avant-garde writing, the *Contact Collection of Contemporary Writers*, containing works by Djuna Barnes, Bryher, Mary Butts, Norman Douglas, Havelock Ellis, Ford Madox Ford, Wallace Gould, Hemingway, Marsden Hartley, H. D., John Herrmann, Joyce, Mina Loy, Pound, Dorothy Richardson, May Sinclair, Edith Sitwell, Gertrude Stein, and Williams. It also included McAlmon's "Spring Leaves to Consider." The

Robert McAlmon in France, 1925

Sylvia Beach Collection

volume offers an ample variety of the writing of the period, with emphasis on McAlmon's own Paris circle.

Though McAlmon spent most of his time with other American expatriates, he was also aware of the French Dadaists and Surrealists he professed to scorn. When Williams visited him and wanted to meet French writers and artists, McAlmon claimed to know very few, but he took Williams to a dinner party where they both enjoyed Valery Larbaud's "quick and responsive" intellect. McAlmon also socialized with a number of French writers and artists, including Jean Cocteau, Jacques Riqaut, Ramon Radiquet, Louis Aragon, Rene Crevel, and Marcel Duchamp. His American and British friends included *Little Review* editor Jane Heap, artists Clotilde and Laurence Vail, poet Nancy Cunard, artist and photographer Man Ray, poet Mina Loy, and novelist Djuna Barnes. McAlmon's ability to drink, dance, and talk was almost incredible; occasionally, he had to leave Paris to recover his health and his sanity. According to Sylvia Beach, any bar or cafe McAlmon frequented soon became the central meeting place for "The Crowd." McAlmon was seldom alone but frequently lonely. One of his few close relationships was with Nancy Cunard, who appears more than once in his poetry.

McAlmon had not abandoned his poetry. In 1926 he published a collection of poems, *The Portrait of a Generation, Including the Revolving Mirror*. Many of them are imagistic lyrics drawing on his life in Paris. The volume consists of two parts: "The Revolving Mirror," a long poem, and a collection of shorter lyrics. Bryher reviewed the work in *Poetry*, claiming that it embodies the values and ideas of McAlmon's generation. She also observed his use of a cinematic technique and called it "the biography of two continents." "The Revolving Mirror" consists largely of quickly presented images or overheard scraps of conversation. There is a deliberate air of randomness to it, intentionally suggesting the chaotic nature of experience. It is a poem made up of different voices, most of them identifiable members of McAlmon's personal world, including his in-laws, Cunard, and Joyce. Ethel Moorhead observed that in this volume McAlmon is "mostly the clever cynical observer" and that his experiment "lacks self-assurance and self-confidence." *The Portrait of a Generation* was McAlmon's first book to be reviewed in a popular American literary journal. In the *Saturday Review of Literature* William Rose Benet denounced the book for its pessimism and confused style. Essentially he found it "excessively tiring." This review did nothing to aid McAlmon in his search for an American publisher.

Paris no longer seemed to have a hold on McAlmon. He was increasingly drawn back to his American material, which had always furnished the basis for his best work. In 1926 he finished *North America Continent of Conjecture*, a 1,200-line epic of the United States, not published until 1929. Perhaps seeking new sources of inspiration, he returned to the United States and traveled to New Mexico. Like his contemporaries D. H. Lawrence and Marsden Hartley, he had particularly admired the Indians of the American Southwest, who were frequently idealized as primitivistic ithyphallic gods of masculine energy. McAlmon's trip to New Mexico in 1927 was a great disappointment to him. He hated the artists' colonies that had been established there and thought he saw his primitive paradise despoiled. He was full of scorn for what he termed the "lavender preciosities" of the artists who had settled there. He left New Mexico and went to New York, where he quickly felt at home because of the many veterans of Montparnasse now living there. He renewed his ties with Williams, met Wallace Stevens, saw Ford Madox Ford, and socialized with Marcel Duchamp and Man Ray. Although he enjoyed New York, McAlmon ·still preferred the less hectic life of Europe. Since he had ended his marriage to Bryher before leaving Paris in 1926 and had received a generous settlement from Sir John Ellerman, he felt ready to return to Paris unencumbered and refreshed.

In spite of his opportunities for a freer life, McAlmon had begun to allow his bitterness and jealousy over his lack of a popular acceptance to interfere in new and old friendships. He had met F. Scott Fitzgerald in 1925, and the two disliked each other at once. In 1926-1927 McAlmon severed all ties with Wyndham Lewis and Hemingway. He was disappointed in his meeting with Wallace Stevens, claiming that Stevens "looked and acted like P. Wyndham Lewis." In 1927, however, he began one friendship which never wavered. McAlmon had met Kay Boyle briefly in 1923, but in 1927 he visited her and Ethel Moorhead in Monte Carlo, carrying with him the typescript of "Deracinated Encounters" for *This Quarter*. Boyle and Moorhead were involved in an ambivalent, painful relationship, for both had loved Ernest Walsh, who had died in October 1926. Kay Boyle and her daughter by Walsh were living with Moorhead when McAlmon visited. He sensed the tension between the two women and offered Boyle financial assistance so that she could leave Monte Carlo and begin a new life. She had long admired McAlmon's work and had agreed with Walsh that McAlmon was one of the best writers of his generation. She accepted his offer of assistance, and thus began a loyal friendship that survived McAlmon's death.

In 1927 *transition*, edited by Eugene Jolas and Elliot Paul, made its first appearance. It was a magazine devoted to experimental literature and art, and McAlmon considered it "a constant example of how not to write." In spite of his disdain, an excerpt from McAlmon's novel "Transcontinental" appeared in the August 1927 number. McAlmon felt, as he confided to Kay Boyle, that the editors included him along with Joyce and Andre Breton and the Surrealists "just to show how bad my writing was." Wanting to disprove this theory, Boyle submitted some of McAlmon's poems to Jolas under the name of Guy Urquhart (McAlmon's mother's maiden name), calling him an unknown young Midwestern poet. Jolas published "The Silver Bull" in the summer of 1928, but when he learned of the deception he was furious. However, in later issues Jolas published two of McAlmon's stories of his childhood and ·his critique of Joyce's *Work in Progress*, later called *Finnegans Wake* (1939).

McAlmon's heavy drinking increased, and he began to write less in the fall of 1927. Sylvia Beach wrote Williams of her concern, but McAlmon appreciated no interference from his friends. In *Time and Western Man*, published that September, Wyndham Lewis wrote savage attacks on Walsh, McAlmon, Boyle, and Carnevali. He calls Walsh an "ideal fool" and especially derides Walsh's great admiration for McAlmon; it was Walsh, after all, who had ranked McAlmon with the likes of Charles Dickens, Joseph Conrad, and William Shakespeare. Lewis's final analysis of McAlmon was that he was a "true primitive," omitting any positive connotations in the term.

In 1928 McAlmon announced to Boyle that "The good days of the Quarter were finished." Few were left from McAlmon's old crowd, and many of his erstwhile friends were now enemies. Rich American tourists were flooding Paris, and their tastes were reflected in the new kinds of bars that appeared. The old fashionable ennui had become permeated with despair, and McAlmon wandered from bar to bar always looking for someone. He became more and more aggressive when he drank, and his friends found him less enjoyable as a social partner. McAlmon published little new material except for a few extracts from works in progress and reprints in avant-garde literary magazines. His reputation was, however, secure enough for him to be the object of two parodies created by a group of repatriated American writers in New York, including Matthew Josephson, Malcolm Cowley, Kenneth Burke, Robert Coates, and Slater Brown, who had contributed a section called "New York: 1928" to an American number of *transition*. The "Occasional Poems" appeared along with "Silver Bull" in the Summer 1928 issue of *transition*:

After Heine

I dreamt that I was Pound himself,
Whom heavenly joy immerses,
And Ten McAlmons sat about
And praised my verses.

Wanton Prejudice

I'd rather live in Oregon and pack salmon
Than live in Nice and write like Robert
McAlmon.

In the fall of 1928 *transition* sent a questionnaire to a number of expatriates in Paris, allowing them to answer the lampoons aimed at them by their countrymen. McAlmon, identifying himself as one of the "deracinated ones," answered that he preferred to live in Europe because "there is less interference with private life here." His vision of himself "in relation to 20th century reality" was "one of remaining myself, or hoping to." Additionally he denied that he saw a revolutionary spirit of any kind in his age; he saw instead conformity and submission.

In 1929 the Contact Publishing Company brought out its last books under McAlmon's direction: Edwin Lanham's *Sailors Don't Care*; *Quaint Tales of the Samurai* by Saikaku Ibara, translated by Ken Sato; and *North America Continent of Conjecture* by McAlmon. *North America* was not particularly well-received. Harriet Monroe criticized its "indiscriminate selection [and] careless understanding." Louis Zukofsky, however, praised the poem as a paradigm of "objectivist" writing and included it with *The Waste Land*, *Spring and All*, and *Harmonium* as "works absolutely necessary to students of poetry." Only 310 copies were printed, and few students of poetry had an opportunity to study it. *North America* is an attempt to define McAlmon's world. Like earlier poems, it is a sort of epic in which McAlmon attempts to present the whole community and its characteristics. Much of the poem seems to be "dressed-up prose," and it, too, suffers from a lack of revision. McAlmon continued to like the poem, and Boyle found it original and potentially influential. *North America*, with its woodcuts by American artist Hilaire Hiler, was the last book McAlmon published

himself, and it was not printed by Darantiere. Instead he sent it to *transition* magazine's printer, Andre Brulliard of Saint-Dizier. In mid-1929 McAlmon closed Contact Publishing Company and left France.

He traveled to Albuquerque, New York, and Mexico City. He found Guadalajara and Sonora, Mexican towns similar to his European retreats, ideal places to work and play; he remained in Mexico for eight months. The rejection slips that continued to pour in depressed him, and he returned to Europe. Williams and Nathanael West resurrected *Contact* magazine in New York and included McAlmon's "It's All Very Complicated" in their first issue (February 1932) and his "Mexican Interval" in the second (May 1932).

In 1932, at Boyle's continued suggestion, Caresse Crosby at the Black Sun Press published McAlmon's *Indefinite Huntress and Other Stories*, a volume containing seven stories, as one of Crosby's new paperback series, the Crosby Continental Editions. The title story is about the bored and empty life of Lily, who suffers from a "despair about action." She leaves behind her friend Helga and becomes involved with a beautiful young boy, Dionisio Granger, and a man, Red Neill, whom she eventually marries. Neill is as moved by Dionisio's beauty as Lily is. After Red's death, Lily feels torn by her feelings for her dead husband, the boy, and her stallion. She eventually decides to return to Helga, for "Helga meant a release into a human relationship." She hopes to find completion and rest with Helga. One of McAlmon's best stories, "The Indefinite Huntress" has sharp, clear characterization, and the rural background is realistic and not oversimplified.

Another important story in this collection is "Green Grow the Grasses." Its subject is the need for passion and the defeat of spontaneity and the instincts. The story is set on the Dakota prairies and tells of two lovers, Antoine and Enid. The narrator tells of their instinctive life, characterized by a naturalness he does not see elsewhere. However, Antoine's prospects are destroyed after he must serve a term in jail, and Enid eventually dies of overwork. A callous world has defeated them, and only a memory of their spontaneity remains for the unsentimental narrator.

A third story, "Mexican Interval," is thinly disguised autobiography. The main character, Kit, goes to a village in Mexico seeking a better world than he has. He sees the spontaneity of the Mexicans and Indians as a quality he lacks and envies. After he watches their rituals more carefully, however, he realizes he has romanticized their lives and finds their world no better than his. The primitive world has its disadvantages also, and Kit's resignation and acceptance are matched in the other stories of the volume. McAlmon's youthful rebellion has faded somewhat into a stoic realization of what the world has to offer. His spirit is not gone, but the vigor of youth is absent. In these stories, too, McAlmon for the first time includes mythological themes and classical references, though with an ironical tone.

In 1938 McAlmon's memoirs, *Being Geniuses Together*, which he had completed in 1934, were published by the London firm of Secker and Warburg. The original manuscript had been greatly edited, and many passages were deleted because the publishers feared prosecution for libel or obscenity. The book did not cause the furor and controversy that McAlmon seems to have hoped for, though several of McAlmon's friends and enemies felt they were unjustly portrayed. In addition to character sketches of many of the famous writers and artists of the twenties, however filled with lapses of memory, a vivid portrait of McAlmon with all his charm and his contradictions emerges. In 1968 Kay Boyle edited the original manuscript and added her own autobiographical interchapters, which describe her early French experiences. Often she provides another perspective on people and events described by McAlmon. When Doubleday published the book in 1968 it was the third of McAlmon's books to be published in the United States. At the urging of William Carlos Williams New Directions had published a volume of McAlmon's poetry, *Not Alone Lost*, in 1937, and in 1963 an expanded version of *Distinguished Air* had been published in New York as an inexpensive paperback under the title *There Was a Rustle of Black Silk Stockings*. McAlmon died, embittered and virtually forgotten, in Desert Hot Springs, California, on 2 February. 1956. He had never achieved the American acceptance he scorned and so greatly desired.

Since McAlmon's death there have been several attempts to revive interest in his work, but almost all claims made for him have to be tempered with the recognition of his weaknesses. Most of his readers have agreed that he is a writer who never realized his own potential. McAlmon's greatest strength was his "Americanness," and he was at his best when he attempted to capture the life he had known in the Dakotas and the Southwest. His own language, although flawed, is capable of evoking the sounds and patterns of American speech. Had McAlmon worked at perfecting this aspect of his style, he might have approached the stature of Sherwood Anderson

or even Hemingway. But McAlmon refused to revise, and his work is marred by a consequent inconsistency of tone and quality. He wanted no artificiality in his prose, but he refused to consider that revision does not necessarily destroy naturalness.

Whatever the fate of McAlmon's literary reputation, he will surely be remembered for his career as a publisher. Although his books never reached a wide audience, his publication of works that would not be accepted. by conservative publishers in the United States provided increased exposure for some of the writers who would later shape the course of American literature. Ironically McAlmon's publishing ventures never launched his own career, and his most valuable contribution to literary history will probably remain his reminiscences about other writers in *Being Geniuses Together*. He was, in his own words, "adrift among geniuses," but he never found a secure mooring.

Other:

Contact Collection of Contemporary Writers, edited by McAlmon (Paris: Contact Editions, 1925).

Biography:

Sanford J. Smoller, *Adrift Among Geniuses Robert McAlmon Writer and Publisher of the Twenties* (University Park & London: Pennsylvania State University Press, 1975).

References:

Kay Boyle, "Brighter than Most," *Prairie Schooner*, 34 (Spring 1960): 1-4;
Hugh Ford, *Published in Paris American and British Writers, Printers, and Publishers in Paris, 1920-1939* (New York: Macmillan, 1975);
Robert E. Knoll, *Robert McAlmon Expatriate Publisher and Writer*, University of Nebraska Studies, new series no. 18 (Lincoln: University of Nebraska, 1957).

Papers:

The largest collection of McAlmon's papers is at Southern Illinois University, Carbondale. The Beinecke Library at Yale University also has a sizeable collection of his manuscripts and letters.

CLAUDE MCKAY
(15 September 1889-22 May 1948)

SELECTED BOOKS: *Home to Harlem* (New York
& London: Harper, 1928);
Banjo, A Story Without a Plot (New York & London:
Harper, 1929);
A Long Way From Home (New York: Furman,
1937);
Selected Poems (New York: Bookman, 1953).

Once, on being asked his nationality, Claude
McKay flippantly answered that he preferred to
think of himself as an "internationalist." Though
lightly given, the answer was not far off the mark.
Born a British subject in Jamaica, McKay
immigrated to the United States in 1912 and in 1914
adopted Harlem as his permanent base. From 1919
until 1924, however, he spent little time in New York
City. From 1919 to 1921 he was in London, and after
a return to New York, he made a pilgrimage to
Russia in 1922-1923, where he was lionized by the
leaders of the revolution and the Russian people.
After Russia he went, by way of Germany, to France,
where, excepting several trips to North Africa, he
would remain until he returned to Harlem in 1934.

Arriving in Paris in the fall of 1923, McKay
found a world of "radicals, esthetes, painters and
writers, pseudo-artists, [and] bohemian tourists—all
mixed tolerantly and congenially enough together,"
but this largely white expatriate world was not to his
personal taste. "I never considered myself identical
with the white expatriates," he writes, though he
confessed, "I was a kind of sympathetic fellow-
traveller in the expatriate caravan." In spite of his
sympathy for them, McKay found the reasons for
expatriation which motivated the white community
too different from his own reasons for exile to make
common cause with them. Unlike those who
repudiated America for a variety of largely cultural
reasons, McKay admits "I was in love with the large
rough unclassical rhythms of American life," and he
did not share the attitudes toward their homeland
that sent most Americans abroad in the twenties.
Rather, he says, "color-consciousness was the
fundamental of my restlessness. And it was
something with which my white fellow-expatriates
could sympathize but which they could not
altogether understand."

This strong sense of color-induced alienation
seems to have characterized much of McKay's
relationship to the Paris literary community. Often
invited to Gertrude Stein's salon, for example, he

Claude McKay in Paris

regularly refused to go because of an "aversion to
cults and disciples" and because he "liked meeting
people as persons, not as divinities in temples." This
same attitude may account for his seeming lack of
interest in meeting either James Joyce or Ernest
Hemingway, both of whose work he admired
immensely but neither of whom he sought out. He
did meet Sinclair Lewis, with whom he spent a long
evening of talk, during which Lewis, "in a shrewd
American way," gave him "a few cardinal and
practical points about the writing of a book or
novel" that McKay says he "did not forget when I got
down to writing *Home to Harlem*."

Just as color isolated McKay in Paris, it
eventually induced him to make his French
headquarters in the Marseilles area. He had
supported himself in Paris by posing nude in
unheated artists' studios, which eventually
undermined his health and led to an attack of
pneumonia. In search of a more tolerable climate, he
went south to the Mediterranean coast, where he
found a community more to his liking than white
Paris. "It was a relief to get to Marseilles," he writes,

to live in among a great gang of black and brown humanity. Negroids from the United States, the West Indies, North Africa and West Africa, all herded together in a warm group. Negroid features and complexions, not exotic, creating curiosity and hostility, but unique and natural to a group. . . . It was good to feel the strength and distinction of a group and the assurance of belonging to it.

McKay seems to have found the South of France more conducive to work than Paris had been. He wrote two of his novels, *Home to Harlem* (1928) and *Banjo* (1929), there using in the latter the waterfront of Marseilles as background. It was Marseilles, rather than Paris, which seems most to have been, as McKay says, "one of those places which stirred me up to creative expression." —*William E. Grant*

Henry Miller

J. D. Brown
University of Oregon

BIRTH: New York City, 26 December 1891, to Louise Marie Nieting and Heinrich Miller.

MARRIAGE: 1917 to Beatrice Sylvas Wickens, divorced; children: Barbara. 1 June 1924 to June Edith Smith, divorced. 18 December 1944 to Janina Martha Lepska, divorced; children: Valentine, Tony. 29 December 1953 to Eve McClure White, divorced. 10 September 1967 to Hoki Hiroko Tokuda.

AWARDS: Elected a member of National Institute of Arts and Letters, 1958.

SELECTED BOOKS: *Tropic of Cancer* (Paris: Obelisk Press, 1934; New York: Medusa, 1940; New York: Grove, 1961; London: Calder, 1963);

What Are You Going to Do About Alf? (Paris: Lecram-Servant, 1935; Berkeley, Cal.: Porter, 1944; London: Turret, 1971);

Aller Retour New York (Paris: Obelisk Press, 1935; New York: Privately printed, 1945);

Black Spring (Paris: Obelisk Press, 1936; New York: Grove, 1963; London: Calder, 1965);

Max and the White Phagocytes (Paris: Obelisk Press, 1938);

Money and How It Gets That Way (Paris: Booster Publications, 1938; Berkeley, Cal.: Porter, 1945);

The Cosmological Eye (Norfolk, Conn.: New Directions, 1939; London: Editions Poetry, 1945);

Tropic of Capricorn (Paris: Obelisk Press, 1939; New York: Grove, 1961; London: Calder, 1964);

The Colossus of Maroussi (San Francisco: Colt Press, 1941; London: Secker & Warburg, 1942);

The Air-Conditioned Nightmare (New York: New Directions, 1945; London: Secker & Warburg, 1947);

Sexus, Book 1 of *The Rosy Crucifixion* (Paris: Obelisk Press, 1949; New York: Grove, 1965; London: Calder & Boyar, 1969);

The Books in My Life (Norfolk, Conn.: New Directions, 1952; London: Owen, 1952);

Plexus, Book 2 of *The Rosy Crucifixion* (Paris: Olympia, 1953; London: Weidenfeld & Nicolson, 1963; New York: Grove, 1965);

The Time of Assassins, A Study of Rimbaud (Norfolk, Conn.: New Directions, 1956; London: Spearman, 1956);

Quiet Days in Clichy (Paris: Olympia, 1956; New York: Grove, 1965; London: Calder & Boyars, 1966);

Big Sur and the Oranges of Hieronymus Bosch (New York: New Directions, 1957; London: Heinemann, 1958);

Nexus, Book 3 of *The Rosy Crucifixion* (Paris: Obelisk Press, 1960; London: Weidenfeld & Nicolson, 1964; New York: Grove, 1965);

Genius and Lust A Journey Through the Major Writings of Henry Miller, edited with commentary by Norman Mailer (New York: Grove, 1976).

No American writer in Paris during the thirties captured so completely the experience of his generation as Henry Miller. He made Paris his permanent residence in 1930, and he stayed until 1939, absorbing and celebrating the city which so many American artists called home in the twenties. By the time Miller arrived, however, Montparnasse was in decline. Under the shadow of the Great Depression, many of the celebrated salons disbanded, and many of the leading expatriate artists and critics abandoned Paris. Henry Miller, alone it seemed, recorded the birth of a terrible beauty in the midst of the ruins of the thirties. The decay of a culture nourished him. His life and art, his actual and imagined experiences, became virtually indistinguishable in Paris. The result, published four years after his arrival, was *Tropic of Cancer* (1934), Miller's narrative of a lost generation which—grown weary of its dreams—woke to a world in violent disintegration. In 1938 Edmund Wilson called *Tropic of Cancer* "the epitaph for the whole generation of American writers and artists that migrated to Paris after the war."

Miller was undoubtedly the leading American artist in the twilight of expatriation in Paris, but he felt that Wilson had misread his work. "I am the hero, and the book is myself," Miller insisted. For the author—the American in exile who had made himself the hero of his own narrative—*Tropic of Cancer* was foremost an act of self-liberation, a new beginning, a celebration of personal rebirth in a dying world. In Paris Miller discovered a new heroic spirit in himself; he translated this as directly as possible into his art. *Tropic of Cancer* was an epitaph—the end of an old phase—but also the beginning of a new phase in American literature.

During the thirties those who could procure copies of *Tropic of Cancer* and the works which followed usually praised Miller's autobiographies in novelistic form. In 1939 Edwin Muir found *Tropic of Cancer* a "shocking book" which pierced "deeper into the disease of our existence than any other." He pronounced it "a work of genius, terrifying and comic." The same year, George Orwell, although repelled by the apolitical nature of Miller's narratives, wrote in "Inside the Whale" that "in the remaining years of free speech any novel worth reading will follow more or less along the lines that Miller has followed." Praising the colloquial style of *Tropic of Cancer*, Orwell argued that Miller was "the only imaginative prose-writer of the slightest value who has appeared among the English-speaking races for some years past." Ezra Pound and T. S. Eliot also expressed great admiration for Miller's work when it first appeared in Paris. Later, Miller's Paris works became more controversial, eliciting highly favorable and unfavorable notices, especially when the prohibition against their publication in America was lifted in the sixties. A fair evaluation of Miller's achievement, however, still requires an understanding of his life in Paris,

the scene and source of nearly all his major work. Expatriation is the central element of Miller's literal and literary quest for meaning. Paris became the capital of individual health in a powerfully rendered landscape of cancer, cataclysm, and death, during a period of disorder between two great wars.

Miller's expatriation and the art which depends so intimately on it also raises a major question in modern literary history, that of the relationship between life and art. Miller's Paris work presents an important solution to this problem. It is often difficult to separate actual events in Paris from Miller's imaginative record. His vast published and unpublished correspondence written between 1930 and 1939, the reminiscences of those who knew him, and Jay Martin's detailed biography seldom challenge the essential truth of Miller's narratives. *Tropic of Cancer*, which recounts Miller's first two years in Paris, is especially factual. After 1932 Miller's life and his art began to diverge, and his achievement as an artist diminishes as Paris gradually ceases to be the only source of material for his art. Miller's expatriation can therefore be conveniently and legitimately divided into two phases with the 1934 publication of *Tropic of Cancer* serving as the dividing line. Before 1934 Miller's life and art in Paris closely correspond; after 1934 Miller's public role changes and his art becomes more dependent on his memory, on the past rather than the immediate experience. In Miller's last years as exile he returns in his art to the life in America which he deliberately rejected when he crossed the Atlantic.

Miller arrived in Paris on 4 March 1930. He had visited Paris two years earlier, but only as a tourist. Resisting the great urge to go abroad which had affected many American artists before 1930, Miller had stayed home, worked a wide variety of jobs in New York City, and struggled without success to find himself as a writer. He knew intimately the litany of complaints earlier expatriates had formulated, and he had lived in the heart of an industrialized, inhuman society far longer than those who had fled to Paris in the twenties. His rejection of America was therefore unequaled in its bitterness, and his late expatriation freed and strengthened him as an artist almost overnight. Yet he still carried with him several third-person novels written in America which he would have to abandon. He had to turn to the unpleasant realities of Paris again and again, even when he dreaded it most, and to record his ongoing sufferings and adventures directly before a new voice emerged. He was already thirty-eight years old in 1930, an unknown writer, without friends or resources in Paris. He had left his second wife, June, in America. She had promised to wire him money, but it never seemed to come. His trunks contained clothes, tailored at his father's shop, which he would soon have to pawn and a worn copy of Walt Whitman's *Leaves of Grass*. It was not an auspicious beginning, and Miller's circumstances would soon worsen.

Front wrapper

He immediately checked in at the Hotel de Paris, where he stayed with his wife during their comfortable tour of 1928; but the next day he had to move to a less expensive hotel on the rue Bonaparte. His day usually began with a fruitless wait at the American Express office for funds from home. Then he took to the streets where his life and art began to merge. An indefatigable walker, Miller was already converting his aimless wanderings in Paris into the rich, energetic prose of the letters he sent friends in America. Walking the streets also prompted Miller to consult the guide books. *Tropic of Cancer* was born when Miller decided to write his own guide to Paris based on his discoveries in the seamier avenues he was then exploring. He deliberately nurtured his Paris book in the long letters he wrote to Emil Schnellock, a commercial artist in New York City who had been a close friend since 1905. The

spontaneous letters a lonely, isolated Miller wrote to Schnellock served as Miller's only workshop. Some of the letters were later published as *Semblance of a Devoted Past* (1944). As George Wickes has demonstrated, many sections of these letters appear a few years later in *Tropic of Cancer* with only slight revision. Miller's Surrealistic evocation of Paris street life, his adventures with prostitutes and local characters of Montparnasse, and his immediate response to the rich, chaotic events of each day were worked out in letters before being redrawn in narrative form.

The letters of 1930 also reveal Miller's sudden, overwhelming release of energies and suggest that the unbounded exuberance of the impoverished exile, portrayed in *Tropic of Cancer*, had a literal as well as literary source. While Miller's actual circumstances in the summer of 1930 were dire—he had no close friends, no job, almost no money, and no fixed residence—he immediately converted his chaotic, hand-to-mouth existence into a voracious grasping for life. Living in cheap hotels, panhandling on the streets and in the cafes he haunted, Miller made his actual sufferings and deprivations the occasion for joyous outbursts in his letters to America. On the first page of *Tropic of Cancer*, Miller compressed his response into a few words: "I have no money, no resources, no hopes. I am the happiest man alive."

If the dark necessities of Paris life produced the anecdotal structure, sordid content, and savage, Dionysian hero of Miller's art, the author was also not long in turning his dismal condition into the means of survival and self-promotion. He deliberately cultivated and exploited his role, that of the expatriate *clochard*, the picaresque desperado. Wambly Bald, an American newspaperman in Paris whose weekly column, "La Vie Boheme," reported the gossip of Montparnasse during the early thirties, soon chose Henry Miller as the subject of one of his light sketches. In Bald's 14 October 1931 column for the European edition of the *Chicago Tribune* (frequently called the Paris *Tribune*), Miller was portrayed as a happy-go-lucky "legitimate child of Montparnasse, the salt of the Quarter," who boldly conned Bald into a handout. Miller had met Bald earlier, assisted him in interviewing other subjects for his column, and probably had a hand in composing Bald's sympathetic portrait of the "Henry Miller-type." Living by his wits, Miller had learned to convert his destitution into self-serving roles.

Nearly every experience served the author as material for his yet unwritten Paris narrative. In

April, for example, three weeks after his arrival, Miller spent the night in an acquaintance's dingy apartment on a mattress saturated with insecticide and lice. This brief episode later found its way into the patchwork structure of *Tropic of Cancer*. During his first summer in Paris, Miller was in actual danger of starving, and he might not have stayed had he not encountered Alfred Perles, an Austrian expatriate writer with an inglorious past. Perles is the hero's boon companion Carl in *Tropic of Cancer*. In Perles's engaging but unreliable reminiscence, *My Friend Henry Miller* (1955), composed with Miller's assistance, their first meeting at a sidewalk cafe in 1930 is recounted. Miller, absolutely broke, was piling saucer on saucer at his table while considering various methods to evade his mounting bill. Perles entered into a long conversation with Miller and offered to pay the tab. "Like Henry, I had been destitute and hungry; like him, I had managed to survive," Perles later explained. "The situations he had to face I had to face as well: we had developed the same desperado philosophy." Perles soon became Miller's closest friend in Paris, the kindred soul who always came to the rescue when bottom was reached. On the very day they first met in Montparnasse, Perles offered to share his room at the Hotel Central on the rue du Maine. Since Perles worked on the night edition of the *Tribune*, Miller could sleep in his bed so long as he avoided Perles's landlord.

The summer of 1930 was a period of intense discovery. Miller visited the prostitutes in the neighborhood often and fell in love with one, Germaine Daugeard, who appears in *Tropic of Cancer*. He also read Andre Breton, Philippe Soupault, and other European Surrealists and Dadaists. His own writing had already anticipated those literary movements, and his absurd, chaotic, comic art remained more visceral, less abstract and programmatic, than that of leading European avant-garde writers.

The abatement of Miller's sufferings after he met Perles was brief. By July, he had moved into a hot windowless room in the Cinema Vanves where he survived on three servings of oatmeal a day. In August he met a rather distasteful character from the past named Nanavati. They had known each other in America when Miller was the rather prosperous employment manager for the Western Union Telegraph Company's messengers. In 1930, however, it was Miller who had to beg for a job. Nanavati made Miller his house servant in a shabby apartment at 54, rue Lafayette. Browbeaten by his condescending master, Miller gave up all hope. His account of life with "Mr. Nonentity" in *Tropic of*

Cancer seethes with bleak, bitter outrage. Miller escaped servitude only when Perles was able to take him in again.

Similar events from the summer of 1930, when Miller was desperate for money, sustenance, and friends, underlie the urgency and rage of *Tropic of Cancer*. An almost morbid fear of starving to death accounts for the phagomania of Miller's Paris narrative. He had left the business world of America, as dramatically as Sherwood Anderson had, in order to devote himself to art, but Miller's need for money and what it would buy often directed his actions. He would survive, but he would not prostitute himself as he felt he had in America. An even deeper source of suffering was Miller's estrangement from his wife June, whom he still loved passionately. When she finally visited Paris in September 1930, she was so repelled by her husband's circumstances that she could stay only a month.

Miller remained. What shocked his wife ultimately strengthened him. If the Paris Miller had discovered in the first six months of 1930 had destroyed his dreams of a glorious future as an artist, the death of this outlandish illusion gradually signaled a new birth. Rather than reject the sordid life he led, Miller embraced it. His acceptance of a dark, sensuous, elemental life was as complete as that of the American author he most respected, Walt Whitman.

Winter, however, promised to be much more dreadful than summer, and Miller made plans to depart Paris; but unable to raise the fare home, Miller was again forced to remain in France. Such lessons become the hero's philosophy in *Tropic of Cancer*. Fate was a most capricious force in Miller's art and life, but it did treat him kindly in the winter of 1930. Fred Kann, an American artist, introduced Miller to Richard Galen Osborn. Osborn, a graduate of Yale Law School, had come to Paris to enjoy himself. Employed by day at the Paris branch of the National City Bank, Osborn led a more riotous nightlife among the idle rich of Bohemia. He could afford a large apartment at 2, rue Auguste-Bartholdi near the Champ de Mars and the Eiffel Tower. It was there that Miller spent the winter in comfort, almost entirely at Richard Osborn's expense.

Osborn's reminiscence of his winter with Henry Miller does not conflict with Miller's narrative version in *Tropic of Cancer*. An episode with a Russian "princess" with whom Osborn lived for a time is essentially the same in both accounts. Osborn does recall, however, Miller's perseverance at the typewriter during the winter of 1930-1931. It was at this time that Miller completed the novel about his life with June Miller which he had begun in America. He also composed his first successful story, "Mademoiselle Claude," in Osborn's cozy study. Although it lacked the fierce vision and bite of later efforts, this first-person account of Miller's relationship. with a Paris prostitute had the characteristic hard-boiled sentimentality and low-life subject matter of his later work. Samuel Putnam, an American expatriate writer and translator, was then editing a small literary magazine, the *New Review*, and he accepted Miller's story for the Fall 1931 issue. "Mademoiselle Claude" was later included in Peter Neagoe's *Americans Abroad* (1931), an anthology of works by Ernest Hemingway, John Dos Passos, Ezra Pound, Conrad Aiken, Gertrude Stein, and others. During the same period, Miller placed sketches of Paris life in the Sunday *Tribune*, which Elliot Paul edited. These successes encouraged Miller but did not free him from financial dependence. In March 1931 Osborn and Miller quarreled. Miller again shared quarters with Alfred Perles.

Miller, always resourceful, devised an ingenious meal schedule, described in *Tropic of Cancer*, whereby he secured one handout dinner a day from a weekly list of seven friends. This sustained him until he landed a job on the *Tribune* with Perles as a $12-a-week proofreader of stock exchange quotations. This monotonous occupation later became the basis for several fine Dadaist passages in *Tropic of Cancer*.

During his brief employment with the *Tribune*, Miller made several important friends. One was Walter Lowenfels, the American experimental poet. Lowenfels and Michael Fraenkel, a writer and sometime publisher, were involved in philosophical discussions of death. Miller became a third party, and in June 1931 he moved in with Fraenkel at 18, Villa Seurat. Here Miller began to compose *Tropic of Cancer*. Fraenkel's influence was undoubtedly strong at first, but Miller eventually concluded that the death instinct was a means to rebirth. He rejected Fraenkel's abstract, disembodied formulation of universal cataclysm and sought personal resurrection in the midst of a dying world. In *Tropic of Cancer*, Fraenkel appears as Boris, the prophet of death, the caricature of the man paralyzed by introspection; Miller, as hero, submerges himself in the life-giving stream of sensuous experience. The first episode of the novel describes Miller's life with Fraenkel, which came to an abrupt end when Fraenkel sublet 18, Villa Seurat in July 1931.

Miller and Perles joined forces shortly afterwards as literary editors, when Samuel Putnam entrusted the *New Review* to these novices while he returned to New York on business. Miller and Perles immediately sabotaged the issue, cutting out Robert McAlmon's lead story, adding their own work, and attaching a manifesto, "The New Instinctivism." In this parody of the literary manifesto, the authors proclaimed their opposition to all movements and *isms* and their support of total "irresponsible" liberation. Putnam's wife discovered their changes as the issue was about to go to the printers and managed to publish the issue minus their manifesto. Putnam did not lecture Miller and Perles; perhaps he sympathized with the ribald, anarchistic thrust of their enterprise. The episode is included in *Tropic of Cancer*, where Putnam is portrayed as Marlowe, the drunken scholar.

In September 1931 June Miller announced she would return to Paris. Miller, however, had just been introduced to a young woman who would replace her in his affections—Anais Nin. Richard Osborn had provided the introduction; Nin's husband, Hugh Guiler, was Osborn's superior at the bank. Opposites in many ways, Henry Miller and Anais Nin were deeply attracted to each other at once. Miller frequently visited Nin's home in Louveciennes, a quiet village west of Paris along the Seine. Their correspondence was immense. By Miller's count, they exchanged over 900 letters during 1931-1932. When Miller's wife arrived, their affair had hardly begun, but she sensed the danger. After a few weeks, the situation was complicated by Nin's advances toward Mrs. Miller. By Christmas Eve, June Miller had walked out on her husband and demanded a divorce. Sensing Miller's agony, Nin arranged through her husband for Miller's appointment as instructor of English at the Lycee Carnot, a preparatory school in Dijon. When Miller left Paris to accept this post, June Miller finally returned to America.

While this triangle does not appear in *Tropic of Cancer*, the Dijon episode receives extended treatment. Miller lasted only the first two months of 1932. His position paid little, the facilities were Spartan, the curriculum uninspired, and Miller felt he had deprived himself of his beloved Paris for nothing. The situation was a nightmare, and Miller later rendered it in a Poesque manner in *Tropic of Cancer*. Nin was supportive, sending lavish gifts to Dijon during this brief exile. By March Miller had escaped to Paris, where he worked on the Paris *Tribune* as assistant finance editor. He moved with Perles into an apartment at 4, avenue Anatole France in Clichy. Although Miller could hold on to his new job only a month, he recalled this period as the most peaceful in Paris. During that quiet summer in

Clichy, Nin paid Miller's share of the rent.

During the same summer, 1932, the events of the final episode of *Tropic of Cancer* unfolded. Richard Osborn (the Fillmore of Miller's narrative) had a nervous breakdown brought on in part by the pregnancy of a young French girl he had taken in while Miller was in Dijon. Miller now came to his former benefactor's aid, deftly ensuring that a broken Osborn evade the girl's angry mother and the French authorities. He shipped the besieged American expatriate home and pocketed at least some of the money Osborn had left for the young woman. The manuscript of Miller's Paris adventures was soon virtually complete.

William Aspenwall Bradley, an American literary agent in Paris, read *Tropic of Cancer*, liked it, and passsed it on to Jack Kahane, an English expatriate who owned the Obelisk Press. Kahane's press was notorious in Paris. It had published risque novels, several composed under pseudonyms by the publisher himself, and a few sexually explicit works of more serious substance, such as Frank Harris's *My Life and Loves*. In *Memoirs of a Booklegger* (1939), Kahane recalled his first reading of Miller's manuscript: "I had read the most terrible, the most sordid, the most magnificent manuscript that had ever fallen into my hands; nothing I had yet received was comparable to it for the splendor of its writing, the fathomless depth of its despair, the savour of its portraiture, the boisterousness of its humour." In October 1932 Miller signed a contract with Kahane, but it would be almost two years before his book was published. Kahane stalled because he feared that the increasing severity of French censorship made *Tropic of Cancer* a poor legal and financial risk.

Although frustrated by Kahane's reluctance, Miller continued to write, revising the manuscript of *Tropic of Cancer* extensively and initiating a series of new literary projects. All work abruptly ceased, however, when June Miller returned to Paris in December 1932. More deeply involved with Anais Nin, but still attached to his wife, Miller was paralyzed. Perles and Nin tried to pack Miller off alone to London for the Christmas holidays, then hid him out in Paris when he was not allowed to cross into England. Nin eventually paid June Miller's passage to America on 26 December 1932, the day Miller turned forty-one years old.

Freed from his wife, Miller devoted himself to several new literary projects in 1933. He worked on what would be his last major Paris work, *Tropic of Capricorn* (1939), and he completed many of the chapters for *Black Spring* (1936). He also began a massive, aborted study of D. H. Lawrence. Kahane

Henry Miller's list of streets and places in Paris

had insisted that such a study should precede *Tropic of Cancer* as evidence of Miller's seriousness and responsibility as a man of letters. The Lawrence book proved disastrous; Miller could not organize his materials in a coherent manner. *Tropic of Cancer* remained unpublished, but Anais Nin, feeling the time was ripe, raised $600, enough to underwrite its publication. She also wrote, in collaboration with Miller, an excellent preface.

Despite Nin's extraordinary efforts, *Tropic of Cancer* did not pass through the presses until 1 September 1934. The same day, Henry Miller moved back into an apartment at 18, Villa Seurat where he had begun to write his Paris book three years earlier. Now he felt he had made his great breakthrough as an artist. Marcel Duchamp embraced *Tropic of Cancer* at once, and just before Christmas 1934, the charismatic French poet-adventurer, Blaise Cendrars—whom Miller worshipped—came to 18, Villa Seurat. Cendrars treated Miller to a lavish dinner; Perles recalled later that Miller was, for once, speechless.

Others soon expressed admiration for *Tropic of Cancer*. Miller received letters of praise from Katherine Anne Porter, Kay Boyle, Aldous Huxley, Stuart Gilbert, Ezra Pound, and T. S. Eliot. Pound judged Miller's work superior to that of James Joyce and Virginia Woolf; Eliot felt Miller had surpassed the achievement of D. H. Lawrence. Although Miller was ecstatic, his work sold far too slowly to gain him financial independence. Between 1934 and 1937 *Tropic of Cancer* sold no more than a thousand copies. The first phase of Miller's expatriation closed on a triumphant note, but Nin continued to pay the rent.

Miller owed Anais Nin other debts as well. She had encouraged him as a fellow artist and broadened his understanding of European art and culture. As Gunther Stuhlmann points out in his introduction to Miller's letters to Nin, the two writers appear at first to have little in common. Miller "gorged himself with the world around him, the world of dirty streets, and dirty people, and spat it out again—transformed, vitalized, reborn in a twentieth-century manner no writer before him had achieved," while Nin "sought to probe for the reality behind the surface, the reality of dream and the endless facets of character" in a world far more "harmonious, beautiful, colorful and richly textured" than the one Miller amalgamated and caricatured. Nevertheless, there were deep affinities. Miller and Nin both rejected the conventional methods of creative expression, ignored current literary movements, and adopted none of the political ideologies which shaped other works of the period. Seeking new literary forms, Miller and Nin both sought self-discovery through new autobiographical forms.

Although Miller translated his literal experience into the narrative of *Tropic of Cancer* and caricatured the people he met and lived with in Paris from 1930 to 1932, his art was not simply a bold roman a clef. Events and characters were altered, exaggerated, and fictionalized—and in this sense Miller's life and his art are distinct—but the author of the narrative could honestly deny that he was a fiction writer. The Henry Miller in *Tropic of Cancer* was the same man the author had felt himself to be in reality. Moreover, this imagined personality was the one Miller had projected to those who knew him in life. The letters, diaries, and accounts of Nin, Perles, Bald, Lowenfels, Putnam, Fraenkel, Kahane, and

others largely confirmed the literalness of the literary hero. Thus, *Tropic of Cancer* can best be classified not as a novel, but as barely fictionalized autobiography—a personal narrative composed in an eclectic, avant-garde manner, true to the life Miller imagined he had lived as he lived it. His work therefore is a part of a long, rich tradition in American autobiographical art which includes the two writers Miller most resembles, Thoreau and Whitman.

In 1931 Michael Fraenkel had advised Miller to abandon the conventional novels he had brought from America, to begin fresh, to write as he lived and felt day by day. By releasing those emotions still pent-up in a third-person narrative, Miller liberated himself and produced a vital, meaningful narrative. In *Tropic of Cancer*, Miller rearranged and embroidered his firsthand experience in response to the imaginative truth it revealed. The result, if not a literal record, was an astonishingly frank, powerful, and essentially truthful account of those first years in exile. Fraenkel came close to capturing the essence of Miller's creative process when he later wrote that "the very manner of his life, the way he had to live it day by day, never sure of a roof over his head, never knowing where his next meal would come from or the next bit of change, the hectic uncertainty and tension all this produced—something which would have broken and rendered inarticulate and frustrate almost any other man—only made and appointed him. It gave the style of the *Tropic of Cancer* its deep, terrible immediacy, its dynamism, its tension, its desperate swing and beat." Nearly all critics have praised Miller's first work, as Osbert Sitwell did, for the "peculiar energy and vision" of its prose style. Here, the style became the man and the man became the style. Miller accepted and celebrated the raw, fundamental, often hideous realities he had discovered in Paris; at the same time his Surreal fantasia could provide a savage, joyous transcendence. At his best as an artist in *Tropic of Cancer*, Miller consistently maintained there a high level of imaginative power, fusing a brutal realism with a stark lyricism, a vernacular amoralism with a darkly serious satire on civilization.

In 1935 Miller returned to America for four months and found that no publisher there would touch his work. It was either too pornographic or too apolitical for the times. When he returned to Paris in May 1935, Miller promptly wrote and published two works in epistolary form. The first, *What Are You Going to Do About Alf?*, was a plea for contributions to support a starving artist in Paris (Alfred Perles). The second, *Aller Retour New York*, an attempt to write the longest letter ever published, was essentially a personal essay on the life-giving power of the renegade artist in a death-dealing world. In November 1935, Miller initiated an even more ambitious venture into correspondence in collaboration with Michael Fraenkel. Called *Hamlet*, the correspondence covered a wide range of subjects, most often the life and art of Henry Miller. By mutual agreement, this work was to terminate at one thousand pages, not a word more or less.

This interest in correspondence as art was only one of many indications that Miller had entered a new phase of his expatriation. After 1934 18, Villa Seurat became the headquarters of a literary circle, and Miller became the new, largely unheralded master. Miller's salon was unlike those which had preceded it a decade earlier, but within its rundown rooms on the Left Bank several significant literary events of the thirties in Paris transpired. Miller was cast in a new role, that of editor, agent, mentor, and businessman. He launched the Siana Series of books, published by Jack Kahane and paid for by Anais Nin, in 1935. Miller's *Aller Retour New York* and Nin's *House of Incest* were the first two entries in the

series; Richard Thoma's *Tragedy in Blue* was the third. An American expatriate who lived in apartment 1 at 18, Villa Seurat, Thoma had been an assistant editor on Putnam's *New Review*. Despite Miller's ability as a self-promoter, however, this venture was unsuccessful. The Siana Series died in 1936.

Another indication of Miller's new direction after *Tropic of Cancer* was his interest in painting. Many of his new acquaintances were artists such as Pablo Picasso, Max Ernst, Joan Miro, and Man Ray. For many years Miller's water colors were a better source of income than his writings. Above all, the second phase of Miller's residence in Paris was marked by his gradual withdrawal from immediate experience as source and subject of his creative expression. *Tropic of Capricorn* is a condensed version of the experiences Miller had unsuccessfully attempted to write about before his exile, and it would be the capstone of his entire expatriation. This shift in time and subject from the Paris of the present to the New York of the past corresponded to a gradual decline in Miller's achievement, suggesting that his best work required a literal immediacy.

Black Spring, however, bridged the two phases of Miller's exile. Miller began writing this work in 1933; he had intended to call it "Self-Portrait." He explained in a letter to Nin that he meant to explore "that large irrational area" of his unconsciousness, to grapple there with the "unseizable." Miller's "Self-Portrait" would proceed "multilaterally in all directions" by recasting the substance of his letters, dreams, memories, "expunged passages from the old *Tropic of Cancer*, and certain extravagant incomprehensible . . . scenes from *Tropic of Capricorn*." The fine Surrealistic chapters of *Black Spring* came in part from a "Dream Book" Miller kept at Nin's insistence in 1932. The even more impressive Dadaistic chapters, such as "Jabberwhorl Cronstadt," a wild, engrossing portrait of Walter Lowenfels, grew out of Miller's conscious observations. Several chapters of reminiscence, composed in a conventional narrative manner, were based on Miller's vivid memories of his life in New York City at the turn of the century. As individual chapters, both experimental and traditional narratives showed Miller at his best. As fragments in a self-portrait, however, they do not cohere.

Just before *Black Spring* went to the presses, Miller's most important new acquaintance introduced himself in an August 1935 letter from Corfu. Lawrence Durrell, a twenty-three-year-old British expatriate, hailed his literary master, the forty-three-year-old author of *Tropic of Cancer* in

Paris. Durrell's first letter termed Miller's *Cancer* "the copy-book for my generation." As Durrell's literary father, Miller was soon to influence the young novelist more thoroughly than any other artist during the thirties. By 1936 Miller and Durrell were discussing many literary enterprises in letters of awesome length and energy. They also exchanged manuscripts frequently, and Miller was especially impressed by Durrell's draft of *Black Book*, a work Miller would later rescue from censorship and virtually publish himself in 1938.

Meanwhile, Miller's own problems with publishing were consuming much of his energy. T. S. Eliot rejected *Black Spring* for Faber and Faber in London. Bennett Cerf and Alfred A. Knopf, who had expressed interest in all of Miller's work, found themselves unable to print anything. Even Huntington Cairns, attorney for the United States Customs Office, one of Miller's many

Front wrapper

correspondents and a fervent supporter of his banned art, was required to advise his superiors that *Tropic of Cancer* could not be legally imported. Miller's friends had smuggled many copies into the United States—Nin held the single trip record of fifty

copies—and Miller had gone to New York himself in 1936 to find a willing publisher. Eventually, censorship itself would make Miller a popular writer. Even before his works were widely distributed, censorship had shaped his reputation among critics and readers. In England during the thirties, favorable reviews by Herbert Read and George Orwell whetted the public's appetite for the contraband narratives. In America intriguing articles in the *New Republic* and *Time* magazine created a similar demand. When the GIs entered Paris in World War II, they devoured Miller's works.

Durrell also ran into censorship problems during this period, and Miller acted on his behalf. In the summer of 1937, Faber and Faber accepted *Black Book* on the condition that certain passages be deleted. Durrell, inclined to accept the publisher's provision, finally honored Miller's strong objections and withdrew the manuscript.

After two years of steady correspondence, Miller and Durrell met face to face at Villa Seurat in September 1937. They immediately seized control of a magazine Alfred Perles edited—the *Booster*, previously the respectable, innocuous house organ of the American Country Club of France. Miller became Fashion Editor, Nin the Society Editor, Michael Fraenkel the head of a Department of Metaphysics and Metempsychosis. Other members of the Villa Seurat circle, including Walter Lowenfels and William Saroyan, were contributors. It was "The New Instinctivism" revisited, and the outraged sponsors quickly disavowed all connection with their magazine. In 1938 the *Booster* was retitled *Delta*, an independent literary magazine which was essentially the house organ of Villa Seurat. At first, Lawrence Durrell did much of the editorial work, and his wife Nancy underwrote the publishing costs.

Nancy Durrell also underwrote Miller's second venture as literary editor, the Villa Seurat Library. The first work in the series, published by Jack Kahane, was Miller's own *Max and the White Phagocytes* (1938), his finest collection of personal essays and sketches. The second work in the Villa Seurat Library was Anais Nin's *Winter of Artifice*. The last work was Durrell's *Black Book*, which Miller saw to press after the Durrells returned to Greece. None of the three books sold enough to recoup their patron's investment.

A German invasion of France seemed imminent by the time the Villa Seurat Library expired in 1938. Miller joined the exodus from Paris in September, but the Munich Crisis passed before he could depart France. The Paris to which Miller returned seemed more deserted each day. Old friends had disappeared or were in transit. Nin moved to New York City. Perles soon took up permanent residence in England. Early in 1939 Miller edited the last issue of *Delta*, appropriately titled the "Peace and Dismemberment Number with Jitterbug-Shag Requiem."

In his last days in Paris, Miller struggled to see *Tropic of Capricorn* to press. After its appearance on 10 May 1939, Miller haunted Paris for several weeks, then left Villa Seurat for good. He reached Athens in July, stayed with the Durrells, then sailed for America the day after his forty-eighth birthday, on 27 December. When he again set foot on his native soil, he was as penniless and nearly as unknown in America as the day he had left for Paris ten years earlier.

Miller's last Paris book, *Tropic of Capricorn*, deals with his experiences in America before his personal liberation in Paris. Viewing the twenties in America from the late thirties in Paris, Miller describes a death-in-life landscape—inhuman, mechanical, oppressive—which he had once known intimately. He does not spare himself, the hero, in this work. *Capricorn* is a negative self-portrait of an unfeeling, brutal outsider at home. The individual idealism and affirmation of *Cancer* are now distorted in a dark, stale world. Violence, nihilism, and aimless sexual explosions express what Miller remembered of his rage and frustration, but even the extended passages of Surrealism do not liberate the hero or suggest a unified Dionysian vision as they do in *Tropic of Cancer*.

This condensation of Miller's experiences before expatriation, while not his finest achievement, far surpasses his later attempts to expand his account of those pre-Paris days. *The Rosy Crucifixion*, a three-volume reminiscence of the twenties, was published in Paris between 1949 and 1960, but it is in no way an expatriate's work. Lawrence Durrell felt that the first volume, *Sexus*, would ruin Miller's reputation. Durrell complained that "all the wild resonance of *Cancer* and *Black Spring* are gone," and that the "new mystical outlines" of Miller's art after 1940 were "lost, lost, damn it, in this shower of lavatory filth which no longer seems tonic and bracing, but just excrementitious and sad." Durrell later retracted this assessment of *Sexus*, *Plexus*, and *Nexus*, but the critics (excepting William Gordon and Norman Mailer) have found *The Rosy Crucifixion* tedious and banal.

The critics were more favorably disposed toward the book which appeared just after Miller left Paris in 1939, *The Colossus of Maroussi*. This was Miller's account of his quest for spiritual illumination in Greece while a guest of Lawrence Durrell. Miller and others later judged it his finest work, but it is a far lesser work than *Tropic of Cancer*. The narrative constantly promises spiritual revelations which it fails to deliver convincingly. As a work of art, and often of bombast, *Colossus* fails to plumb the deeper reservoirs of feeling and symbol which Miller tapped in his early Paris years. A falling off in Miller's power as an autobiographical artist is apparent in the forties, even in the late thirties.

This decline cannot be explained solely in terms of Miller's abandonment of immediate experience as the source of his art. *The Colossus of Maroussi* kept close to the present circumstances of the author, as did *Big Sur and the Oranges of Hieronymus Bosch* (1957) later. The Big Sur book, composed in the fifties when Miller lived on the California coast, is a weak, rambling, often powerless and shapeless narrative of the author's new life in the country he had scorned in the thirties. Yet California was not Paris, and the Henry Miller of 1950 was not the Henry Miller of 1930—and hence not the same artist. Paris provided the perfect catalyst in 1930, and Miller's life and art crossed and ripened as never before or after. It is the legacy of Miller's work in Paris, not his achievements after, which continues to play an important role in recent literary history.

Miller's influence on American literature did not surface until after 1950. The method and vision of Jack Kerouac's *On the Road* (1957), Allen Ginsberg's *Howl* (1956), Richard Brautigan's *Trout Fishing in America* (1967), and Hunter Thompson's *Fear and Loathing in Las Vegas* (1971) are rather direct extensions of the autobiographical, Surrealistic, savage satires which Miller wrote in Paris. Miller can now be seen as an important precursor of recent experiments in novelistic reportage. Norman Mailer's autobiographical art, such as *The Armies of the Night* (1968), is an excellent tribute to the writer Mailer openly acknowledges as a primary influence on post-World War II American artists.

The gradual influence Miller exerted on later generations of writers parallels, and is explained in part by, his long delayed popular reception. *Tropic of Cancer* was difficult to procure in the thirties, and its sales did not skyrocket until the occupation of France in the forties. At the end of the war, Maurice Girodias, who had taken over the Obelisk Press from his father, Jack Kahane, informed Miller that his books had accumulated 410,000 francs ($40,000) in royalties. Two years later in 1947, Girodias reported that those royalties had increased tenfold. Reprints of *Tropic of Cancer* in France sold out quickly even with printings of 10,000 copies. These figures staggered Miller, who was still nearly penniless in America. While he was unable to receive much of the earnings, due to postwar French regulations and the swift devaluation of the franc, Miller profited from the celebrity which resulted. In 1946 Girodias was convicted of selling pornographic materials (Miller's *Tropic*s), but a defense committee of distinguished French writers—including Andre Breton, Albert Camus, Paul Eluard, Andre Gide, and Jean-Paul Sartre—helped reverse the verdict and draw attention to an author whose reputation was still handicapped by prohibitions against his work in most of the world.

Miller often repeated the statement H. L. Mencken had made to him in the thirties: his Paris books would never be published in America during his lifetime. On 24 June 1961, however, Barney Rosset, owner of Grove Press, brought *Tropic of Cancer* home after a twenty-seven-year exile. 68,000 copies sold the first week. By the end of the year Americans had purchased 100,000 copies in hardback and over a million copies in paperback. In 1962 *Tropic of Capricorn* also sold well in America—25,000 copies in hardback during the first three months. Suddenly the prohibitions were removed everywhere. The first British edition of *Tropic of Cancer* sold 40,000 copies the first day. During the sixties Miller achieved unexpected international popularity and prominence.

Although not a pornographer, Miller was perceived as such by the millions who could finally purchase his books over the counter. The publication of *Tropic of Cancer* in America was, at best, a mixed blessing for its author. The censorship trials which erupted in America over Miller's work prompted spirited defenses by many major critics and artists, but the general issue of censorship and art took precedence over a just evaluation of Miller's work. Thus, Miller's achievement as an artist was obscured or distorted by an urgent need to defend the artist against the censor. After the trials ended with a favorable decision by the United States Supreme Court in 1963, many critics revised their extravagant praise of *Tropic of Cancer*. One defender, Harry Levin, later characterized Miller as "an amusing but crude burlesque of .Lawrence" and of far lesser stature than James Joyce. Levin still granted Miller's "undeniable talent," his gusto, and his skill as a "braggart storyteller in the picaresque mode," but he felt that "unfortunately, and increasingly in his other work," Miller's "authentic vein of pungent humor is adulterated by messianic rhapsodies—

Leaves of Grass gone to seed—which prove rather embarrassing." Levin was one of many critics in the sixties who praised Miller's power but judged him as a minor literary figure on the grounds that he was not the equal of Joyce and that his work after Paris indicated that his overall talent was meager. Other critics, however, who devoted themselves to serious extended studies of Miller, saw him as a major literary figure. They usually agreed with Miller's detractors that his work had declined markedly after 1940, and that Miller was not the equal of Joyce or some other monument in the great literature of the world.

Kingsley Widmer was the first to study Miller at some length, and he pointed to an astonishing number of connections between Miller's art and the great literary traditions it served or altered. George Wickes argued in the sixties that Miller was the best American writer of his time during the Paris decade—and perhaps America's greatest literary Surrealist of any decade. William A. Gordon placed Miller at the head of the Romantic movement in twentieth-century literature. Ihab Hassan has viewed Miller as "the first author of anti-literature" and argued that he turned literature into "autobiography of a special kind" in which the effort to record and understand one's life is superseded by "an attempt to *live* it." Hassan's interpretation of Miller's literary achievement is in accord with Miller's own intentions. Abundant, chaotic, aimless, Miller's narratives are what Hassan terms "the act of pure self-expression" through "anti-forms" in which the artist and the man, his life and his art, are unified rather than distinct. *Tropic of Cancer* is Miller's discordant "Song of Myself," artless in the same sense as Whitman's masterpiece, composed now in a minor key in response to a darker stage of American history and individual idealism.

Miller's stature as an artist and his position in twentieth-century literature are far from fixed. No critic would argue that most of his work is first-rate, that his vision is always profound, or that his control over his craft is consistent or firm. Nevertheless, Miller's Paris work has continued to shape our present literature almost a half century after its inauspicious appearance. Miller later explained that his intent in the beginning had been to reveal himself "as openly, nakedly and unashamedly as possible" in order to render back life "enchanted and exalted" to those who read him. In *Tropic of Cancer*, *Black Spring*, and *Tropic of Capricorn*, he succeeds. Out of his sufferings and dreams in Paris Miller has fashioned genuine and lasting works which are almost unrivaled in twentieth-century autobiographical art. In modern literary history, especially in the records of Americans' accomplishments in Paris, Miller's *Tropic of Cancer* takes on a singular importance. As Samuel Putnam observes in his reminiscence, Miller "has summed up for us as no one else has the expatriates' Paris of the second phase: and I think it may be said that the *Tropic of Cancer* is to that phase what *The Sun Also Rises* is to the preceding one." There is no doubt that in the literary history of the American expatriate in Paris Henry Miller's work is of immense importance.

Other:

Hamlet, by Miller and Michael Fraenkel, vol. 1 (Santurce, Puerto Rico: Carrefour, 1939; enlarged edition, New York: Carrefour, 1943); vol. 2 (New York: Carrefour, 1941); vols. 1 and 2 enlarged again as *The Michael Fraenkel-Henry Miller Correspondence Called Hamlet* (London: Edition du Laurier/Carrefour, 1962);

Art and Outrage, by Miller, Lawrence Durrell, and Alfred Perles (London: Putnam's, 1959; New York: Dutton, 1961).

Periodical Publications:

"Bunuel, or Thus Cometh to an End Everywhere the Golden Age," *New Review*, 1 (May-June-July 1931): 157-159;

"Mademoiselle Claude," *New Review*, 1 (August-September-October 1931): 39-45.

Letters:

Semblance of a Devoted Past (Berkeley, Cal.: Porter, 1944);

Lawrence Durrell Henry Miller: A Private Correspondence, ed. George Wickes (New York: Dutton, 1963);

Henry Miller: Letters to Anais Nin, ed. Gunther Stuhlmann (New York: Putnam's, 1965);

Writer and Critic: A Correspondence with Henry Miller (Baton Rouge: Louisiana State University Press, 1967);

Collector's Quest: The Correspondence of Henry Miller and J. Rives Childs, 1947-1965 (Charlottesville: University Press of Virginia, 1968);

Letters of Henry Miller and Wallace Fowlie, 1943-1972, ed. Wallace Fowlie (New York: Grove, 1975);

Henry Miller: Years of Trial and Triumph, 1962-1964: The Correspondence of Henry Miller and Elmer Gertz, ed. Elmer Gertz and Felice F. Lewis (Carbondale & Edwardsville: Southern Illinois University Press, 1978).

Interviews:

George Wickes, "Henry Miller," in *Writers at Work: The Paris Review Interviews*, second series (New York: Viking, 1963), pp. 165-191;

Bernard Wolfe, "Playboy Interview: Henry Miller," *Playboy Magazine*, 11 (September 1964): 77-94;

Georges Belmont, *Henry Miller in Conversation with Georges Belmont*, trans. Anthony Macnabb and Harry Scott (New York: Quadrangle, 1972).

Bibliographies:

Bernard H. Porter, *Henry Miller: A Chronology and Bibliography* (Baltimore: Waverly Press, 1945);

Thomas H. Moore, *Bibliography of Henry Miller* (Minneapolis: Henry Miller Literary Society, 1961).

Biographies:

Kar Baxter, *Henry Miller, Expatriate* (Pittsburgh: University of Pittsburgh Press, 1961);

Jay Martin, *Always Merry and Bright The Life of Henry Miller* (Santa Barbara, Cal.: Capra, 1978);

Alfred Perles, *My Friend Henry Miller: An Intimate Biography* (London: Spearman, 1955).

References:

William A. Gordon, *The Mind and Art of Henry Miller* (Baton Rouge: Louisiana State University Press, 1967);

Ihab Habib Hassan, *The Literature of Silence: Henry Miller and Samuel Beckett* (New York: Knopf, 1967);

Jack Kahane, *Memoirs of a Booklegger* (London: Joseph, 1939);

Edward B. Mitchell, ed., *Henry Miller: Three Decades of Criticism* (New York: New York University Press, 1971);

Bern Porter, ed., *The Happy Rock: A Book About Henry Miller* (Berkeley, Cal.: Porter, 1945);

Samuel Putnam, *Paris Was Our Mistress Memoirs of a Lost & Found Generation* (New York: Viking, 1947);

George Wickes, *Americans in Paris* (Garden City: Doubleday, 1969), pp. 234-276;

Wickes, ed., *Henry Miller and the Critics* (Carbondale: Southern Illinois University Press, 1963);

Kingsley Widmer, *Henry Miller* (New York: Twayne, 1963).

Papers:

The Henry Miller archives at the Library of the University of California, Los Angeles, is the major repository of the author's manuscripts, letters, photographs, and publications. Other important manuscript and correspondence holdings are at the Humanities Research Center Library, University of Texas; Randolph-Macon College; the Barrett Collection, University of Virginia; the Library of Congress; the Brooklyn Public Library; Columbia University; Dartmouth College; Southern Illinois University; Harvard University; Princeton University; and the New York Public Library.

ARTHUR MOSS
(1889-20 February 1969)

SELECTED BOOKS: *Slapstick and Dumbbell A Casual Survey of Clowns and Clowning*, by Moss and Hiler Harzberg (New York: Lawren, 1924);

The Legend of the Latin Quarter Henry Murger and the Birth of Bohemia, by Moss and Evalyn Marvel (New York: Beechhurst, 1946; London: Allen, 1947);

Second Childhood in Villefranche (Villefranche: Editions de la Rade, 1952);

Cancan and Barcarolle The Life and Times of Jacques Offenbach, by Moss and Marvel (New York: Exposition Press, 1954);

Tale of Twelve Cities and Other Poems (Paris: Two Cities Editions, 1963).

Arthur Moss was among the early American expatriates in Paris and a lively participant in Left Bank social and literary activity. With Florence Gilliam, Moss founded and edited *Gargoyle*, the first English-language review of arts and letters on the Continent. He also did free-lance writing and later edited Erskine Gwynne's *Boulevardier*. Moss's friends in Paris included Malcolm Cowley, Robert Coates, Ernest Hemingway, Robert McAlmon, Harold Stearns, Matthew and Hannah Josephson, Claude McKay, Ludwig Lewisohn, James Thurber, Elliot Paul, Harold Loeb, and Kitty Cannell.

Moss was born in Greenwich Village to a Turkish mother and a German-Jewish father, who determined that the family should become completely Americanized. After leaving Cornell without a degree and working as a newspaper reporter in upstate New York, Moss edited the Greenwich Village magazine the *Quill*. According to Gilliam, who was married to Moss for several years, "aside from romantic attachments (he was married several times), he had a notable gift of treating men and women equally as human beings. This endeared him to the feminists of his day, and he marched with the earliest Suffragettes in America. . . . He was a skillful *raconteur* and had a passion for finding a new audience." Gilliam and Moss met while she was working in a New York City bookshop. She became managing editor of the *Quill* in September 1920, and in early 1921 she accompanied Moss to Paris.

Working from their apartment in the rue Campagne Premiere, Moss and Gilliam soon began publication of *Gargoyle*. The first issue (August 1921) had on its cover a chimera instead of a gargoyle, which brought some criticism from French readers, but the mistake was corrected in following issues. Moss contributed book reviews and humorous pieces, and Gilliam reviewed plays and concerts. Commentary in *Gargoyle* focused on the avant-garde in art and letters. Art reproductions represented the work of Pablo Picasso, Henri Matisse, Georges Braque, Andre Derain, Amedeo Modigliani, Paul Cezanne, Albert Gleizes, Juan Gris, Max Weber, and others. Among the writers who contributed to the magazine were Cowley, Coates, Laurence Vail, Hart Crane, Edna St. Vincent Millay, Sinclair Lewis, Matthew Josephson, Stephen Vincent Benet, Gorham Munson, John Reed, H. D. (Hilda Doolittle), and Bryher (Winifred Ellerman). *Gargoyle* never made a profit, however, and it ceased publication in 1922, a little more than a year after it was begun.

Both Moss and Gilliam had done free-lance writing for publications in America to help support themselves during *Gargoyle*'s publication, and they continued to do so after its demise. Moss also contributed articles to the Paris *Times*, an English-language newspaper established in 1924 by the Paris *Herald*'s ex-managing editor Gaston Archambault. For the Paris *Herald* (the European edition of the *New York Herald*), Moss wrote "Over the River," a column containing light social and literary comment on the Left Bank crowd. Another *Herald* editor, Al Laney, called Moss "perhaps the first Boswell of the postwar Quarter . . . , an energetic little man who seemed to know what everybody was doing at all times."

Moss's social contacts not only provided material for his column but also led to other literary projects. The American painter Hiler Harzberg, also known as Hilaire Hiler, was a close friend of Moss and Gilliam. Harzberg's Montparnasse nightclub, The Jockey, was a popular meeting place for Left Bank Americans, and for a time Moss worked as cashier there. In 1924 Harzberg and Moss collaborated on *Slapstick and Dumbbell A Casual Survey of Clowns and Clowning.* Gilliam wrote in her "Faint Note of Introduction" to the book, "Two virtues the writers may well claim for their discourse on clowning ancient and modern. One is a complete freedom from sentimentalizing, which used to be the inevitable accompaniment of any interest in clowns as human beings. The other is a thorough distaste for those aesthetic maunderings which serve so often to turn a healthy appreciation of buffoonery into a languishing intellectual pose." A brisk and enjoyable history of clowns and their art, *Slapstick and Dumbbell* is notable also for its illustrations, including a color frontispiece by Harzberg, a picture by Leger, and several reproductions of works by Heuze, a clown who was an artist. At the request of Robert McAlmon, Moss also contributed a two-page preface, "A Soft Note of Introduction," for *The Eater of Darkness* (1926), a Surrealistic novel written by his friend Robert Coates and published by McAlmon's Contact Publishing Company.

In March 1927 Gwynne established *Boulevardier*, an English-language magazine with a distinct Right Bank flavor. Moss edited the publication and wrote a column called "Books and the Left Bank." Patterned after the *New Yorker* but much inferior, *Boulevardier* printed mainly society news and gossip, but there were stories by Michael Arlen, Noel. Coward, Louis Bromfield, Sinclair Lewis, and Ernest Hemingway. Jed Kiley, Moss's assistant editor, solicited a story from Hemingway, "The Real Spaniard," which was a parody of Louis Bromfield's "The Real French," an earlier *Boulevardier* feature. Moss thought the story could be improved and added his own ending, which angered Hemingway when he saw it in the October 1927 issue. *Boulevardier* ceased publication after the January 1932 issue.

Moss continued to live and write in Paris for most of his life. On 20 February 1969 he died at the American Hospital in Neuilly. —*Jean W. Ross*

References:

Hugh Ford, *Published in Paris American and British Writers, Printers, and Publishers in Paris, 1920-1939* (New York: Macmillan, 1975), pp. 74-75;

Florence Gilliam, "My Years With Arthur Moss," *Lost Generation Journal*, 2 (Fall 1974): 10-13, 32-33; 3 (Winter 1975): 39-42;

Al Laney, *Paris Herald The Incredible Newspaper* (New York & London: Appleton-Century, 1947), p. 151.

PETER NEAGOE
(7 November 1881-28 October 1960)

BOOKS: *Storm A Book of Short Stories* (Paris: New Review Press, 1932; enlarged edition, Paris: Obelisk Press, 1932);

What is Surrealism (Paris: New Review Press, 1932);

Easter Sun (Paris: Obelisk Press, 1934; New York: Coward-McCann, 1934; London: Hutchinson, 1934);

Winning a Wife & Other Stories (New York: Coward-McCann, 1935);

There is My Heart (New York: Coward-McCann, 1936; London: Dent, 1936);

A Time to Keep (New York: Coward-McCann, 1949);

No Time for Tears (New York: Kamin, 1958);

The Saint of Montparnasse (Philadelphia: Chilton, 1965);

A Selection of Stories, ed. John S. Mayfield (Syracuse, N.Y.: Syracuse University, 1969).

Peter Neagoe, American artist and writer, was a native of what is now Romania. Although nearly forgotten by the time of his death, he acquired a small reputation as a writer in the late twenties for his simple, lyrical fiction about his homeland. Neagoe's first stories appeared in *transition* and other Paris little magazines shortly after he abandoned a painting career to write. While in Paris Neagoe also worked as coeditor of the little magazine the *New Review* and edited *Americans Abroad* (1932), an anthology of work by American expatriate writers in Europe.

Neagoe's father was a wealthy notary of a small Transylvania village, and, although he was raised in an intellectual atmosphere, young Neagoe preferred to spend his time among the peasants who herded sheep and farmed in this harsh, rugged region of southeastern Europe. Facts, feelings, and images from his childhood among people he loved and admired became the source material for nearly all of his writings. In *Americans Abroad* Neagoe claims to have begun his writing career as a boy when he became "the scribe of the neighborhood servants" by composing love letters for the illiterate servant girls to send to their boyfriends.

In 1898 Neagoe traveled to nearby Bucharest to study philosophy at the university and painting at the Academy of Fine Arts. In 1901, at the age of twenty, he immigrated to the United States and later became a naturalized citizen. Living in New York City, he continued his art education at the National Academy of Design. At a social gathering to play chess he met Anna Frankeul, a young artist of Lithuanian extraction, whom he married on 31 July 1911. For the next few years Neagoe worked as a translator and served as an illustrator for a large mail-order catalogue.

After World War I the Neagoes, realizing that the lower cost of living in Paris and the inflated value of their American dollars there would enable them to devote themselves full-time to painting, began saving the money they would need to go abroad. In 1926 they settled in Paris, where their neighbors

Peter Neagoe

included artists Georges Braque, Rene Magritte, and Andre Lothe.

Although he was an accomplished artist, Neagoe soon felt outclassed by his wife, who was steadily gaining critical recognition in Paris galleries, and in 1928 he gave up painting to become a writer. His first completed story, "Kaleidoscope," was published in the March 1928 issue of *transition*, edited by Eugene Jolas. The story is a poetic mosaic of childhood memories described in serene, dreamlike images. Subsequent stories that appeared in *transition* between 1928 and 1932 employed this same kind of imagery but within increasingly stricter narrative structures. Neagoe also contributed another story, "It Dawned," to Bob Brown's avant-garde anthology, *Readies for Bob Brown's Machine* (1931), and during the early thirties Neagoe also published several stories in the American magazines *Contact* and *Pagany*, and in *Story*, published in Vienna.

In late 1931 Neagoe began to assist Samuel Putnam with the editing of his magazine, the *New Review*, and in early 1932 he bought a half interest in the magazine, becoming coeditor. At about this same time both the Neagoes and the Putnams settled in Mirmande, an artists' colony in the South of France. Neagoe's links with the *transition* magazine group brought a number of new contributors to the magazine, including Charles Henri Ford, Norman Macleod, Emily Holmes Coleman, Laurence Vail, and, most notably, Kay Boyle. Neagoe also contributed his own work, including his story "The Greenhorn." Because of *transition*'s dislike for Ezra Pound, associate editor of the *New Review*, Pound, who had never been influential in determining the *New Review*'s editorial policy, was pushed further into the background. The fifth and final issue (April 1932) included a poem by Kay Boyle, which, without Putnam's or Neagoe's knowledge, revived an old disagreement about Pound's treatment of Ernest Walsh (the editor of *This Quarter* until his death in 1926), and Pound resigned from the *New Review*'s editorial board. Despite the praise it received from members of the Paris expatriate community, the magazine was disbanded for lack of funds before it published another issue.

Putnam had also put Neagoe to work compiling an anthology of stories and poems by Americans living in Europe, *Americans Abroad An Anthology*, which was published by the Servire Press in December 1932. It contains contributions and brief autobiographies from fifty-two writers. Among those included are Conrad Aiken, Wambly Bald, Djuna Barnes, Kay Boyle, Bob Brown, Kathleen

JANVIER

14 Vendredi. S. Hilaire 14-351 8³⁰ P.M.

JANVIER

15 Samedi. S. Maur 15-350 11³⁰ P.M.

Diary, 1927

Cannell, Emily Holmes Coleman, Malcolm Cowley, Caresse and Harry Crosby, E. E. Cummings, John Dos Passos, James T. Farrell, Charles Henri Ford, A. Lincoln Gillespie, Ernest Hemingway, Eugene Jolas, Alfred Kreymborg, Robert McAlmon, Sherry Mangan, Henry Miller, Ezra Pound, Samuel Putnam, Robert Sage, William Seabrook, Gertrude Stein, Richard Thoma, Laurence Vail, Ernest Walsh, and William Carlos Williams. Neagoe himself contributed his story "Winning a Wife" and a foreword in which he tried to analyze why American writers left America for Paris. He said they were nonconformists escaping the temptation to succeed through compromise, escaping America's notorious desire to standardize everything, even art. He concluded that America has to learn that "art must have freedom and must be appraised with its own criteria and not weighed in the balance of utility."

While Neagoe was working on *Americans Abroad*, the New Review Press published his pamphlet essay, *What is Surrealism* (1932), and his first book of short stories, *Storm* (1932), which had an introduction by Eugene Jolas. Although his tales of Romanian peasant life contained only mildly erotic material, *Storm* was banned by United States customs officials. The banning gave *Storm* a notoriety that tempted book buyers and placed it briefly in a category with James Joyce's *Ulysses* (1922) and other less literary, but more popular, erotic books for which Paris was becoming infamous. A new, enlarged edition of *Storm* was published by Obelisk Press in that same year and was reprinted several times. The stories earned praise not only from Neagoe's mentors Jolas and Putnam but also from Kay Boyle and others.

After it became apparent that the *New Review* would be unable to publish another issue, Neagoe returned to the United States in 1933. The following year his first novel, *Easter Sun*, was published in Paris by Obelisk Press, as well as in New York and London. During World War II Neagoe's knowledge of five European languages made him a valuable staff member of the Office of War Information. His work there included preparing radio broadcasts for the Romanian people. In the years that followed the war, Neagoe and his wife spent their summers in the artists' community of Woodstock, New York, and their winters in Sarasota, Florida. One of his most memorable works, *A Time to Keep* (1949), is an autobiographical chronicle of his childhood years in Romania. He died in Woodstock on 28 October 1960 at the age of seventy-eight. Published posthumously was *The Saint of Montparnasse* (1965), a biographical novel about Neagoe's close friend the Romanian sculptor Constantin Brancusi, whom he knew in Paris.

Although mention of Neagoe's homeland, Transylvania, immediately conjures visions of vampires and werewolves, it is not with these that Neagoe's fiction is concerned but with the simple, hardworking peasants, their customs, problems, and ideals. Neagoe's stories are a combination of realism and romance: his characters are human and genuine, but they are viewed nostalgically as if by a naive child. Many of his stories are like simple fables or folktales; others are more complex and impressionistic. Although multilingual, Neagoe wrote his stories in English; he claimed that it was the language in which he thought best.

The reviewer of *Storm* in the *Saturday Review of Literature* (15 October 1932) declared, "Despite his alliance with those expatriated writers who are gathered together on the Continent, it is not as an experimentalist or eccentric that Neagoe asks to be considered." Indeed, as his fellow expatriate Kay Boyle recognized, Neagoe's stories were at the opposite end of the spectrum from the seemingly formless prose of James Joyce and Gertrude Stein, and in an article written for the Paris *Tribune* (the European edition of the *Chicago Tribune*) she contrasted Neagoe to other writers for *transition* by remarking on "the solemn loyalty Peter Neagoe gives romance." —*Mark Fritz*

Other:

"It Dawned," in *Readies for Bob Brown's Machine*, ed. Bob Brown (Cagnes-sur-Mer: Roving Eye Press, 1931), pp. 44-45;
Americans Abroad An Anthology, edited by Neagoe (The Hague: Servire, 1932).

Periodical Publications:

"Kaleidoscope," *transition*, no. 12 (March 1928): 87-91;
"A Segment of the Whole," *transition*, no. 13 (Summer 1928): 44-49;
"A Fact," *transition*, no. 15 (February 1929): 38-41;
"Dreams," *transition*, no. 18 (November 1929): 64-65;
"Shepherd of the Lord," *Story*, 1 (November-December 1931): 5-26;
"The Village Saint," *transition*, no. 21 (March 1932): 75-81;
"The Greenhorn," *New Review*, 2 (April 1932);

"Holy Remedy," *Pagany*, 3 (July-September 1932): 59-65;

"The Golden Path," *Contact*, 1 (October 1932): 67-74;

"Contentment Is Silent," *Story*, 4 (February 1934): 27-40;

"Then was Hey-Day," *Story*, 8 (April 1936): 50-65;

"A Drum Beat in Harvest Time," *Esquire*, 9 (February 1938): 70-74;

"Ill Winds from the Wide World," *Story*, 17 (July-August 1940): 79-86;

"The Lamb and the Wolves," *Story*, 19 (July-August 1941): 54-64.

References:

Rodica Botoman, "Peter Neagoe's Relations with the American Expatriate Movement in France," *Miorita A Journal of Romanian Studies*, 5 (July 1978): 163-171;

Hugh Ford, *Published in Paris American and British Writers, Printers, and Publishers in Paris, 1920-1939* (New York: Macmillan, 1975), pp. 312-321;

Samuel Putnam, *Paris Was Our Mistress Memoirs of a Lost & Found Generation* (New York: Viking, 1947).

Papers:

Neagoe's papers and some of his paintings are in the Bird Library at Syracuse University.

ANAIS NIN
(21 February 1903-14 January 1977)

SELECTED BOOKS: *D. H. Lawrence An Unprofessional Study* (Paris: Black Manikin Press, 1932; London: Spearman, 1961; Denver: Swallow, 1964);

The House of Incest (Paris: Siana Editions / Obelisk Press, 1936; New York: Gemor, 1947); republished in *Winter of Artifice House of Incest* (London: Owen, 1974);

The Winter of Artifice (Paris: Villa Seurat Editions / Obelisk Press, 1939; New York: Gemor, 1942); enlarged as *Winter of Artifice Three Novelettes* (Denver: Swallow, 1961);

Under a Glass Bell (New York: Gemor, 1944; enlarged edition, London: Editions Poetry, 1947);

Cities of the Interior (n.p., 1959; revised and enlarged edition, Chicago: Swallow, 1974; London: Owen, 1978);

The Diary of Anais Nin 1931-1934, ed. Gunther Stuhlmann (New York: Swallow / Harcourt, Brace & World, 1966); republished as *The Journals of Anais Nin 1931-1934* (London: Owen, 1966);

The Diary of Anais Nin 1934-1939, ed. Stuhlmann (New York: Swallow / Harcourt, Brace & World, 1967); republished as *The Journals of Anais Nin 1934-1939* (London: Owen, 1967);

The Diary of Anais Nin 1939-1944, ed. Stuhlmann (New York: Harcourt, Brace & World, 1969); republished as *The Journals of Anais Nin 1939-1944* (London: Owen, 1970);

The Diary of Anais Nin 1944-1947, ed. Stuhlmann (New York: Harcourt Brace Jovanovich, 1971); republished as *The Journals of Anais Nin 1944-1947* (London: Owen, 1972);

The Diary of Anais Nin 1947-1955, ed. Stuhlmann (New York: Harcourt Brace Jovanovich, 1974); republished as *The Journals of Anais Nin 1947-1955* (London: Owen, 1974);

A Photographic Supplement to the Diary of Anais Nin (New York & London: Harcourt Brace Jovanovich, 1974);

The Diary of Anais Nin 1955-1966, ed. Stuhlmann (New York & London: Harcourt Brace Jovanovich, 1976); republished as *The Journals of Anais Nin 1955-1966* (London: Owen, 1977);

Delta of Venus Erotica (New York: Harcourt Brace Jovanovich, 1977; London: Allen, 1978);

Waste of Timelessness and Other Early Stories (Weston, Conn.: Magic Circle Press, 1977);

Linotte: The Early Diary of Anais Nin 1914-1920, trans. Jean Sherman (New York: Harcourt Brace Jovanovich, 1978);

Little Birds Erotica (New York & London: Harcourt Brace Jovanovich, 1979).

Of all the American expatriates in Paris between 1920 and 1940, Anais Nin was one of the few repatriates. She was born in Neuilly, outside Paris, to artistic parents. Her father, Joaquin, was a pianist and composer; her mother, Rosa, sang. She spent her first eleven years in France, but after Joaquin Nin deserted the family, Mrs. Nin took her children—Anais, Joaquin, and Thorvald—to New York. That separation from her father led Nin to write him a letter that evolved into her most famous literary work, her *Diary*. Nin withdrew from school before completing her formal education. She continued her studies at home and in the public libraries. Around the age of twenty-one she married Hugh Guiler (later known as Ian Hugo), and sometime before 1930 she returned to France. (Her activities between 1920 and 1930 are vague.) She remained there until 1939, when the outbreak of World War II forced her to return to the United States.

By the time she began her literary career in Paris, the group known as the lost generation had dispersed. But Paris is a permanent as well as a movable feast, and it had much to offer her. She drew inspiration not primarily from the writers remaining in Paris, but rather from a strange array of largely unknown characters. Henry Miller was her most intimate friend during that decade in Paris. When they met in 1931, he was a struggling, unpublished author. Even though Nin and Miller were opposites in almost every way, they admired each other as individuals and as writers. Their friendship took most visible form in her preface to his great and infamous *Tropic of Cancer* (1934), his first book, in which she commends his voraciousness, his desire to live life completely, if basically, as others do not: "In a world grown paralyzed with introspection and constipated by delicate mental meals this brutal exposure of the substantial body comes as a vitalizing current of blood." That book was published largely through her efforts. Miller then dedicated *Black Spring* to her in 1936. Their friendship continued until her death, although the true nature of their relationship remains unclear.

While she was most intimate with Miller, Nin had numerous other friends in Paris, and several of them influenced her work. She was a patient of the psychoanalysts Rene Allendy and Otto Rank, and they—especially the latter—and their science had a profound effect on her writing. She became friendly with Antonin Artaud, the mad genius of the theatre. Others with whom she associated were the Peruvian Marxist Gonzalo More and his wife Helba, Conrad Moricand, Michael Fraenkel, and Alfred Perles. Lawrence Durrell became an important member of the Nin-Miller group. Aside from the most significant of these people, and after psychoanalysis, the greatest influences on her work were Surrealism and the writings of D. H. Lawrence, both of which

she evidently discovered and certainly assimilated during her mature years in Paris.

Nin published her first three books during her decade in Paris. The first, *D. H. Lawrence An Unprofessional Study* (1932), is a short critical book; the second, *The House of Incest* (1936), is a prose-poem; and the third, *The Winter of Artifice* (1939), is a collection of novelettes. Individually and collectively they inform the rest of her published work and stand as impressive books at the beginning of a distinguished literary career.

Nin wrote her book on Lawrence in sixteen days, according to her *Diary* published thirty-four years after that earliest effort. Her study is unprofessional, as she openly admitted, but it should not be taken lightly. She was not then nor would she ever become a serious literary critic, but her insights into Lawrence's work are valuable, especially as they anticipate her later publications. She notes, for example, that in order for one to approach Lawrence's world "there must be a threefold desire of intellect, of imagination, and of physical feeling, because he erected his world on a fusion of concepts, on a philosophy that was against division, on a plea for whole vision: 'to see with the soul and the body.'" Similarly a sentence she quotes from Lawrence might well have been her own: "The secret of all life is obedience: obedience to the urge that arises in the soul, the urge that is life itself, urging us to new gestures, new embraces, new emotions, new combinations, new creations." Finally Nin especially applauds Lawrence's observations about women. She believed that of all the male writers he was the one most sensitive to women, particularly in his notion that they are not necessarily well-served in attempting to meet men's conceptions of them. These and many other ideas Nin found valuable in Lawrence's work, and she incorporated them into her own writing.

Nin's next book, in 1936, was her first published fiction, *The House of Incest*. It is the single best work she created. It is important for several reasons, not the least of which is that it proves that from her earliest effort she had a clear perception of what she wished to accomplish in all of her fiction. The prose-poem perfectly illustrates two of her most significant literary tenets. She believed, with Jung, that one should "proceed from the dream outward." *The House of Incest* is all dream until one character finally escapes from the dream and the house. Nin also desired to investigate reality and not realism. By the former she meant real, psychological truth; by the latter, externals, or surface reality. All of her fictions investigate inner truth. She believed so absolutely in the value of her psychological pursuit in fiction that even when she was criticized for not providing enough surface reality—and when she saw that her fiction would never receive a large readership—she steadfastly refused to alter her design. Rather than compromise her art, she quit writing fiction after 1964.

The House of Incest is an unnamed narrator's nightmare. She has obviously had difficulty in life, and to escape it she has withdrawn into her subconscious, or dream, where she hopes to have a painless existence. Her first words suggest her problem: "My first vision of earth was water veiled. I am of the race of men and women who see all things through this curtain of sea and my eyes are the color of water." She psychologically reverts to her prenatal state, finds it comfortable, and wishes not to leave it. She is, in effect, committing a kind of suicide by choosing unalleviated pleasure and comfort over the harshness of life. She also discovers and becomes lost in the Atlantide (Atlantis), a place eternally apart from humanity. It represents an area in which she may participate in "loving without knowingness, moving without effort, in the soft current of water and desire, breathing in an ecstasy of dissolution." She is psychologically dead. Nin implies here and elsewhere that one's dreams are a fertile area that must be cultivated if one is to live as fully as possible. But if one becomes entrapped therein—as this narrator does—great danger ensues.

After leaving the comforts of the Atlantide, the narrator meets Alraune, a woman of great passion whose strength is symbolized by steel. This sensual dancer is active while the narrator—a writer—is passive, and the narrator wants them to join in psychological and physical union. But even though the narrator is eager to fuse with Alraune, she realizes that sacrificing herself entirely to, and losing her identity in, another person is dangerous; as she joins Alraune, she leaves behind "Ariadne's golden thread" by which she may retrace her steps to her own identity. She is beginning to understand the dangers in the existence she thinks she desires.

After concluding her relationship with Alraune and being perplexed by her own distance from life, the narrator encounters another woman, Isolina, who is the antithesis of Alraune. Isolina is soft, inert, and timid, a lame woman who is a "prisoner on earth." The narrator becomes an adviser to Isolina and tells her what she, the narrator, does not yet fully comprehend: that one must experience life's realities if one wishes to live fully. The narrator is now more aware of her own psychological state than she was before she met Alraune. Yet Isolina, like Alraune and the rest of the characters the narrator will meet, is not separate from the narrator. Isolina is rather one aspect of the narrator's multifaceted self. She is therefore an identity that the narrator must recognize and assimilate before she may attain psychological wholeness.

Isolina functions most importantly as the narrator's guide to the house of incest. Isolina loves her brother, and because she is attracted to her likeness she must live in this house of stasis, decay, and death. The narrator discovers there a paralytic and someone called "the modern Christ." They are both outside life's magnetic chain and can exist only in the house of incest. But the narrator also meets one other person, and she—an unnamed dancer—is the most important of all. In her former conscious life, this woman clung selfishly to everything she liked and everyone she loved. As a result she lost her arms and was banished to this house with the others. Unlike her fellow captives, however, she solves her problem, regains her arms, gives and does not possess, and escapes her torment in the house of incest: "And she danced, she danced with the music and with the rhythm of earth's circles, she turned with the earth turning, like a disk, turning all faces to light and to darkness evenly, dancing towards daylight." Since the dancer is a part of the narrator, one assumes that the narrator has taken that first difficult step toward psychological wholeness. Music here and elsewhere in Nin's fiction serves as a kind of panacea for mankind's ills. The Isolina part of the narrator is not yet ready to leave her imprisonment because her guitar string snapped, a frequent Nin symbol for lack of harmony, for isolation, and for psychological despair.

Nin's message is clear. The nature of man's existence is multiple and imperfect. Every individual has many parts, the sum of which is something less than one's ideal self. But if one ignores that multiplicity or demands perfection, that person will not be able to function in life and will have a residence only in something as nonhuman and deadly as the house of incest.

Nin never expressed these basic concerns as eloquently or convincingly as she did in this first volume of her fiction, even though almost all the rest of her fiction is similar to it thematically. It documents her indebtedness to psychoanalysis, Surrealism, and D. H. Lawrence. In all editions of the prose-poem published after 1936, Alraune is named Sabina and Isolina is called Jeanne. Sabina became one of the three major women in Nin's continuous novel, *Cities of the Interior* (1959), and Jeanne became the major character in "Under a

Glass Bell," one of Nin's best stories. *The House of Incest* was the first and it remains the best of Nin's fictions, all of which are substantial. The Parisian cultural ambience of the thirties certainly influenced Nin's creation of this seminal and major work. Such an esoteric book doubtless could not have been written or published in the United States at that time.

The Winter of Artifice, Nin's third book, contains three novelettes. (The contents were revised in subsequent editions.) The first of them, "Djuna," is one of Nin's most realistic fictions. It concerns Johanna, Hans, and Djuna in a menage a trois. Djuna, who recurs throughout *Cities of the Interior* as perhaps the most important of all Nin women, is here reflective, as she would be even more noticeably later. She loves both Hans (based on Henry Miller) and Johanna (who resembles Miller's second wife, June). Nin wisely chose never to republish this piece. It is unwieldy. It resembles certain parts of *The House of Incest* so closely that some of the prose-poem's language is repeated in it. It also looks forward to *Cities of the Interior* and to the first volume of Nin's *Diary* where the relationship among the three major characters is discussed as fact with Nin herself the equivalent of Djuna. She wrote elsewhere much more convincingly than in "Djuna" about the problems of these three principals.

More successful than "Djuna" is "Lilith," a novelette that, revised, became "Winter of Artifice." Here Lilith yearns to be with her father, who deserted his family when she was eleven. Over the years she has idealized him, so when they meet, he naturally disappoints her. This work anticipates other fictional Nin women who seek their lost fathers, and it, like all of Nin's fiction, has its basis in Nin's life, as may be seen throughout her *Diary*.

The last of the novelettes is "The Voice." It is about four troubled characters who attempt to solve their problems through the title character, a psychoanalyst. Djuna is comfortable only when she lives extremely, and she therefore resides outside of life. Lillian is uncertain of her sexuality. Mischa, a cellist, is unable to find his proper role with others and especially with women. Lilith lives too conservatively. All four are aware of their difficulties, but the most pathetic of all is the Voice, who is more in need of unburdening himself than are his patients. But Nin begins to resolve only Djuna's problem. She learns what all of Nin's characters must: that dreams have to be probed, not to the exclusion of conscious reality, but rather to nourish it.

These three books Nin wrote in Paris are all of different genres, yet each focuses on ideas central to everything else (except the erotica) she would write. Her finest literary achievement remains her first fiction, *The House of Incest*.

Nin was also busy contributing to European and North American little magazines during her stay in Paris in the thirties. A few of these pieces are excerpts from *The House of Incest* or *The Winter of Artifice*, but most of the twelve short items look forward rather than backward. Her first publication, other than two juvenile contributions to her school paper in New York in 1918, was "D. H. Lawrence Mystic of Sex" in the *Canadian Forum* (Toronto) in 1930. Therein she makes her first statement on the recently deceased author whose work she would examine in detail two years later. Published in 1938, an article in *Purpose* (London), "Creative Principle in Analysis," is a valuable defense of Otto Rank. "Fragment from a Diary," which appeared the same year in *Seven* (Taunton, England), illustrates how early in her professional career she was interested in publishing the journal she had been keeping for almost a quarter of a century. The first published volume would not appear until 1966.

The most important of her periodical contributions during these years were her first published stories, all of which appeared in 1938. "The Paper Womb" (later "The Labyrinth") appeared in the *Booster* (Paris), "Rag-Time" was published in *Seven*, and "Birth" appeared in *Twice a Year* (New York). Following a book of criticism, a prose-poem, and a collection of novelettes, these stories represent the first efforts in a new genre to which she would devote her creative energies during the next few years. That interest culminated in *Under a Glass Bell*, a collection of her stories (including these three) that she published at her own Gemor Press in New York in 1944. Sixteen unpublished stories from her Paris years were collected in *Waste of Timelessness and Other Early Stories* in 1977. Of all her short fiction, "Birth," one of the earliest, is clearly the best.

Brief mention should be made of two other periodical publications, not because they are substantial items in her literary canon, but rather because of the place in which they—along with "The Paper Womb"—were published. In 1937 Nin published "Le Merle Blanc" (written in French) and "A Boost for *Black Spring*" in the *Booster*. That obscure journal was the enterprise of Henry Miller, Alfred Perles, and others, and Nin served on its editorial board. (It became known as *Delta* in 1938.) She was not an active editor because she thought the undertaking frivolous, as it was. She perceived that it demanded too much of Miller's time and energy that should have been better spent on his serious writing. Still, it served as a focal point for Nin's group of literary friends. They also shared an interest in two publishing ventures—Siana Editions and the Villa Seurat series of books published by the Obelisk Press. The former published *The House of Incest*; the latter, *The Winter of Artifice*, Miller's *Max and the White Phagocytes* (1938), and Durrell's *Black Book* (1938).

Paris was the most important city to Anais Nin. She spent her formative years there, and from her mid-twenties through age thirty-six she cultivated her literature there. She experimented successfully with four different literary genres, and she developed her art to such a level that none of her subsequent fiction differs significantly from what she wrote in Paris. Nor does any of it surpass the quality of *The House of Incest*. Had she not experienced Paris in the thirties, she would not have had the same thoughts on literature or have produced so valuable and unique a literary canon as she did.

—*Benjamin Franklin V*

Periodical Publications:

"Why Every Home Should Own a Liberty Bond," *Criterion*, 5 (March 1918): 9;

"The Password," *Criterion*, 5 (March 1918): 12-13;

"D. H. Lawrence Mystic of Sex," *Canadian Forum*, 11 (October 1930): 15-17;

"Le Merle Blanc," *Booster*, 2 (September 1937): 17-18;

"A Boost for *Black Spring*," *Booster*, 3e Annee, 9 (November 1937): 27;

"The Paper Womb," *Booster*, 4e Annee, 10-11 (December 1937-January 1938): 3-5;

"The House of Incest," *transition*, no. 27 (April-May 1938): 114-118;

"Orchestra," *Phoenix*, 1 (June-August 1938): 95-100;

"Fragment from a Diary," *Seven*, 1 (Summer 1938): 26-27;

"Creative Principle in Analysis," *Purpose*, 10 (July-September 1938): 147-152;

"Rag-Time," *Seven*, 2 (Autumn 1938): 2-4;

"Birth," *Twice a Year*, 1 (Fall-Winter 1938): 132-137;

"Soundless Keyboard Orchestra," *Delta*, 2me Annee, 3 (Xmas 1938): 67-71;

"Mischa's Confession to the Analyst," *Seven*, 4 (Spring 1939): 31-33.

References:

Kenneth C. Dick, *Henry Miller Colossus of One* (The Netherlands: Sittard, Alberts, 1967);

Oliver Evans, *Anais Nin* (Carbondale: Southern Illinois University Press, 1968);

Benjamin Franklin V, *Anais Nin: A Bibliography* (Kent, Ohio: Kent State University Press, 1973);

Franklin and Duane Schneider, *Anais Nin: An Introduction* (Athens: Ohio University Press, 1979);

Evelyn J. Hinz, *The Mirror and the Garden: Realism and Reality in the Writings of Anais Nin* (Columbus: Ohio State University Libraries, 1971);

Mosaic, special Nin issue, 11 (Winter 1978);

Alfred Perles, *My Friend Henry Miller: An Intimate Biography* (London: Spearman, 1955);

Robert Snyder, *Anais Nin Observed From a Film Portrait of a Woman as Artist* (Chicago: Swallow, 1976);

Sharon Spencer, *Collage of Dreams: The Writings of Anais Nin* (Chicago: Swallow, 1977);

Gunther Stuhlmann, ed., *Henry Miller: Letters to Anais Nin* (New York: Putnam's, 1965);

George Wickes, ed., *Lawrence Durrell Henry Miller: A Private Correspondence* (New York: Dutton, 1963);

Robert Zaller, ed., *A Casebook on Anais Nin* (New York: New American Library, 1974).

Elliot Paul

Philip B. Eppard
Providence, Rhode Island

BIRTH: Malden, Massachusetts, 11 February 1891, to Lucy Greenleaf Dowsett and Harold Henry Paul.

EDUCATION: University of Maine, 1908-1909.

MARRIAGE: 20 April 1919 to Rosa Gertrude Brown, divorced. 28 March 1928 to Camille Nesbit Haynes, divorced. 15 April 1935 to Flora Thompson Brown, died 1943. 29 January 1945 to Barbara Ellen Mayock, divorced; children: Leslie Elliot. 13 March 1951 to Serena (Nancy) McMahon Dolan, divorced.

DEATH: Providence, Rhode Island, 7 April 1958.

BOOKS: *Indelible A Story of Life, Love and Music in Five Movements* (Boston & New York: Houghton Mifflin, 1922; London: Jarrolds, 1924);

Impromptu A Novel in Four Movements (New York: Knopf, 1923);

Imperturbe A Novel of Peace Without Victory (New York: Knopf, 1924);

Low Run Tide and Lava Rock (New York: Liveright, 1929);

The Amazon (New York: Liveright, 1930);

The Governor of Massachusetts (New York: Liveright, 1930);

The Life and Death of a Spanish Town (New York: Random House, 1937; London: Peter Davies, 1937);

Concert Pitch (New York: Random House, 1938);

The Stars and Stripes Forever (New York: Random House, 1939);

The Mysterious Mickey Finn or, Murder at the Cafe du Dome (New York: Modern Age, 1939; London: Penguin, 1953);

Hugger-Mugger in the Louvre (New York: Random House, 1940; London: Nicholson & Watson, 1949);

The Death of Lord Haw Haw, as Brett Rutledge (New York: Random House, 1940);

Mayhem in B-Flat (New York: Random House, 1940; London: Transworld, 1951);

Fracas in the Foothills (New York: Random House, 1940);

Intoxication Made Easy, by Paul and Luis Quintanilla (New York: Modern Age, 1941);

The Last Time I Saw Paris (New York: Random House, 1942); republished as *A Narrow Street* (London: Cresset, 1942);

With a Hays Nonny Nonny, by Paul and Luis Quintanilla (New York: Random House, 1942);

I'll Hate Myself in the Morning and Summer in December (New York: Random House, 1945; London: Nicholson & Watson, 1949);

Linden on the Saugus Branch (New York: Random House, 1947; London: Cresset, 1948);

A Ghost Town on the Yellowstone (New York: Random House, 1948; London: Cresset, 1949);

My Old Kentucky Home (New York: Random House, 1949; London: Cresset, 1950);

Springtime in Paris (New York: Random House, 1950; London: Cresset, 1951);

Murder on the Left Bank (New York: Random House, 1951; London: Transworld, 1952);

The Black Gardenia (New York: Random House, 1952);

Waylaid in Boston (New York: Random House, 1953);

Understanding the French (London: Muller, 1954; New York: Random House, 1955);

Desperate Scenery (New York: Random House, 1954; London: Cresset, 1955);

The Black and the Red (New York: Random House, 1956);

Film Flam (London: Muller, 1956);

That Crazy Music: The Story of North American Jazz (London: Muller, 1957); republished as *That Crazy American Music* (Indianapolis & New York: Bobbs-Merrill, 1957).

Of all the American writers who went to Paris in the twenties Elliot Paul may have been the most representative. At least his career has all the elements associated in the popular mind with the expatriate community. A born bon vivant, Paul fit the bohemian cafe society of Montparnasse perfectly. His love of good food and drink showed in his portly figure, and his love of women was legendary. As a coeditor of *transition*, he helped promote the works of Gertrude Stein and James Joyce and became identified with the forces of the avant-garde in literature, art, and music. His Paris years were interrupted by five years spent in Spain, which led to his first commercially successful book, *The Life and Death of a Spanish Town* (1937), containing a powerful indictment of the fascist forces in the Spanish Civil War. That war ended Paul's Spanish sojourn, and he returned to Paris only to be driven back to the United States at last by the advent of World War II. He then celebrated the life in his little corner of Paris in his biggest seller, *The Last Time I Saw Paris* (1942). During his years in Paris he wrote several well-regarded novels of American life. These years also provided the background for a series of popular mystery novels set on Paris's Left Bank.

Elliot Harold Paul's family background was staunchly New England. His mother, Lucy Greenleaf Dowsett Paul, was descended from Richard Tarr, who first settled Rockport, Massachusetts, in 1629. Harold Henry Paul, his father, was from Maine. The Paul family was part of the solid middle class of the Linden section of Malden, Massachusetts, not far north of Boston. Paul's father, who had a checkered career as a businessman, died in 1895 in the Danvers Insane Asylum when Paul was not quite four years old. After graduation from high school in 1907, Paul went west to join his older brother Charles, a civil engineer, who was working for the United States Reclamation Service conducting an irrigation survey on the Yellowstone River in Montana. Paul worked as a timekeeper and a surveyor and decided to pursue a career as an engineer. He returned east and attended the University of Maine briefly in 1908-1909. After leaving school, he went to Louisville, Kentucky, where he worked for a year as an engineer for the city. He then headed west again for a period of vagabondage in Idaho and Wyoming. He was already an accomplished musician and played piano in saloons as well as working at a variety of odd jobs.

Paul eventually found his way back to Boston, where he took up journalism. He worked as a statehouse correspondent, thereby gaining an intimate knowledge of Massachusetts politics. During World War I he went overseas with the 317th Field Signal Battalion and advanced from the rank of private to that of sergeant by the war's end. He returned to Boston, married a hometown girl, and resumed his journalistic career. He also cultivated his interests in music, art, and the theatre and became a member of Boston's bohemian community. With characteristic impulsiveness he quit his job to write a novel. *Indelible A Story of Life, Love and Music in Five Movements* was published by Houghton Mifflin in 1922 and was greeted in the Boston press by lavish articles, at least one of which Paul probably wrote himself. They portrayed him as the young

journalist-vagabond writing in a garret on the shabby side of Beacon Hill. According to Paul he had written *Indelible* in eighteen days. Almost as quickly he produced two other novels: *Impromptu A Novel in Four Movements* (1923) and *Imperturbe A Novel of Peace Without Victory* (1924).

These first three novels were moderately well received, and Paul was regarded as a promising young novelist given to slightly experimental techniques and risque subject matter. The books drew largely on personal experiences and observations in Malden, Boston, the West, and the war. *Indelible* tells the story of two musicians, Samuel Graydon, a native New Englander, and Lena Borofsky, a Russian-Jewish immigrant. The story of their love, the accident that destroys her musical career, and their reconciliation is fairly conventional and even sentimental. Paul's style is striking, however. The perspective shifts from Samuel's first-person narration to the impersonal third-person presentation of Lena's story. Conventional narrative style is mixed with clipped, impressionistic passages. Clearly Paul's idea was to apply some of his knowledge of musical composition to the novel.

This last technique was also employed in *Impromptu*, the story of Irwin Atwood, who, like Paul, comes from a conventional suburb of Boston. He goes overseas during World War I and returns disillusioned, only to find his girl friend driven into prostitution. He can find solitude only back in the army. The story is told in a series of brief vignettes, often with staccato half sentences.

Imperturbe has as its main character Lester Davis, whose career has striking parallels to Paul's own. He leaves New England to work with his older brother on a surveying project in the West, returns to the East to study at the University of Maine, and goes to Louisville, where he works for a while before escaping to the West once more. Some reviewers were shocked by the book's account of Lester's bout with syphilis. He eventually returns to Boston, goes to war, and finds an unsettled peace which leaves him in a condition approaching the voice in Walt Whitman's poem "Me Imperturbe," from which the book gets its title. Reviewers were sometimes critical of Paul's techniques and subject matter in these three novels but praised his skills of characterization and storytelling. Despite the encouraging reception of these three books, Paul retreated from the field of "promising young novelists."

Instead the urge to travel took hold. He left his wife and in the summer of 1923 found himself in Paris. He gained employment eventually with the European edition of the *Chicago Tribune*, often called the Paris *Tribune*, first as a proofreader and subsequently as an occasional literary and music critic. In the paper he had praise for the works of George Antheil, Gertrude Stein, E. E. Cummings, and Ernest Hemingway, but made light of the fiction of Sinclair Lewis and Louis Bromfield. When, late in 1926, Eugene Jolas, another *Tribune* staffer, was planning to launch a new literary review, he invited Paul to join him as coeditor. Together they established *transition*, the most influential expatriate publication in Paris, in April 1927.

It is Paul's association with *transition* that has secured for him a permanent place in literary history. He served as coeditor with Jolas for the first twelve issues, from April 1927 through March 1928. Beginning with the thirteenth issue (Summer 1928) Paul was listed as a contributing editor. In issue number 18 (November 1929) his name was dropped from the masthead, and it was noted that "Elliot Paul whose direct editorial connection with transition ceased in February 1928, is no longer associated in any way with this review." Paul and Jolas apparently parted ways amicably. Paul's erratic life style proved incompatible with the daily requirements of publishing a journal.

During his year as coeditor, however, Paul gave *transition* much of its brash, antibourgeois tone. In an article for the August 1927 issue, "Hands off the Dike," he jibed at those "cautious souls who are constantly on edge for fear some artist or writer will run amuck" and those who feared that innovations in the use of language would somehow topple "the whole structure of logic." His artistic credo was probably summarized in the conclusion of an unsigned editorial for the June 1927 issue in which he defended Stein and Joyce: "We are not troubled by manuscripts we do not understand. When such offerings arrive, we feel at once a certain respect for them. Our fear is that we shall understand them all too well." Paul obviously relished shocking the sensibilities of his native land. In 1929 he had a bill introduced into the Massachusetts legislature which would have required all book and play censors to certify their intelligence and to prove that their sex lives were normal.

Paul was the primary contact between *transition* and Gertrude Stein, so much so that Stein regarded Paul and not Jolas as the moving spirit of the magazine. In *The Autobiography of Alice B. Toklas* (1933) Stein gave the impression that Paul had originated *transition* on his own. This understandably infuriated Jolas and his wife and led to their publishing a pamphlet, *Testimony Against Gertrude Stein*. Paul undoubtedly had a penchant

for self-inflation. Still he should be credited with providing a lucid interpretation of Stein's methods in *transition* and with linking her philosophy to the artistic work of Juan Gris and Pablo Picasso.

Paul's short fiction in *transition* was written in an abstract style notably different from that which he used in his commercially published novels. "The Concert," for example, uses the narrator's stream-of-consciousness to verbalize his mental reactions to a symphony concert. In "Enharmonics" the same method is used to portray the narrator's thoughts of killing his lover. Paul also did translations of pieces by French writers such as Marcel Jouhandeau and Pierre Drieu La Rochelle. One of the editorial goals of *transition* was to forge a link between the progressive writers of Europe and those of the Anglo-American world.

After leaving *transition*, Paul returned to newspaper work, this time for the Paris *Herald* (the European edition of the *New York Herald Tribune*). He also returned to writing novels. After not having a book published for five years, he had three books come out in 1929 and 1930. *Low Run Tide and Lava Rock* (1929) contains two short novels, the first dealing with a decaying coastal town in Maine and the second with the community that surrounds a dam-building project in Idaho. The *New York Times Book Review* noted, "There is nothing in them of the striving after novelty of form which one might have expected from the co-editor of 'Transition.'" This comment can be extended to all of Paul's later fiction. The two novels in *Low Run Tide and Lava Rock* are interesting less for the stories they tell than for the compact portraits they give of contrasting American communities. In *The Amazon* (1930) Paul tells the story of a young woman who desperately desires to go to war and organizes a group of women into a signal corps unit. She contrives to get to France and even to the front lines. The comic opportunities are not missed, but the book is also a convincing portrait of Alberta Snyder's quest for self-realization. The story is told by a foreign correspondent who hears of Alberta's unit and gradually pieces together information on it. In *The Governor of Massachusetts* (1930) Paul returned to the Boston political scene he knew so well from his days as a statehouse correspondent. The governor, Elijah Griffin, is a reticent businessman unsuited for the rough and tumble world of politics he inadvertently gets into. He comes into conflict with Congressman Moore, who epitomizes a new generation of well-polished businessmen in government. The story is told by a young lawyer who works for Asa Perkins, an adviser to Governor

Elliot Paul, inscribed to Sylvia Beach

Sylvia Beach Collection

Reader's Digest. Two years after publication Random House boasted of 150,000 copies in print. Much of its success must be attributed to public interest in the Spanish Civil War. The first half of the book depicts life on Santa Eulalia as Paul knew it during his residence there from 1931 to 1936. The second half shows the gradual destruction of that life as the community is politicized by the approaching war. The book ends with Paul's escape from the island on the day before Italian troops land and set up a fascist government. In reviewing the book for *New York Herald Tribune Books*, William Soskin called it "a lyric work, a heart-felt tribute to a people who won Elliot Paul's heart and to whose youthfulness and true virility he offers almost mystic devotion." He found the poetry more meaningful than the political indignation. Yet it was the idyllic life which Paul evoked so well that made the political indignation so meaningful to readers in 1937.

Paul's technique in this book demonstrates both his reportorial skills and his powers as a storyteller. He is part of the scene he describes, and yet the book is not submerged in authorial intrusion. Freed from the traditional structural restraints of the novel, Paul arranges his portrait of the town as an artist would a painting or a composer a piece of music. Probably he mixed a little fiction with his reportage in the interests of the larger effect. At last he had found a comfortable form as well as a paying audience. It is not surprising, therefore, that he used this same approach in six other books. After 1939, in fact, he abandoned serious fiction altogether and wrote only light mysteries and volumes of autobiographical reportage.

Concert Pitch (1938) combines two of Paul's great loves: music and Paris. He later called it his personal favorite of all his books. It is a psychological novel which Louis Kronenberger saw as suggesting the manner of Henry James. The novel depicts the relationships of a young pianist, his mother, a homosexual music critic who attaches himself to the young man, and the story's narrator, who is in love with the young man's mother. Paul probes the artistic temperament against the background of a modern mechanical age in which the talented individual seems not to have a place. Paul returned to a New England setting for his next novel, *The Stars and Stripes Forever* (1939). Here he examines a small company town racked by labor strife, but in a manner more propagandistic than artistic. The company tries to break the strike and, consequently, to destroy the life of the whole town. The strike-breaking is successful but at the cost of

Griffin and an old-fashioned, upright Boston attorney. The novel is a good study of how social changes were altering politics in New England. On its publication the book aroused added interest because of similarities between Griffin and Calvin Coolidge and between Moore and Alvin T. Fuller, the Massachusetts governor who refused to commute the death sentences of Sacco and Vanzetti.

Again Paul seemed to retreat from the literary field. He took up residence in the little town of Santa Eulalia on the island of Ibiza in the Balearics off the coast of Spain. There he lived quietly, gradually becoming part of the community. He organized an orchestra among the townspeople. The turmoil of the Spanish Civil War drove him out of Spain and led to the writing of what most people consider his best book, *The Life and Death of a Spanish Town* (1937). In writing this book Paul found his most authentic voice. He had earned much of his livelihood as a journalist, yet this was his first nonfiction book. It was a regular selection of the Book-of-the-Month Club and was condensed in support for the company from the town's citizens. Their rallying to the cause of fair treatment for the workers restores the town's faith and represents the spirit of true patriotism.

Paul found a new audience in 1939 when he began writing mysteries in a way that almost suggested a burlesque of the genre. In *The Mysterious Mickey Finn or, Murder at the Cafe du Dome* he introduced the suave detective Homer Evans, an expatriate American in Paris who helps the French authorities in solving a series of bizarre murders. Evans is assisted by the beautiful Miriam Leonard plus an assorted group of Left Bank expatriate writers and artists. The book is filled with violence, and Paul has the chance to display his extensive knowledge of art, music, literature, and cafe life in general, as well as his sense of humor. These outlandish mystery stories were successful enough to become a regular staple of Paul's output. Later Homer Evans mysteries were set in the western United States, in Boston, and in Hollywood.

With his return to the United States, Paul found employment off and on in Hollywood throughout much of the forties. He satirized the censorship policies of the Hays Office in *With a Hays Nonny Nonny* (1942), which presents biblical stories in a form acceptable to the Hollywood censors. That same year he also published his biggest commercial success, *The Last Time I Saw Paris*. Adopting the technique used in *The Life and Death of a Spanish Town*, Paul presents a picture of life in the rue de la Huchette, a small side street on the Left Bank. Just as the Spanish Civil War casts a pall over life in Santa Eulalia in the earlier book, the coming of World War II destroys the life on the rue de la Huchette. Janet Flanner accurately described it as a book "which has the emotional material of the novel but has the stringent actuality of vital statistics." The book cannot be described as a picture of expatriate life in Paris, but Paul's anecdotal style conveys the feeling that the city had for the expatriates. It was bought eagerly by the American public, selling over 200,000 copies in all editions.

After World War II Paul began a series of autobiographical volumes under the general title *Items on the Grand Account*. He included *The Life and Death of a Spanish Town* and *The Last Time I Saw Paris* in the series. The first new volume, and the first in the series chronologically, was *Linden on the Saugus Branch* (1947), which describes the Malden of his boyhood. *A Ghost Town on the Yellowstone* (1948) covers his year in the West after graduation from high school in 1907; *My Old Kentucky Home* (1949) recounts his adventures in Louisville in 1909;

and *Desperate Scenery* (1954) deals with his years as a vagabond in Wyoming and Idaho. The success of *The Last Time I Saw Paris* was undoubtedly a strong inducement to revisit the rue de la Huchette and give a picture of life there after the war. His findings were published in 1950 as *Springtime in Paris*. Winfield Townley Scott's comment about this book could well be applied to all of Paul's volumes of memoirs: "All of it is fun to read and parts of it are no doubt true." Another volume in the series which would cover his years as a statehouse reporter in Boston was apparently planned but never written.

Throughout the years Paul's interest in music continued. He played the piano for President Truman's inauguration and toured with jazz musician Lionel Hampton. His last book, *That Crazy American Music* (1957), reflects this lifelong love. It is a history of popular music in America with an emphasis on jazz and boogie-woogie and with a skeptical look at rock and roll and the rise of Elvis Presley.

Paul had been suffering from heart trouble and had had a series of heart attacks, which took their toll on his famous Falstaffian figure. After a heart attack late in 1957, he returned permanently to Rhode Island, where his younger brother was living. Paul was raised to be a Congregationalist but had abandoned any faith in favor of agnosticism early in his life. In the Veterans Hospital in Providence, however, he joined the Greek Orthodox Church because he was impressed by some of his friends who were members of that church. A month later he was dead of arteriosclerosis. He was virtually penniless when he died.

No account of Elliot Paul's life would be complete without a sampling of the many anecdotes told about him. The most famous dates from the time of his first novel. After receiving his first check from his publisher, he hailed a cab on Beacon Hill and ended up in Montreal with a few friends and a taxi bill of $687. While on the staff of the Paris *Herald*, he left the office for a bite to eat and did not return for several months. Another time, as the big loser in an all-night strip poker game, Paul had to find his way home through the morning rush hour in Paris wearing only his undershorts and a red sash. He was always ready to play the piano or accordion for a drinking party and once played for a day and night with hardly a break. When Horace Liveright returned the manuscript of *The Governor of Massachusetts* requesting that it be cut by 16,000 words, Paul merely held on to it for several weeks, resubmitted it without a single change, and was told that it was now acceptable. He once delivered a manuscript to Random House along with a pair of carrier pigeons to return proofs to him at his home in Connecticut. His fourth wife testified in divorce court that he said good-bye to her in 1948 as if he were going around the corner for a loaf of bread, and then left for New York and Paris. She never saw him again.

The stories are endless, and they undoubtedly have been embellished in the retelling. Still they present an accurate picture of Elliot Paul: an impractical and incurable vagabond, utterly unpredictable, determined to live life for the pleasure to be gained from it. He had a talent for attracting people to him as well as a talent for studying their characters and putting them down on paper. Paul wrote quickly and easily, writing as many as 4,000 words a day. His first draft was his final draft, and he seldom made any revisions. He wrote *Indelible* in eighteen days and the mystery novel *Murder on the Left Bank* (1951) in 1950 during a return trip to the United States on the *Queen Mary*. These were writing habits undoubtedly developed in his journalistic career, and his best books display his reportorial skills. Even in his fiction he claimed that he was writing "current history" and that all of his characters were based on real people. He is remembered best for his association with *transition*, but he might well be resurrected as an appropriate ancestor of the new journalists of the sixties and seventies.

Perhaps the best assessment of Elliot Paul is one he made himself in *Linden on the Saugus Branch*. He was marveling at the difference in character between himself and his two brothers. After describing their rather conventional lives, he said: "I, born of the same parents, and brought up in the same environment, turned out to be a wanderer, without direction or governing philosophy, with no stability or purpose, no achievements which did not come to me easily, impulsive, reckless, impractical and inconsistent, receptive to almost any kind of experience, with limitless curiosity and no standards at all." One might lament the obvious talent squandered in such an approach to life, but in a sense, Paul's contributions to literature stem directly from these characteristics. If the American expatriates in Paris had not had an Elliot Paul, they surely would have had to invent one.

Screenplays:

A Woman's Face, by Paul and Donald Ogden Stewart, Metro-Goldwyn-Mayer, 1941;

It's a Pleasure, by Paul and Lynn Starling, RKO, 1945;

Rhapsody in Blue, by Paul and Howard Kock, Warner Brothers, 1945;

New Orleans, by Paul and Dick Irving Hyland, United Artists, 1947;

My Heart Goes Crazy, by Paul and Sig Herzig, United Artists, 1953.

Other:

Virgil Geddes, *Forty Poems*, introduction by Paul (Paris: Editions des meilleurs livres, 1926);

Luis Quintanilla, *All the Brave*, text by Paul and Jay Allen (New York: Modern Age, 1939);

Fritz Henle, *Paris*, text by Paul (Chicago & New York: Ziff-Davis, 1947).

Periodical Publications:

"Zukunftsmusik," *transition*, no. 1 (April 1927): 147-150;

"The Concert," *transition*, no. 2 (May 1927): 90-93;

"The New Nihilism," *transition*, no. 2 (May 1927): 164-168;

"The Open Shop," *transition*, no. 4 (July 1927): 74-77;

"A Master of Plastic Relations," *transition*, no. 4 (July 1927): 163-165;

"A Rondo," *transition*, no. 5 (August 1927): 61-65;

"Hands off the Dike," *transition*, no. 5 (August 1927): 155-158;

"Simultaneity in Modern Russia," *transition*, no. 5 (August 1927): 159-161;

"Enharmonics," *transition*, no. 6 (September 1927): 40-46;

"No. 4 Commercial Street," *transition*, no. 7 (October 1927): 85-87;

"Honeysuckle Coloured Pyjamas," *transition*, no. 7 (October 1927): 166-170;

"License Three Hundred: Or the Rounder's Conversion to Light Magic," *transition*, no. 9 (December 1927): 29-40;

"First Aid to the Enemy," by Paul, Robert Sage, and Eugene Jolas, *transition*, no. 9 (December 1927): 161-176;

"Mr. Joyce's Treatment of Plot," *transition*, no. 9 (December 1927): 197-203;

"States of Sea," *transition*, no. 10 (January 1928): 30-42;

"Artistic Improvements of the Cinema," by Paul and Sage, *transition*, no. 10 (January 1928): 127-134;

"The Schonberg Legend," *transition*, no. 10 (January 1928): 142-144;

"The Ninety and Nine: A Scenario," *transition*, no. 11 (February 1928): 51-58;

"A Review," by Paul and Jolas, *transition*, no. 12 (March 1928): 139-147;

"The Work of Pablo Picasso," *transition*, no. 13 (Summer 1928): 139-141;

"The Life and Death of Isaac Momblo," *transition*, no. 14 (Fall 1928): 89-96;

"Stuart Davis, American Painter," *transition*, no. 14 (Fall 1928): 146-148;

"Matter over Mind or Every Man His Own Boswell," *transition*, no. 15 (February 1929): 175-183;

"Farthest North, a Study of James Joyce," *Bookman*, 75 (May 1932): 156-163;

"Hemingway and the Critics," *Saturday Review of Literature*, 17 (6 November 1937): 3-4;

" 'Whodunit,' " *Atlantic Monthly*, 168 (July 1941): 36-40;

"Art and Camouflage," *Vogue*, 100 (15 July 1942): 37, 78;

"For Whom, Indeed," *Atlantic Monthly*, 172 (December 1943): 109, 111-112;

" 'Is Happiness Photogenic?,' " *Atlantic Monthly*, 173 (June 1944): 104, 107, 109;

"Looking over the Oscars," *Atlantic Monthly*, 174 (August 1944): 103, 105, 107;

"Concerning Miracles," *Atlantic Monthly*, 174 (December 1944): 110, 113, 115;

" 'Musical and Low,' " *Atlantic Monthly*, 176 (July 1945): 109, 111-112;

"Of Film Propaganda," *Atlantic Monthly*, 176 (September 1945): 123, 127-128;

"Gertrude, Alas, Alas," *Esquire*, 26 (July 1946): 62, 189-193;

"Paris Revisited," *Cosmopolitan*, 128 (April 1950): 52-53, 164-169; 128 (May 1950): 62-64, 179-185;

"The Latin Quarter on Saturday Night," *Atlantic Monthly*, 185 (June 1950): 61-63;

Review of *Across the River and into the Trees* by Ernest Hemingway, *Providence Journal*, 10 September 1950, section 6, p. 8;

"Three Ages of Ageless Paris," *New York Times Magazine*, 22 July 1951, pp. 14, 17.

References:

Ben H. Bagdikian, "Elliot Paul: Writer, Musician, Bon-Vivant," Providence *Evening Bulletin*, 7 April 1958, pp. 12-13;

David Brickman, "Elliot Paul: Another Side to His Bizarre Life," *Malden Evening News*, 31 August 1972, p. 9;

Hugh Ford, *Published in Paris American and British Writers, Printers, and Publishers in Paris, 1920-1939* (New York: Macmillan, 1975);

Eric Hawkins with Robert N. Sturdevant, *Hawkins of the Paris* Herald (New York: Simon & Schuster, 1963), pp. 144-152;

Herbert A. Kenny, "The Last Interview with Elliot Paul," *Boston Daily Globe*, 8 April 1958, pp. 1, 19;

Al Laney, *Paris Herald The Incredible Newspaper* (New York & London: Appleton-Century, 1947);

Dougald McMillan, transition *The History of a Literary Era 1927-1938* (New York: Braziller, 1976);

Shirley Munroe Mullen, "Elliot Paul Plans Return to Hub to Work on Novel," *Malden Press*, 15 March 1951, pp. 1, 13;

"On an Author: Elliot Paul," *New York Herald Tribune Weekly Book Review*, 11 September 1949, p. 2;

Winfield T. Scott, "Lunch with Elliot Paul," *Providence Journal*, 13 August 1950, *Rhode Islander*, p. 7;

Joe Toye, "Genius Burns in Garret on Back of Beacon Hill," *Boston Herald*, 4 June 1922, section C, p. 6;

Robert Van Gelder, "An Interview with Mr. Elliot Paul," *New York Times Book Review*, 1 March 1942, pp. 2, 23.

KATHERINE ANNE PORTER
(15 May 1890-   )

SELECTED BOOKS: *Flowering Judas* (New York: Harcourt, Brace, 1930);

Hacienda (New York: Harrison of Paris, 1934);

Flowering Judas and Other Stories (New York: Harcourt, Brace, 1935; London: Cape, 1936);

Pale Horse, Pale Rider Three Short Novels (New York: Harcourt, Brace, 1939; London: Cape, 1939);

Ship of Fools (Boston & Toronto: Little, Brown / Atlantic Monthly, 1962; London: Secker & Warburg, 1962);

Collected Stories (London: Cape, 1964; New York: Harcourt, Brace, 1965; revised edition, London: Cape, 1967);

The Collected Essays and Occasional Writings of Katherine Anne Porter (New York: Seymour Lawrence / Delacorte, 1970).

Sylvia Beach Collection

Katherine Anne Porter, inscribed to Sylvia Beach

Katherine Anne Porter claimed in later years that during the twenties, when many American writers were hastening to Europe, she felt she had no business there and went to Mexico instead. In fact, she had tried to go to Europe as early as 1918 but was always prevented by financial, medical, and personal obstacles. In August 1931, after her first collection of stories, *Flowering Judas* (1930), had been highly acclaimed and she had received a Guggenheim Fellowship, she finally realized her dream. With her companion, Eugene Pressly, she traveled from Mexico, where she had spent the past eighteen months, to Germany. (The voyage on the German ship the S.S. *Werra* provided the basis for her 1962 novel, *Ship of Fools.*) She intended to go to France, but visa complications prevented her disembarkation, and she was carried on to Bremerhaven. Once settled in a Berlin pension, she decided to stay there and work while Pressly took a secretarial job at the American Embassy in Madrid. Neither Porter's health nor her work prospered in Berlin. She had trouble with the stories in progress, as well as with the reviews she was writing for the *New Republic*, and she finished only a rough account of the three days in July 1931 she had spent at the Hacienda Tetlapayac where Eisenstein was making his movie, *Que Viva Mexico*, later revised and released in the United States as *Thunder Over Mexico* (1933). The greatest benefit of these months was that they supplied the material for "The Leaning Tower," a story she finished ten years later.

In early February she left for Spain, intending to marry Pressly, and stopped briefly in Paris. Her ten-day sojourn there changed completely the course of the next few years of her life. She did travel to Spain but left almost immediately, saying she could never live in Madrid while there was Paris.

During the next four years, apart from a few months when she accompanied Pressly on an embassy posting to Switzerland, and when she made a visit to the United States, she lived in Paris. Pressly took a secretarial job at the American Embassy in Paris; she married him on 15 March 1933 and settled down to a quiet life of domesticity and writing, living first in a small apartment at 166, boulevard Montparnasse and later in the atelier at 70, bis rue Notre Dame des Champs, previously occupied by Ezra Pound.

For Porter, the Paris years have an importance greater than the four-year time span might suggest. In spite of her constant struggle to write a biography of Cotton Mather (which she did not finish), a large portion of her short fiction came to fruition at this time. She reworked the first version of "Hacienda," which had been published in the *Virginia Quarterly Review* in 1932, into its final form. Where each of her earlier Mexican stories had dealt with a single aspect of Mexican life—the native Indian, the Spanish upper class, the artistic community, and the foreign revolutionaries—the final version of the story combines all these strands. The hacienda itself—a pulque producing operation, a movie set, and a feudal manor—provides the central unifying symbol. "Hacienda" is at the same time a portrait of the country and Porter's own personal farewell to it as a place in which to live and as a source of material for her fiction. The story was published separately by Harrison of Paris in 1934, and in 1935 it was included in the expanded version of *Flowering Judas*, which contained all the stories from the earlier edition together with four additional ones, "Theft," "That Tree," "The Cracked Looking Glass," and "Hacienda."

The inspiration for most of the stories she finished in Paris came from her native Texas, and many were mythical, romantic recreations of her family's past. "Two Plantation Portraits" (later entitled "The Witness" and "The Last Leaf"), "The Circus," "The Grave," and "The Old Order" were eventually linked as parts of the long sequence "The Old Order."

Less obvious products of the Paris period are three short novels written in the fall of 1936 after Pressly left his job and Porter returned with him to the United States. Although she wrote "Pale Horse, Pale Rider," "Noon Wine," and "Old Mortality" in an inn in Pennsylvania, they were so complete in her mind when she left France that during two months of seclusion she was able to write them out directly and almost without hesitation.

The three short novels appeared separately and in 1939 were collected in one volume, *Pale Horse, Pale Rider*. This collection received even greater acclaim than her earlier books, and critics compared her with the most distinguished American writers. Her period of sustained productivity had, however, ended, and her few subsequent stories appeared at wide intervals. In spite of its enthusiastic reception, her work was not economically rewarding. She remained a "writer's writer," praised as a brilliant

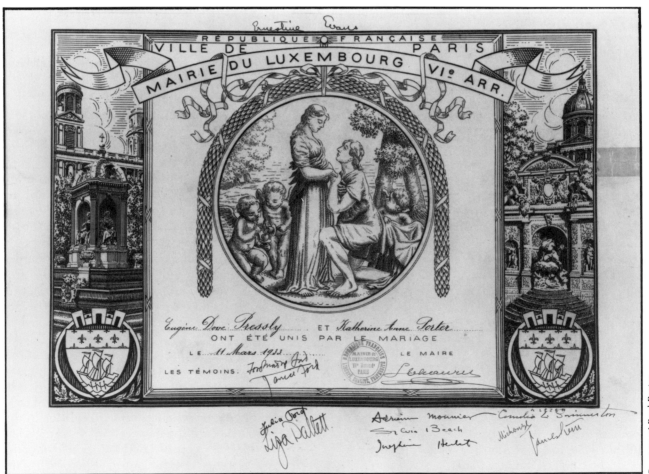

Marriage certificate

stylist with a devoted but relatively small coterie of readers. Accordingly, her energies after 1940 were mostly taken up by efforts to make a living from strenuous lecture tours and teaching jobs. She worked sporadically at *Ship of Fools*, and when it finally appeared in 1962, its reception differed greatly from that of her short stories. It was a great commercial success, but critical opinion of its worth was sharply divided.

Porter often wondered why Paris should have cast such a spell on her and called forth such a flowering of her art. She said she did not love the "cold, drizzling, grey city" for all the obvious reasons—the American bar life, the pretty clothes, the people, theatres, the art shows, and the music. Nevertheless, she did relish these advantages, as a reverie of her character, Mary Treadwell, in *Ship of Fools* well expresses:

> I want to live in that dark alley named l'Impasse des Deux Anges, and have those little pointed jeweled blue velvet shoes at the Cluny copied, and get my perfumes from Molinard's and go to Schiaparelli's spring show to watch her ugly mannequins jerking about as if they were run with push buttons, hitching their belts down in back every time they turn, giving each other hard, theatrical Lesbian stares. I want to light a foot-high candle to Our Lady of Paris for bringing me back, and go out to Chantilly to see if they've turned another page in the Duke's Book of Hours. I'd like to dance again in that little *guinguette* in rue d'Enfert-Rochereau with the good-looking young Marquis—what's his name? descended from Joan of Arc's brother. I want to go again to la Bagatelle and help the moss roses open. . . . I'll go again to Rambouillet through those woods that really do look just as Watteau and Fragonard saw them. And to St. Denis to see again the lovely white marble feet of kings and queens, lying naked together on the roof above their formal figures on the bier, delicate toes turned up side by side. . . . I'm going again to St. Cloud next May to see the first lilies of the valley. . . . Oh God, I'm homesick. I'll never leave Paris again, I promise, if you'll let me just get there this once more. If every soul left it one day and grass grew in the pavements, it would still be Paris to me, I'd want to live there.

Also, while her social life in Paris was not hectic, she renewed her friendships with Caroline Gordon, Allen Tate, Josephine Herbst, Matthew Josephson, and Eugene Jolas, and she had short meetings with Emma Goldman, Caresse Crosby, Djuna Barnes, and Gertrude Stein. Her brief confrontation with Ernest Hemingway is recorded in a humorous essay, "A Little Incident in the Rue de l'Odeon." She formed lasting friendships with Adrienne Monnier and Sylvia Beach, and it was through Sylvia Beach that she made her first public speech, an address to the American Women's Club.

Porter had previously met Ford Madox Ford in New York, and in Paris Porter, Pressly, Ford, and his companion, Janice Biala, became good friends. Ford and Biala were the witnesses at the Presslys' wedding; Pressly typed the manuscript of Ford's memoir *It Was the Nightingale* (1934); and the Presslys were the basis for two characters in Ford's last novel, *Vive Le Roi*. Intense as it was, the friendship was short-lived, and by spring 1934, it had soured.

A more lasting association for Porter began when Ford introduced her to Monroe Wheeler and Glenway Wescott. Wheeler, with Barbara Harrison, a rich patron of the arts, had established a small publishing house, Harrison of Paris, which specialized in elegant limited editions. For them, Porter made the translations of her favorite French songs which they published as *Katherine Anne Porter's French Song-Book*, and she let them publish her final version of "Hacienda." *Hacienda* was Harrison of Paris's last publication, but Porter's friendships with Wescott, Wheeler, and Barbara Harrison Wescott (who married Glenway Wescott's brother) was lifelong. It was both emotionally and materially supportive for Porter because in times of financial distress it was from them she sought help.

The marriage to Pressly must also be counted among the favorable conditions which contributed to Porter's creativity during her Paris period. While the marriage was far from satisfactory, the relationship was the longest she maintained with any man, and it represented the nearest compromise she ever achieved between her conflicting desires for a domestic life and the solitary existence necessary for her work.

Perhaps the most crucial factor in her reaction to Paris was its geographical and cultural distance from her native Texas. No place can have been more antithetical to Texas than Paris, and it gave her a new perspective on her early years. She was able to contemplate her childhood in an atmosphere that revived no painful memories, and she said that her travels in Mexico, Bermuda, and Europe gave her back her own place and her own people, "the native land of the heart." It was in Paris that she started to research her family's roots because she "did not want to feel like an exile," and early in 1936 she returned to her family from Paris for the first time in eighteen years.

Her fiction reflects her reconciliation with her early life. While the stories of "The Old Order" celebrate the family's mythical past, the theme of "Old Mortality" is the effect upon Miranda Gay, Porter's fictional counterpart, of the knowledge that the romantic family history is not in any literal sense "true." In "Noon Wine" her setting is the childhood world she knew at firsthand, that of the plain people, the Texas dirt farmers. In this story she has no fictional representative, but the characters are members of her own family with their names unchanged.

Perhaps the best summary of how external circumstances coincided with Porter's internal development to produce her full maturity as a writer is given in her 29 April 1945 letter to Josephine Herbst:

> I didn't begin to feel contemporary, or as if I had come to my proper time of life until just a few years ago. I think after I went to Europe— Europe was the place for me, somehow, Paris the city, France the country. From there I got a perspective and somehow without struggle my point of view fell into clear focus, right for *me*, at any rate; and what other rightness is there for the individual?

—Joan Givner

Other:

Katherine Anne Porter's French Song-Book, translated by Porter (Paris: Harrison of Paris, 1933).

References:

George Core and Lodwick Hartley, eds., *Katherine Anne Porter: A Critical Symposium* (Athens: University of Georgia Press, 1969);

Joan Givner, *Brave Voyage: The Life of Katherine Anne Porter* (New York: Harper & Row, forthcoming);

John Edward Hardy, *Katherine Anne Porter* (New York: Ungar, 1973);

George Hendrick, *Katherine Anne Porter* (New York: Twayne, 1965);

M. M. Liberman, *Katherine Anne Porter's Fiction* (Detroit: Wayne State University Press, 1971);

William L. Nance, *Katherine Anne Porter and the Art of Rejection* (Chapel Hill: University of North Carolina Press, 1964);

Vida Vliet, "The Shape of Meaning: A Study of the Development of Katherine Anne Porter's Fictional Form," Ph.D. dissertation, Pennsylvania State University, 1968;

Louise Waldrip and Shirley Ann Bauer, *A Bibliography of the Works of Katherine Anne Porter and A Bibliography of the Criticism of the Works of Katherine Anne Porter* (Metuchen, N.J.: Scarecrow Press, 1969).

Papers:

Many of Katherine Anne Porter's papers as well as her personal library are housed in the Katherine Anne Porter Room at the McKeldin Library, University of Maryland.

Ezra Pound

Richard Sieburth
Harvard University

BIRTH: Hailey, Idaho, 30 October 1885, to Isabel Weston and Homer Loomis Pound.

EDUCATION: Ph.B., Hamilton College, 1905; M.A., University of Pennsylvania, 1906.

MARRIAGE: 20 April 1914 to Dorothy Shakespear; children: Mary, Omar.

AWARDS: *Poetry* prize, 1914; *Dial* Award, 1927; Honorary Doctorate, Hamilton College, 1939; Bollingen Award for Poetry, 1948; Harriet Monroe Award, 1962; Academy of American Poets Award, 1963.

DEATH: Venice, Italy, 1 November 1972.

SELECTED BOOKS: *A Lume Spento* (Venice: Privately printed, 1908);

A Quinzaine for this Yule (London: Mathews, 1908);

Personae (London: Mathews, 1909);

Exultations (London: Mathews, 1909);

The Spirit of Romance (London: Dent, 1910; London: Dent; New York: Dutton, 1910);

Canzoni (London: Mathews, 1911);

Ripostes (London: Swift, 1912; Boston: Small, Maynard, 1913);

Gaudier-Breska A Memoir Including the Published Writings of the Sculptor and a Selection from His Letters (London: Lane / Bodley Head; New York: Lane, 1916);

Lustra (London: Mathews, 1916; New York: Knopf, 1917);

Pavannes and Divisions (New York: Knopf, 1918); augmented as *Pavannes and Divagations* (Norfolk, Conn.: New Directions, 1958);

Quia Pauper Amavi (London: Egoist Press, 1919);

Instigations of Ezra Pound Together With An Essay on the Chinese Written Character by Ernest Fenollosa (New York: Boni & Liveright, 1920);

Hugh Selwyn Mauberley (N.p.: Ovid Press, 1920);

Poems 1918-21 (New York: Boni & Liveright, 1922; London: Casanova Society, 1926);

Indiscretions (Paris: Three Mountains Press, 1923);

Antheil and the Treatise on Harmony (Paris: Three Mountains Press, 1924; Chicago: Covici, 1927);

A Draft of XVI. Cantos (Paris: Three Mountains Press, 1925);

Personae The Collected Poems (New York: Boni & Liveright, 1926; London: Faber & Faber, 1952);

A Draft of XXX Cantos (Paris: Hours Press, 1930; New York: Farrar & Rinehart, 1933; London: Faber & Faber, 1933);

Imaginary Letters (Paris: Black Sun Press, 1930);

How To Read (London: Harmondsworth, 1931);

ABC of Economics (London: Faber & Faber, 1933; Norfolk, Conn.: New Directions, 1940);

ABC of Reading (London: Routledge, 1934; New Haven: Yale University Press, 1934);

Make It New (London: Faber & Faber, 1934; New Haven: Yale University Press, 1935);

Eleven New Cantos XXX-XLI (New York: Farrar & Rinehart, 1934; London: Faber & Faber, 1935);

Homage to Sextus Propertius (London: Faber & Faber, 1934);

Jefferson And/Or Mussolini (London: Nott, 1935; New York: Liveright; London: Nott, 1936);

Polite Essays (London: Faber & Faber, 1937; Norfolk, Conn.: New Directions, 1940);

The Fifth Decad of Cantos (London: Faber & Faber, 1937; New York & Toronto: Farrar & Rinehart, 1937);

Confucius Digest of the Analects (Milan: Giovanni Scheiwiller, 1937);

Guide to Kulchur (London: Russell & Russell, 1938; Norfolk, Conn.: New Directions, 1938);

Cantos LII-LXXI (London: Faber & Faber, 1940; Norfolk, Conn.: New Directions, 1940);

The Pisan Cantos (New York: New Directions, 1948; London: Faber & Faber, 1949);

The Cantos (New York: New Directions, 1948; London: Faber & Faber, 1954);

Patria Mia (Chicago: Seymour, 1950);

Literary Essays, edited with an introduction by T. S. Eliot (London: Faber & Faber, 1954; Norfolk, Conn.: New Directions, 1954);

Section: Rock-Drill 85-95 de los cantares (Milan: All'Insegna del Pesce d'Oro, 1955; New York: New Directions, 1956; London: Faber & Faber, 1957);

Thrones 96-109 de los cantares (Milan: All' Insegna del Pesce d'Oro, 1959; New York: New Directions, 1959; London: Faber & Faber, 1960);

Impact Essays on Ignorance and the Decline of American Civilization (Chicago: Regnery, 1960);

Drafts and Fragments of Cantos CX to CXVII (New

Courtesy of Donald Gallup

Opening of the Jockey Club, Paris, ca. 1923 (kneeling: Man Ray, Mina Loy, Tristan Tzara, Jean Cocteau;
second row: far right, Ezra Pound, third from right, Jean Heap; others unidentified)

York: New Directions, 1968; London: Faber & Faber, 1970);

Selected Prose 1909-1965 (New York: New Directions, 1973; London: Faber & Faber, 1973);

Collected Early Poems (New York: New Directions, 1976; London: Faber & Faber, 1977);

Ezra Pound Speaking Radio Speeches of World War II, ed. Leonard Doob (Westport, Conn.: Greenwood Press, 1978).

One of the dominant figures of twentieth-century American literature, Ezra Weston Loomis Pound spent nearly the entirety of his controversial career in exile. Following in the footsteps of Henry James and Whistler, he left America in 1908 to make his literary reputation in London. Leader of the Imagist school and participant in the Vorticist movement, Pound moved to Paris in early 1921, where, for the next three years, he played a prominent role as champion of Joyce and Eliot, editor of little magazines, and mentor to young American expatriates. After leaving Paris in late 1924, Pound settled in Rapallo, Italy, to devote himself to his experimental epic, *The Cantos.* Written over the course of almost half a century, this unfinished "poem including history" has remained one of the most significant and most influential achievements of American literature in this century. During his long years in Italy, Pound became increasingly absorbed in political and economic theory and, optimistically convinced that Mussolini's policies presented an enlightened alternative to modern monopoly capitalism, Pound became an apologist for what he misguidedly construed as Fascist economics. In 1939 he visited America for the first time in twenty-eight years, but returned to Italy, where from 1941 to 1943 he made radio broadcasts against American involvement in the war, which subsequently led to his indictment for treason. Judged medically unfit to stand trial, Pound was placed in St. Elizabeths Hospital in Washington, D.C., where he remained incarcerated from 1946 until 1958. Upon his release, Pound returned to Italy, dividing his time between Rapallo, Merano, and Venice, while continuing work on his *Cantos.*

Pound's career presents an extreme version of the role of expatriation within twentieth-century American letters. Although he initially went abroad as a Jamesian "passionate pilgrim" in search of the holy sites of past cultural achievement, Pound's residence in Europe paradoxically enabled him to discover himself as a contemporary American writer. An early poem addressed "To Whistler, American" might equally typify Pound's own accomplishment in exile: "You had your searches, your uncertainties, / And this is good to know—for us, I mean, / Who bear the brunt of our America / And try to wrench her impulse into art." As in Whistler's case, Paris, the capital of the avant-garde, played a crucial role in shaping Pound's vision of an art which would integrate raw American impulse with the discipline and cosmopolitanism of Continental modernism. Vers libre, Imagism, and Vorticism were all to a certain extent imports from France, and as Malcolm Cowley points out, Pound's poetry and criticism between 1912 and 1920 was influential in determining the intellectual baggage a later generation of American expatriates would carry to Paris. But unlike many of these younger compatriots, Pound would stay on in exile to become, in his own phrase, "the last American living the tragedy of Europe." Displacement came to be the permanent condition of his art; it was his Odyssean fate, as Eliot observed, to be "a squatter everywhere, rootless, ever ready to depart." Ironically, this nomadism was perhaps Pound's deepest American trait.

To understand more fully the place of Paris within Pound's pattern of exile, one has to go back to beginnings, perhaps as far back as his grand tours of England and the Continent in 1898 and 1902: these early glimpses of Old World "kulchur" very likely encouraged the seventeen-year-old Pound to embark on what he would retrospectively term "an examination of comparative European literature." Although this is a rather ambitious description of his undergraduate course of studies at the University of Pennsylvania and Hamilton College, Pound received a respectable enough grounding in the classics, Provencal, French, Italian, and Spanish to go on to graduate work in romance languages at the University of Pennsylvania, where, after earning his M.A., he was awarded a fellowship in the summer of 1906 to do research on the plays of Lope de Vega at the British Museum, the Bibliotheque nationale, and the Royal Library of Madrid. Pound returned from his travels abroad increasingly intolerant of the provincial niceties of American academic life and more assured of his vocation as a poet. As if to play the part more convincingly, he began cultivating a number of Continental eccentricities of dress—black velvet jacket, wide-brimmed hat, and malacca cane. In a sense, Pound never fully abandoned this nineteenth-century Bohemian costume. Later, among the Dadaists of Paris, he would cut a curiously old-fashioned figure; as Paul Rosenfeld remarked, the beard, the cape, the cane appeared to have stepped straight out of the opera *La Boheme.* But what seemed obsolescent in the twenties proved provocative enough in 1907 at Wabash College in Crawfordsville, Indiana, where Pound had been appointed to the Department of Romance Languages. It was perhaps inevitable that his tenure at this small Presbyterian school should be brief. As it turned out, Pound lasted little over a semester, dismissed, according to most versions, for having sheltered an itinerant actress in his rooms overnight, and suspected, moreover, of being a "Latin Quarter type."

Pound's run-in with Midwestern parochialism determined him to try his fortunes in a climate more hospitable to the arts. Accordingly, he set sail for Europe, landing in Gibraltar in early 1908 with $80 to his name. He proceeded on to Venice where, at his own expense, he published his first book of poems, *A Lume Spento*—seventy-two pages of finely wrought "creampuffs" (as he would later call them), notable primarily for their skillful assimilation of the Pre-Raphaelites, Swinburne, Browning, and the early Yeats. From Venice he made his way to London, where his entree into literary circles proved remarkably smooth: *A Lume Spento* received at least one enthusiastic review, and by December 1908 Pound had brought out a second book, *A Quinzaine for this Yule*, with Elkin Mathews, one of the more prestigious publishers of contemporary verse in London. Mathews also printed, in rapid succession, Pound's subsequent volumes: *Personae* (1909), *Exultations* (1909), *Canzoni* (1911), all of which, given their rather idiosyncratic blend of archaism, fin de siecle luxuriance, and Yankee exuberance, were rather well-received by conservative British reviewers. Indeed, after the appearance of *Personae*, Pound was accorded that ultimate privilege of celebrity—satirical mention in *Punch* as "the new

Montana (USA) poet, Mr. Ezekiel Ton, who is the most remarkable thing in poetry since Robert Browning."

Pound had come to London in quest of tradition, and during these early years he cultivated above all the older literary establishment, survivors of the eighteen-nineties Rhymer's Club such as Victor Plarr, Ernest Rhys, Arthur Symons, and William Butler Yeats (whom Pound met through his future mother-in-law, Olivia Shakespear). Although he attended some of the 1909 meetings of the newly formed Poet's Club where T. E. Hulme and F. S. Flint were discussing vers libre and other recent importations from Paris, Pound's own work was still reaching in the opposite direction—back to the France of the troubadours and the Italy of Dante. His volume *Exultations* demonstrated exceptional technical virtuosity, but as several reviewers pointed out, the poems remained too heavily freighted with antiquarian learning. Indeed, Pound was reluctant to give up the persona of the professor entirely, and in late 1909 offered a "Course of Lectures on Medieval Literature" at the Polytechnic Institute. Revised and expanded, these studies on Arnaut Daniel, Cavalcanti, Dante, and Villon were published the following year in England and America as *The Spirit of Romance* (1910), Pound's first major attempt to define the canon of his own poetic tradition.

Although he wrote home that he seemed to "fit better here in London than anywhere else," Pound's rather precarious financial position led him to toy repeatedly with the possibility of resuming his academic career in America, and after a brief tour of the Continent in the spring of 1910, he returned to the United States for an eight-month stay, most of which was spent in New York, where he met up with old college friends William Carlos Williams and Hilda Doolittle (H. D.) and made the acquaintance of his future patron, lawyer John Quinn. Although Pound's description of Seventh Avenue crowds and Manhattan skyscrapers at night ("squares after squares of flame, set and cut into the ether") suggests Apollinaire's or Marinetti's Futurist enthusiasm for modernity, he was dismayed by the lack of direction, by the provincial taste for ersatz evident in American cultural life of 1910. (The Armory Show, which first brought the work of the Futurists and the Cubists to the United States, was still three years off.) In a series of articles published in 1950 as *Patria Mia*, Pound presaged the disaffection with American insularity and complacency of a later generation of expatriates: America tended to dissipate its enormous energy into self-indulgent sprawl; it was shapeless, at once

everywhere and nowhere; it had "no center, no place by which it can be tested," no "city to which all roads lead, and from which there goes out an authority." Its citizens possessed a genuine generosity, "a desire for largeness, a willingness to stand exposed," but "so far as civilization is concerned, America is the great, rich Western province which has sent one or two notable artists [i.e. James and Whistler] to the Eastern capital. And that capital is . . . the double city of London and Paris."

Unhappy with his literary or academic prospects in America, Pound sailed back to that "double city" in early 1911. Upon arriving in England, he immediately set off for Paris, where he spent the next three months completing his volume *Canzoni* and working with his friend the pianist Walter Morse Rummel on troubadour songs. He met up with Yeats and together they visited Parisian sights—as Pound would sardonically recall in Canto LXXXIII, "and Uncle William dawdling around Notre Dame / in search of whatever / paused to admire the symbol / with Notre Dame standing inside it." Together they also attended a number of literary gatherings, but Pound was not impressed: "the crop of poets at present existing in Paris seems a rather gutless lot given over to description." He was more drawn to recent developments in music (Debussy) and the visual arts, though with the exception of Matisse, his tastes still ran to the Impressionists. It was only some years later that he would become fully aware of the modernist achievements of early Cubism, admitting that "We London 1911-14 were subsequent to a great deal of Paris."

For the moment, though, he remained, in Wyndham Lewis's phrase, a man in love with the past. When he left Paris in early June it was to visit Catullus's Sirmione, Renaissance Verona, and the Ambrosian Library in Milan for additional research on Arnaut Daniel. On his way back to England, he passed through Germany to see Ford Madox Ford who, as editor of the *English Review*, had taken an active interest in his work. After reading through *Canzoni*, however, Ford's reaction to Pound's "tertiary archaisms" and stilted diction was to roll on the floor in ridicule. "That roll saved me at least two years, perhaps more," Pound later confessed, "It sent me back to my own proper effort, namely, toward using the living tongue." With Ford's lesson in mind, Pound returned to London in the fall of 1911 prepared to bring himself up to date. He began seeing T. E. Hulme again, attended his lectures on Bergson, and was introduced to A. R. Orage, editor of the *New Age*. Guild Socialist in political temperament, open to a cosmopolitan range of intellectual and artistic experiment, the *New Age* would publish Pound's poetry and prose over the next decade, that is, until Orage himself left for Paris to become a disciple of Gurdjieff. Through the *New Age*, Pound came into contact with the younger London contemporaries—Rupert Brooke, Wyndham Lewis, Katherine Mansfield, John Middleton Murry—and, given the magazine's commitment to importing the best of Continental art and thought into England, he began paying closer attention to developments in Paris. Orage had been publishing Hulme's reflections on such contemporary French thinkers as Sorel, Bergson, and Gourmont, as well as F. S. Flint's accounts of recent Parisian experiments in haiku and vers libre. Assimilating this recent French poetic and linguistic theory to what he had learned from Yeats and the nineties about image and symbol, Pound began to envision a poetry that would combine the suggestiveness of Symbolism, the sonorities of Provencal *motz el son*, the precision of Cavalcanti, and the limpidity of the Greek lyric. Toward the end of 1911, Pound started learning how to write such poetry. By mid-1912, he had found a name for it, Imagism.

Pound chose his "ism" partly with a shrewd eye for publicity and partly to align and contrast his "school" with contemporary vanguard movements on the Continent. Marinetti had been in London in March 1912 to launch the first Futurist Exhibition in England, and later that spring Pound visited Paris with the two other fledgling "Imagistes," the English poet Richard Aldington and the recently transplanted H. D. Significantly enough, it was precisely during these months that the bitter "guerre des deux rives" broke out among Parisian literary circles, leading the Left Bank to secede officially from the traditionalist bastions of the Right. A volley of "ismes" burst forth from the avant-garde presses of the Latin Quarter and Montparnasse— integralisme, impulsionnisme, dynamisme, paroxysme, synchronisme—all of which F. S. Flint dutifully chronicled in his survey of "Contemporary French Poetry" in the August 1912 issue of *Poetry Review*. Flint's inventory of Parisian schools probably decided Pound to invent his own Anglo-American variant, for by the fall of that year he was advertising the existence of "Les Imagistes" in the preface to "The Complete Poetical Works of T. E. Hulme," six poems by Hulme included, half in jest, half in homage, at the back of his own new volume, *Ripostes*.

Although the official program of the Imagists

would not be announced for another six months, many of Pound's poems in *Ripostes* clearly indicated the new direction in which he was traveling: "1. Direct treatment of the 'thing' whether subjective or objective. 2. To use absolutely no word that does not contribute to the presentation. 3. As regarding rhythm: to compose in the sequence of the musical

Sylvia Beach Collection

Ezra Pound at Shakespeare and Company
(photo by Sylvia Beach)

phrase, not in the sequence of the metronome." Compared to the ambitious, polemical manifestoes emanating from Paris, these three ground rules of Imagism constituted a modest enough program. The school did not propose a complete revolution of all existing verse forms, but rather sought to establish a few basic poetic standards "in accordance with the best tradition," a propaideutics oriented toward clear, clean technique: "Use no superfluous word, no adjective which does not reveal something. Don't use such an expression as 'dim lands of *peace*.' It dulls the image. It mixes an abstraction with the concrete. It comes from the writer's not realizing that the natural object is always the *adequate* symbol. Go in fear of abstractions. . . . Don't chop your stuff into separate iambs."

These and other "Don'ts by an Imagiste" were originally published in the March 1913 issue of Harriet Monroe's Chicago-based *Poetry*, to which Pound had been appointed foreign editor six months previously. He had wasted little time securing manuscripts for the newly founded magazine: poems by Aldington and "H. D., Imagiste" were forwarded from London together with contributions by Tagore and Yeats. In his effort to export back home "whatever is most dynamic in artistic thought, either here or in Paris," Pound was especially emphatic that *Poetry* print the "best foreign stuff" and "keep an eye on Paris" by publishing "at least one French poem a month," for until American verse learned to measure itself against contemporary European achievement, its voice would be negligible abroad— and so far, only H. D. had produced "the sort of American stuff I can show here and in Paris without its being ridiculed."

"The important work of the last 25 years has been done in Paris," Pound reiterated to *Poetry*'s readers in January 1913, though in truth he still knew relatively little about contemporary French verse (with the important exceptions of the post-Symbolists Gourmont and Regnier). It was not until a few months later in Paris that Pound actually began meeting some of the newer poets grouped around the magazine *L'Effort Libre*—the *unanimiste* Jules Romains, Pierre Jean Jouve (whose work he had reviewed for *Poetry*), and Charles Vildrac and Georges Duhamel, coauthors of *Notes sur la technique poetique* (1910), a study of verse libre which greatly influenced Pound. Sometime in April, he attended one of the group's gatherings and was invited to take part in a *blague* they were preparing—the election and feting of the "Prince des Penseurs," a certain Jules Brisset, retired railroad inspector and crackpot author of a volume purporting to prove man's descent from the frog. This mystification, aimed at satirizing the recent election by critics and journalists of two mediocrities to the title of "Prince des Poetes" and "Prince des Conteurs" would be remembered by Pound in his *Pisan Cantos* (1948) as a predecessor of later Dadaist tactics of literary provocation.

While in Paris, Pound also met for the first time two American poets, Skipwith Cannell and John Gould Fletcher, as well as Natalie Clifford Barney, wealthy American expatriate and close friend of the French author Pound admired most, Remy de Gourmont. Barney was unable to arrange a meeting between the two, but she did provide an unpublished

English translation of Gourmont's *Les Cheveaux de Diomede* (1897) which Pound in turn convinced the *New Freewoman* to print serially later that fall. Indeed, upon his return to London, Pound threw himself wholeheartedly into his newly discovered role as cultural intermediary among the Left Bank, London, and Chicago. He sent *Poetry* Ford Madox Ford's "Impressionism: Some Speculations," an essay which argued for the straightforward presentation of the "flashed impressions" of modern urban life through the "putting of one thing in juxtaposition with the other" in order to "suggest emotions"—an adumbration of Pound's later "ideogrammic method." If poets were to "register their own times in terms of their time," Ford insisted, they would have to learn, as contemporary French authors had, to write "in a language, roughly speaking, any hatter can use." The new poetry, in short, should be "as well-written as prose"; it should strive for the standard of precision set by the "exact, formal and austere phrases" of Flaubert.

Products of Pound's and Ford's conversations about the French "prose tradition," many of these ideas would be subsequently incorporated into "The Approach to Paris," a seven-part overview of recent developments in French poetry which Pound published in the *New Age* in the fall of 1913. "There

Ezra Pound

are just two great and interesting phenomena: the intellectual life of Paris and the curious teething promise of my own vast occidental nation," he proclaimed in his first installment—the ensuing articles provided a critical survey of the current avant-garde (Romains, Vildrac, Laurent Tailhade, Henri-Martin Barzun, and Andre Spire) while assessing the earlier achievements of Rimbaud, Tristan Corbiere, Paul Fort, and Francis Jammes. While Pound's primary aim was to introduce possible models for new directions in Anglo-American poetry, "The Approach to Paris" also allowed him to define techniques he had been striving to incorporate in his own work. Emile Verhaeren and Barzun were, like himself, working out implications of Whitman, while the *unanimiste* Romains supplied the future author of the *Cantos* with "possibly the nearest approach to true epic that we have had since the middle ages." Vildrac and Jammes, in turn, had "brought the narrative verse into competition with narrative prose," and against the fin de siecle hyperesthesia of Symbolism ("that melange of satin and talcum powder"), there was the satiric vigor of Tailhade and the irony of Corbiere, "as careless of style as a man of swift mordent speech can afford to be." Pound praised this same "prose tradition" in his 1913 reviews of two unknowns, Robert Frost and D. H. Lawrence: the former he compared to Jammes because he had set New England rural life into "natural spoken speech," while the latter seemed closer to Vildrac's "short stories in verse."

Paris, at any rate, had now become for Pound the standard against which all contemporary writing was to be measured. As he summed up the purpose of his "Approach to Paris" series in the October 1913 issue of *Poetry*, "If our writers would keep their eye on Paris instead of on London—the London of today or yesterday—there might be some chance of their doing work that would not be demode before it gets to the press. Practically the whole development of the English verse-art has been achieved by steals from the French, from Chaucer's time to our own, and the French are always twenty to sixty years in advance." As this statement suggests, Pound's contempt for contemporary British letters had grown in proportion to his new enthusiasm for Paris. England, he warned Harriet Monroe, was "dead as mutton"—if American writing was to enter the twentieth-century, it would have to turn to Paris, "or any other center save London." The precise causes of Pound's bitterness toward the British "literary episcopacy" remain unclear: his volume *Ripostes* had, on the whole, been favorably received and,

acknowledged *chef d'ecole* of Imagism, he was by now a recognized figure on the London scene. Still, his experience of Parisian avant-garde pugnacity and his association with the political radicals of the *New Age* led Pound increasingly to conceive of himself as a renegade against the entrenched London literary establishment. Like the young Expressionists in Germany, like the Italian Futurists or the splinter factions of the Left Bank, his work was beginning to register the profound malaise of a generation dimly aware that the nineteenth century was on the verge of a violent close.

Imagism had meanwhile begun to attract attention in America: Pound's celebrated "In a Station of the Metro" ("The apparition of these faces in the crowd; / Petals on a wet, black bough.") had appeared amid other "Contemporania" in *Poetry*'s April 1913 issue, provoking the predictable attacks and parodies; and Amy Lowell had come over to England herself to size up the new "school." An official anthology was in preparation, calculated to counter the success of the *Georgian Poetry* anthologies (which contained the work of such poets as Rupert Brooke and Walter de la Mare and were published by H. H. Munro's Poetry Bookshop in London, with introductions by E. H. Marsh). Containing work by Pound, Aldington, H. D., Flint, Ford, Amy Lowell, Williams, Cannell, John Cournos, Allen Upward, and Joyce (whom Pound had discovered through Yeats), the volume, entitled *Des Imagistes*, finally appeared in America and England in early 1914 after many delays. By this time, however, Pound had already begun to disaffiliate himself from the Imagist label, feeling that its stringent technical standards had been diluted into the flaccid free verse he later renamed "Amygism." His own work, moreover, was moving into other areas: he had spent the winter of 1913-1914 with Yeats working through the manuscript notes of Ernest Fenollosa, whose widow had appointed Pound literary executor, and by late January 1914 he had completed a version of the Noh play *Nishikigi* for *Poetry*—the full text of *'Noh' or Accomplishment* would be published in 1916. He was also growing more and more involved in the new sculpture and painting through the work of his friends Henri Gaudier-Brzeska and Wyndham Lewis—coincidentally or not, Olivia Shakespear's daughter, Dorothy, whom Pound married in April, was herself a painter. At some point during this same spring of 1914, Pound, Lewis, and Gaudier-Brzeska, irked by the flamboyant presence of Marinetti in London, decided they had as much right as the Futurists to consider themselves a movement. That

June, they made their existence officially known with the publication of a hugh calliope pink outrage aggressively titled *BLAST, A Review of the Great English Vortex.*

Like Dadaism later, Vorticism combined put-on with polemic. The inaugural issue of *BLAST* itself parodied both the typography and lyric truculence of Marinetti's and Apollinaire's Futurist manifestoes with a series of iconoclastic "Blasts" and "Blesses" aimed at all and sundry: France, for example, was blasted for its "sentimental Gallic gush," its "poodle temper" and "ubiquitous lines of silly little trees" and in turn blessed for its "masterly pornography," its "combativeness," its "great human sceptics, depths of elegance, female qualities." Ambivalently ethnocentric, Vorticism's grudging respect for France is caught by one of *BLAST*'s characteristic aphorisms: "The nearest thing in England to a great traditional French artist is a great revolutionary English one." The movement, however, most resembled Continental avant-gardes in its proposal for a complete revolution of all the arts—there was to be a Vorticist painting, sculpture, poetry, fiction, and even photography ("Vortograms"). But even though Pound conceded, "we are all futurists to the extent of believing with Guillaume Apollinaire that 'On ne peut pas porter partout avec soi le cadavre de son pere,' " Vorticism loudly dissociated itself from what it considered Marinetti's "accelerated impressionism" and sentimental "automobilism." The Futurists' cult of the ultramodern, Pound and Lewis maintained, was no more than an updated version of nineteenth-century exoticism: they had absorbed the machine into their aesthetic merely on the level of content, whereas Vorticism was above all interested in the machine's implications for artistic *form*—the austere, solid geometries of "planes in relation." For Pound in particular, Vorticism involved a kinetic extension of the "hard light" and "clear edges" of Imagism: where he had previously defined the Image as "that which presents an intellectual and emotional complex in an instant of time," he now spoke of a more dynamic "VORTEX, from which, and through which, and into which, ideas are constantly rushing"—an anticipation of the juxtapositional techniques of the *Cantos.*

But Vorticism represented far more than aesthetic to Pound; it embodied, rather, an entire style of revolt—pugnacious, irreverent, militantly intolerant of all the stagnant *idees recues* of bourgeois culture. No longer content to play the role of craftsman or critical observer, Pound now saw it as the artist's function "to sweep out the past century as surely as Attila swept across Europe." The cool,

ascetic decorum of Imagism gave way to a rhetoric of increasing violence directed against all the "slut-bellied obstructionists" who refused to realize that, as *BLAST* trumpeted, the "Christian Era" was now over. In terms of Pound's future career as poet and provocateur, Vorticism proved to be a seminal engagement: in a sense he went to Paris in the twenties primarily to relive the exuberance and activist camaraderie of "The Men of 1914"—first with the Dadaists, then with the younger American expatriates. Still later, he would put his Vorticist virulence and flair for publicity at the service of another revolution—Fascist Italy.

The "Great English Vortex" was cut short, however, by the outbreak of World War I. Its most promising member, the young sculptor Gaudier-Brzeska, to whom Pound would devote a 1916 study, was killed in action in June 1915, and although a second number of *BLAST* appeared a month later, the whirlpool had lost its centripetal energy. Pound, at any rate, was busy on a number of other fronts. In his capacity as literary editor of the *Egoist* (formerly the *New Freewoman*), he was corresponding with Joyce in early 1914 about the serialization of *A Portrait of the Artist* (1916), and for a number of years thereafter, Pound would act as unofficial literary agent and promoter of this "most significant writer of our decade." With Yeats during the winter of 1914-1915, he again returned to the Fenollosa notebooks. Following the American Orientalist's word-for-word English transcriptions of classical Chinese poems, Pound managed, by a feat of sheer imaginative empathy, to produce a series of translations whose accuracy to the spirit, if not the letter, of the originals Sinologists still admire. Published in the spring of 1915, *Cathay* was also an extraordinarily contemporary work, for in such poems as "Lament of the Frontier Guard" and "Song of the Bowmen of Shu" Pound registered, with eloquent restraint, the harsh grief of exile and war.

The spring of 1915 also saw the publication of T. S. Eliot's "The Love Song of J. Alfred Prufrock" in *Poetry*. Pound had first met its young author in the fall of the previous year (through Conrad Aiken) and had immediately dispatched the manuscript of "Prufrock" to Harriet Monroe with the urgent recommendation that she "get it *in* soon." As it happened, Miss Monroe took some six months to print the poem; not until Pound threatened resignation did she capitulate to publication. The incident is characteristic of Pound's immediate belief in Eliot's importance. He called Eliot the only younger American writer who had actually "trained himself *and* modernized himself *on his own*, and during the war years the two Americans would come to work increasingly in poetical and critical tandem: Pound made his 1915 *Catholic Anthology* a showcase for Eliot's verse, and in the pages of the *Egoist* and the *Little Review* they conspired to mount a twin campaign for French poetry. Eliot had spent 1910-1911 at the Sorbonne and knew the language well enough to have considered abandoning English verse altogether for French vers libre. His "Prufrock" showed, moreover, just how profoundly he had assimilated that ironic distance on language which Pound would describe in his 1917 "Irony, Laforgue and Some Satire" (*Poetry*, November 1917) and later define as *logopoeia*, "the dance of intellect among words." Having experimented with the sophisticated obliquities of Laforgue in their own work, the two Americans went on to share another French poet, Theophile Gautier. Being convinced that "the dilutation of *vers libre*, Amygism, Lee Masterism, general floppiness had gone too far," Pound and Eliot jointly decided that a reversion to rhyme and regular meter was in order, and the chiselled stanzas of Gautier's *Emaux et Camees* (1852) provided the models for the hard, angular satirical verse Eliot would publish in his *Poems* (1920) and Pound in his *Hugh Selwyn Mauberley* (1920).

But of all the French writers the two Americans held in common, it was Remy de Gourmont, more than any other, who shaped Pound's vision of France and French literature during the middle and late teens. Even though the war had interrupted travel across the Channel, Gourmont's work remained Pound's major spiritual tie to Paris. Whereas Eliot tended to view Gourmont almost exclusively as a literary critic, Pound perceived him as a kind of polymath culture hero whose activities as poet, novelist, scholar, critic, editor, and journalist constituted "the best portrait available, the best record that is, of the civilized mind from 1885-1915." He had known Gourmont's oeuvre since 1912 and had imitated the Symbolist strategies of *Litanies de la rose* (1872) in the cadences of his own verse while absorbing the theoretical import of *Le Probleme du style* (1902) into his definitions of Imagism; but Pound revered Gourmont less for specific works than for the entire flavor of his intelligence—its clarity, its urbanity, its irony, its catholicity, its sensuousness, its imperturbable common sense, and its aristocratic refusal to allow itself to be stampeded by *idees recues*, qualities, in short, that made Gourmont "a symbol of so much that is finest in France." Even after Gourmont's death in 1915,

Pound continued to look toward his Paris as the model "laboratory of ideas," as the true center of experiment, a place where "poisons could be tested" and "new modes of sanity be discovered." To a certain extent, Pound invented this Paris. Like China or Provence, it became a locus he inhabited above all in his imagination, an ideal city constructed from the various strata of his readings, capital of a tradition of poetry that stretched from Villon and the Pleiade down through the Symbolists and their modernist offspring, sanctum of critical lucidity, cosmopolitanism, and libertarian respect for individual values.

To praise Paris or France thus became a way of indirectly criticizing England and, until America officially entered the war, an occasion to lambaste the United States for its refusal to come to the support of a beleaguered ally whose achieved civilization provided the major buttress against the onslaught of German Kultur. The phrase "French clarity" became a battle cry of sorts in Pound's journalism of the period; closely related to the "clear, hard prose" that he considered the particular glory of the French language and the ultimate "safeguard of civilization," this clarity had granted her an "inner strength" and, unlike imperialist Britain, America, or Germany, "a means of speaking to people whom she does not govern, and in whose commercial affairs she may have little concern." If France had consistently "held firm," it was because of the "respect for accurate statement" and *mot juste* established by the "solid core in her intellectual life"—that is, the "prose tradition" of Montaigne, Voltaire, Stendhal, Flaubert, Maupassant, and Gourmont. The staying power of French culture showed, in addition, that "literature *pays* a nation." After all, Pound observed, "France spends more on literature than either England or America." She prided herself on the French Academy, honored her writers with a variety of prizes, and, most importantly, "recognized the economy of permitting the special talent to apply itself to the special labor," and hence reserved a special tolerance for the artist or exceptional man inconceivable in America.

"The time when the intellectual affairs of America could be conducted on a monolingual basis is over," Pound proclaimed in 1918, and in his contributions to American periodicals during these years he carried on the French lessons initiated in *Poetry*. Margaret Anderson's New York-based *Little Review* became his most reliable outlet, for John Quinn had arranged for him to act as the magazine's foreign correspondent in early 1917. Pound exercised considerable editorial leverage from the very outset:

the *Little Review* began printing the first installments of Joyce's *Ulysses* in 1917 and over the following years Pound edited special issues devoted to Henry James (1918) and Remy de Gourmont (1919), as well as an anthology entitled "A Study in French Poets" (1918), which brought his earlier "Approach to Paris" series up to date. The *Little Review* printed, moreover, a series of his satirical essays and pastiches which were subsequently gathered under the title *Pavannes and Divisions* (1918). Complimenting the satires of "moeurs contemporaines" in his most recent volume of verse, *Lustra* (1916), the collection shows Pound attempting to astound, confound, and *epater* his American readers in a style that unsuccessfully mimics the wit of Whistler and the dazzling paradoxes of French dandies. Pound's more serious work continued to appear in *Poetry*: since late 1915, he had been working on a "cyselephantine poem of immeasurable length which will occupy me for the next four decades," and in 1917 Miss Monroe published "Three Cantos" (subsequently jettisoned when the poem was completely revised in the early twenties). *Poetry* also printed a number of sections from *Homage to Sextus Propertius* in 1918. A radical retranslation of the Roman poet into the modern urban ironies of a Laforgue, *Propertius*, together with *Cathay* (1915) and *Hugh Selwyn Mauberley*, remains one of Pound's most substantial poetic achievements of the decade.

Pound's multifarious activities as poet, critic, anthologist, and editor educated the tastes and values of the generation of younger writers who had been following his career from America. When Malcolm Cowley lists in *Exile's Return* (1951) the major aesthetic "catchwords" of his generation circa 1920—"form, simplification, strangeness, respect for literature as an art with traditions, abstractness"— the impress of Pound's (and of Eliot's) particular version of modernism is quite evident. And when Cowley remarks that "to young writers like ourselves, a long sojourn in France was almost a pilgrimage to Holy Land," one can assume that Pound's French curriculum played a considerable role in instigating the younger generation's departure for Paris. He had himself returned to France, for the first time in six years, in the spring of 1919, passing through Paris on his way to a walking tour through troubadour Provence with Eliot. While at Toulouse, Pound wrote a number of articles about French provincial life for the *New Age* ("Pastiche: The Regional"), but he was more engrossed in the implications of Joyce's *Ulysses* for his own *Cantos* than in contemporary French writing, and returned

to London that fall to take a post as drama critic. It was not until he was named European correspondent to the *Dial* (New York) in March 1920, on the recommendation of John Quinn and Eliot, that Pound began entertaining the idea of moving to the Continent. After all, his most recent volume of verse, *Quia Pauper Amavi* (which contained *Propertius* as well as the first three Cantos) had been poorly received in England, and his aggressive espousal of the unorthodox economic doctrines of Major Clifford Hugh Douglas made him decidedly unwelcome in most London magazines. Enraged with "usury age-old and age-thick / and liars in public places," now convinced that the war had merely been fought "For an old bitch gone in the teeth, / For a botched civilization," Pound composed *Hugh Selwyn Mauberley* in early 1920. He would later term it "distinctly a farewell to London."

He left for the Continent that spring, partly to gather material for the *Dial*, partly to vacation in Sirmione, where he managed, at long last, to meet the author of *Ulysses*. Ever concerned about the state of Joyce's health, finances, and masterpiece-in-progress, Pound prevailed upon him to quit Trieste for Paris, thus setting in motion one of the major forces that would make Paris the magnet of modernism over the next decade. When Joyce and family arrived in Paris in July, Pound was there to help them settle: he arranged for lodgings and loans, found a translator for *A Portrait of the Artist* (Mme. Ludmilla Bloch-Savitsky), and introduced Joyce (through prewar acquaintance poet Andre Spire) to the future publisher of *Ulysses*, Sylvia Beach. Having installed Joyce in relative comfort, Pound scouted about for contributors to *Dial*. In the space of a single hectic month, he managed to secure "inedited writings of Remy de Gourmont" as well as "acceptable manuscripts or promises of collaboration" from Julien Benda, Marcel Proust, Paul Valery, Louis Aragon, Benedetto Croce, Miguel de Unamuno, Yeats, Eliot, Joyce, and Wyndham Lewis. Upon his return to London late that summer (where he learned he had been fired as the *Athenaeum*'s drama critic), Pound embarked on a series of letters entitled "The Island of Paris," which was published in the October, November, and December issues of the *Dial*.

An invitation to expatriation, this series presented a wide spectrum of recent developments, calculated to provide "a poetic serum to save English letters from postmature and American telegraphics from premature suicide and decomposition." Among the established writers, Pound praised Valery for his *Soiree avec Monsieur Teste* (1896), subsequently published in the *Dial* in Natalie Barney's translation, and cited Proust as "the nearest the French can get to Henry James"; Gide, by contrast, was dismissed as belonging to the *Nouvelle Revue Francaise* crowd, which Pound denigrated as a French variant of Bloomsbury artiness. As for the younger French poets, Pound compared the jazzy colloquialisms of Paul Morand to his own *Lustra*, observed that Aragon was experimenting with "the equivalent of the hokku," and singled out the "vitreous and impeccable versification" of Guy-Charles Cros and the "droll morgue" of painter Maurice Vlaminck's comic verse. He was above all impressed by the range of technical experiment going on in Paris: Andre Wurmser, for example, was exploring the possibilities of verbal orchestration in his half-sung, half-chanted compositions, and Robert de Souza, following the typographical innovations of Mallarme's *Un Coup de des* (1897) and Apollinaire's *Calligrammes* (1918), was trying to develop a system of notation to score the tone and rhythm of verse visually on the page—a technique Pound, like Cummings, would apply in his *Cantos*. But of all the new writers on the Parisian scene, the "young and very ferocious" Dadaists most intrigued ex-Vorticist Pound: "They have satirized the holy church of our century (journalism), they have satirized the sanctimonious attitude toward 'the arts.' They have given up the pretense of impartiality. They have expressed a desire to live and to die, preferring death to a sort of moribund permanence."

The roots of Dada reached back to 1915-1916, with Francis Picabia editing *291* in New York and Tristan Tzara masterminding the anarchistic antics of the Cabaret Voltaire in Zurich. Both men converged on Paris in 1920 and gathered around themselves the young authors associated with the magazine *Litterature*, Aragon, Breton, and Soupault. When Pound arrived in Paris in early 1921 officially to take up residence at 70 bis, rue Notre Dame des Champs, the Dadaists were by far the most boisterous avant-garde on the Left Bank, and he accordingly threw himself into the fray. Much of Pound's involvement in the movement can be ascribed to his extraordinary esteem for poet-painter-impressario Picabia, whom he termed the "dynamic under Dada," a mind capable of "more somersaults than any other writer now living." Dadaism, for Pound, represented the apocalyptic searing away of defunct modes of art and thought, and Picabia appeared to him as the exterminating angel sent to wipe out the old order and usher in the new, "a sort of Socratic or anti-Socratic vacuum cleaner" bent on

the radical *nettoyage* of all the filth of postwar Europe. Picabia, as Pound planned to show in a book entitled "Four Modern Artists" (the other three being Picasso, Wyndham Lewis, and Gaudier-Brzeska), worked neither in the medium of literature nor painting, but rather in the medium of thought itself; his major achievement was to have generated "the excitement of mental peril" by playing with abstract concepts and ideas in such a way as to subvert accepted modes of intellection altogether. Although "Four Modern Artists" was never written, Picabia's particular style of provocation had a considerable impact on Pound. The typographical oddities of Dadaist publications which burlesqued journalistic and advertising devices would find their way into his subsequent prose and poetry, and Dada's aggressive incoherence encouraged a similar tendency in Pound which, in his later polemics of the thirties and forties, often degenerated into mere cantankerousness. Picabia's nihilistic tabula rasa of received values also prompted Pound to conceive his own *Cantos* in a new light: his epic would record his maverick break with modern civilization in search of a new order of culture. Picabia's strategy of "anti-art" furthermore caused Pound to question his residual proclivities toward fin de siecle aestheticism. His inclusion in the *Cantos* of newspaper clippings, historical and economic documents, political slogans, and so forth can be seen as an extrapolation of Dada's attempt to redefine the boundaries and functions of art, to replace the work of art by what Pound called the "act of art," to take the artist out of the safety of the atelier and plunge him back into the immediacy and risk of the world.

Pound participated in a number of Dada stunts (most notably, the mock-trial of reactionary novelist Maurice Barres in May 1921) and contributed to various of its periodicals—Tzara's *Dadaphone* (March 1920), Breton's *Litterature* (September 1920), and Picabia's special issue of *391*, *Le Pilhaou Thibaou* (July 1921). The *Little Review* had also begun leaning toward Dada: in the spring of 1921, it printed the manifesto "Dada souleve tout" with texts by Aragon and Soupault, and later that fall Pound and Picabia jointly edited a "Brancusi Number" for the magazine which contained, in addition to Pound's brilliant appraisal of the Rumanian sculptor's work, Picabia's essay "Fumigations," texts by Paul Morand and Yvan Goll, and a full-length translation by Jean Hugo (with Pound's assitance) of Cocteau's poem "The Cape of Good Hope." The back of the issue featured a number of Dadaist outbursts by "Abel Sanders" (i.e. Ezra

Pound), which parodied the "Baroness" Else von Freytag-Loringhoven's recent review of William Carlos Williams's *Kora in Hell* (1920). Pound and Picabia also collaborated on the *Little Review*'s Spring 1922 number, an issue devoted primarily to the latter's paintings and writings. In addition to a number of playful squibs by "Abel Sanders" ("STOP PRESS / The intellectual capital of America is still Paris"), the number also contained a "Little Review Calendar" concocted by Pound which proclaimed that "the Christian era came definitely to an END at midnight of the 29-30 of October 1921"—the date of Pound's birthday and of *Ulysses*'s completion. Years were henceforth to be denominated "p.s.U." (*post scriptum Ulixi*) and the months were systemically relabeled with Greek mythological names. Superficially a Dadaist joke, Pound's calendar nonetheless expressed his deep conviction that an inaugural age of the modern spirit was at hand.

Picabia, Dada, and the *Little Review* represent, however, only one dimension of Pound's activities during these Paris years, for in addition to acting as intermediary between the French and American avant-garde, he took on a variety of translating jobs. The *Dial* remained his most reliable employer, and during 1920-1921 the magazine published his translations of Gourmont's *Dust for Sparrows*, Morand's *Turkish Night*, and selections from Proust, Jean Giraudoux, and Oscar Milosz. Boni and Liveright in turn commissioned Pound to translate Edouard Estaunie's novel, *L'Appel de la route* (1921), and, more significantly, Gourmont's comparative study of animal sexuality, *Physique de l'amour* (1904), published in America as *The Natural Philosophy of Love* in 1922. Boni and Liveright also brought out Pound's *Poems 1918-21*, which contained, in addition to the contents of *Propertius* and *Mauberley*, four new Cantos recently published in the *Dial*. One of these, Canto VII, is sometimes referred to by critics as Pound's "Paris Canto" (though it was written in 1919). Refracting the novelistic procedures of Henry James and Flaubert through the verbal textures of Eliot's "Gerontion" (1920), the poem presents a ghostly vision of a modern metropolis peopled by "Dry casques of departed locusts / speaking a shell of speech," and cluttered with the tawdry, pretentious furnishings of the Second Empire—an urban hell similar to the one Eliot would explore in his *Waste Land* (1922). Pound, nevertheless, remained relatively unsure of where his *Cantos* were heading. He had discovered the central technical innovation of the poem—the juxtaposition in time and space of "ideogrammic" clusters (as defined by Fenollosa's essay on *The Chinese Written Character as a Medium for Poetry*)—but his epic still lacked a clearly defined shape or direction.

Joyce's *Ulysses* suggested a solution to the problematic structure of the *Cantos*. Although Pound had been closely involved with Joyce's masterpiece since 1917 and had spilled a great deal of ink protesting its American censorship, it was only when he reread it in its entirety upon its publication in 1922 that he was able to grasp the novel's significance as a formal whole. In two important reviews of *Ulysses* published that year (the *Dial* "Paris Letter" of May and "James Joyce et Pecuchet" in the June *Mercure de France*), Pound articulated his sense of Joyce's achievement: *Ulysses* had synthesized the older tradition of epic with its later version, the nineteenth-century realist novel, and had in the process created a new, encyclopedic literary form whose nearest ancestor was Flaubert's comic odyssey of the mind, *Bouvard et Pecuchet* (1881). Following Joyce's Homeric framework, Pound completely recast the opening of his poem in late 1922, making the exile Odysseus the central figure of the *Cantos* and patterning his epic around an encyclopedic voyage of discovery, at once individual and collective, local and universal. The poem now began with Odysseus's descent into the underworld to consult the wisdom of Tiresias, and, like a novel, included history past and present while enacting the modern mind's quest to reconstruct, out of the ruins of its experience, a vision of archetypal beauty and order.

Just as *Ulysses* helped him define his own *Cantos*, so Pound during this same year of 1922 aided Eliot in discovering the form of his *Waste Land*. The tale of Pound's midwifery is well-known—the dropping off of the first draft in Paris in late 1921, the blue-penciling of slack lines and excision of entire sections from the original version, the editorial shaping and pruning, the final shepherding of the manuscript into print. Eliot later handsomely repaid his debt by dedicating the poem to Pound, *"il miglior fabbro"* (as Dante had referred to Arnaut Daniel). A valuable comment on the cinematographic techniques of swift montage employed both by *The Waste Land* and by the *Cantos* is contained in a review Pound wrote of Cocteau's verse in early 1921. The "young aesthetic," he observed, was "partial to a beauty very rapid in kind," largely because of the accelerated tempo of modern urban experience. Whereas the life of a village could accommodate traditional narrative treatment, "in a city the visual impressions suceed each other, overlap, overcross, they are 'cinematographic,' but they are not a simple linear sequence. They are often a flood of nouns without verbal relations." *The Waste Land*, with Pound's help, had achieved precisely this "feel of the age," and he immediately recognized it for the masterpiece it was. Characteristically, Pound felt compelled to assist Eliot in more than an editorial capacity. Realizing that Eliot's health and work were suffering because of the pressures of his job at Lloyds Bank, Pound devised a plan in early 1922 to raise money on Eliot's behalf so that he might devote his full attention to writing. Called "Bel Esprit" and hatched in conjunction with Natalie Barney, who was arranging a similar fund for Paul Valery, the project managed to attract a number of patron-subscribers, but deeply embarrassed by the publicity of the scheme, Eliot asked that "Bel Esprit" be abandoned.

The episode is indicative of Pound's spontaneous generosity toward his friends—and Joyce and Eliot were only two of the many he helped in Paris. Hemingway has said that during these years, Pound devoted only a fifth of his energy to his own work, "with the rest of his time he tries to advance the fortunes, both material and artistic, of his friends. He defends them when they are attacked, he gets them into magazines and out of jail. He loans them money. He sells their pictures. He arranges concerts for them. He writes articles about them. He introduces them to wealthy women. He gets publishers to take their books. He sits up all night with them when they claim to be dying and dissuades them from suicide. And in the end a few of them refrain from knifing him at the first opportunity." Wyndham Lewis's affectionately acid account of the "Pound Circus" in Paris also speaks of his "manic herding of talent," of his tendency "to act as a nursery and lying-in establishment, bureau de renseignement and unofficial agency for unknown literary talent"—especially American talent, given Pound's "tribal attraction for his fellow-countrymen." Indeed, for the first time in over a decade Pound was back in contact with Americans. He seemed to know everybody in Paris. Among the elder expatriates, there was his prewar friend Natalie Barney, at whose elegant salon Americans could rub shoulders with the older generation of French literati and aristocrats. Gertrude Stein's rival gatherings on the rue de Fleurus, on the other hand, Pound did not attend after 1921. According to Hemingway, "she was angry at Ezra because he sat down too quickly on a small, fragile and, doubtless, uncomfortable chair, that it is quite possible he had been given on

purpose, and had either cracked or broken it." There the matter rested.

The list of Pound's acquaintances among the more recent expatriates during 1921-1924 would be long to enumerate. But a brief chronological overview of his American contacts would have to include, from the very outset, Sylvia Beach, for whom Pound's wife Dorothy drew a map to guide new arrivals in town to Shakespeare and Company; he himself did minor carpentry around the bookstore and collected subscriptions for *Ulysses*. Early encounters also included Robert McAlmon and Hemingway, two practitioners of the hard, clean American prose that Pound had long been calling for. Hemingway would remain a lifelong friend: they sparred together at Pound's studio, traveled with their wives through central Italy in 1923, and Pound was instrumental in the publication of Hemingway's *in our time* the following year. Hemingway's work was part of a series William Bird had asked Pound to edit for his newly founded Three Mountains Press. Loosely titled "The Inquest" and designed, in Pound's words, to "tell the truth about *moeurs contemporaines*, without fake, melodrama, conventional ending," the series comprised, in addition to *in our time*, Pound's own autobiographical pastiche, *Indiscretions*, William Carlos Williams's *The Great American Novel*, and three British works, Ford's *Women and Men*, B. C. Windeler's *Elimus*, and B. M. G. Adams's *England*. All but *in our time* were published in 1923. William Bird also agreed to publish a volume of Cantos in a deluxe edition with initials designed by the American artist Henry Strater; work began in 1923, and in January 1925 *A Draft of XVI Cantos of Ezra Pound for the Beginning of a Poem of some Length* finally appeared.

Pound also played intellectual cicerone to a stream of American visitors during these years. Harold Loeb and Alfred Kreymborg, whom he had been in correspondence with since the Imagist days of *Glebe* and *Others*, arrived in Paris in early 1921 in search of material for their new magazine *Broom*. Scofield Thayer, co-owner and editor of the *Dial*, came in July of the same year. Pound took him around to Gertrude Stein's, and Thayer in turn introduced him to visiting E. E. Cummings, whom Pound would feature prominently in his Spring 1923 "Exiles Number" of the *Little Review*. Cummings, too, would remain among the most loyal of Pound's friends, despite their subsequent political divergences. The summer of 1923 saw another influx of visitors: Pound finally met the now aging editor of *Poetry*, Harriet Monroe, who later

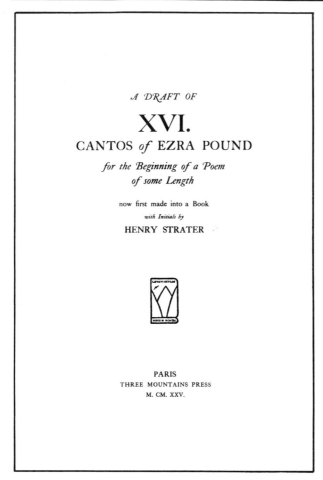

A DRAFT OF

XVI.

CANTOS *of* EZRA POUND

*for the Beginning of a Poem
of some Length*

now first made into a Book
with Initials by
HENRY STRATER

PARIS
THREE MOUNTAINS PRESS
M. CM. XXV.

Title page

remembered that he seemed out "to start civilization again—nothing less" and that he was excited about the "spiritual force" evident in Mussolini's "modern movement." Margaret Anderson of the *Little Review* also dropped by Pound's *pavillon* at 70 bis, rue Notre Dame des Champs that year. She found him high-strung, discomfitingly agitated, and over-elaborate in his attitude toward women: his name was dropped from the masthead of the *Little Review* the following year. The most notable visitor of 1923, however, was John Quinn, powerful and irascible patron of Pound, Eliot, Lewis, Joyce, and the *Little Review*. The Pounds gave a reception for him in their studio which has been memorialized by a group photograph featuring a glowering Quinn, a slouched Pound, and, gingerly seated in chairs designed and built by Pound himself, James Joyce and Ford Madox Ford. Beneath Joyce's vacant gaze, Ford quizzically holds what he later described as a specimen of Poundian sculpture: "Ezra was of the school of Brancusi. He acquired pieces of stone as nearly egg-shaped as possible, hit them with

hammers and laid them about the floor." Quinn's brief passage through Paris produced financial backing for yet another magazine venture. The *transatlantic review*, directed by Ford and assisted by Pound proteges Basil Bunting and Hemingway, with editorial offices above William Bird's press at 29, Quai d'Anjou, made its first appearance in January 1924. The number included two Cantos by Pound, but his contributions to subsequent issues were almost exclusively restricted to music criticism.

An outgrowth of his research into the songs of the troubadours, Pound's interest in music reached back to his earliest days in London with Yeats and Rummel; by the late teens he was publishing music criticism in the *New Age* under the pseudonym of William Atheling. Upon arriving in Paris, he launched himself into his new vocation and began work (aided by Agnes Bedford) on an opera, *Le Testament*, based upon texts of Villon. Natalie Barney lent him the use of her piano and he purchased, moreover, a bassoon whose "deep rumblings and tootings" disquieted even the most sympathetic of friends. His proclivities toward music were further encouraged by the presence in Paris of American-born violinist Olga Rudge and by the arrival in 1923 of wunderkind pianist and composer George Antheil. Pound, sensing there was perhaps another prodigy here of Gaudier-Brzeska's stripe, proceeded to take charge of the career of the "infAntheil terrible." He introduced him to the influential, including Jean Cocteau, fellow "specialist in genius," and arranged concerts, while Antheil in turn helped Pound with his own compositions and discussed musical theory. The fruit of these discussions was *Antheil and the Treatise on Harmony*, a collection of Pound's *transatlantic review* music pieces, published in 1924 by Bird's Three Mountains Press.

Although critics differ on the value of Pound's musical theory, it is best understood as an extension of his Vorticist aesthetic, since what he admired above all in Antheil's percussive compositions was "the cold, the icy, the non-romantic, non-expressive," in short, that same machine hardness he respected in the paintings of Leger. Antheil's most celebrated composition in this mode was the *Ballet Mecanique*, scored for eight pianos, a player piano, electric bells, whistles, xylophones, and airplane propeller. Made into a film by American cameraman Dudley Murphy and Leger in 1924, the piece was first performed on 19 June 1926 at the Theatre des Champs-Elysees, provoking a memorable riot in which Pound apparently took a valiant part. Ten days later, at the Salle Pleyel, Pound's own opera, *Le*

Testament, received its first public performance by Olga Rudge, tenor Yves Tinayre, and bass Robert Maitland. While Hemingway remained skeptical about Pound's music (as did William Carlos Williams, who visited him in Paris at the height of his musical *emballade*), composer Virgil Thomson would later remember it favorably: "The music was not quite a musician's music, though it may well be the finest poet's music since Thomas Campion." Pound, at any rate, thought he had produced something that "ought ultimately to be a French national fete, as Villon is their only substitute for Homer."

But despite this veritable pantechnicon of activity, Pound's Paris years reflect a progressive sense of disillusionment and isolation. In truth, no city could have lived up to the expectations of that ideal capital Pound created for himself and his American readers during the teens—a paradise of experiment and artistic integrity. Once Pound got over the initial ebullience expressed in his early collaborations with Picabia, he began shuttling increasingly between Montparnasse and Italy, where he spent almost half of 1922 and several months of

1923 and 1924 gathering material for his Cantos on the Renaissance condottieri Sigismondo Malatesta and Niccolo d'Este. Although still convinced that Paris remained "the place in which more than in any other there are the greatest number of men and things not for sale," Pound's "Paris Letters" (published regularly in the *Dial* from October 1921 through March 1923) provide a chronicle of his gradual disenchantment with contemporary French literature. He wrote perceptively of the satirical genius of Proust's *Sodome et Gomorrhe* (1921-1922); he praised Cendrars's *Anthologie Negre* (1921) and recent work by Giraudoux, Morand, and Cocteau; he applauded the republication of Jarry's *Ubu Roi* (1896) and extolled French cookbooks ("a complete civilization recognizes all the senses"). But more and more, he returned to earlier French achievements: two letters of 1922 are almost entirely given over to the Flaubert centenary, and by January 1923 he had become convinced that "the latest real news of the French is still Flaubert, Corbiere, Laforgue and Rimbaud." He lamented the lack of a real "chef d'orchestre" in literary Paris—Picabia had more or less faded from the limelight and Andre Breton's star

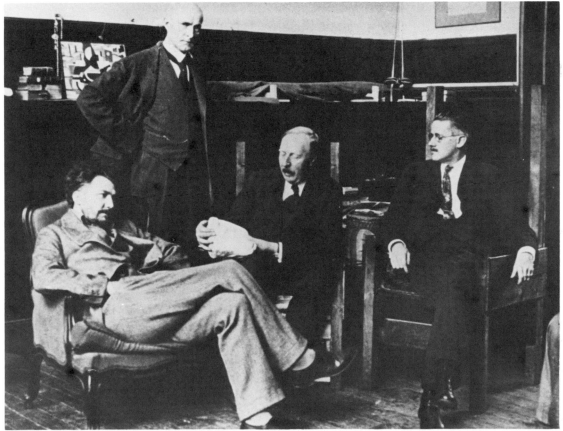

Ezra Pound, John Quinn, Ford Madox Ford, and James Joyce in Paris, 1923

had not yet risen. (The first Surrealist Manifesto was not published until 1924.) Only Cocteau, whose range of activity as musical impressario, poet, artist, playwright, and cineaste equalled Pound's own, remained consistently high in his esteem as the "livest thing in Paris."

Increasingly convinced that it was now time to "build rather than scratch round for remnants and bric-a-brac," Pound found himself turning away from the "indisputable enervation of Paris" to the Italy of such poet-activists as Gabriele D'Annunzio and Marinetti. Mussolini had triumphantly marched on Rome in 1922, and Pound rather naively construed Fascism not for what it was, but rather as yet another modernist movement—not a literary or artistic movement, but rather a political avant-garde dedicated to the construction of the new order out of the ashes of the old. Rhyming Mussolini with those Renaissance culture heroes whose exploits he was documenting in the *Cantos,* Pound idealized Il Duce into a twentieth-century Malatesta devoted to the political and economic regeneration of Italy. He paid dearly for this vision: a direct line can be drawn between Pound's progressive alienation in Paris, his move to Italy, his confused propaganda activities during World War II, and the thirteen years he subsequently spent incarcerated. But behind the public, political implications of Pound's decision to leave Paris in the fall of 1924, there were also more private, more elusive reasons which biographers have been relatively hesitant to discuss. He had been relieved from his editorial post at the *Dial* in May 1923; his association with the *Little Review* had come to an end; and his personal life was growing increasingly complicated. He was named in 1923 as corespondent in divorce proceedings initiated by the husband of Bride Scratton, a friend of Pound's since his early London days. He was also seeing a great deal of Olga Rudge, and his wife Dorothy, disenchanted with the hectic pace of Paris, was anxious to move on to Italy, where, in 1925, Miss Rudge bore Pound a daughter, Mary. His wife had a child of her own, Omar, the following year, thus creating an impossible domestic situation which ultimately tore Pound apart.

"Having rejuvenated by 15 years in going to Paris and added another ten of life by quitting same," Pound settled in Rapallo to devote himself to his *Cantos.* Two publications in early 1925 more or less brought his Paris period to an official close: Bird's sumptuous edition of *A Draft of XVI Cantos* finally appeared, and later that spring Ernest Walsh and Ethel Moorhead dedicated the maiden issue of their magazine *This Quarter* to "Ezra Pound who by

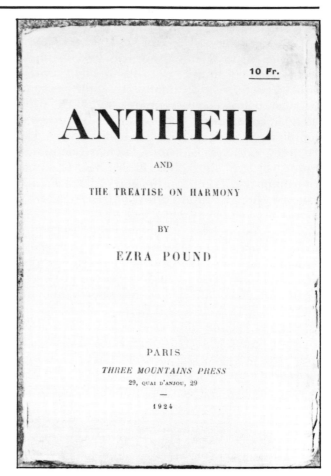

Front wrapper

his creative work, his editorship of several magazines, his helpful friendship for young and unknown artists . . . comes first to our mind as meriting the gratitude of this generation." The issue contained tributes by Joyce and Hemingway as well. In a later issue Moorhead retracted this "too generous dedication" after an editorial squabble with Pound. The incident is perhaps emblematic of Pound's deteriorating rapport with the literary life of Paris. His enthusiasm for Joyce had cooled; after receiving a sample of *Finnegans Wake* in 1926, he wrote to wish Joyce every success but admitted he could make neither head nor tail of it: "nothing short of divine vision or a new cure for the clap can be possibly worth all the circumambient peripherization." As the Joyce cult spread in Paris in the late twenties, Pound grew even more dismissive of "*transition* crap or Jheezus in progress," feeling that it was all mere "diarrhoea of consciousness." Joyce's plunge into what *transition*'s editor Eugene Jolas termed "the language of the night" or Surrealist explorations of the unconscious through automatic writing remained abhorrent to Pound's aesthetic of hard, clear surfaces, of "planes in relation" patterned into luminous forms.

Pound did not entirely disengage himself from Paris, however. After a period of silence, he again erupted briefly onto the scene with a magazine edited from Rapallo. Entitled, aptly, the *Exile*, the first number was printed in Paris and contained John Rodker's "Adolphe 1920," Hemingway's "Nothoemist Poem" (a misprint for "Neo-Thomist Poem") on Cocteau's conversion, part of Canto XX, and Pound's disjointed apercus into the economic significance of the Russian and Fascist revolutions. Three more issues of the magazine appeared, now published by Covici Friede in America; contributors included old friends William Carlos Williams and Yeats, Paris companions Robert McAlmon and Ralph Cheever Dunning, and a new protege, Louis Zukovsky. The first and final magazine over which Pound had complete editorial control, the *Exile* drifted more and more toward political and economic concerns: Pound's experimental twenties were clearly giving way to the harsher ideological climate of the thirties. Pound returned to Paris in 1930 to oversee the publication of *A Draft of XXX Cantos* by Nancy Cunard's Hours Press. His *Imaginary Letters* (originally published in the *Little Review* in 1917) were also brought out by Caresse Crosby's Black Sun Press that year, and Pound contributed a brief introductory note to her posthumous edition of Harry Crosby's *Torchbearer* (1931). After this final spate of publication, Pound more or less disappeared from the Parisian scene: he sent off occasional blasts to the Paris *Tribune* (the European edition of the *Chicago Tribune*), contributed a few items to Samuel Putnam's *New Review*, took an interest in Henry Miller (whose 1936 *Money and How It Gets That Way* is a parody of Pound's economic pamphlets). As for contemporary French writers, only Cocteau, Rene Crevel, and, to a certain extent, Celine, struck him as important, convinced as he now was that France had exhausted herself and could no longer pretend to be "the whole hog and center of European culture."

The center had shifted elsewhere. American writing had finally come of age in Paris and there was a new vortex of talent to attend to back home—a loosely confederated group of Poundian disciples, including Zukovsky, Charles Reznikov, and George Oppen, who called themselves Objectivists. Italy, too, was engaged in a cultural *risorgimento*, and Pound did what he could to introduce new American talent onto the Italian scene. But as his publications of the thirties suggest, Pound's attentions were moving beyond literature. Besides such influential

volumes of literary criticism as *How To Read* (1931), *ABC of Reading* (1934), *Make It New* (1934), *Polite Essays* (1937), one finds *ABC of Economics* (1933), *Jefferson And/Or Mussolini* (1935), *Confucius: Digest of the Analects* (1937), and *Guide to Kulchur* (1938). His Cantos of this period reflect a similar attempt to incorporate aesthetic with political, economic, and cultural vision: *Eleven New Cantos*

Inside front cover, This Quarter, *1 (Spring 1925)*

XXX-XLI (1934) contrasts the ideal America of Jefferson and John Quincy Adams with the hell of contemporary Europe; *The Fifth Decad of Cantos* (1937) deals largely with banking and usury; *Cantos LII-LXXI* (1940) examines, from a Confucian perspective, the dynastic history of China and the career of John Adams. In *The Pisan Cantos*, written in captivity at the U. S. Army Disciplinary Training Center near Pisa and awarded the Bollingen prize for poetry in 1948 amid much public controversy, Pound returns to a more personal, elegiac mode. Among the flood of memories released by his fear of imminent execution, Pound recalls earlier days in Paris, "before the world was given over to wars."

Bursting into occasional French ("Tard, tres tard je t'ai connue, la Tristesse"), Pound revisits the light, the bridges, the friends, and the restaurants of Paris, now transformed by memory into an ideal city of the mind, "now in the heart indestructible." From his subsequent confinement in St. Elizabeths Hospital, Pound continued work on the construction of his increasingly private vision of paradise. *Section: Rock-Drill 85-95 de los cantares* appeared in 1955, followed by *Thrones 96-109 de los cantares* (1959) and *Drafts and Fragments of Cantos CX to CXVII* (1968). Released from St. Elizabeths in 1958, largely through the intervention of Archibald MacLeish, Robert Frost, Ernest Hemingway, and T. S. Eliot, Pound returned to Italy to an old age of doubt, remorse, and silence. He last revisited Paris in 1965 and 1967 for the French publication of his work: he dropped in on Natalie Barney at 20, rue Jacob, toured the Salle Gaudier-Brzeska at the Musee de l'Art Moderne, and apparently was moved by a production of Beckett's *Endgame* (1957).

Translations:

Cathay Translations by Ezra Pound for the Most Part from the Chinese of Rihaku, From the Notes of the Late Ernest Fenollosa, and the Decipherings of the Professors Mori and Ariga (London: Mathews, 1915);

Remy de Gourmont, *The Natural Philsophy of Love*, with postscript by Pound (New York: Boni & Liveright, 1922; London: Casanova Society, 1926);

Confucius The Unwobbling Pivot & the Great Digest, with commentary by Pound, *Pharos*, 4 (Winter 1947);

The Translations of Ezra Pound, ed. Hugh Kenner (London: Faber & Faber, 1953; New York: New Directions, 1953);

The Classic Anthology Defined by Confucius (Cambridge: Harvard University Press, 1954; London: Faber & Faber, 1955);

Sophokles, *Women of Trachis* (London: Spearman, 1956; New York: New Directions, 1957);

Love Poems of Ancient Egypt, translated by Pound and Noel Stock (Norfolk, Conn.: New Directions, 1964).

Other:

Des Imagistes An Anthology, edited with contributions by Pound (New York: A. & C. Boni, 1914; London: Poetry Bookshop, 1914);

Catholic Anthology 1914-1915, edited with contributions by Pound (London: Mathews, 1915);

'Noh' or Accomplishment, by Pound and Ernest Fenollosa (London: Macmillan, 1916; New York: Knopf, 1917);

Harry Crosby, *Torchbearer*, notes by Pound (Paris: Black Sun Press, 1931);

Active Anthology, edited with contributions by Pound (London: Faber & Faber, 1933);

Confucius to Cummings An Anthology of Poetry, edited by Pound and Marcella Spann (New York: New Directions, 1964).

Letters:

The Letters of Ezra Pound 1907-1941, ed. D. D. Paige (New York: Harcourt Brace, 1950);

Pound/Joyce: The Letters of Ezra Pound to James Joyce, ed. Forrest Read (New York: New Directions, 1965).

Bibliography:

Donald Gallup, *A Bibliography of Ezra Pound*, revised edition (London: Hart-Davis, 1969).

Biographies:

Mary De Rachewiltz, *Discretions* (Boston: Little, Brown, 1971);

C. David Heyman, *Ezra Pound: The Last Rower* (New York: Viking, 1976);

Charles Norman, *Ezra Pound*, revised edition (New York: Minerva, 1969);

Noel Stock, *The Life of Ezra Pound* (New York: Pantheon, 1970).

References:

Christine Brooke-Rose, *A ZBC of Ezra Pound* (Berkeley: University of California Press, 1971);

Ronald Bush, *The Genesis of Ezra Pound's Cantos* (Princeton: Princeton University Press, 1977);

Donald Davie, *Ezra Pound: Poet as Sculptor* (New York: Oxford University Press, 1964);

Davie, *Ezra Pound* (New York: Penguin, 1975);

Earle Davis, *Vision Fugitive: Ezra Pound's Economics* (Lawrence: University of Kansas Press, 1968);

L. S. Dembo, *The Confucian Odes of Ezra Pound* (Berkeley: University of California Press, 1963);

John H. Edwards and William Vasse, *Annotated Index to the Cantos of Ezra Pound* (Berkeley: University of California Press, 1957);

T. S. Eliot, *Ezra Pound: His Metric and Poetry* (New York: Knopf, 1917);

Clark Emery, *Ideas Into Action: A Study of Pound's Cantos* (Coral Gables: University of Miami Press, 1958);

J. J. Espey, *Ezra Pound's Mauberley: A Study in Composition* (Berkeley: University of California Press, 1955);

G. S. Fraser, *Ezra Pound* (New York: Grove, 1961);

Eva Hesse, ed., *New Approaches to Ezra Pound* (Berkeley: University of California Press, 1969);

Thomas H. Jackson, *The Early Poetry of Ezra Pound* (Cambridge: Harvard University Press, 1969);

Hugh Kenner, *The Poetry of Ezra Pound* (New York: New Directions, 1951);

Kenner, *The Pound Era* (Berkeley: University of California Press, 1971);

Lewis Leary, ed., *Motive and Method in the Cantos of Ezra Pound* (New York: Columbia University Press, 1954);

Stuart Y. McDougal, *Ezra Pound and the Troubadour Tradition* (Princeton: Princeton University Press, 1972);

Daniel Pearlman, *The Barb of Time: On the Unity of Ezra Pound's Cantos* (New York: Oxford University Press, 1969);

M. L. Rosenthal, *A Primer of Ezra Pound* (New York: Macmillan, 1960);

Peter Rusell, ed., *An Examination of Ezra Pound* (New York: New Directions, 1950);

K. K. Ruthven, *A Guide to Ezra Pound's Personae* (Berkeley: University of California Press, 1969);

R. Murray Schafer, *Ezra Pound and Music* (New York: New Directions, 1977);

Herbert Schneidau, *Ezra Pound: The Image and the Real* (Baton Rouge: Louisiana State University Press, 1969);

Grace Schulman, ed., *Ezra Pound: A Collection of Criticism* (New York: McGraw-Hill, 1974);

Richard Sieburth, *Instigations: Ezra Pound and Remy de Gourmont* (Cambridge: Harvard University Press, 1978);

J. P. Sullivan, *Ezra Pound and Sextus Propertius: A Study in Creative Translation* (Austin: University of Texas Press, 1964);

Hugh Wittmeyer, *The Poetry of Ezra Pound: Forms and Renewal 1908-1920* (Berkeley: University of California Press, 1969);

Wai-lim Yip, *Ezra Pound's Cathay* (Princeton: Princeton University Press, 1969).

Papers:

Most of Pound's papers are in the Ezra Pound Archive at the Beinecke Library, Yale University.

SAMUEL PUTNAM
(10 October 1892-15 January 1950)

SELECTED BOOKS: *Evaporations, a Symposium,* by Putnam and Mark Turbyfill (Winchester, Mass.: Modern Review Press, 1923);

Francois Rabelais Man of the Renaissance, A Spiritual Biography (London & Toronto: Cape; New York: Cape & Smith, 1929);

The Glistening Bridge Leopold Survage and the Spatial Problem in Painting (New York: Covici Friede, 1929);

Direction, a Symposium, by Putnam and others (Paris: New Review Press, 1932);

The World of Jean Bosschere (London: Fortune Press, 1932);

Marguerite of Navarre (New York: Coward-McCann, 1935; London: Jarrolds, 1936);

Paris Was Our Mistress Memoirs of a Lost & Found Generation (New York: Viking, 1947);

Marvelous Journey A Survey of Four Centuries of Brazilian Writing (New York: Knopf, 1948).

Samuel Putnam's love of language and literature served him well in Paris between 1927 and 1933 when his translations of works by French and Italian writers helped to finance his ventures as an editor and publisher. Throughout his career he demonstrated both his wide knowledge of international literature and his love for literary warfare. Although Putnam is justifiably better known for his later, ground-breaking studies of Brazilian literature and for his excellent translations, especially his highly regarded translation of *Don Quixote* (1949), his role as a debunker of both literary conservatism and the "isms" of the avant-garde earned him an important place in expatriate literary circles of the late twenties and early thirties. His memoir of that period, *Paris Was Our Mistress* (1947), documents the activities of a later generation of Americans abroad than those discussed in Malcolm Cowley's *Exile's Return* (1934, 1951) and provides a valuable record for literary historians.

Born in Rossville, Illinois, a small town near the Indiana border, Samuel Whitehall Putnam first became interested in languages at the age of nine when a neighbor taught him a few words of German. Not long afterward he was delighted to discover a French reader in the home of another neighbor. He began to study Latin in school when he was twelve and did so well that a year later his Latin teacher agreed to tutor him in Greek as well. In 1910 Putnam's excellence in Latin earned him a scholarship to the University of Chicago, but ill health forced him to leave school after two years.

Samuel Putnam

In Chicago Putnam held various jobs as reporter, rewrite man, and feature writer for the *Chicago Tribune*, the *Chicago Herald and Examiner*, the *Chicago American*, and the *Chicago Evening Post* before becoming an art and literary critic for the *Evening Post* in 1920. Among his duties as a critic was interviewing visiting literary celebrities, including G. K. Chesterton, William Butler Yeats, Aldous Huxley, and a writer with whom he would become better acquainted in Paris, Ford Madox Ford.

During the early twenties he also served as an editor for the Chicago little magazine *Youth* (1921-1922), and after *Youth* ceased publication, he worked in a similar capacity for another short-lived Chicago little magazine, *Prairie* (1923). In addition, he contributed poems and essays to such little magazines as *Caprice* (1922-1923), *Modern Review* (1922-1924), and *Parnassus* (1924), as well as to two other Chicago magazines, Ben Hecht's *Chicago Literary Times* (1923-1924) and Jack Jones's *Dill Pickler* (1924-1925). A book of poems by Putnam and Mark Turbyfill, *Evaporations, a Symposium*, was published by the Modern Review Press in 1923. (Turbyfill later went to Paris, too, and studied with the Russo-Greek mystic George Gurdjieff.)

Putnam married Riva Sampson in mid-1925, and their son, Hilary, was born in July 1926. A month later Putnam's article in *American Mercury*, "Chicago: An Obituary," involved him in the kind of literary battle that would later characterize his career in Paris. At H. L. Mencken's instigation Putnam proclaimed that the Chicago Renaissance—originally brought about by such writers as Edgar Lee Masters, Carl Sandburg, and Ben Hecht with the aid of Harriet Monroe's *Poetry: A Magazine of Verse*—was dead. Putnam was especially critical of *Poetry*, which he accused of having become "merely a home talent affair. . . . there is always something of a pink-tea flavor to everything connected to it." The article drew immediate criticism from nearly everyone in the Chicago literary establishment, including Sandburg, and Putnam began to think that he might find more congenial company in Paris.

His translations of selections from Arthur Rimbaud, Charles Pierre Baudelaire, Joris Karl Huysmans, and other French writers for several magazines as well as for the *Evening Post* had already attracted the attention of publisher Pascal Covici, who commissioned Putnam to translate works by Huysmans and Pietro Aretino, which were eventually published in 1927 and 1933. When Putnam told Covici of his hope to complete a modern translation of Rabelais, Covici agreed to finance a research trip to Europe. During his years abroad Putnam not only did translations for Covici but also served as an unofficial literary scout for the publisher.

The Putnams arrived in France in early 1927, and after a brief stay in the city of Paris they lived in a series of Paris suburbs—Suresnes, Seaux, and Fontenay-aux-Roses—while Putnam worked at translating. In addition to translating he wrote biographies of Rabelais (1929) and Marguerite of Navarre (1935) during his years in France. He also wrote a Paris art letter for the *Chicago Daily News*, whose Paris office was run by John Gunther, and he occasionally substituted for Ruth Harris, who was the regular art correspondent for the *New York Times*. His interest in the artist Leopold Survage led to an article about Survage for the September 1927 issue of *transition* and later to a book, published in a limited edition of 175 copies by Covici Friede in 1929. Also in 1929 Putnam began writing a weekly Paris letter for the New York *Sun* and occasional Italian letters for the *Saturday Review of Literature*, using information about current trends in Italian literature that he had gathered on several visits to Italy.

Not long after reaching France, Putnam had renewed his acquaintance with Ford Madox Ford, who remembered meeting him in Chicago. Consequently Putnam was included in the frequent teas given by artist Stella Bowen, then Ford's mistress, and later Putnam was invited to Ford's Thursday afternoon gatherings, where he met Allen Tate and Caroline Gordon. Through Ford and other contacts he had made while still a critic in Chicago, he had quickly become part of literary circles in Paris. But, as he points out in *Paris Was Our Mistress*, the first great wave of expatriation was over by the time he reached France. He regularly attended Natalie Barney's salons, went to Sylvia Beach's Shakespeare and Company bookshop, and occasionally visited Gertrude Stein (although he never knew her well and later admitted having been intimidated by her). Despite his acquaintance with these pillars of American literary life in Paris, most of the Americans he met in Paris were different from those he would have met if he had arrived there in 1921.

In *Paris Was Our Mistress* Putnam credits Ernest Hemingway's *The Sun Also Rises*, published in October 1926, with marking "the point of cleavage between the earlier and the later batch of 'exiles,' by embalming in a work of fiction . . . the spirit that animated those who came in 1921 or shortly after. It was a literary post-mortem," because, Putnam says, "Many of the original *emigres* had been in the war or at least had fought and lost the battle of America that followed; whereas those who arrived in the late 'twenties were, frequently, of a still younger, unscarred generation. . . . These latter had no great disillusionment to drown, they were not rebels, and often they were not genuine writers or artists and scarcely pretended to be."

The expatriates' Paris of this second phase is best described for Putnam in a book by a writer whose career he helped to advance, Henry Miller's *Tropic of Cancer* (1934). For him Miller's novel describes "the Montparnasse we knew: a weird little land crowded with artists, alcoholics, prostitutes, pimps, poseurs, college boys, tourists, society slummers, spendthrifts, beggars, homosexuals, drug addicts, nymphomaniacs, sadists, masochists, thieves, gamblers, confidence men, mystics, fakers, paranoiacs, political refugees, anarchists, 'Dukes' and 'Countesses,' men and women without a country; a land filled with a gaiety sometimes real and often feigned, filled with sorrow, suffering, poverty, frustration, bitterness, tragedy, suicide. . . . Montparnassse itself had never been before and never will be again what it was in the 1920's. . . . from 1929

Title page, inscribed to journalist George Seldes by Kiki

on it began dying." Indeed, Putnam says he saw the death of this American expatriate colony foreshadowed only months after his arrival in Paris when on 23 August 1927 he and his wife were nearly caught in a violent anti-American demonstration protesting the execution of Sacco and Vanzetti.

In late 1929, however, Putnam undertook a translating assignment for Edward Titus's Black Manikin Press that linked him to two veterans of the early wave of expatriation he had missed. He agreed to translate into English the memoir of Alice Prin, better known as Kiki, the artists' model who had posed for such artists as Chaim Soutine, Amedeo Modigliani, Moise Kisling, Maurice Utrillo, Tsuguhara Foujita, Per Krogh, and Man Ray and was a captivating member of Montparnasse cafe society. The preface for the book had already been written by Ernest Hemingway, who had read it in the original French. Recognizing Kiki's unique, colloquial French idiom, Hemingway says: "Maybe it won't translate, but if it does not seem any good to you, learn French and read it. . . . It is a crime to translate it. If it shouldn't be any good in English, and reading it just now again and seeing how it goes, I know it is going to be a bad job for whoever translates it, please read it in the original."

Putnam was faced with the problem of

translating a book that would be prefaced with the pronouncement that it could not be adequately translated, and in his rather tongue-in-cheek translator's note, entitled "A Note on Kiki, St. Theresa and the Vulgate," he admits, "I still do not know whether or not it is possible to translate Kiki." He adds, however, that "All translation is a miracle, but the miracle has been known to flower," and he explains that in translating Kiki he has followed the maxim of St. Jerome, the patron saint of translators: "*Non verbum e verba, sed sensum exprimere de sensu.*" That is, he has not translated every word literally but has attempted to present the meaning behind the words. As he says later, "The problem is not to translate Kiki's text, but to translate Kiki. Kiki's prose is deceptively simple, and one has to be constantly on his guard not to betray her with too broad a stroke."

Titus, amused but undoubtedly dismayed at having to sell a translation containing two introductory notes calling it untranslatable, added his own note: "I have a good mind joining in the fray myself and taking up the cudgels, but only to hit both on the head." He goes on, at greater length than either Hemingway or Putnam, to point out that Hemingway had not seen Putnam's translation and to assert that, despite Putnam's disclaimers, he has done "a capital job." Even St. Jerome, he says, would like "the homespun colloquialism of Putnam's English version of the Memoirs. . . ."

Although American customs officials barred its entry into the United States, the English version of *Kiki's Memoirs* (1930) was a success in Paris. In the 7 July 1930 issue of the Paris *Tribune* (the European edition of the *Chicago Tribune*) Wambly Bald calls the book "a translation that has them sounding gongs in Paris," and adds that "Kiki is so satisfied that she has offered to learn English in order to translate anything Putnam writes."

At about the same time he asked Putnam to translate *Kiki's Memoirs*, Titus invited him to help with the editing of *This Quarter*, the little magazine founded by Ernest Walsh and Ethel Moorhead in 1925 and revived by Titus in 1929. The Putnams moved back to the city of Paris, and Putnam joined the magazine as associate editor for the January-February-March 1930 issue, which was devoted to French writing. For the next number Putnam prepared an issue devoted to contemporary Italian writing, one of his interests. The issue included an editorial and a critical article by Putnam about Italian literature as well as "A Miniature Anthology of Contemporary Italian Literature," compiled and edited by Putnam. He translated more than two-

thirds of the contributions himself.

Putnam's association with Titus was based more on financial necessity than on shared literary interests, however. Putnam says in *Paris Was Our Mistress* that Titus's "tastes ran rather to Ludwig Lewisohn and Michael Arlen, and he was especially fond of 'names,' which were about the only thing that would lead him to violate his personal preferences." In the spring of 1930 Putnam started receiving huge packets of short stories from James T. Farrell in Chicago, submissions for publication in *This Quarter*. Putnam remembers that "by every boat, there arrived a fresh batch of stories; I had never seen such an output and with the quality standing up so well to the quantity." He recognized "my own Chicago . . . coming to life in these tales and sketches of back-o-the-yards 'punks.' . . . this was the genuine article." Titus was unconvinced of Farrell's brilliance: " 'This is rot!' was his first reaction. 'Why! This fellow can't even write.' " Putnam did manage to get Farrell's short story "Studs" into the July-August-September 1930 issue of *This Quarter*, but his argument with Titus over Farrell convinced him that he should break with Titus and start his own magazine, the *New Review*, a move he made in the fall of 1930.

His departure from *This Quarter* was far from amicable; Putnam later wrote to Bob Brown, "Some weeks ago, I gave Mr. Titus a verbal kick in the belly, walked out. . . ." Later, when Titus announced his agreement with Edward J. O'Brien to publish some of the stories from O'Brien's annual selection of the best short stories of the year, Putnam published an ad for the *New Review* that announced, "Special Attention! No O'Brien Short Stories," implying that Titus and O'Brien shared a taste for the conventional that was not reflected in the *New Review*. Putnam also attacked *Kiki's Memoirs* in the introduction to his translation of George Rheims's *An Elegant Peccadillo* (1931), calling *Kiki's Memoirs* an overrated book about "saleable nothings" and adding that Rheims's book was a far better book on a similar subject. Titus retaliated by criticizing the quality of Putnam's translation of *An Elegant Peccadillo*.

Sometime in 1930 Putnam began work on *The European Caravan An Anthology of the New Spirit in European Literature*. The volume, containing three sections of writing from France, Spain, and England and Ireland, was published in late 1931. Additional volumes were planned, and, judging from Putnam's introduction, an Italian section was in preparation or perhaps completed, but no other volumes were published. In addition to writing a foreword and a general introduction, entitled "The After-War Spirit in Literature," Putnam edited the French section and did most of the translating with help from Harold J. Salemson and Richard Thoma. Putnam also did some of the editing and translating for the Spanish section.

As the title of Putnam's introduction suggests, most of the writers represented in his anthology began writing after World War I, but he also includes some important prewar modernists. In his introduction Putnam announces that "Contemporary youth prides itself upon its seriousness and upon its confusions, upon the seriousness of its confusions, with the pain of living balanced by the fear of dying, the need of believing by the habit of doubt . . . , and a taste for not believing by the desire to dare to believe in one's unbelief," and he attributes this situation to the breakdown of accepted values following the war. For the writer, he says, the break with social mores is paralleled by a rejection of literary tradition:

> Where the before-the-War aesthete . . . liked to speak of the new art as being a "prolongation" of tradition, his successor of today would throw all tradition overboard. He rejects all words, formulas and limitations. . . . He is opposed to the transcendental and to all absolutes. . . . For the transcendental he would substitute the immanent, and find a psychological (despite his revolt against Nineteenth century psychology) in place of a metaphysical unity. He is animated by a spirit of quest that leaves him no peace. He loves life, but he loves it in much the same fashion as did Job and Schopenhauer. He will dispense with any sort of unity, if needs be,— he has been, very largely, forced to dispense with it,—and he may be heard declaring, "Only the accidental interests us."

Putnam concludes his forty-one page survey of postwar European literature by saying that he has spent eight years reading "the young, their spokesmen and their critics," and while some may accuse him of taking his task too seriously, "That is a good fault for a reporter to have. After all, there was the War. And youth only becomes 'amusing' with the approach of age."

American reviews were mostly good, if not wildly enthusiastic. Angel Flores called the book "an invaluable achievement" (17 April 1932), while the reviewer for the *Boston Evening Transcript* praised Putnam's sympathetic, nonjudgmental approach to the material (13 February 1932). In *Nation* Matthew Josephson called *The European Caravan* "an affair

of extraordinary interest," but he added that "its successful qualities seem rather the result of intuition and happy accident than of design" (17 February 1932). G. M. Acklom, reviewing the anthology for the *Saturday Review of Literature*, said bluntly that Putnam's introduction was excellent, but the selections were mostly "clamorous nonsense and puerile exhibitionism" (6 February 1932). And W. R. Brooks said in the *Outlook* that the book was largely "the work of the extreme left wing in literature," and, he proclaimed, "the only persons who can read these selections with pleasure are their respective authors" (6 January 1932). This criticism is especially curious considering that by the time *The European Caravan* was published, Putnam had been involved in verbal warfare with the literary "left wing," as it was represented by *transition* magazine, for at least a year.

The opening salvo, which also provided the basis for the editorial policy of Putnam's magazine, the *New Review: An International Notebook for the Arts*, was a manifesto that "began as most things did in Montparnasse, around a cafe table" in 1930. It was written in reaction to *transition* magazine's "Revolution of the Word Proclamation," published in the June 1929 issue of Eugene Jolas's magazine. Putnam, Salemson, and Thoma, the signers of the "Direction: For a contemporary expression, not an out-of-date 'modernity,' " had all contributed to *transition*, and Salemson had even signed the "Revolution of the Word Proclamation."

"Direction" proclaimed that "The past decade has been one of pretenders, corpse-raisers, and cheap miracle-men" and that "a Joycean-Stein stutter is now the Shibboleth of the Gileadites," but, the signers added, their statement was "not of necessity a reflection on either Joyce or Stein." They went on to say that, although the "Revolution of the Word Proclamation" called for a break from the literature of the past, its signers' attitudes were not unlike those of the mid-nineteenth-century romantics, and, furthermore, the idea of a revolution in language was part of an ancient tradition that included Aristotle's *Poetics*, Cicero's *De Oratore*, Horace's *Ars Poetica*, and Castiglione's *Il Cortegiano*.

The "Direction" signers' main complaint about the *transition* group was their stress on form: "We call for a return to content." Although Putnam, Salemson, and Thoma believed that the formal characteristics of Joyce and Stein had been imitated too much by inferior talents, they believed that writers should not ignore Joyce and Stein as models any more than they should overlook any other part of literary tradition: "Whatever has been learned from

Joyce, Stein, or any other that may have been of use to the contemporary artist in his task should be, and will be, utilized." The three were convinced that "Good writing does exist," but they were dismayed by some of their contemporaries' shortcomings, which included "lack of knowledge, of orientation, of critical and aesthetic background; lack of feeling for the standard of writing, style (not to have 'a style' but to have 'style'); fruitless groping for the sake of novelty; failure to achieve a synthesis of the unreal and the real; lack of technical equipment, *metier*, which any effective craftsman must possess." They also called for "an American art, not a badly translated and badly garbled European carry-over," but recognized that "America on the other hand needs to become more cosmopolitan. . . ." As the points of their manifesto suggest, the signers of "Direction" were not attempting to start another movement or to set one already existing movement or style above another; rather, they were calling for standards of excellence to be applied to all writing. Their main quarrel with the "Revolution of the Word Proclamation" was that it seemed to emphasize novelty of style and that it presented a narrow definition of what sort of writing should be considered good or modern.

"Direction" was printed on large yellow placards and posted on the walls of all the Montparnasse cafes. It evoked the desired response from Jolas and his followers, beginning what Putnam calls in his memoir the "Battle of the Left Bank." Unlike Putnam's literary battles with Titus, which seem to have been the result of bad feelings on both sides, this battle was conducted with good humor as well as with fervid expressions of literary ideology, and after a while Putnam and Jolas "had a meeting in the cafe Flore, in that No Man's Land that centered about the place Saint-Germain-des-Pres, at which we talked it over very amicably." Despite his differences with Jolas over literary matters, Putnam had great respect for Jolas, and in *Paris Was Our Mistress* he devotes considerable space to discussing the important place of *transition* magazine in the literary history of the period. As he wrote in his autobiographical note for Peter Neagoe's *Americans Abroad An Anthology* (1932), he admired Jolas and disagreed "with him almost always. . . ."

Putnam repeated his call for more emphasis upon content and craftsmanship in the second issue of the *New Review* (May-June-July 1931), and in 1932 he revised the "Direction" manifesto and published it under the imprint of his New Review Press as *Direction, a Symposium*. In *Paris Was Our Mistress* Putnam expands upon his magazine's editorial policy:

> In orientation the *New Review* followed, more or less, the line laid down in the "Direction" manifesto; but my own chief aim as editor was to give a picture of the scene: in other words, *reportage*. . . . it seemed to me that *reportage*, a survey, as the indispensable preliminary to a conceivable stock-taking, was the all-important thing at the particular hour of the clock.

He adds, however, that he "found few who were able to comprehend this attitude." After the magazine's demise Wambly Bald, who had frequently praised the *New Review* earlier, wrote in the Paris *Tribune* that it had been a magazine "conceived in liberty and dedicated to the proposition that almost anyone is literary" (25 July 1933). At the outset Ezra Pound accepted Putnam's offer to make him associate editor. Among the *New Review*'s contributing editors were writers Maxwell Bodenheim and Richard Thoma, composer George Antheil, and artist Hilaire Hiler, who was later named art editor.

The contributors to the first issue of the *New Review* (January-February 1931) include Jean Cocteau, Massimo Bontempelli of the Italian *Novecentisti* or Twentieth-Century Group, and E. Gimenez Caballero, the editor of the *Gaceta Literia* in Madrid, all of whose aesthetics and politics placed them in opposition to the Surrealists currently favored by *transition* (although Gimenez Caballero had contributed to an early issue of *transition* in 1927). The rest of the contents are notably eclectic, however. Other contributions besides those of editors Putnam, Pound, Bodenheim, Antheil, and Thoma include "Maya and the Hunter" by Richard Eberhart, an article on Russian literature after the Revolution by Irish writer George Reavey, an article on Sinclair Lewis by American critic V. F. Calverton, the editor of *Modern Quarterly*, and "From a Work in Static" by Wambly Bald, who frequently mentioned the *New Review* favorably in his weekly Paris *Tribune* column, "La Vie Boheme."

The second issue of the *New Review* (May-June-July 1931) heralded "The New Objectivism"; the most notable example that appears in the issue is " 'A', Third and Fourth Movements" by American Objectivist poet Louis Zukofsky. Other American contributors included Bob Brown and A. Lincoln Gillespie, both of whose work had appeared in *transition*. The issue also included an article on filmmaker Luis Bunuel by the then unknown Henry Miller, an article on Rainer Maria Rilke by Miller's Austrian friend Alfred Perles, and "Commodus" by French poet Georges Hugnet, as well as contributions by Putnam, Pound, Hiler, Antheil, Thoma, and Bald, including Putnam's reworking of the "Direction" manifesto. The issue inspired Bald to support "The New Objectivism": "The champions in *The New Review* seem to agree on the discipline and clarity in letters. This makes for intelligibility and reconstruction. Emphasis is on the 'object,' on the sacramental significance of reality" (14 April 1931).

The August-September-October 1931 issue is undoubtedly the most famous number of the *New Review*, but not entirely because of its contents, which include "Jewboy" by James T. Farrell, whose work Putnam had continued to support, and Henry Miller's important early short story, "Mademoiselle Claude." Other contributors include Samuel Beckett, Alfred Perles, Peter Neagoe, Sherry Mangan, Stella Bowen, Miguel de Unamuno, and Emanuel Carnevali as well as the *New Review* editors. Putnam had returned briefly to the United States before the issue was sent to the printers, leaving Miller and Perles in charge of the remaining editorial duties. While Putnam was in New York showing Miller's "Mademoiselle Claude" to American publishers, Miller and Perles decided to "steal" his magazine. Apparently in reaction to the literary warfare between *transition*'s revolutionaries and the *New Review*'s "Direction" group, Miller and Perles added their own manifesto, "The New Instinctivism," an obscenity-filled spoof on the literary manifesto genre. According to George Wickes, Miller and Perles made the mistake of including some obscenities in French, and, when the French printer noticed them, he alerted Riva Putnam, who brought out the issue minus the manifesto. Putnam, who had been enjoying the warfare with *transition*, took Miller and Perles's attempted sabotage with good humor. A fictionalized version of the episode, in which Putnam is portrayed as Marlowe, appears in Miller's *Tropic of Cancer*.

The last two issues of the *New Review* were published from Mirmande, an artists' colony in the South of France, where the Putnams had moved along with Romanian-American writer Peter Neagoe and his wife, the artist Anna Neagoe. Neagoe, who had bought half-interest in the *New Review*, became coeditor with the fourth number. This change also brought a minor editorial shift. According to Putnam, his good friend Neagoe "definitely belonged to the Jolas-*transition* group, which had always been hostile to Pound.as it was to his favorite, Cocteau. . . ." Pound became advisory editor instead of associate editor. But, although the war with *transition* seems to have ended in a truce, the fourth issue features the Machine Art of the Italian Futurists, whose artistic theory was opposed to that of the Surrealists. Besides the work of Italians Filippo Tommaso Marinetti, Massimo Bontempelli, and Leo Ferrero, the issue indicates the breadth of the editors' interest by also including contributions from Guillaume Apollinaire, Boris Pasternak, Sherry Mangan, James T. Farrell, and Gorham B. Munson. The work of Robert McAlmon appears in the *New Review* for the first time with his story "The Highly Prized Pajamas."

The fifth, and final, issue (April 1932) is further proof of the magazine's eclectic nature. Along with a short story by Neagoe it includes the work of such *transition* contributors as Charles Henri Ford, Norman Macleod, Emily Holmes Coleman, Laurence Vail, and, most notably, Kay Boyle. The issue also includes work by St. Thomas Aquinas, Samuel Beckett, Ford Madox Ford, Sherry Mangan, Kenneth Rexroth, Selden Rodman, and Nancy Cunard. Cunard's article, "Black Man and White Ladyship," defending her relationship with a black man while attacking her mother Lady Cunard and, more generally, all British upper-class society, was considered sensational at the time, and Putnam was given "more than one hint" that he might be able to save his financially troubled magazine "by 'playing up the freak stuff' from Montparnasse."

A different kind of controversy was caused by Kay Boyle's contribution to the April 1932 issue. Unknown to Putnam, Boyle's poem "In Defense of Homosexuality" revived an old quarrel over Pound's treatment of Ernest Walsh, the editor of *This Quarter* until his death in 1926. The poem prompted Pound to request that his name be removed from the list of editors. Putnam implies in *Paris Was Our Mistress* that if the *New Review* had been financially able to publish another issue, Pound's absence from the editorial board would have had no visible effect on the magazine's contents. He describes Pound's literary tastes as having been limited to "Ezra Pound and a handful of old friends and disciples," and he remembers that earlier, when he had asked Pound for a list of French writers whose work should be included in *The European Caravan*, Pound could think of only one name: Cocteau.

Putnam had been reasonably pleased with Pound's first column for the *New Review* (January-February 1931), although he thought some of Pound's comments a bit muddled. By the third number, however, Pound's pronouncements were beginning to alarm him. In *Paris Was Our Mistress* Putnam says that, although Pound could not yet be considered a fascist in 1931, "it was precisely at this period that his views began to change radically, veering from a certain tolerance of the political Left and its cultural manifestations to a pre-fascist mentality. . . ." Pound's "Fungus, Twilight or Dry Rot" in the third issue (August-September-October 1931) contains such statements as "Plutocracy does not favor the arts. . . . Plutocracy hovering above demos favors the second-rate . . . the whole drift of democratic kultur is toward devitalization of letters and scholarship." The solution, Pound continues, is not a revolution of the masses but a "gentlemen's revolution." As Putnam observes in his memoir, his own politics were somewhat confused in the late twenties and early thirties. But, by the time he left France in 1933, he had joined his old literary enemy Eugene Jolas on the political left. After his return to the United States, Putnam wrote an article criticizing Pound and charging that Pound "dwells in a murky Hinterland of his own into which only now and then a fancied ray of light flickers." Called "Ezra Pound: Cracker-Barrel Revolutionist," the article appeared in *Mosaic* for November-December 1934.

In addition to editing the *New Review* Putnam also published a number of books under the New Review imprint during 1931 and 1932. Published in small editions, these books are now rare. In 1931 the New Review Press published *Green Chaos*, poems by Richard Thoma, who was a disciple of Jean Cocteau, and *Pass to the Stars* by Emlen Pope Etting. In 1932 the "Direction" manifesto appeared as *Direction, a Symposium*, and Putnam became involved in another minor literary controversy with Jolas when Neagoe's short story collection *Storm* (1932) appeared under the New Review imprint with an introduction by Jolas. Jolas found in the stories a "complete balance between a sincere telluric sense and its expression," and he praised Neagoe's "very personal abstractions." Putnam responded to Jolas's emphasis on the stories' style in a long review for the final issue of the *New Review* (April 1932). He was mildly critical of Jolas's "rather big and perilously frightening words" and stressed the stories' contents: their characters are immigrant peasants who provide fresh perspectives on American life, which should prove valuable during "an era of crashing stocks and currencies and a seeming deep-setting world's night." *Storm* was banned as obscene by the U.S. Customs Service in Chicago and New York. Putnam and Neagoe collected protests from well-known writers, and Putnam printed a facsimile of the customs department letter with "Banned in America by the U.S. Customs Officials" printed across the top. *Storm* gained notoriety, which helped the sales of the book's expanded edition when it was published by the Obelisk Press in Paris later that

same year, but the *New Review* profited little from Putnam's efforts.

Putnam linked himself to still another literary battle when he published his own translation of Georges Hugnet's poem *Enfances* in 1932. In early 1931 Gertrude Stein's free-form translation of the poem had been published, and author and translator had argued over whose name should appear first on the title page. The brief life of the New Review Press came to an end with the publication of George Reavey's *Faust's Metamorphoses* (1932), a collection of poems for which Putnam wrote a brief foreword.

Another book that Putnam had a small part in producing was Peter Neagoe's *Americans Abroad An Anthology*, published in December 1932 by Servire Press. Putnam had planned the project, but he had assigned to Neagoe the task of compiling the collection. He was pleased with the resulting volume, which included work by nearly all the major American expatriates as well as a host of minor figures. Putnam's "Journey to Riva (An Epic Love-Poem)" is included in the volume. A free-verse poem, replete with mythological allusions, "Journey to Riva" illustrates Putnam's ability to experiment with language without lapsing into the obscurity that he so disliked in the work of some of his contemporaries.

Putnam had not intended the fifth issue (April 1932) of the *New Review* to be the magazine's last. In an article on Dada and Surrealism for the 25 July 1932 issue of *Contempo*, Putnam announced that the autumn 1932 issue would be devoted to the "New Esotericism . . . based upon a feeling for the essentially magic character of the after-War universe in which we live. . . ." Another plan was to have panels of notable Italian and American writers name the three best books of 1932 published in their respective countries. Given the contacts Putnam had made in Italy while working on his Italian letters for the *Saturday Review*, as well as his many acquaintances with American writers and critics, Putnam had no trouble finding people to serve on his two juries. The Italians were enraged, however, by his choice of Ernest Hemingway to be one of the American judges, along with William Faulkner, H. L. Mencken, J. G. Grey, Harry Hansen, Eugene Jolas, R. Ellsworth Larson, and Gorham B. Munson. Mussolini's regime had considered *A Farewell to Arms* (1929) insulting to the Italian people and had suppressed both the book and the recently produced movie.

There was a great uproar in the Italian papers, and at least one newspaper mistakenly stated that Hemingway had been asked to judge Italian books.

Putnam was flooded with letters from Italy, especially from the Italian correspondents for the *New Review*, who asked him to do something to correct the impression that they were consorting with an enemy to the Mussolini government. Putnam decided to call off the whole contest, and he wrote a letter to his Italian contacts pointing out that Hemingway "was a representative, highly popular, and important young American novelist and that he had been asked to pass not upon Italian but upon American works." As far as Putnam was concerned, the entire episode was over, but his "Italian friends, as I called them then" were not willing to drop the matter without first trying to clear themselves of the charges of their political enemies: "They did so by publishing my letter, which would have been all right if they had published it as it stood; but they saw fit to 'edit' it by writing in an abject apology which made me out to be an errant but repentant fascist sympathizer. This letter appeared in the newspapers of Genoa, Rome, and other cities, and nothing that I could do would procure a retraction or correction." Putnam then took his side of the story to Waverley Root of the Paris *Tribune*. The 21 November 1932 issue contains a sympathetic version of the plight of Putnam's contest and includes a list of Hemingway's choices: *1919* by John Dos Passos, *Conquistador* by Archibald MacLeish, and *The American Jitters* by Edmund Wilson.

Putnam had come to Europe "consciously asocial in my attitude toward art and society. . . ." Even though he had been interested in the writings of Karl Marx while a student at the University of Chicago, during his years as a reporter in Chicago he had been more concerned with aesthetics than with politics. Although it was still possible for American writers in France to be basically apolitical when Putnam first arrived there in early 1927, events from 1929 onward tended to make everyone more conscious of politics. In *Paris Was Our Mistress* Putnam describes his growing political consciousness as "just about that of the majority of exiles in those years. We were all of us—or practically all—very, very muddled." His love of the Italian literature of the past had led him to look favorably upon contemporary Italian culture: "I was stubbornly bent upon finding in Mussolini's Italy a literature and a culture that was not there. What I found, in reality, was a desert, a cultural waste land . . . but it took me some little while to realize this." In his editorial comments for the special Italian issue of *This Quarter* (April-May-June 1930) Putnam had wondered "just how far apart . . . the two collectivisms," fascism and communism, were—a not uncommon observation in the early thirties. And in his autobiographical note for *Americans Abroad*, undoubtedly written before the Hemingway episode, he expresses his admiration for both the Italian fascists and the communists. Like many of his contemporaries, Putnam saw the American economic system in ruins and perceived some sort of collectivism to be the answer. The Italians' reaction to his well-intentioned attempt to publicize the best Italian and American books of 1932 cured Putnam of his admiration for fascism. By the time he returned to the United States in 1933, he had moved to the political left. Two days after landing in New York he chaired a meeting of unemployed writers, and the next day he was "one of a committee of three that went down to the Port Authority Building in New York City to demand a writers' project. We were accompanied on our mission by several hundred of our colleagues, and in the crowd I spotted Malcolm Cowley and a number of others of the original band of exiles."

The Putnams loved living in Mirmande, where they had bought a house, but they were becoming increasingly alarmed by the events in Europe, and they were also concerned that their son was growing up speaking a French patois "which the village four miles away, with a patois of its own, did not understand." Another consideration was economic; with funding for the *New Review* no longer available, Putnam took a rush translating job, realizing that, because of worsening economic conditions, it might be "the last job I would be having." With his earnings he went to New York, where he worked at several temporary newspaper jobs until a friend advanced him the passage money for his wife and child.

In 1933-1934 Putnam was involved in editing the short-lived little magazine *New Hope*, which was published in New Hope, Pennsylvania. During the thirties and early forties Putnam was associated with the literary left, writing for such magazines as *Partisan Review* and *New Masses*, which listed him as a contributing editor from 1942 to 1946. From late 1936 to early 1938 he taught at the Philadelphia Workers' School, but tuberculosis, complicated by his always frail health, forced upon him first a stay in a sanatarium and then a two-year convalescence. He continued to write, however, and in 1941, his health somewhat improved, he began contributing frequently to the *Daily Worker*, becoming a regular columnist in August 1942. Also in 1942 he became director of the Tom Paine School of Social Science in Philadelphia.

Putnam had expressed his interest in Latin

America as early as 1935 when he wrote an article for the *Saturday Review* about Brazilian literature, and in 1941 he was approached by the University of Chicago Press to translate Euclydes da Cunha's masterwork, *Os Sertoes*, a project he completed in mid-1943. It was published as *Rebellion in the Backlands* in 1944. Putnam's translation was praised by reviewers, and he became increasingly involved in translating Brazilian literature.

At the same time he became more interested in Latin America, he became decreasingly sympathetic to communism, and he resigned as a regular contributor to the *Daily Worker* on 23 May 1945. Also in 1945 Putnam signed a contract with Knopf to write a history of Brazilian literature, published in 1948 as *Marvelous Journey A Survey of Four Centuries of Brazilian Writing*. In that same year the State Department sent him on a lecture tour to Brazil, and in 1947 he received the Brazilian Government's Pandia Calogeras Prize and was made a member of Brazil's Academy of Letters.

Meanwhile, Putnam's old friend Pascal Covici, now with Viking Press, involved him with new projects, including a translation of *Don Quixote* and the writing of his memoir of his Paris years. His translation of Cervantes's novel appeared in 1949; it was the first modern translation since Robinson Smith's in 1903 and received high praise from the critics. *Paris Was Our Mistress*, published in 1947, was also well-received. Reviewers admired its lack of sentimentality and its attempt to explain the expatriates' leaving and returning to America. They especially liked the sections devoted to Pound, Hemingway, Stein, Cocteau, Aragon, and Pirandello.

Although he continued writing and translating, Putnam's health declined from late 1947 onward. He died in January 1950 at the age of fifty-seven.

—*Karen L. Rood*

Other:

Joris Karl Huysmans, *Down Stream (A vau-l'eau) and Other Works*, translated by Putnam (Chicago: Covici, 1927);

Donatien Alphonse Francois Sade, *Dialogue Between a Priest and a Dying Man*, translated by Putnam (New York: Covici, 1927);

Joseph Delteil, *On the River Amour*, translated by Putnam (New York: Covici Friede, 1929);

Claude Farrere, *Black Opium (Fumee d'opium)*, translated by Putnam (New York: N. L. Brown, 1929);

Francois Mauriac, *The Desert of Love*, translated by Putnam (New York: Covici Friede, 1929);

Francois Rabelais, *All the Extant Works*, translated by Putnam (New York: Covici Friede, 1929);

Jean Cocteau, *Enfants terribles*, translated by Putnam (New York: Brewer & Warren, 1930);

Alice Prin, *Kiki's Memoirs*, translated by Putnam (Paris: Black Manikin Press, 1930); republished as *The Education of a French Model* (New York: Boar's Head Books, 1950);

The European Caravan An Anthology of the New Spirit in European Literature, edited by Putnam and others (New York: Brewer, Warren & Putnam, 1931);

Paul Lacroix, *History of Prostitution Among All the Peoples of the World*, translated by Putnam (New York: Covici Friede, 1931);

Luigi Pirandello, *As You Desire Me (Come tu me vuoi)*, translated by Putnam (New York: Dutton, 1931);

George Rheims, *An Elegant Peccadillo*, translated by Putnam (New York: Holt, 1931);

Georges Hugnet, *Enfances*, translated by Putnam (Paris: New Review Press, 1932);

"Journey to Riva (An Epic Love-Poem)," in *Americans Abroad An Anthology*, ed. Peter Neagoe (The Hague: Servire, 1932);

Pirandello, *Horse in the Moon*, translated by Putnam (New York: Dutton, 1932);

Pirandello, *Tonight We Improvise*, translated by Putnam (New York: Dutton, 1932);

George Reavey, *Faust's Metamorphoses*, foreword by Putnam (Fontenay-aux-Roses, Seine, France: New Review Press, 1932);

Jacques Roberti, *Without Sin*, translated by Putnam (New York: Covici Friede, 1932);

Pietro Aretino, *The Works of Aretino*, translated by Putnam (New York: Covici Friede, 1933);

Pirandello, *One, None and a Hundred-Thousand*, translated by Putnam (New York: Dutton, 1933);

Georges Duhamel, *Papa Pasquier*, translated by Putnam (New York & London: Harper, 1934);

Pierre Nezelof, *The Merry Queen An Historical Story of the Happy and Tragic Life of Marie Antoinette*, translated by Putnam (New York: Liveright, 1934);

Duhamel, *The Fortunes of the Pasquiers*, translated by Putnam (New York & London: Harper, 1935);

Paolo Mantegazza, *The Sexual Relations of Mankind*, translated by Putnam (New York: Eugenics Publishing Company, 1935);

Ignazio Silone, *Mr. Aristotle*, translated by Putnam (New York: McBride, 1935);

Louis Guilloux, *Bitter Victory*, translated by Putnam (New York: McBride, 1936);

Euclydes da Cunha, *Rebellion in the Backlands*, translated by Putnam (Chicago: University of Chicago Press, 1944);

Jorge Amado, *The Violent Land*, translated by Putnam (New York: Knopf, 1945);

Ezio Taddei, *The Pine Tree and The Mole*, translated by Putnam (New York: Dial, 1945);

Gilberto Freyre, *The Masters and the Slaves, (Casagrande & senzala)*, translated by Putnam (New York: Knopf, 1946);

Rabelais, *The Portable Rabelais*, edited and translated by Putnam (New York: Dial, 1946);

Taddei, *The Sowing of the Seed*, translated by Putnam (New York: Dial, 1946);

Magdalena Mondragon, *Someday the Dream*, translated by Putnam (New York: Dial, 1947);

Roger Lemelin, *The Town Below*, translated by Putnam (New York: Reynal & Hitchcock, 1948);

Miguel de Cervantes, *The Ingenious Gentleman Don Quixote de la Mancha*, translated by Putnam (New York: Viking, 1949);

Andre Gide, *Persephone*, translated by Putnam (New York: Gotham Book Mart, 1949);

Cervantes, *Three Exemplary Novels*, translated by Putnam (New York: Viking, 1950).

References:

Hugh Ford, *Published in Paris American and British Writers, Printers, and Publishers in Paris, 1920-1939* (New York: Macmillan, 1975), pp. 162-163, 318-322, 355-356;

C. Harvey Gardiner, *Samuel Putnam, Latin Americanist A Bibliography* (Carbondale & Edwardsville: Southern Illinois University Library, 1970);

George Wickes, *Americans in Paris* (Garden City: Doubleday, 1969), pp. 252-253;

Bertram D. Wolfe, *Strange Communists I Have Known* (New York: Stein & Day, 1965), pp. 72-80.

Papers:

There are collections of Putnam's papers at Princeton University and Southern Illinois University at Carbondale.

ELMER RICE
(28 September 1892-8 May 1967)

SELECTED PLAYS: *On Trial*, New York, Candler Theatre, 19 August 1914 (New York: French, 1919);

The Adding Machine, New York, Garrick Theatre, 19 March 1923 (Garden City: Doubleday Page, 1923; London: French, 1929);

Close Harmony or, The Lady Next Door, by Rice and Dorothy Parker, New York, Gaiety Theatre, 1 December 1924 (New York: French, 1929);

Is He Guilty, 1924;

Life Is Real, 1925, produced in Germany as *Wir im Amerika*;

Cock Robin, by Rice and Philip Barry, New York, 48th Street Theatre, 12 January 1928 (New York & Los Angeles: French, 1929);

Street Scene, New York, The Playhouse, 10 January 1929 (New York & Los Angeles: French, 1929; London: French, 1929);

The Subway, New York, Cherry Lane Theatre, 25 January 1929 (New York & Los Angeles: French, 1929; London: French, 1929);

The Left Bank, New York, Little Theatre, 5 October 1931 (New York & Los Angeles: French, 1931; London: French, 1931);

Dream Girl, New York, Coronet Theatre, 14 December 1945 (New York: Coward-McCann, 1946).

Elmer Rice made his first trip to Paris in 1925, seeking a change of scene in order to revitalize his career after a series of failures in New York. In 1930 he returned to soak up atmosphere for a play about American expatriates living in the Latin Quarter of Paris—an idea which had come to him as a result of his earlier experiences in that city.

A native of New York City, Rice, after receiving his law degree from New York Law School in 1912 and being admitted to the bar, ironically found himself appalled by legal ethics and having serious misgivings about law as a profession. He had already developed an interest in drama and soon resigned his position with a New York law firm to pursue a career as a playwright. In this pursuit he was almost immediately successful. His first Broadway play, *On Trial* (1914), was a smash box-office hit, running for 365 performances and making its twenty-one-year-old author financially secure. His last production came in 1963. During this span of forty-nine years he wrote over fifty plays, more than thirty of which have been published. When one adds to this list four novels, an autobiography, a book on the theatre, a multitude of short stories, book reviews, and articles, plus movie, radio, and television scripts, his literary output and versatility are indeed impressive. As a playwright Rice's dominant concern is with the attainment of "freedom of the body and of the mind through liberation from political autocracy, economic slavery, religious superstition, hereditary prejudice and herd psychology and the attainment of freedom of the soul through liberation from fear, jealousy, hatred, possessiveness and self-delusion."

Rice left for Paris in 1925, taking his wife and children with him. He was not, however, the typical American expatriate. Already financially secure, he did not go to Paris, as did many other expatriates, because he could live cheaply while he wrote. And although he was dissatisfied with the American social and political systems and Americans' treatment of artists, he was critical of those who exiled themselves from their homeland for these reasons. He went there chiefly in the hope that the change would restimulate his creativity after a series of failures in New York. His play *Close Harmony* (1924) had closed after only twenty-four performances. Subsequently, Broadway producer Sam Harris reneged on a promise to produce *Is He Guilty* (1924), Rice's adaptation of Rudolph Lothar's *The Blue Hawaii*, and finally, the coup de grace came with the Actors' Theatre's abandonment of *The Subway* (1929) because of problems with casting and setting.

In Paris Rice lived briefly at a small hotel-pension on the rue de Fleurus and later moved to more permanent quarters in the rue Bonaparte. After a "systematic exploration of the city's museums, churches, monuments," Rice used Paris as a base of operations while he ranged far and wide, first investigating its environs, then moving on to such French cities as Chartres, Rouen, and Reims. Later he visited other areas of France and also traveled to England, Switzerland, Italy, Germany, and Austria. Twice he returned to New York on business.

During his time in Paris Rice was not an habitue of the usual American expatriate gathering places although he did, of course, visit them. Neither did he seek out friendships with the many aspiring young American writers, but he did become acquainted with Elliot Paul, John Dos Passos, E. E. Cummings, Donald Ogden Stewart, and Ernest Hemingway. Sherwood Anderson, however, was the writer with whom Rice formed the closest friendship. Anderson, by then a well-known writer of some critical acclaim, was a frequent visitor at the Rice apartment during his December 1926 to March

Elmer Rice

1927 stay in Paris. Rice also met many non-American writers, among them James Joyce, for whom he signed a strongly worded protest concerning the pirating of *Ulysses* (1922) by New York editor Samuel Roth.

Although Rice had not gone abroad to write, some writing was accomplished. In his Paris apartment he completed a novel, "Papa Looks for Something," that was never published. In Paris, also, Rice worked on a play, *Life Is Real* (1925), which has been produced in Germany but has never been produced in America or published in English. This work led, however, to a chance meeting with Philip Barry and collaboration with him on a play entitled *Cock Robin* (1928) that did reach Broadway. After returning to Paris from an unsuccessful effort to sell his work in New York, Rice met Barry, who was on his way to the Riviera. To pass the time the two decided to write a play, which, as Rice explained it, "was to be a mystery melodrama with comic overtones. The murder was to be cleverly committed in full view of the audience, without their being aware of it." And there would be "such surefire ingredients as a spinsterish detective, a subtle villain and a Helen Hokinson clubwoman." The play progressed much as Rice envisioned it, but little, if any, of the writing was done in Paris. The two playwrights, traveling extensively and to different places, nevertheless managed an active exchange of manuscripts, and in due course the play was completed. At this point Rice's sojourn in Europe had stretched out to two-and-a-half years, and he decided to return home.

The most significant result of Rice's Paris years, however, was still to come. The genesis of a play, *The Left Bank* (1931), had come about while the playwright was living in Paris. Since the setting of the play was to be the Latin Quarter of that city, Rice decided to return there to reacquaint himself with the locale and its expatriate ambience. Thus, in 1930 Rice returned to Paris. *The Left Bank* examines the psychology and behavior of a small group of the American expatriates Rice had come to know during his stay in Paris. Basically he focuses his attention on two married couples, writer John Shelby and his wife Claire and Waldo and Susie Lynde. John and Susie arrange to have an affair and are found out; this discovery, plus various other differences of opinion, leads both couples to divorce. Rice attacks the fragility of American marriages, the double standard of sexual morality, the barrenness of American society, and the puritanism which has blighted it since colonial times. On the latter point John Shelby says that he has left America because he cannot "create in a spiritual vacuum, in an atmosphere that is esthetically sterile." He describes America as a "cultural desert . . . a country that has no traditions and no standards of taste . . . that is wholly absorbed in the problem of material organization . . . where leisure is unknown." Later, in response to Waldo's "Why don't we know how to enjoy ourselves?" Claire Shelby expresses Rice's point of view when she says, "it's because we're essentially a Christian people. We've been taught for centuries to believe in the mortification of the flesh and to look for heaven everywhere except on earth. You can't enjoy the good things in life if you're ashamed of your appetites and have to be a little furtive about satisfying them." The play opened to mixed reviews but was moderately successful, running for 242 performances.

As a playwright Elmer Rice had a remarkably long and productive career. He was both versatile and prolific. His more than fifty plays range in genre through farce, comedy, melodrama, the problem play, fantasy, naturalism, and expressionism. Despite his frequent failures with the critics, he was a serious dramatist, an artist of integrity. In the twenties he contributed two plays to the American theatre which are now secure as classics: *The Adding Machine* (1923), perhaps the best full-length

American expressionistic play, and *Street Scene* (1929), which won a 1929 Pulitzer Prize. A possible revival of interest in Rice may be indicated by the recent republication of *The Adding Machine, Street Scene*, and a later play, *Dream Girl* (1945).

—*Anthony F. Palmieri*

References:

Ralph L. Collins, "The Playwright and the Press: Elmer Rice and His Critics," *Theatre Annual: 1948-1949*, pp. 35-58;

Frank Durham, *Elmer Rice* (New York: Twayne, 1970);

Robert Hogan, *The Independence of Elmer Rice* (Carbondale: Southern Illinois University Press, 1965);

Hogan, "Rice: The Public Life of a Playwright," *Modern Drama*, 8 (February 1966): 426-439;

Meyer Levin, "Elmer Rice," *Theatre Arts*, 16 (January 1932): 54-62;

Anthony F. Palmieri, *Elmer Rice: A Playwright's Vision of America* (Cranbury, N.J.: Fairleigh Dickinson University Press, forthcoming).

WAVERLEY ROOT
(15 April 1903-   )

SELECTED BOOKS: *The Truth About Wagner*, by Root and Philip Dutton Hurn (New York: Stokes, 1930; London: Cassell, 1930);

The Secret History of the War, 2 volumes (New York: Scribners, 1945);

Casablanca to Katyn, volume 3 of *The Secret History of the War* (New York: Scribners, 1946);

The Food of France (New York: Knopf, 1958; London: Cassell, 1958);

The Food of Italy (New York: Atheneum, 1971);

Eating in America, by Root and Richard de Rochemont (New York: Morrow, 1976).

Waverley Root, writer and journalist, began his career in Paris working for the European edition of the *Chicago Tribune*, often called the Paris *Tribune*. As a literary critic for that newspaper he spoke in favor of literary standards and opposed the avant-garde extremism of writers whose experiments led to unintelligibility.

Waverley Lewis Root was born in Providence, Rhode Island, but when he was seven his family moved to Fall River, Massachusetts, where he was educated in the public schools. He attended Tufts College, now Tufts University, for three years, and although he did not complete the requirements for graduation, in 1940 Tufts gave Root his B.A. *ex ordinem*, as an earned degree. While at Tufts he was campus correspondent for a Boston newspaper during his first year and for the Associated Press during his second and third years. He also worked on the Tufts student newspaper and was its editor during his final year at school.

After leaving Tufts Root moved to New York, where he worked for a variety of trade publications; he wrote music and theatre criticism for one magazine and short, short book reviews for the New York *World*. He also worked for Samuel Roth's *Two Worlds Quarterly* while Roth was publishing a serialized version of *Ulysses* (1922). Roth told Root he was paying Joyce for the publishing rights, but when Root arrived in Paris in May 1927, he discovered that Roth had made no agreement with either Joyce or the publisher of *Ulysses*, Sylvia Beach. Root's only full article in *transition* magazine was an extremely unflattering description of Roth, which appeared in the December 1927 issue. In his article Root warns Joyce of Roth's "long and honorable record of promise breaking."

When Root arrived in Paris in 1927, he applied to Bernhard Ragner, then managing editor of the Paris *Tribune*, for a job. Ragner was impressed by the fact that Root had worked for the New York *World* and hired him immediately. Root did not tell Ragner that his only work for the *World* had been the brief book reviews. Among those on the staff of the Paris *Tribune* when Root arrived were Elliot Paul, coeditor of *transition*, Robert Sage, who would soon become *transition*'s associate editor, William L. Shirer, Edgar Calmer, and music critic Irving Schwerke. The founder and coeditor of *transition*, Eugene Jolas, had also been on the *Tribune*'s staff but had left the paper to devote his full time to the magazine.

From the start Root distinguished himself by his energy and speed. Of all the paper's rewrite men he was the most adept at taking a mass of clippings from various French newspapers and weaving them into a comprehensive, readable story for Americans. In addition he wrote literary and art criticism and did profiles for a feature column called "Who's Who in Paris" about notable visitors to Paris. In May 1928 Root and his French wife went to London, where Root worked for the Chicago *Tribune*'s London bureau.

From London he wrote to Jolas in reaction to a questionnaire that had appeared in the Fall 1928 issue of *transition*. "Why Do Americans Live In Europe?" reports the answers of a number of expatriate Americans, many of whom were regular contributors to *transition*, to four questions about their visions of reality and their perceptions of the relationship of art to the spirit of their age. In "An Open Letter to the Editor," published in the February 1929 issue of *transition*, Root criticizes the questionnaire, which, he says, asked silly, unanswerable questions. In his opinion pompous questions such as "What particular vision do you have of yourself in relation to twentieth century reality?" are bound to provoke self-conscious exhibitionism:

> The selfconscious artist makes me sick. . . . God knows that an artist, even properly discouraged, is selfconscious enough without assistance. This business of asking him to to [*sic*] indulge in soulsearching in answer to questionnaires only aggravates a vicious habit peculiar to the breed. The artist is generally a pretty distasteful sort anyway: I don't suppose his average is any worse than the average among non-artists, except that his defects are handed out for inspection of his fellows with much greater freedom. I am against encouraging him to make any more exposition of himself than is necessary.

Root finds *transition* "the most interesting magazine published in the English language," but, he says, "its interest is often that of an irritant."

In December 1929 Ralph Jules Frantz became managing editor of the Paris *Tribune* and hired Root as night editor, making him second in command in the editorial department. Root was also chief book reviewer and editor of the literary pages. Returning to Paris in May 1930, Root remained with the *Tribune* until it merged with the European edition of the *New York Herald Tribune* (the Paris *Herald*) on 1 December 1934.

In his 1929 letter to *transition* Root was critical of those writers who were overly concerned with literary style at the expense of content. He expresses a similar point of view in a 17 November 1930 *Tribune* article in which he argues that the recently awarded Nobel Prize should have gone to Theodore Dreiser rather than to Sinclair Lewis: "Those who put Dreiser below Lewis are evidently confusing craftsmanship with art. Lewis reads more smoothly than Dreiser, but . . . the test of great writing is not the ease with which it glides into the mind—and out again. It would be more accurate to gauge its greatness by the turmoil which it causes in forcing its way into the mind; and for that purpose rough edges are no handicap."

A few months later he found *Lucy Church*

Amiably (1930), written and published by Gertrude Stein, to be a prime offender of his injunction against self-conscious literary experimentation. In a 9 February 1931 review, which parodies Stein's style, he comes to the conclusion that the only comprehensible part of the novel is Stein's "Advertisement" printed in the front of the book:

> This is less difficult than other parts. This is more simple. But it is all simple. She said by repeating you can change the meaning you can actually change the meaning.
> Repeat.
> But then it it it is all simple. It is all simple. It is all simple. It is all.
> Simple.

In his reviews for the *Tribune* Root was not critical of all expatriate writing and publishing, however. For example, he admired the attractive appearance of the books published by Harrison of Paris (16 February 1931) and found *Year Before Last* (1932) by Kay Boyle to be "as near perfect as any novel which has been discussed on this page since William Faulkner's *Sanctuary*. . . ." He admired her writing because, "despite her technical skill, her language remains always a tool, a means of expression, and not the end in itself" (21 November 1932). He also expressed admiration for Peter Neagoe's *Americans Abroad An Anthology* (1932) because the "merely freakish and the out-and-out idiotic . . . are kept to a minimum in this volume . . ." (10 December 1932). Root even praised Stein's far more accessible book, *The Autobiography of Alice B. Toklas* (1933). In a long review he commented that "There is no ambiguity about her words. . . . Her vocabulary is simple and precise. It is directed to the intellect, not to the emotions" (9 October 1933).

During these years in France Root and Philip Dutton Hurn wrote *The Truth About. Wagner* (1930), based on documents preserved by the illegitimate daughter of Richard Wagner's first wife. The book was highly controversial and was criticized by many of Wagner's admirers. From 1932 to 1940 Root was also Paris correspondent for the Danish newspaper *Politiken*, published in Copenhagen,

and before the last issue of the Paris *Tribune* appeared on 30 November 1934, he had already begun working for the Paris bureau of the United Press.

After the demise of the European edition of the *Chicago Tribune*, Root began editing a weekly newspaper, called the *Paris Tribune*, that was in no way connected to the *Chicago Tribune*, although a number of the old Paris *Tribune*'s staff members wrote for the new weekly. Because of pressure from the Paris *Herald*, which sought a monopoly on American readership in Paris, and because many of the contributors either found other jobs in Paris or returned to the United States, the weekly *Paris Tribune* ceased publication after two months.

In 1938 Root was fired by the United Press for a story he filed on 20 January 1938 predicting that the Nazis would invade Austria around 15 May. Under pressure from the Nazi Propaganda Ministry all German newspapers canceled their United Press contracts, which were renewed after Root was fired. (Root missed the date of the German takeover of Austria, 13 May 1938, by only two days.) Root joined the Paris bureau of *Time* for the rest of 1938, and the next year he became a broadcaster for the Mutual Broadcasting System. He made his last radio broadcast from Bordeaux on 22 June 1940, the day that Petain announced the armistice with Germany.

Returning to the United States, Root worked at a number of newspaper and broadcasting jobs. He also wrote *The Secret History of the War*, three volumes published in 1945 and 1946. He went back to France in 1950 and lived at Villefranche-sur-Mer, where he worked at ghostwriting a number of books. From 1952 to 1955 he lived in The Hague, editing Fodor's travel guides. He returned to Paris in 1955 and worked for a small news syndicate before becoming the Paris correspondent for the *Washington Post* in 1958. After retiring from the *Post* in 1967, he served as Paris editor for *Holiday* magazine from 1968 to 1971. Between 1956 and 1971 Root wrote a number of books, one on European winter sports and several volumes on French, Italian, and American cooking. He continues to live and write in Paris. —*Ralph Jules Frantz*

ROBERT SAGE
(1899-27 October 1962)

Robert Sage, journalist, editor, and translator, worked in the Paris, Vienna, Rome, and London offices of the *Chicago Tribune* and the *New York Herald* for most of his life; from September 1927 to June 1929 he was also an editor for *transition*, the important little magazine founded by Eugene Jolas and Elliot Paul in 1927. A fine literary critic, Sage contributed to the success of *transition* and its mission to disseminate some of the best experimental prose and verse being written during the late twenties and early thirties.

Sage was born in Detroit, Michigan, and graduated from the University of Michigan in 1922. After working for the *Detroit Times* for a year, he left for Paris where he began his association with the European edition of the *Chicago Tribune*, often called the Paris *Tribune*. Here he met Eugene Jolas and Elliot Paul, fellow Americans also working for the *Tribune*. When Jolas and Paul, with the assistance of Jolas's wife Maria, brought out the first

issue of their new literary magazine, *transition*, in April 1927, Sage wrote a glowing review for the *Tribune*'s 20 March 1927 issue in which he praised the editors' "tolerance and good judgment" and "creative editorship" and summarized the editorial principles they had stated in the first number. He concluded: "The April number of *transition* has about it nothing of the belligerent radicalism of *Secession* nor the passive correctness of T. S. Eliot's *Criterion Quarterly*. In range it extends from the advanced writing which represents the latest stage of James Joyce's evolution to the conservative but richly woven prose of Ludwig Lewisohn. Each narrative and poetic contribution represents a personal tendency caught at a high degree of perfection. This insistence on uniform quality rather than uniform style is the most reassuring sign that *transition* is well immunized from arteriosclerosis."

Sage did indeed have much to praise in the new journal, and during its ten-year, erratic life *transition* became a leading literary magazine, publishing an international group of authors who were for the most part intent upon experimentation in prose and verse. Controversial because of its often bizarre contents and radical views, the journal was soon an outlet for almost every literary movement in Paris, other European capitals, and America. Sage recognized the importance of *transition* before its reputation was secure, and even though he kept his job with the *Tribune*, he contributed reviews, short stories, and essays to most of the first twenty issues. His book reviews of such works as H. D.'s *Palimpsest* (1926), Robert Coates's *The Eater of Darkness* (1926), E. E. Cummings's *is 5* (1926), and Pierre Drieu La Rochelle's *Le Jeune Européen* (1927) began to appear in the first number. With *transition* 6 Sage became associate editor, and the editors announced that he would "assume direction of the critical section." He also clearly recognized the tensions between the Jolases and Paul which led to Paul's leaving *transition* amicably after the twelfth number (March 1928) and thus to Sage's increased editorial responsibilities, beginning with the Summer 1928 issue. As Sage later told Eric Hawkins, Paul, who had always worked quickly, seldom stayed long at the Jolases' house in Colombey-Les-Deux-Eglises, where most of the editorial work was done, and he was often unavailable when Jolas, who worked more slowly, wanted to consult him. The two coeditors also differed temperamentally and philosophically, and Sage evidently worked far more successfully with the Jolases than Paul had. (Sage's French wife Maeve had also been hired as secretary and receptionist at *transition*'s hotel-room business office in the rue Fabert in Paris.)

The philosophical compatibility between Sage and Jolas is especially evident in *transition* 8 (November 1927). In Sage's critical article, "Lilies for Realism," he decries the American refusal to accept experimental novels, such as Conrad Aiken's *Blue Voyage* (1927), and concludes: "Believing in the elastic and thorough-expressive capacities of the novel, one might only hope for a few more brave Andersons, Franks and Hechts and Aikens to recognize the defunctness of realism. A mob of unjailed imaginations would be as intolerable as the present situation, but there is no hazard of this phenomenon chasing advanced writers into new roads of escape. It will, happily, never be generally recognized that art cannot linger and that revolt, far from requiring justification, is the sole duty an artist can admit." For Sage, James Joyce's work epitomized that revolt as it did for most of *transition*'s regular contributors. In *transition* 14 Sage added to the critical praise found largely in *transition* of the fragments of Joyce's *Work in Progress* (published as *Finnegans Wake* in 1939). Reviewing "Anna Livia Plurabelle," reprinted in *transition* 8, he considers whether this fragment is the most beautiful yet to appear and decides that at least "it illustrates as perfectly as a fragment may the difficulties and miracles of the Joycian writing." Finally in *transition* 18, Sage added his argument in "Word Lore" to the "Revolution of the Word" debate which Jolas had initiated in transition 16/17 with a proclamation signed by Sage, among others. "And I, for one, hope within the next few years to see the english language—and, above all, the american language—begin, thanks to the efforts of the new writers of today, to shed some of its many obstinate tags and reassemble itself into a new form more nearly in tune with the rhythm of the century."

Sage's position with *transition*, however, had to change because his job with the *Tribune* took him away from Paris. After he and Jolas edited *Transition Stories* (1929), a collection of twenty-four prose selections which had appeared in *transition*, he was called contributing editor in *transition* 15 (February 1929) and advisory editor in 16/17 (June 1929). Then in 19/20 (June 1930), when *transition* was temporarily ended, Jolas announced that Sage was now stationed in London as a correspondent for the *Tribune*. In 19/20, which was intended to be *transition*'s final issue, Jolas also published Sage's "Farewell to Transition," a letter dated 20 March 1930. "In any case it is useless to regret: better to be thankful that *transition* has existed, with its discoveries, its battles, its controversies, its ideas and its superb work in revivifying literature. . . . Life for me has been pleasanter since 1927 because of *transition*'s existence, and I feel certain that many others can honestly say the same thing. Possibly I am unjustifiably prejudiced, but I suspect that after the twenty numbers of *transition* american literature will be a little different just as all literature has been a little different since the publication of *Ulysses*."

Jolas revived *transition* in early 1932, but Sage did not contribute. He continued to work as a rewrite man for the *Tribune* until 1934 when he joined the *Herald*'s editorial staff. During World War II he and his wife stayed in Brittany, and he rejoined the *Herald* in the mid-forties as travel editor. In 1954 he published an English translation of Stendhal's private diaries. He died of a heart attack in Paris on 27 October 1962. —*Thomas E. Dasher*

Publications:

Transition Stories, edited by Sage and Eugene Jolas (New York: W. V. McKee, 1929);
"Salvage from Limbo," in *Americans Abroad An Anthology*, ed. Peter Neagoe (The Hague: Servire, 1932), pp. 359-374;
Eugene Jolas, ed., *Transition Workshop*, includes contributions by Sage (New York: Vanguard, 1949);
The Private Diaries of Stendhal, edited and translated by Sage (Garden City: Doubleday, 1954).

References:

Eric Hawkins, with Robert N. Sturdevant, *Hawkins of the Paris Herald* (New York: Simon & Schuster, 1963), pp. 149-150;
Dougald McMillan, transition *The History of a Literary Era 1927-1938* (New York: Braziller, 1976), pp. 19-182.

HAROLD J. SALEMSON
(30 September 1910-   )

BOOKS: *Ou est mon pere* (Liege, Belgium: Anthologie, 1929);
Communisme de l'Oeil (Paris: Tambour, 1930).

Harold J. Salemson was a very young American writer in Paris at the close of the twenties and one of the few whose work grew largely out of a French education. Unlike the expatriates who went to Paris "to live cheaply and be able to write an American book," Salemson went to France twice as a boy for extended periods of schooling and returned to Paris as a free-lance writer and critic. His wide range of literary and artistic interests placed him in the company of such writers as *transition* magazine publisher Eugene Jolas, novelist and *transition* editor Elliot Paul, poet Richard Thoma, novelist and critic Ludwig Lewisohn, and editor Samuel Putnam. Although he relished the spirit of tolerance in Paris, Salemson viewed his work there from an American orientation. He wrote in *transition* 14 (Fall 1928): "Those who, like myself, feel that they are here to imbibe everything they can and then help to forge an American entity in the superior elements of life must feel, with me, that they are in a way spies." His critical essays and translations from English to French and French to English helped make the writing of each culture accessible to the other, and his short-lived magazine, *Tambour*, provided an intelligent perspective on the expatriate writing of the twenties.

Salemson was born in Chicago. His father, a neighborhood physician on the Northwest Side, traveled to house calls by streetcar, and Salemson began his education at an early age by adding up the numbers on the transfers. His parents were allowed by the school authorities to teach him at home until. he was eight, when he began his public schooling in the fifth grade. After graduating from grammar school at age eleven, he spent four of the next six years studying in France. In 1927 he was enrolled in the Experimental College at the University of Wisconsin, but he stayed there only one semester. Since several of his articles had already been published in French periodicals, his professors agreed that he should write independently rather than remain in college. Salemson returned to Paris in 1928, not quite eighteen years old.

Mrs. Salemson gave her son the money no longer needed for tuition to publish the French-English magazine *Tambour*, which contained both original work and translations of previously published work. It came out irregularly in eight issues from February 1929 to June 1930. Salemson recalls that production costs were only eighty to one hundred dollars an issue: "Nobody got paid anything; there were just the printer's costs." *Tambour* had a circulation of about fifteen hundred copies, of which some eight hundred went to subscribers; copies were also on sale at Sylvia Beach's Shakespeare and Company in Paris and at Brentano's and the Gotham Book Mart in New York. *Tambour* 1 featured the work of Andre Spire, Ralph Cheever Dunning, Philippe Soupault, Countee Cullen, Blaise Cendrars, Stuart Gilbert, and others. Subsequent issues included that of Pierre MacOrlan, Maxwell Bodenheim, Jean Cocteau, Julian L. Shapiro (later known as John Sanford), Richard Thoma, Paul Bowles, and Parker Tyler. *Tambour* 5 was a special issue on Anatole France. Among the contributors of work in English were Theodore Dreiser, H. L. Mencken, William Carlos Williams, Edmund Wilson, and George Bernard Shaw; French articles were written by Andre Gide, Victor Llona, and Andre Maurois. *Tambour* 7 featured a group of Italian poets in French translation, and the last issue contained prose fiction by James T. Farrell.

Salemson was one of the signers of Eugene and Maria Jolas's "Revolution of the Word Proclamation," which appeared in *transition* 16/17 (June 1929) and clarified the Jolases' philosophy of experimentation with language and form in literature. In "Essential: 1930 (A Manifesto)" for *Tambour* 7, Salemson discussed the results of the experimental writing of the twenties. In their effort to break away from traditional forms, he explained, the modernists had "achieved a classicism of anti-form." It was now time for a new point of view. "We demand that the artist look at his day with the point-of-view of his day, as he understands it, and without making us feel his presence in it." Salemson elaborated on this point of view in "James Joyce and the New Word," a critical essay in *Modern Quarterly* (1928-1930): " . . . we of the younger generation will have to return to the crossroads from which our elders took the wrong path, and seek our direction on another road. That road will be the Revolution of the Idea, the new point-of-view, an entirely renovated outlook, purely ideological, which may be correlated with but will be independent of both the Revolution of the Word and the Revolution of the Act." In 1930 Salemson, Richard Thoma, and Samuel Putnam signed "Direction," a manifesto which set the editorial policy for Putnam's *New Review* and, like "Essential: 1930," advocated a return to content in writing. These two statements reflected Salemson's

Harold J. Salemson, 1930s

developing political interests and foreshadowed the proletarian literature of the thirties.

A series of distorted articles about life and literary personalities in Paris has been unjustly attributed to Salemson. After poet and publisher Harry Crosby's suicide in New York on 10 December 1929, Salemson received a cable from an uncle who was an editor on the Hearst papers asking for information about Crosby and others. He naively supplied what he felt to be basic information; without his prior knowledge, this went into the composition of four articles "by Harold Salemson as told to Nigel Trask," an office name used to cover ghostwritten material. Although the articles bore little resemblance to the material Salemson had provided and were published without his consent, he is still mentioned in some sources as their author.

While he was publishing *Tambour*, Salemson also contributed criticism to *transition*, *This Quarter*, *Poetry*, and Charles Henri Ford's *Blues*. He wrote the column "Lettres anglo-americaines" (quarterly reports on American books) for *Mercure de France* and acted as regular film critic for the weekly *Monde*. One of his poems, "Chicago," appeared in *Blues*, and articles were published in *Bifur*, the French avant-garde magazine for which William Carlos Williams was American editor. Translations were an important part of Salemson's work. His translation into English of Cocteau's

poem "Angel Wuthercut" was published in the *New Review* and reprinted in Putnam's *The European Caravan* (1931). Others include translations for French periodicals of Eugene O'Neill's "Moon of the Caribbees" and "Bound East for Cardiff," the novellas of V. F. Calverton, and an early piece by Eric Blair (later known as George Orwell) for *Monde*.

Salemson returned to the United States in November 1930. Pursuing his interest in movies, he went to Hollywood in 1931 as critic and correspondent for *L'Intransigeant*, then the leading Paris evening newspaper, and its affiliated publications, including the movie weekly *Pour Vous* and the sports weekly *Match* (later *Paris-Match*). These properties were bought in 1938 by *Paris-Soir*, and Salemson was retained on the staff as Hollywood bureau head until the fall of Paris to the Nazis in 1940. During the same period he worked in several capacities on films and contributed extensively to periodicals in the United States and abroad. He was then one of the few writers in English giving films the serious critical attention they later came to receive generally. In World War II he was involved in the Mediterranean Theatre during the invasion of Sicily and the Italian mainland, and he wrote the leaflets dropped by plane throughout the landings in the South of France. Although he was blacklisted in the late forties and the fifties, he continued to work in both the artistic and executive ends of the movie industry. Salemson and his wife live in Glen Cove, Long Island. He has taught film courses, subtitled foreign films, worked at free-lance writing and editing assignments, and continues to translate French books into English. —*Jean W. Ross*

Other:

Thought Control in U.S.A., edited by Salemson (Hollywood, Cal.: Hollywood A.S.P. Council, P.C.A., 1947);

Salvador Dali, with Andre Parinaud, *The Unspeakable Confessions of Salvador Dali*, translated with notes by Salemson (New York: Morrow, 1976);

Pierre Cabanne, *Pablo Picasso: His Life and Times*, translated with notes by Salemson (New York: Morrow, 1977).

Periodical Publications:

"The Poetry of Paul Valery," *Poetry*, 32 (April 1928): 36-41;

"Why Do Americans Live in Europe?," by Salemson and others, *transition*, no. 14 (Fall 1928): 97-119;

"Paris Letter," *transition*, no. 15 (February 1929): 103-112;

"Chicago," *Blues*, 1 (July 1929): 147;

"On Current French Reviews," *This Quarter*, 2 (July-August-September 1929): 181-183;

"Paris Letter," *Blues*, 2 (Fall 1929): 35-38;

"James Joyce and the New Word," *Modern Quarterly*, 5 (1928-1930): 294-312;

"Essential: 1930 (A Manifesto)," *Tambour*, no. 7 (1930): 5-7;

Jean Cocteau, "Angel Wuthercut," translated by Salemson, *New Review*, 1 (January-February 1931): 10-14; republished in *The European Caravan An Anthology of the New Spirit in European Literature*, ed. Samuel Putnam and others (New York: Brewer, Warren & Putnam, 1931), pp. 282-287.

References:

Samuel Putnam, *Paris Was Our Mistress Memoirs of a Lost & Found Generation* (New York: Viking, 1947), pp. 220, 227-229;

Frederick J. Hoffman, Charles Allen, and Carolyn F. Ulrich, eds., *The Little Magazine A History and a Bibliography* (Princeton, N.J.: Princeton University Press, 1947), pp. 80, 84, 293;

Hugh Ford, *Published in Paris American and British Writers, Printers, and Publishers in Paris, 1920-1939* (New York: Macmillan, 1975), pp. 318-321.

WILLIAM SEABROOK
(22 February 1886-20 September 1945)

SELECTED BOOKS: *Adventures in Arabia* (New York: Harcourt, Brace, 1927; London: Harrap, 1928);

The Magic Island (New York: Harcourt, Brace, 1929; London: Harrap, 1929);

Jungle Ways (New York: Harcourt, Brace, 1931; London: Harrap, 1931);

Air Adventure (New York: Harcourt, Brace, 1933; London: Harrap, 1933);

The White Monk of Timbuctoo (New York: Harcourt, Brace, 1934; London: Harrap, 1934);

Asylum (New York: Harcourt, Brace, 1935; London: Harrap, 1935);

These Foreigners (New York: Harcourt, Brace, 1938);

Witchcraft (New York: Harcourt, Brace, 1940; London: Harrap, 1941);

Dr. Wood (New York: Harcourt, Brace, 1941);

No Hiding Place (Philadelphia & New York: Lippincott, 1942).

William Buehler Seabrook achieved fleeting celebrity with two of his ten books: *The Magic Island* (1929), one of the first revelations of the voodoo cults in backwoods Haiti that introduced the zombie to presumably civilized audiences, and *Asylum* (1935), an unsparing account of Seabrook's experiences in Bloomingdale Hospital, White Plains, New York, where he had voluntarily committed himself to be treated for acute alcoholism. Seabrook spent scattered years in France, but despite his many friendships in the American literary community, none of his books were about Paris, and only one grew out of his connections there.

Son of a poorly paid Lutheran minister who preached in small southern coastal towns, Seabrook was born in Westminster, Maryland, and attended Newberry College in South Carolina, graduating with a Ph.B. in 1905, followed by an A.M. in 1906. Upon graduation he worked for the *Augusta Chronicle* in Georgia and used his small savings to finance his first trip to Europe around 1908. After returning to the United States he worked for the *Atlanta Journal* and became a founding partner in the Lewis-Seabrook Advertising Agency. At the outbreak of World War I he volunteered to fly with the Lafayette Escadrille, but failing to pass the eye test, he joined other Americans driving ambulances for the American Field Service. After the war he tried the life of a gentleman farmer in Georgia at his wife's uncle's expense, but soon he moved to New York to work for the *New York Times*. He found his true career, however, when some friends from the Middle East suggested an expedition there that resulted in *Adventures in Arabia* (1927). He spent most of the twenties in New York before going to Toulon on the French Riviera, where from 1930 to 1933 he resided with his second wife, novelist Marjorie Worthington, who was later his biographer.

Seabrook's book about Haiti, *The Magic Island*, attracted the attention of French diplomat and writer Paul Morand, who insisted that Seabrook must follow up this account of a primitive society's rituals with an even more startling one about the cannibal tribes in Western African jungles. Seabrook's attempt to lend authenticity to *Jungle Ways* (1931), the report of his experiences in the Ivory Coast, also brought him brief notoriety. Morand had advised him that during his expedition he must eat human flesh, but his jungle hosts substituted a great ape in a ritualistic dinner. After returning to France he claims that he carried out the experiment with the aid of medical friends who had access to cadavers. He reports eating a considerable quantity of the meat, which "didn't taste like pork," as he had heard, "but mature veal or young beef." His autobiography, *No Hiding Place* (1942), suggests that he produced many of his sensational writings in a successful effort to shock his hysterically proper mother.

Seabrook never went back to France after returning to the United States in 1933 to battle against the alcoholism that he never entirely conquered. He settled at Rhinebeck, New York, in the Hudson River Valley and contributed to the *Reader's Digest*, among other publications. His last major expose, *Witchcraft* (1940), attracted less attention than earlier ones, and he was not able to carry out a planned return to France to help during World War II. In September 1945 he was found dead of an overdose of sleeping pills.

Two useful sources of biographical information are Seabrook's autobiographical note in Peter Neagoe's *Americans Abroad An Anthology* (1932), which contains an excerpt from *The Magic Island*, and Marjorie Worthington's *The Strange World of Willie Seabrook* (1966). Both, however, are factually unreliable. —*Warren French*

Other:

"Goat-Cry Girl-Cry," in *Americans Abroad An Anthology*, ed. Peter Neagoe (The Hague: Servire, 1932), pp. 403-417.

Reference:

Marjorie Worthington, *The Strange World of Willie Seabrook* (New York: Harcourt, Brace & World, 1966).

WILLIAM L. SHIRER
(23 February 1904-   )

SELECTED BOOKS: *Berlin Diary The Journal of a Foreign Correspondent, 1934-1941* (New York: Knopf, 1941; London: Hamilton, 1941);

End of a Berlin Diary (New York: Knopf, 1947; London: Hamilton, 1947);

The Traitor (New York: Farrar, Straus, 1950);

Midcentury Journey The Western World Through Its Years of Conflict (New York: Farrar, Straus & Young, 1952; London: Hale, 1952);

Stranger Come Home (Boston: Little, Brown, 1954; London: Hale, 1955);

The Consul's Wife (Boston: Little, Brown, 1956);

The Rise and Fall of the Third Reich A History of Nazi Germany (New York: Simon & Schuster, 1960; London: Secker & Warburg, 1960);

The Rise and Fall of Adolf Hitler (New York: Random House, 1961); republished as *All About the Rise and Fall of Adolf Hitler* (London: Allen, 1962);

The Sinking of the Bismarck (New York: Random House, 1962); republished as *All About the Sinking of the Bismarck* (London: Allen, 1963);

The Collapse of the Third Republic An Inquiry into the Fall of France in 1940 (New York: Simon & Schuster, 1969; London: Heinemann, 1970);

20th Century Journey A Memoir of a Life and the Times The Start 1904-1930 (New York: Simon & Schuster, 1976).

William Lawrence Shirer, historian and novelist, was born in Chicago to Seward Smith Shirer, a United States assistant district attorney, and Josephine Tanner Shirer. After his father's death in 1913, Shirer's family moved to Cedar Rapids, Iowa, where Shirer graduated from Coe College in 1925. Following graduation Shirer went to Paris with a friend for the summer, planning to return to the United States in the fall to work, but his enthusiasm for Paris, which seemed intellectually stimulating and less personally restrictive than the United States, led him to apply for jobs with the European editions of two American newspapers in Paris. His experience as editor of his college paper and as sports editor of the *Cedar Rapids Republican* was probably a factor in his being hired as a copywriter for the European edition of the *Chicago Tribune*, usually called the Paris *Tribune*.

Among Shirer's coworkers at the *Tribune* when he started work in August 1925 were James Thurber, Elliot Paul, Eugene Jolas, and Virgil Geddes, who at the time were all aspiring writers although Paul and Jolas are now more often remembered for founding *transition* in 1927. Through these friends Shirer met a number of other writers, including Harold Stearns, Ezra Pound, Ernest Hemingway, Sinclair Lewis, John Dos Passos, Theodore Dreiser, F. Scott Fitzgerald, and Sherwood Anderson. Shirer lived at the Hotel de Lisbonne, which was the home of many Americans on the Left Bank, especially employees of the *Tribune*.

Although the Paris *Tribune* had been started in 1917 by Colonel Robert McCormick to give American soldiers in Paris a touch of home, by 1925 it had become, according to Shirer, a journal of American expatriates, written and read by Left Bank writers and artists. Shirer and the other copywriters regularly had to expand brief news cablegrams from New York and London to full columns of detailed news, relying on background knowledge as well as imagination. Shirer became known as the paper's disaster expert, writing long columns on air and sea tragedies based on short cablegram reports. Scores from intercollegiate and professional athletic contests were similarly turned into play-by-play accounts by Shirer and other reporters of the *Tribune* to satisfy the demands of Americans in Paris for the details of such events as the Harvard-Yale games.

When Shirer arrived in Paris, he hoped to become a writer of poetry and fiction. His early attempts remained unpublished, but his interests gradually changed to reporting foreign political news. Since Elliot Paul and Eugene Jolas usually wrote the literary articles for the Paris *Tribune*, Shirer's assignments were more likely to be sports, financial, and political stories. He maintained a strong concern for literature, but was more interested in reading French authors than English-language writers. He occasionally attended readings by James Joyce at Sylvia Beach's Shakespeare and Company bookshop, but he spent more time across the street at the French bookshop, Adrienne Monnier's La Maison des Amis des Livres. Here he met Andre Gide, Jules Romains, Paul Claudel, Louis Aragon, Andre Breton, and Valery Larbaud, all of whose works he read enthusiastically. Shirer's interest in French civilization was also reflected in his attending lectures at the College of France, which he preferred to the Sorbonne, where he also went occasionally. He frequently wrote articles for the Sunday issue of the Paris *Tribune*, under the heading "Review of Reviews," which summarized the major ideas and criticism appearing in such French journals as *Les Nouvelles Litteraires*, *La Revue des Vivants*, and *Les Annales*. He was particularly interested in articles by French critics on American authors and in articles about the international political situation. He was concerned that Americans were unaware of the threat of war in Europe and unwilling to read serious articles by overseas correspondents. Shirer agreed, in a review of an article in the *American Mercury* by H. L. Mencken, that "think stuff" was not wanted by American editors, who preferred articles about parrots committing suicide or jazz concerts at funerals.

Three of the women whom Shirer was asked to interview during these years in Paris made a strong impression on him. He was enchanted by Mary Garden and Isadora Duncan but unfavorably impressed by Gertrude Stein. He viewed Stein as a publicity seeker with an inflated sense of her own importance. She described herself to Shirer as the only living representative of the "Big Four" writers

William L. Shirer in Paris, 1927

of American literature—Poe, Whitman, Henry James, and herself. She had just completed a lecture tour at Cambridge and Oxford Universities in England and was disappointed that there had been no coverage in the Paris papers. She gave Shirer a copy of her lecture, entitled "Composition as Explanation," as a basis for his article. He found her explanations unintelligible and repetitive. Her statement that "The time of the composition is the time of the composition" reminded Shirer of Thurber's article about President Coolidge, in which Thurber has Coolidge say that a praying man was a man who prayed. When Stein advised Shirer to stop writing newspaper articles so he would not ruin his style, he considered the advice to be useless. A later interview with her in 1934, when he was working briefly for the Paris *Herald*, described Stein's pleasure at becoming a celebrity with the success of *The Autobiography of Alice B. Toklas* (1933).

By the summer of 1927 Shirer's articles on important sports events and human interest stories, such as the Lindbergh landing in Le Bourget and the Sacco-Vanzetti riots at the American Embassy in Paris, had attracted the attention of Henry Wales, chief of the foreign service of the *Chicago Tribune*, and Shirer was asked to become a foreign correspondent for the home paper. Although his friends James Thurber and artist Grant Wood became dissatisfied with the expatriate's life in France in the summer of 1926 and returned to the United States, Shirer continued to be stimulated by life in Paris throughout his two years there from 1925 to 1927. The new position of European correspondent for the *Chicago Tribune*, however, meant that he would spend the next years traveling from city to city. His two years in Paris had been most influential in broadening his interests and developing his skills as a reporter. Although he did not again live in Paris for such an extended period, he returned for shorter visits or work assignments many times. These years in Paris he considered to be both a highlight and a turning point in his life. The most colorful and evocative writing in his memoirs, *20th Century Journey* (1976), is found in the chapters dealing with these two years.

From 1927 to 1929 Shirer wrote stories from London, Paris, Geneva, Rome, Dublin, Vienna, and Prague for the *Chicago Tribune*. He was then named chief of the *Tribune*'s Central European bureau, which was located in Vienna, and reported the rise of Hitler and the Nazi party during the critical years from 1929 to 1932. A special assignment to India during these years enabled him to meet Mahatma Gandhi and develop an interest in the Civil Disobedience movement. He left central Europe for Spain in 1932, following a skiing accident which resulted in the loss of sight in one eye. He and his Viennese wife, Theresa Stiberitz, whom he had married in 1931, lived in a village in Spain while Shirer recuperated and worked on a novel on India.

In 1934 Shirer resumed his work as a European correspondent, writing briefly for the Paris *Herald* and then going to the Universal News Service in Berlin. When the UNS was disbanded in 1937, Shirer was asked by Edward R. Murrow to open a Vienna office and arrange radio broadcasts for the Columbia Broadcasting System from that city. After Hitler annexed Austria in 1938, Shirer broadcast from Prague and Berlin until December 1940, when he returned to the United States for his first extended visit to his home since he left in the summer of 1925.

In addition to lecturing Shirer prepared for publication the diary which he had kept while in Berlin and was able to bring out of Germany. It was published in 1941 as *Berlin Diary The Journal of a Foreign Correspondent, 1934-1941* and quickly became a best-seller. It was a Book-of-the-Month Club selection and was translated into several European languages. During World War II Shirer worked in the United States as a radio commentator for the CBS network and as a columnist for the *New York Herald Tribune*. He was awarded the George Foster Peabody Award for outstanding interpretation of the news in 1946. However, a dispute with Edward R. Murrow, a longtime friend who was at that time a vice-president of CBS, led to his resignation from the network in 1947. He joined the Mutual Broadcasting System as a commentator and wrote a sequel to his first book on Germany, called *End of a Berlin Diary* (1947). It deals with the end of World War II in Germany and the events immediately following the war.

Shirer also used his experiences and acquaintances in Berlin and Vienna in the thirties as the basis for a novel about an American correspondent who becomes a traitor to his country and joins the Nazis. *The Traitor* (1950) is generally considered to be a portrait of the United Press correspondent, Bob Best. Aside from its historical interest the book did not attract wide comment by literary critics. Although Shirer wrote two more novels, *Stranger Come Home* (1954) and *The Consul's Wife* (1956), his nonfiction works were both more popular and more highly praised by critics.

In 1952 Shirer published a book about Paris in the twenties, *Midcentury Journey The Western World Through Its Years of Conflict*, which was a Literary Guild selection. In this book he investigates the changes which had taken place in the quarter of a century since his first trip to Paris. He stresses the "magic and light" of Paris in the twenties, as well as the freedom of thought, speech, and action which had characterized the city when he first arrived. The rapid disintegration of France and the failure of will to resist Germany, which he had witnessed in the late thirties and in 1940, had made a profound impression on him. The two central chapters of *Midcentury Journey*, "The Waning Star of France" and "The Master Race," offer some tentative answers to the questions he poses about the fall of France and the rise of Hitler, themes which would continue to be important in his future writing.

Detailed research on Germany and France occupied much of Shirer's time during the fifties and sixties and resulted in the publication of the two books with which his name is most often associated, *The Rise and Fall of the Third Reich* (1960) and *The Collapse of the Third Republic* (1969). Both books became best-sellers; *The Rise and Fall of the Third Reich* became the first ten-dollar book to head the best-seller list in the United States. It was a Book-of-the-Month Club selection and winner of a National Book Award in 1960. It was generally praised by American critics for its thoroughness and lively writing style. Some German critics, on the other hand, felt that it reflected an anti-German bias.

Shirer's next major project was a return to a study of the reasons for the decline of France from the position as a European leader in the twenties to the weak, spiritless country it seemed to be in 1940. *The Collapse of the Third Republic* again showed that Shirer was a tireless researcher whose work was aided by the contacts made during the years in which he was a reporter and radio commentator in Europe. Many critics considered the book to be the best one-volume study of recent French history.

In 1973 Shirer completed the first volume of his memoirs. Entitled *20th Century Journey* the book recaptures the excitement that the young Bill Shirer felt when he arrived in Paris from a small Midwestern college. It provides an outstanding picture of the contrast between the two cultures, as seen through the eyes of an intelligent, observant young man. Shirer is currently working on the second volume of these memoirs.

Although Shirer did not publish any poetry or fiction during the years he lived in Paris, as he had originally hoped to do, his Paris experience was pivotal in his life. It changed him from a relatively inexperienced, although well-read, youth to a journalist with wide interests and a concern for careful research. These traits, combined with a clear and vigorous writing style gave him unprecedented success as a journalist-historian. —*Alice Henderson*

References:

Malcolm Cowley, review of *20th Century Journey*, *New York Times Book Review*, 10 October 1976, p. 2;

J. L. Hess, "William Shirer: A Matter of Character," *New York Times Book Review*, 24 July 1977, p. 3.

SOLITA SOLANO
(1888-22 November 1975)

BOOKS: *The Uncertain Feast* (New York & London: Putnam's, 1924);

The Happy Failure (New York & London: Putnam's, 1925);

This Way Up (New York & London: Putnam's, 1927);

Statue in a Field (Paris?, 1934).

Solita Solano was born in New England in 1888. Both in youth and maturity she was strong-willed, inquisitive, and independent. Expressing her dislike for educational systems and her love of travel early in life, she spent three years in the Philippines instead of going to college. There she helped to survey and build coral roads. After her return to America, she began her writing career in 1914 as a cub reporter for the *Boston Herald-Traveler*, where she was soon promoted to the post of drama editor and critic (becoming the first woman to hold that position on a major daily U.S. newspaper). Five years later Solano went to work for the *New York Tribune*, where she served as drama editor for one year before departing in 1921 for Europe and the Near East with her friend Janet Flanner.

Solano spent time traveling in Greece, Crete, Turkey, and Vienna before settling in Paris in 1922. Once settled in Paris she mingled freely with the literary vanguard and was acquainted with many of its luminaries, including Sylvia Beach, Gertrude Stein, Margaret Anderson, the Fitzgeralds, Ernest Hemingway, James Joyce, and Ezra Pound. Her closest and longest friendships, however, were with Nancy Cunard, British poet and founder of the Hours Press, and with Flanner, who in 1925 became Paris correspondent for the *New Yorker*. Their enduring friendship she later described as "a fixed triangle . . . forty-two years of modern female fidelity." Solano lived with Flanner for twenty years.

Solano was not a prolific writer: she published only three novels and one book of poetry, *Statue in a Field* (1934?), all within the first twelve years of her life in Paris. Her fiction is best characterized as psychological realism, but it also displays a somewhat romantic affinity for the exotic, the Oriental, and the flamboyant in her choice of image, metaphor, and minutely detailed description. She seems obsessed with the failures of human relationships. Her three novels explore unrequited love and distraught marriage relationships and involve strong-willed characters (the men often neurotic and the women raffish) whose obsessions and self-indulgences result in self-destruction and whose stormy affairs end in bitterness and disillusionment.

The Uncertain Feast (1924), her first novel, is set in New York and is about Daniel Greer, a man whose hard work and determination in the face of extreme odds win him the editorship of a thriving newspaper, but whose weak, neurotic personality results in the failure of his much longed-for marriage to Amy Fiske, a socialite from Boston. She becomes indifferent and lazy; he selfish and even brutal. His efforts to get from life all that he can without regard for others result in bitter triumphs and successes without rewards. He seems, paradoxically, both a giant and a pygmy.

The Happy Failure (1925) repeats the themes of a sour marriage and the misfit personality. Its hero, Timothy Doan, struggles between the conflicting influences of his money-making father, his society-loving mother and sister, his wife's wish that he go into business, and his own dream to live a secluded life in the country where he would have time to write. An irreparable gulf widens between father and son and between husband and wife. The couple separates after one year of marriage. The hero, however, sees his failure as the beginning of a new freedom.

The third novel, *This Way Up* (1927), involves yet another bad marriage and a childish, self-centered character. Anthony, an American architect, returns to Paris ostensibly to study but actually to pursue Rosario, a pert Catalonian dancer who has led him on for two years. When in Paris she flaunts a new lover in his face, he, in a fit of anger and despair, marries a girl whom he met on the liner. The marriage ends in heartbreak; Rosario alone remains untouched by the havoc she has helped to create.

Solano's work, in the words of *transition*'s editors (who published an excerpt from *This Way Up* in the September 1927 issue), "had the honor of not pleasing" most American critics, who criticized her "sophisticated" use of classical allusions, her stark amorous detail, and her "execrable" and "abhorrent" style. A few critics, however, lauded her fictional realism for its "impeccable psychology" and "absolute ruthlessness," comparing her to Theodore Dreiser and Ben Hecht. Reviewer Lillian

Hellman appreciated *This Way Up* for its acute observations and intelligence and admired its young author for treating Paris not with "that palsy of admiration which strikes so many American writers" but "as if it were founded by human beings." Solano's prose is frequently over detailed, but it does convey with fidelity and vigor what she perceived as a fundamental ugliness and decay in the hearts and minds of modern human beings.

Solano's feelings about the Paris literary scene and her own career were ambivalent. In her response to the questionnaire that appeared in the final issue of the *Little Review* (May 1929), she said that she considered art "pleasant but unimportant" and that she disliked "the stupidity and vileness of human relations" as well as "stories (both dirty and clean), what passes for art, reality (except for laboratory data) . . . the theatre, novels" and "banal conversation." After 1930 her literary output declined, and she led an increasingly quieter life. In the mid-thirties she, along with Margaret Anderson and her friend Georgette Leblanc, became a disciple of the Russo-Greek mystic George Gurdjieff who had established a spiritual retreat at Fontainebleau-Avon, and for five years she served as Gurdjieff's secretary. In her later years she worked at times as an editor and involved herself in her special interest, etymology. She died at the age of eighty-six in the Paris suburb of Orgeval. —*JoAnn Balingit*

Other:

"Nancy Cunard: Brave Poet, Indomitable Rebel," in *Nancy Cunard Brave Poet, Indomitable Rebel*, ed. Hugh Ford (Philadelphia: Chilton, 1968), pp. 76-77.

Periodical Publications:

"Constantinople Today," *National Geographic*, 41 (June 1922): 647-680;
"This Way Up," *transition*, no. 6 (September 1927): 68-74;
Answer to Questionnaire, *Little Review*, 12 (May 1929): 81-82.

Papers:

Solano's and Flanner's papers are at the Library of Congress.

HAROLD E. STEARNS
(7 May 1891-13 August 1943)

BOOKS: *Liberalism in America Its Origin, Its Temporary Collapse, Its Future* (New York: Boni & Liveright, 1919);
America and the Young Intellectual (New York: Doran, 1921);
Rediscovering America (New York: Liveright, 1934);
The Street I Know (New York: Lee Furman, 1935);
America A Re-appraisal (New York: Hillman, Curl, 1937).

Harold Edmund Stearns was a prolific journalist and editor of the influential *Civilization in the United States An Inquiry by Thirty Americans* (1922), the book that inspired many dissatisfied young Americans to go abroad. When Stearns sailed for an extended stay in Europe on 4 July 1921, he was already known as a spokesman for the younger generation in America.

Stearns's father died shortly before his son's birth in Barre, Massachusetts. As a result Stearns's mother, a nurse, brought the boy up in straitened financial circumstances in several small New England towns. Stearns was determined to get an education, and his high school years were financed largely by his own ingenuity. In 1909, shortly before graduating from high school, Stearns began reviewing books for the *Boston Evening Transcript*, the beginning of a long and often successful career in journalism.

Surmounting formidable financial obstacles, Stearns entered Harvard in 1909 and finished the requirements for his degree in 1912, graduating with honors in 1913. In the summer of 1911 he became a reporter for the *Boston Herald*, and in 1912 he went to New York and immediately found a job as a feature writer with the New York *Evening Sun*. After a few months he joined the staff of the *Dramatic Mirror* and in the late summer of 1913 met Carl Van Vechten, then dramatic critic for the *New York Press*. Van Vechten persuaded Stearns to become a Sunday theatrical feature writer for the *Press*. During his association with the *Press*, Stearns met Somerset Maugham and Djuna Barnes, forming a friendship with Barnes that he would continue in Paris. In addition to his newspaper writing, Stearns contributed occasional articles to *Harper's Weekly*, *Forum*, and *Colliers*.

In the summer of 1914 Stearns made his first trip to Europe. After his arrival in London, Maugham befriended him and introduced him to the city. Stearns traveled to France with Walter Lippmann,

and his introduction to Paris was memorable. He knew that war in Europe was imminent, but he was shocked to find himself present in France and England when each entered World War I. Though his feelings about war were complex, Stearns was essentially a pacifist who hated the hysterical patriotism he found in his own country and the human slaughter he read about in Europe. He continued his newspaper writing, but he had no desire to be a war correspondent and generally shunned the subject of war.

After his return to the United States, Stearns moved to Greenwich Village and eventually became a salaried contributor for the *New Republic*. When America entered the war, Stearns managed to avoid being drafted, having no sympathy with "Wilson's war for democracy." In December 1917 he went to Chicago as editor of the prestigious literary magazine the *Dial* and remained there for six months until the *Dial* was moved to New York in June 1918. Stearns continued working on the *Dial* in New York, and when the war ended, he began his first book, *Liberalism in America Its Origin, Its Temporary Collapse, Its Future* (1919). In early 1919 he married Alice Macdougal, an editorial assistant to Horace Liveright. About the time Stearns's first book went to press, his wife died in San Francisco from complications of childbirth. Stearns's son, Philip, remained in Carmel, California, to be brought up by Alice Stearns's parents.

Grief over the loss of his wife dimmed Stearns's interest in the reception of *Liberalism in America*. The book, an attack on President Wilson's liberalism, was praised by H. L. Mencken and Senator William E. Borah, a Republican from Idaho, but it was criticized by Walter Lippmann. Stearns's second book, *America and the Young Intellectual* (1921), a defense of the younger generation's disenchantment with current conditions, stressed particularly the unjustified witch-hunts that were taking place soon after the end of the war. Stearns made it evident that he had not turned his interest from literature to politics completely when he took on a respected and formidable opponent, one of the leaders of the New Humanists, Stuart P. Sherman. Responding to Sherman's attack on the younger generation in the January 1921 issue of the *Atlantic Monthly*, Stearns defended the "moral idealism" of the young in an article marked by great dignity of style and the humanistic outlook that Sherman himself had defended. Stearns's article, "America and the Young Intellectual," published in *Bookman*, contained the manifesto of exile: "We of the younger generation make our plans for leaving the country of our birth and early affection."

After working with Albert Jay Nock on the *Freeman* during 1920 and early 1921, Stearns began to assemble the essays for his anthology *Civilization in the United States*. He secured contributions from some of the best-known writers of his day—Conrad Aiken, H. L. Mencken, Lewis Mumford, George Jean Nathan, Ring Lardner, Van Wyck Brooks, and authorities in virtually every field of American life—to contribute to his symposium. Published in 1922 and critical of America for its materialism and puritanism, the book was influential in the exodus to Europe that followed thereafter. The essays suggested that the vulgar, materialistic life in America was anathema to the creative individual. The artist and writer must flee abroad, therefore, to protect their creative potential.

Stearns sailed for Europe in July 1921, telling reporters that he might stay forever. Before leaving New York, he was careful to provide himself with sources of income once he arrived in Paris. Ready cash came from Doran, who contracted to publish *America and the Young Intellectual*, and Mencken secured him a job as correspondent for the *Baltimore Sun*, a position he held for five years. Stearns first went to London, where he looked up Sinclair Lewis, who financed a trip for both of them to Paris. What began as a vacation became a five-year stay for Stearns, for Lewis had loaned him enough money to stay in Paris for some time.

After Lewis's money was gone, Stearns began the habit of borrowing in times of need from his various American friends, a habit that led to Hemingway's portrayal of him as the indigent Harvey Stone in *The Sun Also Rises* (1926). In late 1921 Stearns took a job at the copy desk of the European edition of the *New York Herald* and also became the Paris correspondent for *Town and Country*, covering politics, wines, prohibition, morality, and the French sense of humor. He remained with that magazine for the next four years. Stearns soon became a fixture in Montparnasse and almost a symbol of the expatriate life in Paris. Shortly before Christmas of 1922, Stearns left his job with the *Herald*, and in June 1923 he attended his first thoroughbred horse race, the Grand Prix de Paris. This event was the beginning of his subsequent enduring fascination with racing.

In December 1924 Stearns returned to America on a brief visit, arriving in California for his son's fifth birthday. The visit did not establish any close relationship, and Stearns soon left for New York, where he visited with Mencken and Malcolm Cowley. While there, he also urged Horace Liveright

to publish Hemingway's *In Our Time* (1925). In early 1925 Stearns returned to Paris and found himself unemployed and virtually destitute, dependent on the good will of friends and acquaintances. These circumstances gave rise to the widespread view that Stearns was merely a hanger-on at cafes. Criticizing American expatriates in the October 1925 issue of the *American Mercury*, Sinclair Lewis singled out one person as "very father and seer of the Dome . . . authority on living without laboring." Although he did not mention this person by name, most of the Left Bank literary community recognized his portrait of Stearns. Stearns's response in the 10 December 1925 issue of the Paris *Tribune* (the European edition of the *Chicago Tribune*) was that Lewis's article was "cheap, inaccurate, and absurd." Stearns did not deny that he was the target of the attack; he maintained instead that Lewis misunderstood the Montparnasse colony.

The employment that Stearns finally gained at the end of 1925 did little to repair his damaged reputation. He filled the role of "Peter Pickem," the traditional name for the forecaster of races whose column in the Paris *Tribune* was well-known to turf fans. He held this job until 1930, when he moved to take a similar post with the London *Daily Mail* under the traditional pseudonym of "Lutetius." From the latter part of 1925 until late 1931 Stearns's life was intellectually and creatively unproductive. He spent most of his time at the horse races, attending one almost every day of the year. Stearns was often without money, and the funds to finance his champagne generally came from fellow workers, friends, or generous American tourists. John Dos Passos remembers in *The Best Times* (1966) that Stearns had a "certain sallow charm" and was still "an entertaining talker," but also that he eked out a pathetic living "selling tips on the ponies to American tourists he picked up in the various ginmills he frequented." William L. Shirer, in *20th Century Journey* (1976), remembers his dismay at seeing his former hero in Paris; he felt sad, as did many of Stearns's friends, watching "the slow degeneration of one once so splendidly endowed and so promising." Because of his long silences and paradoxical dignity, Stearns was given the nickname "Hippique Buddah" by some of his coworkers.

In 1931 Stearns was afflicted with temporary blindness, and he lost his job with the *Daily Mail*. Again he was destitute, but with the help of friends he returned to the United States in the early part of 1932. By the end of that year he had finished an article on the French for the *Baltimore Sun*, an article for *Harper's* on racing, and an article for

Scribner's, significantly entitled "A Prodigal Returns."

No longer "a prodigal," Stearns was to publish four more books before his death. *Rediscovering America* (1934) received wide critical acclaim and established its author as having truly returned home. Stearns's autobiography, *The Street I Know* (1935), is in many ways a confessional of his wasted years abroad. Though he never denies his fascination with Paris and the expatriate life, he does maintain that the creativity he left America to foster was virtually destroyed during his residence in Montparnasse. *America A Re-appraisal* (1937) was a reversal of Stearns's position in the symposium that had made him famous in 1922. In it he defends America against its Marxist critics in a manner that reflects philosophical training and psychological insight.

In 1937 Stearns married Elizabeth Chalifoux Chapin. His last book, *America Now An Inquiry Into Civilization in the United States* (1938), was another collection of essays, this time thirty-six, which explored the entire spectrum of American life. Stearns's essay in the volume, "The Intellectual Life," discusses Americans' willingness to hear new ideas and also their readiness to destroy the fantasy found in them. The tone of the volume, unlike that of his first, is one of optimism about America's future. Stearns resided with his new wife in Locust Valley, Long Island, until his death on 13 August 1943.

Stearns always did his best work in the United States. Though he is sometimes credited with leading the exodus of the young intellectuals abroad, his defiance of American repressions did little to further his career. Unfortunately, Hemingway's one-sided fictional portrait of Stearns in *The Sun Also Rises* is the one which persists; Kay Boyle's rather gentle portrayal of Stearns in *Monday Night* (1938) is less well-known. Stearns's importance still rests primarily on his early career, when he was, as Eugene Jolas described him in the Paris *Tribune* for 3 May 1925, the *"enfant terrible* of American journalism."

—*Kerin R. Sarason and Ruth L. Strickland*

Other:

"America and the Young Intellectual," *Bookman,* 53 (March 1921): 42-48;

Civilization in the United States An Inquiry by Thirty Americans, edited by Stearns (New York: Harcourt, Brace, 1922; London: Cape, 1922);

America Now An Inquiry Into Civilization in the United States, edited by Stearns (New York & London: Scribners, 1938).

Gertrude Stein

James R. Mellow
Clinton, Connecticut

BIRTH: Allegheny, Pennsylvania, 3 February 1874, to Amelia Keyser and Daniel Stein.

EDUCATION: B.A., Harvard University, 1897; Johns Hopkins Medical School, 1897-1901.

DEATH: Neuilly-sur-Seine, 27 July 1946.

SELECTED BOOKS: *Three Lives* (New York: Grafton Press, 1909; London: Bodley Head, 1915);

Portrait of Mabel Dodge at the Villa Curonia (Florence, Italy: Privately printed, 1912);

Tender Buttons (New York: Claire Marie, 1914);

Geography and Plays (Boston: Four Seas, 1922);

The Making of Americans (Paris: Contact Editions, 1925; New York: Boni, 1926; London: Owen, 1968);

Composition as Explanation (London: Leonard & Virginia Woolf at the Hogarth Press, 1926);

A Book Concluding with As A Wife Has a Cow A Love Story, illustrated by Juan Gris (Paris: Editions de la Galerie Simon, 1926; Barton, Millerton & Berlin: Something Else Press, 1973);

A Village Are You Ready Yet Not Yet A Play in Four Acts, illustrated by Elie Lascaux (Paris: Editions de la Galerie Simon, 1928);

Useful Knowledge (New York: Payson & Clarke, 1928; London: Bodley Head, 1929);

Lucy Church Amiably (Paris: Plain Edition, 1930; New York: Something Else Press, 1969);

Dix Portraits, by Stein, with translations by Georges Hugnet and Virgil Thomson and illustrations by Pablo Picasso, Pavel Tchelitchew, Eugene Berman, Christian Berard, and Kristians Tonny (Paris: Libraire Gallimard, 1930);

Before the Flowers of Friendship Faded Friendship Faded (Paris: Plain Edition, 1931);

How to Write (Paris: Plain Edition, 1931; Barton: Something Else Press, 1971);

Operas and Plays (Paris: Plain Edition, 1932);

Matisse Picasso and Gertrude Stein With Two Shorter Stories (Paris: Plain Edition, 1933; Barton, Berlin & Millerton: Something Else Press, 1972);

The Autobiography of Alice B. Toklas (New York: Harcourt, Brace, 1933; London: Bodley Head, 1933);

Four Saints in Three Acts, An Opera To Be Sung (New York: Random House, 1934);

Portraits and Prayers (New York: Random House, 1934);

Lectures in America (New York: Random House, 1935);

Narration (Chicago: University of Chicago Press, 1935);

The Geographical History of America (New York: Random House, 1936);

Everybody's Autobiography (New York: Random House, 1937; London & Toronto: Heinemann, 1938);

Picasso (Paris: Libraire Floury, 1938); republished in English, trans. Alice B. Toklas (London: Batsford, 1938; New York: Scribners; London: Batsford, 1939);

The World is Round (New York: William R. Scott, 1939; London: Batsford, 1939);

Paris France (London: Batsford, 1940; New York: Scribners; London: Batsford, 1940);

What Are Masterpieces (California: Conference Press, 1940);

Ida (New York: Random House, 1941);

Petits Poemes Pour Un Livre de Lecture, trans. Madame la Baronne d'Aiguy (Charlot, France: Collection Fontaine, 1944); republished in English as *The First Reader & Three Plays* (Dublin & London: Maurice Fridberg, 1946; Boston: Houghton Mifflin, 1948);

Wars I Have Seen (New York: Random House, 1945; enlarged edition, London: Batsford, 1945);

Brewsie and Willie (New York: Random House, 1946);

Selected Writings of Gertrude Stein, ed. Carl Van Vechten (New York: Random House, 1946);

Four in America (New Haven: Yale University Press, 1947);

The Mother of Us All, by Stein and Virgil Thomson (New York: Music Press, 1947);

Blood on the Dining Room Floor (Pawlet, Vt.: Banyan Press, 1948);

Last Operas and Plays, ed. Van Vechten (New York & Toronto: Rinehart, 1949);

Things as They Are (Pawlet, Vt.: Banyan Press, 1950);

Two: Gertrude Stein and Her Brother and Other Early Portraits[1908-12] (New Haven: Yale University Press; London: Cumberlege / Oxford University Press, 1951);

Mrs. Reynolds and Five Earlier Novelettes (New Haven: Yale University Press; London: Cumberlege / Oxford University Press, 1952);

Bee Time Vine and Other Pieces 1913-1927 (New Haven: Yale University Press; London: Cumberlege / Oxford University Press, 1953);

As Fine as Melanctha (1914-1930) (New Haven: Yale University Press; London: Cumberlege / Oxford University Press, 1954);

Painted Lace and Other Pieces (1914-1937) (New Haven: Yale University Press; London: Cumberlege, 1956);

Stanzas in Meditation and Other Poems[1929-1933] (New Haven: Yale University Press; London: Cumberlege / Oxford University Press, 1956);

Alphabets & Birthdays (New Haven: Yale University Press; London: Oxford University Press, 1957);

A Novel of Thank You (New Haven: Yale University Press, 1958; London: Oxford University Press, 1959);

Gertrude Stein on Picasso, ed. Edward Burns (New York: Liveright, 1970);

Fernhurst, Q.E.D., and Other Early Writings (New York: Liveright, 1971; London: Owen, 1971);

Reflection on the Atomic Bomb, ed. Robert Bartlett Haas (Los Angeles: Black Sparrow Press, 1973);

Money (Los Angeles: Black Sparrow Press, 1973);

How Writing is Written (Los Angeles: Black Sparrow Press, 1974).

"It was not what France gave you but what it did not take away from you that was important," Gertrude Stein once remarked by way of explaining her long-term residence in Paris. She had found in the French capital the privacy and freedom to live and write as she pleased. She was one of the most celebrated expatriates of her time, living in a standard of modest luxury with her lifetime companion, Alice B. Toklas. As the hostess of a well-publicized salon, Stein included among her friends and acquaintances many of the great and near-great men and women of her time—artists, writers, composers, critics, and publishers.

She needed two civilizations, she claimed: America had made her, but it was in Paris that she became a writer. It was, indeed, during her forty-three years abroad that she produced—and promoted—the idiosyncratic and experimental poems, plays, "word-portraits," and novels which admirers regarded as innovations in the use of

language and critics denounced as childish twaddle. (In later years she would also write three of the most vital and comprehensible memoirs of the period.) Throughout her career she was to remain a self-proclaimed genius whom the broad public and many critics regarded as a coterie writer, easily dismissed as the "Mama of Dada," or "The Mother Goose of Montparnasse." Still, it says something for Gertrude Stein's perseverance that from the distance of Paris she managed to court, direct, and sustain her American reputation as a quintessentially modern writer. Her famous line, "Rose is a rose is a rose is a rose," was endlessly quoted, misquoted, and ridiculed, but it kept the name and the image of the plump, cropped-haired author firmly before the public. Asked once how she had managed a publicity campaign that even a practiced press agent might envy, Gertrude Stein countered, "By cultivating a small audience."

Stein arrived in Paris in the fall of 1903 to take up residence with her brother Leo in the combined studio and pavilion at 27, rue de Fleurus, which was soon to become the mecca for visiting tourists and artists of all nations who wanted a glimpse of modern art. The Steins, including their older brother Michael and his wife Sarah—who lived nearby on the rue Madame—amassed a collection of modernist art, prime works by Henri Matisse, Pablo Picasso, Pierre Bonnard, Juan Gris, as well as works by Edouard Manet and the Postimpressionists Paul Cezanne, Paul Gauguin, and Henri Toulouse-Lautrec, that was overshadowed only by the collections of the far wealthier Russian merchants Shchukin and Morosov. The distinction was that the Stein collections were accessible in Paris, and the Steins themselves were fierce propagandists for the modern movement.

The unconventionality of Gertrude Stein's lifestyle and her openness to vanguard trends may have been encouraged by her erratic family life. Shortly after her birth, her family traveled abroad for a period of five years, settling largely in Vienna and Paris. After their return to the United States, Daniel Stein, having invested in street railroads and real estate in the San Francisco area, moved his family to California in 1880. At best, the education of both Leo and Gertrude Stein was spotty; a matter of shuttling between public schools and private tutors, according to the whims of their father, supplemented by whatever reading they cared to engage in. Gertrude Stein had a taste for Wordsworth and the English poets, as well as for Jules Verne. She read Henry Fielding and Tobias Smollett and was especially fond of Samuel Richardson's *Clarissa Harlowe*

Paintings at 27, rue de Fleurus

(1747-1748). She laid claim to having read every line of William Lecky's *History of England in the 18th Century* (1878-1890) and Thomas Carlyle's *History of Frederick II of Prussia, Called Frederick the Great* (1858-1865). She and Leo Stein regularly attended the theatre and the opera in San Francisco, and they saw their first "masterpiece" of French painting when Jean Millet's *Man with a Hoe* was exhibited there in 1880. With the deaths of Amelia Stein (1842-1888) and Daniel Stein (1832-1891), family discipline became even more relaxed; Michael Stein (1865-1938) served as the indulgent guardian of both Leo and Gertrude.

Throughout her early career, Gertrude Stein exhibited a profound dependence upon her brother Leo. In 1892 Leo Stein went to Harvard; the following year, she enrolled at Radcliffe. Her literary efforts during this period consisted of a number of indifferently written themes for William Vaughn Moody's course in English composition. (Instructors complained of her wayward syntax.) But she developed an abiding interest in psychology, became a favorite pupil of William James, and engaged in research that resulted in two papers for the Harvard *Psychological Review*, "Normal Motor Automatism" (1896) and "Cultivated Motor Automatism" (1898). After her graduation from

Harvard, again following in her brother's footsteps—and acting upon the advice of William James—she moved to Baltimore to pursue a medical career at Johns Hopkins. But aside from her independent research conducted for the neurological specialist Dr. Llewellys Barker and her casework in obstetrics which took her to Baltimore's Negro quarter, Stein confessed she was unconsolably bored with medical practice and pathological psychology. It was with a feeling of profound relief that she gave up her medical career and moved to Paris, where Leo Stein, planning to take up a career as an artist, had settled early in 1903.

Although her first decade in Paris was given over to the visual arts and her growing relationships with such artists as Matisse, Picasso, Georges Braque, Robert Delaunay, and Marie Laurencin, Stein also became acquainted with several vanguard French writers—notably Max Jacob and Guillaume Apollinaire, the extravagant poet, boulevardier, art critic, and promoter of his friends the Cubists. Later, through Picasso, she was also to meet Jean Cocteau, who professed an admiration for some of her more hermetic works such as *Tender Buttons* (1914). Throughout that decade, Gertrude Stein devoted considerable energy and thought to her own writing, working at night in the privacy of her studio, after her guests had departed. It was in the rue de Fleurus studio in October 1903 that she completed her first known novella, *Q.E.D.* (posthumously published in 1950 as *Things As They Are*), an account of an unhappy lesbian relationship drawn from her Baltimore experiences, that is all the more moving for the clinical straightforwardness of its style. In it, an ebullient young woman named Adele is initiated into the mysteries of sex in the course of a passionate affair with Helen Thomas, "the American version of the English handsome girl." Helen, in turn, is dominated by the wealthy and manipulative Mabel Neathe, a spinster "possessed by a nature of the tropics."

Stein's first published book, *Three Lives* (1909), a series of three *contes*, written somewhat in the manner of Gustave Flaubert, whom Leo had encouraged her to read and translate, was published in America at her expense. For a first book by an unknown writer, it received considerable praise: the critic for the *Brooklyn Daily Eagle* called it "an extraordinary piece of realism," while the anonymous reviewer of the *Kansas City Star* claimed, "Here is a literary artist of such originality that it is not easy to conjecture what special influences have gone into the making of her." Her story "Melanctha," one of the earliest and most sensitive treatments of Negro experience, was particularly singled out for praise. Although the love affair between the mulatto girl Melanctha and the black doctor, Jefferson Campbell, is clearly a reworking of the love affair in *Q.E.D.*, the success of the tale derives from the racy, almost vernacular style of the dialogue.

Stein's major literary effort during her early years in Paris, however, was *The Making of Americans* (1925), ostensibly a history of the Dehning and Hersland families, but an enormous, wordy, intolerably repetitious outpouring of descriptive vignettes and increasingly abstracted character analyses. Midway, in response to some psychological compulsion, the book takes on the impossible task of analyzing the "bottom nature" or essential character of "every kind of men and women, every kind there is of men and women." Against all reason, Gertrude Stein steadfastly maintained that it was her masterpiece, a book to be compared with Marcel Proust's *Remembrance of Things Past* (1912-1927) and James Joyce's *Ulysses* (1922). The writing of it occupied her for approximately five years, from 1906 to 1911, though in its jerry-built fashion, it also incorporated fragments, such as the "Fernhurst" episode written earlier. Each evening's stint of writing was faithfully

typed by Alice B. Toklas, who had recently arrived in Paris and in 1910 had moved into the rue de Fleurus to become Gertrude Stein's "wife," lifetime companion, occasional secretary, and staunchest supporter.

Despite the best efforts of Gertrude Stein and her friends, no American or English publisher would take *The Making of Americans*, considering it far too long and too eccentric to be profitable. It was not published in book form until 1925. But it did give rise to the full-blown literary experiments that first brought her fame—and notoriety—as a literary expatriate. Throughout the writing of *The Making of Americans*, Stein kept notebooks in which she set down her rambling assessments of various character types she had encountered. These provided the source for her later "word-portraits," in which repetitions, suggestive allusions, verbal color, and insistent rhythm were intended to approximate her subjects—usually her friends and the visitors to her salon. From collections of such portraits, she also developed her earliest theatrical pieces, "What Happened, A Play" (1913) and "For The Country Entirely. A Play in Letters" (1916). In time she discarded all the conventional dramatic devices—scenery, plot lines, and character development—relying solely upon the spoken word, an innovation that anticipated certain developments of the Theatre of the Absurd.

Prior to World War I, a few of these experiments were published. Her *Portrait of Mabel Dodge at the Villa Curonia* (1912), a word-portrait of the exuberant and avant-garde American hostess, was circulated in a privately printed edition by Mabel Dodge herself. It was also reprinted, along with her word-portraits of her artist friends "Matisse" and "Picasso" (both written in 1909), in the early issues of Alfred Stieglitz's avant-garde publication *Camera Work*. In New York her name was being promoted by two critics, Henry McBride, art critic for the New York *Sun*, who often wrote about her and her work in his columns, and Carl Van Vechten, cultural critic and novelist, who for years served as her unofficial and unpaid literary agent. Her contributions had also begun to appear in *Vanity Fair* as well as in such ephemeral literary magazines as *Rogue* and *Soil*. Probably her oddest and most difficult book, and the one that established for decades her image as a literary eccentric, is *Tender Buttons*, a volume of her most hermetic poems published in a small edition in New York just before the outbreak of World War I.

Stein and Toklas were stranded in England when war was declared. They had gone there during the summer of 1914 in hopes of persuading the English publisher John Lane to take on her work. (He had tentatively agreed to publish an English edition of *Three Lives*.) For eleven weeks they remained with Alfred North Whitehead and his family at his country home, Lockeridge. It was not until mid-October that they were able to arrange passage to France. In wartime Paris they were confronted by zeppelin raids as well as food and fuel shortages and decided to travel to the Mediterranean. They spent a year in neutral Majorca, where Stein continued writing her sometimes cryptic, sometimes idyllic, poems dealing with their daily life on the island, their acquaintances, and excursions. Occasionally, in a lyric vein, she referred to her affection for Toklas and their "marriage," as in "Lifting Belly" and "I Have No Title To Be Successful," poems which were eventually published in the posthumous volumes *Bee Time*

Vine (1953) and *Painted Lace* (1956). By the summer of 1916 both Stein and Toklas had grown weary of their enforced vacation and returned to France. Hoping to serve the war effort, Stein arranged for the purchase of a Ford truck, christened it "Auntie," and learned to drive. She and Toklas offered their services to the American Fund for French Wounded and for the remainder of the war transported hospital supplies and set up depots throughout France. Stein's first contact with soldiers—both French and American—at army installations and along the road encouraged a camaraderie that she found enjoyable. Her experiences became the subject of some of her more intelligible lyrics of the period. "Soldiers like a fuss," she reported in one of her wartime ruminations, "Give them their way." The lines come from the poem "Work Again," which, along with "Accents in Alsace," appeared in *Geography and Plays* (1922), the first of her postwar volumes to be published in America—as usual at her own expense.

The two decades between World War I and World War II were, for Stein, the period of her most consistent literary production and of her greatest literary influence and reputation. Her contributions were sought after by the editors of the new—and usually nonpaying—little magazines of the time. Her friendships during this period were more literary than artistic. She could no longer afford the paintings of the successful Cubists, but she remained on the warmest of terms (despite occasional differences) with Picasso and consolidated her friendship with Juan Gris. (About Gris she wrote a simple and touching elegy, "The Life and Death of Juan Gris," which appeared in the July 1927 issue of *transition*.) Throughout the twenties and thirties she befriended certain of the Surrealist artists and writers. Although her poetic methods might seem related to or antecedent to the Surrealists' interest in Freudian associations and in the subconscious, Stein was never enthusiastic about the movement and distrusted its attempts at shock tactics. Some of it she regarded as pornographic or worse—"girls' high school stuff." Although she was warmly appreciative of the young Surrealist Rene Crevel, as with her relationships to other French writers such as Apollinaire, Cocteau, and Georges Hugnet, her interest was more apt to be personal than literary. It is questionable whether her command of French literature, as distinct from the spoken language, enabled her to appreciate fully the works of the French writers with whom she associated. More to the point, her complacent egotism as a writer made her somewhat insular.

Gertrude Stein

There can be no question, however, about her interest in the younger American and English writers who flocked to Paris after the war and whom she dubbed "The Lost Generation." (She acknowledged frankly that the epithet had been invented by a French innkeeper who claimed that all young men between the ages of eighteen and twenty-five were in need of a civilizing experience—usually an affair with an older woman—but that the young men who had gone to war had lost their opportunity and so were a lost generation.) Stein was never interested in the bohemian life-style—the cafes and the nightlife—of the young expatriates in Paris. Nor was she ever involved in the summer exodus to the French Riviera, which was just coming into vogue among the fashionable. Conservative in their habits, she and Toklas lived the life of a modestly comfortable bourgeois couple, entertaining their friends at teas and dinners in their Left Bank apartment. (Toklas had become one of the notable cooks of her time; she also served as a watchdog at the rue de Fleurus, screening the visitors—and sitting with the wives of the visitors—before they were allowed to share in Stein's conversations.) After 1924 their summers were spent in the unfashionable rural town of Belley, in the department of Ain. From 1929 until World War II, they rented a seventeenth-century villa in the nearby farming community of Bilignin. It became a "summer palace" for brief visits from such notables as Picasso, Andre Breton, Thornton Wilder, Cecil Beaton, Clare Boothe Luce, and her publisher husband Henry Luce.

Her major literary friendships with other writers during this period were with Ernest Hemingway, F. Scott Fitzgerald, and Sherwood Anderson. Although Stein may have advised Hemingway to give up journalism, live frugally, and cut back on his use of descriptive adjectives, she did not blue-pencil the manuscripts of younger writers in the fashion of Ezra Pound. She preferred to talk about a writer's general vision, "the way of seeing what the writer chooses to see," and the relation between that vision and the way it was put down on paper. Hemingway had written her early in their relationship: "It used to be easy before I met you. I certainly was bad, gosh, I'm awfully bad now but it's a different kind of bad," but in his hard-boiled, dissembling fashion he was both appreciative and critical of Stein as a writer. He acknowledged the value of her use of rhythm and repetition in writing, but he could also tell Allen Tate that Gertrude Stein was lazy and vain as a writer and that she had invented a private style for herself, for which there were no standards of judgment so there could be no comparisons with her rivals. Hemingway's taut, declarative style had already been formed in the practice of journalism, and it is doubtful that Stein had any profound influence upon his work. Their relationship became a casualty of the literary life, precipitated by what she considered Hemingway's shabby treatment of Sherwood Anderson. In *The Autobiography of Alice B. Toklas* (1933), while describing a conversation with Anderson, she remarks that Hemingway was "yellow," implying that he was so concerned about his career and his image that he could never write honestly from his experience. Hemingway was to have a final revenge in his scathing portrait of Stein and Toklas in his posthumously published Parisian memoir, *A Moveable Feast* (1964).

Sherwood Anderson, too, was already an established writer when he met Stein on a visit to Paris in 1921; their relationship was one of mutual admiration and respect. Anderson publicly praised her innovations with language and was privately flattering. Out of his own weaknesses he seems to have responded to the weaknesses in her style—a tendency to discursiveness and repetition—but beyond certain superficial mannerisms, Anderson was not deeply influenced by Stein's writing. More often than not it was Stein's single-minded commitment to literature and her perseverance in spite of ridicule and neglect which impressed other writers. In the strictly literary sense, hers was a hard act to follow; blatant imitations of her manner were usually disastrous. Stein had even less direct literary influence on Fitzgerald, whom she saw on his frequent visits to Paris. Throughout her life she maintained a great respect for Fitzgerald's writing and was particularly encouraging with the writer who, whatever his drunken bravado, always had feelings of insecurity about his work. She remained convinced that in *This Side of Paradise* (1920) and *The Great Gatsby* (1925), Fitzgerald had really created his own age as a writer, the age of Gatsby and the lost generation, and that he would still be read "when many of his well known contemporaries are forgotten."

During the twenties and thirties, Stein's often friendly, sometimes quarrelsome relations with other celebrated writers of the period extended to such figures as Ford Madox Ford, Edith Sitwell, Lincoln Steffens, Robert Coates, Janet Flanner, Bravig Imbs, William Carlos Williams, Glenway Wescott, Paul Bowles, Thornton Wilder, and Louis Bromfield. More often than not, her cordial relationships with such writers depended upon their being socially entertaining or professionally useful

Beinecke Library

Bravig Imbs, Alice B. Toklas, and Gertrude Stein at Aix-les-Bains, 1928

or only intermittent, admiring visitors. Seldom was there any question of Stein's dominant influence upon them as writers; although there is a possibility that Stein's antic plays may have offered some encouragement to Wilder's theatrical experiments in *Our Town* (1938) and *The Skin of Our Teeth* (1942). Ezra Pound was too contentious a personality to serve as one of Stein's promoters, and he was not encouraged to call at the rue de Fleurus—particularly after he had accidentally broken an

antique chair in the course of an animated discussion. Stein was to have a very cordial relationship with Sylvia Beach, proprietor of the bookstore Shakespeare and Company, even though Beach was the publisher of James Joyce, whom Stein regarded as her principal rival among the moderns. Although the two writers were longtime residents of Paris, they met only once, at a party, and found they had little to say to one another. Stein had been equally wary of meeting T. S. Eliot, who made a brief call at the rue de Fleurus in 1924 and asked for a contribution to his magazine, the *New Criterion*. Stein supplied "The Fifteenth of November," a poem commemorating the American poet's visit, but had to wait more than a year before Eliot printed it. Eliot's opinion, she learned by way of the grapevine, was that "the work of Gertrude Stein was very fine but not for us."

Stein had a strictly limited appreciation of music. As a child she had liked Wagner, but then she came to feel "that music was made for adolescents and not for adults." Nonetheless she had a passing acquaintance with the French composer Erik Satie, and knew the young American composers George Antheil and Aaron Copland. Her real musical friendship during this period was with the American composer Virgil Thomson. But Thomson, besides being a composer, had distinct literary interests. When he visited Stein in 1925, he was already an established music critic, having written for the *Dial*, the *New Republic*, and H. L. Mencken's *American Mercury*. Their friendship was quickly cemented when he began setting a number of her poems to music—notably, "Preciosilla," the "Portrait of F. B.," and "Capitals Capitals." He also began to create impromptu musical "portraits" of his friends, borrowing the idea from Stein's word-portraits. The major collaborative efforts of the pair, however, were two celebrated operas: *Four Saints in Three Acts*, first performed in February 1934, with an all-Negro cast, at the Wadsworth Atheneum in Hartford, Connecticut, and *The Mother of Us All*, commissioned by Columbia University and produced there in 1947, the year after Stein's death. For the first, Stein drew upon her enthusiasm for the Spanish saints, Teresa of Avila and Ignatius of Loyola, to create a kind of timeless sequence of arias and tableaux which, in the scenario developed by the painter Maurice Grosser, bore some relationship to the rituals of the Catholic Church. Her last opera, based loosely on the life of Susan B. Anthony and her companionship with Dr. Anna Howard Shaw, another nineteenth-century feminist, carried echoes of Stein's long-term relationship with Toklas. She also introduced a number of other unrelated historical figures—Daniel Webster, Thaddeus Stevens, and Lillian Russell. In Thomson's words, his score was "an evocation of nineteenth-century America, with its gospel hymns and cocky marches, its sentimental ballads, waltzes, darn-fool ditties and intoned sermons."

Throughout the twenties Stein relied upon the little magazines to bring her work before the public. Beginning with "Vacation in Brittany," which appeared in the Spring 1922 number of the *Little Review*, Stein appeared with some regularity in that controversial publication edited by Margaret Anderson and Jane Heap, who had courageously published installments of Joyce's *Ulysses*. The editors of virtually every vanguard literary magazine of the period expected contributions from Stein to launch their publications, and Stein readily supplied poetry and prose for such exotically titled reviews as *Broom, This Quarter, Black & Blue Jay, larus The Celestial Visitor, Close Up, Blues,* and *Pagany*. Her relationships with the editors were often short-lived, partly because the magazines were transient, folding after a few months or a season, but also because she was extremely jealous of her reputation and took offense when an editor seemed too eager to court such rivals as Joyce or Pound. Her affiliation with *transition* lasted for several years, although Stein was inclined to feel that coeditor Elliot Paul was the operative intelligence behind the magazine rather than its founders, Eugene and Maria Jolas. For several years the Jolases generously published a good deal of her work, including the text of her opera *Four Saints*, a reprint of *Tender Buttons*, and a bibliography of her work. The association ended when Stein became a best-selling author with *The Autobiography of Alice B. Toklas*. Angered at her description of *transition*, the Jolases printed a "Testimony against Gertrude Stein" (February 1935) with contributions by Matisse, Braque, Tristan Tzara, and Andre Salmon, claiming that Stein had clearly not understood the events she had written about in her memoirs and denouncing the book's "hollow, tinsel bohemianism." In 1930, when *transition* suspended publication for two years, Stein, somewhat fatuously, decided that it was her contributions that had kept the publication alive and that when the Jolases failed to publish her, *transition* died.

Hemingway engineered the publication of Stein's long overdue novel, *The Making of Americans*, in Ford Madox Ford's magazine, the *transatlantic review*, where it appeared in regular installments from the April 1924 issue until the magazine's demise in January 1925. It was Robert McAlmon who, with some misgivings, agreed to publish the novel in book form. The publication of *The Making of Americans* by McAlmon's Contact Publishing Company in 1925 was a major failure; by December 1926 only 103 copies had been sold. Edmund Wilson, a critic usually receptive to Stein's work, maintained in the *New Republic* that he had been unable to finish reading it and doubted that anyone could. A reviewer for the *Irish Statesman* was convinced that it was "among the seven longest books in the world." Only Marianne Moore, writing in the *Dial,* had a kind word, calling it "distinctly American," but she compared it to Bunyan's *Pilgrim's Progress* (1678). Stein, who hoped for great things from the book, became increasingly dissatisfied with its distribution and sale, and McAlmon, exasperated with her meddling, threatened to get rid of the edition "by the pulping proposition." The business venture ended in a bitter break which Stein, unsuccessfully, tried to mend.

Two collections of Stein's works appeared in the twenties: *Geography and Plays,* published in 1922 at her own expense, and *Useful Knowledge,* brought out by the small New York firm Payson & Clarke in 1928. It included a number of early pieces, among them "Farragut or A Husband's Recompense," written during her wartime sojourn in Majorca. In 1926 Leonard and Virginia Woolf's Hogarth Press published *Composition as Explanation,* a lecture that Stein had delivered to appreciative undergraduate audiences at both Oxford and Cambridge earlier in the year. In collaboration with Daniel-Henry Kahnweiler, Picasso's dealer, there were two luxury editions of her works: *A Book Concluding with As a Wife Has a Cow* (1926), with lithographs by Juan Gris, and *A Village Are You Ready Yet Not Yet A Play in Four Acts* (1928), illustrated by Elie Lascaux. A third volume, *A Birthday Book,* fell through when Picasso failed to supply the expected engravings. The young French poet Georges Hugnet, acting as publisher (and translator, together with Virgil Thomson), produced a luxury volume of Stein's word-portraits, *Dix Portraits* (1930), with illustrations by Picasso and the new young artists of her circle, Pavel Tchelitchew, Eugene Berman, Christian Berard, and Kristians Tonny. Her friendship with Hugnet ended in another literary quarrel. She had made a free adaptation of Hugnet's poem sequence "Enfances" and proposed that the two works be published as a book. The arrangement broke down, however, over a question of equal billing. Hugnet was afraid that his work would be overshadowed by Stein's greater reputation; Stein huffily withdrew her text but allowed it to be printed—or misprinted, as "Poem Pritten on Pfances of Georges Hugnet"—in the Winter 1931 issue of *Pagany.*

In the quarrel with Robert McAlmon the irate publisher had challenged Stein, claiming that if she were so concerned about her "art," she could well afford to publish her works herself. Dissatisfied with her lack of recognition, aware of the successes of younger writers like Hemingway and Fitzgerald,

Stein decided to do just that. In 1930 she and Toklas initiated the Plain Edition, intended to publish "all the work not yet printed of Gertrude Stein," and in that year they produced her rambling and unfocused tale *Lucy Church Amiably,* billed as "A Novel of Romantic beauty and nature and which Looks Like an Engraving." Over the next three years, in printings ranging from 1000 to 500 copies, they published a series of Stein's most hermetic works:

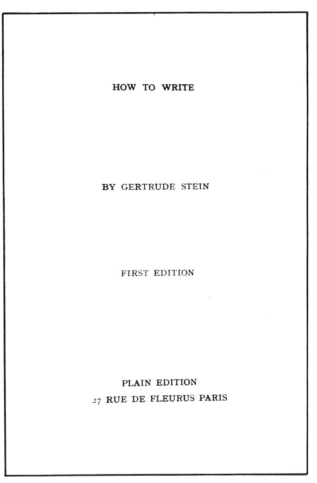

HOW TO WRITE

BY GERTRUDE STEIN

FIRST EDITION

PLAIN EDITION
27 RUE DE FLEURUS PARIS

Title page

How to Write (1931), *Operas and Plays* (1932), and *Matisse Picasso and Gertrude Stein* (1933). They also published a limited edition of Stein's ill-fated Hugnet translation, meaningfully titled *Before the Flowers of Friendship Faded Friendship Faded* (1931). None of the volumes was a success, although the editions, for which Toklas carefully selected the papers, typefaces, and bindings, have become collectors' items.

Asked once what a writer most wanted, Stein threw up her hands and exclaimed, "Oh, praise, praise, praise, praise, praise." Throughout her career she had been courting *"la gloire."* It came with the publication of *The Autobiography of Alice B. Toklas,* written as the reminiscences of her lifetime companion and covering the early, heroic years of the Cubist revolution and the Rousseau banquet, and the no less exciting decade of the twenties with its literary squabbles and its literary celebrities—Hemingway, Fitzgerald, Anderson, Joyce, Eliot, Ford Madox Ford, and Djuna Barnes. From the outset, the best-seller potential of the book was recognized by Stein's shrewd Parisian agent, William Aspenwall Bradley, who began receiving chapters of the memoir in the late summer of 1932. Harcourt, Brace readily agreed to publish the American edition, with John Lane's Bodley Head contracting for the English edition. The Literary Guild bought it for its September 1933 selection. Stein also realized a lifetime ambition, publication in the staid *Atlantic Monthly,* which serialized the book in four abridged installments beginning in May 1933. Seemingly overnight she had become famous.

With some trepidation, after a thirty-year absence, she agreed to make a lecture tour of the United States. The ground had been well-prepared by the extraordinary reception of her book and by Virgil Thomson's well-publicized performances of their opera, *Four Saints.* Reporters and newsreel photographers crowded aboard the deck of the *Champlain* when it pulled into New York Harbor on the morning of 24 October 1934. Stein's return was front page news for all of the major dailies. She saw her name in lights coursing around the Times Building. Throughout her six-month tour she was relentlessly interviewed and photographed. Her lectures on modern art, poetry and grammar, her own literary methods, and the forbidding subject "What is English Literature," delivered at the Colony Club and at East Coast colleges and universities from Harvard to the University of Virginia, were always well-attended and thoroughly reported in the press. She had tea at the White House with Eleanor Roosevelt and a sad Christmas meeting with Fitzgerald in Baltimore. In Richmond she dined with Ellen Glasgow and a slightly stunned James Branch Cabell, who wondered if Stein could be serious about her writing. At the University of Chicago she lectured Chancellor Robert Hutchins and Mortimer Adler on the subject of education, met Thornton Wilder, and delivered a series of four specially written lectures on "Narration." Despite her busy schedule, she found time to do a good deal of other writing as well. For the *New York Herald Tribune,* in the spring of 1935, she wrote a series of

six weekly articles, discoursing on such subjects as American education and American crimes. (Her astonishing publicity also gave her entree to another bastion of respectability, the *Saturday Evening Post,* which in the following year published five of her articles on the most unlikely of subjects—"Money." A Republican in matters of economics, she was convinced that Roosevelt was trying to spend money out of existence.) In California she met William Saroyan, Charlie Chaplin, and Dashiell Hammett, all of whom she admired, and resolutely snubbed Mabel Dodge Luhan, Robinson Jeffers, and the entire artistic colony at Carmel, declaring in an interview, "I like ordinary people who don't bore me. Highbrows, you know, always do." By the time she sailed for Europe on 4 May 1935, it was clear that her American tour had been a resounding success. She had acquired a publisher, Bennett Cerf of Random House, who agreed to publish one book by her each year. Cerf welcomed her highly readable account of her American tour, *Everybody's Autobiography* (1937), and kept his word by first publishing her far less popular productions— *Portraits and Prayers* (1934), *Lectures in America* (1935), *The Geographical History of America* (1936)—and later her hodgepodge novel *Ida* (1941), based loosely and very improbably on the life of the Duchess of Windsor.

Stein's *Picasso* (1938), her homage to her painter friend, was published on the eve of World War II. A warmhearted and affectionate memoir of their relationship, it was also an evocative portrait of an era in life and art that was passing from the scene. Stein was convinced there would be no war on the grounds that a full-scale European war was unthinkable. Nevertheless, it came. In September 1939 she and Toklas were settled in Bilignin. Lulled by the "phony war," they decided to remain in their corner of France, close to the Swiss border. When France fell, she and Toklas lingered on in a state of indecision. Ironically, her tribute to her second country, *Paris France,* was published in 1940. Finally they decided to stay on in France until the end of the war. Although they were in purportedly Unoccupied France and could count on the protection of their neighbors and of their friend the historian Bernard Fay, a Vichy official and director of the Bibliotheque nationale, it was still a dangerous decision. As Jews—and as enemy nationals, once America had entered the war—they could easily have been shipped off to concentration camps. At first in Bilignin and then at nearby Culoz, where they were obliged to move in 1943, they endured the food and fuel shortages, waiting for their liberation. They lived quietly; Toklas gardened, Stein walked, meditated, sawed wood. There were some dangerous moments, as in 1943 when a German officer was billeted in their home.

For Stein the wartime years in France provided a delayed education in politics. She grew to understand, as she never quite had before, the value of personal liberty. In her memoir, *Wars I Have Seen* (1945), she offers a vivid and moving account of daily life in France during those troubled years: the bitter enmities among her French neighbors, the hardships and fears of the times, the small acts of generosity, and the heroic acts of the Maquis.

With the liberation, she returned to Paris in December 1944. She was grateful to find that her valuable collection of paintings had not been vandalized or stolen. She renewed old acquaintances with Picasso and Parisian friends and even had a cordial meeting with Hemingway, one of the more celebrated liberators of the French capital. With the end of the war, she was launched on a new wave of celebrity; American GIs flocked to her apartment on the rue Christine, where she and Toklas had moved before the war. Under the auspices of *Life* magazine, she was flown to Germany with a contingent of GIs and photographed on the terrace of Hitler's Berchtesgaden retreat. She wrote about the experience for *Life* and wrote about the GIs in a thin little volume, *Brewsie and Willie* (1946), a plea for individualism in the face of the growing conformity of industrial life, written in the lingo of the American soldier.

Given the pace of her life, she had begun to grow increasingly tired and irritable. She quarreled with an army group over a production of her wartime play, *Yes is For a Very Young Man*. (It was eventually produced in the Pasadena Playhouse in March 1946.) While on a vacation in Luceau, she became seriously ill and was advised to see a specialist immediately. She entered the American Hospital at Neuilly, where, after an unsuccessful operation for cancer, she lapsed into a coma and died on the evening of 27 July 1946. She was buried in Paris in Pere Lachaise Cemetery, the resting place of the eminent dead, a repository of French life and letters. Twenty-one years later Toklas was buried by her side.

Stein's public image had always been newsworthy; but her writing—especially her "difficult" works—even during her lifetime seemed *hors concours*, of little concern to literary critics and academicians. Following her death, her innovations in the use of language were always given a polite nod of recognition, but her emphasis on the abstract qualities of language—the color, sound, and rhythm of words—did not lend itself readily to the kind of textual explications which, under the guidance of the New Criticism, came to dominate American literary studies. Although her difficult works offered stray hints of meaning, they offered far fewer textual opportunities than the writings of James Joyce. Beginning in 1951 and continuing through 1958, Yale University, to which Stein had left her papers and manuscripts, began publishing the Yale Edition of the Unpublished Writings of Gertrude Stein, but without any great critical response. The pioneering critical studies are still few: Donald Sutherland's *Gertrude Stein: A Biography of Her Work* (1951), Michael J. Hoffman's *The Development of Abstractionism in the Writings of Gertrude Stein* (1965), and more recently, Richard Bridgman's *Gertrude Stein in Pieces* (1970). Benjamin L. Reid's *Art by Subtraction* (1958) offers a sharply argued dissenting opinion. With the centenary of Stein's birth in 1974, however, there has been a marked revival of interest—both public and academic—in her life and her work.

Periodical Publications:

"Normal Motor Automatism," by Stein and Leo M. Solomons, *Psychological Review*, 3 (September 1896): 492-512;

"Cultivated Motor Automatism," *Psychological Review*, 5 (May 1898): 295-306;

"Henri Matisse," *Camera Work*, Special Number (August 1912): 23-25;

"Pablo Picasso," *Camera Work*, Special Number (August 1912): 29-30;

"Aux Galeries Lafayette," *Rogue*, 1 (March 1915): 13-14;

"M. Vollard et Cezanne," New York *Sun*, 10 October 1915, Section 5, p. 12;

"Mrs. Th_____y," *Soil*, 1 (December 1916): 16;

"Have They Attacked Mary. He Giggled.," *Vanity Fair*, 8 (June 1917): 55;

"Two Cubist Poems. The Peace Conference, I and II," *Oxford Magazine*, 38 (7 May 1920): 309;

"If You Had Three Husbands," *Broom*, 1 (January 1922): 211-215; 1 (April 1922): 74-77; 2 (June 1922): 242-246;

"Vacation in Brittany," *Little Review*, 8 (Spring 1922): 5-6;

Review of *Three Stories & Ten Poems* by Ernest Hemingway, *Chicago Tribune*, European edition, 27 November 1923, p. 2;

"The Making of Americans," *transatlantic review*, 1 (April 1924): 127-142; 1 (May-June 1924): 297-

309; 1 (July 1924): 392-405; 2 (August 1924): 27-38; 2 (September 1924): 188-202; 2 (October 1924): 284-294; 2 (November 1924): 405-414; 2 (December 1924): 527-536; 2 (January 1925): 662-670;

"The Fifteenth of November," *New Criterion*, 4 (January 1926): 71-75;

"Composition as Explanation," *Dial*, 81 (October 1926): 327-336;

"An Elucidation," *transition*, no. 1 (April 1927): 64-78;

"The Life of Juan Gris. The Life and Death of Juan Gris," *transition*, no. 4 (July 1927): 160-162;

"Mrs. Emerson," *Close Up*, 2 (August 1927): 23-29;

"Georges Hugnet," *Blues*, 1 (July 1929): 133;

"Five Words in a Line," *Pagany*, 1 (Winter 1930): 39-40;

"Scenery and George Washington," *Hound & Horn*, 5 (July/September 1932): 606-611;

"American Newspapers," *New York Herald Tribune*, 3 March 1935, section 4, p. 10; 23 March 1935, p. 16;

"The Capital and the Capitals of the United States of America," *New York Herald Tribune*, 9 March 1935, p. 11;

"American Education and Colleges," *New York Herald Tribune*, 16 March 1935, p. 15;

"American Crimes and How They Matter," *New York Herald Tribune*, 30 March 1935, p. 13;

"American States and Cities and How They Differ from Each Other," *New York Herald Tribune*, 6 April 1935, p. 13;

"American Food and American Houses," *New York Herald Tribune*, 13 April 1935, p. 13;

"Butter Will Melt," *Atlantic Monthly*, 159 (February 1937): 156-157;

"The Situation in American Writing," *Partisan Review*, 6 (Summer 1939): 40-41;

"Stanzas in Meditation," *Poetry*, 55 (February 1940): 229-235;

"The Winner Loses: a Picture of Occupied France," *Atlantic Monthly*, 166 (November 1940): 571-583;

"Off We All Went To See Germany," *Life*, 19 (6 August 1945): 54-58.

Letters:

Sherwood Anderson/Gertrude Stein Correspondence and Personal Essays, ed. Ray Lewis White (Chapel Hill: University of North Carolina Press, 1972);

Dear Sammy Letters from Gertrude Stein & Alice B. Toklas, ed. Samuel M. Steward (Boston: Houghton Mifflin, 1977).

Bibliographies:

Robert Bartlett Haas and Donald Clifford Gallup, *A Catalogue of the Published and Unpublished Writings of Gertrude Stein* (New Haven: Yale University Library, 1941);

Robert A. Wilson, *Gertrude Stein: A Bibliography* (New York: Phoenix Bookshop, 1974).

Biographies:

John Malcolm Brinnin, *The Third Rose Gertrude Stein and Her World* (Boston: Little, Brown, 1959);

Four Americans in Paris: The Collections of Gertrude Stein and Her Family (New York: Museum of Modern Art, 1970);

Janet Hobhouse, *Everybody Who Was Anybody: A Biography of Gertrude Stein* (New York: Putnam's, 1975);

James R. Mellow, *Charmed Circle Gertrude Stein & Company* (New York & Washington: Praeger, 1974);

W. G. Rogers, *When this you see remember me Gertrude Stein in person* (New York & Toronto: Rinehart, 1948);

Linda Simon, ed., *Gertrude Stein: A Composite Portrait* (New York: Avon, 1974);

Elizabeth Sprigge, *Gertrude Stein: Her Life and Work* (New York: Harper, 1957);

Alice B. Toklas, *What is Remembered* (New York, Chicago & San Francisco: Holt, Rinehart & Winston, 1963).

References:

Richard Bridgman, *The Colloquial Style in America* (New York: Oxford University Press, 1966);

Bridgman, *Gertrude Stein in Pieces* (New York: Oxford University Press, 1970);

Donald Gallup, ed., *The Flowers of Friendship Letters Written to Gertrude Stein* (New York: Knopf, 1953);

Frederick J. Hoffman, *Gertrude Stein* (Minneapolis: University of Minnesota Press, 1961);

Michael J. Hoffman, *The Development of Abstractionism in the Writings of Gertrude Stein* (Philadelphia: University of Pennsylvania Press, 1965);

Michael J. Hoffman, *Gertrude Stein* (Boston: Twayne, 1976);

Bruce F. Kawin, *Telling it Again and Again* (Ithaca: Cornell University Press, 1972);

Rosalind Miller, *Gertrude Stein: Form and*

Intelligibility (New York: Exposition Press, 1949);

Benjamin L. Reid, *Art by Subtraction: A Dissenting Opinion of Gertrude Stein* (Norman: University of Oklahoma Press, 1958);

Wendy Steiner, *Exact Resemblance to Exact Resemblance: The Literary Portraiture of Gertrude Stein* (New Haven: Yale University Press, 1978);

Allegra Stewart, *Gertrude Stein and the Present* (Cambridge: Harvard University Press, 1967);

Donald Sutherland, *Gertrude Stein: A Biography of Her Work* (New Haven: Yale University Press, 1951);

Edmund Wilson, *Axel's Castle A Study In the Imaginative Literature of 1890-1930* (New York & London: Scribners, 1931).

Papers:

The major repository for Stein materials is the Beinecke Library, Yale University, which has most of Stein's manuscripts and correspondence and her unpublished notebooks. There are also significant collections at the Bancroft Library, University of California at Berkeley, and the University of Texas at Austin.

LEO STEIN
(11 May 1872-29 July 1947)

BOOKS: *The A-B-C of Aesthetics* (New York: Boni & Liveright, 1927);

Appreciation: Painting, Poetry and Prose (New York: Crown, 1947);

Journey Into the Self being the letters, papers & journals of Leo Stein, ed. Edmund Fuller (New York: Crown, 1950).

Leo Stein had little direct influence on the generation of writers and painters who gathered in Paris during the twenties. Yet between 1904 and 1910 Stein was the primary collector of and propagandist for the modern art hung at 27, rue de Fleurus, the residence which he shared with his younger sister, Gertrude Stein. During these years he dominated their Saturday evening gatherings with his analytical lectures on such figures as Pierre Auguste Renoir, Paul Cezanne, Henri Matisse, and Pablo Picasso. Though he soon lost faith in the direction of most modern art, including his sister's writing, he was clearly instrumental in establishing both a subject matter and an important setting for the artistic and literary renaissance of the twenties.

Born to Daniel and Amelia Keyser Stein in Pittsburgh, Pennsylvania, and raised primarily in Oakland, California, Stein spent much of his childhood traveling with his family in Europe. He studied history at Harvard, from which he received his degree in 1895, and following a round-the-world trip he enrolled as a biology student at Johns Hopkins in Baltimore, where he shared an apartment with his younger sister. In 1900 Stein left the United States to live in Italy, England, and France. He took up residence at 27, rue de Fleurus in early 1903; Gertrude Stein joined him there in the fall of that year.

During the early period of their life together in Paris, Leo Stein, not his sister, was the discerning connoisseur and collector of modern art. Under his direction the pair purchased their first Cezannes, Matisses, and Picassos, and as Stein later recalled in his *Appreciation: Painting, Poetry and Prose* (1947), "I was the only person anywhere, so far as I know, who in those early days recognized Picasso *and* Matisse. Picasso had some admirers, and Matisse had some, but I was alone in recognizing those two as the two important men." As the collection grew to include Renoirs, Gauguins, Vallottons, Manguins, and at least one work each by Daumier, El Greco, and Toulouse-Lautrec, Stein became chief propagandist for the new art: "I expounded and explained." By all accounts his prolonged monologues were zestful and incisive but also too stridently dogmatic to please all of his listeners.

With the waning of the decade Stein's dedication to the new art died: "in the six years from the time I bought that first Cezanne, I had had enough of intensive concern with so-called modern art. I had come to find it only occasionally good enough." Picasso's movement into Cubism, an artistic method that Gertrude Stein was trying to imitate in her writings, offended Leo Stein's more conservative conceptions of significance, form, and beauty. As his *Journey Into the Self* (1950) documents, he regarded the two Cubist experimenters and their works as "stupid," "damned nonsense," "Godalmighty rubbish," and "oodles of bosh." The painter and the writer were, in Stein's opinion, substituting eccentric style for genuine substance and vision: "Picasso was for essentials a feeble, not a powerful artist. He tried to circumvent

Leo Stein in Paris, 1926

this by novel inventions of form. Gertrude couldn't make ordinary syntax and words in their ordinary meanings have any punch, and like Picasso she wanted Cezanne's power without Cezanne's gift. So she perverted the syntax.'' As the Steins became more divergent in tastes and interests—his demand for stringently classical standards in painting and literature conflicting with her commitment to experimentation, his extreme preoccupation with his work-constricting neurosis contrasting with her creatively productive celebrations of self—their parting was inevitable. Their ''disaggregation'' occurred in 1913, Leo Stein taking with him most of the Renoir and Matisse paintings and Gertrude Stein retaining at 27, rue de Fleurus the majority of the Picassos and almost every other piece in the art collection.

Following his break with his sister, Stein moved to Florence. He spent World War I in the United States but returned to Italy in 1919. In March 1921 he married Nina Auzias, with whom he had maintained a long, rather complicated relationship, and the couple lived primarily in Florence, at his villa in Settignano, near Stein's close friend Bernard Berenson. They also kept an apartment in Paris, and although he never saw his sister after 1920, Stein, according to the memoirs of Samuel Putnam and Harold Loeb, frequented the same Left Bank cafes as the writers of the younger generation. Yet, as Virgil Geddes testifies, Stein's influence as aesthetic theorist was practically nil. His first book, *The A-B-C of Aesthetics* (1927), with its insistence upon such qualities as ''intensity and comprehensiveness of [the painter's] unifying perception,'' was generally not well received or understood by either critics or artists.

Stein spent the remainder of his life honing his aesthetic theories and plumbing his own neurosis. Following World War II, which he and his wife spent in Settignano, he published *Appreciation: Painting, Poetry and Prose.* The book, a further elucidation of his aesthetic principles, received much critical praise. Its most engaging sections recount his development as an appreciator of art and offer a version of life at 27, rue de Fleurus which counters the ''fictions'' set down in his sister's *Autobiography of Alice B. Toklas* (1933). Stein died of cancer only months after the publication of *Appreciation*, but in 1950 a third collection of his writings, *Journey Into the Self*, appeared. Composed of letters, journal entries, and autobiographical fragments, the book chronicles Stein's intense investigations into his crippling neurosis, which he finally conquered at the end of his life, describes for a third time his development as an aesthetic theorist, and abundantly documents his responses to Gertrude Stein, Picasso, T. S. Eliot, and other modern painters and writers. *Journey Into the Self*, which was highly praised on its publication, remains the most accessible and appealing of Stein's works.

Although Stein was not in tune with the literary and artistic movements dominating Paris in the twenties, he did help establish the background against which that renaissance could occur. As a supporter of modern art in the prewar period, he helped define ideas and techniques which the postwar writers and painters brought to full realization.

—*Judith S. Baughman and Virgil Geddes*

References:

John Malcolm Brinnin, *The Third Rose Gertrude*

Stein and Her World (Boston: Little, Brown, 1959);

Virgil Geddes, "Leo and Gertrude," *Lost Generation Journal*, 2 (Winter 1974): 16-17;

Aline B. Saarinen, "The Steins in Paris," *American Scholar*, 27 (Autumn 1958): 437-448.

DONALD OGDEN STEWART
(30 November 1894-   )

BOOKS: *A Parody Outline of History* (New York: Doran, 1921);

Perfect Behavior (New York: Doran, 1922);

Aunt Polly's Story of Mankind (New York: Doran, 1923; London: Brentano, 1927);

Mr. and Mrs. Haddock Abroad (New York: Doran, 1924; reprinted, Carbondale & Edwardsville: Southern Illinois University Press, 1975—adds an afterword by Stewart);

The Crazy Fool (New York: Boni, 1925);

Mr. and Mrs. Haddock in Paris, France (New York & London: Harper, 1926);

Father William (New York & London: Harper, 1929);

Rebound (New York, Los Angeles & London: French, 1931);

By a Stroke of Luck! An Autobiography (London: Paddington Press; New York: Paddington Press / Two Continents, 1975).

Donald Ogden Stewart was already the author of the highly successful work *A Parody Outline of History* (1921) before he went to Paris for the first time in 1922, but it was in Paris that Stewart developed his own brand of "crazy humor," previously used by Ring Lardner, and employed it in the novel *Mr. and Mrs. Haddock Abroad* (1924).

A native of Columbus, Ohio, Stewart attended Phillips Exeter Academy and Yale University. After graduating from Yale in 1916, Stewart worked for the American Telephone and Telegraph Company before entering the navy in early 1918. Because of his poor eyesight, he spent World War I as an instructor in Chicago. After his discharge in April 1919, he returned to the telephone company and was transferred to Minneapolis, Minnesota, where he lived across the river in St. Paul and became friendly with F. Scott Fitzgerald, who was at home finishing his first novel, *This Side of Paradise* (1920). In the spring of 1920 Stewart went to Dayton, Ohio, to work for a company owned by the family of a fellow Yale graduate, but by November 1920 both Stewart and his employers had decided that he was not a businessman.

Stewart went to New York and renewed his acquaintance with Fitzgerald, now married and living in New York after the success of *This Side of Paradise*. Fitzgerald's connections with Edmund Wilson and John Peale Bishop at *Vanity Fair* helped Stewart to place some parodies in this magazine. Also at this time Stewart published a series of pieces in the *Bookman* that were collected in *A Parody Outline of History*—American history retold in the styles of James Branch Cabell, Sinclair Lewis, F. Scott Fitzgerald, Ring Lardner, Edith Wharton, and other popular writers.

In early 1922 Stewart's resolve to go to Paris was strengthened when he read the recently published *Civilization in the United States*, edited by Harold Stearns. He arrived in Paris in the spring of 1922 and spent the early part of his year abroad working on a series of parodies of best-selling etiquette books, conceived before he left New York. The pieces were published in *Harper's Bazaar* and *Vanity Fair* before they were published as *Perfect Behavior* (1922).

Between the spring of 1922 and April 1923 Stewart met some notable expatriates, savored French life, read *Ulysses* (1922), stayed some months in Vienna, became fascinated with H. G. Wells's *Outline of History* (1920), and spent the winter in Capri. In Capri the idea came to him for his next book, *Aunt Polly's Story of Mankind* (1923), a view of history largely influenced by H. G. Wells. In 1923 Stewart returned to Paris, where he read T. S. Eliot's *The Waste Land* (1922) and met Ernest Hemingway, both at the recommendation of John Peale Bishop. John Dos Passos and Gilbert Seldes were in Paris at the time, and with them Stewart met the founder of Dada, Tristan Tzara, writer Pierre Drieu de la Rochelle, and composer Darius Milhaud. The excitement of this visit to Paris was also enhanced by his association with fellow Yale graduate Gerald Murphy and his wife, Sara, both of whom Stewart greatly admired.

Returning to America, Stewart went to the MacDowell Colony in New Hampshire to complete his work on *Aunt Polly's Story of Mankind*, uninterrupted by his always active social life. By this time Stewart already had an established reputation as a wit, both publicly and privately. John Dos Passos remembers in *The Best Times* (1966): "Conversation in the early twenties had to be one wisecrack after another. . . . One of the most skilled at this exhilarating sport . . . was Donald Ogden Stewart. . . . In spite of a certain obsession with social status, Don managed to be funny about almost

Mr. and Mrs. Haddock Abroad
by Donald Ogden Stewart
Chapter I

Please return to
D.O. Stewart
159 Bd Montparnasse
Paris.

Mr. and Mrs. Haddock were very excited about going abroad. It was the first time either of them had ever been abroad to Europe, although Mr. Haddock had been to Chicago 8 times, Kansas City 5 times, Kansas City (Kan). 5 times, St Louis 4 times, Denver 4 times and New York City twice but it had rained four days out of five.

Mrs. Haddock had been to St. Louis once and Chicago twice, in pullman cars named respectively Edgar Allen Poe, Sweet Juniper and Spaulding oolis. She had not slept very well the first two times and the third time she had not slept at all. She slept very well at home though, mostly on her back and left side. Her mother's maiden name had been Quetch.

Mr. and Mrs. Haddock had been married twenty five odd years and their grandparents were all dead on both sides. So they were quite alone in the world except for Mr. Haddock's father and mother and Mrs. Haddock's father and mother, who were, however, quite old, their combined ages totalling 329 or several score years.

They also had a son, Frank (Haddock) but he wasn't going abroad although he could have gone abroad if he had wanted to, but he didn't want to, and they also had a young daughter Mildred.

That ought to give you a pretty fair idea of the city in which Mr and Mrs. Haddock lived. It was everything. We laughed like fools whenever we saw each other." When Stewart finished his book, he believed that it would firmly establish him as the leading satirist of his time. The work satirizes religious hypocrisy, middle-class smugness, and the greed of munitions makers. Self-satisfied Aunt Polly, satirically represented as the fulfillment of the evolutionary process, has planned a celebration of Peace and Progress. The celebration, undertaken by juveniles, ends in a brawl in which David, Uncle Frederick's son, makes his fortune by selling guns to the combatants. Instead of the loud denunciation and social ostracism Stewart expected as results of his "bombshell," all he received was a "resounding silence" when *Aunt Polly's Story of Mankind* appeared. Booksellers, critics, and fans felt disappointed in their humorist; only Stewart's friends, such as Dorothy Parker and Robert Benchley, were appreciative and encouraging. Discouraged by his failure as a satirist, Stewart decided to remain with his brand of "crazy humor" and carefree fun.

In April 1924 Stewart returned to Paris with Philip and Ellen Barry. Hemingway liked Stewart's never-published novel in progress, "John Brown's Body," and included an excerpt from it in the *transatlantic review*. Hemingway, the Murphys, Seldes, Dos Passos, and Archibald MacLeish also encouraged Stewart in his composition of *Mr. and Mrs. Haddock Abroad*, a book in the nonsense idiom that he had decided to write after arriving in Paris. With his friends' laughter as support he finished it in about a month. Mr. and Mrs. Haddock and their daughter, Mildred, compose an ordinary, representative American family who are making their first trip abroad. The humor comes largely from non sequiturs, and the world which the Haddocks inhabit is anything but representative of reality: it is rather, as Stewart describes it, a "cloud-cuckoo land." Unlike *Aunt Polly's Story of Mankind, Mr. and Mrs. Haddock Abroad* has no biting satire, and its sole purpose is to amuse and entertain.

In July 1924 Stewart made his first trip to Pamplona for the fiesta of San Fermin. The party included Dos Passos, the Hemingways, William and Sally Bird, and Robert McAlmon. After his trip to Spain he stopped off at the Riviera to visit the Murphys before returning to New York. Stewart had encouraged Hemingway to seek an American publisher for *In Our Time* (1925) after reading the stories in Paris. In September Hemingway sent the typescript to Stewart at the Yale Club in New York to engage Stewart's assistance in finding an American publisher. Stewart submitted the typescript first to Doran, his own publishers, and to soften Hemingway's disappointment when Doran rejected the stories, Stewart sent Hemingway a large personal check. Stewart then took the typescript to H. L. Mencken in the hope that Knopf might publish it. The book was finally accepted by Boni & Liveright, and early in February Stewart cabled Hemingway that the book had been accepted. Meanwhile, Stewart's own book, *Mr. and Mrs. Haddock Abroad*, was well received, and Stewart accepted the offer of a lecture tour of the United States, which gave him his first exposure to Hollywood.

Stewart again returned to Paris in the summer of 1925. Shortly after his arrival, he received the news that his most recent book, *The Crazy Fool* (1925), was doing quite well immediately after its publication. It is the story of a man who inherits a run-down insane asylum of which he must make a success before he can marry the banker's daughter. Stewart intended the work as a satire of his own drive for business success in those years following his graduation from Yale. He also had a Hollywood contract in mind when he wrote the story, and his first contact with the movie industry came when Hollywood bought the screen rights.

After a tour of Vienna and Budapest with Robert Benchley, Stewart again went to Pamplona. This time the famous party included Lady Duff Twysden, Harold Loeb, Bill Smith, and the Hemingways. As a result of this memorable reunion, Stewart, together with Bill Smith, was fictionalized by Hemingway as Bill Gorton in *The Sun Also Rises* (1926). During a visit to the Murphys at Antibes, Stewart conceived the idea of a sequel to *Mr. and Mrs. Haddock Abroad* and returned to Paris to work on it. However, he soon received his summons to Hollywood and completed the sequel, *Mr. and Mrs. Haddock in Paris, France* (1926), there. In this novel he abandoned carefree humor for a message: America would some day become "the great beautiful soul of the commercial scientific age."

On 24 July 1926 Stewart married Beatrice Ames in Montecito, California. He had also recently signed a contract with the *Chicago Tribune* syndicate to write a series of humorous articles. Stewart took his bride to France on their honeymoon to see many of his old friends, but in the fall of 1926 he and Hemingway had a disagreement over an unkind poem Hemingway had written about Dorothy Parker and read at a party at the MacLeishes' apartment. Stewart protested, and the nature of their friendship was changed forever. Though Stewart continued to admire Hemingway, the two men were never again more than casual friends.

The rest of Stewart's career centered largely around several plays and movies. He was a successful actor in Philip Barry's *Holiday* (1928); he wrote *Rebound* (1931), one of the ten best plays of 1929-1930; and he won an Oscar for the screenplay of *The Philadelphia Story* (1940). By the time he was divorced on 8 September 1938, Stewart had become a Communist sympathizer, to the surprise of all his wealthy, socially elite friends. At a political rally he met Ella Winter Steffens, widow of Lincoln Steffens, whom he married on 4 March 1939. After being blacklisted for his political activities, Stewart moved with his wife to London in 1951, and they continued to live there. Stewart was not one of the giants of expatriate literature, but he was a gifted humorist who could Americanize Dada in his "crazy humor," as Gilbert Seldes once urged him to do. Such humor

was his *metier*, and that talent was one reason for his success as a playwright and screenwriter.

—*Bertram D. Sarason and Ruth L. Strickland*

Other:

"Fragment IV," *transatlantic review*, 2 (July 1924): 116-120.

References:

Carlos Baker, *Ernest Hemingway A Life Story* (New York: Scribners, 1969), pp. 127-130, 148-152, 176-179;

John Dos Passos, *The Best Times* (New York: New American Library, 1966), pp. 157-179;

Bertram D. Sarason, *Hemingway and* The Sun *Set* (Washington, D.C.: Bruccoli Clark / NCR Microcard Editions, 1972).

ALLEN TATE
(19 November 1896-9 February 1979)

SELECTED BOOKS: *Stonewall Jackson The Good Soldier* (New York: Minton, Balch, 1928; London, Toronto, Melbourne & Sydney: Cassell, 1930);

Jefferson Davis: His Rise and Fall (New York: Minton, Balch, 1929);

Poems: 1928-1931 (New York & London: Scribners, 1932);

The Mediterranean and Other Poems (New York: Alcestis Press, 1936);

Reactionary Essays on Poetry and Ideas (New York: Scribners; London: Scribners Ltd., 1936);

The Fathers (New York: Putnam's, 1938; London: Eyre & Spottiswode, 1939);

Memoirs and Opinions 1926-1974 (Chicago: Swallow, 1975); republished as *Memories & Essays old and new 1926-1974* (Manchester, England: Carcanet Press, 1976).

John Orley Allen Tate was born in Clark County, Kentucky. After an uneven preparatory education, he entered Vanderbilt University in September 1918. During the course of his studies, he became a student of John Crowe Ransom, who remembers Tate in those days as a student who "was reading Baudelaire and Mallarme . . . [and] already quoting de Gourmont on the 'dissociation of ideas.' " Tate was the only undergraduate invited by

Donald Davidson to join the Fugitives and to work on their literary journal. Writing under the pseudonym Henry Feathertop, Tate published poems in the *Fugitive* that already showed the influence of his reading of French poets.

Moreover, Tate seems to have derived his attitude toward writing from the French. As Andrew Lytle says of him, "He, more than any other writer, has upheld this professionalism of letters. This attitude is obviously more French than English and is, I feel, unique in the English-speaking world, at least to the extent he carried and carries it." Tate's actual experiences in Paris influenced him little, however, for a number of reasons, including his solid grounding in classics (part of his undergraduate education), his passionate devotion to the beleaguered South of the twenties and thirties, and the odd historical fact that many expatriates were basically uninfluenced by their Parisian experiences. As Ernest Earnst remarks, the American expatriates of the twenties "tried so hard to shake off the dust of their native land; yet perhaps no group of expatriates was so thoroughly American."

Tate, his wife (the novelist Caroline Gordon), and his daughter first went to Paris on Tate's Guggenheim Fellowship in 1928-1929. This fellowship had been procured for Tate through the influence of Ford Madox Ford, to whom Gordon had become secretary in 1927 and whom she persuaded to move in with them at 27 Bank Street in New York City. Tate was at this time working as a free-lance

Allen Tate

Sylvia Beach Collection

writer and subeditor of the pulp magazine *Telling Tales*. Ford was appalled at what he perceived to be the Tates' miserable standard of living (though Tate himself was quite content with it) and wrote a letter to Henry Moe at the Guggenheim Foundation urging that Tate be given a fellowship to go abroad, which was duly awarded. The Tates sailed for England in September 1928, and, after spending some time there, they crossed the English Channel to France in November.

Thirty years later Tate remarked of his decision to go to Paris: "Our generation thought England a little tiresome, so Paris was the place—and that's where we went. It was a little like Brigham Young seeing the desert: This Is The Place. This was the place we were headed for—our spiritual home. I had come from a small provincial university, a university which nevertheless provided a world view which a classical education makes possible; I was now, at the end of the Twenties, suddenly plunged into the world of the expatriates." One may here perceive the youthful enthusiasm of a twenty-nine-year-old writer who had suddenly arrived at what, in his opinion, was the true home of literature. Shortly after their arrival in France, the Tates entered

wholeheartedly into the life-style of the expatriates. Tate was never entirely happy in Europe, however, for in a letter to Mark Van Doren on 6 November 1928 Tate was already wishing he were back in the United States.

A significant part of their life in Paris included renewing old acquaintances and making new ones. The old acquaintances were those of the "New York period," particularly John Peale Bishop and Ford, whom Tate describes as "one of the great men of the Twenties." Tate had met Bishop in New York in 1925, though he did not particularly note the encounter because of other preoccupations at the time. Their renewed acquaintance in Paris soon became a lasting friendship, however. The Bishops had rented a country house, Chateau du Petit Tressancourt, about fourteen miles northeast of Paris, in a village named Orgeval. Tate was a frequent visitor at Petit Tressancourt, where the circle often included such people as Robert Penn Warren, Ernest Hemingway, F. Scott Fitzgerald, and Archibald MacLeish. Tate was obviously pleased to be admitted to the group. It was at Orgeval that Tate and Warren were the first to hear the draft of "Many Thousands Gone," which Bishop read to them in December 1928. (Bishop would later confess to Tate that the sympathetic hearings often given him by the two were a major turning point in his life.)

Ford and Tate's friendship also continued in Paris. Tate was writing a great deal, and Tate's presence in Paris led Ford to renew his former practice of holding sonnet-writing contests on Saturday nights. Ford handed out the subjects, which had to be turned into sonnets within a specified time. Although Tate was the "major-domo on these occasions," it was Ford himself who was the final arbiter. The prize, as Tate recalled, "was always a stale cake provided by Ford, which he always won but gave to the runner-up." When Ford departed for the United States in January 1929, he left the Tates and poet Leonie Adams, who had been their constant companion in France, in rent-free possession of his apartment at 32, rue Vaugirard for six months. Ford also helped Tate from time to time by other financial assistance. Tate's respect for Ford remained genuine and constant even long after Ford died. As he would remark in 1960 of Ford, "He was the last great European man of letters. They don't produce them anymore—anywhere." Tate seems to have also earned the admiration and respect of his older mentor, for Ford paid the Tates several visits after their return to the States.

Tate also met other prominent novelists, including F. Scott Fitzgerald, to whom he was introduced by Bishop at a dinner party. Fitzgerald, upon their introduction, discomfited Tate by asking him, "Do you enjoy sleeping with your wife?" to which Tate responded, "It's none of your damn business." (Bishop later told Tate that Fitzgerald asked all men that question when he first met them.) Tate's acquaintance with Fitzgerald continued the whole of his stay in Paris, however, despite its startling and unorthodox beginning.

Tate also made the acquaintance of Hemingway, to whom he was introduced by Sylvia Beach at Shakespeare and Company. Tate considered Hemingway one of the better-read men he knew during that time and admired him, despite the fact that the novelist once severely reviled Ford to Tate's face. During the fall of 1929 Tate accompanied Hemingway on Sundays to the bicycle races at the Velodrome d'Hiver. He never went with Hemingway to a bullfight, however, a lapse he later regretted.

Tate's introduction to Gertrude Stein was a summons to come to tea on a Thursday, which was waiting for Tate and Gordon when they first arrived in Paris. The invitation was apparently arranged through Ford's good offices. Tate became a regular at Stein's literary conclaves, where she followed the custom of segregating the men and women, sending the women off to talk with her companion Alice B. Toklas while she talked to the men. In a 29 January 1929 letter to Van Doren Tate characterized Stein as "really a delightful woman," but, despite this initial burst of enthusiasm, he never grew genuinely fond of Stein, as he later admitted: "I didn't really like Miss Stein and I have never been able to read her works with either pleasure or edification."

Although Tate and his friends were all busy writing, it is clear that not all was work. The expatriates tended to stick together, and, as Tate himself remarks, the group might as well have been "in Harlem, or Minneapolis, because they all get together and don't see anybody else. It's like living in a small town." Tate often joined the expatriates in purely nonliterary activities. In addition to the times spent with the Fitzgeralds and Hemingway, Tate also passed many nights at the Cafe des Deux Magots with Ford.

Despite his friendships with such novelists as Hemingway, Ford, and Fitzgerald, Tate's only novel, *The Fathers* (1938), does not admit comparison to the works of his Parisian contemporaries and shows no signs of their influence. The works which immediately followed his first stay in Paris were two Southern Agrarian works—a biography of Jefferson Davis (1929) and

his essay on religion in *I'll Take My Stand* (1930). It was not until 1932 that the first group of poems of this period would appear as *Poems: 1928-1931*. The second group of poems which would seem likely to show Parisian influences did not appear until 1936 as *The Mediterranean and Other Poems*. In the same year he contributed an essay on economics to another Agrarian work, *Who Owns America?*, and published his first book of critical essays, *Reactionary Essays on Poetry and Ideas*. In all these works Tate shows the independence of his experience in Paris, his fondness for his original education at Vanderbilt, and his love for the South.

Tate had proposed for his Guggenheim Fellowship that he would compose a long poem of around one thousand lines. Tate worked assiduously at this poem after he and Gordon moved into Ford's apartment and even wrote Van Doren in January 1929 that he had completed 500 lines of it. This poem was so difficult for Tate, however, that it was apparently never finished. As he remarked to Van Doren: "I've got to write it, but no one I daresay will force me to publish it. There's hope of sanity in that." Much of Tate's time in Paris was also spent writing his biography of Jefferson Davis, a companion to his earlier biography of Stonewall Jackson (1928), indicating that Tate's mind was far from the Champs Elysees and the Rive Gauche. Tate finished his work on this book in July 1929, just as he and Gordon were vacating Ford's apartment.

Poems: 1928-1931 is further proof of the sturdiness of Tate's ties to the South. These poems reflect Tate's frustration and discontent with life in France, for, as Radcliffe Squires notes, "the poems he wrote in late 1928 and in 1929 do not rank with his best," a situation which cannot be entirely ascribed to Tate's youthfulness. "Mother and Son," one such poem, perhaps reaches back to his relationship with his own mother, but arises as well to some degree from the "cultural disorientation" he felt at the time. Despite the fact that the subject of the poem must be accepted for what it is, a poem literally about mothers and sons, one may not readily reject Squires's thesis that it is also indicative of "a dominant mood of cultural shock and homesickness."

During this time Tate seems to have wrestled with the problem of religion in his personal life. His religious background was an amalgam of Presbyterianism, Episcopalianism, and Roman Catholicism. Tate believed that art could not survive without religion; yet, he was seized by religious doubts that occasioned much perplexity and bemusement. As Squires remarks, "If he felt the need for religion he could not quite feel religion itself." It was from this confusion that arose Tate's poem "The Cross," which he had originally entitled "The Pit." Behind this poem lie associations expressing the imperfections of the present life and the longing for a more blissful, less confused state. This state is not really achievable, however, in a post-Crucifixion era, for the Crucifixion itself is indicative of the profound nature of the flaw in man's existence—had man been happy, it would all have been unnecessary. It would be years before he could reconcile his life to his religion.

The time in France was ended with a stay in Brittany, where the Tates moved after leaving Ford's apartment and from whence they sailed for New York on 1 January 1930. Whatever unpleasantness Tate felt at his experience in France was deepened by his mother's death in July 1929, of which he learned shortly after arriving in Brittany. Once back in the United States, however, Tate readily resumed his former life, plunging enthusiastically into the Agrarian movement once more.

In 1932 Gordon was the recipient of a Guggenheim Fellowship, and the Tates returned to France in July. Instead of going to Paris, the Tates moved to Villa Les Hortensias at Cap Brun, a domicile Ford had found them quite near his own. Tate's chief acquaintances during this period continued to be the Fords and the Bishops. Though the Bishops continued to live in Orgeval, they came in September to visit the Tates, when they all went to Monte Carlo.

Despite feelings of frustration and boredom, Tate continued to work on his biography of Robert E. Lee, which was supposed to be in a series with his two earlier works on Confederate figures. This book was never finished. It reflects the continuation, between his trips to France, of his activities in the Agrarian movement. The Agrarians' defense of the South had risen to a fever pitch between 1929 and 1932, and Tate had made significant contributions to the movement during that time and had written many of his better early poems under its influence. Some of these poems, such as "Sonnets of the Blood," finished in July 1931, strongly evoke his Southern background. It was natural, therefore, that his literary activities continue in this vein on his return to France.

In 1932, while living at Cap Brun, Tate composed "The Mediterranean," one of his better early poems and one of the extraordinary literary documents of modern poetry. The poem was occasioned by a sumptuous picnic given for Ford at Cassis in 1932. During the picnic Ford remarked that the magnificent cove where it was held must have resembled those at which Aeneas and his band stopped to eat. After rereading the *Aeneid*, Tate began to compose his poem in September. Despite the obvious connection between France and the piece's composition, Squires points out that "the poem comes back—like a mind coming back from immediate pleasure to a thought that worries it—to the center of Tate's social beliefs, his uneasy Agrarianism." The poem is more a reflection of Tate's heritage and his grounding in classics than it is of any French influence. As Tate contemplated the poem, he even changed the title to better reflect the poem's emotional and intellectual underpinnings: it had originally been entitled "Picnic at Cassis," a title Tate apparently found too narrow. He would later transfer his inspiration to the United States in a companion piece called "Aeneas at Washington," thus closing the circle.

The Tates, restless and financially insecure, moved to Paris late in 1932, primarily because Tate felt that he might get more work done in the capital city, where he would at least have easy access to books. (He had had to go to Toulon to purchase his *Aeneid*.) Matters did not improve, however, and the Tates, now disillusioned, left France in February 1933. Once back in the United States, Tate resumed his former activities and wrote Bishop in April that now that he had taken up life at his farm, Benfolly, Europe was "very far away, remote, and unattainable . . . all the emotions of this country clicked back into place, and life now goes on."

Tate's experiences in Paris are basically interludes in a literary career that was devoted largely to his native South. During the years he was in France, the South was under particularly bitter attack from the North as an area backward in industrial development and benighted intellectually. Such acerbic attacks, especially those by H. L. Mencken, only aroused the South to action, and at that point in his career Tate felt more inclined to devote his energies to the defense of his own section of the country than to pursue literary fashions. Also, Paris in the late twenties was losing some of its vitality and energy as a home for expatriates; hence, Tate did not experience the expatriate movement in its full vigor, and its influence on him was thus further reduced. Finally, Tate, having genuinely liked the United States, found it difficult to turn on his native country, for to have done so would have been to have attacked implicitly the South as well. He therefore concentrated on themes that rose above the petty criticisms of his native land. Neither is it certain that he was entirely in agreement with the theory of American decline held by many expatriates. Despite his initial enthusiasm and eagerness for the expatriate movement, he came away from France disenchanted. In this sense Edmund Wilson was prescient when he wrote to Tate in 1928, "It is our high destiny to step in and speak the true prophetic words to declining Europe."

Tate was influenced by Europe in general as opposed to being overly influenced by one particular section of it or one particular experience in it. In the words of Pier Francesco Listri, translated by Radcliffe Squires, Tate's "cultural world is double-stitched. One thread secures him to Europe, the other to the defeated South, so that his poetic imagination redounds with an exquisite metaphysics blended with generals, region, and the Confederate flag. Within this farrago, however, we can discern a great intellectual (after the model of Eliot who for a time constituted his god on earth), encumbered with a weighty tradition, fixed in his illustrious position of an authentic conservative, and favored (O rare occurrence) with an inexhaustible sense of irony." Tate has achieved such stature precisely because he was vigorous and independent in his pursuit of his poetry. —*Everett C. Wilkie, Jr.*

Other:

I'll Take My Stand: The South and The Agrarian Tradition By Twelve Southerners, by Tate and others (New York & London: Harper, 1930);

Who Owns America? A New Declaration of Independence (Boston & New York: Houghton Mifflin, 1936);

John Peale Bishop, *The Collected Poems*, edited with an introduction by Tate (New York: Scribners, 1948);

"Random Thoughts on the 1920's," *Minnesota Review*, 1 (Fall 1960): 46-56.

References:

Ferman Bishop, *Allen Tate* (New York: Twayne, 1967);

Lillian Feder, "Allen Tate's Use of Classical Literature," *Centennial Review of Arts & Science*, 4 (Winter 1960): 89-114;

R. K. Meiners, "The Art of Allen Tate: A Reading of 'The Mediterranean,'" *University of Kansas City Review*, 27 (December 1960): 155-159;

Meiners, *The Last Alternatives: A Study of the Works of Allen Tate* (Denver: Swallow Press, 1963);

Radcliffe Squires, *Allen Tate A Literary Biography* (New York: Pegasus, 1971).

RICHARD THOMA
(17 June 1902-   )

BOOKS: *Green Chaos* (Fontenay-aux-Roses, Seine, France: New Review Press, 1931);
The Promised Land (Paris, 1935?);
Tragedy in Blue (Paris: Obelisk Press, 1936);
August 18, 1944 (Los Angeles, 1944?);
Green Death (Los Angeles, 1945);
The Book of Lambda (Newington, Conn., 1952?).

Although little is known about Richard Thoma's early life, he was fairly well-known in Paris as a poet and editor by the time Peter Neagoe included an essay by Thoma in *Americans Abroad An Anthology* in 1932. In 1930 Thoma, Samuel Putnam, and Harold J. Salemson had signed "Direction," a manifesto responding to *transition* magazine editor Eugene Jolas's "Revolution of the Word Proclamation," which called for a radical restructuring of the written word. For the next two years, as an associate editor of Putnam's *New Review*, he was involved in much of the *New Review*'s warfare against Edward Titus's conservative *This Quarter* on the one hand, and Jolas's avant-garde *transition* on the other. Thoma's poems are rather formal in style, yet some are relentlessly homosexual in subject. His obscurity is in part due to the unavailability of his books, all of which were published in limited editions.

Poems included in Thoma's first book, *Green Chaos*, published in an edition of 100 signed copies by the New Review Press on 10 November 1931, had appeared previously in *Morada*, *Blues*, *Pagany*, and the *New Review*; he had also contributed to *Tambour*, *This Quarter*, and *transition*. Most of the poems in *Green Chaos* are addressed to specific acquaintances: for example, "Afric Blues" is to Ezra Pound and "Tropic Song" to Aldous Huxley. "To a Suicide" is Thoma's response to Harry Crosby's death: "Was it worth the destruction of a known caress?" The book ends with a long poem, "Fin du Monde," dedicated to Thoma's mentor, Jean Cocteau:

I have set women aside and apart forever—
men still erect what no woman can sunder.
The cold women shall die and men shall burn
   together,
brightly in the night with a freed green fever

The colors blue and green recur throughout Thoma's writing. In his essay "Consideration of Mayo," published in *Americans Abroad*, he talks of blue and green as "the colours of tragedy, magic, and poetry." "Fin du Monde" ends: "Across the blue melody / The green chaos of the sailors forms me." "Poem for Lillian" begins: "I will write you a pale-green poem set in Morocco, / full of depraved women and moonlight and oh! splendour!"

At the time Neagoe's anthology was compiled, Thoma was already working on his "evocation of the middle ages, their splendor, their abomination, and their God." *Tragedy in Blue* was published in May 1936 by the Obelisk Press as the second volume in the Siana Series, inaugurated by Henry Miller and Anais Nin. In a 17 January 1979 letter Miller remembers knowing Thoma slightly and adds that he and Thoma were interested in Gilles de Rais, a French nobleman who fought with Joan of Arc. *Tragedy in Blue* details the moral deterioration of Gilles de Rais following the martyrdom of Joan of Arc. Gilles, who allies his forces with the soldier-maiden Jehanne, falls in love with both Jehanne and her faith. However, Gilles's vanity leads him to use Jehanne's martyrdom to test God's will, so that when Jehanne is burned at the stake, Gilles loses his faith:

> No thought of Jehanne now. No more white fires. No celestial sinning. No love. No mystic fires. Instead, the dangers of poetry, the daemon of the fallen morning, the songs of loneliness by two, the dark crimes of Tiffauges.

His disillusionment first turns to homosexual depravity: "Now there were only daemons to pursue. They were present and vivid and had mocking eyes and short guttural cries that promised quick experienced hands ready to practise many kinds of love." He stages fantastic stage productions, the last of which reenacts the life of Jehanne, with Gilles playing himself; the play successfully outrages King Charles. At this point Gilles, now bankrupt, turns to alchemy and actively solicits the aid of Satan: he takes a fancy to young boys, possessing them once, then disposing of them. Meanwhile he falls in love with a young Italian mystic and conjurer named Francesco Prelati: "They never erred, never mistook, never misunderstood. They went very fast. They went, as fast as the dead." Together Gilles and

Francesco commit more atrocities. Eventually, though, Gilles is arrested by the Bishop of Nantes, loses his vanity, and is rewarded by a vision of Jehanne just as Prelati attempts to conjure up Satan; Gilles regains his faith, dismisses Prelati, and makes a full confession. Oddly enough, the reader first learns that Gilles has a wife and daughter when they come to his execution. The book touches on the elusive nature of faith—even Satan never appears, though Gilles and Francesco Prelati do everything in their power to enlist his aid.

While in Paris Thoma also earned money by translating. Harry and Caresse Crosby hired him to do the translation for their Black Sun Press edition of *47 Unpublished Letters from Marcel Proust* (1930), but, according to Hugh Ford, Thoma quit before finishing the project. He also did some of the translations for Samuel Putnam's anthology, *The European Caravan* (1931), and in 1932 when Edward Titus turned over the last issue of *This Quarter* to Andre Breton and the Surrealists, Thoma and Samuel Beckett were hired to translate the contributions. Other of his translations of poetry and fiction appeared in *Life and Letters*, *Sewanee Review*, and *transition*.

Thoma had one other book of poetry privately printed in Paris and two more in America. *The Promised Land* (1935?) appeared in an edition of 100 copies, with a foreword by Stuart Gilbert and drawings by Mayo. Reading Thoma's later books, one finds lines or stanzas revised from earlier poems, so that *The Book of Lambda* (1952?) incorporates much of the material in *Green Chaos* and *The Promised Land*; *Green Death* (1945) also includes bits of earlier material.

Henry Miller's friend Lawrence Clark Powell recalls that Richard Thoma was living in Beverly Glen, California, in the early forties and that Thoma was working, and frustrated, as an accountant with a manufacturing or office supply firm in Los Angeles. Miller stayed for a while in an apartment above the garage of the house Thoma rented in Beverly Glen. In August 1944, when Thoma considered writing a book about Miller, he wrote a long letter to Miller, and later thought well enough of it to publish it himself. Perhaps in this letter he speaks best for himself:

> One of the things that drove me away from Paris was people in the cafes coming up to me whom they knew to be an intimate of Cocteau and wanting to argue about this or that phase of the poet's life, or propound, or expound, or whatever the hell it is. After all there are rocks. And either they shelter, or they crush. One

doesn't argue about rocks. I am no intellectual, no clerk, no peterman. Please explain this to anyone who makes odd noises about me. Or else don't explain it! To hell with explanations. Sapristi! Quoi?

—*James Hejna*

Other:

"Elagabalus," in *Americana Esoterica* (New York: Macy-Massius, 1927);

"Consideration of Mayo," in *Americans Abroad An Anthology*, ed. Peter Neagoe (The Hague: Servire, 1932), pp. 424-427.

References:

Hugh Ford, *Published in Paris American and British Writers, Printers, and Publishers in Paris, 1920-1939* (New York: Macmillan, 1975), pp. 166, 213, 318-321;

Jay Martin, *Always Merry and Bright The Life of Henry Miller* (Santa Barbara, Cal.: Capra, 1978), pp. 315, 397-398;

Samuel Putnam, *Paris Was Our Mistress Memoirs of a Lost & Found Generation* (New York: Viking, 1947), pp. 227-229.

JOHN THOMAS
(1900-12 March 1932)

BOOK: *Dry Martini* (New York: Doran, 1926; reprinted, Carbondale & Edwardsville: Southern Illinois University Press, 1974—adds an afterword by Morrill Cody).

John A. M. Thomas went to Paris to write a novel, but he did not ally himself with the writers and intellectuals of Montparnasse. Instead he became an habitue of the Right Bank and a regular at the Ritz Hotel bar on the rue Cambon. In Thomas's novel, *Dry Martini* (1926), Willoughby Quimby's favorite bar, the Garden of Allah, is based upon the Ritz Bar. Thomas could afford to indulge his taste for what Morrill Cody calls "the romantic and decadent remains of the Edwardian era which he found on the Right Bank."

The son of socially prominent New Yorkers, Dr. and Mrs. Allen M. Thomas, he graduated from Yale University in 1922. At Yale, he was chairman of the *Yale Literary Magazine* and won the Metcalf Prize

for a dramatic essay. After graduation, he went to Paris to study at the Sorbonne and to write. Unlike many other young American writers in Paris, he did not have to work to support himself, and he was sufficiently well-off to afford the prices in the expensive Right Bank bars where he fraternized with successful writers such as F. Scott Fitzgerald, Louis Bromfield, and later Ernest Hemingway.

Dry Martini is an honest attempt to depict American life on both sides of the Seine, despite its decidedly Right Bank point of view. Thomas's disdain for the Left Bank is apparent in a chapter called "La Vie de Boheme," where one of his characters comments that the only virtue of the typical Left Bank artist is that he lacks false pride: "Not one of them is at all reticent about the fact that he is dead broke, that he gets drunk every night, that he would be glad to have you pay for his drink or his dinner, that he would be even more delighted to borrow some money from you. Those things are corner-stones of Anglo-Saxon Bohemia in Paris."

The expatriates of Thomas's novel are Edwardian decadents, rather than the rebellious intellectuals of the twenties. Willoughby Quimby, a wealthy, middle-aged man-about-town, tries to reform in order to set an example for his twenty-year-old daughter Elizabeth, who arrives unexpectedly to live with him. Elizabeth is intent upon adventure, however, and her father's efforts to protect her from the influences of his own friends are ineffectual. She is seduced by the unprincipled roue, Conway Cross, but is rescued by another of Willoughby's drinking companions, Freddy Fletcher. Meanwhile, Willoughby has decided that marriage would be a pleasant alternative to the endless round of bars his life has become, but after he has been spurned by his daughter's best friend, the great love of his youth, and his ex-wife, he returns to his old routine. In a time of pervasive experimentation with narrative technique, the omniscient narrator of *Dry Martini* seems closer to Thackeray's satiric "puppet master" than to the more limited, deeply ironic points of view in the novels of Thomas's contemporaries. When *Dry Martini* was published in 1926, reviews were mixed. Reviewers called it "light," "amusing," "sophisticated," and "a promising debut with unpromising material." But despite its unenthusiastic reception it was popular enough to be made into a movie, starring Mary Astor as Elizabeth, which opened in New York in November 1928.

Thomas returned to New York in 1925 and married Josephine Scott in April of that year. After an extended honeymoon in Europe, they settled in New York. They were divorced in 1930. For several years before his death in 1932, Thomas did research in New York on a book which, according to Morrill Cody, was intended to describe the "history of 58th Street from the East River to the Hudson." But, says Cody, Thomas "only got as far as Dan Moriarty's place at 216 East 58th and thereafter made it his drinking headquarters." In March 1932, Thomas died of acute chronic alcoholism. —*Karen L. Rood*

JAMES THURBER
(8 December 1894-2 November 1961)

SELECTED BOOKS: *Is Sex Necessary? Or Why You Feel the Way You Do*, by Thurber and E. B. White (New York & London: Harper, 1929; London: Heinemann, 1930);

The Seal in the Bedroom & Other Predicaments (New York & London: Harper, 1932; London: Hamilton, 1951);

My Life and Hard Times (New York & London: Harper, 1933; London: Harper, 1934);

The Middle-Aged Man on the Flying Trapeze (New York & London: Harper, 1935; London: Hamilton, 1935);

Let Your Mind Alone! And Other More or Less Inspirational Pieces (New York & London: Harper, 1937; London: Hamilton, 1937);

The Male Animal, by Thurber and Elliott Nugent (New York: Random House, 1940);

My World—And Welcome To It (New York: Harcourt, Brace, 1942; London: Hamilton, 1942);

Fables for Our Time and Famous Poems (New York & London: Harper, 1940; London: Hamilton, 1940);

The Thurber Carnival (New York & London: Harper, 1945; London: Hamilton, 1945);

The Beast in Me and Other Animals (New York: Harcourt, Brace, 1948; London: Hamilton, 1949);

Thurber Country (New York: Simon & Schuster, 1953; London: Hamilton, 1953);

Further Fables for Our Time (New York: Simon & Schuster, 1956; London: Hamilton, 1956);

Alarms and Diversions (London: Hamilton, 1957; New York: Harper, 1957);

The Years With Ross (Boston & Toronto: Atlantic Monthly Press / Little, Brown, 1959);

Lanterns & Lances (New York: Harper, 1961; London: Hamilton, 1961);

Credos and Curios (London: Hamilton, 1962; New York & Evanston: Harper & Row, 1962);

A Thurber Carnival (New York, Hollywood, London & Toronto: French, 1962).

France does not figure prominently as a subject in James Thurber's works. Yet his three longest European sojourns—from November 1918 to March 1920, from May 1925 to May 1926, and from May 1937 to August 1938—proved influential to his development as a writer. His first Parisian stay dislodged some of his early provincial views; his second unleashed the comic voice that attained full maturity during the *New Yorker* years. All three visits to the Continent provided Thurber with norms against which to measure the American attitudes and manners examined in his best essays, stories, and drawings.

James Grover Thurber was the second of three sons born to Mary Fisher Thurber and Charles L. Thurber in Columbus, Ohio. Although he was blinded in the left eye by a childhood accident, Thurber was an excellent, but introverted, public school student. He dropped out of Ohio State University after the 1913-1914 school year, but in the fall of 1915 he reentered the university, where, encouraged by his friend Elliott Nugent, he plunged into campus life as a writer for the university newspaper, the humor magazine, and the music and drama clubs. He left Ohio State without a degree in June 1918.

From November 1918 until March 1920 Thurber served as a code clerk for the state department in Paris. His assignment to France rather than to Switzerland occurred, he later claimed, because an urgent request for code books was mistranslated as an appeal for code clerks. His letters of the period to Nugent cast Thurber as the American innocent at once enticed and offended by the mores of postwar Paris; his letters to his family frequently exhibit a streak of Babbitt-like chauvinism. Yet in such retrospective examinations of his 1918-1920 experiences as "The Hiding Generation" (1936), "An Afternoon in Paris" (1937), "Exhibit X" (1948), and "The First Time I Saw Paris" (1957), Thurber emphasizes the wonderful, liberating chaos enjoyed by Parisians and Americans alike following the Armistice.

Returning to Ohio in the spring of 1920, Thurber became a reporter for the *Columbus Evening Dispatch*. He married Althea Adams in 1922 and supplemented his newspaperman's income by writing and directing musical comedies for the Ohio State University drama club. In 1924 he left the *Dispatch* to attempt a career as a free-lance writer in Jay, New York. After a few unproductive months the Thurbers returned to Columbus, where he worked primarily as a publicity agent for several local business and civic organizations.

In May 1925 Thurber and his wife embarked for

France. Landing in Normandy, they rented a room in a farmhouse, where Thurber worked on a novel. He abandoned the project after 5,000 words but later described, in "Remembrance of Things Past" (1936), certain of his adventures in Normandy. Moving to the French capital in September, Thurber got a job as a rewrite man for the Paris *Tribune* (the European edition of the *Chicago Tribune*). City editor David Darrah hired him over dozens of other applicants,

James Thurber

Thurber remembered in *The Years With Ross* (1959), because he introduced himself not as a poet, a painter, or a novelist but instead as a newspaperman with five years of experience.

Among Thurber's associates on the *Tribune* were aspiring writers William L. Shirer, Eugene Jolas, Elliot Paul, and Virgil Geddes. From a few lines of cable delivered each evening, the *Tribune* staffers were expected to produce a respectable newspaper; prodigious memories and fertile imaginations seemed to be their primary resources for the job. Thurber, for example, once transformed a six-word dispatch announcing the death of baseball player Christy Mathewson into an amazingly accurate and perceptive obituary. On other occasions he created vivid expansions upon the skeletal news of sporting events and air disasters, and according to Shirer he was a genius at "reporting"

President Coolidge's speeches, with perfect imitations of his cliched sentiments and hackneyed diction.

During his stay in Paris Thurber seems not to have met such writers as Ernest Hemingway, John Dos Passos, F. Scott Fitzgerald, or Gertrude Stein, although he did know Robert Coates. If Thurber was not an intimate of the better-known Left Bank writers, he was quite familiar with their work, discussing it for hours at a time with the other *Tribune* staffers, Shirer says. Thurber himself managed during 1925-1926 to produce eight freelance articles, the majority of which came out in Sunday supplements of the New York *World*, the *New York Herald Tribune*, or the *Kansas City Star*. The most significant of these publications was "A Sock on the Jaw—French Style," which appeared in *Harper's Magazine* for February 1926 and which, besides netting the writer the substantial sum of $90, introduced themes and techniques later refined in Thurber's *New Yorker* essays. A genuinely funny piece, "A Sock on the Jaw—French Style" contrasts French and American modes of disputation and celebrates the elaborate chaos resulting from the French method.

In December 1925 Thurber was sent to Nice to serve as coeditor of the *Tribune*'s Riviera edition. According to Shirer, Thurber's handling of the news for the Riviera *Tribune* was even more fantastic than it had been for the Paris edition. Thurber's account of the Nice experience in "Memoirs of a Drudge" (1942) confirms Shirer's assessment. Whether he was analyzing the 1926 Helen Wills-Suzanne Lenglen tennis match, conducting interviews with Isadora Duncan and Rudolph Valentino, or creating bogus social notes for Althea Thurber, his social editor, Thurber let his imagination soar. He seemed influenced in his writing by the *bagarre*, the pervasive disorder and hilarious uproar which he defined in "La Grande Ville de Plaisir" (1938) as the governing spirit of the city itself. Yet despite the creative opportunities afforded by Paris and Nice and the considerable encouragement provided by "A Sock on the Jaw—French Style," Thurber still regarded himself, Shirer declares, as a failed writer or, at best, as a thirty-one-year-old novice. He therefore determined in May 1926 to leave France and to pursue his desired career in New York.

Thurber arrived in New York in June 1926 and persistently submitted manuscripts to prospective publishers, among them a new magazine named the *New Yorker*. After showering him with rejection slips, the magazine finally accepted three of his pieces, and in February 1927 Harold Ross hired

Thurber as a *New Yorker* editor, shortly thereafter demoting him to the more congenial position of staff writer. Thurber's office mate at the magazine was E. B. White, who greatly influenced the new staffer's prose style and enthusiastically promoted his drawings. At White's insistence, Thurber illustrations appeared in their coauthored book, *Is Sex Necessary?* (1929).

Between 1927 and 1935 Thurber became one of the most prolific and best known of the *New Yorker* writers. Among the volumes published during this period were the first of Thurber's books composed entirely of drawings, *The Seal in the Bedroom & Other Predicaments* (1932); his reminiscences of Columbus, *My Life and Hard Times* (1933), for which Hemingway wrote a dust-jacket blurb reading, "Even when Thurber was writing under the name of Alice B. Toklas, we knew he had it in him if he could only get it out"; and the generally darker-toned miscellany, *The Middle-Aged Man on the Flying Trapeze* (1935). These three volumes illustrated the various facets of Thurber's talent and established several of his most important subjects: the perpetual battle between dominant, unimaginative women and neurotic, fantasy-embracing men; the constant conflict between man and machinery; the general superiority, in character and good sense, of animals over humans; the bewildering but liberating powers of chaos, idiosyncrasy, and imagination.

These works reflected currents in Thurber's personal life during this period. On 7 October 1931 Althea Thurber bore him a daughter, Rosemary, but in May 1935 their always difficult marriage ended in divorce. The following month Thurber married a former editor of slick magazines, Helen Wismer, whom he later labeled his "seeing eye wife." Shortly after his marriage to Helen Thurber, Thurber resigned his full-time staff position at the *New Yorker*, although he remained a regular contributor to the magazine for many years.

Between May 1937 and August 1938 Thurber made his last extended visit to the Continent. The impetus for the trip was a one-man show of his drawings at the Storran Gallery in London, but his itinerary also included stays in Scotland, Italy, Normandy, the Riviera, and Paris. June 1937 found the Thurbers enjoying cafe society with Hemingway, Vincent Sheean, Janet Flanner, Aristide and Mary Mian, Dorothy Parker, and Lillian Hellman. Much of the conversation of those evenings focused on the Spanish Civil War, in which many American writers and artists had become actively involved on the Loyalist side; opposing his

friends' political fervor, Thurber argued that writers should simply write and not allow themselves to be caught up in war and factionalism.

In early 1938 the Thurbers settled for several months at the Villa Tamisier on the Riviera, where he wrote the majority of the eight travel pieces, most with French subjects, later collected in *My World— And Welcome To It* (1942). Among these essays are the reminiscences of his earlier stays in Paris and Nice—"An Afternoon in Paris" and "La Grande Ville de Plaisir"; celebrations of the chaos implicit in French politics and in French interpretations of other cultures—"You Know How the French Are" (1937), "La Fleur des Guides Francais" (1938), and "There's No Place Like Home" (1937); a straightforward travel account—"Journey to the Pyrenees" (1942); and two pieces concerning the vagaries of European drivers—"After Cato, What?" (1938) and "A Ride With Olympy" (1938). Olympy and Maria Sementzoff, who were respectively gardener-chauffeur and housekeeper-cook at the Villa Tamisier, also appear as central figures in "Joyeux Noel, Mr. Durning" (1949) and "The Girls in the Closet" (1951), works collected in *Thurber Country* (1953). Another essay, probably written before Thurber's 1937 departure for the Continent and featured in *Let Your Mind Alone!* (1937), is "Wild Bird Hickok and His Friends," a riotous account of the French treatment of American frontier heroes. The 1937-1938 European visit clearly provided Thurber with materials important to his examinations of the human comedy, whether French or American.

Upon his return to the United States, Thurber, in collaboration with his former Ohio State classmate Elliott Nugent, began work on *The Male Animal* (1940). During the writing of the play he suffered serious visual problems. He underwent several difficult eye operations during 1940 and 1941, but his impaired vision progressively diminished to total blindness by the end of the decade. Yet despite his shaken health, Thurber continued to produce works of high quality. *My World—And Welcome To It* contained several acknowledged masterpieces, and *The Thurber Carnival* (1945) became his greatest single artistic and financial success.

Thurber's interest in fables and fairy tales, reflected by his production of seven such volumes, began with the onset of his blindness, as did the increased emphasis upon word-game comedy, conversation pieces, and communications problems which dominated *The Beast in Me and Other Animals* (1948) and *Thurber Country*. Only *The Years With Ross* and the montage play *A Thurber*

Carnival (1962), both drawing upon earlier experiences and materials, broke the pattern of ever-increasing pessimism which characterized such works of the final period as *Further Fables for Our Time* (1956) and *Lanterns & Lances* (1961). In these bitter volumes, chaos—whether social, political, cultural, or linguistic—is neither funny nor liberating but is instead the mark of a terrible decline in the modern world. Even in the last two stories to employ Paris settings, "Brother Endicott" (1962) and "The Other Room" (1962), both published posthumously and collected in *Credos and Curios* (1962), the tone is muted and the vision quite grim. After attending a party for Noel Coward, Thurber, on 4 October 1961, suffered a massive stroke; he lay hospitalized in a state of semiconsciousness until 2 November 1961, when he died of pneumonia.

The bulk of Thurber's literary achievements neither occurred in France nor treated French subjects. Yet his three extended stays in Paris and on the Riviera clearly influenced his development as a writer. His experiences both as a code clerk and as a *Tribune* reporter gave him a broader perspective on life than Columbus, Ohio, could provide, and in Paris and Nice he was forced to compare his talents to those of some of the finest writers of his generation. If his actual writing accomplishments during 1925-1926 were slight, they did introduce the comic voice that was fully developed during the *New Yorker* years. Thurber's 1937-1938 return to the Continent initiated the steady trickle of French pieces that continued to appear until his death. Implicit in these essays and stories are contrasts between the cultures of France and America. Yet in the best of these pieces, national differences are overshadowed by international similarities. The writer's most memorable French figures, like their American counterparts, confront and embrace chaos, idiosyncrasy, and fantasy, thus revealing the universality of the human comedy as Thurber perceived it. —*Judith S. Baughman*

References:

Burton Bernstein, *Thurber* (New York: Dodd, Mead, 1975);

Edwin T. Bowden, *James Thurber: A Bibliography* (Columbus: Ohio State University Press, 1968);

Charles S. Holmes, *The Clocks of Columbus: The Literary Career of James Thurber* (New York: Atheneum, 1972);

William L. Shirer, *20th Century Journey A Memoir of a Life and the Times The Start 1904-1930* (New York: Simon & Schuster, 1976).

EDWARD WILLIAM TITUS
(1870-27 January 1952)

A Polish-born American citizen who spent his childhood in New Orleans, Edward William Titus had lived in Paris with his wife and children for a brief time before World War I. In 1918 he returned and rented a small apartment on the rue Delambre in Montparnasse, close to the Cafe du Dome. He was separated from his wife, Helena Rubinstein, whose profits from her cosmetics business allowed him to occupy himself as a litterateur and bibliophile. In 1924 he set up a bookshop at 4, rue Delambre, in the rooms below his apartment. Enigmatically naming the shop At the Sign of the Black Manikin, he stocked it with current works from American and English publishers, limited editions of the classics, and rare books. The shop was not profitable, and, as with all of Titus's literary efforts, it had to be subsidized by his wife. To him the shop was a hobby rather than a business; moreover, though it was highly regarded, the bookshop's esoteric atmosphere, as part gallery and part rare book room, kept it from becoming the gathering place for writers Titus had planned. In early 1926, when almost the entire stock of current books had been sold, Titus became a publisher, arranging for his printing to be done at the Crete Printery at 24, rue Delambre.

Between mid-1926 and spring 1932, the Black Manikin Press produced twenty-five books. Most were published in limited editions, and some included introductions by writers of the caliber of Ernest Hemingway and Thomas Mann while others were illustrated by artists of the stature of Jean Cocteau. During his first year as a publisher, Titus brought out three books by American expatriates. The first was *Rococo* by Keatsian poet and recluse Ralph Cheever Dunning, whose work was admired by both Titus and Ezra Pound. In 1929 Titus published a second collection of Dunning's verse, *Windfalls*. These two volumes caused a considerable critical stir, which, as Sisley Huddleston recalls, "did a great deal to make Ralph Cheever Dunning known." The second book to bear the Black Manikin imprint was Ludwig Lewisohn's *The Case of Mr. Crump* (1926). Published in a deluxe edition of 500 copies, the book was so popular that Titus republished it, adding a preface by Thomas Mann, in 1931. In that same year he published another book by Lewisohn, *The Romantic*. Titus's final publication in 1926 was *The Frog*, a play by Virgil Geddes, then financial editor for the European edition of the *Chicago Tribune* (the Paris *Tribune*).

The seven Black Manikin books for 1927 were

Edward W. Titus

largely undistinguished with the exception of Arthur Schnitzler's *Couples (Der Reigen)*, translated by Titus and Lily Wolfe, and Manuel Komroff's *The Voice of Fire*. Komroff's anticlerical tale was beautifully illustrated by Polish artist Polia Chentoff, who later drew the frontispiece portrait for Dunning's *Windfalls*. The three Black Manikin offerings for 1928 included Mary Butts's *Imaginary Letters*, with copperplate engravings made from drawings by Jean Cocteau. Also published in 1928 was William Van Wyck's *Some Gentlemen of the Renaissance*, which was printed in an outsized format by masterprinter Maurice Darentiere in Dijon and consisted of four free-verse sketches of Giotto, Michelangelo, Galileo, and Richelieu. Titus had also announced his plans to publish Djuna Barnes's *Ladies Almanack* in 1928, but a disagreement over finances caused him to withdraw his support for the book.

In 1929 Titus published D. H. Lawrence's *Lady Chatterley's Lover*, a reprint of the original 1928 edition published in Florence by Giuseppe Orioli, to which was added a new introduction by Lawrence. Titus knew that he was risking legal difficulties by publishing the book, and his edition does not bear the imprint of the Black Manikin Press. The first printing of 3,000 copies sold out quickly and was followed by two more printings of 3,000 and 5,000 copies respectively. The profits made on *Lady Chatterley's Lover* helped to offset the losses on less popular Black Manikin books. *The Legend of Ermengarde*, ostensibly by the fourteenth-century troubadour Uc Saine (Hugh Saxon) and translated into modern verse by Homer Rigaut, was also published in 1929. The poem was actually the work of American poet Ramon Guthrie.

The following year Titus published the English translation of *Kiki's Memoirs* by Montparnasse artists' model Alice Prin, better known as Kiki. For Titus she expanded her original memoir published in French in 1928 by Parisian Henri Broca. Titus's edition contains an introduction by Ernest Hemingway, who had read the book in French and who wrote that it was untranslatable. The translator, Samuel Putnam, said in his note that all translations were miracles and that although he felt he had been somewhat successful with Kiki's book, Hemingway might be right. Titus added his own note, suggesting that both men were merely "decanting poppycock." Besides the two books by Lewisohn published in 1931, the Black Manikin Press offerings for the year included *No Man's Meat* by Canadian novelist Morley Callaghan. The final book to appear under the Black Manikin imprint was Anais Nin's first book, *D. H. Lawrence An Unprofessional Study*, published in the spring of 1932. Nin's work became one of the most sought-after Black Manikin books.

Titus's marriage to Helena Rubinstein had been disintegrating even before his arrival in Paris. In 1929 affairs reached a crisis because of Rubinstein's preoccupation with the growth of her cosmetics empire and her suspicions about Titus's infidelity. In a last attempt at reconciliation, Titus had proposed the construction of a set of studio apartments where they could live surrounded by artists, and below it a "little American theater" where new plays could be performed. The site chosen was 216, boulevard Raspail in the heart of the Left Bank district. The apartments were never finished, though some plays were performed there. As Rubinstein recalls: "This is what we did. After the scripts had been read, each of the plays was produced in English, French and Italian . . . we enjoyed many delightful evenings there—until, unfortunately, the police intervened. They alleged that some of the plays were too outspoken and that the playwrights . . . were using our private stage to attack the government! The theatre was closed by order of the

Prefecture." When the project collapsed, the separation between Titus and Rubinstein became permanent.

In the spring of 1929 Titus decided to take over the defunct little magazine *This Quarter*. Between spring 1925 and spring 1927, Ethel Moorhead and Ernest Walsh had produced three issues of the magazine, but after Walsh's death in 1926, the magazine suspended publication. In early 1929 Titus assumed both ownership and editorship. As he said in his first editorial for *This Quarter* (July-August-September 1929), he did so from a desire to perpetuate the name of a fine and "courageous" magazine and from an admiration for Ethel Moorhead, who, in the spring 1927 issue of *This Quarter*, had strongly criticized Ezra Pound for callously ignoring Walsh's death, despite Walsh's profound esteem for Pound. More importantly he had a sense that the magazine, regardless of its quality, had lacked editorial direction. "To tell the truth," Titus wrote, "although we have been watching *This Quarter* from its inception under the courageous editorship of our predecessors, we were never quite sure whither its footsteps led." While Titus admitted that greater editorial direction was not essential, he strongly implied that it would be worthwhile; and his lengthy editorials for *This Quarter* and his own regular feature, "The Flying Column," indicate the presence of a controlling hand, which, in Sisley Huddleston's words, "took up the cudgels against the cult of unintelligibility."

Furthermore, the editorship of the magazine gave Titus a chance both to extend his literary patronage beyond the bounds of the Black Manikin Press and to involve himself more closely in the creation of literature. He was soon telling Sylvia Beach and others to send him "young meritorious writers who find it difficult to get their work published." Then in his second issue of *This Quarter* (October-November-December 1929), he announced the creation of the Richard Aldington American Poetry Prize (first 2,500 francs and later 10,000 francs) for the "ablest young American poet whose work has appeared in *This Quarter*." In the next number (January-February-March 1930) he offered a similar prize for "the ablest English poet" and the William Van Wyck Prize of 2,500 francs for the better of the two poets. Finally, in the March 1932 issue came the announcement of the Heinemann prize of fifty guineas for the best short story to appear in *This Quarter* during the year. After a heated debate between Titus and Aldington, the Richard Aldington Prize was divided between E. E. Cummings and Walter Lowenfels. The English poet

who received *This Quarter*'s prize was John Collier, who also received the William Van Wyck Prize. Leslie Reid was given the Heinemann Prize for his story "Across the Heath," which appeared in the March 1932 issue of *This Quarter*. Titus's own literary aspirations were at least partly satisfied by his translations of the poetry of Johann Wolfgang von Goethe, Arthur Rimbaud, Rainer Maria Rilke, Hermann Hesse, and Stefan George which appeared regularly in the magazine and which were praised by Ludwig Lewisohn for being "filled by both the stringency and the subtlety of his taste."

In the first anniversary issue of *This Quarter* (April-May-June 1930) Titus wrote in his editorial: "We venture to say that no periodical published in the English language, certainly none published in that language in a foreign country, has within the covers of four issues brought together such a constellation of contributors as it has been our pleasure to put before our readers this past year." These issues included works by D. H. Lawrence, Liam O'Flaherty, Allen Tate, Robert McAlmon, Robert Penn Warren, and Richard Aldington. Later issues included poetry from E. E. Cummings, Aldous Huxley, and Louis MacNeice; criticism by Paul Valery and Joseph Wood Krutch; and fiction from Ernest Hemingway and James T. Farrell. Though Titus certainly preferred well-known artists, he was prepared to publish new talent, and, encouraged by Samuel Putnam, he devoted a series of issues to the writing of a number of European countries: French literature in March 1930, Italian in June, Russian in September, German in December, the literature of Austria in March 1931, and of Poland in September 1931. Finally, in the penultimate issue (September 1932), he handed over the magazine to the guest editorship of Andre Breton, who produced a definitive analysis of Surrealism.

Despite the plaudits from Parisian literary circles, *This Quarter* was to Titus, as the bookshop and the press had been, never anything more than a bibliophile's expensive hobby, and it clearly became irksome to him at times. He shared the editorial burden during 1929 with the Pierre Lovings. When they left for America, he appointed Samuel Putnam as associate editor. Putnam worked on the issues of March and June 1930, until he and Titus quarreled over the merits of James T. Farrell. Titus used an impromptu editorial committee from the fall of 1930 until December 1932, when *This Quarter*'s final issue was published.

Earlier in 1932 the Black Manikin Press had closed down, and with *This Quarter*'s last issue Edward Titus's contribution to Parisian literary and intellectual life abruptly ceased. He moved to the resort of Cagnes-sur-Mer, where, after his divorce from Helena Rubinstein in 1937, he lived in comfortable seclusion with his second wife. As Hugh Ford has put it, "Titus' exodus from Montparnasse was eerily complete." He died in 1952, at the age of eighty-two. —*Toby Widdicombe*

References:

Hugh Ford, *Published in Paris American and British Writers, Printers, and Publishers in Paris, 1920-1939* (New York: Macmillan, 1975), pp. 117-167;

Sisley Huddleston, *Back to Montparnasse* (London: Lippincott, 1931), pp. 100-108;

Ludwig Lewisohn, "Tribute to Edward Titus," letter to the editor, *New York Times*, 12 February 1952, p. 26;

Helena Rubinstein, *My Life for Beauty* (New York: Simon & Schuster, 1964).

ALICE B. TOKLAS
(30 April 1877-7 March 1967)

BOOKS: *The Alice B. Toklas Cookbook* (New York: Harper, 1954; London: Joseph, 1954);

Aromas and Flavors of Past and Present, ed. Poppy Cannon (New York: Harper, 1958; London: Joseph, 1958);

What Is Remembered (New York: Holt, Rinehart & Winston, 1963; London: Joseph, 1963).

Alice Babette Toklas was born in San Francisco to Ferdinand and Emma Levinsky Toklas and grew up in San Francisco and Seattle, where her father was a merchant. Her family was of the Jewish middle class, and she was educated in private schools and at the University of Seattle. She was given piano lessons, and when she was in her mid-twenties, she thought seriously of becoming a concert pianist. She described herself as being on the fringe of San Francisco's "Bohemians," the literary and artistic group which flourished at the turn of the century.

Her life changed considerably after the San Francisco earthquake of 1906. In the spring of that year, she met Michael and Sarah Stein, the brother and sister-in-law of Gertrude Stein, when they came to San Francisco to assess damage done by the earthquake to property which they owned in the city. The couple, along with their brother Leo and sister Gertrude, were making their home in Paris, and their description of the city convinced Toklas to journey to France.

Little enticement was necessary, however, since Toklas's life in San Francisco was by then depressing and even stultifying. Her mother had died when Toklas was in her late teens, and she became cook and housekeeper for a group of male relatives which included her father, grandfather, younger brother, and assorted uncles and cousins. Because of her family obligations, she was forced to withdraw from social life; by the age of twenty-nine, she was living a dull, spinsterish existence.

With a journalist friend, Harriet Levy, Toklas left home, hoping never to return. She arrived in Paris in September 1907 and on the evening of her arrival met Gertrude Stein. Toklas was immediately fascinated by Stein, describing her later as "a golden brown presence" who emanated a deep and rich inner life. For her part, Stein was interested in Toklas and had been for some time. She had read and analyzed letters which Toklas had written to a friend in Paris, and she felt that she already knew her.

The two women saw a great deal of each other throughout the fall, winter, and spring, and Toklas began to offer encouragement for Stein's writing. At the time, Stein was suffering from a break in her relationship with her brother Leo, with whom she was living and to whom she had been close. In many ways, Toklas replaced Stein's brother in her affections and filled his role of confidant and emotional support.

By the summer of 1908, a genuine love was evident between the two women. Toklas joined the Steins when they all vacationed in Fiesole, Italy, and it was there that Stein proposed a lifelong relationship with Toklas which was, in effect, a marriage. As Stein later described the relationship, she was to be the "husband" and Toklas the "wife."

Alice Toklas claimed that a bell rang each time she encountered a genius, and she was aware of the distinct chiming when she met Gertrude Stein. She did not consider herself an artist or writer, but she was wholly sympathetic to Stein's experiments in language and to her artistic sensibilities. Although Leo Stein had become increasingly disgusted with his sister's convoluted, sometimes unintelligible prose, Toklas could reply with conviction, "Yes." She understood, and Stein needed her sanction. Furthermore, they shared the joy of dissecting the personalities of many of their friends and relatives, something Stein termed finding the "bottom nature" of an individual.

Soon, Leo Stein moved out of the house which

he and his sister rented at 27, rue de Fleurus in the Montparnasse district of Paris, and Toklas moved in. She has been described as Stein's housekeeper, secretary, cook, typist, and friend. She was all of these, and without her ability to keep the household running smoothly, to oversee the maid, to bring some order to Stein's life, to be ever-watchful of new friends, it is doubtful that Stein would have produced the work she did.

Stein was the center of one of the most famous salons in Paris in the twenties and thirties. In the atelier on the rue de Fleurus, Alice Toklas was content to sit with the wives, while her companion was surrounded by the artists: Picasso, Matisse, Hemingway, Bravig Imbs, Virgil Thomson, Ezra Pound, Thornton Wilder, Francis Rose, Braque, George Antheil, and Man Ray.

But Toklas exerted a strong influence over who was allowed to remain friends and who was barred from continuing a relationship with Stein. The most notorious example of Toklas's will came when Stein met Ernest Hemingway in 1921. From the beginning, Toklas disliked him and tried to convince her friend that Hemingway was using her, was not sincere in his effusive praise, and was vulgar, childish, selfish. She warned Stein to break off the friendship and even threatened to leave her if she did not. Years later, Toklas admitted her real reason for disliking Hemingway: she feared he might seduce Stein. Hemingway, on his part, later admitted that he had been sexually attracted to Stein. By the late twenties, after the publication of Hemingway's *The Sun Also Rises* (1926) with Stein's famous epigraph about the "lost generation," he was no longer welcome at the rue de Fleurus. Toklas had succeeded in getting rid of him. "And when you think of all the wives he had," she said later, "I think I was right."

Toklas was not only protector, but also served as impresario. When Stein could not find a publisher to handle her work, Toklas proposed to be both publisher and distributor. She found a printer, chose endpapers, read proof, and contacted booksellers to make their publishing company, Plain Editions, a small success. In January 1931, Stein's lyrical novel, *Lucy Church Amiably*, was ready for the public, and she took to wandering about Paris, looking for copies of the book in shop windows, and reporting back to Toklas. "This event," Toklas said, "gave Gertrude Stein a childish delight amounting almost to ecstasy."

Toklas's own works were written after Stein died. While Stein was alive, Toklas never would have presumed to compete as a writer, though Stein herself had often jokingly suggested that she write a

book. One idea they discussed was Toklas's compiling a cookbook, filled with the succulent recipes for which she was well-known and complemented by anecdotes about their many illustrious dinner guests. One day, sitting on the terrace of their summer house at Bilignin, she mentioned the possibility of her writing the book to Thornton Wilder. "But Alice," he cautioned, "have you ever tried to write?" Always remembering the slight (Toklas neither forgave nor forgot), she went on to write *The Alice B. Toklas Cookbook*, which was published in 1954. The cookbook's most famous recipe is that for hashish fudge, contributed by her artist friend, Brion Gysin. Toklas, who had decided not to test any of her friends' contributions, allowed the recipe to slip by because she did not realize what the ingredients were. Later, she was troubled to think that readers might find in the fudge an explanation for Stein's strange writing. The book achieved popularity as a delightful memoir of Toklas's life with Stein and of the many artists they knew. Her recipes, which are usually rich and expensive to prepare, take on a special glamour when one knows they were enjoyed by such guests as Pablo Picasso, Francis Picabia, Francis Rose, Dora Maar, Pierre Balmain, Carl Van Vechten, and Cecil Beaton.

The book is written in the spare, distilled style which Gertrude Stein had imitated so well in *The Autobiography of Alice B. Toklas* (1934). And like *The Autobiography*, the *Cookbook*'s anecdotes center largely around Stein: her likes and dislikes, her eccentricities, her adventures. All of Toklas's culinary inventions, it appears, were subject to Stein's approval. When Stein could not decide whether she wanted chestnuts, mushrooms, or oysters in her Thanksgiving turkey, Toklas was moved to concoct a stuffing which combined all three. Only when her piecrust met her companion's standard did she proceed to mincemeat.

The *Cookbook* is ample evidence that Toklas's life was intertwined with some of the most flamboyant writers and artists of the twentieth century, and even her smaller literary contributions, several articles published in the fifties, attest to her enviable life.

The *New York Times Book Review* featured her article "They Who Came to Paris to Write," which gave her opinions of writers beginning with Stein and ending with those she had met as late as 1950. After World War I, she noted, "American lady novelists, poetesses and fashion writers had gone home and after the peace were replaced by a younger generation of Americans": Sherwood Anderson, F. Scott Fitzgerald, John Dos Passos, Glenway Wescott, even Hemingway. She had known them all. Anderson, she thought, was always a gentleman. Fitzgerald, in *This Side of Paradise*, had given "the definitive portrait of his generation." Dos Passos had great "Latin charm." Hemingway was dismissed briefly: "I feel that about Hemingway, that is that neither reading nor writing is a natural inevitable necessity for him."

Toklas had always taken Fitzgerald's part in the one-sided rivalry between Fitzgerald and Hemingway, and her protectiveness extended to a *New York Times* review of Malcolm Cowley's 1951 edition of Fitzgerald's short stories. Reading his stories, she said, was "a melancholy pleasure, for Fitzgerald had become a legend and the epoch he created is history." Other articles by Alice Toklas appeared in major magazines. "Fifty Years of French Fashions," published in the *Atlantic Monthly* in June 1958, offered her view of haute couture from the time she visited Paris as a child with her parents to her current friendship with Pierre Balmain. Balmain, she revealed, had designed several suits and dresses for both her and Stein, though the public had no idea that they were so fashionably dressed. "Be sure you don't tell anybody that we are wearing clothes made by Pierre Balmain," Stein once told her. "We look like gypsies." Toklas commented not only about fashion, but also about politics. She described the uneasy political atmosphere in Paris during the spring of 1958 in "The Rue Dauphine Refuses the Revolution," which appeared in the *New Republic* for 18 August 1958. There would be no revolution, she predicted, and De Gaulle would soon rise to power once again. In this case, she was correct.

A second cookbook bearing Toklas's name, *Aromas and Flavors of Past and Present*, was begun in 1956 and published in 1958. Her motivation was not as inspired as with her first cookbook. This one was written to fulfill her contractual obligations with one publisher so she could move on to another, and her creative effort was minimal. She had only to supply the recipes, and another writer, Poppy Cannon, would do the rest. Cannon was an advocate of shortcut cooking, but Toklas would rise at five to begin to dice, blend, simmer, and stew for a dinner party—if she had not already begun the evening before.

The book Toklas was more interested in writing was a memoir which she planned to call *Things I Have Seen*. She never wanted to exploit her life with Stein, but by 1958, at eighty-one, she was often in financial difficulty and hoped that the book would help. Her health, however, did not enable her to work on the project alone, and a writer who had been

her friend and Stein's was enlisted to assist. Max White began taking notes and attempting to piece together what should have been Toklas's autobiography, but he found his task insurmountable. She would do nothing but repeat the already often-told stories about Stein. In her mind, the purpose of the book would be to burnish Stein's image, to keep alive the legend which she had helped to create. She wanted all references to herself discarded. Finally, White was so frustrated he refused to continue, tore up the few notes he had taken, and left her alone with her memories. Only with the help of secretaries and other friends did the book finally appear, in the spring of 1963, with the more apt title: *What Is Remembered*.

Alice Toklas spent her last years in ill health, suffering from arthritis and cataracts. For a time she lived in Rome, at the Sisters of the Precious Blood. Her last few years were spent in an apartment in Paris where she was forbidden to drive a nail into the walls. No pictures could be hung, but her portrait by Dora Maar was leaned against a wall. Still, she lived with her memories and her belief in a reunion, after her death, with Gertrude Stein. She had converted to Catholicism in 1957 hoping, she admitted to friends, to find Stein in heaven.

On 7 March 1967, Alice B. Toklas died.

—Linda Simon

Periodical Publications:

"They Who Came to Paris to Write," *New York Times Book Review*, 6 August 1950, pp. 1, 25;

"Between Classics," review of *The Stories of F. Scott Fitzgerald*, ed. Malcolm Cowley, *New York Times Book Review*, 4 March 1951, p. 4;

"Some Memories of Henri Matisse: 1907-1922," *Yale Literary Magazine*, 123 (Fall 1955): 15-16;

"Fifty Years of French Fashions," *Atlantic Monthly*, 201 (June 1958): 55-57;

"The Rue Dauphine Refuses the Revolution," *New Republic*, 139 (18 August 1958): 8;

"Sylvia and Her Friends," *New Republic*, 160 (19 October 1959): 24.

Letters:

Staying On Alone: Letters of Alice B. Toklas, ed. Edward Burns (New York: Liveright, 1973).

Biography:

Linda Simon, *The Biography of Alice B. Toklas* (Garden City: Doubleday, 1977).

References:

Richard Bridgman, *Gertrude Stein in Pieces* (New York: Oxford University Press, 1966);

John Malcolm Brinnin, *The Third Rose: Gertrude Stein & Her World* (New York: Grove Press, 1959);

Harriet Levy, *920 O'Farrell Street* (Garden City: Doubleday, 1947);

James R. Mellow, *Charmed Circle Gertrude Stein & Company* (New York & Washington: Praeger, 1974);

W. G. Rogers, *When This You See Remember Me: Gertrude Stein in Person* (New York: Rinehart, 1948);

Elizabeth Sprigge, *Gertrude Stein, Her Life and Work* (New York: Harper, 1957);

Gertrude Stein, *The Autobiography of Alice B. Toklas* (New York: Random House, 1933);

Stein, *Everybody's Autobiography* (New York: Random House, 1937);

Stein, *Paris France* (London: Batsford, 1940);

Stein, *Wars I Have Seen* (New York: Random House, 1945).

Note: References to Toklas appear throughout Stein's work. See Simon and Bridgman.

Papers:

Most of Toklas's papers are at the Beinecke Library, Yale University. Material about her early years in San Francisco is at the Bancroft Library, University of California at Berkeley. The Bancroft Library has recently acquired some later material.

LAURENCE VAIL
(28 January 1891-16 April 1968)

BOOKS: *Piri and I* (New York: Lieber & Lewis, 1923);

Murder! Murder! (London: Peter Davies, 1931);

365 Days, by Vail, Kay Boyle, and Nina Conarain (London: Cape, 1936; New York: Harcourt, Brace, 1936);

Two Poems (New York: Modern Editions, n.d.).

Laurence Vail, novelist, poet, painter, and sculptor, was born in Paris on 28 January 1891 and died in Cannes on 16 April 1968. Known variously as the King of Montparnasse or the King of Bohemia, he is important for his Surrealist prose and his avant-garde art. He was described by Peggy Guggenheim as "always bursting with ideas," and he exerted a catalytic force on his many friends, among them Djuna Barnes, Hart Crane, Ernest Hemingway, James Joyce, and Ezra Pound.

His family had been connected with France for many generations: his great-grandfather had been a friend of Lafayette; his paternal grandfather, Adam Vail of New York, knew Vicomte Ferdinand de Lesseps and married a girl from Brittany; Vail's father, the commercially successful painter Eugene Lawrence Vail, was born in Paris and brought his son up to live like a Frenchman but think like an American. The most significant parts of Vail's education did not occur during his often-interrupted formal schooling in Paris, in Connecticut, or at Oxford, but in the summers spent with his father in Venice or in the French Alps.

Laurence Vail served during 1918 in the American army as an officer assigned to the Corps of Interpreters. He met heiress Peggy Guggenheim in Manhattan in 1921 and married her the next year in Paris. They had two children, quarreled, gave marathon parties, and separated in 1929. In December 1928, Vail had met Kay Boyle at the Coupole, and soon a relationship developed which lasted until 1941. This marriage produced three children and the short story collection *365 Days*, coedited and coauthored by Kay Boyle, Vail, and Nina Conarain. Boyle credits Vail with being one of the most important influences on her development as a writer: he encouraged her in the cross-country skiing and mountain climbing which were to figure in several of her novels, and he introduced her to many American and French writers. During the war years in Connecticut and New York, Vail was heartsick for Europe; he crossed the Atlantic again after the war, to spend the rest of his life mainly in France.

Vail's creative life was extremely varied. Perhaps he best characterized his own course in "Grey Crust," a poem published in *Poetry* in 1921: "I would be fused into anyone going new ways." Tristan Tzara considered him one of the fathers of Dada, and he was an early practitioner of Surrealism in art and literature. He experimented with form, diction, and style. He was one of the signers, along with Kay Boyle, Hart Crane, Harry Crosby, Eugene

Laurence Vail, 1920s

Jolas, and others, of the "Proclamation" which announced the "Revolution of the Word" in *transition* (June 1929) and stated that the undersigned were "tired of the spectacle of short stories, poems and plays still under the hegemony of the banal word, monotonous syntax, static psychology, descriptive naturalism."

Piri and I (1923), Vail's first novel, is a fantasy based in part on his life from age eleven onward and treats his very close relationship with his sister, Clotilde, as the romance of two people, Piri Riminieff and Michael Lafosse, the narrator. *Piri and I* defies simplistic categorizing, since the fictional modes change to suit the author's purpose. At first it is quite frankly a sensitive story of childhood and adolescence, then it becomes a novel of manners, and finally it turns self-consciously philosophical. Vail's narrator looks back nostalgically upon his early loves: "Where is she now—the marvellous Lili, once the pride and terror of nurses, the tyrant of the child-speckled avenue?" Occasionally Vail, trying to see the world through a child's eyes, becomes trapped in an overwrought simile: "Slatternly words fall from her heavy lips like frogs from the lips of the princess in the fairy tale." He reveals himself as a word painter who, at his best, can achieve images which move with the authority his friend Marcel Duchamp produced on canvas. As Piri and Michael climb, "The mist falls away from them, tumbling gently like the skirts of a ballet dancer."

The novel of manners section begins with the descriptions of spas and ski resorts, of balls and tennis tournaments. Some of the characters recall eighteenth-century English stage figures: "Now it is a buxom blonde, striving to demonstrate by a simpering laugh and coy little steps that her heart is as young as the night." Vail's narrator describes himself in terms that clearly fit Vail himself; he is "a blond lad with large and uncertain blue eyes, an acquiline nose, and a slightly irregular mouth." Soon the narrator's philosophy emerges; in a false society, the clever person assumes the mask of the *pierrot* to safeguard his integrity: "He is the amateur actor let loose in the world. . . . The real artist is essentially the amateur. This young man's poses are both intuitive and intellectual." This passage could describe the outward show put on by Laurence Vail and his friends Harry Crosby and Robert McAlmon.

Piri and I is fairly traditional in form and gives little hint of the various styles, from Victorian sentimental realism to Surrealism, to appear in *Murder! Murder!* (1931), and of the interior monologue mode which dominates the later novel. *Murder! Murder!* contains portraits and events for which the originals are easily recognizable: Polly is Peggy Guggenheim; Martin Asp, the protagonist and narrator, is Vail himself; Nell, the "queen of Montparnasse," owes a lot to Florence Martin, Gerald Burns to Harold Stearns, and Miriam Oon probably to Mina Loy. Vail also exploits the banalities of his tourist countrymen: two young women are defined by their assertion that "We might do both Louvres before lunch."

The book begins with a section entitled "Advertisement" which gives excerpts from confessions of murder, ranging from the Victorian-chaste admission of a fratricide complete with "deathly pallor," feminine sympathy, and invocations of the Maker, to the blunt "Killed her? I should say I did."

The action is frankly Surrealistic: a murder has been—may have been?—committed by the narrator. In an excerpt published in *transition* (June 1929), the murderer/narrator, M, is pursued around the world by a detective, D, who is the narrator's double and alter ego. Reality and dream, sobriety and drunkenness alternate. Vail experiments with relativity: the dream-events of several days' duration turn out to have lasted only a few hours. Then both D and M become drunk on Prohibition liquor in a Manhattan speakeasy, and time lags. A slow-motion chase ensues which takes six hours and thirty-eight minutes and covers eight blocks. Even the dialogue is expanded visually: "P---pp---er---er---haps-------if---I---t---t---tt-----ake-----a-----s-----s---sh---ort-----n---ap-----I---m---may---be---a---a---able-----to---cr---cr---awl---or---h---h---hob-------ble-------." Later the pace challenges time itself: "At the same time, to judge by rude chronometer, M is at Washington Square and at the Battery. He dives. A minute later D follows him into the puddle. And, indeed, for swimmers like M and D, the Atlantic is a puddle."

There is a Rabelaisian quality to much of Vail's humor and to his prose style. Lists expand simple statements into pages: "Outraged, as you say. Fondled, petted, taken liberties with, chucked under the chin, osculated, bitten, caressed in all sorts of places, cuddled, bussed, clasped, muzzled. . . ." Beneath all his buffoonery and word-wizardry, Vail has a serious purpose in *Murder! Murder!*. He has shown man's despair at his loss of individuality. As Martin Asp laments, after an unsuccessful attempt to have himself arrested for his real or imagined murder, "No doubt of it: I am a null, a zero." He needs desperately to assert himself, and in this Kafkaesque attempt he is denied success by wife, friends, and officials. Asp approaches the stature of a modern Everyman in the last lines of the novel as, in a final attempt to become "something," he says, "I smash a tumbler. I smash a bottle. Filling my hands with broken glass, I rush out of the cafe . . . into the night . . . across the street. . . ."

Vail did not publish the many other novels he wrote. According to Kay Boyle, he destroyed seven or eight manuscripts. He may have been haunted by his own cry, "Why should we, living poems, fuss about with ink?" His other writings show considerable promise, but they are relatively few. An early play, *What Do You Want?*, was produced by the Provincetown Players in 1919. A few poems and short stories appeared in Peter Neagoe's *Americans Abroad, Bellman, Broom, Dial*, the *New Review*, Bob Brown's *Readies* anthology, and the *Smart Set*. His verse tends to lapse into prosaic utterance, but there are occasional effective images:

> Wine starts a glissade of words
> We will meet again   Maud Trevylyan
> When the gutter is choked with leaves.

His essay on "Mutation in Language" in *transition* (July 1935) reflects the diction of *Finnegans Wake* and looks forward to Lucky's speech in *Waiting for Godot*:

> Referring to glummarians and deams of Acaca old blanketters and aulde douchers roting the rechauffe with comas and semicomas, arsestericks & hystarisks & Nobel Prize periods—you know, the fool stop when the pintellect stoops to pickpocket slime from old Messachusetts
>
> the word wormed
> He was not the lowest poochpooet who hardly sang.

Vail was also a versatile linguist who produced translations into English from French, German, and Italian. In his first important effort, Madeleine Clemenceau-Jacquemaire's *The Life of Madame Roland* (1930), he achieved a dignified and controlled prose suited to the original. His second translation from French, Charles-Louis Philippe's *Bubu of Montparnasse* (1932), was published by the Black Sun Press with a preface by T. S. Eliot. Eliot had complained privately about the language of Vail's translation, and indeed, though it reads well, the street-tough quality of the original is not consistently maintained. Robert Neumann's *On the Make* (1931), which Vail translated from German, is rendered in a racy, rather British English: "I've too much to do to waste my time twaddling fiddlesticks." Laurence Vail also had "too much to do" in too many creative fields for him to fulfill all the promise he showed, but he deserves to be remembered for his contributions to the life, art, and literature of his generation. Thus far, he has been largely neglected by critics and historians.

—*Ian S. MacNiven*

Other:

Madeleine Clemenceau-Jacquemaire, *The Life of Madame Roland*, translated by Vail (London & New York: Longmans, Green, 1930);

"Always Gentleman - To God - Aria di Maria - Envoi - Pogrom?," in *Readies for Bob Brown's Machine*, ed. Bob Brown (Cagnes-sur-Mer: Roving Eye Press, 1931), pp. 9-15;

Robert Neumann, *On the Make*, translated by Vail (London: Peter Davies, 1931);

"Buster Bourbon, Private," in *Americans Abroad An Anthology*, ed. Peter Neagoe (The Hague: Servire, 1932), pp. 428-457;

Charles-Louis Philippe, *Bubu of Montparnasse*, translated by Vail (Paris: Black Sun Press, 1932).

Periodical Publications:

"Americans," *Dial*, 70 (February 1921): 163;

"Grey Crust," *Poetry*, 19 (December 1921): 136-137;

"A Great One," *transition*, no. 14 (Fall 1928): 151-163;

"Revolution of the Word Proclamation," signed by Vail and others, *transition*, no. 16/17 (June 1929): 13;

"Murder, Murder," *transition*, no. 16/17 (June 1929): 108-119;

"Inquiry on the Malady of Language," by Vail and others, *transition*, no. 23 (July 1935): 168-171;

"Fragment from a Novel," *transition*, no. 27 (April/May 1938): 138-141.

References:

Hugh Ford, *Published in Paris American and British Writers, Printers, and Publishers in Paris, 1920-1939* (New York: Macmillan, 1975);

Peggy Guggenheim, *Out of this Century* (New York: Dial, 1946);

Robert McAlmon, *Being Geniuses Together 1920-1930*, revised edition with additional material by Kay Boyle (Garden City: Doubleday, 1968).

CARL VAN VECHTEN
(17 June 1880-21 December 1964)

BOOKS: *Music After the Great War* (New York: Schirmer, 1915);

Music and Bad Manners (New York: Knopf, 1916);

Interpreters and Interpretations (New York: Knopf, 1917); revised and republished as *Interpreters* (New York: Knopf, 1920);

The Merry-Go-Round (New York: Knopf, 1918);

The Music of Spain (New York: Knopf, 1918; London: Kegan Paul, Trench, Trucbner, 1920);

In the Garret (New York: Knopf, 1920);

The Tiger in the House (New York: Knopf, 1920; London: Heinemann, 1921);

Peter Whiffle His Life and Works (New York: Knopf, 1922; London: Richards, 1923);

The Blind Bow-Boy (New York: Knopf, 1923; London: Richards, 1923);

The Tattoed Countess (New York: Knopf, 1924; London: Knopf, 1926);

Red (New York: Knopf, 1925);

Firecrackers (New York: Knopf, 1925; London: Knopf, 1927);

Nigger Heaven (New York: Knopf, 1926; London: Knopf, 1926);

Excavations (New York: Knopf, 1926);

Spider Boy (New York & London: Knopf, 1928; London: Knopf, 1928);

Parties (New York: Knopf, 1930; London: Knopf, 1930);

Feathers (New York: Random House, 1930);

Sacred and Profane Memories (New York: Knopf, 1932; London, Toronto, Melbourne & Sydney: Cassell, 1932).

Carl Van Vechten, one of America's most eclectic men of letters, published six novels, two works on cats, and eleven collections of his critical essays on the arts. Although comfortable enough as the youngest son of prosperous parents in Cedar Rapids, Iowa, where he was born and raised, Van Vechten yearned for more exciting and exotic influences even as a child. In his continual search for expressions of genius in the art world, Van Vechten never discovered a more satisfying place than Paris.

As a writer of novels suffused with civilized humor, Van Vechten concentrated, he said, on "treating extremely serious themes as frivolously as possible." His first novel, published in 1922, perfectly blends these aims, presenting a whimsical chronicle of the author's experiences in Paris, Florence, and New York high society, thinly disguised as the story of a dissatisfied young genius known by Van Vechten. *Peter Whiffle His Life and Works* has been acclaimed by critics as Van Vechten's best novel. Readers have especially enjoyed descriptions of prewar Paris seen through the eyes of a dazzled young man.

Van Vechten first visited Paris in 1908, motivated by a burning need to attend opera on the Continent. The young correspondent for the *New York Times* carried back to America the bright picture of Europe's city of enchantments he presented in *Peter Whiffle*: "The aroma of the chestnuts, the melting grey of the buildings, the legions of carriages and buses, filled with happy, chattering people, the glitter of electricity, all the mystic wonder of this enchanting night will always stay with me." In other passages Van Vechten portrays the young artists of Paris through such characters as Martha Baker, a masterful portrait artist reduced to painting society ladies for a living; Frederic Richards, a blond giant who sketches telling likenesses on napkins which are snapped up by his fans; and, of course, Peter Whiffle, a young

Werther with the giddy abandon of the fin de siecle in his blood and the concentration span of a five-year-old. In short, *Peter Whiffle* admirably evokes a Paris filled with young Americans, independent and sometimes talented, who contributed so much to the myth that "Americans go to Paris when they die."

Experimenters in form and theme dominated those prewar years in France. Van Vechten's work, both as critic and novelist, was influenced by poets such as Joris Karl Huysmans and Arthur Rimbaud, painter Edgar Degas, and British writer on the Symbolists Arthur Symons. His conception of Paris, and life in general, was always fundamentally romantic. Except in a later work on life in New York's Harlem, *Nigger Heaven* (1926), his prose was rarely concerned with world affairs, poverty, or violence. Unlike those who experienced the war firsthand, such as Ford Madox Ford and John Dos Passos, Van Vechten echoed the bohemian glitter of prewar Paris in the brightly colored surfaces of his novels.

By inclination and training a critic, Van Vechten expanded the role to suit his taste for the new, the exotic, and the neglected. The critical essays he wrote while working for a number of newspapers in Chicago and later New York are most impressive when fueled with his enthusiasm for the excellence of such new talents as Waslaw Nijinsky, Arnold Schoenberg, and Ethel Waters, all of whom he helped introduce to the public. He was the first major music critic to recognize jazz as a peculiarly American contribution to European musical tradition, an early pioneer for social equality for Negroes, and the first to study thoroughly the music of Spain, publishing a major collection of essays on the subject. Several fine essays on Paris also found their way into his collections, foremost among them an enchanting description of the *bal musette*.

When Van Vechten visited Paris in 1913 for the second time, with Fania Marinoff, his fiancee, it was expressly to see Diaghilev's ballet and to visit Gertrude Stein, about whom he had heard from Mabel Dodge, a mutual friend. Stein and Van Vechten, or that "young man of the soft much-pleated evening shirt" as she called him later in *The Autobiography of Alice B. Toklas* (1933), hit it off immediately. Van Vechten not only became her good friend, but he championed her work in America, helping her to place one of her earliest works, *Tender Buttons* (1914), with Donald Evan's Claire Marie Press. As Edward Lueders says, "Through the years when her work provoked either derision or polite

Alice B. Toklas, Carl Van Vechten, and Gertrude Stein, 1934 (photo by Van Vechten)

bewilderment, Van Vechten . . . kept it alive and in print." As an admirer of those artists whose writings were intentionally obscure or difficult, Van Vechten championed many literary causes, yet never with the love he accorded Stein. In 1930 Van Vechten again visited Paris. During this time Stein wrote in his autograph book: "Carl is here which is a pleasure we are here which is a pleasure, and we all like nougat." Upon her death in 1946 Van Vechten became Stein's literary executor.

After renouncing his own literary career except to write introductions to books on subjects that interested him, Van Vechten took up photography in 1932. Although the craft had been one of his many pastimes, his hobby now became a serious art. He photographed many well-known people of his age, among them Stein. He once boasted, "I've photographed everybody from Matisse to Isamu Noguchi."

Although Van Vechten visited Paris several times both before and after World War I, his primary arena was New York. While living there with Fania Marinoff, he sent friends to visit Stein and received visits from European celebrities and American expatriates in exchange. The fame of those Van Vechten encouraged and championed has far exceeded his own renown. He was not simply a frivolous child of the twenties whose novels and critical works can be viewed as artifacts of a past decade. Although he is often remembered solely as Gertrude Stein's American friend, or as the man who awakened interest in the later works of Herman Melville, his own writing deserves recognition.

—*Carol Gunther*

Other:

Lords of the Housetops, Thirteen Cat Tales, edited with a preface by Van Vechten (New York: Knopf, 1921);

Ronald Firbank, *Prancing Nigger*, introduction by Van Vechten (New York: Brentano's, 1924);

Langston Hughes, *The Weary Blues*, introduction by Van Vechten (New York: Knopf, 1926);

Gertrude Stein, *Three Lives*, introduction by Van Vechten (New York: Modern Library, 1933);

Stein, *Selected Writings*, edited by Van Vechten (New York: Random House, 1946);

Stein, *Last Operas and Plays*, edited by Van Vechten (New York & Toronto: Rinehart, 1949);

Stein, *Two: Gertrude Stein and Her Brother and Other Early Portraits [1908-12]*, includes a note by Van Vechten (New Haven: Yale University Press; London: G. Cumberlege, Oxford University Press, 1951);

Padraic Colum and Margaret Freeman Cabell, eds., *Between Friends Letters of James Branch Cabell and Others*, introduction by Van Vechten (New York: Harcourt, Brace & World, 1962).

References:

Joseph Warren Beach, "The Peacock's Tail," in his *The Outlook for American Prose* (Chicago: University of Chicago Press, 1926);

Donald Gallup, "Carl Van Vechten's Gertrude Stein," *Yale University Library Gazette*, 27 (October 1952): 77-86;

Hugh M. Gloster, "The Van Vechten Vogue," *Phylon*, 6 (Fourth Quarter 1945): 310-314;

Alfred Kazin, "The Exquisites: Coda," in his *On Native Grounds* (New York: Reynal & Hitchcock, 1942);

Edward Lueders, *Carl Van Vechten* (New York: Twayne, 1965);

Lueders, *Carl Van Vechten and the Twenties* (Albuquerque: University of New Mexico Press, 1955);

Mabel Dodge Luhan, *Intimate Memories*, volumes 2 and 3 (New York: Harcourt, Brace, 1935, 1936).

Papers:

Van Vechten's papers are in the Beinecke Library at Yale University.

ERNEST WALSH
(10 August 1895-16 October 1926)

BOOK: *Poems and Sonnets* (New York: Harcourt, Brace, 1934).

Ernest Walsh, expatriate American poet and coeditor of the small, but influential, experimental magazine *This Quarter*, was born in Detroit, Michigan. As a child he lived in Cuba, where his father, James Walsh, was a tea and coffee wholesaler. After the family returned to Detroit, his father died, and Walsh subsequently ran away from home at the age of fourteen. At seventeen he was diagnosed as tubercular and spent two years in a sanatorium at Lake Saranac, New York, from which he was discharged, supposedly cured. From 1914 to 1917 he wandered about the country in and out of work. Finally he enlisted in the army as an air cadet, and he was severely injured in the crash of the plane he was piloting during a training flight in Texas. The lung damage that he suffered as a result of the accident was complicated by the consumption from which he had never recovered.

Walsh began writing poetry while undergoing treatment at the United States Public Health Service Hospital #64 at Camp Kearney, California, in 1921. Fortunately he came to the attention of Harriet Monroe, who published four of his poems in her magazine *Poetry: A Magazine of Verse* for January 1922. Then, pronounced incurable and dismissed from the hospital with a government pension, he decided to spend his few remaining years in Europe living among the writers and artists he admired. Armed with letters of introduction from Monroe to Ezra Pound and other writers, Walsh journeyed to Paris. There, installed at the fashionable Claridge Hotel, his belongings impounded because he could not pay his bill, he was befriended by Ethel Moorhead, a Scottish painter and suffragette, who became his friend and benefactress.

Together they determined to publish a quarterly of their own, one which would "publish the artist's work while it is still fresh." The first issue of *This Quarter* appeared in January 1925, and it was dedicated to Ezra Pound, "who by his creative work, his editorship of several magazines, his helpful friendship for young and unknown artists, his many and untiring efforts to win better appreciation of what is first-rate in art comes first to our mind as meriting the gratitude of this generation." Published here were works by H. D., Kay Boyle, Gertrude Stein, Emanuel Carnevali, Ernest Hemingway, Robert McAlmon, and William Carlos Williams. The second issue included an extract of James Joyce's *Work in Progress*, the evolving opus which was to become *Finnegans Wake* (1939). The magazine attracted a good deal of attention because of its fresh critical stance and its rebellious denunciation of the literary establishment. Walsh, however, was able to edit only the first two numbers of the journal, for in Monte Carlo on 16 October 1926, nursed by his friends Ethel Moorhead and Kay Boyle, he died of tuberculosis at the age of thirty-one and was buried in Monaco. The third issue of *This Quarter*, published by Ethel Moorhead as a memorial to her coeditor, contains a blistering editorial accusing Pound of ignoring Walsh and his magazine and retracting the extravagant dedication printed in the first number. After Walsh's death Boyle, who had lived with him during the last year of his life and had assisted him in his editorial duties, gave birth to his daughter. Boyle's second novel, *Year Before Last* (1932), is based in part on her romance with Walsh in the months prior to his death. In addition the material which she appended

Front cover, This Quarter, *1 (Spring 1925)*

Ernest Walsh and Ethel Moorhead in Chillon, 1925

to her edition of Robert McAlmon's *Being Geniuses Together* (1968) is a moving recollection of their time together and the subsequent birth of their daughter.

Virtually all of Walsh's poems that were published in the twenties appeared in the pages of *Poetry* and *This Quarter*. Eight years after his death they were collected and published with a memoir by Ethel Moorhead, but the edition sold only 500 copies and was out of print within two years. His poetry consists of short lyrics written, with the exception of some experimental sonnets, in free verse. The subject matter is frequently erotic, and the imagery is shockingly vivid and sensual. "Leave that sow your mother," he blusters in "Venus In A Pension," a bold restatement of the carpe diem theme, "before your buttocks / are no longer bold / And your belly / is the concern / of three doctors / and one nurse / Rather than one poet / and many songs / . . . / I will make a song for you / like a white screen / On which the words / are written / beautiful / and strange / as / sleep." Other verses are encomiums to the circle of literary acquaintances whom Walsh admired, including Pound, Carnevali, and Hemingway. Toward the end of his short career Walsh showed signs of a maturing poetic genius, and he developed an easy, conversational style which is fresh and

compelling. His experiments with language also include poems written in a pseudoarchaic English. An example is "Sonnete," which begins, "She is a powdery morsel bond titely / In brite colers. I expectt her to explode / Into a shower of lingerie anytime."

Walsh's editorials and reviews of such books as Hemingway's *In Our Time* (1925) and McAlmon's *Distinguished Air* (1925), published in the first three issues of *This Quarter*, attack the literary establishment, which he variously defines as the *Dial*, the *New Criterion*, *Poetry*, T. S. Eliot, and William Butler Yeats. He praises what he feels is a new, lively breed of writers. "Ezra Pound, James Joyce, Robert McAlmon, Carl Sandburg, William Carlos Williams, and Emanuel Carnevali," he declares, "are the six greatest living literary artists"; "unrhymed verse, everything else being equal, is always superior to rhymed verse"; and T. S. Eliot, an historian rather than a critic, "has been dead a long time." Such criticism is, like Walsh himself, erratic and extravagant, but it is also perceptive and vigorous. After his death the magazine was published from 1929 to 1932 under the more conservative editorship of Edward Titus, but it had lost its lively appeal.

The significance of Ernest Walsh's contribution to American literature is in part historical, for as editor of *This Quarter* he published writers of greater stature than his own. However, the value of his poetry may not be discounted. Produced during a span of only five years, it is limited in its breadth, but many of the poems, particularly his last ones, possess a fresh and enduring quality that should recommend them to contemporary readers. —*Donald R. Knight*

References:

Sylvia Beach, *Shakespeare and Company* (New York: Harcourt, Brace & World, 1959), pp. 138-140;

Emanuel Carnevali, *The Autobiography of Emanuel Carnevali*, ed. Kay Boyle (New York: Horizon, 1967), pp. 231-235;

Edward Dahlberg, "The Expatriates: A Memoir," *Texas Quarterly*, 6 (Summer 1963): 50-55;

Ernest Hemingway, *A Moveable Feast* (New York: Scribners, 1964), pp. 123-129;

Robert McAlmon, *Being Geniuses Together 1920-1930*, revised edition with additional material by Kay Boyle (Garden City: Doubleday, 1968);

Harriet Monroe, "Ernest Walsh," *Poetry*, 41 (December 1932): 208-214;

Charles Norman, *Ezra Pound* (New York: Macmillan, 1960), pp. 274-278;

Winfield Townley Scott, "Ernest Walsh: The Poet Against Despair," *Decision*, 11 (August 1941): 36-46;

William Wasserstrom, "Hemingway, the *Dial*, and Ernest .Walsh," *South Atlantic Quarterly*, 65 (Spring 1966): 171-177.

GLENWAY WESCOTT
(11 April 1901-   )

SELECTED BOOKS: *The Bitterns A Book of Twelve Poems* (Evanston: Monroe Wheeler, 1920);

The Apple of the Eye (New York: Lincoln MacVeagh / Dial, 1924; London: Butterworth, 1926);

Natives of Rock: XX Poems: 1921-1922 (New York: Francesco Bianco, 1925);

Like A Lover (Macon & Villefrance-sur-Mer: Monroe Wheeler, 1926);

The Grandmothers A Family Portrait (New York & London: Harper, 1927; London: Butterworth, 1927);

Good-Bye Wisconsin (New York & London: Harper, 1928; London: Cape, 1929);

The Babe's Bed (Paris: Harrison of Paris, 1930; New York: Minton Balch, 1930; London: Simkin, 1930);

Fear and Trembling (New York & London: Harper, 1932);

A Calendar of Saints for Unbelievers (Paris: Harrison of Paris, 1932; New York: Minton Balch, 1932; London: Simkin, 1932);

The Pilgrim Hawk (New York & London: Harper, 1940; London: Hamilton, 1946);

Apartment in Athens (New York & London: Harper, 1945); republished as *Household in Athens* (London: Hamilton, 1945);

12 Fables of Aesop (New York: Museum of Modern Art, 1954);

Images of Truth Remembrances and Criticism (New York & Evanston: Harper & Row, 1962; London: Hamilton, 1963).

Glenway Wescott, novelist, short-story writer, essayist, poet, and critic, is a native of Wisconsin. In 1919 he withdrew from the University of Chicago after less than two years' attendance, launching his career as a writer. After several years of travel in the United States and Europe, Wescott settled in France in 1925 and remained for eight years. Though often in Paris during this period, he lived mainly in Villefranche-sur-Mer in the South of France. In 1933 he returned to New York City and divided his time between a New York apartment and the family farm in New Jersey. From 1943 to the present he has lived in rural New Jersey, publishing occasionally, but in no way matching the creative work of his earlier years. Wescott was elected to the National Institute of Arts and Letters in 1947, initiating a period of public service which has continued to the present. In later years he has been active as a reviewer, and as a lecturer and commentator on both his expatriate years and the work of other writers.

Wescott's major contributions to American literature were made in the twenties, especially during his years in France. France was his workshop, though his subject invariably was rural Wisconsin. His best-known novel, *The Grandmothers* (1927), was written and published during his years abroad. Selected as a Harper Prize novel, it enjoyed both public and critical success. *Good-Bye Wisconsin* (1928), a collection of short stories, along with *The Grandmothers*, made Wescott's literary reputation almost as luminous as those of his famous contemporaries F. Scott Fitzgerald and Ernest Hemingway. Other works published during the years in France include *The Babe's Bed* (1930), *Fear and Trembling* (1932), a collection of essays, and *A Calendar of Saints for Unbelievers* (1932). *The Pilgrim Hawk* (1940), one of his most artistically accomplished works, was an outgrowth of his experiences in France, as were two retrospective short stories: "Mr. Auerbach in Paris" and "The Frenchman Six Foot Three," both published in *Harper's* in 1942. The first is set mainly in Paris in 1923 and the second in and around Paris in 1938.

Wescott began his professional writing career as a young poet, publishing two books of poetry, *The Bitterns* (1920) and *Natives of Rock: XX Poems: 1921-1922* (1925). The poems are lyrics, written in the style of the Imagist poets. Although the poems provide abundant evidence of Wescott's image-making ability, characteristic of his lyrical and poetic prose, it was in the short story and novel, rather than in poetry, that he earned his literary reputation.

In *The Apple of the Eye* (1924), *The Grandmothers*, *Good-Bye Wisconsin*, and *The Babe's Bed*, Wescott's themes and techniques interrelate to form a series of commentaries and evaluations of America and American character. In the highly evocative lyric prose of these works, rich in imagery and sensuous in detail, Wescott employs a central young narrator: Dan Strane in *The Apple of the Eye*; Alwyn Tower in *The Grandmothers*; a nameless, expatriate son visiting his Wisconsin home in *The Babe's Bed*; and Alwyn, again, in *The Pilgrim Hawk*. Nostalgically and elegiacally, each of these narrators imaginatively recreates the American past, as symbolized in rural characters from Wisconsin, and in so doing he reveals the involvement, and, ultimately, the rebellion of his own mind and sensibility. Although sensitive to and sometimes admiring of the staunchness and endurance of his family and other rural characters, the narrator also comes to see the narrowness of their perspectives and aspirations, their emotional repressions, and the grotesque configurations of their lives under the pressures of harsh, rigid circumstances and attitudes. The testimony of these fictional works, often thinly masked autobiography, explains why Wescott, like his persona Alwyn Tower, abjured Wisconsin, and finally America, and sought a life abroad more hospitable to the young artist. Although these works of the twenties are an indictment of family, region, and even country, they also constitute a chronicle of loving tribute and regret for all that is remembered but necessarily abandoned. The narrators cannot totally escape the past, nor their regret or guilt, as suggested in Wescott's haunting and nostalgic narrative tone. Only in *The Pilgrim Hawk* does the narrator attain a measure of objectivity.

Wescott's first novel, *The Apple of the Eye*, recounts the initiation of fifteen-year-old Dan Strane into the ambiguities and complexities of rural Wisconsin life. The novel is divided into three books, and each is the story of different characters who advance Dan's informal education about local life. Their stories inspire Dan to break away from the puritanical inhibitions and harsh codes that weigh so heavily on the people of the region in order to seek a different destiny. The novel attracted serious critical commentary, which credited the book with giving a fresh, valuable dimension to the image and myth of the Middle West.

A few weeks after his arrival in Paris in 1925 Wescott began writing his best-known work, *The Grandmothers*. After several months in Paris on the Left Bank he moved, in April, to Villefranche-sur-Mer on the southern coast where he completed the novel late in 1926. Villefranche-sur-Mer was to become his home until his return to the United States in 1933 although he traveled throughout France and other parts of Europe during this period.

Although Wescott spent much of his time at Villefranche-sur-Mer on the Riviera, he was acquainted with Gertrude Stein and the writers and artists in her circle. Ernest Hemingway depicts Wescott as the effete character Robert Prentiss in the early Paris sections of *The Sun Also Rises* (1926). Wescott was sometimes joined at Villefranche-sur-Mer by his close friend Monroe Wheeler, who had

Glenway Wescott

published Wescott's first book, *The Bitterns*, in 1920. Wheeler and Barbara Harrison ran Harrison of Paris, a publishing house which published Wescott's *The Babe's Bed* and *A Calendar of Saints for Unbelievers*. (Barbara Harrison married Wescott's brother in 1935.) On the Riviera, Wescott also met F. Scott Fitzgerald, whose work he admired.

Wescott first conceived *The Grandmothers* as a history of his own family rather than a work of fiction, but as the work grew, it compelled his imagination to transcend memory, and the work was transmuted from a personal memoir to a skillful and successful novel. Twelve of the fifteen chapters of *The Grandmothers* present histories and portraits of members of Alwyn Tower's family. Taken together the members of the Tower family form a many-faceted symbol of midwest history and ultimately represent characteristic American types. The first two chapters and the last chapter frame this family album; in them Alwyn ruminates about the significance of the peoples' lives and carries to conclusion his lifelong desire to understand and evaluate his heritage. Also, in the last chapter, Alwyn discovers the full significance of his expatriation. He sees his life abroad as a form of pioneering, a thrust toward new experience. At the same time, because expatriation imposes loneliness, it is also a form of punishment for his abandonment of his homeland and for his continuing enchantment with the past. With the completion of this novel Wescott gave his most elaborate farewell to his family, his past, and his work of the twenties. Though some contemporary critics found *The Grandmothers* overwrought in style and effeminate, especially in comparison to the work of Hemingway, Fitzgerald, and Sinclair Lewis, many more celebrated the novel for its inventive form, elegant style, and lyrical evocation of the past as an effective way of assessing American character and heritage.

Good-Bye Wisconsin is a collection of ten short stories and an introductory essay from which the book takes its title. In the essay Wescott explains that Wisconsin's melancholy atmosphere, its materialism and moral taboos, its unimaginative and depressing towns make it an inhospitable place in which to live. The ten stories, many of them written in France, form a series of country fables, giving an impressionistic interpretation of the grievances set forth in the lead essay. Among the themes explored in this collection of stories are the problems of flight and expatriation, and their dubious, at best ambiguous, rewards. Looking back over the collection just before publication, Wescott felt it defined, be it Wisconsin's fault or his own, "a strangely limited moral order."

Wescott's last work dealing with Wisconsin is *The Babe's Bed*. It was written in Paris in November 1929 and published in an edition of 393 copies by Barbara Harrison of Harrison of Paris, who was to be the prototype for the young woman in *The Pilgrim Hawk*. In *The Babe's Bed*, a thirty-five page short story, Wescott closed the book on his midwest materials, and it was not until ten years later, with *The Pilgrim Hawk*, that he again published a sustained work of fiction. In *The Babe's Bed* an unnamed narrator from abroad, reminiscent of Alwyn Tower, visits his Wisconsin family and sees his sister's new baby as a symbol of himself. Bound by its crib, the baby appears to the narrator as an emblem of how he was bound by the region, crying to escape. The family has moved to town and to the

narrator's despair seems diminished by its removal from the land and the related myths and dreams of the region. The emotional burden of interpersonal relationships in the family also impresses itself upon the observer-narrator, and he realizes how fragile, distorted, and incomplete an artistic rendering of the external world becomes when translated into story. The theme of the relationship of truth and image informs this story, and in Wescott's subsequent writing it was a matter of increasing, and paralyzing, philosophical and aesthetic concern. The story is a complex statement which rounds out and brings up to date a decade of testimony about Wescott's Wisconsin, and it also poses problems as to how fiction, and the imagination that engenders it, may respond to the passion for truth.

During his years in France Wescott published two other books, *A Calendar of Saints for Unbelievers* and *Fear and Trembling*. The first, published by Harrison of Paris, is a series of ironic, pithy commentaries on the lives of the saints. The latter is a collection of essays stemming from Wescott's motor trip through Germany with Monroe Wheeler, Barbara Harrison, and George Platt Lynes in August and September 1931. This gracefully written book reveals a sharp and appreciative eye for the European scene, and its presentation of the political and emotional atmosphere warns against the impending World War. The book was poorly received by its reviewers, while the *Calendar* received scant attention. By the end of the twenties Wescott had exhausted the Midwest as material for his fiction. Since 1940 Wescott has published two works of fiction: *The Pilgrim Hawk* and *Apartment in Athens* (1945). In addition there has been a collection of essays, *Images of Truth Remembrances and Criticism* (1962), and the *12 Fables of Aesop* (1954), newly narrated by Wescott.

The Pilgrim Hawk is generally considered by critics as one of Wescott's finest works and an exemplary use of the novella form. An older, more sophisticated Alwyn Tower narrates the 20,000-word story, and he discovers in the hawk a unifying, multifaceted symbol of the novella's themes: the psychological complexities of love, the problems of growing older, the painful wisdom on the other side of innocence. Wescott was always concerned with using fiction as a means of expressing the truth, as he understood it. As his career progressed, however, he found the reverie by which he evoked the past increasingly suspect, as being too personal and dangerously distorting. In *The Pilgrim Hawk* he develops a more objective mode of narration, putting more aesthetic distance between himself and his work in the interest of greater truth. The work did much to reclaim Wescott from literary obscurity and to recall his earlier accomplishment. Wescott's final novel, *Apartment in Athens*, employs the technique of omniscient narration. It was a popular success but is considerably below the artistic achievement of his two most distinguished works, *The Grandmothers* and *The Pilgrim Hawk*.

As critics have often observed, Wescott's career was meteoric during his expatriate years, and, though he showed flashes of brilliance in subsequent work, the promise was never realized. His most enduring works were either written in France or reflected something of his experience there. Consequently any serious consideration of the work of expatriate American writers during the twenties must soon discover Wescott. Many literary experiments and techniques of his time converge in Wescott's poetry and fiction. With Wisconsin as metaphor Wescott's fiction provides insight into the Midwest and also explains the impulses motivating intellectual pioneering and the dilemmas of the writer who chooses to live abroad. In Wescott's recreation of a locale and a personal past, the dimensions of his work extend beyond regional boundaries and individual experience and suggest a fable of America. As stylist as well as regional writer, Wescott makes an important literary contribution. Trained in the disciplines of Imagist poetry, he employs a precise diction and lyrical style to evoke the past; the style is a perfected instrument for communicating states of mind and nostalgic recollection. His work unfailingly testifies to his ideals of literary excellence. —*Sy M. Kahn*

Other:

"The Dream of Audubon, Libretto of a Ballet in Three Scenes," in *The Best One-Act Plays of 1940*, ed. Margaret Mayorga (New York: Dodd, Mead, 1941), pp. 361-374;

The Maugham Reader, introduction by Wescott (Garden City: Doubleday, 1950);

Short Novels of Colette, introduction by Wescott (New York: Dial / Permanent Library, 1951).

Periodical Publications:

"Mr. Auerbach in Paris," *Harper's*, 184 (April 1942): 469-473;

"The Frenchman Six Foot Three," *Harper's*, 185 (July 1942): 131-140.

References:

Ira D. Johnson, *Glenway Wescott: The Paradox of Voice* (Port Washington, N.Y. & London: Kennikat, 1971);

Sy M. Kahn, "Glenway Wescott: A Critical and Biographical Study," Ph.D. dissertation, University of Wisconsin, 1957;

Kahn, "Glenway Wescott: The Artist at Work," *Papers on English Language and Literature*, 1 (Summer 1965): 250-258;

Kahn, "Glenway Wescott's Variations on *The Waste Land* Image," in *The Twenties: Fiction, Poetry, Drama*, ed. Warren French (DeLand, Fla.: Everett / Edwards, 1975);

William H. Rueckert, *Glenway Wescott* (New York: Twayne, 1965);

C. E. Schorer, "The Maturing of Glenway Wescott," *College English*, 18 (March 1957): 320-326;

Morton Darwen Zabel, "The Whisper of the Devil," in his *Craft and Character in Modern Fiction* (New York: Viking, 1957), pp. 304-308.

NATHANAEL WEST
(17 October 1903-22 December 1940)

BOOKS: *The Dream Life of Balso Snell* (Paris & New York: Contact Editions, 1931);

Miss Lonelyhearts (New York: Liveright, 1933; London: Grey Walls, 1949);

A Cool Million (New York: Covici Friede, 1934; London: Spearman, 1954);

The Day of the Locust (New York: Random House, 1939; London: Grey Walls, 1951);

The Complete Works (New York: Farrar, Straus & Cudahy, 1957; London: Secker & Warburg, 1957).

The writer who was to become known as Nathanael West was born Nathan Weinstein in New York City; he was the first son of Russian-Jewish immigrants. His individuality early exhibited itself in his indifference toward school; his interest in the arts, books, and theatre; and his reluctance to follow his father in a business career. While he did not graduate from high school, by a series of creative manipulations of transcripts he was eventually admitted to Brown University with advanced standing and graduated in 1924. By this time he had already written and drawn illustrations for his college and summer camp magazines and was bent upon becoming a writer.

When he died at the age of thirty-seven, he had produced four books, at least two of which, *Miss Lonelyhearts* (1933) and *The Day of the Locust* (1939), are regarded as American classics. All of his books are marked by a deep understanding of the collective life of society, imaginative insights, a sense of the grotesque, and a style brilliantly suited to his material.

In common with many of his literary contemporaries who graduated from college in the mid-twenties, West tended to turn his back on American traditions of realism and to find his inspiration and models in such older French writers of fiction as Gustave Flaubert, Joris Karl Huysmans, and Anatole France; in such Symbolist poets as Arthur Rimbaud, Charles Baudelaire, and Jules Laforgue; and in such contemporaries as Andre Breton, Guillaume Apollinaire, Jean Cocteau, and Marcel Proust.

Soon after he graduated from Brown University in 1924, he set out to persuade his family to send him to Paris to work on a novel. Before applying for a passport he decided to change his name; and in August 1926 he took the name Nathanael West. In October 1926 he sailed for Paris, where he remained for three months, fully on his own for the first time. Though he wrote relatively little, West's experience in Paris had a permanent influence on his understanding of the writer's life, and it solidified his preferences in fiction.

To be sure, he did work on his first book, *The Dream Life of Balso Snell* (1931), during the time he was in Paris. This short Surrealist novella concerns the adventures of a young skeptic as he wanders about in the bowels of the Trojan Horse—symbolic for West of the Western tradition. There he meets and satirizes a series of self-styled artists representing the major writers of the twentieth century. One section of the novel consists of an account of the betrayal of Janey Davenport by a poet named Beagle Darwin, an American who is living a phony bohemian life in Paris. This episode was written in West's room in the Hotel Liberia on the rue de la Grande Chaumiere. Some of the descriptions in this episode reflect the scene, overlooking the Cafe Carcas, which West saw from his window as he wrote.

West later told the newspaper reporter A. J. Liebling that he had finished *The Dream Life of Balso Snell* in Paris. While this statement was not literally true, he does seem to have consolidated his plans for the novel while he was there and to have sketched out several of its sections. More important, this book, which gave a permanent bent to the direction of West's career, was conceived, outlined, and finally completed under the influence of the modern French spirit in literature. In a comment on his own book West deliberately distinguished its kind of comedy from that of "English humor," but added: "With the French, however, West can be compared. . . . he is much like Guillaume Apollinaire, Jarry, Ribemont-Dessaignes, Raymond Roussel, and certain of the surrealists." *The Dream Life of Balso Snell* was published by the Contact Publishing Company and was the last book to appear under that imprint, originally created in Paris by Robert McAlmon. The work of the press was now being carried out by William Carlos Williams with New

Nathanael West en route to Paris, 1926

York booksellers David Moss and Martin Kamin. Although McAlmon was not involved with its publication, West's book aptly reflects and summarizes the spirit of avant-garde literary experiment that was the principle of Contact Editions. Unfortunately the book was published in a limited edition, was hardly reviewed, and attracted little public attention; it did, however, call West's talent to the attention of a few discriminating critics such as Edmund Wilson and Malcolm Cowley. Between 1931 and 1933 West and Williams also revived and coedited the magazine *Contact*, founded in 1920 by Williams and McAlmon. Many writers published in the earlier *Contact* also appeared in this magazine.

During his brief stay in Paris West was also influenced by the theories and practice of modern art. The impact of Max Ernst was particularly evident. He also became close friends with the American artist Hilaire Hiler. The influence that Surrealist painting had upon him in Paris is attested to by the fact that his best short story—one that is still unpublished—concerns the doings of an expatriate American artist in Paris. In this tale, titled "The Imposter," a painter tells about his meeting with an insane bohemian sculptor named Beano Walsh and, in the same spirit as that of *The Dream Life of Balso Snell*, he brings art, deception, and fantasy into violent confrontation.

Perhaps most important of all for West, Paris remained a symbol of liberation, personally and artistically. For years he told stories—mostly fantasies—about his adventures there. He continued to be influenced by French writing and Surrealist art. His next three novels, *Miss Lonelyhearts*, *A Cool Million* (1934), and *The Day of the Locust*, are all influenced by French writing, and in the latter two, explicit references to the influence of his Paris experience may be found.

West's second novel, *Miss Lonelyhearts*, is much less satirical than his first. The story of a newspaperman who writes a lovelorn column, it brilliantly fuses the tragic and comic spirits in what West was calling American "super-realism." In his third novel, *A Cool Million*, West returned to burlesque comedy, but with an underlying concern with the deceptions engendered by the American Horatio Alger myth of success. Neither of these books sold well, and West was forced to find another means of support. The last five years of his life were spent in Hollywood, where he worked as a screenwriter on grade-B movies. Over a period of several years he planned and wrote a novel reflecting his life in Hollywood, *The Day of the Locust*. Probably his best book, this novel emphasizes the frustrations of the modern men whose lives are so empty they can find satisfaction only in monstrous fantasies.

In the seventies West was recognized by critics in America and Europe as one of the major American novelists of this century, and he is likely to hold this place both with critics and even with a fairly widespread popular audience. —*Jay Martin*

References:

Victor Comerchero, *Nathanael West, The Ironic Prophet* (Syracuse, N.Y.: Syracuse University Press, 1964);

Stanley Edgar Hyman, *Nathanael West* (Minneapolis: University of Minnesota Press, 1962);

James F. Light, *Nathanael West An Interpretive Study*, second edition (Evanston, Ill.: Northwestern University Press, 1971);

Irving Malin, *Nathanael West's Novels* (Carbondale: Southern Illinois University Press, 1972);

Jay Martin, *Nathanael West The Art of His Life* (New York: Farrar, Straus & Giroux, 1970);

Randall Reid, *The Fiction of Nathanael West No Redeemer, No Promised Land* (Chicago: University of Chicago Press, 1967).

Edith Wharton

Margaret B. McDowell
University of Iowa

BIRTH: New York, New York, 24 January 1862, to Lucretia Rhinelander and George Frederic Jones.

MARRIAGE: 29 April 1885 to Edward Robbins Wharton, divorced.

AWARDS: Legion d'Honneur, 1916; Order of Leopold (Belgium), 1919; Pulitzer Prize for *The Age of Innocence*, 1921; honorary doctorate from Yale University, 1923; membership in the American Academy of Arts and Letters, 1930.

DEATH: Pavillon Colombe, Saint Brice-sous-Foret, France, 11 August 1937.

SELECTED BOOKS: *Italian Villas and Their Gardens* (New York: Century, 1904; London: Lane / Bodley Head, 1904);
Italian Backgrounds (New York: Scribners, 1905; London: Macmillan, 1905);
The House of Mirth (New York: Scribners, 1905; London: Macmillan Ltd. / New York: Macmillan, 1905);
Madame de Treymes (New York: Scribners, 1907; London: Macmillan, 1907);
Ethan Frome (New York: Scribners, 1911; London: Macmillan, 1911);
The Reef (New York: Appleton, 1912; London: Macmillan, 1912);
The Custom of the Country (New York: Scribners, 1913; London: Macmillan, 1913);
Fighting France from Dunkerque to Belfort (New York: Scribners, 1915; London: Macmillan, 1915);
The Marne (New York: Appleton, 1918; London: Macmillan, 1918);
French Ways and Their Meanings (New York & London: Appleton, 1919; London: Macmillan, 1919);
The Age of Innocence (New York & London: Appleton, 1920);
A Son at the Front (New York: Scribners, 1923; London: Macmillan, 1923);
Twilight Sleep (New York & London: Appleton, 1927; London & New York: Appleton, 1927);
The Children (New York & London: Appleton, 1928; London & New York: Appleton, 1928);
Hudson River Bracketed (New York & London: Appleton, 1929; London & New York: Appleton, 1930);
The Gods Arrive (New York & London: Appleton, 1932);
The Buccaneers (New York & London: Appleton-Century, 1938);
The Collected Short Stories, ed. R. W. B. Lewis, 2 volumes (New York: Scribners, 1968).

The breadth of Edith Wharton's achievement makes definition of her place in literary history difficult. For fifty years she wrote prolifically, and her audience ranged from scholars to readers of popular magazines. She produced short stories, ghost tales, novellas, novels, autobiography, literary criticism, and books on travel, landscape gardening, Italian architectural history, and interior decorating. Like Nathaniel Hawthorne and Henry James she explored the ambiguities of inner experience and of human behavior as her characters attempt to achieve moral illumination and are inhibited from so doing by social convention. Like her friend Henry James she sought to relate values and patterns in American life to those in European cultures. Like the younger writers she admired, F. Scott Fitzgerald and Sinclair Lewis, she produced excellent fictional commentaries on the values of contemporary American society although, unlike them, she lived only in Europe after 1912.

Wharton was at home with European culture. Her childhood was spent in Europe, and she returned to France with her parents for two years at the age of eighteen. Following her marriage in 1885 she continued to travel extensively—an Aegean cruise on a chartered yacht in 1888, springs in Italy, summers in Newport, Rhode Island, and winters in New York, England, or France. She spent the entire year abroad in 1909. After she sold The Mount, her estate in Lenox, Massachusetts, in 1911, and filed for divorce from Edward Wharton in 1912, she became a permanent resident of Paris. In the remaining twenty-five years of her life she returned to America for only a few days, in 1923 to receive the first honorary degree given to a woman by Yale University. She journeyed to Florence many times to visit the Bernard Berensons and enjoyed travel in

England and continental Europe almost every year. Wharton even toured behind the enemy lines during World War I with French officials. Throughout World War I she dedicated her days to administration of facilities for refugees and her evenings to projects to raise funds for war relief. She headed the American division of the *Accueil Franco-Americain*, which lodged 30,000 refugees, established four colonies for children and old people, and treated 100,000 military personnel afflicted with tuberculosis. Responding to the personal request of the queen of Belgium, she established the Children of Flanders Rescue Committee, which placed 650 orphans with foster families.

Although she lived in France during so much of her life, she continued throughout her career to write only in English and to create primarily American characters. Only two of her novels are set entirely in France. *Madame de Treymes* (1907), the first, is also the first of her books strongly influenced by James. Madame Christiane de Treymes represents the decadence and the authoritarian inflexibility of a French-Catholic aristocratic family and is contrasted with her brother's widow, Fanny Malrive, a young American woman. Fanny fears that marriage to her American fiance will jeopardize her custody of her son because her French in-laws might object to his leaving Paris. When Madame de Treymes tells Fanny's fiance, Durham, that she will gain family approval of the marriage if he pays her own lover's debts, Durham leaves rather than involve Fanny in a sordid agreement.

In the longer novel set exclusively in France, *The Reef* (1912), Wharton uses Jamesian stylistic devices to tell the story of another American widow of a Frenchman. Anna Leath is also engaged to an American and maintains a guarded relationship with her husband's wealthy elderly relatives to insure her stepson's inheritance. Anna gradually realizes that her fiance, Darrow, has been the lover of her daughter's American governess, Sophy Viner, who is the stepson's fiance. Anna's resentment of the adventurous American governess may foreshadow Wharton's moralistically negative view of American youth in the twenties, but she later reversed this attitude in her presentation of the "adventurers" in *The Buccaneers* (1938), in which American girls, much like Sophy in their impulsiveness and lighthearted affection, emerge victorious over the rigidity of class and convention. James regarded *The Reef* as a masterpiece, admiring Wharton's moral insight and aesthetic control.

Still another young American woman married to a Frenchman is the heroine of *The Custom of the Country* (1913). The novel describes Undine Spragg's social and economic conquests as she successfully overcomes the restrictions placed on women, first by New York high society and later, after her marriage to a Frenchman, by French

Edith Wharton

aristocracy. Beautiful, ruthless, and triumphant, she is "the monstrously perfect result of the system," unlike Lily Bart in Wharton's earlier novel *The House of Mirth* (1905), who is the victim of the same social and economic forces. Undine is an insatiably ambitious woman in a world where only men are supposed to be so ambitious and materialistic. She confronts effectively with her force and energy the paternalism and the materialism which form the custom of her country, where women are the possessions of wealthy men and men must slave to satisfy the women they have won.

In the best of her postwar novels, *The Age of Innocence* (1920), Wharton, who so often in her fiction questioned the value of conventions, celebrates the worth of aristocratic values and rituals in the New York of the 1870s. Family responsibility and loyalty further self-development rather than deny it in this book. *A Son at the Front* (1923) also presents more conventional attitudes than do the novels of some of Wharton's younger contemporaries who criticized traditional values in their war novels. In her novel Wharton glorifies French patriotism and courage, as she does in her less distinguished war writings—*Fighting France* (1915), *The Marne* (1918), *French Ways and Their Meanings* (1919)—concentrating not on the soldiers so much as on the relatives fighting battles of the spirit at home.

In the late twenties Wharton successfully returned to the satiric comedy of manners she had used in *The Custom of the Country. Twilight Sleep* (1927) and *The Children* (1928) develop similar themes—destructive materialism, irresponsible pursuit of pleasure, oppression of women, and disregard of children by their divorced parents. These novels indicate her continuing creative development, as do her many short stories written in the last two decades of her life. One third of her stories appeared after World War I, including the excellent "Miss Mary Pask," "Bewitched," "Atrophy," "A Bottle of Perrier," "After Holbein," "The Day of the Funeral," "Joy in the House," "Pomegranate Seed," and "Roman Fever."

In her last two completed novels, *Hudson River Bracketed* (1929) and *The Gods Arrive* (1932), Wharton traces the career of an aspiring author, Vance Weston, who loses his perspective amid the materialism of the New York publishing world and the bohemian atmosphere of Paris. Only solitude, suffering, and exhausting work seem to hold promise for him at the end of the second book. *The Buccaneers* is considerably more impressive than these novels, even though Wharton's death left it in fragmentary form.

Wharton was a commanding, yet attractive, person who enjoyed the friendship of many distinguished and famous people over the decades despite her own apprehension about meeting new people and the fears her formidable manner sometimes aroused in others. Privileged by birth, Wharton knew such well-known American families as the Roosevelts, Lodges, Tafts, and Vanderbilts. Although she always enjoyed mingling with the notable, she reached out to a variety of people, including younger writers. Since she was democratic in spite of her aristocratic heritage, she enjoyed the comment circulating in Paris in 1912: "Edith Wharton and Teddy Roosevelt are both self-made men."

If she grew up in a society given to elaborate social festivities, she limited her own gatherings in Paris usually to about eight people, carefully chosen for their common interests and temperamental compatibility. Her entertaining, though informal, was meticulously and graciously planned. In her later years at Hyeres on the Riviera, guests wandered to rocky areas above her home to enjoy winter picnics. She left her many houseguests to their own resources until noon while she wrote in bed.

Many of Wharton's famous associates during her years in Paris were friends whom she had known since the turn of the century. Her closest companion was Walter Berry, an international judge, head of the American Chamber of Commerce in Paris, and a friend of Proust and James. He advised her on the details of her books for over thirty years. They both read insatiably in several languages and fields and sometimes traveled together. At his death on 12 October 1927 she wrote: "The stone closed over all my life." When Wharton died in 1937, she was buried next to him.

Berry's death brought Wharton in conflict with one of the younger American expatriates in Paris when Berry's cousin, poet and publisher Harry Crosby, became executor of the estate. In his will Berry left Crosby "All the rest of the books in my appartement (except those bequeathed by Articles First and Second above, and those books which Edith Wharton may desire to take, as provided by Article Third above). . . ." Crosby later asked Wharton to return at least half of the books she had taken. Wharton, who had borne all the expenses of Berry's funeral, eventually took only seventy-three books and sets of books which, according to Crosby's biographer Geoffrey Wolff, were valued at about what she had spent for the funeral. Crosby took the rest of Berry's library, which numbered nearly eight thousand books.

After living in a spacious, eighteenth-century apartment in Faubourg Saint Germaine in Paris for part of the year from 1907 to 1912, Wharton had moved to 53, rue de Varenne in Paris, where she lived exclusively from 1912 to 1919. After World War I she took up residence at Pavillon Colombe, a country estate in the village of Saint Brice-sous-Foret, twelve miles north of the city. In 1920 she established her winter home in the ancient convent of Sainte Claire at Hyeres. In Paris she knew many of the French aristocrats in the Faubourg section of the city, where she had set *Madame de Treymes* (written the year before she moved there), but she also soon came to know the intellectuals who had moved to the area. Near her were friends she had met in 1893, writer Paul Bourget and his wife Minnie; another French novelist, Charles du Bos, who had translated the

French edition of *The House of Mirth* and later helped with her war relief efforts; and Rosa de Fitz-James, who welcomed her to her salon. Through them, she soon included among her friends others living nearby: Rainer Maria Rilke, Auguste Rodin, Jean Cocteau, Andre Gide, Paul Valery, and Andre Maurois. Maurois pleased her with his biography of General Hubert Lyautey, who had been her host in Morocco. Cocteau's effervescent romanticism also delighted her; for her he was one "to whom every great line of poetry was a sunrise." In the twenties she became increasingly interested in the theatre and enjoyed the friendship of Edouard Bourdet, whose comedies she greatly admired.

One Newport neighbor of Wharton's youth, Consuelo Vanderbilt, who had reluctantly married the Duke of Marlborough in 1895, became Wharton's friend in Paris, though she continued to regard Wharton as a cold, proud woman. Nevertheless, they visited one another often for over thirty years. On one of her visits to the Duchess of Marlborough at Blenheim, Wharton met the young Winston Churchill. Other important friends who lived in England, some of whom were expatriate Americans, often visited her in Paris. Henry James, who died in 1916, had come to know her apartment as "the house of mirth." For Howard Overing Sturgis, she became part of his intellectual "family" that gathered at Queen's Acre near Windsor. James's death in 1916 and Sturgis's death in 1920 left a void in Wharton's life. In 1904 she met Gaillard Lapsley, a Cambridge don, and in 1937 he became her literary executor and editor of *The Buccaneers*. John Hugh Smith, a banker, and Robert Norton, a watercolor painter, joined Wharton's group of intimates at Christmas at Hyeres for twenty years. In a sense she presided over a salon each year at Hyeres. About 1930 the winter group at Hyeres began including two other younger Englishmen of note and their wives— the novelist Aldous Huxley and Berenson's prize apprentice, Kenneth Clark, now a well-known art critic and museum curator at Oxford.

The most intellectually significant of her late friendships were those with Bernard Berenson; his wife, Mary; his brother-in-law, Logan Pearsall Smith; and his assistant, Nikki Mariano. She had met them while in Italy in 1903 doing research for *Italian Villas and Their Gardens* (1904) and *Italian Backgrounds* (1905), but she offended the Berensons so greatly by her coldness that for six years they avoided gatherings where she might be present. In 1909, however, Henry Adams conspired to place Wharton next to Berenson in a dimly lit room. The result: before recognizing the woman beside him,

Berenson became "enthralled by the wit and sensitiveness . . . the freedom of her spirit, her reading, and her sense of fun." A friendship ensued, and for thirty years Berenson, the great art critic of the Renaissance, became "dearest B. B.," and hundreds of letters passed between them. On the day of Walter Berry's death, she wrote the Berensons, who rushed to Paris to support her in this crisis, and Bernard Berenson stayed for over two months.

Wharton illustrated in her personal relationships a collocation of personality traits which at first baffled the people who later became her friends. Smith explained this startling contrast in Edith Wharton of haughtiness and warmth: she "terrified those of whom she stood in terror. . . . But at a gleam of sympathy and consideration, there would emerge . . . one of the most intelligent, witty, and freest of human beings . . . and one of the most tender and loyal of friends. She loved good conversation and ribaldry and laughter." Despite the formidable impression that she conveyed, Wharton was, in fact, diffident toward strangers and sometimes terrified by them. She once confided to her old friend Daisy Chanler that, when a stranger approached her, her terror sometimes distorted the person's face so that all imperfections in it were magnified to horrible proportions.

Wharton's haughtiness and sophistication had a frightening effect on F. Scott Fitzgerald, who sent her a copy of his recently published novel, *The Great Gatsby*, in 1925. After she read it, Wharton sent him a note expressing her gratitude and praising the book, but she mentioned an alternative method she herself might have used in the early characterizing of Gatsby. She invited Fitzgerald and his wife for lunch or tea that week. Perhaps one of the more reliable of the conflicting accounts of the meeting, which Zelda Fitzgerald did not attend, is that of Theodore Chanler, an American composer whose mother was one of Wharton's lifelong friends and who brought Fitzgerald to Pavillon Colombe from Paris and drove him back. Chanler contends that Fitzgerald was not drunk, as other reports have indicated, but he had consumed a bottle of white wine on the trip from Paris and was tense about meeting Wharton. At their meeting he banteringly complimented her, while she remained stiffly formal. The result was that he became still more tense. Then, according to Chanler, he told a story of his living by mistake in a brothel during his first two weeks in Paris. Wharton did not realize the story was a hoax but inquired in all seriousness as to what went on while they were in the brothel. Her sophistication may have disconcerted Fitzgerald, but on the return trip he did not appear squelched and did not speak as if he and Wharton had been adversaries. Consequently Chanler discounts the report that Fitzgerald sobbed to Zelda, "They beat me!"

Though the anecdote became exaggerated to the detriment of both authors, it suggests Edith Wharton's lifelong problem in relaxing with new acquaintances, in spite of her remarkable ability to maintain and to consolidate friendships not only with renowned people but also with the most humble. Hamlin Garland recalls of his visit in the twenties that, as they walked from the station, every child and woman in the village smiled and spoke to her as if they were close friends. Malcolm Cowley, furthermore, in *Exile's Return* (1951), observes that Wharton, in fact, did understand Fitzgerald, because she, like most young writers of the 1890s, had been in revolt against conventions just as the writers in the twenties were.

Wharton's meetings with Sinclair Lewis during the twenties were more successful. When Lewis congratulated her on winning the Pulitzer Prize in 1921, she wrote of her "despair" in having got an honor that should have been his. After they had had lunch several times at the Pavillon Colombe and in Paris, he asked permission to dedicate *Babbitt* (1922) to her, and she accepted the dedication with great pleasure. Although she praised *Babbitt* in her correspondence to him, she remarked that she preferred *Main Street* (1920) because Carol Kennicott, more than Babbitt, stayed somewhat detached from the milieu that Lewis was satirizing. Her reaching out to Fitzgerald and to Lewis suggests significantly that Wharton saw herself and her work as part of American culture, although she had become so remote geographically from it. At the same time she extravagantly praised a minor writer of satirical comedies, Anita Loos, seeing in Lorelei Lee of *Gentlemen Prefer Blondes* (1925) a new Undine Spragg. Although Wharton hated the Ritz Hotel in Paris, she made a special trip there to attend a luncheon for Loos.

Wharton's friendships spanned more than one decade and included a great variety of artists and musicians, but the people who gathered at her homes seldom included those who met at Gertrude Stein's house in Paris, nor, for the most part, those intellectuals who were affiliated with Bloomsbury in London. Wharton was, finally, too conservative in outlook and the practice of her art to appreciate the work of modern writers such as Stein, James Joyce, T. S. Eliot, or Virginia Woolf. From the Bloomsbury group, however, Lytton Strachey became her good

friend after his brother married Mary Berenson's daughter, and Desmond MacCarthy, introduced by Logan Pearsall Smith, became her close friend until her death.

When Edith Wharton was nominated for the Nobel Prize in 1927, Chief Justice Howard Taft wrote that, as a writer of fiction, she had "sustained a higher level of distinction than that of any other contemporary in her own country." Seven professors at Yale University signed a document declaring her to be "the foremost living creative literary artist of America." Although she did not win the prize, such claims for her fiction are not excessive.

Bibliographies:

Vito J. Brenni, *Edith Wharton A Bibliography* (Morgantown: West Virginia University Library, 1966);

James W. Tuttleton, "Edith Wharton: An Essay in Bibliography," *Resources for American Literary Study* (Fall 1973): 163-202;

Marlene Springer, *Edith Wharton and Kate Chopin A Reference Guide* (Boston: G. K. Hall, 1976).

Biography:

R. W. B. Lewis, *Edith Wharton A Biography* (New York, Evanston, San Francisco & London: Harper & Row, 1975).

References:

Louis Auchincloss, *Edith Wharton* (Minneapolis: University of Minnesota Press, 1961);

Millicent Bell, *Edith Wharton & Henry James The Story of Their Friendship* (New York: Braziller, 1965);

Irving Howe, ed., *Edith Wharton: A Collection of Critical Essays* (Englewood Cliffs, N.J.: Prentice-Hall, 1962);

Margaret B. McDowell, *Edith Wharton* (Boston: Twayne / G. K. Hall, 1975);

Blake Nevius, *Edith Wharton A Study of Her Fiction* (Berkeley: University of California Press, 1953);

Geoffrey Walton, *Edith Wharton A Critical Interpretation* (Rutherford, N.J.: Fairleigh Dickinson University Press, 1971);

Cynthia Wolff, *A Feast of Words the Triumph of Edith Wharton* (New York: Oxford University Press, 1977).

Papers:

The major depository of Wharton's letters, diaries, notebooks, and manuscripts is the Beinecke Library at Yale University.

MONROE WHEELER
(13 February 1900-   )

SELECTED BOOKS: *Twentieth Century Portraits* (New York: Museum of Modern Art, 1942);

The Last Works of Henri Matisse (New York: Museum of Modern Art / Chicago: Art Institute of Chicago / San Francisco: San Francisco Museum of Art, 1961).

A native of Evanston, Illinois, Monroe Wheeler spent most of the twenties traveling through Europe with his friend from their days at the University of Chicago, Glenway Wescott. Wheeler studied in England, France, and Germany in 1922-1923 and began a career in typographical design and book production that was to bring him critical recognition in Parisian literary circles in the early thirties. Wheeler had begun his career by publishing Wescott's *The Bitterns* in 1920, and he continued to publish books throughout the twenties. Of particular interest are the three books of poetry Wheeler published in the Manikin series: Janet Lewis's *The Indians in the Woods* (1922), William Carlos Williams's *Go Go* (1923), and Marianne Moore's *Marriage* (1923). While at Villefranche-sur-Mer on the Riviera he published another book by Wescott, *Like a Lover* (1926).

In 1930 Wheeler settled in Paris, and he and Barbara Harrison established Harrison of Paris, announcing that they would produce high quality limited editions to be sold at reasonable prices. Harrison provided the financial backing; Wheeler contributed his experience in typographical design and book production. Although Wescott was not officially a partner, he helped Wheeler select manuscripts for publication. Between October 1930 and December 1934 Harrison of Paris published thirteen books, twelve of which were produced in Paris. (The last, Katherine Anne Porter's *Hacienda*, was published in New York.) All displayed what Waverley Root of the Paris *Tribune* (the European edition of the *Chicago Tribune*) termed "uniform good taste, intelligence and artistic sensibility" (16 February 1931).

Harrison of Paris's first venture, in October 1930, was the publication of Shakespeare's poem *Venus and Adonis*, with a cover design by Wescott. It was followed in the same month by a collection of seven tales by Bret Harte, *The Wild West*, with illustrations by Pierre Falke. In November 1930 they published the first English translation of Thomas Mann's autobiography, *A Sketch of My Life*, and the first edition of Wescott's *The Babe's Bed*, which was dedicated to Barbara Harrison.

In 1931 the number of titles for publication was increased to five. *The Fables of Aesop* in Sir Roger L'Estrange's witty Elizabethan translation was published in October, with Alexander Calder's spare line drawings complementing the text. Next, Wheeler and Harrison published their own translation of Merimee's opera libretto *Carmen*, to which they appended a series of Merimee's letters, containing early sketches for the libretto. The book was illustrated by Swiss painter Maurice Barraud. Wheeler also translated the third work to be published that October, Madame de La Fayette's description of the death of Charles I's daughter, *The Death of Madame*. Wheeler and Wescott then decided to publish Constance Garnett's translation of Fedor Dostoevski's *A Gentle Spirit: A Fantastic Story* (November 1931), with original drawings by Christian Berard, thus continuing Wheeler's practice of using highly talented but lesser known artists to illustrate the press's books. Harrison of Paris's last venture that year was also its largest edition to date: 700 copies of Byron's *Childe Harold's Pilgrimage* (November 1931), 35 of which were bound in Moroccan leather by the master craftsman, Huser of Paris. The volume contained twenty-eight illustrations by Sir Francis Cyril Rose.

During the next three years Wheeler published only four more books. The reasons for such a curtailment in production are not altogether clear, though the poor sale of Wheeler's most ambitious project, *Childe Harold's Pilgrimage*, may have been partly to blame. In 1932 Harrison of Paris published two delightful and ingenious typographical experiments: Wheeler's *A Typographical Commonplace-Book* and Wescott's *A Calendar of Saints for Unbelievers*. Wheeler's book was a typographer's tour de force: a compilation of literary anecdotes and purple passages in a bewildering variety of type styles, intended, Wheeler said, to "exploit the possibilities of certain European typefaces" that were "for the most part unsuitable for book-printing." Wescott's book, the longest ever published by Harrison of Paris, was set by hand at the Enschede foundry in Haarlem and consisted of a series of irreverent portraits of saints, illustrated with zodiac signs by Pavel Tchelitchew. In 1933 Wheeler commissioned Katherine Anne Porter to compile and to translate a selection of French songs spanning nearly six hundred years. *Katherine Anne Porter's French Song-Book* was a masterpiece of design, harmonizing poetry, prose, and musical notation in an aesthetic whole.

In early 1934 Harrison of Paris transferred its operations to New York. After the publication of Porter's *Hacienda*, the partners agreed that prohibitive costs and inadequate facilities for carrying on their publishing ventures in the United States meant that the enterprise had to be abandoned, and in December 1934 Harrison of Paris closed down. Wheeler continued to be involved in publishing and book design, working for the American Institute of Graphic Arts and the Museum of Modern Art in various capacities. He has written books on such subjects as illustration and modern art, and among his publishing projects was directing the Museum of Modern Art's publication of Wescott's *12 Fables of Aesop* (1954). At present he

lives in New Jersey. —*Toby Widdicombe*

Other:

A Typographical Commonplace-Book, compiled by Wheeler (Paris: Harrison of Paris, 1932);

Modern Painters and Sculptors as Illustrators, edited by Wheeler (New York: Museum of Modern Art, 1936);

Britain at War, edited by Wheeler (New York: Museum of Modern Art, 1941);

Modern Drawings, edited by Wheeler (New York: Museum of Modern Art, 1947);

Bonnard and His Environment, by Wheeler and others (New York: Museum of Modern Art, 1964).

Reference:

Hugh Ford, *Published in Paris American and British Writers, Printers, and Publishers in Paris, 1920-1939* (New York: Macmillan, 1975), pp. 323-344.

THORNTON WILDER
(17 April 1897-7 December 1975)

SELECTED BOOKS: *The Cabala* (New York: A. & C. Boni, 1926; London: Longmans, Green, 1926);

The Woman of Andros (New York: A. & C. Boni, 1930; London: Longmans, Green, 1930);

Our Town (New York: Coward, McCann, 1938; London: Longmans, Green, 1956);

The Merchant of Yonkers (New York & London: Harper, 1939);

The Skin of Our Teeth (New York & London: Harper, 1942; London: Longmans, Green, 1958);

The Ides of March (New York & London: Harper, 1948; London: Longmans, Green, 1948);

The Matchmaker (New York, Hollywood, London & Toronto: French, 1957).

Thornton Wilder, the only writer to receive Pulitzer Prizes for both plays and a novel, once observed, "I guess I was the only writer of my generation who didn't 'go to Paris!' " For him the road abroad led to Rome, which he first visited in the summer of 1920, after graduating from Yale, as a

resident visitor at the American Academy. The influence of Greco-Roman culture and his Italian friendships is apparent in his novels *The Cabala* (1926), *The Woman of Andros* (1930), and *The Ides of March* (1948).

Wilder did visit Paris several times during the twenties, however, beginning in the spring of 1921 when he wished to brush up on his French before returning to teach at Lawrenceville Academy. On another trip in 1926, Sylvia Beach introduced him to Ernest Hemingway, with whom he became friendly. But none of these brief visits affected his work. He did not become a part of the American literary enclave in Paris until after one of Gertrude Stein's infrequent visits to her native country after she had settled in France in 1903. In November 1934, she came to lecture at the University of Chicago, where Wilder was teaching, and though he had not been impressed with her writings previously, they became good friends. He agreed to write a foreword to *Narration* (1935), based on her lectures in Chicago; and on 6 July 1935, he arrived in Paris to visit with Stein and Alice B. Toklas there and at their country house in Bilignin, where Stein unfolded plans for future collaborations. Although Wilder refused to become involved in all her schemes, he was profoundly influenced by his association with her. As Richard Goldstone explains in his biography of Wilder, "He left Bilignin, more determined than ever that he would write plays"—plays influenced by Stein's pioneering efforts to renounce traditional plot and dramatic action and "to express human

Gertrude Stein and Thornton Wilder at Bilignin, 1937

emotions as they are, rather than in the heightened and strained state produced by the conventional dramatic situations."

The immediate fruit of Wilder's Parisian experience was *Our Town* (1938), in which he returned to a technique that he had employed in some earlier one-act plays. Set on a bare stage with a minimum of props, *Our Town* is a universal tale of love and death presented in the microcosm of a New Hampshire village. Many European influences combined to shape *The Merchant of Yonkers* (1939), a comedy based on a nineteenth-century British version of an Austrian farce. The play was not successful at first, but revised as *The Matchmaker* in 1955, it served as the basis for the enormously successful musical comedy, *Hello, Dolly.* The Parisian influences of Gertrude Stein and Irish expatriate James Joyce are strongest in *The Skin of*

Our Teeth (1942), where Wilder presents through the Antrobus family the archetypal history of the triumph of the human spirit over catastrophes like glaciers, floods, and wars.

Wilder returned to Paris briefly in 1937 and again in 1939 to plead with Gertrude Stein to return to the United States before the German invasion. Although he spent little time in France, the plays influenced by his Parisian experience epitomize the freedom, individuality, experimentation, and faith in man's indomitable spirit that was shared by many of the American writers in France. —*Warren French*

References:

Rex Burbank, *Thornton Wilder* (New York: Twayne, 1961; revised edition, Boston: Twayne, 1978);

Richard H. Goldstone, *Thornton Wilder: An Intimate Portrait* (New York: Saturday Review / Dutton, 1975);

Donald Haberman, *The Plays of Thornton Wilder* (Middletown, Conn.: Wesleyan University Press, 1967).

WILLIAM CARLOS WILLIAMS
(17 September 1883-4 March 1963)

SELECTED BOOKS: *The Great American Novel* (Paris: Three Mountains Press, 1923);
Spring and All (Paris: Contact Editions, 1923; West Newburyport, Mass.: Frontier Press, 1970);
In The American Grain (New York: A. & C. Boni, 1925; London: MacGibbon & Kee, 1967);
A Voyage to Pagany (New York: Macaulay, 1928);
The Autobiography of William Carlos Williams (New York: Random House, 1951; London: MacGibbon & Kee, 1968);
I Wanted to Write a Poem (Boston: Beacon Press, 1958; London: Cape, 1967);
The Embodiment of Knowledge, ed. Ron Loewinsohn (New York: New Directions, 1974);
A Recognizable Image William Carlos Williams on Art and Artists, ed. Bram Dijkstra (New York: New Directions, 1979).

William Carlos Williams has been considered one of America's foremost modernists, perhaps the quintessential avant-gardist, one who has had a profound influence on subsequent generations of writers. Throughout his life Williams espoused the

William Carlos Williams

take a "sabbatical" year's leave from his medical practice. Leaving their two young sons with family and friends, the doctor and his wife disengaged themselves from domestic routine by taking an apartment in New York for six months. Then they sailed for Europe aboard the *Rochambeau* on 9 January 1924.

In keeping with the duality of the poet's sensibility it was fitting that the Williamses divided their sabbatical time between New York and Paris. New York was the American center for modernism. From his outpost in Rutherford, New Jersey, the doctor had been accustomed to quick trips into New York to participate on the edges of artistic activity. But New York in turn was a satellite of Paris, the social fount and source of the avant-garde.

After a nine-day voyage the Williamses arrived at Le Havre and went immediately to Paris for ten days. February was spent in southern France, March in Italy, April in Vienna for medical studies, and May in Paris again. On 12 June 1924 they left for the United States. The Williamses had stayed in Paris for approximately six weeks, a time taken up with wine tasting, choice dining, and sight-seeing. But their greatest pleasure clearly came from meeting a full roster of expatriates congregated in Paris.

In some instances Williams simply renewed old acquaintances, including his close friend Ezra Pound, who returned to Paris from Rapallo. With Pound Williams shared a rivalry over poetry; not so with Robert McAlmon, whom Williams had met in Greenwich Village while McAlmon was working as an artists' model. In 1920 the two had started a mimeographed magazine called *Contact*, which advocated an American art. Prospects looked fine until McAlmon unexpectedly married British writer and heiress Winifred Ellerman, known as Bryher, and promptly left for Europe. He set up the Contact Publishing Company in Paris, publishing Williams's *Spring and All* in 1923. This volume of prose and poetry went virtually unnoticed at the time, but it dramatized Williams's concern for the possibilities of poetic creation arising out of a dialectic with the destruction of tradition and convention. *Spring and All* epitomized Williams's desire for "Contact," the immediacy of fresh experience.

McAlmon served as energetic host to the Williamses in Paris. He introduced them to James Joyce, the young American composer George Antheil, the British novelist Ford Madox Ford, Ernest Hemingway, the sculptor Constantin Brancusi, and Man Ray and his young assistant Berenice Abbott, who photographed the poet and

creation of a unique American art at the same time that he was keenly interested in avant-garde developments from abroad. Paris in particular was a part of his imagination from an early age. His mother had studied painting there as a young woman, only to be called home to the Caribbean when the family money ran out. Marriage and children in alien New Jersey frustrated her ambition to be a portraitist. In 1897 she took her two sons abroad for a year, part of which time they were schooled in Paris. The 1913 Armory Show in New York introduced Williams to the painters of the French avant-garde, and he actually met a number of them when they were in New York during World War I. Thus for someone who called himself "a United Stateser" Williams was inordinately attracted to Europe. This rueful self-portrait appeared in *The Great American Novel*, published in Paris in 1923, a year prior to the poet's first trip abroad with his wife Flossie. The two had decided to then had a misunderstanding over the fee. Through McAlmon they also met Nancy Cunard, the British heiress, who came to the United States in 1931 during the course of compiling her *Negro Anthology* (1934) and visited the Williamses in Rutherford, and William Bird, whose Three Mountains Press had published *The Great American Novel* in 1923 as part of Ezra Pound's *"Inquest* into the state of contemporary English prose," a series which also included Ernest Hemingway's *in our time* (1924).

Williams did not meet many of the French Surrealists at this time, even though they were the most highly publicized avant-garde group in Paris. Despite his friend's entreaties McAlmon refused to make the necessary introductions on the erroneous grounds that the Surrealists were inconsequential. (However, Williams did meet Philippe Soupault, whose Surrealist novel *Last Nights of Paris* he translated in 1929.) A meeting with Gertrude Stein was postponed until Williams's second, and last, brief trip to Europe in 1927.

Despite such omissions and short though it was, the 1924 trip to Paris eventually led to the poet's essays on Joyce, Antheil, Brancusi, and Kay Boyle, a close friend of McAlmon's whom Williams had first met in New York. In 1928 Williams published *A Voyage to Pagany*, his first novel, based upon the itinerary of his trip in 1924 and drawing upon the theme of an innocent American in Europe. With its straightforward plot and conventional characterization *A Voyage to Pagany* stood in marked contrast to the earlier *The Great American Novel*, which celebrated opacity in its pursuit of words in their experiential immediacy. If *The Great American Novel* is "about" anything, Williams once said, it is about a little Ford falling in love with a truck. It is about an American writer's use of words.

But the most immediate impact of Paris was on *In The American Grain* (1925), a collection of writings on important figures in American history. Although the poet and his wife researched a number of chapters in New York during the six months prior to their European visit, the trip itself allowed Williams to gain the necessary distance to discern the texture of the American past, as Williams himself recognized, "to hear myself above the boilermakers in and about New York." In the eleventh chapter, at the center of the book, Williams visits the critic Valery Larbaud in Paris and explains the need for an American identity derived from an awareness and understanding of the American past. Separate chapters were published in *Broom* in 1923 and 1924, and the book itself was brought out in 1925 by Albert and Charles Boni, the poet's first commercial

publisher. A handsome volume that had small sales at the time, *In The American Grain* has since been recognized as a major essay on American culture.

The significance of Paris for Williams's general development as a writer went beyond these tangible achievements. Paris offered Williams an environment in which to see more visual art, always a stimulus for his poetry. He was also able to meet those whom he had known only through their works. They confirmed for him the possibility of a community of artists. But characteristically he drew back from complete immersion in Parisian life. Williams dramatized this ambivalence in "Gulls," a poem written in Paris but set in Rutherford: "My townspeople, beyond in the great world, / are many with whom it were far more / profitable for me to live than here with you." He admonishes them to listen, "for you will not soon have another singer." The city of Paterson and industrial New Jersey were the unlikely materials of his songs.

—*Dickran L. Tashjian*

Other:

Philippe Soupault, *Last Nights of Paris*, translated by Williams (New York: Macaulay, 1929).

Periodical Publications:

"A Note on the Recent Work of James Joyce," *transition*, no. 9 (November 1927): 149-154;

"George Antheil and the Cantilene Critics: A Note on the First Performance of Antheil's Music in NYC; April 10, 1927," *transition*, no. 13 (Summer 1928): 237-240;

"A Point for American Criticism," *transition*, no. 15 (February 1929): 157-166;

"L'Illegalite aux Etats-Unis," *Bifur*, no. 2 (25 July 1929): 95-103;

"The Somnambulists," *transition*, no. 18 (November 1929): 147-151;

"The Work of Gertrude Stein," *Pagany*, 1 (Winter 1930): 41-46;

"A 1 Pound Stein," *Rocking Horse*, 2 (Spring 1935): 3-5;

"Rome," ed. Steven Ross Levy, *Iowa Review*, 9 (Summer 1978): 12-65.

Letters:

The Selected Letters of William Carlos Williams, ed. John C. Thirlwall (New York: McDowell, Obolensky, 1957).

References:

James E. Breslin, *William Carlos Williams, An American Artist* (New York: Oxford University Press, 1970);

Bram Dijkstra, *The Hieroglyphics of a New Speech: Cubism, Stieglitz, and the Early Poetry of William Carlos Williams* (Princeton: Princeton University Press, 1969);

Hugh Ford, *Published in Paris American and British Writers, Printers, and Publishers in Paris, 1920-1939* (New York: Macmillan, 1975);

Robert McAlmon, *Being Geniuses Together 1920-1930,* revised edition with additional material by Kay Boyle (Garden City: Doubleday, 1968);

Paul L. Mariani, *William Carlos Williams: The Poet and His Critics* (Chicago: American Library Association, 1976);

Hillis J. Miller, *Poets of Reality: Six Twentieth-Century Writers* (Cambridge: Harvard University Press, 1965);

Dickran Tashjian, *Skyscraper Primitives: Dada and the American Avant-Garde, 1910-1925* (Middletown, Conn.: Wesleyan University Press, 1975);

Tashjian, *William Carlos Williams and the American Scene, 1920-1940* (New York & Berkeley: Whitney Museum of American Art / University of California Press, 1978);

Linda Wagner, *The Prose of William Carlos Williams* (Middletown, Conn.: Wesleyan University Press, 1970);

Wagner, ed., *Interviews with William Carlos Williams* (New York: New Directions, 1976);

Emily Mitchell Wallace, *A Bibliography of William Carlos Williams* (Middletown, Conn.: Wesleyan University Press, 1968);

Mike Weaver, *William Carlos Williams: The American Background* (Cambridge, England: Cambridge University Press, 1971);

Reed Whittemore, *William Carlos Williams: Poet from Jersey* (Boston: Houghton Mifflin, 1975).

Papers:

Major collections of Williams's papers are in the Beinecke Library, Yale University, and in the Poetry Collection of the Lockwood Memorial Library, State University of New York at Buffalo.

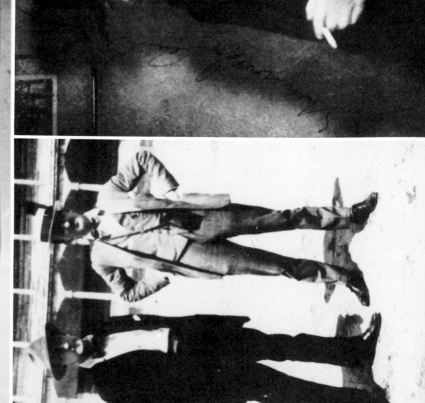

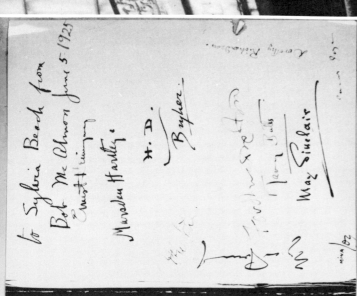

CONTACT COLLECTION OF
CONTEMPORARY WRITERS

Appendix I

Selected English-Language
Little Magazines and Newspapers

Magazines

The Little Review
Chicago, New York, Paris. March 1914-May 1929. Editors: Margaret Anderson, Jane Heap. Moved to Paris in 1922.

Gargoyle
Paris. August 1921-November 1922? Editor: Arthur Moss.

Broom
Rome, Berlin, New York. November 1921-January 1924. Editors: Harold Loeb, Alfred Kreymborg, Matthew Josephson.

Secession
Vienna; Berlin; Reutte, Austria; Florence; New York. Spring 1922-April 1924. Editors: Gorham B. Munson, Matthew Josephson, Kenneth Burke.

transatlantic review
Paris. January 1924-January 1925. Editor: Ford Madox Ford. Published in separate editions for distribution in Paris and New York.

This Quarter
Paris, Milan, Monte Carlo. Spring 1925-October/December 1932. Editors: Ernest Walsh (1925-1926), Ethel Moorhead (1925-1927), Edward Titus (1929-1932). Suspended publication, Summer 1927-June 1929.

The Exile
Dijon, Chicago. Spring 1927-Autumn 1928. Editor: Ezra Pound.

Boulevardier
Paris. March 1927-January 1932. Editors: Arthur Moss, Jed Kiley. Published by Erskine Gwynne.

transition
Paris, The Hague. April 1927-Spring 1938. Editors: Eugene Jolas, Elliot Paul, Robert Sage. Suspended publication, July 1930-February 1932.

Tambour
Paris. February 1929-June 1930. Editor: Harold J. Salemson.

Front
 The Hague. December 1930-June 1931. Editors: Sonja Prins, Norman Macleod.

New Review
 Paris. January 1931-April 1932. Editors: Samuel Putnam, Peter Neagoe, Ezra Pound, Richard Thoma.

Caravel
 Majorca. Summer 1934-March 1936. Editors: Sydney Salt, Jean Rivers, Charles Henri Ford.

Plastique
 Paris. Spring 1937-1939? Editor not established.

The Booster
 Paris. September 1937-Christmas 1938. Editors: Alfred Perles, Lawrence Durrell, Henry Miller, William Saroyan. Became *Delta* in April 1938.

Verve
 Paris. December 1937-September/November 1940. Editor: E. Teriade.

Paris Newspapers

New York Herald, European Edition (Paris *Herald*)
 (After 19 March 1924: *New York Herald*, European Edition of the *New York Herald Tribune*.) 1887-1966.

Chicago Tribune, European Edition (Paris *Tribune*)
 1917-1934.

Paris *Times*
 1924-1929.

Appendix II

Books for Further Reading

This list contains books of general interest to students of the American literary community in Paris during the twenties and thirties.

Allan, Tony. *Americans in Paris*. Chicago: Contemporary Books, 1977.

Anderson, Margaret. *The Fiery Fountains*. New York: Hermitage House, 1951.

Anderson. *My Thirty Years' War*. New York: Covici Friede, 1930.

Anderson. *The Unknowable Gurdjieff*. London: Routledge & Paul, 1962.

Antheil, George. *Bad Boy of Music*. Garden City: Doubleday, Doran, 1945.

Beach, Sylvia. *Shakespeare and Company*. New York: Harcourt, Brace, 1959.

Callaghan, Morley. *That Summer in Paris*. New York: Coward-McCann, 1963.

Charters, James, with Morrill Cody. *This Must Be the Place Memoirs of Montparnasse*. London: Joseph, 1934.

Cowley, Malcolm. *—And I Worked At the Writer's Trade*. New York: Viking, 1978.

Cowley. *Exile's Return*, revised edition. New York: Viking, 1951.

Cowley. *A Second Flowering Works and Days of the Lost Generation*. New York: Viking, 1973.

Crosby, Caresse. *The Passionate Years*. New York: Dial, 1953.

Cunard, Nancy. *These Were the Hours Memoirs of My Hours Press Reanville and Paris 1928-1931*. Ed. Hugh Ford. Carbondale & Edwardsville: Southern Illinois University Press, 1969.

Dos Passos, John. *The Best Times*. New York: New American Library, 1966.

Duncan, Isadora. *My Life*. New York: Boni & Liveright, 1927.

Flanner, Janet. *Paris Was Yesterday 1925-1939*. Ed. Irving Drutman. New York: Viking, 1972.

Ford, Ford Madox. *It Was the Nightingale*. Philadelphia: Lippincott, 1933.

Ford, Hugh, ed. *The Left Bank Revisited: Selections from the Paris* Tribune *1917-1934*. University Park & London: Pennsylvania State University Press, 1972.

Ford, Hugh, ed. *Nancy Cunard Brave Poet, Indomitable Rebel*. Philadelphia: Chilton, 1968.

Ford, Hugh. *Published in Paris American and British Writers, Printers, and Publishers in Paris, 1920-1939*. New York: Macmillan, 1975.

Gallup, Donald, ed. *The Flowers of Friendship Letters Written to Gertrude Stein*. New York: Knopf, 1953.

Guggenheim, Peggy. *Out of This Century*. New York: Dial, 1946.

Hawkins, Eric, with Robert N. Sturdevant. *Hawkins of the Paris* Herald. New York: Simon & Schuster, 1963.

Hemingway, Ernest. *A Moveable Feast*. New York: Scribners, 1964.

Hoffman, Frederick J., Charles Allen, and Carolyn F. Ulrich. *The Little Magazine A History and a Bibliography*. Princeton: Princeton University Press, 1947.

Hoffman. *The Twenties American Writing in the Postwar Decade*, revised edition. New York: Collier, 1962.

Huddleston, Sisley. *Back to Montparnasse Glimpses of Broadway in Bohemia*. Philadelphia: Lippincott, 1931.

Imbs, Bravig. *Confessions of Another Young Man*. New York: Henkle-Yewdale House, 1936.

Josephson, Matthew. *Life Among the Surrealists*. New York: Holt, Rinehart & Winston, 1962.

Kahane, Jack. *Memoirs of a Booklegger*. London: Joseph, 1939.

Laney, Al. *Paris Herald The Incredible Newspaper*. New York & London: Appleton-Century, 1947.

Loeb, Harold. *The Way It Was*. New York: Criterion, 1959.

Longstreet, Stephen. *We All Went to Paris Americans in the City of Light 1776-1971*. New York: Macmillan, 1972.

McAlmon, Robert. *Being Geniuses Together 1920-1930*, revised with additional material by Kay Boyle. Garden City: Doubleday, 1968.

McMillan, Dougald. transition *The History of a Literary Era 1927-1938*. New York: Braziller, 1976.

Mellow, James R. *Charmed Circle Gertrude Stein & Company*. New York & Washington: Praeger, 1974.

Minkoff, George Robert. *A Bibliography of* The Black Sun Press. Great Neck, N.Y.: Minkoff, 1970.

Neagoe, Peter, ed. *Americans Abroad An Anthology*. The Hague: Servire, 1932.

Poli, Bernard J. *Ford Madox Ford and the* TRANSATLANTIC REVIEW. Syracuse: Syracuse University Press, 1967.

Putnam, Samuel. *Paris Was Our Mistress Memoirs of a Lost & Found Generation*. New York: Viking, 1947.

Sarason, Bertram D. *Hemingway and* The Sun *Set*. Washington, D.C.: Bruccoli Clark / NCR Microcard Editions, 1972.

Shirer, William L. *20th Century Journey A Memoir of a Life and the Times The Start 1904-1930*. New York: Simon & Schuster, 1976.

Stein, Gertrude. *The Autobiography of Alice B. Toklas*. New York: Random House, 1933.

Wickes, George. *The Amazon of Letters The Life and Loves of Natalie Barney*. New York: Putnam's, 1976.

Wickes. *Americans in Paris*. Garden City: Doubleday, 1969.

Wolff, Geoffrey. *Black Sun The Brief Transit and Violent Eclipse of Harry Crosby*. New York: Random House, 1976.

Contributors

W. R. Anderson	*Huntingdon College*
JoAnn Balingit	*The American School, Tangiers*
Judith S. Baughman	*University of South Carolina*
Ronald Baughman	*University of South Carolina*
Winifred Farrant Bevilacqua	*Universita Degli Studi di Torino*
Edgar M. Branch	*Miami University*
J. D. Brown	*University of Oregon*
Carolyn Burke	*University of California, Santa Cruz*
Richard Collins	*University of California, Irvine*
David Cowart	*University of South Carolina*
Leland H. Cox, Jr.	*Columbia, South Carolina*
Victor P. Dalmas, Jr.	*Fayetteville, North Carolina*
Thomas E. Dasher	*Georgia Southern College*
Elizabeth Davidson	*University of South Carolina, Spartanburg*
John M. Dunaway	*Mercer University*
Philip B. Eppard	*Providence, Rhode Island*
Paula R. Feldman	*University of South Carolina*
Edward Fisher	*Washington, D.C.*
Noel Riley Fitch	*Point Loma College*
Joseph M. Flora	*University of North Carolina, Chapel Hill*
Benjamin Franklin V	*University of South Carolina*
Ralph Jules Frantz	*Fair Lawn, New Jersey*
Warren French	*Indiana/Purdue Universities, Indianapolis*
Mark Fritz	*Pennsylvania State University*
Sally Moore Gall	*New York University*
Minna Besser Geddes	*Atlantic, Maine*
Virgil Geddes	*Atlantic, Maine*
Nicholas Gerogiannis	*Auburn University, Montgomery*
Joan Givner	*University of Regina*
William E. Grant	*Bowling Green State University*
Carol Gunther	*University of California, Irvine*
James Hejna	*University of California, Irvine*
Alice Henderson	*University of South Carolina, Spartanburg*
Sy M. Kahn	*University of the Pacific*
Louis F. Kannenstine	*New York, New York*
Donald R. Knight	*University of South Carolina, Spartanburg*
David V. Koch	*Southern Illinois University*
Thomas S. W. Lewis	*Skidmore College*
Ian S. MacNiven	*Maritime College, State University of New York*
Jay Martin	*University of California, Irvine*
Robert K. Martin	*Concordia University*
Howard McCord	*Bowling Green State University*
Margaret B. McDowell	*University of Iowa*
James R. Mellow	*Clinton, Connecticut*

Contributors

Eva B. Mills	*Winthrop College*
Anthony F. Palmieri	*George Mason University*
Donald G. Parker	*Orange County Community College,*
	State University of New York
Constance Pierce	*Pennsylvania State University*
Cynthia H. Rogers	*Columbia, South Carolina*
Karen L. Rood	*Columbia, South Carolina*
Jean W. Ross	*Columbia, South Carolina*
Bertram D. Sarason	*Southern Connecticut State College*
Kerin R. Sarason	*South Central Community College*
David E. Shi	*Davidson College*
Richard Sieburth	*Harvard University*
Linda Simon	*Concord, Massachusetts*
David Sours	*Pennsylvania State University*
Edna B. Stephens	*East Texas State University*
Ruth L. Strickland	*University of South Carolina*
Dickran L. Tashjian	*University of California, Irvine*
C. F. Terrell	*University of Maine, Orono*
Stephen Thomas	*University of California, Irvine*
Creath S. Thorne	*Southern Illinois University*
Seymour I. Toll	*Bala-Cynwyd, Pennsylvania*
Alan Wald	*University of Michigan*
Robert Lee White	*York University*
George Wickes	*University of Oregon*
Toby Widdicombe	*University of California, Irvine*
Everett C. Wilkie, Jr.	*Brown University*
Melody M. Zajdel	*Michigan State University*